Hollywood Musicals Nominated for Best Picture

Hollywood Musicals Nominated for Best Picture

by FREDERICK G. VOGEL

McFarland & Company, Inc., Publishers
Jefferson, North Carolina, and London

Publisher's Note

Frederick G. Vogel died in 1998, a few
months after completing the manuscript
of this book. Its publication has been
accomplished with the help of his wife, Mary.

Library of Congress Cataloguing-in-Publication Data

Vogel, Frederick G., 1933–
Hollywood musicals nominated for best picture / by Frederick G. Vogel
p.   cm.
Includes bibliographical references and index.

ISBN 0-7864-1290-9 (illustrated case binding : 50# alkaline paper) ∞

1. Musical films—United States—History and criticism.
2. Academy Awards (Motion pictures)   I. Title.
PN1995.9.M86V64   2003   791.43'6—dc21   2002015412

British Library cataloguing data are available

On the cover: Charles King, Joan Crawford,
Conrad Nagle, and Cliff ("Ukulele Ike") Edwards
in MGM's *The Hollywood Revue of 1929*

Manufactured in the United States of America

*McFarland & Company, Inc., Publishers
Box 611, Jefferson, North Carolina 28640
www.mcfarlandpub.com*

To Mary, invaluable helpmate,

with love

Acknowledgments

Collecting and verifying material for a book on a subject as vast as the Oscar-nominated musical films puts the author deeply in debt to the many other authors of earlier works on the Hollywood musical. It is now seven decades since the release of the very first partially "talking" song-and-dance movie, and over that time numerous astute chroniclers have written extensively of the progress and eventual decline of this film phenomenon. Every conceivable aspect of musical production has been covered by newspaper and magazine critics and by biographers of many of the behind-the-camera giants who created them, the stars who appeared in them, and the composers and versifiers who wrote the songs for them.

He or she who undertakes a review of the most honored of musical films must also acknowledge the splendid assistance of such invaluable institutions as the Library of Congress, the Billy Rose Theatre Collection in the New York Public Library for the Performing Arts, the Academy of Motion Picture Arts and Sciences, and the American Film Institute for maintaining vast collections of documents and memorabilia relating to the subject at hand.

Also deserving of tribute is the videocassette, which permitted the author to replay as many times as necessary the 34 nominated musicals currently available on that miracle of late-20th-century technology. The plots of the four films not on videocassette were condensed from contemporary reviews that appeared in *The New York Times*, *The New York Herald-Tribune*, and *Variety*.

Special thanks are due—and happily extended—to Sheldon Harnick, the immensely helpful lyricist for the songs in *Fiddler on the Roof*; John Kander, whose music highlighted both the stage and the screen version of *Cabaret*; Joseph Stein, who wrote the libretto and screenplay of *Fiddler on the Roof*; Margaret Whiting, the gracious singer of popular songs, who contributed recollections of the artistic association between Maurice Chevalier and her songwriter father, Richard A. Whiting; and Tory L. Robinson, executive director of Dorothy's House in Liberal, Kansas. Very active in their respective fields, the above individuals when asked for assistance, offered it instantly and in as complete a form as one could wish for.

Most deserving of citation for his unstinting efforts to assist me after I was hospitalized as this project drew to its conclusion is dear friend Stewart Siegel, whose invaluable help in escorting me to various Manhattan sites and performing various fact-verification duties enabled me to complete these labors long before I otherwise could have, if left on my own to ferret out the source material and make the necessary adjustments.

It is safe to say that without the activities of Mr. Siegel and my wife, Mary, filling in for me at critical junctures of the completion process, this book would never have seen the light of day.

Also worthy of recognition, if only in memoriam, are about two dozen deceased contributors to Hollywood musicals, ranging from such composers as Harold Arlen, Jule Styne, and Harry Warren to such lyricists as E.Y. Harburg, Sam Coslow, and Sammy Cahn, all of whom similarly took time away from their busy schedules to share with me memories of various incidents in their professional lives. Their Hollywood experiences were of particular value in enriching my attempt to reconstruct the earliest and middle years of the film musical, as well as in gaining greater insight into the goals they hoped to achieve through their participation in such noteworthy examples as *42nd Street*, *One Hundred Men and a*

Girl, The Wizard of Oz, Anchors Aweigh, and *Funny Girl.*

What follows is a tour of the Hollywood musical from its golden years of 1929 to 1958 up to the present.*

If only one author presumes to act as guide along the way, he does so with full knowledge that he himself had been enticed onto the yellow brick road by the many film commentators and historians who went before him.

Frederick G. Vogel
Maplewood, New Jersey
1997

---

*As of 2001, no movie musical after 1991 had received an Academy Award nomination for best picture; Moulin Rouge was nominated in 2002, but one might agree that it does not meet the criteria established by the author.— The Editors.

Contents

Preface

Only one year after the presentation of the first series of Academy Awards, on May 16, 1929, two musicals joined the select group of five films that had received nomination as best picture of the 1929-30 season. The winner was *The Broadway Melody*, the most influential of all of Hollywood's song-and-dance films centering on backstage Broadway, and the source of two immensely popular songs that have outlived everything associated with that trend-setting film except the studio that produced it. Also nominated was *The Hollywood Revue of 1929*, even less professionally mounted than *Melody*, but capable of fascinating 1990s viewers by virtue of its preserving old-time vaudeville on film.

Since then, 36 additional musicals have been nominated as best picture of the year, the most recent, *Beauty and the Beast*, in 1991. Indicative of the post–1958 decline in Hollywood's musical production, that film was the first feature to compete for the award in 12 years, since *All That Jazz* in 1979. Meanwhile, no musical had won the award since *Oliver!*, 23 years earlier. King of the film-musical hill is Metro-Goldwyn-Mayer, with 10 nominees to its credit, including producer Arthur Freed's two Oscar winners. Six carried the 20th Century–Fox logo (one of the pictures was co-produced by Columbia Pictures), and five each were brought to the screen by Paramount and Warner Bros.

Considering the hundreds of musical movies, both original and borrowed from Broadway's extensive repertoire, since *The Jazz Singer* taught the studios how to sing as well as speak in 1927, the 38 that have competed for the award are actually only a slim sampling of the industry's output. Few would argue that at least a dozen—*42nd Street, Top Hat, The Wizard of Oz, Yankee Doodle Dandy, An American in Paris, The King and I, West Side Story, Mary Poppins, My Fair Lady, The Sound of Music, Oliver!, Fiddler on the Roof, Cabaret*—are excellent films, expertly directed, photographed, and acted, and for the most part towering over the stage shows on which seven of them were based.

Conversely, some viewers very well might complain that several other nominees were unworthy to compete—*She Done Him Wrong* and *Doctor Doolittle*, for example—while faulting the Academy of Motion Picture Arts and Science voters for ignoring such classic musical pictures as director Rouben Mamoulian's *Love Me Tonight* (1932); Mervyn LeRoy's *Gold Diggers of 1933*, a remake with a new Al Dubin-Harry Warren score of *Gold Diggers of Broadway*; Mark Sandrich's *Holiday Inn*; Alfred E. Green's *The Jolson Story* (1946); Gene Kelly and Stanley Donen's *Singin' in the Rain* (nominated only for Lennie Hayton's musical direction and Jean Hagen's supporting role, and loser of both in 1952); Vincente Minnelli's *The Band Wagon* (1953); and Donen's *Funny Face* (1957).

Of the 38 musical nominees, nine—or less than one-fourth—won the best picture award. That is a respectable total as compared to, say, the number of winning war, Western, and gangster movies, three other categories that Hollywood has released by the hundreds over the Academy's 70-year history. Only six war films have won the award: *Wings* (recipient of the first best picture Oscar), *All Quiet on the Western Front, Bridge on the River Kwai, Patton, The Deer Hunter*, and *Platoon*. Three Westerns copped the prize, *Cimarron, Unforgiven*, and *Dances with Wolves*; *High Noon* lost out, as did *Shane*, along with every one of John Ford's impressive Westward Ho! adventure films, including *Stagecoach* in 1939. A mere two gangster movies have been voted best picture: *The Godfather* and its sequel, *The Godfather Part II*.

As might be expected, recalling Holly-

1

wood's intense interest in musical pictures in the 1930s, most of the musical nominees—16—were released during that decade. Included was *The Great Ziegfeld*, the second musical to be voted best picture and the first to co-star the year's best actress. Three each were nominated during the 1929, 1934 and 1935 seasons, matching the 1929 record that no other year has equaled. Ranking second to the 1930s, the 1960s gave birth to nine musical nominees, a rather spectacular achievement for a decade in which the film musical spent most of the second half in an iron lung awaiting a renaissance that never came.

Equally curious is the fact that the 1940s, when Hollywood expended a massive amount of time and effort on cheering up World War II Americans on the battlefield and on the home front, released only three musical nominees. Also deficient were the 1950s, when Metro-Goldwyn-Mayer's Leo the Lion roared his greeting to movie fans at the beginning of some of the best made musicals ever to emerge from that fabled studio. Only four films competed for best picture in that ten-year period, three from MGM and the other from Fox, but two managed to win the award for a .500 batting average, the highest-ever percentage of nominees *vs.* winners. Only the 1960s, with four winning state-of-the-art translations of Broadway blockbusters among the nine contestants, has challenged that record.

Among the oldest of all the Academy Award classifications, and the only one on which the entire Academy membership votes, the best picture designation was a pivotal part of the 1929 ceremony. For some unaccountable reason, the awards for best song and best scoring were not initiated until 1935 (for the 1934 calendar year), an egregious oversight that precluded the Academy's honoring such earlier valentines as "Marie," "Louise," "You Were Meant for Me," "Sunny Side Up," "My Ideal," "You Brought a New Kind of Love to Me," "Please," and dozens of other movie gems written by such esteemed lyricists and composers as Irving Berlin, Richard Rodgers and Lorenz Hart, Richard A. Whiting, Nacio Herb Brown, Ray Henderson, and Leo Robin and Ralph Rainger.

This book is a study of all the musical films honored over the years by the Academy of Motion Picture Arts and Sciences.

Omitted from this text are best picture nominees *The Red Shoes* (1948) and *Amadeus* (1984), which, although filled with beautiful music, cannot be considered musical comedies, or even musical plays (like *Fiddler on the Roof* and *All That Jazz*), the two categories into which all the motion pictures under discussion in this text fall.

Similarly excluded because the drama of their screenplays takes such heavy precedence over the songs are such other nominees as *Love Affair* (1939), *The Bells of St. Mary's* (1945), *The Country Girl* (1954), and *Nashville* (1975). Although all of these films contains at least one original song, it was their interweaving of drama and human comedy that earned them Academy recognition. In a large sense, the music is incidental, not a primary character or plot motivator. Especially in *Nashville*, which centers on the lives of 24 major characters whose destinies are altered forever over a five-day period, the music is used as embellishment consistent with the film's setting in the country music capital of the world. This film and the other three would have succeeded as a human interest stories without including a single song throughout their entire running time.

Brief biographical notes on the major songwriters who worked on nominated musical films are presented as indicators of their impressive and influential service to both films and the musical theater. The same attention is paid to the most renowned of the film-musical stars mentioned, as well as to the most familiar of the character actors and actresses whose usually brief appearances in musicals added greatly to the films' humor and audience enjoyment.

Despite their shortcomings and the inability of all but a few to withstand the rigorous weathering of time, the films discussed in this book still stand as monuments to the men and women before and behind the camera who brought them to the screen. Unique in many ways, they gave audiences the precious gift of laughter, performers to cherish, songs to sing, dreams to dream, and welcome respites from the troubles of day-to-day living.

And, as most of the original viewers of these treasured heirlooms of recollection would attest, that *was* entertainment!

THE HOLLYWOOD MUSICALS

Introduction

The great surge of musical pictures that began emanating from Hollywood in early 1929 brought to audiences the world over a unique art form that no other country has ever rivaled in either quantity or quality. Their immediate popularity naturally gave rise to over-abundance, and except for the stagnant mid-1930 to early 1933 period, they inundated movie houses up to 1958, before ebbing to a sustained trickle. Musical films opened to worldwide view the inestimable talents of numerous skillful performers, from tap dancer Fred Astaire to ballerina Vera Zorina. Although many of these stars had begun their careers on the bandstand, stage, or radio, it was their film appearances that turned them into household names.

The musical is the only film category that owes its existence exclusively to Hollywood's ability to record music and lyrics. War, Western, romance, and adventure movies were staples of the silent era, as were fantasies, swashbucklers, farces, comedies of manners, detective stories and Biblical-based dramas, some with walk-ons and extras numbering in the hundreds, others with only one or two stars and a handful of supporting players.

Pre-*Jazz Singer* Hollywood occasionally tampered with translations of Broadway musicals, but all were bereft of sound, save for excerpts from the original scores provided by in-theater orchestras, organists, or pianists as background music. It was the generally amusing librettos, simplistic as most were, and star power of the leading players that carried the films. Reading printed dialogue and ignoring the absence of songs, however, were poor substitutes for hearing the human voice, and so silent musicals never enticed huge audiences, particularly among persons who had seen the stage originals.

The consensus among critics and moviegoers that the musical film is dead is an exaggeration comparable to the supposed demise of the happy endings that brought the overwhelming majority of all Hollywood pictures to their conclusion during the Great Depression, the hot war against the Axis federation, and then the Cold War against the Soviet Union. Dormant is the more appropriate word. The number of musical pictures has surely been curtailed since *Gigi* came along in 1958, and the rather weak attempts to pump a heartbeat into the art form by resuscitating Broadway's problem musicals have been hit-and-miss at best. And throughout those succeeding decades there was scant evidence that the popularity of chorus line extravaganzas like *The Broadway Melody* and its descendants, which so captivated film fans during the first 30 eventful years of the "all-talking" musical, would ever return.

The disappointing film versions of director John Huston's *Annie* (1982), which sought to spin a web of untrue-to-life, Depression-era optimism, and *A Chorus Line* (1985), an introspective seminar in the *42nd Street* mold on the psychological hazards of competing for even anonymous roles in a Broadway-bound production, failed to nurse the genre back to health, even though each was based on a Broadway megahit. Nor did *Star!* or best picture nominees *Doctor Doolittle* and *Hello, Dolly!*, each bogged down with Ziegfeldian excess baggage, convince the new generation of moviegoers that substance had at last replaced shallowness, or that subtlety was now preferred over spectacle. Unfortunately, not even the occasional stage-based pictures were able to contradict the belief that Broadway musical successes, themselves growing fewer and fewer by the 1970s, could always be relied on to provide creditable sources for celluloid interpretation, a profound reversal of film history. Even *Grease* (1978), the last truly successful Hollywood musical, was followed in typical Movieland fashion four years later by a weak reprise bearing an identification number, *Grease II*, which stumbled at capitalizing on the popularity of its predecessor.

No longer, it seemed, could 90 minutes' worth of watching and hearing pretty people perform pretty tunes suffice to insure healthy box office revenue. That was the musicals' major selling point of yesteryear, back when the studios had at their disposal both the production and the distribution facilities needed to grind them out, with only an infrequent fan rebellion to deter them from releasing still more of them. Most of their films were made entirely in Hollywood, and under the roofs of such powerhouses as MGM, Fox, and Warner Bros. were clustered many of the greatest musical personalities and technicians of the time, along with the props and special effects designed to enhance their pictorial professionalism. For 30 years, from the dismal thirties to almost the end of the button-down fifties, musical films were accepted as part of America's DNA, as hereditary as munching hot dogs at a Fourth of July picnic.

Besides talent, the studios also owned the theaters, assuring a consistent outlet for their products, which up to the late forties had yet to feel the sharp competitive sting of television. Movies were the family's sole entertainment on a night out, made even more enjoyable by viewing them in stately entertainment mansions holding 2,000 and more spectators. As late as 1947, there were 669 motion picture theaters in the five boroughs of New York. They could seat a combined 811,003 persons, roughly equivalent to one-tenth of the city's population. That was only the largest concentration of Hollywood's huge market, which the moguls seemed able to satisfy regardless of how many times their manufactured goods were cut from cloth that even back then carried the distinct odor of mothballs.

Although the studios switched the backlot settings of their musical pictures now and then, both story lines and conflict resolutions remained impervious to drastic alteration. In short, the old musical comedy structure became so rickety that collapse was inevitable. Like the overwhelming majority of their Broadway counterparts, Hollywood's musicals historically eschewed reflecting society as it was in favor of glorifying it as Americans wished it to be.

Throughout the Depression and World War II years especially, they performed the invaluable duty of alleviating the national nervousness by opening viewers' eyes to numerous scenes of happiness unbound. Like heroine Mia Farrow in the 1985 comedy-fantasy *The Purple Rose of Cairo*, moviegoers experienced the glamorous life while sitting motionless in the dark. Over and over, survivors of want and war derived vicarious enjoyment from seeing angst-free youngsters successfully combat the fatigue and disillusionment of their elders by remaining true to the conviction that the future was destined to be far, far greater than the present. Whether on Broadway itself (*42nd Street*) or aboard a ship (*Follow the Fleet*, 1936), in the ramshackle remains of a decaying theater (*Babes on Broadway*, 1943) or on the makeshift stage of an abandoned warehouse (*Two Girls and a Sailor*, 1944), Hollywood stars paraded across the screen to entertain and uplift.

The characters were virtually impossible to dislike, what with their spit-and-polish grooming, enthusiasm for life, sunny smiles, and resolute high spirits that not even the lack of money could dampen for very long. Usually inordinately talented, they were cheerful under stress and ambitious but rarely backbiting, or when occasionally so, capable of reformation. Congenital optimists, they never doubted that whatever endeavor they undertook would culminate in success, while remaining mindful that it would be attained only through determination, hard work, and luck, the latter always sailing into the plot at the most opportune moment. Like fairy tale princes and princesses without portfolio, the stars were preordained to realize their goals, no matter whether they happened to be putting on their shows in the face of formidable obstacles or marrying the ideal albeit elusive lover.

Unremittingly, they respected authority, as anyone who remembers Gene Kelly's "Singin' in the Rain" routine can verify. After splashing with merry abandon along puddle-filled gutters, he is approached by a suspicious policeman. Although Kelly's dancing spree was not the least bit threatening to himself or anyone else, he docilely winds it up quickly under the stern glare of the officer, salutes him with an innocent smile, and sashays away from him down the street. Along the way, Kelly presents the umbrella as a gift to a drenched pedestrian who happens to pass by.

Movie-musical fans gave the latest of their

periodic goodbyes to the genre in the late sixties, and that one seems to be sticking. Musicals continue to reappear, but on what seems to be a trial basis. The two or three that are released each year have been droning the same 40 year-old message, even if they are imported from contemporary Broadway. In effect, the film musical has become too geriatric to amuse, an endangered species on the verge of extinction. If there are signs of impending recovery, they are shadowy at best, resting somewhere between negligible and improbable.

Relatively few original musicals made their movie debuts over the 1968–1996 time period. Of a vastly different breed from those that had preceded them, none significantly furthered the cause of increasing film-musical production. Exemplified by such essentially dramatic films as *American Graffiti* and *Let the Good Times Roll* (both 1973), *American Hot Wax* and *Coming Home* (both 1978), *Pennies from Heaven* (1981), and *Dirty Dancing* (1987), they featured 20 and sometimes even more songs that were typically inserted to provide a platform for exhibiting the talents of musical stars or groups, rarely to integrate the lyrics into the plot.

The scores were often blends of old and new tunes performed randomly both on- and off-screen by a host of celebrities who usually appeared only momentarily to complete their stints, never to be seen again. As before, less care was devoted to the plots than to the musical interludes, and rarely did any single performer dominate the cast as, say, Deanna Durbin or Bing Crosby during the film-musical's heyday. Not since the late 1930s, when Hollywood began the periodic release of biomusicals of songwriters and singers, had musical films contained quite so many different songs; not since the all-star World War II spectacles had they crammed so many cameos of popular personalities into a single film.

Hollywood's Largesse. The standard definition of a film musical is a comedy or fluffy romance with at least one original song or a filmed version of a Broadway musical, even if no new songs are interpolated into it. Sometimes, as with nominees *One Night of Love* and *One Hundred Men and a Girl*, one new song is sufficient to qualify a film as a musical, provided that the star sings three or four classical arias along the way. "Biographies" of retired or deceased show business icons also fit the bill, as does such a pleasant animated songbook as *An American in Paris*, which in 1951 featured not a single tune written after 1938.

In the 67 years between *The Broadway Melody* and Andrew Lloyd Webber's rock opera *Evita* (1996), Hollywood has bequeathed about 1,500 musical pictures, despite the gaping hiatus of the early 1930s, when the public temporarily tired of them and forced the studios to forfeit their budget-busting proclivities for sober acceptance of the financial realities of the Depression. About 135 musicals had been released between February 1929 and June 1930, 40 more up to the end of 1932. Another 500 or so went to market between March 1933 and the late summer of 1939, when exhaustion again drove customers away from them. Another revival that continued from late 1940 to mid-1946 powered the production of 450 more musicals along the assembly line. About 350 were released between 1947 and 1960, followed by 110 or so between 1961 and 1996.

Throughout the better part of 1929–58, Hollywood had enjoyed the quid of vast public support of musicals without the quo of rewarding such faithfulness with originality. Most of its musical pictures lacked that vital asset, whether home grown or plucked from Broadway, which itself was equally deficient in breaking through new plot barriers. Already stale by late 1929, the eclectic film-musical plots nonetheless continued on their largely winning way, with studio executives surmounting occasional fan rebellions by pausing to figure out new ways to drop the same single-dimension characters into the same timeworn stories in practically identical surroundings.

The names of the stars changed as newcomers replaced their elders, but they, too, became inevitably trapped in tradition. The studios' pretense of injecting new life, along with the new faces, into the thoroughly familiar usually worked. Musical pictures made more comebacks than actress Sarah Bernhardt, whose series of "farewell" performances continued unabated for three years even after one of her legs was amputated in 1915.

In recent decades Broadway, too, has witnessed a severe diminution of musical production, although it has yet to entirely relinquish its age-old role as a source of musical films. But the massive cost of mounting a stage musical, a handicap shared by the Hollywood studios, burgeoned so outlandishly that producing one, chancy in even the most pullish of times, became almost prohibitive. Prompted by the death of established musical stars and songwriters, and the generational gaps that consigned old-fashioned musicals and show tunes to sentimental aging Americans, Broadway producers were forced into bomb-proofing the box office by concentrating on properties rich in flashy special effects or on "safe" properties long admired by the public.

For the most part, 1995–96 theatergoers were treated to respectable musical rehashes of respectable vehicles written years ago, in several instances as far back as the twenties and thirties. Of the 38 plays and musicals opening on Broadway by May 1, 1996, the official end of the 1995-96 season, only six were original works produced specifically for the New York stage. Of the six, two were based on hit movies, *Victor/Victoria*, which continued into 1997, and *Big*, which failed despite an intense promotional campaign. The rest were revivals (18 in all), one-person shows like comedian Jackie Mason's *Love Thy Neighbor*, or original plays created elsewhere, by non-profit, regional, or London theatrical groups—that subsequently were produced on Broadway.

As even loyalists must admit, even if grudgingly, the old-fashioned film musical did approximate a passport to magical lands, giving fans a sort of escape hatch out of the distressing present by reviving the past, when vaudeville was king, Lillian Russell serenaded her vast public with "Come Down Ma Evening Star," and even a first world war seemed inconceivable. The plots were unashamedly derivative and frequently mindless, short on suspense and realism, too often interrupted by vaudeville-bred comedy routines, and irrevocably tethered to the Broadway musical comedy dictum that the audience must leave the theater with a smile on its collective face.

Stock-in-trade artificialities rather than creativity pervaded pre-1970s musical pictures, as well as all other film categories. The ill-timed knock at a door or ring of a telephone that interrupts the leading players' all-important first kiss ... the star actor's inability to leave a room

without aiming a final acerbic or plaintive comment at his lover just before closing the door behind him ... the inadvertent fall into a swimming pool, assumed to be all the more hilarious if the victim is fully dressed and pushed ... the match held too long till it burns the fingers ... the abrupt spitting out of a drink, be it coffee or champagne, indicating the drinker's inappropriate response to an unexpected remark or unforeseen circumstance ... the mispronunciation of surnames, especially if non-Anglo-Saxon ... the endless bumping into furniture by the smitten but girl-shy young man on his visit to the object of his affection. So often were these rituals repeated in all types of films that they qualified, in the eyes of many observers, as generic to the medium.

Confined solely to musicals was the frequent pairing of the young aspiring actress and mature star or producer on the balcony of his penthouse, both transfixed by the bright lights of midtown Manhattan, she dreaming of seeing her name spelled out in them, he vowing to do all he can to help her along the treadmill to stardom (Evelyn Keyes and Larry Parks in *The Jolson Story*, 1946, among many notable examples). The lump in the throat of the startled female performer when she catches midsong sight of her one-time lover, up to that point believed to be beyond recall (Judy Garland in *For Me and My Gal*, 1942, Deanna Durbin in *His Butler's Sister*, 1943).

Frequently in evidence was the emotional suffering of the ingenue after learning that "our song"—the one her boyfriend had written exclusively for her—is to be introduced instead by a singer with a heftier show business reputation (Judy again in *Strike Up the Band* and Alice Faye in *Tin Pan Alley*, both 1940). The naïve youngster, newly arrived in New York from the sticks, animated by stubborn, chin-up determination to succeed in the Big Time come what may (Ruby Keeler in *42nd Street*, Eleanor Powell in *The Broadway Melody* of 1936 and 1938.) The completion within minutes of the newest bestselling song by an experienced composer and a young female amateur with a knack for writing lines that rhyme (Bing Crosby and Mary Martin in *Rhythm on the River*, 1940, Robert Young and Ann Southern in *Lady Be Good*, 1941).

Like the mysterious turning of the hands of

a clock or tearing off the pages of a calendar to denote the passing of time, career crises in the lives of leading musical players were reported in montages, typically via 220-point boldface newspaper headlines, partly to justify their importance in the screenplay, partly to condense what otherwise would involve numerous trips to a courthouse. When the courtroom was shown, there sat the cantankerous judge, forever banging his gavel and threatening to throw everybody out unless order were restored. Meanwhile, reporters stampeded en masse up the aisle to grab the nearest telephone, demand that the operator "gimme rewrite," and shout fast-breaking news into the ear of the unlucky fellow or gal at the other end of the line.

Such a contrivance was palatable at, say, the beginning of *Mr. Smith Goes to Washington* (1939). Those newsmen were reporting a truly "big story"—the unexpected death of a U.S. Senator. But its modified use in such a musical as *Happy Landing* (1937) is ludicrous. There a succession of broadcast journalists speaking a variety of languages over a battery of microphones informs the hushed world that bandleader Cesar Romero is actually piloting a plane from New York to Paris, where he is scheduled to put on a show. True, the incident spurs plot development since, as anticipated, Romero lands not in the French capital, but in Norway, which opens the door of opportunity for pal Don Ameche to meet Sonja Henie and embark on the rocky road to romance. Trite, yes, but durable, too. Inserted with rarely a daylight of difference among them, all of these visual and auditory tricks were deemed integral to moving the screenplays forward or breathing life into the most ordinary of them. If their repetition disturbed anybody, it was only the finicky, who most likely did not care for musicals anyway, and sat with eyes and ears closed while awaiting the gangster co-feature to show up. In short, the moguls were gatekeepers of the traditional, more custodians than innovators.

Ranking second in musical-screenplay importance—and third in the cast listings—was the manipulative "other woman," more glamorous than the girl-next-door heroine but fated to suffer eventual defeat because of her deviousness, a major impediment to attracting audience sympathy when she finally got her comeuppance. Particularly adept at playing the overbearing femme fatale was Lynn Bari, whose duplicitous efforts to ensnare John Payne from Sonja Henie in *Sun Valley Serenade* (1941), George Montgomery from Ann Rutherford in *Orchestra Wives* (1942), and then Payne again from Alice Faye in *Hello Frisco, Hello* (1943), resulted in well-deserved failure, even if she had managed to tempt Payne into a quickly dissolved marriage. Equally unsuccessful, and even more assertive, was Binnie Barnes, who surfaced as the scheming contender for the love of wealthy stockbroker Charles Winninger in *Three Smart Girls* and as the rival of Eleanor Powell for the affection of Robert Taylor in *The Broadway Melody of 1938*.

Also inserted with redundancy into musical comedy plots was the female bosom buddy of the leading lady, ever available to console whenever fortune frowned on her friend's progress toward stardom. Her typical "Aw, gee, honey" treatises on the value of sticking to one's guns under stress were recited by such able Tess Truehearts as Winnie Lightener in *Dancing Lady* (1933), Ruth Donnelly in *Cain and Mabel* (1936), and Carole Landis in *Footlight Serenade* (1942). Particularly gifted at portraying the heroine's helpmate was Joan Blondell, whose gold-plated heart was very much in evidence in *Dames* (1934) and *Colleen* (1936).

Always on tap to wrap security blankets around distressed damsels, often at the expense of her own ambition, she was excessively devoted to take-charge guys, like producer James Cagney in *Footlight Parade* (1933), who failed to appreciate her immense contributions to his success till the end of the picture. As with all these confidence-building character actresses, Miss Blondell tended to dismiss her acts of kindliness with a shrug rather than subject herself to the ridicule she knew would result from exposing the mellow side of her nature.

Male actors were frequently assigned the part of the "other man," although disaster was etched into their faces from the outset. Unlike the ladies, whom they matched in number of appearances, these affable ciphers were unworthy competitors of the leading men in looks, personality, talent, wit, energy, and dialogue. Born losers, they treated the leading lady with an obeisance that approached abject humility.

Their love for her was undoubtedly sincere, but too fawning to arouse fascination, too tepid to enflame passion. In fact the male also-rans, like Maurice Murphy, whose youthful pining for Rochelle Hudson is outmaneuvered by the mature John Boles in *Curly Top* (1935); Ralph Bellamy *vs.* Fred Astaire *vis-à-vis* Ginger Rogers in *Carefree* (1938); poor Lyle Talbot *vs.* Tyrone Power for the hand of Sonja Henie in *Second Fiddle* (1939); and dancer Gene Nelson in film after film had but one thing in common: they were boring.

These men, however, did have one advantage denied to frustrated lovers in tragedy: they all lost well. The lady losers generally stormed off the screen in a huff after their forward passes had been intercepted; the men almost always bowed out in gentlemanly fashion after wishing the winning male and bride-to-be long life and happiness. But then, what else could they do? Foolhardy indeed was the apprentice lover who would pit himself against such upholders of dapper masculinity as Bing Crosby, Nelson Eddy, Gene Kelly, and Don Ameche, even if some of them were quite pleasing in demeanor and polished as a diplomat.

But musical comedy format dictated that at the end they be left at the altar, notwithstanding any progress their misguided attempts at wooing might have made over the previous 75 or so minutes of running time. Cast many times in this role was Cesar Romero, his appetite constantly whetted to little avail for an affair with Betty Grable. In *It Happened in Brooklyn* (1947), Frank Sinatra loses Kathryn Grayson to the aristocratic Peter Lawford with the same aplomb he had exhibited when he lost her two years earlier to Gene Kelly in *Anchors Aweigh*. And handsome George Murphy, an accomplished dancer and better-than-average stage-trained singer and actor, twice saw his dream of joining Eleanor Powell in wedlock flicker out, first because of the presence of Robert Taylor in *The Broadway Melody of 1938* and then because of Astaire in *The Broadway Melody of 1940*.

More Familiar Faces—and Roles. The subsidiary characters, those upholsterers of fraying musical comedy plots on stage as well as on screen, were typically worked into the productions for comic relief. Having patented their quirky mannerisms long before becoming

recognizable to moviegoers, they were often the most interesting members of the cast. Highly skillful at double-takes, and pratfalls, and projecting idiosyncracies and alternating between pathos and slapstick, many had learned their trade playing almost identical parts in vaudeville or legitimate stage comedies. They were of two major types. The most common was the laid-back adviser to the excitable hero or heroine, ready and always willing to guide them along the correct path of conduct, basing their recommendations on a lifetime of experience dealing with temperamental folks involved in similar problems.

Played by both men and women—for example, Jackie Gleason in *Springtime in the Rockies* (1942), Milton Berle, as advance man for Glenn Miller's Orchestra, in *Sun Valley Serenade,* and Robert Benchley in *The Sky's the Limit* (1943)—they were usually portrayed as hard-driving show biz publicists or agents, tough and demanding but basically benevolent. Identical services were provided by such other gloom-chasers as Phil Silvers, who revealed much of his Sgt. Bilko craftiness while remaining faithful to Victor Mature and Betty Grable in *Footlight Serenade* and Gene Kelly in *Cover Girl* (1944). One of the best of the lot was Eve Arden, whose breezy *sotto voce* wisecracks pumped most of the life into *Stage Door* (1937), as well as into the aforementioned *Cover Girl, My Dream Is Yours* (1948), and *Tea for Two* (1950). Despite Miss Arden's apparent delight in deflating the balloon of ego with an occasional caustic comment, both she and her less acidic counterparts were devoted to their moon-faced, starry-eyed female clients, whom they regarded as close friends and served with all-consuming passion.

At the opposite end of the musical comedy pole was the elderly lady socialite determined to keep family members from producing a stage play or appearing in one (Helen Westley in *Dimples* [1936] and *Rebecca of Sunnybrook Farm* [1938]), and Edna Mae Oliver in *Little Miss Broadway* [also 1938]. These and other anti-show biz harridans vied for frequency of appearances with the irascible male industrial magnate who, although indifferent to show business, is conned into funding a production; the downbeat performer angling for a comeback; and the fog-bound aging playboy hoping to gain a foothold in what he believes to be the easy-virtue world of the theater.

An almost totally unknown but ideal representative of the dyspeptic executive, Claude Gillingwater, Sr., wisely backs away from his aversion to show people in *The Poor Little Rich Girl* (1936) and *Just Around the Corner* (1939). In between, playing a judge, he permits one of the contestants in a lawsuit to rehearse a musical in his own courtroom (*Little Miss Broadway*) as a means of testing its suitability for the Great White Way. In *42nd Street* and *Dames* (1934) the ever-reliable Guy Kibbee, like Raymond Walburn a specialist in depicting certified dullards, masterfully played the well-healed Broadway angel with visions of receptive chorines dancing in his head. The superb character actor Charles Winninger practically owned the sympathetic role of the over-the-hill oldster eager to revive his career, even though its death coincided with that of vaudeville (*Babes in Arms*, 1939, *Ziegfeld Girl*, 1941, *Give My Regards to Broadway*, 1948). Similarly effective was the pudgy but still effervescent Jack Oakie in such bittersweet 1940s excursions into the vaudeville of yesteryear as *Young People* (1940), *The Merry Monahans* (1944), and *When My Baby Smiles at Me* (1948).

Among the most dependable character actresses, as sure to show up in musical pictures as Esther Williams in a bathing suit, was the racy, scatterbrained chum of the prim and proper female lead. Besides inserting comedy into the pictures—often the only evidence of it—her *raison d'etre* was the relatively simple one of heightening the beauty and charm of the leading lady by inviting the audience to compare their respective physical and personality attributes. Needless to stress, the comedienne's roughhouse antics and generally plain-vanilla appearance emphasized the attractiveness and demureness of the heroine. The latter always got her man; the former, almost never. The wallflower female was personified to advantage in the mid- to late thirties by Joan Davis for Fox and Martha Raye, whose delirious cry of "Oh, boy!" announced the opening of another front in the war between the sexes, for Paramount.

This musical comedy edict was enforced even if the target of her affection happened to be equally unglamourous as she: Bob Burns in *Waikiki Wedding*, Buddy Ebsen in *My Lucky Star* (both 1937), Bert Lahr in *Just Around the Corner*. To the leading lady (or man) was given the hit ballads to perform either solo or in a duet, while the loud-mouth lady sidekick was confined to undistinguished novelty tunes, which she delivered with a raucousness that complemented her persona. Star Shirley Ross, not Martha, for example, sings Leo Robin and Ralph Rainger's "Sweet Leilani" and "Sweet Is the Word for You" in *Waikiki*. In *Star*, Sonja Henie charmingly glides across the ice to Mack Gordon and Harry Revel's "By a Garden Wall" and joins a chorus of college-age youngsters to sing "This Could Be the Night"; Miss Davis's duet with Ebsen was the lively and ephemeral "Could You Pass in Love?"

Although she could sing with effortless grace and warmth, as in her September 17, 1939, recording of "Body and Soul," Martha Raye further displayed her rough-hewn vocal gymnastics in 1938, attacking the elusive Lynne Overman in *The Big Broadcast of 1938* with Robin and Rainger's lively "Mama, That Moon's Here Again," Bob Burns in *Rhythm on the Range* (1936) with Sam Coslow's "Mister Paganini," and, in *College Swing* (1938) duetting "How'dya Like to Love Me?" in concert with Bob Hope, then at the threshold of a notable career. Joan had already foreshadowed her own bouncy singing style, which she merged with a penchant for slapstick, with her comical rendition of "Olga from the Volga," an untypical lackluster tune by Gordon and Revel, in *Thin Ice* (1937). Naturally, male leads were usually teamed up with their own basically crackpot but amusing comrades, among the best of whom was Sid Silvers, who, besides adding much-needed humor to *Born to Dance* (1936), complemented Jack Benny's own comic relief appearance in *The Broadway Melody of 1936*.

That all the foregoing elements, overused since shortly after the inception of musical films, could be anticipated by audiences contributed mightily to the decline of the genre. It was stalled in the mid-fifties, however, when musicals began marching along Hollywood Boulevard to the strains of a different drummer. The studios undertook the filming of such meaty successes as *Carousel* (1956) and *The King and I*. Once again musical pictures expe-

rienced a popularity surge that culminated in
the breaking of new ground in setting, incident, and characterization in *West Side Story,
My Fair Lady, The Sound of Music, Fiddler on
the Roof,* and *Cabaret.*

Except for *The Great Ziegfeld,* these films
had the longest running times among the nominated musicals, partly, one suspects, to compensate for the lack of a B-picture co-feature on
the same bill. It mattered little that the publicity surrounding the original stage versions
during their lengthy Broadway runs had long
since removed all the suspense, or that many of
the songs were already widely known. Their
stories and treatment were so compelling that
most viewers even failed to notice that hum-
mable melodies, those mainstays of earlier stage
and screen musicals, were often sacrificed by
contemporary songwriters wanting to make almost every song define character personality or
heighten plot development rather than seek hit
status.

Some stars of these later pictures were not
musically trained, resulting in the dubbing of
their singing voices, a contrivance frequently
called upon since 1930 and involving such
1940s performers as Marjorie Reynolds (in *Holiday Inn*) and Rita Hayworth (in all her musicals). And although most of the subsidiary
actors in post-1950 musical pictures were excellent, very few have reappeared on the screen
either in musicals or in dramas. Nor has a genuine musical star, like Liza Minnelli, who
shortly after *Cabaret* in 1972 became a notable
casualty of the abrupt drop in film-musical production.

Asset Side of the Ledger. What made
Hollywood popcorn musicals so popular for so
long is easy to identify. Foremost among the assets was the music, which was typically written
in the 1929–58 period by many of the finest
composers in pop music history. One of them,
Harry Warren, set the *Your Hit Parade* record
by placing 42 of his screen songs, written for
Warner Bros., Fox, MGM, and finally Paramount, on that weekly radio (and later television) barometer of the nation's biggest-selling
and most requested songs. Richard A. Whiting
and Ralph Rainger, and later James Van
Heusen and partners Ray Evans and Jay Livingston, were responsible for most of the songs

introduced in Paramount films. Harry Revel
turned out popular ballads on an almost pic-
ture-by-picture basis for Fox, as did James
McHugh for Universal.

Alternating between Broadway and Hollywood were such melodic masters as George
Gershwin, Jerome Kern, Richard Rodgers, Irving Berlin, Cole Porter, Harold Arlen, and Jule
Styne. Collaborating with them were masterful
word merchants including Lorenz Hart, Oscar
Hammerstein II, Ira Gershwin, Harold Adamson, Frank Loesser, Leo Robin, Mack Gordon,
Al Dubin, Johnny Mercer, Johnny Burke, and
Sammy Cahn—who holds the record for most
best song nominations with 26—these lyricists
made certain that film musicals provided highly
literate top-of-the-line songs from 1929 through
1958.

However boilerplate the story lines, they
were generally acted out by talented performers. If the leads were often not exactly spell-
binding in the dramatic scenes, they consistently excelled in the musical numbers, which
was the purpose of starring them in these picture in the first place. Watching their artistry
was enjoyed by so many that the studios consistently built new musicals around these
charismatic personalities, providing concrete
evidence of their gigantic audience pull.

Excluding performers like Bob Hope and
Jerry Lewis, who sang in many of their pictures
but were primarily comic actors, and crooning
cowboys Gene Autry and Roy Rogers, some 30
musical stars have gained admission to the annual roll call of Hollywood's "Top Ten" moneymakers over the past 63 years. A respectable
percentage—Crosby, Shirley Temple, Doris
Day, Jane Withers, Miss Henie, and Julie Andrews—achieved significant multiple-year listings.

Although not often challenged to do so in
musical pictures, a number of actors and actresses were indeed capable of rendering first-
rate dramatic performances when required.
Luise Rainer's portrayal of Anna Held in *The
Great Ziegfeld,* for example, won her the 1936
best actress award, while James Cagney's role as
George M. Cohan in *Yankee Doodle Dandy* is
about as superb an acting job as ever seen on
the screen. Three other male and female stars
would subsequently win the Oscar for best actress or actor in a musical picture.

Both sexes fared even better in receiving nominations for the top acting award, even if they all lost out to competitors who appeared in Hollywood dramas. Such female musical stars as Grace Moore, Leslie Caron, Dorothy Dandridge, Judy Garland, Debbie Reynolds, and Diana Ross were nominated once, and Bette Midler and Miss Andrews twice. Fourteen musical actors were nominated for the top prize, including Maurice Chevalier, opera star Lawrence Tibbett, Mickey Rooney, Gene Kelly, Dan Dailey, and Frank Sinatra. Some dramatic stars—Barry Fitzgerald, Larry Parks, James Mason, and Roy Scheider among them —were nominated for their roles in musicals, thereby adding prestige to the films as well as to their own careers.

One-time or occasional musical stars nominated for best actress/actor are quite plentiful, indicating that genuine talent, hidden for so long until they were graduated into dramatic films, bubbled beneath the surface of their singing and dancing roles. Foremost among them was Irene Dunne, with five nominations and no wins, followed by Jane Wyman, whose first picture was the minor musical *Pigskin Parade* in 1936, and Joan Crawford, each with three nominations and one win.

The best supporting actor/actress classification, initiated in 1936, boasts a creditable number of musical-performer nominees, with 18 character actresses and 25 actors receiving nomination and 8 winning the award. Then there were the non-musical subsidiary players nominated for the supporting award, whose presence in musicals added to the stature of both themselves and the films—Thelma Ritter, for example, in *With a Song in My Heart* (1952), the "biography" of singer Jane Froman.

Essential to the artistic and commercial success of musical films was the professionalism of the directors, cinematographers, choreographers, and other craftsmen and women assigned to negotiate them along the perilous route to completion. Fortunately for everybody concerned, including viewers, the pictures as a whole were supervised by some of the highest-caliber directors in the motion picture business. Among the most gifted old-timers, only John Ford, William Wellman, and William Wyler never became involved in musical productions. Alfred Hitchcock also kept his distance from them even if he did permit a music hall orchestra to play Richard Rodgers and Lorenz Hart's minor "Tinkle, Tinkle," written for the 1931 British musical *Evergreen*, at the end of *The 39 Steps* (1935), when Mr. Memory lies dying backstage.

The roster of directors who did, however, is quite impressive, ranging from George Stevens (*Swing Time*, 1936) and Frank Capra (*Riding High*, 1950; *Here Comes the Groom*, 1951) to Lewis Milestone (*Hallelujah I'm a Bum*, 1933) and Henry King (*Alexander's Ragtime Band*, 1938). The directors of 17 of the 38 musical films nominated for best picture were also nominated for their own Academy Award, among them such giants as Ernst Lubitsch, Frank Borzage, Michael Curtiz, Walter Lang, and Norman Jewison. Robert Wise won two directing awards; one each was won by Leo McCarey, Vincente Minnelli, Jerome Robbins, George Cukor, Carol Reed, and Bob Fosse. The great King Vidor was the only director to receive nomination for a non-contending film musical, *Hallelujah*, a 1929 MGM picture with an all-black cast and original songs by Irving Berlin.

The nominated musicals' cinematographers were an especially talented lot, many of them, like the directors, having honed their skills during the silent era. Particularly adept at creating atmosphere and uniquely deploying the camera so that it seemed to be a participant in the film was Harry Stradling, who photographed numerous MGM musicals, including *Till the Clouds Roll By* (1946), *Easter Parade* (1948), and *The Barkleys of Broadway* (1949), and won the Academy Award for *My Fair Lady*.

It was perhaps natural for Irving Berlin to satirize use of the fancy word "Choreography" to designate what once was known as dance direction in the 1954 song he wrote for Danny Kaye to perform in *White Christmas*. The songwriter, after all, had been long accustomed to watching phalanxes of chorus girls strutting their attractiveness and pounding out their steps with metronomic precision in pretty much the same way since Ziegfeld's time. But that era was all but over by the early fifties. Blending drama with ballet, the new switch in dance routines was indeed a remarkable—and overdue—development that delighted the new generation of ensemble dance enthusiasts, even while disconcerting toe-tapping traditionalists like Berlin. Aptly representing the old school of dance directors over the years were such masters as Seymour Felix and Bobby Connolly; from the new school of choreographers came such meritorious practitioners as Gene Kelly and Bob Fosse.

Likewise deserving of praise for their contributions to Oscar-nominated musicals, as well as to many other films neglected by Academy voters, are the virtually unknown cadres of editors, like Thomas Pratt (*42nd Street*) in the distant past and two talented women, Blanche Sewell and Adrienne Fazan, in more recent decades. Integral to streamlining miles of jumbled, often inchoate, film into a presentable 90 minutes or so, they were largely responsible for the admirable pacing of their films. Costume designers of the stature of Dorothy Jeakins (*The Music Man*, *The Sound of Music*), Gwen Wakeling, and Irene Sharaff, and art directors from Cedric Gibbons and Van Nest Polglase to Philip Rosenberg took on the largely unsung chores of beautifying the pictures with sumptuous evening dresses and interior sets bursting with creativity. Special thanks must be given to such a first-rate hair stylist as Sydney Guilaroff, who gave Claudette Colbert her bangs, turned Lucille Ball into a redhead, gave Judy Garland her *Wizard of Oz* braids, and designed some of the most celebrated coiffeurs in movie history between 1934 and the late 1970s. Beneficiaries of his artistry ranged from Garbo to Garson to Monroe. His *Marie Antoinette* in 1938 required 2,000 court wigs, lesser models for 3,000 extras, and star Norma Shearer's memorable bejeweled and feathered skyscraper creation. Then there were such inestimable orchestrators and arrangers as Ray Heindorf, Conrad Salinger, Lennie Hayton, John Williams, and Ralph Burns, whose decades of services on the scoring stage soared beyond craftsmanship often into the realm of sheer genius.

The Broadway Melody (1929)

A Metro-Goldwyn-Mayer picture. DIRECTOR: Harry Beaumont. PRODUCER: Laurence Weingarten. STORY: Edmund Goulding. CONTINUITY: Sarah Y. Mason. DIALOGUE: Norman Houston and James Gleason. CINEMATOGRAPHER: John Arnold. FILM EDITORS: Sam S. Zimbalist and William LeVanway. CHOREOG-RAPHER: George Cunningham. ART DIRECTOR: Cedric Gibbons. RECORDING ENGINEER: Douglas Shearer. COSTUMES: David Cox. SONGS: Lyrics by Arthur Freed, music by Nacio Herb Brown. RUNNING TIME (SOUND VERSION): 1 hour and 50 minutes. *Principal Players*: Charles King (Eddie Kerns). Anita Page (Queenie). Bessie Love (Hank). Jed Prouty (Uncle Jed). Kenneth Thomson (Jacques Warriner). Eddie Kane (Francis Zanfield). James Gleason (Himself). *Major Academy Award*: Best Picture. *Nominations*: Best Director; Actress (Bessie Love).

Released February 1, 1929, *The Broadway Melody* ultimately shared the same dismal fate as many other pivotal works of the distant past—movies with titles that are far better known than their content. Their cinematic influence once powerful, dimmed over succeeding decades, and the innovative touches that made them unique no longer startle or impress. This venerable warhorse is acknowledged to be an American primitive landmark—in fact, *the* landmark, without hesitation or qualification—in the development of the movie musical. Film historians have largely agreed that it is the best of all the very early "all-talking, all-singing, all-dancing" movies, and most people have been content to let the matter rest. In effect, *Melody's* prestige continues to feed off its reputation, with its textbook lessons and groundbreaking attributes either underappreciated or ignored.

Contemporary viewers seeing it for the first time will be astounded that a film carrying such impressive credentials could be so stilted and devoid of the creative and technical refinements that characterized motion pictures of only several years later. It is depressingly studio-bound, never venturing even for a moment beyond the four walls of a room or a theater onto Broadway or any of the midtown side streets. Only three brief scenes, of Anita Page and Kenneth Thomson climbing into a taxicab and the final two newsreel-like action shots of Times Square anchored by the Hotel Astor, pretend to give viewers exterior glimpses. The tracking of characters as they move is virtually non-existent, except for the few rare instances when the camera pulls back from a medium shot or closeup into a long shot to permit some character maneuverability. For the most part, the actors walk into set scenes as if from the wings of a proscenium, and huddle together in order to avoid being sliced out of the individual frames by an almost inflexible camera.

Toleration of these and other deficiencies of this lovable dinosaur must be exercised in much the same way that one overlooks the even greater shortcomings of *The Birth of a Nation* and *The Jazz Singer*. Each of these two films is very much a product of its time, and no amount of accumulated praise can conceal their identity as artifacts from Hollywood's Dark Ages. Each also qualifies as a classic, like *The Broadway Melody*, pitiful but pioneering, outstanding in concept but only marginally successful as indicators of the movie-making wizardry that soon would distinguish Hollywood films after decades of experimentation.

The fact remains that *Melody*, begun in the summer of 1928, or only about eight months into the talking-picture era, represented the film capital's first major effort to bring to the screen the formulaic backstage song-and-dance showcase so common to 1920s Broadway. The praise lavished on *Melody* by many critics and spectators is fully justified. The picture did its job quite well, integrating music, dance, and dialogue in a plot that was far more realistic than any of its few precursors and, in fact, all but a handful of successors. Galvanizing it is not; endearing it remains.

Charles King, as the brash Eddie Kerns, and Anita Page, the Queenie half of the Mahoney Sisters, in *The Broadway Melody*, MGM's landmark 1929 musical.

Of supreme impact on the development of the film musical was the innovation introduced by Douglas Shearer at the outset of *Melody*'s production cycle. MGM's all-time superstar sound engineer, and future winner of 12 Academy Awards for best sound recording, Shearer came up with the idea of filming and recording song sequences separately. Permitting singers and dancers to dub lyrics and taps by listening to playbacks after the musical sequences were filmed enhanced camera mobility while raising *Melody*'s professionalism to comparatively significant heights.

Although the picture, which contains far more drama than comedy, is 100 percent all-talking, as advertised, it is less than 25 percent all-singing and all-dancing. A huge amount of dialogue separates the renditions of the songs, among the most tuneful written for any pre-1933 film. The dialogue is quite respectable for the time, excluding Charles King's cry of de-

light—"Hot Dog!" at the finish of his first "Broadway Melody" solo.

The film capital was very much alert to *Melody*'s assets, placing it among the most commercially successful films of the period. The newly established Academy of Motion Picture Arts and Sciences nominated the feminine lead, Bessie Love, as best actress of 1928-29, and Harry Beaumont as best director. Neither won, with Miss Love losing out to the formidable Mary Pickford (for her performance as Norma Besant in *Coquette*), and Beaumont to Frank Lloyd, who won for *The Divine Lady*, and was nominated for two other 1929 dramas, *Drag* and *Weary River*. The musical, however, gave MGM one of its first two major Academy Awards, winning the best picture Oscar over four comparatively minor competitors, *Alibi*, with Chester Morris; *The Hollywood Revue of 1929*, another MGM musical with an all-star cast; *In Old Arizona*, the first talkie with outdoor scenes shot in two-strip Technicolor; and *The Patriot*, starring Lewis Stone.

From the twin standpoints of foreshadowing the soon-to-be dominating presence of the film musical and substantially weakening Broadway's lock on musical comedy, *Melody* unquestionably deserved its Academy accolades and subsequent designation as the "granddaddy of film musicals." Despite its rare non-happy ending, the picture served as inspiration for literally scores of later Hollywood musicals, practically all of them slavishly committed to varying only slightly its plot and characterizations up to the virtual demise of the conventional movie musical in the late 1950s. It even spawned a direct descendant in the form of the 1940 remake, *Two Girls on Broadway*, with Joan Blondell and Lana Turner as the two backwoods sisters hellbound on becoming Broadway headliners, and George Murphy as the friend and lover of both. The few new songs, by Nacio Herb Brown and Walter Donaldson, were as undistinguished as the picture.

Films centering on the excitement associated with Broadway's backstage life became so thoroughly annotated over the next few years that most moviegoers were convinced that beyond the borders of Manhattan, all was Bridgeport. What the musical moguls did not recognize was that they would soon run out of the few variations on a single theme. For the most part, all the story lines were so similar that all the conclusions were foreseeable.

Not that *Melody* was the first attempt at building box office revenues by enticing the public into enjoyment of big-budget musical dramas interspersed with chorus line cavorting and lovers' serenades. *The Jazz Singer*, released in October of 1927, was the first partially talking motion picture to trace the often sidetracked efforts of a never-say-die entertainer to carve a name for himself on the Great White Way. It covered much of the same territory as *Melody*, even if far less gracefully.

That the jazz singer (Al Jolson) embarked on his show business career from a synagogue, while the singing Mahoney Sisters blew into New York from Midwest vaudeville houses, is irrelevant. So many other film musicals followed *The Broadway Melody* that it is difficult to distinguish one from the other, even if their settings changed every so often from the legitimate theater to nightclubs, bandstands, even burlesque houses. Unlike *Melody*, most relied on old songs, often resung by the singers who had introduced them years earlier, for example, Fanny Brice's reprise of "My Man," Sophie Tucker's "Some of These Days," and Rudy Vallee's "I'm Just a Vagabond Lover."

Of the 125 or so musical films that went to market between the winter of 1928-29 and the late spring of 1930, practically all of them dealt with the struggles of theatrical amateurs to gain a beachhead in stone-hearted Manhattan. All except *Melody* were quickly forgotten, and understandably so, once the unique experience of hearing vocalists sing and dancers tap out their love messages had lost its novelty value. Musical pictures were released at such a furious clip that artists and technicians, inexperienced with the workings of the equipment that had made sound pictures possible, were overwhelmed by the constant modifications needed to incorporate the newest techniques of filmmaking. Yet, the pictures were so alike in content that it seemed the moguls had conspired to produce one gigantic musical comedy split into installments.

Despite the professionalism that went into *The Broadway Melody*, it is readily apparent that the film was released too early to take advantage of the movie-making advances then on the threshold of discovery or refinement. Unlike good wine, it has not aged gracefully. Except for Miss Love, who began her film career as a child performer in 1910, the acting is poor, and the movements of the cast studied and usually as awkward as the chorus work. In *The Matinee Idol*, one of the seven films directed by Frank Capra in 1928, Love had played a part roughly similar to that of Hank Mahoney, appearing as Ginger Bolivar, an unusually incompetent actress in a totally untalented theatrical troupe. What mostly accounted for *Melody*'s best picture award and historical significance was its dispensing with the typical happily-ever-after ending that concluded the overwhelming majority of its imitators.

Added to this realistic touch, undeniably reflective of the average novice's humiliating experiences on Broadway, was the dialogue, redolent with show biz patois, and a top-notch original score. Three of the songs attained instant popularity—the jaunty title tune, the ballad "You Were Meant for Me," and the playful "Wedding of the Painted Doll." The first standards to emerge from an MGM sound track, all were reprised to advantage in *Singin' in the Rain* (1952), which bundled together the studio's own nostalgic recollections of the hazards it had faced 24 years earlier while discarding silent pictures for the talkies.

As is evident in most MGM musicals through the years, the studio was not the least hesitant to mount the most spectacular sets and fill them with chorus lines that were only slightly less awkward than those assembled by other studios. It assigned some of its most prized talents to *Melody* in the hope of lifting it to the highest state of perfection to which the industry of the time was capable. True, the goal was reached partly because of the absence of any earlier musical film to challenge its supremacy.

The Serial Musicals. Released six months before Warner Bros.' *Gold Diggers of Broadway*, the MGM musical laid the foundation for its own and other studios' series of song-and-dance extravaganzas carrying identical titles, but updated by inserting the year of production. Three Broadway Melodies followed, in 1936, 1938, and 1940. (A proposed "Broadway Melody of 1944" was changed to *Broadway Rhythm* before release.) There were also three successors to Warner's Gold Diggers, in 1933, 1935, and 1937, plus *Gold Diggers in Paris* in 1938. Paramount followed suit with four Big Broadcasts, the first in 1932 and another in 1936, 1937, and 1938.

Whether revolving around the world of radio or the stage, these serial pictures were roughly similar in plot to the original *Melody*. Different leading and subsidiary players were usually assigned parts, and the songs were always new. They, plus specialty acts, took precedence over the stories, which were wispy and at times absurd. For example, the silly plot of *The Big Broadcast of 1938* consists of a transatlantic race between two ocean liners from New York to London. As usual, it was the vaudeville routines and musical sequences that made the picture popular. Particularly memorable in the sentimental department was Leo Robin and Ralph Rainger's Oscar-winning "Thanks for the Memory," which provided the foundation for recounting the happier days shared by a recently divorced couple, played by Bob Hope and Shirley Ross.

Much as these serials owed to the archaic Broadway revues of the teens and twenties, they were indebted to *The Broadway Melody* to an even greater degree. The 1929 film blazed a unique trail by adding a plot with subsidiary offshoots that appeared intermittently throughout the screenplay and involved all the major characters. It was, in Broadway parlance, a "book show" rather than a *Hollywood Revue* collection of short skits separated by songs.

Like their stage counterparts, the movies' brand of serial musicals depended for appeal exclusively on the stars and songs, sometimes helped along by the sets and occasional two-strip Technicolor sequences. Fortunately for the movie industry, the decision to film backstagers coincided with the availability of some highly talented songwriters, all of whom had at least some stage training. MGM never tired of relating each subsequent Broadway Melody to the 1929 original by briefly repeating the title song during presentation of the credits in each of the three followups. But the pictures also contained a plot, rarely fresh and usually unduly complicated, and it was the stories that unified the individual scenes while what passed for character development was under way.

In practically all the Broadway Melody and Gold Diggers pictures the plot was the same: the young girl comes to the Big Town, makes some headway on her march to stardom, which proves to be elusive until she falls under the aegis of a handsome producer, composer, or actor, falls in love with him, and captures theatergoers' hearts with her debut in his new show. It would have been inconceivable for producers of the time to deviate from the formula by setting their musical pictures, as later moguls would, in a Catholic Church rectory, for example, or in the Oregon wilderness, Siam, the London townhouse of a professor of linguistics, or pre-revolution Russia.

The script of *The Broadway Melody* was better than those written for its feeble Broadway-based film contemporaries, which were almost immediately relegated to obscurity. Like all of them, the setbacks and heartbreaks associated with the outsize striving of unknowns for fame and fortune are present; in an unlikely coda, however, neither *Melody* heroine has gained either by the time the picture ends. The London-born writer of the story, Edmund Goulding, had already secured a measure of success as actor, playwright, and screenwriter before 1929. Adroitly complementing his plot was the mostly mundane but sometimes incisive dialogue supplied by Norman Houston and James Gleason, the latter a veteran actor and playwrite, and therefore most likely familiar with the vicissitudes that befall practitioners of both professions.

Goulding went on to become a first-rate director of dramas (*Grand Hotel*, 1932; *The Dawn Patrol*, 1938; *Dark Victory* and *The Old Maid*, both 1939; and *Nightmare Alley*, 1947) and occasional composer of popular songs, like "Mam'selle," which appeared in his own *The Razor's Edge* in 1946. Gleason, a film actor since 1922, by the 1940s would become one of Hollywood's most appealing and skillful character actors. Usually cast as the tough but sympathetic theatrical producer (*Babes on Broadway* and *Footlight Serenade*, both 1942), he is perhaps best remembered as the half-grumpy, half-grandfatherly milkman who befriends the newly married Judy Garland and Robert Walker in *The Clock* (1945).

The Broadway Melody marked the film debut of the new songwriting team of Arthur Freed and Nacio Herb Brown, who were to serve as MGM's chief contract songwriters up to mid-1939. A one-time vaudevillian and revue writer, Freed wrote the words to his first song hit, "I Cried for You," with Gus Arnheim as composer, in 1923. Along with Brown, his ASCAP catalogue bulges with contributions to MGM dramas, adventures, and musicals, ranging from "The Pagan Love Song" (1929) to "Good Morning" (1939). In later life the producer of a score of MGM musicals (*An American in Paris*, *On the Town*, *Singin' in the Rain*, *Gigi*), Freed served as president of the Academy of Motion Picture Arts and Sciences in 1964.

Brown's early career differed from Freed's to such an extent that it must have been with surprise that Hollywood received the news that the 32-year-old had been hired to compose the music for the Grade A *Melody*. MGM, already renowned as the "Tiffany of Hollywood studios," in lyricist E.Y. Harburg's estimation, usually sought only established craftsmen and

women to participate in its projects, and it was willing to pay whatever fees their services commanded. Although a trained musician, Brown was the owner of a tailoring business and later a realtor before turning to songwriting for a livelihood.

When he moved to Hollywood in 1928, he had but two minor song hits to his credit, the non-production "When Buddah Smiles" and the intricate instrumental "Doll Dance." Among the most difficult of popular piano pieces since Felix Arndt, a charter member of the American Society of Composers, Authors and Publishers, wrote "Nola" in honor of his wife in 1913, "Doll Dance" was debuted in *Carter DeHaven's Fancies*, a mild Los Angeles stage success of 1926. (Actor-director DeHaven was the father of Gloria DeHaven, a popular MGM actress of the 1940s. She holds the rare Hollywood distinction of having played her own real-life mother, Flora [Parker] DeHaven, in *Three Little Words* in 1950).

After the dissolution of his partnership with Freed in 1939, Brown wrote the score for Fox's *Wintertime* (1943) and *The Kissing Bandit*, a spectacular 1948 MGM box office bomb starring Frank Sinatra and Kathryn Grayson. A first-rate melody-maker, he never received a single Oscar nomination, despite his long-term employment with Hollywood's most prestigious studio and impressive collection of screen tunes. Freed, who wrote with other composers after 1939, received but two best song nominations, for "Our Love Affair" in 1940 and "How About You?" in 1942.

They'll Take Manhattan. The aerial overviews of Manhattan that open *The Broadway Melody* provide a proper salutation to the fabled City of Dreams. Looking downward, the camera glides above the spires, steeples, and flat-top roofs clustered on and around Wall Street, projecting a series of panels worthy of a book of fairy tales illustrated by J. P. Morgan. It proceeds north only as far as the Woolworth Building, then looking every inch the cathedral of office towers that its architects had envisioned in 1913. Although George M. Cohan's "Give My Regards to Broadway" is heard in the background, it is the Broadway of Lower Manhattan, not of Herald or Times Square so beloved by the songwriter, that appears on the screen. The brief views of Times Square, where the screenplay action takes place, are postponed till just before the end. The delay is appropriate. It is the sights and sounds of the theatrical district that have been etched indelibly in the memory of the departing Bessie Love, whose valiant attempts to stake out a claim there has ended in failure.

As far as moviegoers were concerned, the opening documentary pictorials of the downtown skyscraper-studded financial center were sufficient to impress out-of-town viewers with the concrete and mortar majesty of Manhattan in the final year of the Roaring twenties. Eight months would elapse between the release of *Melody* and the outbreak of the Great Depression, which muted the hum of the ticker-tape machines to an anguished drone. With the Chrysler and Empire State buildings still to be constructed in midtown, it was left to the Lower Manhattan skyline to make the film's major point: it is a gigantic city, at once alluring and forbidding, the compelling citadel of aggressiveness, never shy about proclaiming its leadership in commerce and the arts, rarely bothering to acknowledge the presence of even the boldest of newcomers.

Like the similar preludes to 42nd Street and, above all, to *West Side Story*, *The Broadway Melody*'s introduction shuns the slums that had encroached on all Manhattan neighborhoods. Excluded are views of the squatty tenement-tombs housing the vast majority of residents who played their negligible parts in the Symphony of Six Million in silence rather than to applause. Nor does the magnetic splendor of New York's architectural trappings give the slightest indication that America's Emerald City can be destructively impersonal while decoupling the relationship of dreamer from dream. The ambition that drove the Mahoneys to Manhattan would never let them settle for a walk-up flat and ho-hum job. Like so many other youngsters who went there before and after them, the sisters measured success by the degree of stardom they achieved, assuming that their transition from hopeful to toast of the town was preordained.

The self-confidence that drove them there was fortified by the example set by Eddie Kerns, a singing songwriter friend who had earlier left his Midwestern stamping grounds for the East and was now succeeding on Broadway. Played by Charles King, a one-time musical comedy and vaudeville performer whom MGM would cast as co-star in two other 1929-30 musical extravaganzas, *The Hollywood Revue of 1929* and *It's a Great Life*, he had urged the sisters to follow his lead and shoot for the moon in Manhattan. In love with Bessie Love, he had promised to help both her and her sister upon their arrival.

The hustle and bustle that characterized the Times Square of the late 1920s is very much in evidence at the offices of Gleason Music Publishing Co., owned and operated by namesake actor Gleason himself. About a dozen singers and "ponies"—Broadway slang for chorus dancers—are auditioning in separate cubicles to the cacophony of loud, jumbled noises that earned such musical-publishing centers as West 28th Street, and later the Brill Building, still at the southeast corner of 49th Street and Broadway, the descriptive nickname of Tin Pan Alley. Judging their potential is Gleason, who focuses his attention on King and persuades him to sing his newest song, which has been earmarked to appear in a forthcoming Broadway revue carrying the same title as the song. The positioning of "The Broadway Melody," so early in the film was another departure from normal movie-musical practice, then and now. Typically, renditions of title tunes, hits or not, were reserved for the end of the picture, when the stars and huge assemblies of dancers were combined to perform them in a splashy finale.

"The Broadway Melody" is sung twice by King within five minutes after the completion of the credits. His almost identical solos are upbeat throughout, giving the tune an inappropriate jazzy touch that tends to detract from the lyric's dramatic implication that Broadway is entirely capable of smiling even as it crushes the optimism of its latest victim. Actually, there was nothing new in the warning. Howard Johnson and Fred Fisher's "There's a Broken Heart for Every Light on Broadway" related a similar cruel tale 14 years earlier, explaining that "those lights above you think nothing of you." Unfortunately for Bessie, and to a lesser extent her sister, Anita Page (Queenie), two of the millions of new broken hearts about to be broken will be theirs.

One of King's two accompanists is composer Brown, who plays the piano. In neither solo does King make any attempt to conceal his vaudeville background, nor, apparently, did director Harry Beaumont ask him to. The singer's ungainly gestures, together with his use of Jazz Age body undulations to maintain the tempo, more closely approximate the agitated style of Al Jolson than the melancholy reminiscing of lost love by Rudy Vallee, whose balladeering was then coming into fashion. King's delivery clearly resembles that of a performer before a live audience who is intent on holding the attention of persons sitting in the farthest reaches of the second balcony. Particularly indebted to Jolson as mammy singer is King's repetitious clasp of hands over his heart at the conclusion. The song, however, withstood the singer's excesses to rank alongside Dubin and Warren's "Lullaby of Broadway," from *The Gold Diggers of 1935*, as the finest anthem to that fabulous thoroughfare ever written for a movie musical.

Besieged with offers from the assembled auditioners to perform the song in the show, King refuses. It is reserved for the Mahoney Sisters, he tells everybody, leading several disappointed showgirls to vent their jealousy by deriding the Mahoneys as a "small-time sister act" in what was to be merely the opening volley in a barrage of catty remarks aimed at the two by their rivals.

The story shifts to a room in a theatrical hotel on West 46th Street—possibly the Remington—labeled as such by an intertitle, a narrative device carried over from silent films. Considering that up to mid-1930 Hollywood movies were released in both sound and silent versions to accommodate theaters that were not wired for talking pictures, the inclusion of scene-setting titles would not have raised viewers' eyebrows. Into the room stride the new immigrants, Bessie and Anita. Complying with backstage-musical tradition, they are already financially strapped but thrilled with their new environment. Ordering but one breakfast to conserve their diminishing bankroll, Bessie avoids tipping the bellboy by joining Anita at the window to gape dreamily into the panorama of surrounding office towers. It is apparent that Bessie, her eyes radiating with the fire of unshakable determination, is the stronger of the two, the strict disciplinarian averse to allowing anything to impede realization of the goal she has set for both.

The view from the window actually frightens her chubby and taller sister, who suggests that they return to the Midwest and practice their craft for at least one more season. Bessie demurs, exclaiming that they are in New York, "the place we've dreamed about and talked about!" Why, she asks, should such a talented twosome have to contend with "smelly day coaches" and the other inconveniences of touring the sticks to play for hicks just to earn enough money to get them back to where they already are. Worry not, she assures nervous Anita. Before long they will see their names in lights where it counts—right here on Broadway.

Up the Ladder. The next day, while Bessie is washing their undies with Lux Flakes in the bathroom sink, the sisters are visited by their Uncle Jed, played by Jed Prouty, one of Hollywood's most popular character actors who, from 1936 to 1940, would team up with Spring Byington to play the parents in the Jones Family series. Amusing as those pictures usually were, they failed in their goal to make mincemeat of the competitive Andy Hardy pictures. Since *Melody* was made at a time when personality handicaps were expected to produce belly laughs, Prouty stammers his way through much of his dialogue, often substituting synonyms for words that are blocked by his inability to speak them. (A similar offense is inflicted later by the unbilled actor who plays producer Zanfield's dress designer, whose effeminacy borders on the absurd.)

Now a New York-based theatrical agent, Prouty brings news that he can guarantee the girls 30 weeks of bookings back in the Midwest. Encouraging them to accept, he verifies Anita's estimation of New York as a place that delights in trashing newcomers. She welcomes the offer as a means of escaping the harsh reality she fears will soon break their spirit, but Bessie refuses to succumb to despair, at least not this early in the game. The Duncan Sisters made it big, she notes, and so shall the Mahoney Sisters.

The second visitor is King, who was Bessie's lover when he was traveling the Midwest circuit with the sisters. She spurns his offer of marriage, reminding him that it was she who had urged him to go East, where he has achieved the stardom that she and Anita hope to duplicate. Unfazed by the rebuff, which one assumes is only the latest in a long series, King vows to recommend both girls for parts in his new show and join him in introducing "The Broadway Melody." He again sings it solo and then reprises it in a hot-cha dance version. It is apparent during the number that King is becoming attracted to Anita.

As many other male leads were to acknowledge to other younger ladies on the screen, the little girl with the gangly legs and freckles has miraculously grown up behind his back into a most attractive full-blown young woman. Thus does the certainty that Anita will sow seeds of discord between her and her sister arise, and not all that subtly. But that highly overworked plot development is three reels away and, out of Anita's sight, King resumes ogling Bessie. His love for her may be so far unrequited, but at least there is always the chance that after she has acquired a Broadway reputation, she may respond to his overtures with sweet surrender. For all King knows, Anita never will.

In the following scene, set in a theater, the audience is introduced to the spiteful chorus youngsters and the prickly dance director who is rehearsing them in the routines to be featured in the latest of producer Zanfield's revues, an obvious word play on Ziegfeld. Clustered together in auditorium seats are the archetypical middle-age backers of the show, contentedly surveying the chorus girls, and the dictatorial producer, Francis Zanfield himself, his booming voice already trembling with impatience at the slow progress the show is making. Appearing in the role is Eddie Kane, who over the next two decades, as his wavy black hair turned to silver, would personify the perfect headwaiter, charming but businesslike, in scores of bit appearances for practically all the Hollywood studios.

Hoping to open the door of opportunity for the sisters, King asks Kane to audition them. The producer prefers not to, but after casting a cliched leer at Anita, reverses his decision. Elated, bossy Bessie horns in to issue commands to the pianist on how to play the song to the girls' advantage, and together they sing off-key while swaying arm-in-arm to the picture's first throwaway song, the virtually tuneless "Harmony Babies."

Their act, as inadvertently awkward as any ever seen on the screen, does pay at least a partial dividend. Impressed with Anita's looks, Kane proposes to hire her, but not Bessie— until, that is, Anita begs him to take her sister, too. He finally agrees, prompted by Anita's willingness to work for no salary, provided that Bessie receives the money instead. Overhearing the deal, King sympathetically promises Anita not to tell Bessie, sealing the bargain with a kiss.

Refusing to allow herself to dally with her sister's boyfriend, Anita backs away from King, pleading that he do nothing that would hurt Bessie. He agrees, reluctantly. Miss Page falters in this sequence, her first attempt in sound at dramatic acting. Suitable as decoration for any lightweight film as a chorus girl or walk-on, she had only minor appearances in five silents to her credit when she was hired for *Melody*, and her career would come to an abrupt conclusion four years later, despite her marriage to composer Brown, who continued to pour out MGM melodies. Then 19, Miss Page was a "Wampas Baby Star"—a starlet most likely to succeed as a future full-fledged movie star. The title, coined by the Western Association of Motion Picture Advertisers in 1922, was also bestowed on Miss Love, Joan Crawford, Janet Gaynor, Joan Blondell, Rochelle Hudson, and Ginger Rogers before the competition went defunct in 1934. Bessie was clearly far superior as an actress in a film awash in poor performances; in fact her acting rivals the music as the highlight of the picture.

Hustle and Heartbreak. Stubbornly insistent that she be allowed remain in the show, Bessie is given another chance by Kane, and rejoins her sister at the show's first dress rehearsal. Anita becomes progressively worried while the various performers, from star to spear carrier, display their pettiness by trading insults and demanding special treatment from the technicians, in particular the keeper of the spotlight. The infighting, assumed to be representative of stage performers vying for attention, is undoubtedly overbaked, but it did have the effect of influencing backstage relationships in musical films for decades, revealing most of the participants as having far more temperament than talent.

King sings "The Broadway Melody" again

while Bessie and Anita sway to it in the background, confirming the well-founded suspicion that dance direction still had a long road to travel before it met up with professionalism. Supposed to reflect the Manhattan skyline at night, the sets are blatantly artificial, surely unworthy of a would-be Ziegfeldian type of production, but typical of the 1929 period. The producer wisely scorns the sisters' tepid dancing and orders the removal of both from the skit. Despite Bessie's fiery protest—she has taken on the additional burden of the twosome's business manager—a chorus of 12 highkickers dressed in egregious costumes replaces them, providing the live backdrop to still another King reprise of the title tune—his sixth, and still the record for repetitions of the same song by a single singer in any film musical. Conforming with the era's perception of beauty are the girls' quivering, beefy thighs, which up to about 1935 were as much a part of their credentials as their clumsy footwork.

It is during the practice session of an outlandish sketch that looks like an out-take from MGM's own *Ben-Hur* that the picture reaches the first of its "defining" moments. A chorus girl, frozen like a statue on a pedestal high above the stage floor, swoons and falls. Undisturbed, Kane dismisses the accident as probably inevitable and gives the part to Anita. Although her sole job is to stand stiffly, arms outstretched above her head and smile, she is wildly praised by the rest of the cast, who unaccountably detect rays of talent shining from the young lady's motionless, speechless replica of a ship's prow. The only exception is Bessie, who expresses the accurate opinion that her sister got the job solely because of Kane's appreciation of her figure. Stage struck though she is, Bessie is not one to be blinded from reality by Broadway's bright lights. The theme song of the skit, "The Love Boat," is sung by tenor James Burroughs, whose vocalizing, like the song itself, is a disaster.

Neither sister is invited to the cast party that night, and so King offers to take them out for a chop suey dinner. Anita, her ego disclosing signs of puffing up from the plaudits bestowed on her by her easily impressed co-workers, excuses herself because of a headache, suggesting that she will try to join them later. Unwilling to accept her limp excuse, King becomes further infuriated when he overhears Anita accept a date with Kenneth Thomson (Jacques Warriner), who had gone backstage to compliment Anita on her "performance." With mischief in his eyes and lust in his heart, Thomson exudes the on-the-make raunchiness of the typical movie-musical's wealthy Broadwayite while failing to exhibit a single redeeming quality as compensation. With just enough nimbleness and polish to conceal his smarmy intentions, Thomson's character was to reappear again and again under different names in film musicals until 1934, when stern application of the Motion Picture Production Code transformed the cavalier skirt-chaser into a respectable dabbler in the arts, elderly buffoon, or faithful counsel to his actress friends, warm but never passionate, helpful but never intrusive.

With a shout of "It's my life and I'll live it as I see fit!" Anita storms out of her dressing room, leaving a depressed King and Bessie alone to contemplate the sorry consequences certain to accrue to Anita from playing around with an experienced wolf in tuxedo clothing. "The bright lights got under her skin," King utters dourly, mostly to himself. Unknown to him, and to Bessie till she returns to their hotel room and finds Anita in bed, her wavering sister had decided not to go out with Thomson after all.

The Broadway playboy, however, is not one to quit after a single frustrating turn of events. He sends Anita a love note embedded in a bouquet of flowers in a further attempt to entice her to his luxurious apartment. Gradually, Anita's regard for her pursuer changes from aloofness to infatuation, resulting in her defying King by accepting Thomson's invitation to celebrate her birthday in a speakeasy.

King's response is to sing of his love for her in the still-familiar ballad "You Were Meant for Me," one of the biggest hits on the short list of instantly recognizable 1920s Hollywood songs. King's delivery, straightforward and practically devoid of emotion, is naturally no match for the *Singin' in the Rain* version, sung by Gene Kelly to Debbie Reynolds in a backlot sound stage, and then followed by one of the screen's most romantic dance duets, showing how greatly movie making had progressed over the intervening two decades.

King's musical confession backfires, however, when Anita refuses to be tempted into his arms, reminding him that he is Bessie's boyfriend, and therefore impossible to become hers. Suddenly, into their presence burst Bessie and friends bearing a birthday cake and gifts. Finding the room too small for the birthday celebration, they decide to transfer it to a larger suite in the hotel. Bessie follows the crowd, but Anita slips away to attend Thomson's party at an ornately decorated bistro instead. Adding to the festivities is a bandstand rendition of "Truthful Parson Brown," already a modest song hit written by Willard Robison and performed by Earl Burnett's Los Angeles Hotel Biltmore Orchestra. The words are sung by the male Biltmore Trio, actually a quartet of negligible distinction.

Later, slithering over to Anita like a cobra, Thomson, the self-styled "expert" at judging women, pulls flattery from his bag of tricks. He informs the gullible backwoodswoman that her rare beauty entitles her to rapid advancement up the show business ladder—with his invaluable help, of course. As a means of further documenting his love, he presents her with a diamond bracelet and promise to give her a Rolls Royce and Park Avenue apartment of her own.

As expected, Anita's awareness of the countless benefits to be derived from kept womanhood far outweighs the fear of the stigma attached to it. Returning to her hotel room at 5 the next morning, she delights in showing off the bracelet to her thoroughly dejected sister, who realizes that her evening prayer to God to help Anita "stay on the right path" will not be answered satisfactorily. Adding to Bessie's disillusionment is Anita's eagerness to engage in verbal fisticuffs to defend what she terms her right to get "everything in the world I want," regardless of the method.

Goodbye, Broadway. The opening night of "Zanfield's Revue" features a cluster of about 30 pretty and proficient tap and ballet dancers who accompany James Burroughs's singing of "The Wedding of the Painted Doll," one of the more delightful novelty tunes of the late twenties. Relying more on acrobatics than artistry for effect, the production number is quite professional for the time. The sequence was to have been released in two-strip Technicolor, as were many individual scenes in other 1929 films, but disappointed by the shoddy results, MGM production chief Irving Thalberg ordered that it be converted to black and white.

Immediately following the song, the Mahoneys sing and dance to the skittish and wholly lackluster number "The Boy Friend," while Bessie strums a ukelele. Despite the girls' trademark wrapping of arms around each other, their feud over Thomson continues to rankle both, as well as King, who ratchets up the controversy by warning Anita that marriage is the last thing on the playboy's mind. Even after King forces her to admit that she loves only him, Anita insists that she will keep her cardboard lover's latest gift of a fur coat and move into her own subsidized Park Avenue apartment to boot.

Actually sparked in part to fend off further romancing by King and send him back into Bessie's arms, Anita's intoxication with Thomson upsets King far more than the young lady had anticipated. He turns for consolation to Bessie, who now realizes that her chances for stardom are as bleak as King's romancing her ever again. In fact, she is willing to sacrifice both dreams for the good of King and her sister, and she urges him stand up like a man and claim Anita as his own. Jealous enough to kill Thomson, or at least make him "suffer as he has made me suffer," King accepts the challenge and vows to confront his sleazy rival. Shortly after he leaves, Bessie telephones Prouty to accept his 30-week offer. Her agent uncle is not seen during the conversation, only a closeup of Bebe's Pagliacci-like face, tears of desperation cutting squiggly paths through her makeup. Adept at projecting inner turmoil by facial expression and voice modulation, Bessie alternately displays intense disappointment over her career and marriage setbacks and lost hope for a bright show business future.

Although not so powerful a "telephone scene" as Luise Rainer's expanded version in MGM's *The Great Ziegfeld*, it clearly foreshadows it and succeeds in lifting *Melody* to its dramatic apex. To cement the new arrangement with her uncle, Bessie agrees to team up with Flo (Mary Doran), a blonde singer whom she had earlier pummeled in a hair-pulling contest at the theater. The two may still be carrying on a Hatfield and McCoy relationship, but Bessie intends to do her best to convey the illusion of a happy show biz partnership.

In her new apartment Anita is undergoing a reformation totally in tune with late 1920s morality. Feeling estranged from King and Bessie, and lonely amid the splendor of her new surroundings, she rejects Thomson's advances, shouting that he can take back his baubles and look elsewhere for a lover. Turning angry, he reasserts his claim to her and demands that she agree to be his mistress. A struggle ensues, and Anita is unable to extricate herself from his clutches.

An ally comes to her rescue in the person of King, who attacks Thomson. In a unique reversal of the conventional fight between good and evil, a quick right to the jaw drops King to the floor, where he suffers further humiliation by being ejected from the apartment by two of Thomson's boorish bullies. He is comforted in the corridor by Anita, however, who offers him sympathy tinged with admiration for his attempted heroism. She accepts his declaration of eternal love, happy at last to be relieved of further contact with Thomson.

A short time later, fresh from their honeymoon, Anita and King reappear in Bessie's hotel room. All three have reconciled their differences. Her ambition hardened by adversity into rock-ribbed determination to succeed at making a comeback, Bessie bears no grudge against either her sister or her former boyfriend. She most likely never really loved him anyway, and is sincerely pleased at her sister's deliverance from evil. Anita announces that she has quit the stage, content to trade in the life of a vagabond for the tamer one of suburban housewife.

Into the room comes Mary Doran, Bessie's new "bimbo" partner, the feathers of her florid dress flapping with every step. She promptly intensifies Bessie's contempt by suggesting to King that he keep her in mind for a part in his next show. The two girls then perform a spirited reprise of "Harmony Babies" that is no worse than the Bessie-Anita original. Nor is it any better, suggesting (1) that Mary is as poor a singer and dancer as Anita, and (2) that Bessie's musical talents have not improved very much despite her having acquired a smidgen of Broadway exposure.

The final scene shows Bessie and Uncle Prouty, seated uncomfortably in a cramped back seat of a taxicab, on their way to the railroad station, where she is to embark for Peoria, the first leg on her decidedly non-triumphant return to her entertainment roots. Emotionally scarred, she stoically insists to Prouty that she'll be back in New York "in six months." But for the present, she concedes, it's surely "better to star in Oshkosh than starve on Broadway." Whether Bessie's fierce ambition will make it possible for her to overcome the demotion and replant her feet on the road to glory is left to the viewer to decide. A ground-level view of Times Square, where, according to the title song, millions of lights flicker and the hearts of hopefuls beat a little quicker, marks the end of the film.

But, as Prouty had explained to Anita in the previous hotel room scene, show biz "troupers are all tramps," without home, family, or much of anything else to call their own. Bessie "never had a real break," he continued, but she is bound to get one—eventually. "She'll be much happier on the road," he assured Anita. "That's her life, the only life she can live."

Never again would a backstage-based musical film close on a more bittersweet note, or more dramatically underscore the truism that happiness postponed is not necessarily happiness lost. Chances are pretty good that Bessie will make the grade the next time around.

The Hollywood Revue of 1929 (1929)

A Metro-Goldwyn-Mayer picture. DIRECTOR: Charles F. Reisner; ASSISTANTS: Jack Cummings, Sandy Roth, and Al Shenberg. PRODUCER: Harry Rapf. DIALOGUE WRITERS: Al Boasberg, Joe Farnham, and Robert E. Hopkins. FILM EDITORS: William S. Gray and Cameron K. Wood. CINEMATOGRAPHERS: John Arnold, Irving Ries, Maximilian Fabian, and John M. Nickolaus. ART DIRECTORS: Cedric Gibbons and Richard Day. CHOREOGRAPHERS: Sammy Lee and George Cunningham. SOUND: Douglas Shearer, Russell Franks, William Clark, Wesley Miller, and A.T. Taylor. COSTUMES: David Cox, Henrietta Fraser, and Joe Rapf. MUSICAL ARRANGERS: Arthur Lange, Ernest Klapholtz, and Ray Heindorf. MUSIC: Various lyricists and composers, including Arthur Freed and Nacio Herb Brown. RUNNING TIME: 1 hour and 56 minutes. *Principal Performers (as themselves, in alphabetical order):* Nils Asther, Lionel Barrymore, Joan Crawford, Marion Davies,

Marie Dressler, Cliff Edwards, Gus Edwards, John Gilbert, Oliver Hardy, Buster Keaton, Charles King, Stan Laurel, Bessie Love, Polly Moran, Anita Page, and Norma Shearer. Jack Benny and Conrad Nagle: Masters of Ceremonies. *Major Academy Award Nominations:* Best Picture; Art Direction.

From their inception, Hollywood's talking pictures drew heavily from the Broadway theater, as well as nightclubs, burlesque, and vaudeville, for material and inspiration. According to Edwin M. Bradley's excellent coverage of *The First Hollywood Musicals*, 62, or 36 percent, of 171 musical features from *The Jazz Singer* (1927) to the end of 1932 were based on plays, dramatic and musical, most of them produced in New York and more than a few of pre-World War I vintage.

So it was a natural consequence of the arrival of sound stages that the moguls or their representatives, many of whom had not anticipated the public's quick, almost unanimous fascination with the talkies, would embark on trips back East for recruiting purposes. What they deliberately sought was the long-term loan of performers with experience in reciting dialogue and singing lyrics, as well as the professionals who wrote their words, decorated the productions with attractive sets and costumes, and whipped what had begun as vague concepts into finished products in presentable film format.

And there they went, scouring the sidewalks of New York, bringing back to their entertainment factories cadres of performers, songwriters, librettists, and choreographers (then called dance directors), who reconstituted the industry's silent "shadow plays" into the semi-respectable talk-a-thons and sing-alongs of the late twenties. That most of the expatriate Easterners had little or no acquaintance with films failed to concern the studio heads. All of the newcomers were accustomed to dealing with audible dialogue, and that was exactly what the movies needed if they were to successfully compete with Broadway and touring companies for box office revenues. Quite a few of their movies had failed on stage, but that mattered little. No studio expected to produce hits of the magnitude of *No, No, Nanette, The Desert Song, Rio Rita, Show Boat,* or *Good News* every time out. Even Broadway was rarely able to outdo itself.

No better than their Great White Way counterparts at devising sure-fire gimmicks to unerringly separate the wheat of inspiration from the chaff of mediocrity, the moguls gleefully went on picking up properties and then picking them apart in hopes of satisfying the less critical movie audiences. Chances, they assumed, were pretty good that even the least distinguished of their films would at least resonate with occasional professional touches inserted by their experienced creators. Actually, very few did.

At the end of 1929, Irving Berlin, Walter Donaldson, Richard A. Whiting, Vincent Youmans, James F. Hanley, Harry Tierney, Ralph Rainger, James V. Monaco, and the trio of [Buddy] DeSylva, [Lew] Brown, and [Ray] Henderson were among the Broadway-based composers working feverishly in the studios' stables. Jolson had made history with *The Jazz Singer,* based on the 1925 Broadway play by Samson Raphaelson and starring George Jessel. Also from the stage and other entertainment media came Fanny Brice, Sophie Tucker, "Texas" Guinan, the Four Marx Brothers, Helen Morgan, John Boles, Bing Crosby, Charles and Dennis King, Jeanette MacDonald, and Gertrude Lawrence.

Some of the biggest silent picture stars had learned their craft on the legitimate stage, but they were far less numerous than the legion of personalities who responded to the allure of the talkies. The three Barrymores alternated between New York and Hollywood throughout the teens and twenties. Valentino and Lon Chaney appeared in roadshow musicals before falling in the lap of luxury and adulation, courtesy of motion pictures. And movie versions of stage pieces were not exactly unknown in pre-1927 Hollywood, especially the classics, such as *Hamlet.* Possibly because no author's royalties were involved, the Shakespeare drama was filmed no fewer than 12 times before 1920.

With their chorus lines, solo singers, and off-screen instrumentalists, musicals naturally presented more challenges than dramas to the new school of movie makers. Although a handful from Broadway had been made into silents, like Donaldson's *Kid Boots* and Sigmund Romberg's *The Student Prince,* they were outshone by talking pictures, which permitted performers or their dubbers to sing from sound

Charles King, left, Joan Crawford, Conrad Nagle, and Cliff ("Ukulele Ike") Edwards were only four of the headliners in MGM's all-star *The Hollywood Revue of 1929*.

tracks. From about January of 1929 to June of 1930, studios and fans became so enamored of this innovation that Hollywood poured musicals out at a furious clip in the mistaken belief that the public would never tire of listening to songs and still more songs, watching chorus girls cavort to them and handsome crooners and beautiful ladies pledge their love with them. As was so often the case, the moguls were wrong. In order to cater to what they sensed was an insatiable demand for operettas, musical comedies, and backstagers, they released such an overwhelming glut of second-rate musicals that the public finally rebelled and, made even more money-conscious by the ravages of the Depression, temporarily relegated song-and-dance films to the back burner of their creative departments.

Also unfortunate in the 1929-30 period was the studios' casting many of their own leftover stars from the silent era in new blockbusters in an attempt to boost their sagging popularity. The oldtimers' transition to talking pictures rarely succeeded, and the inability of many to adapt to the new technology denied them additional opportunities to learn the tricks of the trade. In company with their Broadway colleagues, they were soon either dismissed outright or given small parts in later minor talkies as a sort of gratuity for past services.

The Hollywood Revue of 1929 is a telling example of the film capital's frenzy to rush musicals into production to take advantage of what was perceived as a huge demand for them. Teams of directors, screenwriters, cinematographers (better known as directors of photography), and songwriters were quickly assembled to cobble them out without recourse to differentiating one plot from another or the latest hero and heroine from those who had preceded them. The result was that, of all of Hollywood's Dark Age productions, the musicals most closely resemble what later generations would consider to be the Theater of the Absurd. Only a small percentage were granted sufficient time to improve on their source material or display very much originality.

Reflective of Its Era. Despite the production challenges it faced, *The Hollywood Revue of 1929* is, if not a polished gem, a diamond in the rough that both mirrored its era and helped greatly to influence the all-star musical pictures produced throughout much of the succeeding two decades. This sometimes charming antique began showing its age not very long after its release that June, slightly more than four months after MGM's sturdier *The Broadway Melody*. Offering priceless glimpses into the typically trite vaudeville turns of late twenties comedians, dancers, singers, and "straight" men—those successors of the old minstrel show interlocutors—it is easily the best of the early textless extravaganzas that depended solely on star power, ballads and novelties, and two-strip Technicolor to attract huge audiences.

In his August 18, 1929, review, the *New York Times'* chief film critic, Mordaunt Hall, found that *Revue* "trots gayly along from beginning to end with a wonderful fund of amusement, and its clever and lavish staging is enhanced by imaginative camera work." At times a "trifle amateurish" and not above inserting slapstick here and there, the film seemed to Hall to be aimed primarily at the folks seated in the gallery of the Astor Theatre rather than those in the orchestra. But, he added, all the stars contributed to keeping the "pot of fun simmering throughout the whole show." Much of the material, displayed in specialty acts, was greeted by roars of laughter from the first-night audience. A September critique in the same newspaper by Brooks Atkinson, then bylined as J. Brooks Atkinson, also looked with favor on the MGM movie while pointing out the obvious inability of vaudeville movies to duplicate the intimacy between live performer and audience that exists in regular theatrical presentations in legitimate houses.

Not the first in this pioneering series of musicals, *Revue* faced stiff competition from Warner Bros.' *Gold Diggers of Broadway* and

Show of Shows, and Fox's *Movietone Follies*, also released in 1929, and Universal's *The King of Jazz* and Paramount's *Paramount on Parade*, both of which traveled the movie house circuit beginning in mid-April 1930. The moguls had surely latched onto a briefly winning formula for attracting customers, which by its very nature was not predestined to last very long. Moviegoers of the time might well have tired of watching musicals with warmed-over plots and copycat dialogue while patiently awaiting the next song or dance, but the strain of sitting through a feature picture without any story line at all became even more monotonous.

Too many songs were inserted into these diversions, and exceedingly few of them merited the attention of "Singin' in the Rain." To fill out their usual 90-minute running time, many timeworn songs—Harry Dacre's "A Bicycle Built for Two" and Joe Young, Sam M. Lewis and M.K. Jerome's "Rock-a-Bye Your Baby with a Dixie Melody"—were interpolated, along with numerous minor tunes written on the spot by largely undistinguished lyricists and composers, placed at random throughout the pictures, and performed mostly in amateurish fashion by even the most professional of the stars. Here and there a catchy phrase is discernible, but on average the songs show the effects of being written at record speed to meet tight production deadlines.

The skits typically lacked originality, especially to persons who frequented vaudeville houses, and although often repeated on screen by experienced two-a-day headliners, the performers' lack of intimacy with the essentials of movie acting is sometimes painful to watch. In fact, very few of the household-name stage actors and actresses who appeared in these extravaganzas were given the chance to develop into movie stars; by mid-1930 both they and their plotless pictures had disappeared from movie houses.

Superstar spectacles would not return to the screen till the first Big Broadcast serial musical in 1932 revived the tradition of stacking celebrities from radio, the stage and opera to cabarets and concert halls one atop the other in much the same manner as Ed Sullivan would at the dawn of the television variety show almost two decades later. Predating Sullivan's role as master of ceremonies were Jack Benny and Conrad Nagle (in *The Hollywood Revue*), comedian Frank Fay (in *Show of Shows*), Leon Errol, Skeets [Richard] Gallagher, and Jack Oakie (in *Paramount on Parade*), and bandleader Paul Whiteman in *King of Jazz*. As with the Ben Vereen character in *All That Jazz* some half-century later, the excessive praise that rolls off the tongues of these celebrity introducers tends to reek with insincerity, detracting from rather than enhancing the acknowledged talents of the crowd-pleasers these two pitchmen were assigned to highlight.

Throughout much of the thirties, Movieland was enamored of such ephemera as Paramount's *Big Broadcast of 1937*, with songs by Leo Robin and Ralph Rainger and a huge cast that included Leopold Stokowski, Larry Adler, Benny Fields, Shirley Ross, Bob Burns, Benny Goodman, George Burns and Gracie Allen, and Martha Raye. In the forties the third tidal wave of all-star extravaganzas flooded movie houses with the onset of World War II. As in days of yore, the best of the lot, Warner Bros.' *Thank Your Lucky Stars*, MGM's *Thousands Cheer,* Universal's *Follow the Boys*, and Paramount's *Star Spangled Rhythm*, interpolated songs and sketches into weak but vastly popular films that centered for the most part on the struggles of professional entertainers to put on a show for servicemen and women.

Updating Yesteryear. Like its sister films, *The Hollywood Revue of 1929* found its inspiration on Broadway, but it was the Broadway of Florenz Ziegfeld and John Murray Anderson, who for years had been inviting vaudevillians into their stage revues and glamorizing their routines by adding spectacular lighting, costumes and scenery, which the vaudeville theaters could never hope to emulate. The first edition of the *Ziegfeld Follies*, in 1907, consisted of set pieces performed by veteran vaudeville comedians and musical numbers by top-drawer musical comedy stars, backed up by the producer's typical battalions of garishly garbed hoofers. The formula clicked, encouraging Ziegfeld to add the Midnight Frolics and Nine O'Clock Revues to his roster of annual

confections. Their success attracted an assortment of rivals into the arena, each quite similar in format but rarely fearsome as Follies competitors, such as producer Ned Wayburn's *Town Topics*; the Shuberts' *Passing Shows*, *Music Box Revues*, and *Artists and Models*; George White's *Scandals*; Earl Carroll's *Vanities* and *Sketch Book*; and the *Hitchy Coo*, *Greenwich Village Follies*, *Cotton Club*, and *Little Show* series.

Since it was produced by MGM, *The Hollywood Revue of 1929* was expected to outdistance its competitors in the all-important areas of spectacle, stars, songs, and script. Curiously, the result was a mixed bag of virtues and flaws. All six of the major extravaganzas proudly showed off their studios' two-strip Technicolor processes, but MGM's was no clearer or brighter than the others. Nor was it used throughout, as happened with *Gold Diggers of Broadway*, *The Show of Shows*, and *The King of Jazz*, being confined largely to the impressive "Orange Blossom Time" finale. Even the infrequent expertise displayed by some of its many stars was unable to salvage hopelessly unfunny skits. Indeed, it still surprises to witness that proud Culver City institution's dismal crusade to reverse the decline of vaudeville by perpetuating the worst of it. Rather than lifting it back into favor, *Revue* helped to hasten its death.

Revue's artistic slipshoddiness is all the more disappointing when one realizes the immense talent, either on the bud or in full flower, at MGM's disposal. The cast of behind-the-camera specialists and performers reads like an honor roll of Hollywood's best, even though the former were shortchanged from doing their very best by only scant familiarity with talking musicals and the latter by the faulty material handed to them. Director Charles F. Reisner, a one-time film comedian and screenwriter, piloted 11 pictures before *Revue* and 27 afterward, up to 1950. Assistant director Jack Cummings would later produce MGM musicals of the caliber of *Born to Dance* (1936), *The Broadway Melody of 1940*, *Three Little Words* (1950), *Kiss Me Kate* (1953), and the best musical nominee *Seven Brides for Seven Brothers*.

Co-choreographer Sammy Lee, who had directed the dances for the original 1927 *Show*

Boat, would continue contributing his talent to many later musical films for practically all of the major studios. Also at the threshold of their talking picture careers were musical arrangers Arthur Lange, soon to win Oscars for *The Great Ziegfeld* and *The Great Victor Herbert* (1939), and Ray Heindorf, another future recipient of Academy Awards for *Yankee Doodle Dandy*, *This Is the Army* (1943), and *The Music Man*. Also on hand were the always reliable Cedric Gibbons, designer of the Oscar statuette, and Douglas Shearer, brother of actress Norma. Then as later absolute masters of their craft, they would win 23 Academy Awards between them for art direction and sound recording up to the mid-fifties.

The appearance of Marie Dressler, who sings Andy Rice and Martin Broones's inconsequential "For I'm the Queen," for instance, did little to enhance the reputation of that grand old symbol of the clownish but aspiring lady aristocrat deprived of full membership in the upper echelons of society by her snide outspokenness. Her long and varied career had included stardom as a turn-of-the-century vaudeville trouper and a brilliant movie debut alongside Charlie Chaplin in *Tillie's Punctured Romance* in 1914, which was based on one of her earlier legitimate stage successes. Two post-1929 best actress nominations were to follow, one for *Min and Bill* (1933), which she won, the other for *Emma*, which eluded her in favor of Helen Hayes as Madelon in *The Sin of Madelon Claudet*.

Marie fared better in her joint effort with Bessie Love, Charles King, Cliff and Gus Edwards, and Polly Moran on the slightly more amusing and tuneful "Marie, Polly and Bess," by Joe Goodwin and Gus Edwards. The song marked her first association with one-time vaudeville comedienne Polly, with whom she would co-star in five lighthearted film flings from late 1929 to 1933, the year that Marie ranked number one on the "Top Ten" list of Hollywood's biggest moneymaking stars (Will Rogers was second). Joining her on the list were five other MGM stars: Wallace Beery (in fifth place), Jean Harlow (sixth), Clark Gable (seventh), and two of Marie's *Revue* co-stars, Norma Shearer (ninth), and Joan Crawford (tenth). Dressler's third song, Ed Haley and Robert A. Keiser's "While Strolling through the

Park One Day," is also performed in company with Polly, along with Cliff and Gus Edwards, Bessie Love, and Charles King.

Buster Keaton's cameo appearance alongside a submarine in *Revue's* "Dance of the Sea" sequence skirted total disaster only by its brevity. One of silent Hollywood's greatest comedians—and acrobats—he was given little chance to indicate his adaptability to sound, even though his stony, noncommital face, worthy of inclusion on Mount Rushmore, remained intact to good effect. Keaton was still another graduate of vaudeville, which, like George M. Cohan, he joined as a member of his family's act while still a child. He continued making films well into the mid-sixties, sinking along the way into gradual oblivion, no doubt helped along by the pitiful 1957 "biographical" film, *The Buster Keaton Story*, with Donald O'Connor in the title role.

Similarly appearing to disadvantage were Stan Laurel [Arthur Stanley Jefferson] and Oliver Hardy [Oliver Norvell Hardy, Jr.], the movies' still unsurpassed comedy duo. Apart from two minor films, *Lucky Day* (1917) and *45 Minutes from Hollywood* (1926), in which both appeared but not as a team, they co-starred in more than 100 silent and sound shorts and 27 feature-length films between 1927 and 1950. Troupers that they were, the boys did their best in the unmemorable "Magicians" skit, which provides few chuckles from start to finish.

Although she was a passable but minor musical performer who had once won a Charleston contest, Joan Crawford [Lucille Fay Le Sueur] was to enter the ranks of Hollywood's most highly adaptable actresses by virtue of alternating from gloom to doom in a wide range of dramatic parts, as her Oscar-winning performance in *Mildred Pierce* was to verify in 1945. The spirited personification of mid-twenties misguided youth, she developed into the talkies' archetypal femme fatale, first as the scheming working girl with an over-ambitious agenda of goals, then as the lonely mature woman desperately seeking true love, and finally as the harridan victimized by revenge-minded persons she had once alienated. Her portrayals were usually excellent, something that no one in the *Revue* audience would suspect.

Her appearance in the singing and dancing routine "Gotta Feelin' for You" was notable only for introducing the first screen song composed by Louis Alter, recently made famous by virtue of his six-minute instrumental "Manhattan Serenade," a section of which became a vastly popular song in 1942 after Harold Adamson added a lyric to it. Alter later would receive two Academy Award nominations, losing each time to Jerome Kern, for "A Melody from the Sky" in 1936 and "Dolores" in 1941.

Also faring poorly was Marion Davies, a former Ziegfeld girl and still paramour of William Randolph Hearst, whose participation in "Tommy Atkins on Parade" was an early example of MGM's tendency to camouflage faulty production values by overwhelming the eyes and ears with fanciful pyrotechnics so bloated as to appear ridiculous. The song itself is also a forgettable contribution on the part of Arthur Freed and Nacio Herb Brown, who were certainly capable of far better work. As if to indicate the wide range of special effects available to the studios, Miss Davies appears with a chorus of men dressed as Grenadier Guards. At first merely a lilliputian among brobdingnagian soldiers, she subsequently grows up to natural size. The same effect is used when Bessie Love is introduced as a tiny figure who is lodged in the pocket where Jack Benny keeps his walking-around money. The miniature actress steps out of the pocket and is soon exhibited in her normal height on the palm of Benny's hand.

Even less distinguished in their *Revue* appearances were the studio's dramatic stars. Lionel Barrymore, soon to win the Oscar for best actor as Stephen Ashe in *A Free Soul* (1931), is adequate in his brief sequence as a crotchety authoritarian figure, a part he would perfect over the next two decades, especially as Dr. Gillespie in the Dr. Kildare series. Almost totally wasted is Nils Asther, who not that much earlier had co-starred with Joan Crawford (in *Our Dancing Daughters*, 1928) and with fellow Swede Greta Garbo (in *Wild Orchids*, 1929). On the downside of his career when *Revue* opened, his gig failed to reverse his fortunes, although in 1933 his last hit picture, *The Bitter Tea of General Yen*, was se

lected as the first movie to be shown on the screen of the newly opened Radio City Music Hall.

Norma Shearer was an attractive and talented MGM star from 1927 to 1942. A six-time nominee for best actress (she would win the award in 1930 as Jerry in *The Divorcée*), she was the wife of Irving Thalberg, MGM's wunderkind, and therefore entitled by marriage to prominence in any of the studio's all-star bonanzas. In *Revue* she does manage to maintain viewer interest in a respectable rendering of the balcony scene from *Romeo and Juliet*. With partner John Gilbert, whose weak speaking voice ended his movie career soon after the talkies replaced the silents, she engages in an often amusing attempt to recite her lines despite constant interruptions from *A Chorus Line* type of director (Lionel Barrymore) who is dissatisfied with their performances and demands that they speak the dialogue in colloquial English. In a curious twist of Movieland fate, Miss Shearer would play Juliet seven years later, at age 36, opposite 43-year-old Leslie Howard, in MGM's stunning version of the Shakespeare drama, for which she received her fifth Academy Award nomination.

Whether *Revue*'s respectable lineup of movie stars was the most impressive among the six blockbusters is debatable. It certainly bested those who appeared in *Gold Diggers of Broadway* and *Fox Movietone Follies,* neither of which featured a single performer bearing impressive credentials, either in 1929 or since. Far more competitive were *The Show of Shows* (with John Barrymore, Douglas Fairbanks, Jr., bandleader-singer Ted Lewis, Beatrice Lillie, Myrna Loy, Chester Morris, canine superstar Rin Tin Tin, Ann Southern [then known as Harriette Lake], Ben Turpin, and Loretta Young); *Paramount on Parade* (Jean Arthur, Mischa Auer, Clara Bow, Virginia Bruce, Maurice Chevalier, Gary Cooper, Kay Francis, Fredric March, William Powell, and Lillian Roth); and *The King of Jazz* (John Boles, Walter Brennan, the future winner of three Oscars as best supporting actor, Bing Crosby, one-time Keystone Cop Slim Summerville, and Paul Whiteman).

Hit of the Score. With 17 songs by 14 lyricists and composers, *Revue* fell about midway between the seven in *Fox Movietone Follies* and the almost 20 in *King of Jazz*, which included excerpts from George Gershwin's five-year-old "Rhapsody in Blue." None of the *Revue* songs—or any from its five rivals—has managed to triumph over the test of time as well as "Singin' in the Rain," the movie's sole song success. Admittedly, this still well-known Freed and Brown tune has received booster shots over succeeding years, ranging from Judy Garland's rendition in *Little Nellie Kelly* (1940) to the magnificent Gene Kelly version in the 1952 MGM film of the same name, to sustain its popularity. *Gold Diggers of Broadway* managed to debut two popular but transitory ditties, the often-ridiculed "Tip-Toe through the Tulips (with Me)" and "Painting the Clouds with Sunshine," both by Al Dubin and Joe Burke and sung by recording star Nick Lucas. From *The King of Jazz* came Billy Rose and Mabel Wayne's pretty "It Happened in Monterey" and Jack Yellen and Milton Ager's "The Song of the Dawn," both sung by John Boles. Thanks to Chevalier, Sam Coslow's "Sweepin' the Clouds Away" captured the fancy of music fans—briefly— in *Paramount on Parade*.

Although intimately identified with dancer Kelly over the past four and one-half decades, "Singin' in the Rain" was performed in *Revue* by Cliff Edwards, better known as "Ukulele Ike," along with an awkward assortment of MGM chorus girls wearing raincoats and the Brox Sisters, who also appeared momentarily in *The King of Jazz*. After singing his way through a few more musical pictures, Edwards joined the ranks of supporting actor in numerous dramas, including a bit part as a wounded Confederate soldier in *Gone with the Wind*. In 1941, as the off-screen voice of Jiminy Crickett in Disney's *Pinocchio*, Edwards introduced the year's winning movie song, "When You Wish Upon a Star."

Like Charles King, Bessie Love, Anita Page, and James Burroughs, Freed and Brown's "You Were Meant for Me" was carried over from *The Broadway Melody* into the all-star revue, where it is mouthed by Conrad Nagle using King's voice. Nagle, a co-founder of the American Academy of Motion Picture Arts and Sciences, was one of MGM's smoothest dramatic stars, equipped with a mellifluous speaking voice and the looks of a distinguished statesman. Star of such prestigious silent dramas as *Quality Street*

(1927) and *Glorious Betsy* (1928), he was definitely out of place in a bantam-weight musical, serving as co-introducer of the various acts, and easily outshone by Jack Benny in his feature-movie debut.

But even Benny, despite intimations of the trademark stance and gestures of a genuinely inspired comedian, seems embarrassed when called upon to utter a nonsensical introductory sentence or two. He would make his radio debut on May 2, 1931, on the *Ed Sullivan Show*. By the end of the next year, he was firmly ensconced as a master comedian on his own weekly program—the fellow who remained a perpetual 39 years old (he was 35 when *Revue* was released), refused to replace his ancient Maxwell motor car, kept his money locked in a vault in the basement of his house, and scratched out melodies on his out-of-tune violin.

The other Edwards in the cast—Gus— wrote seven of the *Revue* songs and participates in the delivery of four of them. Of surprisingly weak caliber for the man who had written such admirable chestnuts as "School Days," "Sunbonnet Sue," "By the Light of the Silvery Moon," "In My Merry Oldsmobile," and "If I Were a Millionaire," his *Revue* tunes included "I Never Knew I Could Do a Thing Like That," "Minstrel Days," "Nobody but You," the mandatory mammy song, "Your Mother and Mine," a sentimental nightmare sung by Charles King, "Lon Chaney's Going to Get You, If You Don't Watch Out," and the aforementioned "Marie, Polly and Bess" and "Orange Blossom Time." A most discerning judge of talent, Gus Edwards was responsible for handing out the first big break to a host of wannabe entertainers, including the Duncan Sisters, whose lives may well have provided the story for *The Broadway Melody*, and future MGM stars Eleanor Powell and Ray Bolger.

Ranking second in supplying the most new *Revue* songs was another established composer, Fred Fisher. Like Gus, Fred was hardly at the pinnacle of his powers in 1929, as his "Bones and Tambourines," "Strike Up the Band" (not to be confused with the Gershwin march), and "Tableaux of Jewels" prove. But he could console himself with the knowledge that many of his earlier compositions—"Come, Josephine, in My Flying Machine," "Chicago," "Dardanella,"

"And the Band Played On," and "Oui Oui, Marie"—would continue to uphold his reputation as a superior writer of perennially popular songs from the pre-1920 era. Another song, "Low Down Rhythm," was a minor effort on the part of partners Raymond Klages and Jesse Greer, who nonetheless scored a major victory by writing "Just You, Just Me," one of 1929's better-remembered tunes, which appeared originally in *Blondy*.

With all its faults, *The Hollywood Revue of 1929* is well worth viewing by anyone lucky enough to find it listed in the daily roundups of television programs. One of the four best picture nominees yet to be transferred to videocassette, the film is definitely the kind that Hollywood doesn't make any more and never will again. It is for this reason that *Revue* qualifies as both historic and unique in the annals of the American film.

The Love Parade (1930)

A Paramount picture. DIRECTOR: Ernst Lubitsch. PRODUCER: Ernst Lubitsch. SCREENWRITER: Guy Bolton. STORY: Ernest Vajda, based on the play *Le Prince Consort*, by Léon Xanrof and Jules Chancel. DIALOGUE DIRECTOR: Perry Ivins. CINEMATOGRAPHER: Victor Milner. FILM EDITOR: Merrill White. ART DIRECTOR: Hans Dreier. SOUND: Franklin Hansen. COSTUMES: Travis Banton. MUSICAL DIRECTOR: Victor Schertzinger. SONGS: Lyrics by Clifford Grey, music by Victor Schertzinger. RUNNING TIME: 1 hour, 52 minutes. *Principal Players:* Maurice Chevalier (Count Alfred Renard). Jeanette MacDonald (Queen Louise). Lupino Lane (Jacques). Lillian Roth (Lulu). Eugene Pallette (Minister of War). Lionel Belmore (Prime Minister). Carl Stockdale (Admiral). *Academy Award Nominations*: Best Picture, Director, Actor (*Maurice Chevalier*), Cinematography, Art Director, Sound.

For the only time in Academy Award history, three musicals produced by the same studio and starring the same actor, Maurice Chevalier, were nominated for best picture for three consecutive years. Released between November 1929 and March 1932, the Paramount films in fact were the only musicals to receive the nomination during that three-year period. The first, *The Love Parade*, was so crammed with delights that it is a fit competitor with *The Broadway Melody* for landmark designation as the best and most prestigious movie musical between *The Jazz Singer* and *42nd Street*.

Overlooking its technical deficiencies, the natural byproducts of being released while talking pictures were still in their infancy, it exudes craftsmanship at every single level. The first musical best picture candidate to receive more than three Oscar nominations, *The Love Parade* failed to win in any of the six categories in which it was entered, but that was to be expected when its chief competitor for major honors was *All Quiet on the Western Front*, which won the best picture award for Universal and the best director award for Lewis Milestone. Winning as best actor that year was George Arliss for his peerless performance as British Prime Minister Benjamin Disraeli in Warner Bros.' *Disraeli*. Like Arliss, Chevalier received best actor nomination for his role in two 1929–30 films. The other one was as Pierre Mirande in *The Big Pond;* Arliss' second nomination cited his appearance as the tongue-twisting Oxonian, the Rajah of Rukh, in *The Green Goddess*.

As with most Hollywood films between late 1927 and early 1930, *The Love Parade* was shipped to movie houses in one of two versions. Silent prints went to theaters that had not been wired for sound, all-talking prints to houses equipped to handle them. Since the immense popularity of *The Love Parade* was derived largely from the caliber of its songs and often witty and risqué dialogue, it is doubtful that viewers of the silent version could really appreciate its rare quality. Yet, considering that Ernst Lubitsch's silent version of *Lady Windemere's Fan* (1925) had achieved distinction as a comedy of manners without invoking slapstick to compensate for the lack of Oscar Wilde's aphoristic dialogue testified to the master director's uniqueness at turning out classic films under difficult circumstances that would inhibit others from even attempting such a project. Lubitsch did the same two years later with *The Student Prince*, which though shorn of the score (except in the background), he was able to turn into an utterly charming story of love between a young nobleman and a peasant girl. Alone among directors of the time, Lubitsch was as adept at making musical pictures as he was at straight comedies.

Born in Berlin, Germany, he began his career as a comedian, gradually proving his virtuosity by writing and then occupying the

The object of two ladies' affections, Maurice Chevalier finds it difficult to choose between Jeanette Mac-Donald, left, and Lillian Roth in *The Love Parade.*

director's chair while with the Bioscope film studio. Concentrating on directing shorts and features beginning in 1914, he acquired an international reputation only four years later with *The Eyes of the Mummy* (*Die Augen der Mummie Ma*) and *Gypsy Blood* (*Carmen*), both starring Poli Negri. The first inkling of his gift for satire appeared in *The Oyster Princess* (*Die Austern-prinzessin*) in 1919, in which he ridiculed American manners that he felt were hypocritical. He was to zero in on the same theme throughout his years in Hollywood, which began in 1923 with *Rosita*, treating character defects particularly among the idle well-to-do as comedy rather than tragedy.

Few other directors of the time matched his mildly caustic commentaries on contemporary life, which often involved the rituals of courtship between two sophisticates angling to add to their individual fortunes by merging them through marriage. He eschewed coarse-

ness in his exposés, however, always relying on cool detachment rather than the crusader's zeal to right all wrongs. Subtlety, which in his musicals turned suggestiveness into an art and gave substance to his style, was one of the most cherished hallmarks of all his pictures. Besides firming up the shaky foundation on which most of his screenplays rested, that all-important commodity underwent improvement over time, culminating in such films as *The Merry Widow* (1934), also with Chevalier and Jeanette Mac-Donald; *Bluebeard's Eighth Wife* (1938), with Gary Cooper and Claudette Colbert; *Ninotchka* (1939), with Greta Garbo and Melvyn Douglas; and above all *To Be or Not to Be* (1942), with Jack Benny and Carole Lombard as the Polish husband-and-wife acting team, in which he cleverly paired anti-Nazi propaganda with the hilarious sideshow of Benny's erroneous belief that Carole is engaging in love affairs with attractive male members of their audiences.

Despite his fascination with laying bare humankind's romantic and pecuniary frailties, Lubitsch was basically a sentimentalist, more willing to excuse than condemn. His most untypical American film, *The Shop Around the Corner* (1940), is an uncomplicated love story involving two lonely working-class clerks (James Stewart and Margaret Sullivan) in a Budapest leather goods store owned by Frank Morgan. Quite possibly the gentlest romantic comedy on film, it seemed to summarize the Lubitsch philosophy that despite the unwelcome intrusion of schemers into the lives of ordinary people, they who play by the rules of acceptable conduct can find happiness without demeaning themselves in any way. And, like the stern but forgiving father he was, he seems to imply with exultant good humor that that's indeed a beautiful sight to behold!

The Love Parade was Lubitsch's third talking picture for Paramount, which kept him on the payroll throughout most his career. His first, *The Patriot* (1928), had also been nominated for an Academy Award, as would *Heaven Can Wait* 15 years later. It was also the second American film with Maurice Chevalier, the other half of the multi-talented Franco-German partnership, if one skips the humdrum three-reel travelogue, *Bonjour New York!* (1928). Like Lubitsch, Chevalier had appeared in film shorts between 1908 and 1928, when he left France at age 40 for the United States and the leading role of Maurice Marny in Paramount's *Innocents of Paris*. Actually a minor musical with a Lubitsch story, mediocre sets, and stiff acting that resembled amateur night at the local high school, it nonetheless survives as a classic example of how a highly personable performer with one of the most ingratiating smiles in movie history can soar above his material.

Chevalier certainly was capable of measuring up to the demands of his roles, even if they were pretty much the same throughout his early movie career. More the entertainer than the actor, he was possessed of one of the screen's most engaging personalities, and it was his through his charm that he captured and retained his enormous fan following. He could sing and speak dialogue convincingly. After all, he had been France's most celebrated entertainer, a veritable bundle of *joie de vivre*, who

since adolescence had entranced patrons of Parisian music and variety halls and then as partner with the equally legendary Mistinguette at the *Folies-Bergère*. *Innocents of Paris,* in which he was billed as the world's greatest entertainer, belonged solely to Chevalier, since without his presence, it would have quickly evaporated into a curiosity. All of his irresistible Continental mannerisms are on display to advantage—the eyes that twinkle at the sight of a beautiful woman, the swagger that promises her the thrill of romance, the lips that curve into a mischievous little boy pout to tempt her into his arms, the amicable shrug of the shoulders when his advances meet with temporary disfavor—all of it delivered with the temperament of a cultivated man of the world whether playing a common junk dealer or an aristocrat.

Many of Chevalier's French-language signature songs had preceded him across the Atlantic: "Ma Pomme," "Place Pigalle," "A Barcelone," "Valentine," "Un Tout P'Tit Peu," and "Dites-Moi, Ma Mère," the latter by Maurice Yvain, who also composed "My Man." Combined with the singing actor's appearance in some of the finest musicals of the 1929–34 period, these and later tunes provided by American songwriters enabled him to cast a magnetic spell over audiences that few other performers were able to match. The songs became as prominent a part of Hollywood's aural landscape as they were of his own repertoire. In 1928 he was hired by the Chase and Sanborn coffee company to star in its radio variety show at the then unheard salary of $5,000 a week. (In September 1931, Eddie Cantor succeeded him in the starring role.)

Composer of *The Love Parade* songs was Victor Schertzinger, a rare combination of director and songwriter, who had written background music for silent films, including "The Civilization Peace March" for the antiwar *Civilization* in 1916. Best known today for "Marcheta," or possibly "Tangerine," Schertzinger continued writing screen songs up to his death in 1941. Among them was the title song for *One Night of Love*, which, like *The Love Parade*, received a best picture nomination. The lyricist for *The Love Parade* was Clifford Grey, a Britisher who, like Schertzinger, had won acclaim from World War I audiences for the verses to such love songs as "If You Were the

Only Girl in the World," and in the twenties for "The March of the Musketeers" and "Hallelujah."

The Love Parade marked the movie debut of Jeanette MacDonald, a one-time Broadway chorus girl and musical comedy starlet. Lubitsch himself selected her for the role of Queen Louise after viewing her screen test, which actor Richard Dix had recommended to Paramount executives. The film was an auspicious debut for the 28-year-old singing actress, leading to a succession of musical pictures that moved her into the limelight some five years before MGM coupled her with Nelson Eddy for the filmed operettas that brought great fame to both as "America's Sweethearts."

Following *The Love Parade*, Miss Mac-Donald appeared in Rudolf Friml's *The Vagabond King* and disappointing but original *The Lottery Bride* (both 1930) and Jerome Kern's *Cat and the Fiddle* (1934). Again in company with Chevalier, she made *Love Me Tonight* (1932), *One Hour with You*, and *The Merry Widow*, the two co-stars' final outing under Lubitsch's direction. Her third film for Paramount, the superior *Monte Carlo* (1930), ranks with *Love Me Tonight* and *Maytime* (1937) as her finest picture. Produced and directed by Lubitsch, *Monte Carlo* paired Miss MacDonald with Jack Buchanan, that reliable standard bearer of British musical comedy and films, as the count and countess lovers. Together in 1931 they introduced the everlasting hit "Beyond the Blue Horizon," one of the first musical antidotes to the nationwide hopelessness created by the Great Depression.

Chevalier's heftiest acting competitor in *The Love Parade* was not Miss MacDonald, but vivacious 18-year-old Lillian Roth in her second of 11 talking pictures. A one-time child actress on Broadway and in silent films, she lucked out in the part of Lulu the maid by duetting one of the earliest and best of Hollywood's truly comic songs, "Let's Be Common." (Her second number, "Gossip," is almost as good.) Her singing partner for each song, Lupino [Henry] Lane, was a member of a prominent family of English thespians and a distant relative of actress Ida Lupino. Soon to descend into a regrettable life of alcoholism and divorce, Miss Roth was portrayed in the 1956 "autobiographical" film *I'll Cry Tomorrow* by

Susan Hayward, who was nominated for best actress for her sterling performance.

Before dropping out of films in 1933, Miss Roth introduced two very popular 1930 songs, Bert Kalmar and Harry Ruby's "Why Am I So Romantic?," with Harold Thompson in *Animal Crackers*, and Sam Coslow and W. Franke Harling's "Sing You Sinners" in *Honey*. The writer of *The Love Parade* screenplay was Guy Bolton, one of the most prolific and successful musical comedy librettists, who alone or in collaboration was responsible for 50 Broadway and London musical librettos, including *Sally*, *Lady, Be Good!*, *Rio Rita*, and *Anything Goes*. Particularly rewarding to attentive watchers of the film are fleeting glimpses of teenagers Virginia Bruce and Jean Harlow, as well as of silent screen comedian Ben Turpin as a cross-eyed man.

Although *The Hollywood Revue of 1929* is available on lazer disc in both American NTSC and British PAL formats, three other early best picture nominees have yet to be released for home viewing. Besides *The Love Parade*, they include *The Smiling Lieutenant* and *One Hour with You*. With luck, one may catch all but *Lieutenant* on cable television or at movie-revival houses, but such occasions rarely pop up. As regards *Lieutenant*, many parts of it are believed to be irrevocably lost or otherwise impossible to obtain and piece together into a certified whole. Whether an unabridged version exists in any single location is doubtful.

That this picture, regarded as inestimable by contemporary accounts, should have become a victim of such negligence is lamentable. But, along with the presumed loss of numerous other early dramatic and musical pictures, its disappearance underscores the indifference of the studio heads toward safeguarding their own artifacts. Such cavalier treatment was widespread well into the 1930s. If the pictures held up reasonably well to complete their first-run schedules, the executives were content. What happened to them after withdrawal was apparently of slight significance.

Up to about 1950, movies were photographed on nitrate stock, a fragile and volatile substance unfit to guard against the defects of long-term storage. From that year forward, acetate and polyester, known as "safety film," was used enhancing preservation but not guaranteeing it. The original negative of *My Fair Lady*, for example, almost decomposed entirely in Warner Bros.' vaults, requiring noted restorers Robert A. Harris and James C. Katz to spend six months and $600,000 to save the 1964 movie that had won eight Academy Awards.

Setting the Standard. It is safe to say that few directors' talking picture debut measured up to the brilliance of Ernst Lubitsch's *The Love Parade*. Easily the best of all the numerous Hollywood operettas of the 1929–30 period, it is appealing throughout, charming and tuneful as any picture of the time, and distinguished by literate, at times epigrammatic, dialogue and genuinely talented performers. Of special delight is the captivating ballad, "Dream Lover," sung beautifully by the loveless Jeanette MacDonald. Trailing close behind are the catchy "My Love Parade," in which Maurice Chevalier revives succulent memories of Mistinguette and Mitzi and other members of his extensive gallery of past lovers, and the militaristic "March of the Grenadiers," delivered with uncommon lustiness by Miss MacDonald and a huge chorus.

Similarly noteworthy, though far less familiar over the years, are the lively "Anything to Please the Queen," "Nobody's Using It Now," "Champagne," "The Queen Is Always Right," and the little gem of wistfulness entitled "Paris, Stay the Same," shared by Chevalier, his valet, Lupino Lane, and his dog as they prepare to leave the City of Light under duress. These Clifford Grey–Victor Schertzinger songs never managed to rise to the acclaim generated by the melodies of Romberg, Victor Herbert, or Rudolf Friml, but they are unquestionably superior to the majority of other songs written expressly for pre–1932 Hollywood operettas. That Schertzinger preferred to concentrate more on directing than supplying songs and background scores to motion pictures proved in the long run to be a loss, even if several of the films he directed were very good indeed.

Like *Gigi*, far more Continental European than American in spirit, *The Love Parade* is set in Paris, where it was presumed that people of all classes consistently engaged in what even in New York would be regarded as naughty conduct. A satire revolving around the imaginary

kingdom of Sylvania, the picture shines most noticeably when its typically complicated operetta plot is ignored and the director's satiric touches are permitted to take center stage. Up to the challenge of poking fun at Americans' notoriety for respecting the monetary value of a work of art, as opposed to its artistic worth, Lubitsch provides an especially well-known example in the scene showing a bus full of tourists busily reading their newspapers—presumably the financial pages—as a guide rattles off the impressive cultural history of the royal palace. The newspapers are shunted aside and the readers regard the guide's narrative with special interest only after learning that the palace is worth an estimated 110 million dollars.

Like the many comedies and melodramas concerning the upper echelons of society, *The Love Parade* echoes the determination of the wealthy and privileged to suppress scandal at all costs. Lubitsch goes one giant's step further, however, by implying that scandalous conduct is usually tolerated provided that subtlety marks its presence and that no one of importance suffers because of it.

Very much a creature of his times, despite his originality of plot and direction, Lubitsch was not up to fashioning what people of today might describe as the self-sufficient woman, both career-oriented and able to function quite nicely without men, although such an opportunity presents itself throughout *The Love Parade*. Clearly, Lubitsch was not a devotee of the liberated woman, as George Cukor and others were in the 1940s with such female-based films as *Woman of the Year* and *Adam's Rib*, in which Katharine Hepburn is depicted as every bit as accomplished as Spencer Tracy. Although a capable ruler, Miss MacDonald is popular with her subjects despite her smugness, but she is not permitted to reign with the assertiveness of a Rosalind Russell, either after the fashion of the older, dominate sister in *My Sister Eileen,* or as the woman executive in *Take a Letter, Darling* (both 1942). Notwithstanding her wealth and skill at issuing edicts and orders, Queen Jeanette is a woman in desperate need of a man to love and obey.

The film smacks a little of the drama *Forbidden Paradise*, Lubitsch's own 1924 pictorial essay on Catherine of Russia. Comedy raises its welcome head, however, in the operetta when

Count Alfred Renard (Maurice Chevalier), the Sylvanian envoy to France, is recalled by his government when it discovers that his fondness for the ladies is interfering with his diplomatic duties. The chief instigator of the count's forced removal from his beloved Paris is one Paulette, played by Yola D'Avril, an unfaithful wife who accuses the count of being unfaithful to her. When her husband appears, she apparently shoots herself and falls to the floor. The angry husband picks up the weapon and fires it at the count, only to find that it is loaded with blanks, a fact known to Chevalier and Yola all along. So happy is the husband that his wife is still living that he fails to observe the count's ambling to a dresser drawer, where he drops the pistol alongside dozens of others, a testament to his wide-ranging experiences in such jealous-husband episodes.

An enigma to her courtiers and advisers, Queen Jeanette constantly confounds them by refusing every suitor they arrange for her to meet. But, one must remember, she has yet to come across Chevalier, which she does when he appears before her to be punished for permitting *affaires de coeur* to monopolize his attention at the expense of conducting Sylvania's official business. This fellow, she seems to say, even if with extreme reluctance at first, is her vision of the ideal dream lover.

The palace soon becomes abuzz with gossip about the love between the Queen and the diplomat. Since Sylvania law dictates that the man who weds a Queen can only be her consort, with nothing whatever to say concerning affairs of the kingdom, it is Jeanette who takes the initiative during the ceremony, even to placing the ring on his finger. It will be her final authoritative gesture.

Queen Louise soon learns that her earthy paradise has not been freed from petty annoyances, most of the newer ones caused by her prince consort husband. Expecting to show him off before her countrymen in all his finery, replete with decorations and medals, at the opera, she is chagrined at his absence. Chevalier does show up finally, but only when he wants to. To Jeanette's surprise, he is greeted with rousing cheers from the opera audience. It is becoming quite clear that Chevalier is the better liked and admired of the two. Henceforth, his goal will be to convince the Queen

of the importance of his inestimable help in winning the hearts of her local enemies and Continental rivals. Gradually, she begins to succumb meekly to his frequent orders, a sign that Chevalier's power continues on the rise as Jeanette's declines. "Now bow!," commands Chevalier at one point. The Queen obeys. "Now smile!," he demands, and again she follows directions. That's the way a good marriage, among commoners or royalty, should be conducted, Lubitsch implies, and the surest guarantee that a couple will live happily forever.

Critic Mordaunt Hall summarized the salutary impact of *The Love Parade* as well as anyone when he wrote at the end of his review: "It is a delightful entertainment, this *Love Parade*, one that makes the spectator hopeful that the silly diatribes that have so recently been seen on the screen will be cast in the background for this sophisticated, intelligent fun."

The Smiling Lieutenant (1931)

A Paramount picture. DIRECTOR: Ernst Lubitsch. PRODUCER: Ernst Lubitsch. SCREENWRITERS: Ernest Vajda, Samson Raphaelson, and Ernst Lubitsch. CINEMATOGRAPHER: George Folsey. FILM EDITOR: Merrill White. ART DIRECTION: Hans Dreier. SOUND: Ernest F. Zatorsky and C.A. Tuthill. MUSICAL DIRECTOR: Adolph Deutsch. MUSICAL ARRANGERS: John W. [Johnny] Green and Conrad Salinger. SONGS: Lyrics by Clifford Grey, music by Oscar Straus. RUNNING TIME: 1 hour, 28 minutes. *Principal Players*: Maurice Chevalier (Niki). Claudette Colbert (Franzi). Miriam Hopkins (Princess Anna). George Barbier (King Adolf). Charles Ruggles (Max). Elizabeth Patterson (Baroness von Schwedel). *Major Academy Award Nomination*: Best Picture.

Again focusing his pair of roguish eyes on beautiful women while strolling through the park, or anywhere else, for that matter, Maurice Chevalier surpassed every other role he ever played as Niki in *The Smiling Lieutenant*. The picture itself is a singularly effective blend of operetta and musical comedy that neatly balances the traditional courtliness of Old World royalty with sly touches of late twenties morality that invest the story line with uncommon distinction. This affable, sometimes wistful officer in the Austrian Royal Guards indeed possesses a ready and winning smile that lights up his face and heightens his appeal to the opposite sex, particularly titled or talented young

Maurice Chevalier, attentive and exuding military decorum, as he appeared in *The Smiling Lieutenant.*

ladies more interested in affairs with an attractive man than in the politics or the concert hall.

Even at the age of 42, which Chevalier passed during the filming of the picture, he had

lost little of his beguiling presence, if any at all. Still an entertainment icon in his native France, he rewarded his far-flung fans for their faithfulness by appearing in French-language versions of *The Smiling Lieutenant,* as he had with *Innocents of Paris, The Love Parade, The Big Pond, Playboy of Paris,* and later with *One Hour with You, The Way to Love, The Merry Widow,* and *Folies-Bergère.* Fortunately, like the Marx Brothers, he was able to circumvent overexposure by never appearing in more than two American films a year.

That number was exceedingly small for a star of his stature, but absolutely necessary to preventing his basically similar characterizations from listing toward routine rather than amusing his vast public. Moviegoers expected Groucho to wisecrack his way through the plot, Chico to fail at every endeavor except playing the piano, and Harpo to pull a storehouse of items—a cup of coffee, a hatchet, a lighted candle—from under his overcoat, only to subside into seriousness when strumming the strings of his harp. They never tired of the brothers' antics, nor did audiences evince either surprise or irritation when Chevalier again and again reverted to his typical gusto in pursuing women acquaintances.

The Smiling Lieutenant was his only American feature-length film in 1931 compared with Clark Gable's 12. But Gable could get away with overextending himself; his directness and blunt masculinity at love making was just what the doctor ordered at a time when realism was beginning to inundate motion pictures, temporarily eclipsing the refined extravagances of operetta.

If not exactly championing free love, the Chevalier of 1931 still needed little more than the vision of a lovely and vulnerable lady to prod him into anticipating a liaison. Marriage may well have been her objective, but only rarely did matrimony enter into the happy-go-lucky lieutenant's plans, and usually only as a last resort to securing the companionship of a skittish female. What Chevalier's screen persona most desired was basking in the delights of wedded life without becoming enmeshed in the responsibilities.

Filmed at Paramount's Long Island Studio in Astoria, Queens, operated specifically to be within easy commuting distance of actors appearing on Broadway, *Lieutenant* was based on the 1907 operetta *Ein Waltzertraum* and the contemporaneous novel *Nux, der Prinzgemahl* by Hans Müller. Some of the Oscar Straus songs were carried over from the operetta, others were added to the film, one of them a jewel of new-generation waltzes, "While Hearts Are Singing," sung twice by Claudette Colbert, a passable but evanescent singer. Subsequently, it is through humming a waltz that Niki, the smiling lieutenant (Maurice Chevalier), succeeds in stealing Franzi (Claudette Colbert), an attractive violinist, from his comrade Max (Charles Ruggles).

Competent but relatively inactive, Straus was, and still is, remembered as the composer of "My Hero," which he wrote in 1909 for *The Chocolate Soldier.* On a par with Romberg's "Will You Remember?" as a heroic love song, it was reprised by Nelson Eddy and Risë Stevens in *The Chocolate Soldier* (1941), a mild movie success that was based not on the original Straus operetta but on Ferenc Molnar's 1924 nonmusical soufflé, *The Guardsman,* released in 1931 as the only film co-starring Alfred Lunt and Lynn Fontanne in 1931.

Typically, the guiding hand of director-producer Lubitsch is evident throughout the picture. This time he participated on the screenplay with Ernest Vajda, who had written the story for *The Love Parade,* and Samson Raphaelson, already an accredited screenwriter. He also staffed *Lieutenant* with acting heavyweights. Among them was the Paris-born Miss Colbert, a stage and screen actress who had changed her name from Lily Claudette Chauchoin for her first Broadway role in *The Wild Wescotts* in 1923. *Lieutenant* was her eighth film and second opposite Chevalier, with whom she had appeared the previous year in *The Big Pond.* An exemplary performer, she developed quickly into one of Hollywood's most accomplished screwball comediennes and dramatic actresses.

Also in the cast was Miriam Hopkins, another Broadway veteran, always a pleasure to watch, especially when vying for attention with Bette Davis, her *bete noire* in such later movies as *The Old Maid* (1939) and *Old Acquaintance* (1943). *Lieutenant* was her second film and the first of her three musicals, which also included *Dancers in the Dark* (1932), released shortly after she had been scared out of her wits by Fredric March in Rouben Mamoulian's *Dr. Jekyll and Mr. Hyde,* and *She Loves Me Not* (1934), which also featured Bing Crosby. Like

Miss Colbert, she was far better in nonmusical pictures. Her singing voice was not very good, as is quite evident in "One More Hour of Love" and "Jazz Up Your Lingerie." Like Miss Colbert, she was far better in nonmusical pictures, with Miss Colbert winning the best actress Oscar for *It Happened One Night* (1934), a part that, ironically, Miss Hopkins turned down.

The next year, Miss Colbert lost the Oscar for *Private Worlds*, a *Snake Pit*-like drama set in a mental institution, and again in 1944, despite her sturdy performance in David O. Selznick's *Since You Went Away*. Miss Hopkins also suffered a defeat at the hands of Academy voters, losing out in 1935 to Miss Davis, of all people, as the lead in *Becky Sharp*, the first feature film to be shot entirely in the new three-strip Technicolor.

Lieutenant is notable for serving as springboard for virtuoso Johnny Green's meteoric rise as musical arranger for major motion pictures. He had become associated with Paramount as a rehearsal pianist in 1929, and in years to come he would exhibit an unusually well-rounded talent for composing, conducting, and scoring. As an early thirties songwriter, though rarely for the movies, Green wrote such perennials as "Coquette" (not the same as Irving Berlin's title song for Mary Pickford's 1931 film of the same name), "I'm Yours," "Out of Nowhere," "I Cover the Waterfront," "You're Mine, You," and "Body and Soul," one the period's foremost torch songs. He served as MGM's general music director during that studio's second golden age of musicals, 1949-58, winning Academy Awards for scoring *Easter Parade* (1948), *An American in Paris*, *West Side Story*, and *Oliver!* Assisting him on *Lieutenant* was Conrad Salinger, a remarkably proficient musical arranger and orchestrator whose name, like Green's, would be appended to the credit cards of numerous MGM musicals, particularly from the late forties to the late fifties.

The Mischievous Officer. This middle picture in the string of three cinematic jewels piloted by Lubitsch is generally regarded as the best of them, although its unavailability prevents critical comparison with the master director's other two Oscar-nominated operettas.

Permeated with satire, whether dealing with romance or royalty, the picture is thoroughly enjoyable as both a comedy of manners and as an operetta, a unique claim to fame that few films of the time, or later, are qualified to make.

The first sound uttered by Chevalier in the picture is a yawn that, as a number of reviewers noted, failed to infect audiences, which remained alert to the plot twists and innuendoes Lubitsch worked into the theme. Sitting on his bed as a buglar is heard blowing the wake-up call, Chevalier enters into a new day with his first song, the slightly risqué "Toujours l'Amour in the Army" as a celebration of the importance of a spiffy uniform to a soldier's success at attracting women. Chevalier has been as successful as any of his buddies, quick to smile and maybe wink at any pretty girl, regardless of what the consequences of his friendly nature might be.

The scene shifts to a view of the special royal train transporting King Adolf XV of Flausenthurm, who is on his way to visit the Emperor of Austria. With him is his then frumpish daughter, Princess Anna (Miriam Hopkins), who is again reminded of her father's frequent outbursts of temper when vexed, which occurs again when he notices that the name of his country on a boundary-line sign post is spelled without an h. One of the better character actor exponents of inevitable irritability, George Barbier plays the pompous King to perfection, a result of his long experience on Broadway that would turn him into one of the most agreeable of disagreeable old men in dozens of 1930s films.

Informed by telegram while aboard the train that the Emperor will be unable to meet Adolf in Vienna because of a earlier commitment to attend a cattle show, the King is again forced to vent his displeasure, which is increased by a clever Lubitsch touch. A cattle train happens to pass Adolf's special, and the cows are all mooing as if gloating over the fact that the Emperor had elected to pay attention to them instead of meeting with the visiting monarch from Flausenthurm.

Still more complications arise, however, when Adolf and his princess daughter reach Vienna. Chevalier's penchant for smiling at ladies he finds attractive lands him in serious trouble when he smiles just as the royal carriage passes him. Princess Miriam thinks the smile was directed at her, whereas Chevalier was actually sending it to Claudette Colbert, who is watching the procession on the opposite side of the street. Angrily, Miriam demands that a court-martial be instituted against Chevalier, but her father refuses, preferring to dole out the punishment for Chevalier's supposed impertinence himself.

Chevalier is adequate to the challenge posed by the King, and he appears to lie his way out of trouble by informing the princess that he had smiled at her only because she is so beautiful. What he failed to consider was the extent of the gratitude to be felt by the unpretty princess, who had regarded the smile and wink as insulting, in her despairing father's praise. Rarely ever having heard such flattery before, Miriam secretly becomes so delighted that observant Adolf decides that Chevalier is just the man to marry his daughter.

Miriam is willing and is happy while confiding to her feminine coterie of Chevalier's modesty and gentleness. The groom, meanwhile, is telling Claudette that there is dynamite in her kisses and sharing such a delightful song as "Breakfast Table Love." Also happy is Father Adolf, who telephones the Austrian Emperor to tell him the good news:

"Listen, Emp, I want to tell you something very confidential. Now keep this under your crown: my little Anna is in love. What? You know all about it? The whole palace knows? Yes, she wants to marry him. What do you think of Anna marrying an ordinary lieutenant? What?—What? You think it is a great thing for Flausenthurm? Well, let me tell you it's a great thing for Austria, too."

After the wedding, Niki discovers that Claudette is scheduled to perform in the capital city of Flausenthurm, and he orders the police to halt the concert and deliver her to him in a secluded spot, only the first in a series of rendezvous between Chevalier and the woman he truly loves. Miriam, of course, learns of their meetings and becomes somewhat friendly with her worldly rival, who in the song "Jazz Up Your Lingerie" even offers advice on how to spruce up her appearance—and intensify Chevalier's interest in her. Essentially, Claudette is a good girl; she has accepted the

loss of Chevalier as husband, even though she is unquestionably the ideal lifelong partner for him, and is planning to return to Vienna for good. Miriam, meantime, is content in the marriage, certain that it will prove to be her major source of happiness, and sincerely wants to be a good wife to her cosmopolitan husband.

In the best Lubitsch tradition, Chevalier's growing perception that Miriam's alterations in appearance are transforming her into a new, and far sexier, woman brings the couple closer and closer together. Looking at her one afternoon as she plays the piano and smokes a cigarette, he is convinced that the transition is due to the new brand of liquor he has been drinking lately. As if to fortify his opinion and preserve the vision of loveliness that the princess has become, he strides to the portable bar and pours a few shots down his throat. Life with Anna, he is certain, will surely be a glamorous one after all.

One Hour with You (1932)

A Paramount picture. DIRECTOR: Ernst Lubitsch; ASSISTANT: George Cukor. PRODUCER: Ernst Lubitsch. SCREENWRITER: Samson Raphaelson, based on the 1909 play *Nur ein Traum*, by Lothar Schmidt. CINEMATOGRAPHER: Victor Milner. FILM EDITOR: William Shea. ART DIRECTOR: Hans Dreier. COSTUMES: Travis Banton. SOUND: M.M. Paggi. MUSICAL DIRECTOR: Nat Finston. SONGS: Lyrics by Leo Robin, music by Richard A. Whiting and Oscar Straus. RUNNING TIME: 1 hour, 20 minutes. *Principal Players*: Maurice Chevalier: Dr. André Bertier. Jeanette MacDonald: Colette Bertier. Genevieve Tobin (Mitzi Oliver), Charles Ruggles (Adolph), Roland Young (Professor Olivier), George Barbier (Police Commissioner), Josephine Dunn (Mme. Martel), Richard Carle (Detective). *Major Academy Award Nomination*: Best Picture.

Paramount bowled another strike in early 1932 by reuniting Lubitsch, Chevalier, and Jeanette MacDonald for the second time in three years for their most highly sophisticated comedy of manners, as frothy a picture as any one of them was ever involved in. More sensuous than *The Love Parade,* even *The Smiling Lieutenant,* but handled with the gifted director's traditional deftness, it emerged as a minor classic of sexual innuendo, which only a few years later would be practically expunged from the screen under the watchful eyes of Joseph Breen, a former policeman who became the sole

Married couples Maurice Chevalier and Jeanette MacDonald, left, and Genevieve Tobin and Roland Young in *One Hour with You*.

judge of movie morality as director of the newly inaugurated Motion Picture Production Code Administration.

All the familiar Chevalier trademarks—the arched eyebrows above the playful leer, the undisguised exultation at finding another candidate for conquest— are very much present, as is the virtuous heroine's emotional turmoil over whether to submit to entreaties or reject them—and, if the latter, for how much longer. No Fred Astaire type of lover, incessantly proclaiming his love for a young woman whose chastity he is willing to preserve until after he slips a wedding ring on her finger, the magnetic Chevalier is again cast as the middle-age provocateur with the soul of an incurable romantic and a heart bubbling over with songs. That his depiction of the would-be merry philanderer succeeded once more was the crux of the contemporary review of *One Hour with You* in the *Philadelphia Inquirer*. Applauding Lu-

bitsch in particular, the unnamed critic regarded the film as "something so delightful that it places the circle of golden leaves jauntily upon the knowing head of Hollywood's most original director."

Taking as his sources both his own 1924 silent comedy, *The Marriage Circle*, and Samson Raphaelson's rewrite of Lothar Schmidt's 1909 play, *Nur ein Traum* (*Only a Dream*), Lubitsch skillfully welded them into an updated musical comedy laced with irony, wit, and nine songs to add sparkle that very well might have been lacking had another hand guided the conversion of the two basically trite sources into film. Sporting as professional a lineup of actors, technicians, and songwriters as any Hollywood musical of the pre-*42nd Street* years, *One Hour with You* was as big on talent as it was ahead of its time in satirizing upper-class mores.

The performers were uniformly endowed

by nature and training to play their individual parts. Chevalier, appearing in his third nominated musical—the most ever by any star, with still another, *Gigi*, to arrive on the scene 36 years later—is perfect. (The actor was also the model for the suave cartoon character Lumiere, in *Beauty and the Beast* in 1991.) So is Jeanette MacDonald, who was actually quite adept at comedy, an asset rarely on view in her later films opposite Nelson Eddy. Her playfulness beautifully complements Chevalier's, even though she recognizes his amorous intentions and vows to stand in his way of achieving them.

Two of Paramount's mightiest character actors, Charles Ruggles and Roland Young, add to the overall merriment to such a degree that one wishes the studio had found a part for the dour, always low-key Charles Butterworth, the third member of its triumvirate of master comedians. Genevieve Tobin, a talented actress who had accrued a wealth of stage experience since World War I, when she co-starred with her sister, Vivian, in vaudeville, is a delight as Young's spouse.

Assisting Lubitsch, if only marginally, in the director's chair was George Cukor, who like Raphaelson, had only recently been recruited from Broadway. Cukor, of course, developed into one of Hollywood's great directors, much as Raphaelson was to become renowned for his screenplays for a widely diverse assortment of works, ranging from *Trouble in Paradise* (also 1932), *The Merry Widow, Angel* (1937), *Suspicion* (1941), *Heaven Can Wait*, and *The Harvey Girls* (1945) to *But Not for Me* (1959), one of Clark Gable's final films.

Lovely to Listen To. Three of the nine *One Hour with You* songs were composed by Richard A. Whiting, among the earliest and most active of the East Coast songwriters to decamp to Hollywood after the industry's forays into musical production created an intense need for them. An excellent but sadly neglected tunesmith, Whiting began his career during World War I. His first hit, "It's Tulip Time in Holland" (reprised 27 years later in *Hello Frisco, Hello*), was followed in 1918 by such powerhouse songs as the non-production "Till We Meet Again," along with

George M. Cohan's "Over There" the only World War I song to enjoy a strong revival at the outset of World War II as well, and "Japanese Sandman," "Ain't We Got Fun?," "Breezin' Along with the Breeze," and "(I'm in Love with You) Honey." His novelty "Horses" was unique in reproducing the clomping of horses hooves in the melody line, while the ballads "Sleepy Time Gal" and "She's Funny That Way" increased his professional stature as the twenties came to their end.

One of the first original theme songs to appear in a 1929 film, "Yo Te Amo Means I Love You," from *Wolf Song*, was his, along with "Louise," sung by Chavalier to Sylvia Beecher in the aforementioned *Innocents of Paris*. Other popular Whiting movie melodies from 1929 include "My Sweeter Than Sweet," the highlight of *Sweetie*, one of the first college musicals, with Nancy Carroll, Jack Oakie, and Helen ("boop-boop-a-doop") Kane. Hal Skelley introduced his "True Blue Lou" in *The Dance of Life*, which marked the first film appearance of Oscar Levant.

In the thirties, numerous other highly successful movie songs flowed from the pen of Paramount's chief contract composer. Mostly writing in collaboration with Leo Robin, another Broadway expatriate and as gifted a lyricist as ever labored in the Hollywood vineyard, and at rare times with fellow composers W. Franke Harling, J. Newell Chase, Ralph Rainger, Whiting was responsible for one or more songs in some 20 movies from 1929 to 1937. In 1930, his most productive film year, Whiting supplied Chevalier with the mildly successful "All I Want Is Just One Girl," for *Paramount on Parade*, as well as "It's a Great Life If You Don't Weaken" and the beautiful "My Ideal" for *Playboy of Paris*. "Beyond the Blue Horizon" and "Give Me a Moment, Please" (the themesong of violinist Dave Rubinoff) were both sung by Miss MacDonald in *Monte Carlo* (1931), along with the lovely ballads "My Future Just Passed" in *Safety in Numbers*, and "It Seems to Be Spring" in *Let's Go Native* (1930).

Despite his knack for composing hit movie and non-production melodies, Whiting was responsible for only a few pre–1929 interpolations in a handful of stage shows ("Where the

Black-Eyed Susans Grow," in Al Jolson's *Robinson Crusoe, Jr.,* 1916, and "I've Got the Blue Ridge Blues" for another Jolson show, *Sinbad,* 1918). He wrote one song each for *A Lonely Romeo* and *The Greenwich Village Follies,* as well as about a dozen for the George White Scandals, the military show *Toot Sweet,* and *Chatter Box Revue,* all 1919. He took temporary leave of Hollywood in 1931 to collaborate with Oscar Hammerstein II on the score of Broadway's disappointing 15-performance run of *Free for All,* starring Jack Haley, and then joined with fellow songwriters Nacio Herb Brown, Vincent Youmans, and Roger Edens for *Take a Chance* (1932), in which Haley and Ethel Merman duetted "Eadie Was a Lady" and "You're an Old Smoothie." That musical fared far better, remaining on the Great White Way for 243 performances.

Returning to the film capital in 1933, Whiting wrote individual songs and complete scores for such films as *Adorable,* Janet Gaynor's final film musical; *Bottoms Up* ("Waitin' at the Gate for Katy"); *Bright Eyes* ("On the Good Ship Lollipop"); *Coronado* ("You Took My Breath Away"); *Big Broadcast of 1936* ("Miss Brown to You," "Double Trouble"); and *Sing, Baby, Sing* (the Oscar-nominated "When Did You Leave Heaven?"). In 1936-37, with able newcomer Johnny Mercer as lyricist, he brightened such movies as *The Cowboy from Brooklyn* ("Ride, Tenderfoot, Ride" and "I'll Dream Tonight"); *Hollywood Hotel* ("Hooray for Hollywood," widely regarded as the official Movieland theme song, introduced by Frances Langford and Johnny ["Scat"] Davis, "Silhouetted in the Moonlight," and "I'm Like a Fish Out of Water"); *Varsity Show* ("Have You Got Any Castles, Baby," "We're Working Our Way Through College"), and *Ready, Willing and Able* ("Too Marvelous for Words").

When he died at age 47 on February 10, 1938, Whiting not only left behind a large legacy of long-lasting songs written for Fox and Warner Bros. as well as Paramount, but also his gifted daughter, Margaret, one of the finest of the many popular female vocalists of the 1940s and 50s. Gaining a firm show business foothold by appearing on radio's *Eddie Cantor Show* and with bandleader Bob Crosby's "Bobcats" on *Club Fifteen,* she paid

exquisite homage to her father by recording many of his songs, including two very pretty non-production tunes, "Guilty" and "Sorry" in the 1940s.

Miss Whiting noted recently that her father "adored Chevalier" and ranked him high among the "most talented and brilliant performers he'd ever known." One day in 1929, when Whiting and lyricist Robin were sharing a suite at the Hollywood Roosevelt, where they munched on sandwiches and cheese and crackers while working on *Innocents of Paris,* Chevalier rang them from the lobby and asked whether he could come up and visit them. "They put all their goodies in drawers and cleaned up as quickly as they could. Chevalier stepped into the room, sat for a few minutes, and asked, 'What's that aroma—cheese? Oh, I'd love some!'," she recalled recently. "The writing partners whipped out the cheese and crackers, ordered a bottle of wine, and had a great time." Only a young child at the time of Chevalier's glory days, Miss Whiting got to know the fabulous Frenchman and to this day remembers going to a Hollywood theater and hearing him sing 'Louise' and 'My Ideal,' which he graciously dedicated to her.

Whiting's title tune for *One Hour with You,* the best known of the songs, was picked up the next year by Eddie Cantor, who added greatly to its popularity by installing it as the sign-off theme song of his weekly radio program, assuring listeners that he loved "to spend each Sunday with you." Whiting's other contributions were "Three Times a Day" and "What Would You Do?"

Of the picture's other six songs, all but one—John Leipold's "Police Number"—were by Robin and Oscar Straus. Deserving special mention are their pretty waltz "We Will Always Be Sweethearts," sung by Chevalier and Miss MacDonald, and the jubilant "What a Little Thing Like a Wedding Ring Can Do," also sung by the two stars as a tribute to the socially acceptable sexual joys available to marriage partners.

Second Time Around. The source of the picture, Lothar Schmidt's play, *Only a Dream,* had already been filmed by Lubitsch in 1924 as his first American comedy, the silent *The Marriage Circle.* Good as the picture was, it is unable to hold a candle to the scintillating 1932 frou-frou that remade it as *One Hour with You*. Critics do not place it on a par with *The Love Parade* and *The Smiling Lieutenant*, but it remains a sly and saucy example of the director's later playful approach to the boudoir adventures of the rich and famous.

Unlike the earlier two musical movies, *One Hour with You* finds Maurice Chevalier as his usual debonair self in the role of Dr. André Bertier, happily married at the beginning, as at the end, to Jeanette MacDonald, who is utterly bracing as the eventually wronged wife.

Chevalier plays a prominent Paris physician; MacDonald portrays his fair and graceful wife, Colette. They poke fun at their "lawful...and awful nice" situation with a rendition of the Robin and Straus song, "What a Little Thing Like a Wedding Ring Can Do."

As Mitzi Olivier (Tobin), an old friend of Colette's married to a stuffy college professor (Young), sets her sights on a resistant André, the plot begins to unfold. It quickly becomes clear that the romantically inept Adolph (Ruggles) has an eye for Colette. At a swank dinner party given by the Bertiers, Colette watches as André attempts to change the seating arrangements of Mitzi and Mademoiselle Martel (Dunn). And—to the great merriment of the audience—Colette wrongfully assumes that her husband is involved in an affair with the latter. Shortly after dinner, the mischievous Mitzi, the real flirt, moves into action. She becomes André's partner on the dance floor after dinner, and tries to maneuver him outside onto the balcony.

Professor Olivier, not unaware of his wife's flirtatious conduct, is having her tailed by a detective, who, in due time, presents Bertier with a full report on what has happened during the evening. Bertier thinks that he must confess all to his wife, who, as it turns out, never for a moment suspects him of involvement with Mitzi. The real shock as far as Colette is concerned, was the near-affair between herself and Adolph.

Throughout the film, action stops and the characters take the audience into their confidence to conduct personal asides: Here, Colette, holding Mlle. Martel accountable for her husband's absence, is so distraught she can not take seriously the feeble post-party overtures of Adolph:

HE: Any man who leaves a woman like you on a night like this with a man like me deserves it.

SHE (sobbing): But it was my fault! I was wrong!

HE: You have a right to be wrong. You're a woman. Women are born to be wrong. (He leans closer to her in a flash of passion.)...I like my women wrong!

In the film's best song, André jubilantly shows that he bears some affection for Mitzi. He enthuses: "Oh, That Mitzi." But, of course, he loves Colette too much to stray. Still, he has been found out through the work of the sleuth (Carle) hired by the professor. He is called as a witness in a divorce suit brought against Mitzi. Again, as often happens throughout the film, Chevalier confidentially turns to the audience. This time, he plaintively asks in Whiting's song, "What would you do?"

He decides to admit a brief "indiscretion." Colette responds by saving face. But, of course, she has had a fling with Adolph, and is forced to confess her "sins," declaring, "An eye for an eye; an Adolph for an Adolph." The film winds up with Colette and André importuning the audience:

SHE: Ladies—
HE: And gentlemen—
SHE: If he were your husband.
HE: And she were your wife.
SHE: And he is a Don Juan.
HE: And she has dreams.
SHE: And he confesses.
HE: And she admits—
SHE: But you like him—.
HE: And you love her.
SHE: And you adore him.
HE: And you're crazy about her.
SHE: What would you do?
HE: What could you do? (Then, a kiss.)

The frothy finish fully met the expectations of Depression-era audiences. Curiously, a second conclusion that had André admit to being unfaithful was filmed. Lubitsch had André explain to the audience that something happened after the party. Fadeout came just as André got to the part where "we went into Mitzi's apartment and sat down in the living room." Obviously, the dark ending would have put a damper on all the mirthfulness. It was wisely dropped.

42nd Street (1933)

A Warner Bros. picture. DIRECTOR: Lloyd Bacon. SCREENWRITERS: Rian James and James Seymour, based on the novel by Bradford Ropes. CINEMATOGRAPHER: Sol Polito. FILM EDITORS: Frank Ware and Thomas Pratt. CHOREOGRAPHER: Busby Berkeley. ART DIRECTOR: Jack Okey. SOUND: Nathan Levinson. GOWNS: Orry-Kelly. VITAPHONE ORCHESTRA CONDUCTOR: Leo Forbstein. SONGS: Lyrics by Al Dubin, music by Harry Warren. RUNNING TIME: 1 hour and 29 minutes. *Principal Players*: Warner Baxter (Julian Marsh), Bebe Daniels (Dorothy Brock), George Brent (Pat Denning), Ruby Keeler (Peggy Sawyer), Guy Kibbee (Abner Dillon), Una Merkel (Lorraine Fleming), Ginger Rogers (Ann Lowell), Ned Sparks (Barry), Dick Powell (Billy Lawler), Allen Jenkins (Mac Elroy), George E. Stone (Andy Lee). *Major Academy Award Nominations*: Best Picture; Sound.

Fresh from a small town somewhere in the hinterlands and looking every inch the sweet innocent, Ruby Keeler (Peggy Sawyer) readily admits her professional limitations while hoping for the chance to try out for the chorus of a new Broadway musical. She has little in common with her hard-bitten, through-the-mill female competitors, accustomed as they are to conspiring to graduate from chorine to soubriquet with a few lines to speak to second female lead with their names printed in large boldface type on the program. Or, failing in that endeavor, to end their days of existing on short rations courtesy of stage door Johnnies with bulging wallets.

Impervious to her competitors' wisecracks, Ruby cherishes the less ambitious hope of qualifying to dance alongside them in total anonymity behind the footlights, knowing that her presence will add but momentary luster to the musical numbers in which she may participate. Braced for rejection, she is in no hurry to achieve greatness, conscious of the fact that she has much to learn about her adopted profession, and she is willing to submit to the judgment of her betters. She is docile and unhesitatingly obedient to the authoritarian Warner Baxter (Julian Marsh), the testy taskmaster producer of the forthcoming Broadway show *Pretty Lady*. Possessed of a

heady reputation as the most successful impresario of musical comedy in America, as well as a holy terror to work for, he has devoted his adult life to the stage at the exclusion of everything else. Throughout the picture he shows no interest in women, perpetually expending whatever amount of blood, sweat, and tears is required of him and his underlings to achieve professional perfection.

But fortune takes an unexpected turn on Ruby's behalf. A broken ankle incapacitates the show's leading lady, Bebe Daniels (Dorothy Brock), on the very night before the show is scheduled to open on 42nd Street. The next afternoon, Baxter takes a million-to-one chance by selecting Ruby to substitute for the wounded Bebe. Equally doubtful that a raw amateur with only five weeks of rehearsal as a chorus girl could carry even a community theater production, Ruby is nonplused. Her big chance has fallen in her lap, but far too early. Undoubtedly, the other girls would snap up the part with nary a second's hesitation while congratulating Baxter for discerning their talent, hidden for so long by servitude as high-kicking puppets.

But Baxter has no alternative this late in the game. Either the show opens on time or he suffers a humiliation that could cost him his livelihood, maybe his life. He tries to squelch his own doubts about Ruby's potential by assuring her that she is definitely up to the challenge. The speech he delivers to her in the frenetic tones of a college football coach just before the opening night curtain is still among the best known in the annals of film, concluding with one of the most effective lines to emerge from a film-musical sound track. Holding on to her shoulders as if for dear life, his eyes overflowing with anxiety while his voice exudes counterfeit confidence, Baxter tells the apprehensive Ruby: "You're going out a youngster but you've got to come back a star!" Like other bits of the dialogue, Baxter's words have been much parodied ever since; if his and the other actors' lines were not a collection of clichés when they spoke them—and they probably were—they have descended to that level after years of imitation, an unenviable fate that the film shares with *Casablanca*.

Far more than another potboiler with panache, *42nd Street* to this day is regarded as

Warner Baxter, right, barks out instructions to dance director George E. Stone in a sequence from *42nd Street*. Fifth in the right row of chorines is Ginger Rogers, who played the part of the slightly dishonorable "Anytime Annie."

one of America's few truly monumental musical pictures. Both the prelude and the peak of the musical-film revival of 1933, it is superbly enhanced by impeccable casting, tone, songs, and pace that made it virtually bomb-proof at the box office. *42nd Street* clearly represented a towering improvement in style and substance over the outpouring of backstage-based musicals since *The Broadway Melody* showed Hollywood how to make them.

Compared with that early MGM musical, *42nd Street* is far less studio-bound. Besides providing a gratifying mix of closeups and medium and long shots, the camera actually tracks characters as they walk, mostly from the side, but a few times very briefly from the front and back. One scene actually includes a reaction shots, where the camera focuses on the listener rather than the speaker during an exchange of dialogue. It arrives when the audience sees a silent Baxter reacting to the words spoken off-screen by Robert McWade

(Jones). Less significant is the medium shot of Miss Daniels's bare legs while Guy Kibbee rambles on about his fixation for her.

42nd Street's plot was not original, repeating familiar settings and deploying typical Broadway types to act out their individual frustrations and triumphs. Nor does it contain any real hair-trigger tension. Audiences had been conditioned to musicals' overcoming all obstacles after wringing a few tears from the eyes and putting a few lumps in the throat. The classic play *Broadway*, although revolving around a group of chorines in a nightclub, minted practically every one of *42nd Street*'s plot and dialogue nuances as far back as 1926.

In fact, Warner Bros.' own *On with the Show*, released almost exactly four years earlier, roughly covered the same territory in two-strip Technicolor, although the link between these two films ends there. The source of *42nd Street* is different from that of *On with the Show*, which was based on *Shoestring*, an unpublished play by

Humphrey Pearson. So are the director, cast, choreographer, and cinematographer. The one hit song written for *On with the Show*—Grant Clarke and Harry Akst's "Am I Blue?"—is not heard in *42nd Street*, which sported its own brand new, and far better, score with lyrics by Al Dubin and music by Harry Warren.

The most significant difference between the two films is the treatment: *On with the Show* is draggy, pot-marked with poor performances, sound, and dance routines, all caused by the participants' lack of experience with the new picture-making technology rather than by a common deficiency in professionalism. So realistic is *42nd Street* that one can almost smell the greasepaint. Its lightning-like progression from scene to scene and avoidance of excessive sentimentalism are other compelling attributes it shares with *Casablanca*.

Instead of "Pretty Lady," *On with the Show*'s production in progress was called "Phantom Sweetheart," and the little waif with the Broadway aspirations, played by Sally O'Neil, was a native New Yorker hatcheck girl. Its comedy arose not from the chorines' sarcastic exchanges, but from the antics of Joe E. Brown, capable even in his film debut of tickling the nation's funny bone. The boyishly handsome juvenile was played not by Dick Powell, who would not enter films until 1932, but partly by the almost instantly forgotten William Bakewell and partly by one-time child actor Arthur Lake, who beginning in 1938 would appear as Dagwood Bumstead opposite Penny Singleton on the radio and in an interminable series of *Blondie* pictures based on Chic Young's popular comic strip. The line accompanying Sally's exit from backstage to proscenium as substitute star was the far less dramatic "Go on and give them everything you've got!"

Following along under the shadow of the commonplace *On with the Show* and the dozens of other pre–1933 backstagers was *42nd Street*'s reintroduction of the tough, energetic director, the temperamental leading lady, and such other stereotypes as the on-the-make production staff. The redundant "I don't know nothin' about show business" financial backer also shows up, as incompetent as he is jealous of the prerogatives to which he feels his funding entitles him.

But so shrewdly are these characters worked into *42nd Street*'s main and five subsidiary plots, all as old as talking pictures themselves, that its bromidic incidents, personalities, and dialogue seem remarkably fresh, thanks mostly to the superlative performance handed in by Baxter, who won the best actor Academy Award in 1929 for his portrayal of O. Henry's Cisco Kid in *In Old Arizona*, as the high-anxiety director. Not until William Powell played Florenz Ziegfeld in 1936 would a non-musical actor so dominate the screenplay of a musical. Most of the dialogue is his, and he appears in most of the scenes.

Equally responsible for *42nd Street*'s glory were the so-called "minor" actors, who as usual are first-rate in their short stints. Ned Sparks (Barry), his monotone and unsmiling face having already lifted his comic style to an art, is perfect in his brief role as the hard-nosed co-producer who punctuates his edicts and complaints with chomps on an unlighted cigar. The uncharismatic Allen Jenkins, as Baxter's dour chief assistant, Mac Elroy, reprises his customary role as the deadpan fatalist, made memorable as Paul Muni's fellow inmate in *I Am a Fugitive from a Chain Gang* in 1932, always hoping for the best but expecting the worst. Whatever happens, happens, aptly summarizes his philosophy; errors of commission and omission are inevitable and no cause for alarm. "We all make mistakes, Boss. That's why they put rubber on the ends of pencils," he will tell gangster Humphrey Bogart in 1937 in *Dead End*. George E. Stone (Andy Lee), who entered films as a child actor during World War I, again made the most of his part as the mousy lower-echelon executive whose hopes for advancement depend more on catering to his boss' whims than on talent.

As steered by the prolific director Lloyd Bacon, whose résumé included two primitive Al Jolson musicals, *The Singing Fool*, one of the most commercially successful of musical pictures, and *Say It with Songs* (both 1928), *42nd Street* made such a salutary impact—one is shy about describing it as profound—on the public that it immediately raised, Lazarus-like, the movie musical from the doldrums of the 1930-33 period. By itself it reinvigorated audiences into embarking once again on trips to movie houses for another Hollywood vision of the world of the Broadway theater.

Among its many assets, the most impressive is *42nd Street*'s powerhouse score. Composer Warren, acknowledged as the "Father of the Hollywood Musical," had written only one other screen musical—and very few for Broadway—before signing the contract to collaborate with lyricist Al Dubin on this one. The earlier musical, a 1929 revamp of Rodgers and Hart's *Spring Is Here*, introduced Warren's "Cryin' for the Carolines" and "Have a Little Faith in Me." Workhorse Harry, as he called himself, would continue pouring out songs, from ballads and waltzes to novelties and rumbas, for such household-name stars as James Cagney, Marion Davies, Eddie Cantor, Al Jolson, Eleanor Powell, Alice Faye, Glenn Miller, Betty Grable, Astaire and Rogers, Bing Crosby, and Dean Martin over the next 38 years, compiling a record 309 songs for 79 movies, mostly for Warner's. Eleven of his songs were nominated for Academy Awards, the second highest total in history after James Van Heusen's 14. Three won the Oscar, one each for three different studios. The Brooklyn-born melody-maker might have won still more awards, possibly for "Forty-Second Street" and "Shadow Waltz," had the Academy of Motion Picture Arts and Sciences awarded Oscars for best song in 1933. As it is, his total is stupefying when one considers that for much of his career he was competing with the likes of Porter, Gershwin, Rodgers, Berlin, Kern, and Arlen for assignments.

Despite his success in the motion picture industry, Warren looked upon it with hostility, if not absolute contempt. To him, as with a number of other artists, though usually with far less antagonism, the industry was run for the most part by untalented autocrats forever seeking praise from incompetent sycophants. His most vivid memory of his *42nd Street* days, as expressed in a 1976 interview, was the "unbearable" heat he had to withstand from August to October 1932 to complete the score. But he remained in Southern California for the rest of his life, dying there at the age of 88 in 1981.

Later Influences. Reversing the long-established trend of shipping Broadway musicals to the West Coast for remakes as films, producer David Merrick reconstituted *42nd Street* as a stage vehicle in 1980.

Starring Tammy Grimes as Dorothy Brock and Jerry Ohrbach as Julian Marsh, the show broadly followed the Bradford Ropes novel and Rian James–James Seymour screenplay. The four hit Dubin and Warren screen songs were retained, and eight other Warren tunes from six additional 1930s film musicals were inserted, including the show-stopping "Lullaby of Broadway." Gower Champion, who had appeared with his wife, Marge, in several 1950s Hollywood musicals, including *Show Boat*, was director and choreographer. Two comparative unknowns, Wanda Richert and Lee Roy Ream, played the Ruby Keeler and Dick Powell parts. James Congdon appeared in George Brent's role, Don Crabtree in Guy Kibbee's. Karen Prunczill was the modernized but equally brainless "Anytime Annie," practically immortalized by Ginger Rogers.

In the spring of 1975, the stage musical most often cited as the modern-day successor to the 1933 film opened at the Newman Theatre, part of Joseph Papp's Public Theater complex, deserting it three months later, on July 15, for the uptown Shubert. There it remained for almost 15 years, eventually elevating *A Chorus Line* into the longest-running show in Broadway history, until being replaced in the summer of 1977 by the musical Cats. Actually, it has little in common with the movie, and is far better in every aspect, except for the Edward Kleban–Marvin Hamlisch score. Two of their minor songs, "I Hope I Get It" and "I Can Do That," however, are unquestionably the best musical expressions of the grit and determination all stage aspirants need to succeed.

Taking place entirely on the stage of a theater while the unseen director decides which of 31 boy and girl applicants he will select to fill eight chorus line vacancies, the musical was actually based on true-life experiences. It resembled a movie only in that it was performed without an intermission. The psychological probing into the dancers' characters as they verbalize or sing their biographies, serve the purpose of helping the director pick and choose from among them. Such an actionless plot would have been inconceivable in 1933 or, if attempted at all, the biographies would have been reduced in number and acted out in flashbacks.

That the original *A Chorus Line* was untranslatable into celluloid was proved by the 1985 film version, one of the screen's greatest examples of the ruination of a classic stage show. Nominated for but three Academy Awards, for best film editing, song, and sound, the picture starred Michael Douglas, who brought the director to life as a shallow and petulant man with a consistent growl and sanctimonious presence. Warner Baxter was equally rough as sandpaper, but he was also merciful at crucial moments and always on the lookout for an opportunity to praise the deserving. Few people would care to work for Baxter, but even they would admit their admiration for him.

The World's Crossroads. If by 1933 the American public did not automatically identify Times Square as the nation's entertainment capital, the movies were not to blame. For years Hollywood had set numerous musicals on the west side of midtown Manhattan, where, as the scripts pointed out, all the important music publishers, agents, and producers made deals with performers, songwriters, and librettists, and the names of many of the most honored stars in show business exploded in crescendos of light on scores of marquees.

Once known as the Longacre, the little triangle of concrete between Broadway and Seventh Avenue that formerly held the Pabst Hotel, owned by the brewery, became the home of *The New York Times* on January 18, 1904. Three months later, on April 19, Mayor George McClellan, son of the famous Civil War general, signed a resolution that officially switched the name of the site of the new 375-foot-high Times Tower, modeled after a Renaissance Florentine building, and surrounding blocks to Times Square. Helped by the opening of the city's first subway line on October 27, 1904, Broadway became the undisputed main street of the Square. At the end of the 1920s it boasted the city's most impressive theaters, even though the largest were devoted to movies-cum-vaudeville rather than to plays.

It was on the side streets from 42nd to 52st Street, between Sixth and Eighth Avenues, that the majority of the legitimate theaters settled.

And of all these streets, none surpassed the number of stage houses crammed onto both sides of West 42nd Street, each separated from its nearest competitor by only a few feet. Like Broadway in Los Angeles, especially between 3rd and 9th streets, which still boasts the largest concentration of pre-World War II movie houses in America, 42nd Street remains a window on a long-deceased world that was determined to create total entertainment environments by designing ticket booths, lobbies, auditoriums, staircases, and even restrooms to put patrons into as many exotic worlds as the plays and musicals themselves. Little wonder that the intense rivalry to fill those seats led historian Carol Willis to term that single block of 42nd Street the "capital of capitalism."

Although some of the theaters hosted films once in a while—*The Birth of a Nation*, for example, had its premiere in 1915 at the Liberty Theatre, where it ran for 44 weeks—it was not until the early Depression years that showing films became a full-time industry on 42nd Street. Much as the owners of the bankrupt-darkened theaters were happy to admit Hollywood's ready-made fare into their properties to survive, they laid out unwelcome mats to the newly arrived burlesque troupes, like Billy Minsky's, which performed on two runways installed in the Republic in 1933, along with such other unsavory enterprises as shooting galleries and a flea circus that set up shop nearby.

The economic woes of the time, of course, had a devastating impact on the Broadway theater, reducing the number of productions from 239 in 1929-30 to 187 in 1930-31, 100 in 1938-39, and a mere 72 in 1940-41. Ironically, by the time *42nd Street* made its debut in March 1933, it was canned rather than live presentations that kept open such theaters as the Victory, the city's oldest surviving theater, built in 1900, renamed the Republic in 1902, and restored and reopened as the New Victory in 1996, and the Apollo, which for a time operated under the name of The Academy. Other of the street's theaters included the Harris, Lyric, Selwyn, and Times Square. The America Theatre was torn down in 1932.

The best known of them, then as now, was the Amsterdam, an Art Nouveau playhouse opened in 1903. It was purchased ten years later by Florenz Ziegfeld, who renamed it the New

Amsterdam, and into which he moved his *Follies*, which played there from 1913 to 1927, when the shows were moved to his newly constructed namesake palace some 14 blocks to the north. It was in the roof garden supper club of the 42nd Street property, officially known as Aerial Gardens, that Ziegfeld produced his subsidiary musicals, the *Nine O'Clock Revues* and the *Midnight Frolics*.

The Plot Unfolds. *42nd Street* begins as a modest travelogue, simulating the route taken by many an East Side swell either to see a stage show or to appear in one. Still photographs of signs spell out the juncture of avenues and cross streets from Third Avenue and East 42nd Street westward to Times Square. They are not presented in precise geographical order, but who would quibble with such a minor inconsistency? Thankfully, the visual jaunt ends before reminders of the elegance that once characterized 42nd Street are overshadowed by the slums of Hell's Kitchen (now called Clinton) on the other side of Eighth Avenue.

In patented Warner Bros. style, the film begins in breathless fashion, with various spokesmen announcing the news that "Jones and Barry are doing a show!" A closeup of a contract dated August 29, 1932, verifies the rumor. The camera then enters the office of Guy Kibbee (Abner Dillon), an aging, short, chubby, bald kiddie car manufacturer and backer of stage properties with a boyish twinkle in his eyes that he reserves for actresses, none of whom takes seriously his attempts to romance them. Unlike the oily Jacques Warriner in *The Broadway Melody*, Kibbee has yet to pass his first lesson in the art of seduction, being neither subtle nor suave enough to impress. His attempts at attracting the opposite sex range from comic to pathetic to petty when repulsed. The earliest example of his congenital awkwardness is his flirtation with Bebe Daniels (Dorothy Brock), whom he reminds that it was on his recommendation that Jones and Barry gave her the lead in their new musical. He expects payment and offers her a proposition. "Call me Abner," he coos, a mild directive that amuses rather than inflames the actress, who wisely catalogues him as a harmless would-be dandy who can be strip-mined

for goodies with ease—and without any commitment on her part.

Warner Baxter is an altogether different case. Unlike Kibbee, whose investment is the only thing on the line every time one of his shows opens, it is Baxter's prized reputation that he wishes to preserve by participating in the new musical show. A veteran of Broadway bouts, he is quite accomplished at picking himself up off the canvas and punching his way to victory. He is first seen in the producing firm's office nervously treading the floorboards while admitting to the partners that he is broke and tired. The only reason he has accepted their offer to serve as general stage director is to make money. Almost wiped out by the Depression, he is determined to recoup his losses, and this time salt enough away for these rainier days bound to come.

Even a telephone call from his physician fails to dissuade Baxter from undertaking the new assignment. He drives himself too hard, the doctor says, warning that the strain of directing another show will not result in just another nervous breakdown, but may prove to be fatal. Looking the partners squarely in the eyes, Baxter admits to the doctor that the struggle for perfection he brings to every show is killing him, but that the new one will be his "last shot" on Broadway. He simply cannot afford to let the producers and himself down by relaxing his standards and giving them anything less than a first-rate show. By now eager to face the daunting task ahead, Baxter hangs up and tells Jones and Barry to issue a chorus call tomorrow morning at 10 sharp.

At the appointed hour, the camera provides a long shot of a stage jammed with youngsters, mostly female, anxious for a job, since like Baxter, they are broke and, in spite of their inbred cynicism, enamored of the theater. Faithful to custom, the troupers are presented as callous individualists, jealous of one another, critical, resentful, and ever on the alert to ridicule their opponents. Chattering like birds of prey scanning the ground for a meal of bones, the *42nd Street* chorus is far more germane to the plot, and to its humor, than the ladies in *The Broadway Melody*.

Two of the chorus applicants were budding

movie stars in real life, equally entitled to more than walk-on roles because of their adeptness as comediennes. This talent was quite evident in Una Merkel, another of the film's carryovers from the silents and Broadway, whose string of comedy appearances would make her face one of the most familiar to 1930s audiences. The other was Ginger Rogers, *42nd Street*'s most obvious young woman of apparent easy virtue whose avocation had earned her the tell-tale moniker of "Anytime Annie." She is defined with precision, if not grace, by dance director Stone, who wryly observes that in Ginger's constant alternating between auditions and bedrooms, "She never said no, and then she didn't hear the question."

Into the scene steps Ruby Keeler, wearing her acolytism to advantage, threading her way through the crowd and timorously asking for the "gentleman in charge." Several of the more acid chorines direct her, first, to the men's room and then to the dressing room of Billy Lawler, a young man seeking the part of the third-ranking male lead, or juvenile. Luckily for Ruby and the Warners, the fellow in the room is Dick Powell, with whom Ruby would team in seven subsequent musical films that turned the twosome into the movies' most popular romantic couple between Janet Gaynor and Charles Farrell and Jeanette MacDonald and Nelson Eddy. Ruby beats a hasty retreat from the dressing room when she discovers he is stripping down to his skivvies to climb into his costume. But the connection has been made. Their mutual attraction glows instantly from the screen, so much so that the handsome tenor offers to introduce the sing-and-dance maiden to Baxter.

Agony and Ecstasy. Hours later, after the applicants have been winnowed down to a fortunate few, Stone notices that he is one girl short. Under Powell's prodding, Baxter agrees to test Ruby, whom he had previously eliminated from consideration, in a routine solo. "She'll do," he mutters while moving to center stage to address the assembly. Like a drill sergeant bellowing orders to draftees, Baxter warns them of the hardships they must endure over the next five weeks. They will work, sweat,

and work some more…They will dance till their feet fall off…They will go though the roughest time they have ever lived, adding that those unable to bear up under such pressure should quit now.

No one leaves the auditorium, however, and all egos are propped up by Baxter's single upbeat promise that when opening night is over, they will be proud to be associated with a hit show that bespeaks professionalism at every level.

The optimism that underlay Baxter's admonition changes to gloom after the first song rehearsal. Purposely derivative and sugar sweet in lyric and melody, "It Must Be June" is embarrassingly typical of many such banalities inserted into low-budget stage and screen shows of the 1929–32 period. Still worse is the choreography, which groups the chorus girls into platoons of nymphs walking aimlessly about the stage carrying hoops of flowers above their heads in an untoward attempt to suggest the arrival of spring.

"It smells!" cries the exasperated albeit acutely observant Baxter, "It's out!" His abrupt dismissal of the number results in protests by lyricist Al Dubin and composer Harry Warren, who appear briefly to play themselves. Warren began his career as a bit actor, "usually as a gangster," in Biograph silent films, and would appear once more, in *Go into Your Dance* (1935). Baxter ignores the complainers, and the scene fades to the outside of the theater to introduce the third of the film's intertwined subplots, this one involving the secret love affair between Bebe and George Brent (Pat Denning).

She had picked him up in her car, where Brent, born George Nolan in Ireland in 1904 and later to co-star with Bette Davis in 11 Warner Bros. dramas, voices his discontent with their clandestine meetings. Like Bessie Love and Charles King in *The Broadway Melody*, Bebe and Brent had once been partners in vaudeville, and it was she who had coached him and laid the plans for both to chase after stardom in New York. She has made it big, Brent has not. Still in love with him, Bebe has been supporting him while he looks for work, in effect demeaning his self-esteem by casting him as a gigolo, a role he is becoming increasingly reluctant to play.

The couple's latest rendezvous has been witnessed by Kibbee, sending out danger signals to be ignored at Baxter's peril. Jones and Barry race over to him and present their already harried director with another production problem. Kibbee, they inform Baxter, is growing fonder of Bebe, and he very well may withdraw his $70,000 financial interest in the show if he learns that the lady is two-timing him with Brent. "No vaudeville chump is going to wreck my show!," Baxter barks, telephoning a gangster acquaintance named Slim Murphy, who is to offer Brent the choice of ending his relationship with the actress or suffering a beating at the hands of Murphy's coterie of thugs.

The next day, during another of Baxter's frequent in-theater fulminations at the dancers' inadequacies, he demands that the chorus dance faster and faster till they are able to perform the routines in their sleep. Unaccustomed to such hectic activity, Ruby passes out. She is carried from the stage floor to an adjoining hallway, where she meets Brent, who is waiting for Bebe. Displaying his innate kindliness, he helps to revive Ruby, comforting her with advice to take things a little easier. He is obviously enchanted with the youngster, whose girlish naïvete stands in stark contrast with the mature, fleeting charms of jaded Bebe. Delighted by his solicitousness, Ruby unwittingly becomes entangled in a four-sided love affair involving Brent, Bebe, Kibbee, and now her.

Bebe, meanwhile, has introduced the film's first song hit, "You're Getting to Be a Habit with Me," one of the finest entries in the extensive Dubin-Warren catalogue. A competent actress as well as singer, she delivers the song while perched in Helen Morgan-style on a piano, remaining respectfully faithful to the lighthearted lyric and tempo throughout. Unaware of Brent's and Ruby's presence, she passes through the corridor a few minutes later on her way to meet the tuxedo-clad Kibbee for a night on the town. Brent watches them climb into a taxi with a mixture of jealousy and resignation, assuming that she is tired of paying his debts while waiting for him to rebuild his career.

Activated more by genuine fondness than retaliation, Brent asks Ruby to have dinner with him. Later that evening, after escorting her to her brownstone walkup, he is confronted by ganglord Murphy, who warns him to "lay off" Bebe. His henchmen then proceed to rough up Brent to give him a sample of the punishment to come his way if refuses to obey the edict. The commotion brings Ruby back down the stairs and over to Brent, sprawled on the sidewalk. She helps him into her apartment, much to the irritation of her Irish landlady, who upbraids her for bringing a man into her room. Insulted, Ruby declares her intention to move out forthwith, a risky decision since she and Brent have only $1.50 between them. Without thinking, Ruby snaps up his offer to share his apartment for the night. After all, they agree, a bed is preferable to a park bench.

At first relaxed and secure in Brent's company, she becomes fearful of being compromised when her benefactor carries his sleepy guest into his bedroom. Although a pauper, Brent is still a gentleman. She will sleep there, alone, while he beds down on the living room sofa. Ruby is pleased with the arrangement, but she is careful to lock the bedroom door anyway.

Next morning, after she has left the apartment for the theater, Brent is visited by Bebe, who notices his packed luggage stacked up at the door. They must part at least temporarily, he explains, adding that he has found a job in Philadelphia. Rather than protesting the separation, Bebe surprisingly accepts it with enthusiasm. She says that she had only wanted to help him financially while he sought that elusive Lucky Break. But she now realizes she has hurt him instead by depriving him of his manhood. There will be no more secret rendezvous, she continues. The time has come for him to make a career for himself under his own steam. Brent agrees, elated by her vow that someday they will be back together again.

Another Openin', Another Show. Meanwhile, the allotted five weeks of rehearsal have elapsed, and although even the latest practice session reminds Baxter of "amateur night," his show will give its pre–Broadway performance the next evening. The site will be the Arch Street Theatre in Philadelphia, not Atlantic City as planned. The mention of Philadelphia naturally gives rise to a series of W.C. Fields–like jabs at its alleged dullness by the chorus, but it causes Bebe to object angrily. Knowing that Brent is there and that work still eludes him, she refuses to go. Baxter's flattering appraisal of her vital importance to the success of the show, however, finally changes her mind.

Actually, Baxter's most recent criticism of his exhausted crew was unfair. Vast improvement is easily detected at the final dress rehearsal, beginning with Bebe's singing and dancing reprise of "You're Getting to Be a Habit with Me," this time with four chorus boys in tow. Constrained from enjoying himself by his self-imposed work regimen and constant worry, Baxter is unable to relax that night by attending the pre-opening parties given by Bebe and by the cast in different suites in a Philadelphia hotel.

Longing for companionship to assure him that the show has all the earmarks of another hit, he calls on Stone to accompany him to his hotel room. For the first time, Baxter is presented as more human than machine, politely questioning the dance director on whether he believes the performers are prepared to face a paying audience and the newspaper critics. Yet he can do no more; the deadline has arrived. Though far less devoted to perfection than his boss, Stone reluctantly breaks a date with miffed Una to while away a few hours trying to console the uptight, self-styled "sick man" still hoping to retain his foothold at the top of his profession.

At Bebe's party, Kibbee makes a pest of himself, much to her chagrin. That the nerves of all her guests are frayed almost to the breaking point fails to dissuade the old man, drunk and crass, from offending almost everyone. More exhausted than anyone else, Bebe finally explodes after Kibbee openly accuses her of giving him the air even though it was he who had finagled her into the leading part. She orders him out of the suite, and slaps him when he refuses her demand. He and her other guests finally do leave when Bessie shows no willingness to control her temper tantrum, underscoring her anger by throwing various pieces of crockery at them to propel their departure.

Her argument with Kibbee results in Bebe's hurrying to Brent's lower-floor hotel room and begging him to take her back. Kibbee, meanwhile, has stormed into Baxter's room with the demand that he drop Bebe from the show. Bax-ter is up to the challenge, reminding the "pot-bellied sap" that it is far too late to make any cast changes, and moreover that any profit Kibbee hopes to make on his investment depends almost entirely on her professionalism and popularity. Kibbee relents. Bebe can go on as scheduled, but only if she apologizes to him for her outburst—and tonight.

At the cast party, Ruby flees the suite after being pawed by a chorus boy (Edward J. Nugent). On the way down the stairs, she catches sight of Bebe kissing Brent on her way into his room. Showing no disappointment that the two are apparently lovers, Ruby knocks at the door to tell Brent that she has heard from gossipy colleagues that trouble is heading his way. Having received no apology from anyone, Kibbee is back on the warpath. Bebe, wrongly inferring that Ruby is in love with Brent, struggles to pull him away from the youngster, falling to the floor in the ensuing shoving match. Worried when she is unable to stand up, Brent calls Baxter, who arrives at his room just in time to hear the house doctor (George Irving) confirm Brent's own prognosis that Bebe has fractured her ankle. From her moans and pained expression, Baxter surmises that his leading lady's broken ankle will not permit her to live up to her well-wishers' customary sendoff that she "break a leg" on stage that evening. More disillusioned than ever, he cancels the opening night performance.

With Kibbee now courting Ginger, he and his new protégée visit Baxter the next morning. The harried director refuses Kibbee's demand that Ginger replace Bebe, and, curiously, so does the lady. She admits she wants the part, but she also knows that she has neither the talent nor the charisma to support an entire Broadway production. But there is someone who can—Ruby! She pleads with Baxter to give the girl the part. "I've been waiting years for a break like this," Ginger confides. "So Peggy must be really good to make me recommend her for it."

Ruby is stunned when Baxter asks whether she feels able to substitute for Bebe, and that the role is hers if she wants it. He reminds her that she is already familiar with the songs and dialogue; all she needs is an intensive five hours of rehearsal to put them in proper perspective. Dazed, Ruby nods wary agreement. True to his work ethic, Baxter rushes her into Bebe's former dressing room and through an excruciating crash course in what it takes for an apprentice chorus girl to qualify as a leading lady in one afternoon. Ruby proves to be a quick study, and one hour before the show is to open, Baxter announces to the tense crew that the show will definitely go on.

Ruby then receives two visitors, both intent on priming her confidence. The first is Powell, who confesses his love for her and happily receives acknowledgment that she feels the same way about him. He leaves as Bebe, contrite and sympathetic, limps into the room. She admits she had planned to pull out Ruby's hair for usurping her role. Yet, she continues in the halting voice of a thoroughly tired-out veteran of theatrical wars, she's been given many chances to excel, and now it's Ruby's turn. Like Anita Page in *The Broadway Melody*, Bebe is entirely willing to forgo future theatrical triumphs. Despite all the adulation, publicity, and money, her years in the spotlight have prevented her from getting the only thing in life that really matters to her. But no longer. She will be marrying Brent tomorrow and happily become his co-star for life in bed. As for Ruby, the ailing ex-star expresses certainty that her youth, beauty, and freshness are all she'll need to click in the role thrust upon her.

Final Examination. The house is filled that night by the time the pit orchestra strikes up the overture. While on her way to the stage, Ruby is called aside by Baxter, who demands that she give the best performance she is capable of. Since the film was released in a Depression year, it was entirely appropriate that Baxter would solemnly impress upon her the importance of succeeding by linking it to the fortunes of the entire company. "Two hundred people, two hundred jobs, two hundred thousand dollars, five weeks of grind and blood and sweat depend upon you. It's the lives of all these people who've worked with you. You've got to go on, and you've got to give and give and give…. You can't fall down. You can't because your future's in it, my future, and everything all of us have is staked in you." It is not only for her sake, but for that of the anonymous behind-the-footlights stage hands and technicians as well as the performers that Ruby has to come back a star. Their livelihood depends on her, as does the survival of their families. Weighty indeed is the burden he has placed on the youngster's shoulders, but she accepts it as a duty that the largely out-of-work audiences of the time would readily appreciate and silently applaud.

As in *Footlight Parade*, which followed *42nd Street* by five months, the three production numbers come in rapid succession near the end of the film. The first, the peppy "Young and Healthy," became noted as one of dance director Busby Berkeley's earliest Warner Bros. sequences that depended for spectacle on the arrangement of the chorus in geometric patterns suggesting flower petals. It was also the first time that Berkeley dollied the camera between the legs of standing chorus girls, an inventive if somewhat bizarre angle that was effectively satirized in *The Boy Friend* 38 years later. A delightful tune, though nowhere nearly so popular as the other three *42nd Street* songs, "Young and Healthy" is crooned by Powell to an unbilled blonde with one of the prettiest faces ever to decorate a Hollywood chorus line. She reappears even more briefly in the next song.

Under the watchful eyes of Baxter, Ruby enters the show in a replica of Grand Central Station, where a train platform divides in half to reveal the interior of a Niagara Falls–bound train. On it are newlyweds Ruby and Clarence Nordstrom, who duet one of Warner Bros.' biggest and best hits, "Shuffle Off to Buffalo." Warren's bouncy melody is enlivened still further by Dubin's exceptional, and mildly suggestive, three sets of lyrics, alternating between the frivolous and the saucy, between the young marrieds' joyful anticipation of their honeymoon (first chorus) and the cynical divorcées' sour recollections of wedded life (second and third choruses), all of them sounding off from their berths in Pullman cars.

The third and final number, consisting of the toe-tapping title tune, several vignettes, and about 100 dancers, provides a highly stylized survey of some of the offbeat characters and activities that most out-of-towners assumed were typical of Times Square at a time when the atmosphere was more carnival that sleazy. The song is introduced by Ruby, dressed in top hat, tights, long black stockings, and what appear to be orthopedic shoes, who sings and then dances it. Although some critics have judged her dancing as bordering on the amateurish because of her habit of looking down at her feet instead of at the audience, she was by no means the only dancing celebrity who did. Two better-known exponents of this clumsiness were Joan Crawford, who rarely raises her head while performing Harold Adamson-Burton Lane's "Everything I Have Is Yours" in *Dancing Lady*, and Marion Davies in *Going Hollywood* (both 1933).

Ruby's rendition is followed by a brief camera tour of the street, crowded with panhandlers, peddlers, and passers-by, and hairdressers, porters, shoeshiners, clerks at work, black children dancing on the sidewalk, men-about-town strolling arm in arm with ladies of the night, a drunk or two, and an occasional taxicab. The clearly artificial set, which included a surreal representation of the elevated subway station at the corner of Sixth Avenue and 42nd Street, was typical of the kind mounted for all the screen musicals of the era. Not until he choreographed Gold Diggers of 1933 later in the year would Berkeley stray from the manageable and suggestive to the outlandish, placing showgirls and boys on huge, complicated backdrops so incapable of duplication on any stage that they seemed to represent sheer absurdity for its own sake, eye- catching as his excesses undoubtedly were.

About midway through the slice-of-life tour of 42nd Street, a woman battles inside her flat to keep an attacking man at bay. She jumps from the balcony to escape his lurches only to die on the street from her paramour's stabs in the back. The chorus then enters, along with Powell and Ruby, who reprise the song and end the sequence clasped in each other's arms above a pasteboard high-rise office building. The model for the skyscraper must have stood on another street, since, save for two medium-height structures, 42nd Street between Sixth and Eighth Avenues contained no really tall buildings then or now.

The inaugural performance of "Pretty Lady" over, it is a brain- and bone-weary Baxter who ambles out the stage door into the alley.

That the show is a hit is verified from the comments of departing theatergoers; but the fact that his reputation has not been sullied by anyone in the cast means little to him. He has just passed through a five-week orgy that has siphoned all pride and life out of him. Besides, some of the comments he hears do not exactly massage the ego. "Without a talented girl like Peggy Sawyer, there'd be no show at all," one woman declares, while a man opines that "Marsh'll probably take all the credit by claiming he discovered her." Says another, "Some guys get all the breaks," downgrading the time and effort expended by Baxter to refine the show through endless rehearsals, keeping the cast constantly on its collective toes, and injecting a sense of professionalism into the arteries of misfits who only a few short weeks ago had answered a chorus call as disgruntled neophytes.

Baxter slumps to the bottom step of an adjoining stairwell with only a cigarette to keep him company, disheveled, dejected despite his latest success, too much alone to celebrate, too exhausted to care, an extinct volcano.

Not the typical ending to a musical comedy, certainly, but one of the most persuasively realistic ever to appear on a movie screen.

She Done Him Wrong (1933)

A Paramount picture. DIRECTOR: Lowell Sherman. PRODUCER: William LeBaron. SCREENWRITERS: Harvey Thew and John Bright, based on the play *Diamond Lil*, by Mae West. CINEMATOGRAPHER: Charles Lang. FILM EDITOR: Al Hall. ART DIRECTOR: Robert Usher. CHOREOGRAPHER: Harold Hecht. COSTUMES: Edith Head. ORIGINAL SONGS: lyrics and music by Ralph Rainger. RUNNING TIME: 1 hour, 6 minutes. *Principal Players*: Mae West (Lady Lou). Cary Grant (Captain Cummings). Owen Moore (Chick Clark). Gilbert Roland (Serge Stanieff). Noah Berry, Sr. (Gus Jordan). Rafaela Ottiano (Russian Rita). Dewey Robinson (Spider Kane). David Landau (Dan Flynn). Rochelle Hudson (Sally Glynn). Tammany Young (Chuck Connors). Louise Beavers (Pearl). *Major Academy Award Nomination*: Best Picture.

That Mae West's entrance line would be memorable was a foregone conclusion. Already renowned on both coasts as the undisputed mistress of one-liners waist deep in sexual innuendo delivered in lower-register tones, she was determined from the outset of *She Done*

Mae West ogles an unbilled actor while Cary Grant ogles her during the filming of *She Done Him Wrong*.

Him Wrong not to disappoint. And she doesn't. Sweeping into Gus Jordan's combination saloon and cabaret in The Bowery, she is complimented by a woman on the garish, plumed garments draped over her statuesque figure.

Mae nods her head in complete agreement, explaining that her fastidious finery and regal demeanor long ago earned her the deserved reputation as "one of the finest women who ever walked the streets." In that single line, the tone of the picture as a virtual kama sutra of dou-ble-entendres is set, as is her role as a plump heartbreaker and bistro chanteuse, her indeli-cate gestures and swagger as overcooked—and hilarious—as ever.

Although she lacked the vitality of Sophie Tucker and the enlightened buffoonery of Marie Dressler, only Mae could have replaced these two entertainers as a stout, sometimes risqué, fan favorite. Her buxomness, which during World War II provided ample justification for nicknaming a popular inflatable life jacket the "Mae West," was one of her biggest assets, and one that the other two en-tertainers were unable to match. When she sang, she sounded like Sophie, whose career was in serious decline in 1933, and she domi-nated her films, as had Marie, who died that year. So in Mae West, Hollywood found the perfect successor to the "Last of the Red Hot Mammas," as well as to the peerless MGM comedienne, uniquely able to tantalize the op-posite sex while deflating pomposity with dia-logue directness. Women were not exactly en-amored of the blonde bombshell. In the first place, her colorful, florid costumes were widely regarded as unappealing when compared with the plain brown felt chapeaux and unfrilly frocks worn by most mid–1930s ladies. And it is doubtful that they appreciated her attrac-tiveness to men.

In all her early pictures, Mae played char-acters who were not exactly models of virtue: a lower-economic-class temptress in *Night After Night*; a burlesque queen in *Belle of the Nineties*; a Bowery con artist who specialized in selling the Brooklyn Bridge in *Every Day's a Holiday*; a dance hall hostess in *Goin' to Town*; and a small-time circus performer in *I'm No Angel*. But her male fans never took umbrage at any-thing she said or did, rallying to her defense by buying enough tickets to suggest widespread approval of her roles and the desire to see more of the same. So numerous were her supporters that she was twice included in the list of Hol-lywood's Top Ten moneymakers, ranking eighth in 1933 and fifth the next year.

Her specific job in *She Done Him Wrong*, at which she excelled, was to further intoxicate the male patrons of the bar with her exagger-ated glamour and inimitable singing of torch songs. With the exception of "Frankie and Johnny," of unknown authorship, Mae's two other songs were written by Ralph Rainger, Paramount's long-term and ever on-call com-poser who this time out also wrote the lyrics. An early sound-movie composer, Rainger at the time specialized in sober, blues-like melodies, like "Moanin' Low" and "Here Lies Love," written at the outset of his career, the first for Broadway, the other for Paramount. Neither of his *She Done Him Wrong* tunes ranks among his best compositions, nor did they de-velop into hits. But they fit Mae's serio-comic singing style like a slinky satin glove. Her role as instigator of sexual fantasies was the same one she had played for years on the Broadway stage, sometimes witnessing the abrupt closing of her shows by the police for alleged im-morality. She would continue to supply ener-gizing plasma to seven more films up to her temporary retirement after *The Heat's On* in 1943.

It was natural that The Bowery should serve as the site of her *She Done Him Wrong* dalliances. Her mild Brooklyn accent and in-nate cynicism instantly identified her as an am-bitious native of that backroom borough who had crossed the East River to acquire fame and fortune. The character she plays naturally adopts that Lower Manhattan neighborhood as her personal stamping ground, what with its adeptness at luring residents and visitors into partaking of its imposing array of honky-tonk attractions, some of which actually matched the notoriety of "Lady Lou" herself. So many and varied were these pleasure dens that two late-19th-century popular songwriters, Charles H. Hoyt and Percy Gaunt, were compelled to lament their shock value in the familiar lines, "The Bowery! The Bowery! / I'll never go there any more." For some people, it seems, once was enough.

At one time a country lane that ran be-tween the "bouweries," or farms, of Dutch and Walloon burghers, including Peter Stuyvesant, director general of what was then known as New Netherland, The Bowery was one of the Big Town's biggest carnival centers even be-fore Mae got there. Block after block was lined with freak shows, from which vaudeville arose, penny arcades, bars that featured live musical performers, and a scattering of theaters. Not noted for observing all the moral tenets of the day, the Coney Islandesque community was far different from the disreputable slum it became in the 1930s, when every tour bus in Manhattan carried visitors south along Third Avenue to view a veritable boulevard of broken dreams. By then the Bowery was America's best-known Skid Row, crammed with cheap men's hotels, missions and flop houses, pawn shops and greasy spoons, and drunks passed out on the sidewalk or in the gutter.

The buzz of activity that turned Mae's Bowery into march routes for curious and carefree browsers was duplicated above ground, where steam-powered Third Avenue Elevated Railroad cars, some heading south on one side of the street, some in the opposite direction on the other side, permitted only slivers of daylight to drop through the slim open spaces between the rails onto the sidewalk. Black, it might be said, was The Bowery's dominant color, brightened only when Mae paraded along it decked out in her starched Easter finery, which she wore throughout the year. Noise was another dominant characteristic, much of it arising from pedestrians and amusement show barkers forced to shout their messages to be heard above the raucous rattle of the electrified streetcars than ran up and down the cobblestoned street.

But The Bowery boasted at least one incontestable attraction to libidinous and virtuous alike, especially of the penny-pinching variety. Its restaurants were uniformly good, if not grand, and the prices were dirt cheap. As late as 1900, according to a menu preserved in the New York Public Library's Buttolph Collection, the Squirrel Inn, a most respectable eatery at 131 Bowery, offered "regular" breakfasts, dinners, and suppers for pocket change. Early morning diners, for example, could partake of griddle cakes or an egg omelet for 15 cents, with bread and butter and either coffee, tea, cocoa, or milk thrown in. Around noontime, a small steak or liver and bacon, along with soup, beverage, and dessert, cost the same.

Come supper time, they could avail themselves of ham and beans, corned beef hash, or beef stew for a dime. For an extra nickel they could order a choice of pie or pudding, or if still hungry for meat, any kind of sandwich.

The jewels that Mae acquired from uptown admirers were therefore of incalculable worth, beyond the comprehension of people accustomed to 1990s prices. Little wonder the fleshy lady's chief goal was to accumulate as many as possible, thereby adding greed to her laundry list of vices. The proceeds from a pawned diamond ring could easily support her for a lifetime, considering that she could be fed well three times a day for a whole week for seven dollars, and still have some change left over to tip or keep.

Short and Sultry. Reviewing the film, the shortest of all the nominated musicals (about one-third the length of *Fiddler on the Roof*), more than 60 years after its debut forces one to question why it was considered for an Academy Award instead of, say, the far superior Gold Diggers of 1933 or *Footlight Parade*. Disinclination to nominate three Warner Bros. musicals in the same year was possibly the major reason, especially in light of the fact that Warners had practically no competitors in the field throughout 1933. No fewer than four Paramount pictures, however, had been put up for grabs in the 1927-28 season.

The plot of *She Done Him Wrong* is trivial, unduly complicated, and peopled by the same kind of men—short, slim, mean, and jittery—who wore those black hats in the new rash of talking Westerns beginning to flood movie screens. Fleshing out these broadly drawn characters were subsidiary actors who, for all their facial familiarity, could hardly be classified as more than third-level "stars" drifting toward the fringes of obscurity.

Gilbert Roland's career was in temporary eclipse after almost 15 years of screen experience, as was that of Noah Beery, Sr., brother of Wallace and father of Noah, Jr., who would carry the family name into numerous B-picture Westerns and thrillers of the thirties and forties. Owen Moore, a film actor since 1908 and one time husband of Mary Pickford, had been relegated to minor roles in co-features for more than a decade, while a stiff and humorless Cary Grant was given no opportunity to display the natural flair for unruffled sophistication that was to be his most engaging trait beginning with *Big Brown Eyes* three years later.

The picture is inadequate in everything except comedy, and even that is apparent only when Mae is on the screen, a fact that underscores the magnetic spell that a true star, even one with only one film behind her in 1933, can cast over the box office. Without the spice Mae adds to this Paramount confection, it would be little more than a tasteless 19th-century melodrama so out of tune with 1930s America as to confound critics trying to determine why it was made. And melodramatic the film surely is, but intentionally. Lowell Sherman, an actor as well as director, refused to allow any of the performers to camp his or her role, stultifying as they all are, wisely permitting them to infuse their characterizations with a seriousness that lent at least a modicum of credence to the proceedings.

The excellent cinematography by Charles Lang was not exactly groundbreaking, but its smooth transitions from closeups to medium and long shots overcame the abruptness that had marred changes of view in many earlier musical pictures. In a rare retreat from the normal, his camera generously tracks Mae and others along Paramount's backlot facsimile of The Bowery, supplying both visual variety and flow to a movie that otherwise would have been statically confined to the bar, Mae's apartment, and a jail cell.

The extent to which the resurrective power of cinematography can be abetted by creativity of set and costume design is quite apparent in *She Done Him Wrong*. Combined, they project a realistic "Gay Nineties" atmosphere, when waiters sang in lattice-wrought bistros and men wearing derbies and spats bellied up to the bar for five-cent schooners of lager beer and free lunches. Particular favorites, the film indicates, were Eben E. Rexford and Hart Pease Danks' "Silver Threads among the Gold," Theodore Metz's "Ta-ra-ra Boom-de-Ree," and Charles K. Harris's "After the Ball," more than any other song certain to be heard in any film reenactment of that period. The care the studio's craftsmen and women devoted to mirroring these sights and sounds of that bygone era made it easy for the middle-aged and elderly in the audience to relive their own youth.

Superb at playing the eternal temptress, Mae's screen persona was more akin to that of the worldly-wise, 40-something woman than of the curvaceous "Betty Boop" cutie. Few other actresses of the time would point with pride to the painting above Gus's bar of a reclining nude blonde of voluptuous Italian Renaissance proportions and admit that she had posed for it. But Mae remained aloof while on the prey for male companionship, choosing one, dismissing the other with the indifference of a grocer discarding smudged apples from his bins of edible fruit.

To flex her charms, she allowed her eyes to promise delectable interludes of illegitimate love that her innate strain of morality prevented her from fulfilling—usually. She was a born flirt, turning susceptible men into panting sycophants. An unrivaled purveyor of sexual fantasies, she reveled in raising male passion only to deflate it with the flimsy excuse that the suitor had either misread her intentions or wildly misjudged their own appeal.

She soon tired of her men, quickly ending any relationship that threatened her virtue, which for the most part was unassailable, by deriding their efforts and finally driving them into the ground like human spikes. What she mostly longed for was attention, even adulation, of the kind that the lowliest citizen bestows on the unapproachable empress. Or at least to receive such a compliment as the one to be uttered seven years later by an enamored W.C. Fields in *My Little Chickadee*, when he described Mae as "easy on the ears and a banquet for the eyes."

It was most likely her calculated attempts to decoy would-be lovers into sexual satisfaction and then deceive them, leaving them as mere shells of the men they once were, that prompted the ironic title of the film, which was based on her own Broadway play. As the "Frankie and Johnny" lyric points out, men had long done women wrong. But now Mae was about to turn the tables on them. This time it was to be a woman who would do them wrong.

A kind of reverse morality play, *She Done Him Wrong* presents Mae in her truest light. Self-centered to a fault, she takes advantage of no one, except scheming male acquaintances who deserve the fleecing she gives them. She unapologetically lives life to satisfy only herself, and is swift to peel away social cant and expose hypocrisy. As in all of her early films, the usually stone-hearted Mae gains audience sympathy by her readiness to act as intermediary between the defenseless and those who would do them wrong.

Her multi-layered dialogue naturally played havoc with the censors, who were usually at a loss over what to delete from her pictures and for what reason. The result was that they allowed her to run full throttle through her pictures, since sensuous as Mae was, she never veered into salaciousness, although she had a knack for hinting at it without speaking a word. As Mae herself explains at her deadpan best at the beginning of the film, she likes things to be a "little spicy, but not too raw, you know what I mean?"

An unreconstructed Jazz Age woman, she was more or less permitted to drift at leisure from man to man, from music hall to boudoir as she wished up to 1935, when the newly strengthened Motion Picture Production Code forced even her to sing, in *Goin' to Town*, that "Now I'm a Lady." Unfortunately, she returned to her former wastrel ways with uncharacteristic vengeance in 1978 in the self-destructive film disaster *Sextette*. She died two years later at the age of 85. The respectable, often insightful 1982 television movie *Mae West* starred Ann Jillian in the title role.

Selfish and Selfless. Like most thirties musicals, regardless of what era they were set in, *She Done Him Wrong* has a show business background and the pretty, innocent young girl destined to learn the evils of the Big Town the hard way. With more accuracy than usual, the prologue to the film defines the 1890s not as a "Gilded Age"—which it was, if only for the wealthy—but as a "lusty, brawling, florid decade," to which histories of the period attest. From that point on, it is up to Mae to prove the validity of that verdict.

The will-o'-the-wisp plot begins when bar owner Noah Beery, Sr. (Gus Jordan) tells Mae (Lady Lou) that he is danger of losing his business because of the frequent intrusions of Cary Grant (Captain Cummings), commandant of the Bowery Mission, situated next door, and a formidable crusader against any establishment that caters to wine, women, and song. He adds that he has warned the handsome young reformer to stay away, but to no avail, and that

she should tone down her stage performances whenever he comes into view. On the way to her dressing room, Mae greets her friend Rafaela Ottiano (Russian Rita), who introduces Mae to Gilbert Roland (Serge Stanieff). "I've heard so much about you," he oozes after confirming in his mind that it is Mae's likeness that hangs on the bar room wall. "Yeah, but you can't prove it," Mae quips with a wink. She obviously welcomes his lecherous appraisal of her charms while enjoying her own usual top-to-bottom inspection of her latest conquest.

As she is about to walk to her upstairs apartment, which like Mae herself is stuffed with an oversupply of luxurious trinkets, young and distraught Rochelle Hudson (Sally Glynn) enters the bar. Mae's mood changes from detached observer of saloon life to concerned confidante when Rochelle seems about to faint. Mae escorts the young woman to her apartment, where she attributes the swoon to man trouble. Mae, of course, knows all about that; her vast exposure to the malady has made her an expert at recognizing the symptoms in other women.

Deserted by her lover, Rochelle admits that until recently she had not been aware that he was married all the time. Mae nods sagely and orders her maid, Louise Beavers, in her customary role as the amiable Aunt Jemima of black domestics, to launch the uplifting of Rochelle's morale by replacing her drab clothing with an assortment of Mae's leftovers. "When a woman goes wrong, men go right after them," Mae comments, sizing Rochelle up as immature, vulnerable, and in need of a sprucing up to attract replacement suitors.

Mae's concern for the girl is understandable and for a much stronger reason than the one about how opposites attract. Then 19, the black-haired actress with the eyes of blue was perfection as another dainty innocent whose hopes would be dashed on the rocks of big-city reality, and yet spunky enough to assert herself when absolutely necessary. It was with surprise, or more likely shock, that fans observed this soft-spoken youngster, who had played Shirley Temple's older sister in *Curly Top* (1935), in roles as a gangster's moll, even as a machine gun-wielding member of the mob, in a collection of B-level shoot-'em-up thrillers, like *Show Then No Mercy*, beginning in the late thirties.

But Mae is able to offer only temporary solace. Rochelle is so far along on the path to emotional breakdown that she becomes a willing victim of the scheming Rafaela, who befriends the young woman with promises of material help. Can you sing, she asks. If so, Rafaela adds, she can assure Rochelle of a lucrative job on San Francisco's Barbary Coast, at the time widely regarded as The Bowery West.

As they talk, into the bar strolls Grant. That he looks upon bar owner Gus with anything less than total contempt is quickly dispelled when he shields a derelict who has just broken the front display window in an alcoholic rage. The mission captain tells the police that the man had been with him all day, a falsehood cheerily backed up by cop-hating Mae, who appreciates Grant's deception as much as his good looks and tight-fitting uniform. Her sexual antennae starting to quiver, she clearly labels him as her next seductee, partly out of genuine appreciation of his attractiveness, partly to romance him out of curtailing her employment opportunities by shutting the bar and other iniquitous establishments scattered throughout the neighborhood.

Although probably not the grande dame of Bowery seediness, Gus's place is a powerful magnet for as mangy a clientele as Captain Grant could ever hope to lock up. Moore, Roland, and Rafaela are crooked as a W.C. Fields pool cue. Fellow habitues Dewey Robinson (Spider Kane) and Tammany Young (Chuck Connors) are devious and corrupt. And David Landau (Dan Flynn), who learned little the previous year from his agonizing defeat at fixing football games at the hands of an even cleverer Harpo Marx in *Horse Feathers*, is a scheming political hack.

Maybe Next Time? At the moment, Mae is unaware that the captain's mission house is suffering from a shortage of contributions that threatens its ability to pay the rent. Ever the straight-arrow gentleman, Grant declines her irreverent invitation to accompany her to her apartment. Bouncing back from the unaccustomed rebuff, Mae confirms in her best-known film line that the invitation is open-ended: "Why don't you come up and see me sometime?," frequently misquoted as "Why don't you come up sometime and see me?"

Alone in her quarters and avidly perusing the guardedly prurient pages of *The Policemen's Gazette*, Mae learns from Dewey Robinson that a disreputable old flame, Owen Moore (Chick Clark) desperately wants her to visit him in jail, where he has been confined for stealing bangles and baubles on her behalf. The news disturbs the usually phlegmatic Mae, who has no interest in stoking the embers of a dead romance.

She agrees to make the trip, however, when Robinson informs her that Moore is becoming quite perturbed, to put it mildly, at her absence. The jail scene is extraneous to the plot, which is not exactly nail-biting to begin with. But it does underline the breadth of Mae's underworld liaisons when all of Moore's cellmates greet her warmly as an old friend. Already suspicious of Mae's vow to love only him, Moore warns that he will kill her if he ever learns she has been false to him.

Like Dolly Levi some 50 years later, Mae is relieved to be back where she belongs. Regaling herself in her comfortable apartment and dismissive of Moore's threat, Mae for a second time reveals her marshmallow heart by offering to purchase the mission house from its Simon Legree landlord for $12,000 in cash, which she intends to raise by pawning bits and pieces from her storehouse of jewels. She again confronts Grant, who this time obligingly follows her up the stairs for a brief, but strictly platonic, visit. Her next guest is ward-heeling Landau, another old flame dropped cold turkey by Mae the minute he became more pesty than amorous. He surprises her with the information that Beery is bankrupt, a distressing state of affairs that has left him without funds to subsidize political payoffs, which Mae correctly translates into a virtual guarantee that the bar will be closed by the legendary New York City policeman nicknamed "The Hawk."

Still hopeful of convincing Mae of his irresistibility, Landau discloses a plan to keep her in her job as resident diva and in the luxury she regards as a birthright. He will facilitate Gus's arrest by The Hawk and take over the bar himself. Delighted at the prospect of insuring her professional and lifestyle security, Mae revs up her interest in Landau and begins cozying up to him. Like the rest of her male targets, Landau interprets as charm what the ladies instantly recognized as guile.

Her love campaign is interrupted, however, by the unannounced appearance of Robinson, who informs Mae that Moore has broken out of jail. How he managed to do so is only the first in a long list of imponderables in a script with enough holes to sink a light cruiser. Grant adds to her nervousness by paying a second visit to ask what has happened to the missing Rochelle, whose father, wondering what became of Sally, had inquired of her whereabouts at the mission.

Unable to provide any information, Mae shrugs off the young woman's fate to resume her one-sided courtship with businesslike Grant. She is unable to bulldoze his rock-hard standoffishness, but a few cracks begin to appear as she continues to turn up the heat. Only moderately disappointed when he retreats back to the mission, she summarizes her progress to date with the leering observation, "Well, it won't be long now." No other lady of the screen was so enamored of herself or, for that matter, more certain of trumping adversity with patience.

Mae's next visitor of the evening is escapee Moore, who demands that she accompany him on a trip to a new life far away from The Bowery. When she refuses, and in addition tells him that she never loved him, he tries to strangle her. But he pauses, unable to follow through; he still loves her despite all the unhappiness she has caused him. Besides, the attempted murder is thwarted by Roland, who barges in and throws Moore aside in his rush to aid Mae and repeat his fascination for her by declaring that she was obviously "made for love," his in particular.

Rafaela is next to burst into the room, where she catches her lover in Mae's embrace and upbraids Roland for unfaithfulness and Mae for betraying a friend. A second struggle ensues, this one between Rafaela and Mae, who is twice her opponent's size. Further infuriating Rafaela is the discovery of a diamond pin she once owned swinging on Mae's bodice. Pulling a knife from her purse, she inadvertently stabs herself instead and dies moments later.

Beery and a policeman race into Mae's quarters, which by this time resembles a waiting room in Grand Central Terminal, in hopes of recapturing Moore. Alert as ever to potential danger, Mae seats Rafaela's corpse on a chair, props it up like a dummy, and pretends to be combing her hair until everybody leaves. She then wraps Rafaela into a loose package, presumably for later burial. Having regained her customary cool after all these encounters, Mae swishes down the stairs, cooly takes her place on the stage, and serenades her attentive audience with the sexually implicit lyric of "A Guy What Takes His Time," which, like her earlier rendition of "Easy Rider," holds a variety of interpretations, depending on the mood of the listener.

As soon as the applause dies away, Mae saunters over to Beery and asks whether he knows what has happened to the missing Rochelle. Playing up to him to elicit an answer, she first has to assure the jealous bar owner that Roland means nothing to her. Unexpectedly, Moore reappears in the bar and shoots Landau, whom he recognizes as a rival for Mae's hand. The gunfire leads to the dispatch of Grant and a squad of policemen to the scene. They arrest Beery, who, now it can be told, had been a partner all along with Rafaela and Roland in a counterfeiting ring. Also arrested is Roland, fingered by Rochelle, who bursts out of nowhere and charges him with transporting girls like herself to San Francisco for purposes unquestionably immoral.

Assuming that Mae is somehow involved in at least one of these illegal enterprises, Grant takes the shady lady into custody but acquiesces to her demand that she not be forced to suffer the indignity of being transported along her beloved Bowery with the other captives in a police wagon. She contends that her exalted status on the Strip entitles her to make the trip in a hansom cab, and also to adorn herself with her ermine wrap.

Joining her in the cab, Grant tries his hand at love-making, but now it is Mae's turn to exhibit lacerating disinterestedness. Seeking to gain her confidence, he confirms her fear that the police will confiscate all her ill-gotten goods, but insists that she will not be sent to prison. Maintaining that she is his prisoner as he slides a ring down her finger, he adds that he'll happily be her official "jailer" for a long, long time. Grant's vows of clemency and life commitment as husband can be taken at face value. His is the voice of authority that speaks nothing but the truth. A master of disguise, he is widely respected by the police and city fathers, and therefore accustomed to having his own way. He is also a shrewdy, the personality asset most admired by Mae.

Besides, who else would have been clever enough to conceal from her his true identity as The Hawk till the very end—even if everyone in the audience had coupled them together as early as the third reel?

Flirtation Walk (1934)

A First National picture. DIRECTOR: Frank Borzage. SCREENWRITER: Delmer Davies, from an original story by Daves and Lou Edelman. CINEMATOGRAPHERS: Sol Polito and George Barnes. FILM EDITOR: William Holmes. CHOREOGRAPHER: Bobby Connolly. MUSICAL CONDUCTOR: Leo F. Forbstein. ORIGINAL SONGS: lyrics by Mort Dixon, music by Allie Wrubel. RUNNING TIME: 1 hour, 37 minutes. *Principal Players*: Dick Powell (Dick ["Canary"] Dorcy, Jr.) Ruby Keeler (Kit Fitts). Pat O'Brien (Scrapper Thornhill). Ross Alexander (Oskie). John Eldredge (Lieutenant Ben Biddle). Henry O'Neill (General John Brent Fitts). Guinn Williams (Sleepy). *Major Academy Award Nomination*: Best Picture.

One of the three musical films nominated for best picture of 1934, *Flirtation Walk* suffers in comparison with its rival candidates, *The Gay Divorcee* and *One Night of Love*, in plot and acting, if not in characterization, which throughout the three films clearly adheres to standard musical comedy format by reducing both leading and subsidiary players to single-dimension status. All the *Flirtation Walk* participants are motivated by a single determinant that spurs them to action, be it ambition, jealousy, endlessly striving for perfection, or valuing friendship as the most rewarding of all male relationships. With its brisk pace and pleasing personnel, the film qualifies as an important forerunner of the multitude of contrived World War II comedies and dramas revolving around the reformation of the anti-hero, who is eventually converted from balky recruit to effective leader proud to wear the uniform of his particular military service. The producing studio, First National Pictures, had been founded as

First National Exhibitors' Circuit in 1917 and became a part of Warner Bros. in 1925.

Interest in the characters in *Flirtation Walk* is sustained for a longer period than in the other two nominees. Few persons in the audience were wealthy enough to pursue a love affair amid the opulent resort surroundings that made *The Gay Divorcee* such an engaging excursion into Depression-era escapism. Nor did many moviegoers know an aspiring opera star or plan to vacation in such a seductive site as Milan, Italy, where much of *One Night of Love* is set.

A great number, however, were familiar with military life. With World War I fewer than a score of years in the past, a great number of older viewers had fought in it and maintained a justifiable respect for the Army, if not fond recollections of the officers schooled at West Point, to which *Flirtation Walk* is "respectfully dedicated." Then, too, it was becoming increasingly apparent that Adolf Hitler, who succeeded Paul von Hindenburg as leader of Germany on August 2, 1934, about the same time that *Flirtation Walk* was released, was entirely capable of threatening world peace with a clear and present danger.

Thanks to the glut of love stories making the rounds of film houses, viewers had become well acquainted with short-circuited love affairs, a rather common screenplay occurrence made transitory by the perpetual happy endings that the Hollywood of the time tacked on to its products. And a second glut—the recent revival of peeks at backstage Broadway like—had taught them that producing a stage musical was fraught with perils involving ego and artistic integrity.

As appeared so often in other film genres, the basic incompatibility existing between the two leading male characters gives *Flirtation Walk* all of its comedy and most of its sentimentality. Set almost totally in the refined and disciplined precincts of West Point, that renowned Hudson River enclave a short distance north of New York, the film has as much in common with male-oriented adventure yarns as with musical comedy's conventional romantic buildup to the final-reel uniting of hero and heroine. The picture is, in fact, the first Grade A musical to combine a seemingly incongruous Don Quixote-Sancho Panza relationship and a boy-meets-girl love affair in the same plot.

Dick Powell, holding the upraised sword, and Ruby Keeler as the "Lady General" during the "No Horse, No Wife, No Mustache" musical skit in *Flirtation Walk.*

Starkly different as the typical male partners in Hollywood's adventure films were, and still are, in personality, lifestyle, and goals, their pairing on picaresque voyages has always appealed to a huge market of action film fans. Each is selfish yet selfless, too. The antagonism that often strains their relationship is overcome by compatibility in crises. The handsome, basically non-violent partner—the star of the film—is well groomed and gentle of bearing. Introspective and analytical, he is capable of rendering his opponents ineffectual by devising the most ingenious of ploys to circumvent their hostility. Yet, beneath the veneer of self-sufficiency lie doubts that he can vanquish them completely in a society that places scant premium on reasoning one's way out of difficulty. His amiable sidekick, ever suspicious of the intellectual's preference for meditation over brashness, is the worldly-wise, virile street fighter accustomed to bullying his opponents into submission. When life-and-death show-

downs occur, his rough-and-tumble services prove to be invaluable to wreaking justice on the bad guys.

Each man is burdened by his own peculiar set of flaws. Alone, they most likely would succumb in time to the forces leagued against them. Operating in unison, however, they inevitably prevail over all challenges, the thinking man's tendency to deliberate overruled by his partner's boldness when it becomes evident that confrontation rather than compromise is definitely the better part of valor.

Firmly rooted in the literature of ages long passed, this welding of two such dissimilar characters in an irreversible bond of fellowship is the stuff that a huge number of comedy and adventure films have been made of. In the silent days, Raymond Hatton (the plotter) was teamed to stunning effect with the burly Wallace Beery (the activist). Stan Laurel, slight of build and sleight of hand, co-starred with the ill-tempered Oliver Hardy in one of the finest of all screen partnerships involving the timid mouse and overpowering bulldog. What made their antics so unsettling was Laurel's tendency to disregard Hardy's sturdy advice, which far more often than not would have precluded their stumbling into predicaments in the first place, or at least have extricated them from disaster while there was still time to compensate for Laurel's judgmental errors.

Later years witnessed the meteoric rise of Bud Abbott and Lou Costello, the former slim, neatly garbed, and level-headed, the latter a roly-poly, baggy-pants clown who led both into troubles that would have been averted if Abbott's coolness of head had prevailed over Costello's instant replays of excitability. Placid Bing Crosby performed an identical service *vis-à-vis* the easily agitated Bob Hope in seven "Road" pictures, which began with *Road to Singapore* in 1940 and ended with *Road to Hong Kong* 22 years later. In the 1950s another crooner, Dean Martin, in film after film up to the dissolution of the partnership in 1956, regularly redressed the wrongs perpetrated on bumpkin Jerry Lewis, whose inability to distinguish friend from foe, illusion from reality resulted in frenzied reactions that were inconsistent with the phlegmatic Martin's Crosby-like knack for deflating tension by singing a soothing ballad.

Western films, of course, were chief among the vehicles used to link two disparate characters as collaborators on sagebrush adventures while adding credence to the old saw that friendship makes for strange bedfellows. Superbly fulfilling his role in scores of cheapie "B" Westerns as the brain-dead compatriot of the gentlemanly, mature William Boyd was Andy Clyde. A veteran of extensive practice sessions in numerous two-reel comedies that sharpened his slapstick skills even before sound replaced the silents, he was the best horse soldier ever to ride alongside novelist Clarence E. Mulford's Hopalong Cassidy. Cut from the same cloth were [John] Fuzzy Knight (who played piano-playing Rag Time Kelly in *She Done Him Wrong*) and Al [Fuzzy] St. John, among the most active of the Depression children's Saturday matinee buffoons. Crusty Smiley Burnett appeared in about 200 minor Westerns opposite such Cactusland glamour boys as Charles Starrett, Johnny Mack Brown, and Gene Autry.

Leo Carrillo was far the most jovial and prepossessing of the cowboy second bananas, dutifully accompanying the chivalrous Mexican bandit played by Duncan Renaldo, and later by dashing Cesar Romero, on their Cisco (or "Ceesco") Kid travels. Toothless cowpoke George ("Gabby") Hayes easily overcame a face that was gnarled and stubbled as a cactus by his unswerving loyalty, becoming a fixture in company with Boyd and Roy Rogers. So did Andy Devine, he of the wide girth and croaky voice, who also frequently accompanied Rogers on 70-minute crusades for frontier justice. The teaming of Errol Flynn and Alan Hale in 13 action films, including *Dodge City* (1939) and *Virginia City* (1940), remains the most spectacular example of undying comradeship between the patrician hero and the rough-hewn but ever-faithful comrade. Luckily, their pictures benefitted from the fact that both Flynn and especially Hale, who began his film career in the 1911 Western *The Cowboy and the Lady*, were first-rate actors and the scripts far above average.

The favorable fan reaction to odd-couple pairings was most likely responsible to a large degree for 20th Century–Fox's, and later Universal's, uniting Basil Rathbone and Nigel Bruce in the lucrative 14-installment Sherlock Holmes series of 1939–46. As readers of the detective stories are aware, Dr. Watson, in the creative hands of Arthur Conan Doyle, was a stolid medical man whose obtuseness was tolerated with amusement by the Victorian supersleuth the good doctor tried his best to assist.

As the quintessential Holmes, Rathbone shone as the intellectual at work, alert, lucid, and painstakingly attentive to detail. The choice of Bruce as Watson was likewise fortunate. He was sometimes cast in other roles in which he exercised sound judgment, but from the beginning of his film-acting days he was typically presented as the doddering dullard (*Stand Up and Cheer!*, 1934) or oafish aristocrat (*The Rains Came*, 1939, *The Blue Bird*, 1940). Like Inspector Lestrade, Scotland Yard's premier dunce, played by Dennis Hoey, Watson was neither nimble nor quick, and rarely articulate. His frequent descent into churlishness at evidence of Holmes's renown and authoritative analyses of the criminal mind is mitigated, however, by sincere astonishment at his friend's latest stroke of deductive brilliance. Yet Bruce's portrait of Watson as perplexed helpmate struck a receptive chord with moviegoers, the majority of whom would most likely acknowledge that they, too, would be awed trying to compete with a superior mind that regarded the piecing together of the most complex crime puzzle as merely elementary.

In musical films, odd-couple pairings were personalized most often by straight man John Payne and jovial Jack Oakie. Equally ambitious to succeed in show business, the pudgy Oakie could always be depended on to coerce his tall, dark, and handsome co-star into trading in his moodiness for another crack at building their careers regardless of how many times they had been sabotaged by setbacks. Together, they were invincible, skipping over obstacles to confound the odds-makers by becoming stars in the music publishing field (*Tin Pan Alley*), in radio (*The Great American Broadcast*), and as nightclub tycoons (*Hello Frisco, Hello*). As fellow U.S. Marines in *Iceland* (1942), Oakie even helped to smooth the way for Payne's romance with Sonja Henie by selflessly—and wisely—taking himself out of the competition for her hand.

Soft-Hearted Disciplinarian. Few actors of the 1930s better displayed the qualities of tough but tender comrade to their impulsive co-stars than Pat O'Brien. One of the most reliable members of the Warner Bros. stock company, he was so proficient and popular that he was assigned parts in 17 feature films between 1933 and 1936. Neatly balancing the belligerency of the authoritarian with the sentimentality of the Father Confessor, his characters were intolerant of disloyalty in any form, whether it be to established codes of conduct or to a friend. Directness and sacrifice were virtues, dereliction of duty and self-centeredness major flaws. To O'Brien, life was little more than an endless series of challenges that separates man from boy, hero from coward. The immature flee from disappointments, the adult remains steadfast as the stars, facing and finally overcoming them. To him, challenges were always opportunities in disguise. Curiously, O'Brien was consistently

shunted aside by the Academy of Motion Picture Arts and Sciences, which never nominated him for any acting award, an inexcusable omission.

Clean as hound's teeth, the characters he played demanded or sought to persuade their associates to lead lives free from pettiness and insincerity. If showering them with invective did not do the trick, perhaps a calm *tête-à-tête* would. Either way, it was instilling the values of teamwork that consumed much of the actor's screen life. Setting an example of reasonableness in even the most adverse situations, and refusing to hold a grudge against persons unable or unwilling to measure up to his standards, the avuncular O'Brien was appreciated by all the characters he reformed in picture after picture.

Evidence of the actor's adept balancing of hard-nosed realist and compassionate buddy arose at the outset of his Hollywood days. His role as the dynamic newspaperman with a heart (*The Front Page*, 1931, and *The Final Edition*, 1932) compared favorably with that of the gifted Edward G. Robinson in *Five Star Final* (1931). Although O'Brien had racked up some experience singing and dancing on the stage, he exhibited neither talent in his six musical films between 1934 and 1938, being confined to peppering the plots with his portrayals of the rough-talking agent with a mushy spot reserved for the youngsters placed in his care.

Especially in pictures with James Cagney—they co-starred in nine between 1934 and 1940—O'Brien personified the paternalistic friend in need who tamps down Cagney's inclination to explode at the slightest provocation. With a speech pattern that frequently infringed on Cagney's own copyrighted Gatling gun delivery, O'Brien cultivated a gift for consoling the rebellious while escorting them along the route to salvation that inevitably elevated him, along with Spencer Tracy and Bing Crosby, to the priesthood. He played the role of priest twice opposite Cagney, first as his boyhood friend in *Angels with Dirty Faces* in 1938, and then as his only friend in *The Fighting 69th* two years later. As *Fighting Father Dunne* (1948), he proved to be as effective a helpmate to misguided boys as had Tracy 10 years earlier in *Boys Town*. The reverential decorum that fit O'Brien like a custom-tailored suit was also apparent in several of his non-religious portrayals, notably as the strict but sympathetic warden in *San Quentin* (1937) and as the competitive but considerate football coach in *Knute Rockne—All American* (1940).

All of these O'Brien attributes were combined to advantage in *Flirtation Walk*. His advance-warning nickname of "Scrapper" clearly indicated the willingness of this career non- com to uphold Army discipline even at the price of alienating the men in his charge. But his rule-book conduct supported his preference for nurturing soldierly pride in them through non-confrontational means, thereby exposing the same split Jekyll and Hyde personality that reformed Cagney in *Here Comes the Navy*, also 1934, *Devil Dogs of the Air* the next year, and *Ceiling Zero* in 1936.

Confrontation and Fisticuffs. We first meet O'Brien about two minutes into *Flirtation Walk* during a mock defense of the Hawaiian Islands by the U.S. Navy, Army Air Corps, and Field Artillery. In film musicals' earliest ironic foreshadowing of what seven years later would be the Japanese attack on Pearl Harbor, the opening scene consists of a closeup of a War Department memo ordering troops stationed at "Schofield Barracks" to hold practice maneuvers for repelling an invasion of the Islands. Naturally, viewers were as unaware as studio executives of the significance of Hawaii to the future course of United States history. Had they guessed at what would happen there, the film's brief sequences of preparedness in action would have qualified as propaganda by stiffening America's resolve to beef up its armed services in order to fend off any potential enemy's daring to launch an attack in the Pacific. Thus do the opening scenes make abundantly clear that the film was not to be a visual echo of such light-hearted military vehicles as *Hit the Deck*, which MGM had transferred almost intact from stage to screen in 1930, or the farcical *Shipmates* in 1931.

Interspersed with documentary film clips of battleships on the prow and double-tier airplanes zooming across the wild blue yonder are the actors' frenzied motions, set against realistic studio backdrops that convey the illusion of men and materiél in combat. Immediately obvious is O'Brien's gruff professionalism and Powell's cavalier attitude toward the operation and dislike of O'Brien. Assigned to an anti-aircraft unit, Private Powell performs his duties without enthusiasm, which results in the first of gung-ho Sergeant O'Brien's battery of complaints against his conduct.

Later, at the Army's Honolulu post, Powell wisecracks to a buddy that O'Brien is not only a "monster in uniform," but also the "slowest thinking guy I've ever seen." As occurred many times in Hollywood stories of friendly enemies, Powell's smart-alecky critique is overheard by its source. O'Brien, his feathers ruffled by further evidence of his subordinate's refusal to conform to his own deeply ingrained sense of Army camaraderie, pummels Powell in the ensuing altercation in a latrine.

The result is O'Brien's ordering Powell to police his barracks and a few private rooms that are reserved for special guests. Hoping to find a contrite sufferer, dust rag in one hand, broom in the other, during a follow-up inspection, O'Brien is startled to discover Powell lying fully dressed in an empty bathtub, manicuring his nails with a cleaning brush, a doggerel song on his lips. More disappointed than angry, O'Brien senses that Powell's hostility toward both him and Army discipline is irremediable. He seems to be more interested in being the Rudy Vallee of the regiment, O'Brien grunts, than moving up in the ranks.

Then, with the same parental concern he displayed in the latrine, where he suggested that the nosebleed he had inflicted on Powell was sufficient cause for the younger man to repair to the post hospital, O'Brien issues the challenge that summarizes the primary plot of the picture. "If you don't want to take orders, go to West Point and learn how to give them!," he shouts before exiting the room in disgust. Meanwhile, Powell is to suffer additional degradation by serving as chauffeur for a military bigwig due to arrive aboard ship that afternoon for a brief Honolulu stopover on his way to Manila.

With their personalities now established— the brusque yet solicitous non-com *vs.* the likable yet carefree enlistee—the screenplay introduces the subordinate on-again, off-again love affair involving the attractive young twosome who had first met in *42nd Street*. Again cast as Powell's sweetheart, as she had been in each of her first four pictures, was Ruby Keeler. And young they were, with Dick not quite 30 and Ruby only 24. Largely because of the maturity of his roles and sagacity of his advice, the 34-year-old O'Brien always appeared much older than the boyish, prank-loving Powell and Cagney.

The scene shifts to the Port of Honolulu as a steamship pulls into a dock. Aboard it are Ruby, as Kit Fitts; Henry O'Neill, a thoroughly competent bit actor who, like Jonathan Hale, Samuel S. Hinds, Russell Hicks, and Minor Watson, appeared in hundreds of films from the early 1930s to the late 1950s, as her father, General John Brent Fitts; and John Eldredge, aide to the general and boyfriend of the daughter, as Lieutenant Ben Biddle, stuffy, humorless, and cranky. Once on land, they are approached by Powell, who accommodates Ruby by carrying her baggage to his parked car, where he inadvertently drops a suitcase, exposing the lady's undergarments. As embarrassed as Ruby, Dick hurriedly repacks them and proceeds to drive the party to post headquarters.

It is while Ruby is settling herself in a guest room that romance makes its debut, a subtle one to be sure, and a rare reversal of the standard aggressive male-timid female routine. Ruby gingerly tries to break the ice by nonchalantly dismissing Powell's dockside awkwardness with cooing voice and occasional come-hither glances, hoping to stimulate his ardor. Powell remains passive, however, regarding her as inimical to his bias toward sidestepping commitments, whether they entail his career or personal life. But the screenplay has succeeded in coupling the love-hate relationship between Powell and O'Brien with Powell and Ruby's own periodic disenchantment with each another. Powell's petulance is to remain the source of O'Brien's and Ruby's irritation and mutual insistence that he begin to act responsibly.

Several cuts above his usual role as wavy-haired warbler of pretty tunes, the role permits Powell to demonstrate his largely overlooked dramatic competence. He measures up to the split-personality nuances of his characterization, which required a higher degree of acting ability than that of the stage-struck troubadour in *42nd Street* and Gold Diggers of 1933. The finest examples of Powell's acting prowess would not surface for another decade, when as hard-boiled private detectives and government agents in *Murder My Sweet* (1945), *Johnny O'-Clock* (1947), and above all in the tingling tales of drug smuggling, *To the Ends of the Earth* (1948), and the potential assassination of newly elected President Lincoln, *The Tall Target* (1951), he won plaudits from fans and critics alike.

One of filmdom's earliest and best crooners of popular songs, the tenor introduced dozens of movie hits, from Dubin and Warren's "The Shadow Waltz" in 1933 and "I Only Have Eyes for You" in 1934, both with Ruby at his side, and Irving Berlin's "I've Got My Love to Keep Me Warm" (with Alice Faye) in 1937 to Johnny Mercer and Harold Arlen's "Hit the Road to Dreamland" (with Mary Martin) in 1943. Powell helped to popularize many other tunes as host of the late–1930's radio program *Hollywood Hotel* (also the name of one of his 1937 films). In 1940–41 his Decca recordings of college football songs were immense bestsellers.

On a Beach in Hawaii. Unable to crack Powell's aloofness, Ruby talks him into driving her not to the officers' reception she is obliged to attend, but deep into the Hawaiian countryside. It is while on their way to a secluded fishing village that Powell reveals his blood relationship to several "well-connected" military dignitaries whose names Ruby recognizes. Why, she asks, with such important people presumably on call to dispense favors is he still a mere private. Rather than taking offense, Powell concedes that his lowly rank befits his lack of effort toward promotion.

The picture's first musical scene occurs during a luau being held by the villagers. Differing from the typical Hollywood musical of the period, it is the dancing that highlights the sequence. None of the tunes was original, all being long associated with Hawaii and the hula. Professionally choreographed by Bobby Connolly, the dance routines capture the romantic aggressiveness of the foot-stomping chorus boys and the lyrical loveliness of the girls' undulating hands and hips. Invited by the friendly natives to join them in song, Powell sings "Aloha Oe, (Farewell to Thee)," the traditional Hawaiian Islands parting anthem heard in countless films set in Hawaii. Also known as "Until We Meet Again," the words and music were written by [Lydia Kamakaeha] Liliuokalani, Hawaii's last queen, who composed more than 150 songs and ruled for about two years beginning in 1891.

Not surprisingly, Powell's rendition is superb, verifying the appropriateness of his "Canary" nickname. Powell's solo is rewarded with admiring glances from Ruby. Demure as they are, they also radiate a bottled-up sexual desire that was about as steamy as the Hollywood of 1934 was willing to permit. (As if to boldly announce that *Flirtation Walk* contained no offensive scenes or dialogue, which trod lightly into some pre–1935 musicals, notification that the film had been approved by the National Board of Review appears in unusually large type on its own credit card. Typically, this information was printed in small type at the bottom of the title card.)

Powell appreciates the devilment in the lady's eyes, and together they depart the village for a deserted moonlit beach. In the midst of their shy overtures to love, however, they are interrupted by one of musical films' most common—and often reviled—characters, the "other man," who is destined to lose the girl of his dreams minutes before the film ends. The abrupt intruder is John Eldredge (Lieutenant Ben Biddle), pompous as ever, trying his best to conceal his anger by treating Powell with the commissioned officer's courtly disdain of an errant private. He orders Powell back to the post, where he is to await the lieutenant's presence, and offers to take Ruby to the reception himself.

When next in O'Brien's company, Powell is enmeshed in self-pity and worry. He had committed one of the most mortal of military sins by talking back to Eldredge while the officer was reprimanding him for endangering Ruby's reputation by driving her to the fishing village. Powell's reaction to the dressing down is to desert the army, a decision that shocks O'Brien. Then, summoning up his ritualistic father-to-son mannerism, he confesses that he likes Powell too much not to help him, and the sergeant offers to assist him to escape from the island.

Instead, he locks Powell in the barracks and scurries away to visit Ruby in the hope that together they might somehow calm Eldredge's anger and deter Powell from deserting. Ruby comes through by agreeing to see the young man and do what she can to help him salvage his career. Following O'Brien's suggestion, Powell goes to her room, where he admits his love for her at the outset of their meeting. Delighted as Ruby is to hear the news, she dismisses it by referring to her trip to the beach as merely a "crazy impulse" that for a brief time caused her to "forget myself." He means nothing to her, she adds, strongly implying that he never will. She further recommends that Powell forget that evening, as she has.

Her stinging remarks stun the baffled young man back to his senses, and he stalks out of the room. After he has gone, she writes a note to Eldredge in which she takes all the blame for lapsing into uncharacteristic behavior on the beach. Then, having been faithful to the musical heroine's penchant for sacrificing her love for the good of her man, Ruby falls sobbing on her bed.

Change of Heart. O'Brien's quest to help his friend has succeeded in dampening Powell's obsession with Ruby, while her note has succeeded in placating Eldredge, who informs Powell that he is now willing to drop the matter to save Ruby from further embarrassment. Without Ruby to distract him, Powell decides not to desert after all and jeopardize his future. He turns down O'Brien's offer to accompany him on an assignment in China in favor of devoting his off-duty hours to studying whatever subjects are needed to qualify him for admittance to West Point. He is certain that Ruby prefers to dally with officers and gentlemen, like Eldredge, not with dime-a-dozen enlisted men.

Powell's intention to become a cadet is not influenced solely by the hope of impressing Ruby, whom he has managed to dismiss from his mind. Rather, it springs from the longing to acquire upper-class qualities in order to impress some later lady who, apparently like Ruby, judges the worth of a suitor by the bars on his collar (the officer half of the West Point equation) and his mannerliness (the gentleman half). Although sorry to lose his companionship, O'Brien encourages Powell to strive toward his goal, adding that proud as the sergeant is of the enlisted man's ability to carry out orders, the officer also shares in battlefield glory by issuing only wise ones after due deliberation. According to the sergeant, the one complements the other, with the officer's role clearly of greater importance than the common soldier's. In Powell's stead on the China trip is Guinn Williams (Sleepy), a well-known Hollywood specialist in portraying muscle-bound, usually affable dunces, whose bulk and loudmouth portrayals earned him the nickname of "Big Boy."

With Ruby, her father, and Eldredge back aboard ship on their way to Manila, and O'Brien en route to China, Powell is relieved of personality conflicts that might interfere with achieving his objective. Having misjudged the lady's motive for rejecting him—the film musical's most cherished device for temporarily sundering love affairs—he successfully submerges memories of her in heavy concentration on his studies.

Powell succeeds in his mission, and a little less than halfway through the film, the backdrop shifts to West Point. It will remain there to the end, interrupted intermittently by brief glimpses of O'Brien and Williams, who are called upon solely to flesh out the main plot by (1) giving a running account of Powell's advancement up the cadet ranks through the letters he writes to the sergeant, and (2) showing O'Brien's burgeoning pride in following his protégé's step-by-step progress.

Not particularly original in text or treatment, the highs and lows of the young officer-in-training fail to differ significantly from the conventional tale of the bad boy reformed into a model of military proficiency. From the outset of his four-year tenure at the Academy, Powell follows all the rules, hits the books, accepts the gratuitous upper-classmen hazing to which all plebes are heir, and forms firm fellowship with his mischievous bunkmates, especially one Oskie, engagingly played by Ross Alexander, whose suicide in 1937 at the age of 30 ended a promising career. With an obvious gift for comedy, Alexander serves in O'Brien's absence as Powell's conscience, encouraging him to overcome infrequent periods of depression by finding rainbows in the clouds.

What mostly distinguish the West Point scenes in *Flirtation Walk* are the realistic interpolations of cadets on the march—to the mess hall, to assembly, to their quarters. Especially noteworthy is the sight of them in full-dress uniform stepping lively to the beat of military music along the parade grounds, ever in unison, as if a dance director with Busby Berkeley credentials had assembled a first-rate, all-male chorus line.

The marchers, of course, were actual cadets filmed earlier by West Point cameramen for publicity purposes. But the scenes showing Powell participating in the parades are so deftly integrated that it takes scant suspension of disbelief to accept the men in formation and the music in the background as having been filmed and recorded entirely on the West Coast. Only in the other major 1930s West Point musical, Cole Porter's *Rosalie* (1937), would such half–West Point, half–Hollywood artistry match that of *Flirtation Walk*.

Powell's eagerness to become an officer seems well on the way to fulfillment when he is promoted to corporal and finally regimental commander. It is during his senior year that Eldredge reappears, along with Ruby and her father, who has been appointed West Point superintendent. Unfazed by neither seeing nor hearing from Powell for almost four years, Ruby is delighted at spotting him in a parade organized to welcome her father to the Academy. If it is difficult to fathom the instantaneous delight that flutters her heart, considering the time lapse since their last unpleasant meeting in Hawaii, still more mysterious is Eldredge's lack of progression from suitor to husband, or failure to shift his affection to a more receptive lady. Unappealing as his stilted mannerisms and rhetoric are, he would certainly be regarded as a model husband by many other military daughters.

Ruby, however, is fated to suffer the same rejection she had inflicted on Powell. Her attempt to renew acquaintances is disdainfully ignored after she hurries over to him at the conclusion of the parade. He surprises her by neglecting to make any reference to the coolness that marked their last encounter, but it is his pretending not even to remember her, surely the quickest way to stifle romance, that truly offends her.

As every good Hollywood musical should, *Flirtation Walk* incorporates a show business background, brief as it is, that is sited in a theater at West Point instead of on Broadway. Assigned by his buddies to write and direct a play for the 1934 edition of the Academy's traditional "100th Night from June" pre-graduation celebration, the sulking Powell refuses their insistence that Ruby appear in it. But he finally agrees, as does her father, whose approval must be obtained, since no female had ever been admitted into the cast of a West Point show. Bowing to the pressure of her cadet supporters, Ruby accepts the offer, and Powell is forced to write her into his revised script. The task is not to his liking, but he completes it while soothing his ruffled artistic feathers by carping at Ruby's tardiness in showing up for the first rehearsal.

Although Powell defines his play as a comedy, it is in fact patently unfunny in both incident and dialogue, with the three-song score its only virtue. Entitled "Femme Trouble," the show is set in the "far distant" future and based on the "ridiculous assumption," in Powell's words, that the Academy has come under the control of a woman. Playing the "Lady General" is Ruby, who takes pleasure in snapping out directives to her male subordinates while powder puffing to her nose. Asking which specific Academy regulation most pesters cadets, she is informed in the opening song by Powell and a male chorus that it is the one that prohibits them from enjoying certain civilian privileges. Not one of composer Allie Wrubel's better songs, "No Horse, No Wife, No Mustache" is nonetheless not so bad as one might infer from the title, and its march-like tempo has an underlying attractiveness.

Far better is the second song, again delivered by Powell, along with Ruby, and a chorus of young men and women. Sung after she has rescinded the Academy's regulation against cadet marriages, "Mr. and Mrs. Is the Name" highlights the skit entitled "The West Point Wedding Day." In it Powell marries Ruby and about 30 other cadets get their own wives, garbed in bridal gowns when the skit opens.

The third and final tune is the singable "Flirtation Walk," one of the catchiest popular songs of 1934 as well as one of Wrubel's best, being particularly distinguished by the melodic variations that end each of the three stanzas. It is not nearly so spectacular a production number as, say, Dubin and Warren's "Pettin' in the Park" (in Gold Diggers of 1933) or Irving Kahal and Sammy Fain's aquatic "By a Waterfall" (in *Footlight Parade*). But unlike *Flirtation Walk*, those two earlier musical films failed to impose a single limitation on the flamboyant indulgences that underlay Berkeley's choreography. Connolly's routines always displayed far greater restraint than those devised by Busby the Great.

The song charmingly escorts Dick and Ruby along the Academy's Flirtation Walk, the lover's lane that leads to the equally romantic enclave known as Kissing Rock. The inclusion of two artificial, squealing cats in the first reprise detracts from the song's romantic underpinnings, but compensation quickly arrives in the chorus' superlative vocal reprise, which tends to erase from memory the caterwauling that preceded it. It is during the song that Powell finally admits his love for Ruby in an unrehearsed aside. The play ends with her admission that she loves him, too, and that yes, she wants him to give all the orders from now on. A military career and bossiness are simply not for her or, it is assumed, should they be for any other young American woman.

In earlier film-musical years, their proclamation of love would herald the end of the picture, with the strains of the chief ballad trailing them along the path to eternal happiness. Not so in *Flirtation Walk*; there is still Eldredge to deal with. During their love-making interlude on stage, Ruby had failed to tell Dick that the long-term "understanding" between her and Eldredge had resulted in her recent acceptance of his proposal of marriage. The cantankerous officer had sat in the audience unsmiling and uneasy throughout the play, visibly embarrassed that the butt of most of the jokes bore the name of "Quibble," a jestful substitute for his own surname of Biddle. Even less to his liking was the mock marriage between Powell and his fiancée.

Later that night, after reading of their engagement in the West Point newspaper, Powell visits Ruby and proposes that she marry him instead. An unexpected knock at the front door announces the entry of the lieutenant, who escorts Powell out of Ruby's house and threatens him with a court martial for visiting her without permission, and after taps, both unpardonable cadet misfires. Powell, disillusioned over her rejection and fearful of endangering her reputation once again, returns to his room and writes a letter of resignation from the Academy.

It is at this point that O'Brien, his tour of duty in China concluded, appears on the grounds of West Point as an uninvited guest at the forthcoming graduation ceremony. He meets Powell and expresses pride in him and the desire to enlist in the young officer-to-be's first command. His suitcase open and dressed in civilian clothes, Powell has little choice other than to admit that he is resigning. He hopes to remain in the Army, however, and is willing to begin his career all over again as a private. He echoes O'Brien's high opinion of enlisted men, adding that it is they, not the officers, who are the backbone of the Army.

Disappointed is the word for O'Brien, who can hardly believe his ears. After almost four years of deprivation and hard work, his young friend for unknown reasons is about to jettison his career. He is further distressed when Powell relates his decision without rancor, commenting matter of factly that "I guess I just wasn't cut out to be either an officer or a gentleman."

Another knock at the door. Eldredge interrupts the two men to tell Powell that the superintendent has elected to overlook Powell's visit to his daughter. Furthermore, Ruby has returned Eldredge's ring and professed her love for Powell. Another specimen of the gracious loser, Eldredge congratulates his rival, warmly shakes his hand, and departs, his unrequited presence no longer needed. All that is required to end *Flirtation Walk* on a cheery note is quickly marshaled: Powell is graduated to officer rank, he and Ruby will wed, and everything will be well with everybody, at least until December 7, 1941.

Rather than instructing Dick and Ruby to share a smothering hug and kiss to close the film, the sentimental albeit extremely talented Frank Borzage, director of such classics as *Seventh Heaven* (1927), *Street Angel* (1928), *A*

Farewell to Arms (1932), *Three Comrades* (1938), and *The Mortal Storm* (1940), called on O'Brien to wind things up. No longer Powell's friendly antagonist, the sergeant realizes that each has remained loyal to the other, despite their philosophical differences. His face, in a long closeup, follows Powell as he ascends the platform steps and accepts his degree. Also in the audience are a little girl and her mother. The camera zeroes in on the child as she stares up at O'Brien and whispers, "Look, Mama, that man's crying." But it is tears of happiness he sheds. His once-troublesome young friend has measured up to the demands of an exacting profession and become a man.

An agreeable if not memorable film, *Flirtation Walk* owes much of its success to the consummate skill of the cadre of behind-the-scenes professionals like cinematographer Sol Polito. A master director of photography with 17 years' experience behind him in 1934, Polito was responsible for filming such other Warner Bros. favorites as *I Am a Fugitive from a Chain Gang*, *42nd Street*, and Gold Diggers of 1933. The man who photographed the magnificent charge of the Light Brigade in 1936, he added *G-Men*, *The Petrified Forest*, *The Adventures of Robin Hood* (his first in Technicolor), *The Sea Hawk*, *Now, Voyager*, and the 1945 Gershwin-based musical *Rhapsody in Blue* to his list of credits.

The equally experienced co-cinematographer, George Barnes, entered motion pictures in 1919 and would win the Academy Award in 1940 for *Rebecca*. Especially talented at filming musicals, Barnes photographed *Footlight Parade*, *Dames*, *Gold Diggers of 1935* (with Polito), *In Caliente*, *Broadway Gondolier*, *Cain and Mabel*, and several others. Both polished craftsmen, Polito and Barnes accomplished their goal of alternating effortlessly from the stark to the sensuous in framing their films.

Complementing the camera work was the expert editing of William Holmes. The individual scenes are expertly paced, permitting the film to proceed along its predictable course without indulging in unnecessary gestures, superfluous movements, or any other excess baggage. Likewise, the straightforward dialogue, shorn of verbiage, moves the story along without needless commentary.

Delmer Davies, co-author of the story and

sole screenwriter, is far better known as the director of such impressive World War II films as *Destination Tokyo* and *Pride of the Marines*, both featuring John Garfield, one of the anonymous dancing sailors in *Footlight Parade*. By the time of *Flirtation Walk*, Davies had already written the screenplay for *Dames*, a slightly earlier Powell-Keeler musical that briefly carried the working title of Gold Diggers of 1934. The experience he gained from that exercise unquestionably influenced his *Flirtation Walk* script in that both stars were handed almost identical roles—the devil-may-care, often brash Powell in pursuit of the practical-minded Ruby, who patiently awaits the time when her beau will out-wrestle his personal problems and pop the question.

The producing of a musical play is central to both *Dames* and *Flirtation Walk*. Dick and Ruby appear in them, and the one troublesome *Dames* character (Hugh Herbert) who endangers the young couple's happiness is reformed, as is Eldredge in *Flirtation Walk*. Davies' skill in braiding the threads of both plots and tidying up their tangled love affairs satisfied viewers unwilling to deal with life's complexities.

The storyline of *Flirtation Walk* is more complex than that of the earlier piece, holding interest by dissecting the characters in real-world conflicts rather than by featherdusting redundant situations for them to reveal their essentially uncomplicated responses to trivial matters. Davies's artistry had progressed in the intervening four months between the two films: *Dames* is much too lightweight to retain very much of its original appeal in the 1990s; *Flirtation Walk* still provides valid insights into relations between novice and professional, nonconformist and traditionalist, and, above all, self-absorption *vs.* friendship and love.

In short, the film is far better than one would deduce from *New York Times* critic André Sennwald's unflattering 1934 review. He did correctly encapsulate the few strengths and many weaknesses of *Flirtation Walk*, but he also overstepped himself by condensing its sole values as "a rousing recruiting poster ... and a splendid laboratory specimen of the adolescent cinema."

The Gay Divorcee (1934)

An RKO Radio picture. DIRECTOR: Mark Sandrich; ASSISTANT: Argyle Nelson. PRODUCER: Pandro S. Berman. SCREENWRITERS: George Marion, Jr., Dorothy Yost, and Edward Kaufman, based on the stage musical *The Gay Divorce*, by Dwight Taylor. CINEMATOGRAPHER: David Abel; SPECIAL EFFECTS: Vernon Walker. FILM EDITOR: William Hamilton. ART DIRECTORS: Van Nest Polglase and Carroll Clark. CHOREOGRAPHERS: Dave Gould, Fred Astaire, and Hermes Pan. COSTUMES: Walter Plunkett. RECORDING: Hugh McDowell, Jr. SOUND: Carl Dreher. SOUND CUTTER: George Marsh. MUSICAL DIRECTOR: Max Steiner. MUSICAL ADAPTATIONS: Kenneth Webb and Samuel Hoffenstein. MUSIC RECORDING: Murray Spivak and P.J. Faulkner, Jr. PRODUCTION ASSOCIATE: Zion Myers. ORIGINAL SONGS: Lyrics by Mack Gordon and Herb Magidson, music by Harry Revel and Con Conrad. RUNNING TIME: 1 hour, 47 minutes. *Principal Players*: Fred Astaire (Guy Holden). Ginger Rogers (Mimi Glossop). Alice Brady (Hortense Ditherwell). Edward Everett Horton (Egbert Fitzgerald). Erik Rhodes (Rodolpho Tonetti). Eric Blore (A Waiter). William Austin (Cyril Glossop). Betty Grable (A Hotel Guest). *Major Academy Award*: Best Song ("The Continental"). *Nominations*: Best Picture; Art Direction; Sound; Musical Direction and Adaptations.

Entering vaudeville as children in an act called "An Electric Toe-Dancing Novelty," Fred Astaire appeared in ten stage musicals with his sister Adele, and later in the same number of films opposite Ginger Rogers. Musical comedy's chief exponent of nonchalant elegance, he had developed into Broadway's mightiest male dancer before appearing in the minor role of Fred in his first film, MGM's *Dancing Lady*, in 1933. Sharing dancing credit was Joan Crawford, the first of his Hollywood partners, who over the next 34 years would include Eleanor Powell, Paulette Goddard, Rita Hayworth, Joan Fontaine, Marjorie Reynolds, Virginia Dale, Olga San Juan, Joan Leslie, Lucille Bremer, Ann Miller, Betty Hutton, Cyd Charisse, Leslie Caron, Audrey Hepburn, Judy Garland, Jane Powell, and Vera-Ellen, in addition to Miss Rogers, about as glamorous and talented a constellation of beauties as any star, musical or otherwise, could hope for. He even did a brief stint with Gene Kelly in *Ziegfeld Follies* (1946) and with Sarah Churchill, daughter of Britain's wartime Prime Minister, Winston, in *Royal Wedding* in 1951.

Born of an immigrant stage-struck father who changed his surname to Astaire from Austerlitz, Fred and Adele won their first New

Fred Astaire and Ginger Rogers at the conclusion of their "Night and Day" dance duet in *The Gay Divorcee*.

York booking in 1911 at Proctor's 5th Avenue Theatre, appearing in the comedy sketch "A Rainy Saturday." The brother especially went on to amass enviable experience as singer and actor as well as dancer before retiring from the stage to enter the movies. His first minor role on Broadway was in *Over the Top* in 1916, and two years later he appeared in The Passing Show of 1918, his first hit show, both with music mostly by Sigmund Romberg. His final starring role was in *The Gay Divorce*, not re-garded as among his more successful outings, even though it ran for 248 performances at Broadway's Ethel Barrymore Theatre in 1932, another 108 times at the Palace the next year, and fared even better in London. His leading lady, Claire Luce, also left for Hollywood after the show closed.

Astaire's mastery of the intricate art of syn-chronizing toe taps with the beat of pit or-chestras was easily duplicated with playbacks upon his arrival in Hollywood. He was equally adept at measuring up to the demands of vo-calizing songs in a wide assortment of tempos, especially the upbeat, like "Fascinating Rhythm," "Funny Face," and "'S Wonderful." Naturally his dancing took precedence over his singing in the public's estimation, but Astaire's voice combined the richness of Crosby's and the felicitous phrasing, if not the mellowness, of Sinatra's.

On stage, as in films, Astaire was the re-cipient of a huge bequest of first-rate songs written by the cream of American lyricists and composers. Fortunately for the multitude of new fans intoxicated with his movie majesty and magnetism, almost all of his major stage composers contributed songs to his Hollywood musicals. Vincent Youmans, who had provided the Broadway score for *Smiles* in 1931 (even though Astaire did not perform the hit, "Time on My Hands"), also wrote the songs for the dancer's second film, *Flying Down to Rio* (1933), which included the sprightly title song, "The Carioca," and the tango "Orchids in the Moonlight."

The Gershwin brothers in 1922 con-tributed three songs to *For Goodness Sake* (rechristened *Stop Flirting* for its London run) and then the complete scores for *Lady Be Good!* (1924) and *Funny Face* (1927), all of which added significantly to Astaire's Broadway song-and-dance reputation. They furthered his film career in 1937 with 12 more songs ranging from the bouncy "Things Are Looking Up" to the dramatic Oscar-nominated "They Can't Take That Away from Me" for the films *A Damsel in Distress* and *Shall We Dance*, respectively. Cole Porter, who supplied the songs for *The Gay Di-vorce*, wrote eight new ones for The Broadway Melody of 1940 and *You'll Never Get Rich* (1941). Jerome Kern, composer of the score for

Astaire's *The Bunch and Judy* in 1920, gave him three Academy Award-nominated ballads, "Lovely to Look At" (*Roberta*, 1935), "The Way You Look Tonight" (*Swing Time*, 1936), and "Dearly Beloved" (*You Were Never Lovelier*, 1942).

From Irving Berlin came the 1935–48 scores for *Top Hat*, *Follow the Fleet*, *Carefree*, *Holiday Inn*, *Blue Skies*, and *Easter Parade*, each of them containing at least one mammoth hit. Harold Arlen wrote the tunes for *The Sky's the Limit* (1943), and Harry Warren for Ziegfeld Follies, *Yolanda and the Thief*, *The Barkleys of Broadway*, and *The Belle of New York*. Frank Loesser provided both lyrics and music for *Let's Dance* in 1952, and Johnny Mercer did the same for *Daddy Long Legs* in 1955. Alan Jay Lerner collaborated with Burton Lane for the songs in *Royal Wedding* (1951).

In 1953 the agile performer made the best film of his middle years, *The Band Wagon*, orig-inally a 1931 stage hit, with songs by Howard Dietz and Arthur Schwartz. This time around, Astaire performed "Dancing in the Dark," with Cyd Charisse. In the original Broadway revue, he played no part in introducing the classic song. Also from *The Band Wagon* came "I Love Louisa" and the anti–Depression "New Sun in the Sky." As a bonus for the renewal of their long-dormant partnership with Astaire, the two songwriters added a new tune to the film, "That's Entertainment," which he sang in tan-dem with Nanette Fabray and Jack Buchanan.

Typically, the film remakes of Astaire's Broadway musicals, mostly produced by Charles Dillingham, bore only the slightest re-semblance to the original productions. That was as true of *The Band Wagon* and *The Gay Divorcee* as it was of *Funny Face* (1957), *Silk Stockings* (also 1957), based on Garbo's *Ninotchka*, with music by Cole Porter, and *Fin-ian's Rainbow* (1968), with music by Burton Lane.

Not even Bing Crosby, Betty Grable, and Alice Faye were able to avail themselves of so many high-caliber hits from such a gallery of songwriting royalty. Perhaps Astaire's long as-sociation with them induced him to try his own hand at composing melodies. He wrote about 25 published songs, including "I'm Building Up to an Awful Let-Down" (with Johnny Mer-cer's lyric), which found its way into the 1936

British stage musical *Rise and Shine*, and from there onto *Your Hit Parade*. His single melodic contribution to *Ziegfeld Follies*, "If Swing Goes, I Go Too," however, was unceremoniously dropped. This happy combination of working with great writers and Astaire's own genius as a performer placed the dancer high on the list of the film industry's most popular stars. Together with Ginger Rogers, he placed fourth among the Top Ten box office champions in 1935, third in 1936, and seventh in 1938.

He was a very competent actor, but the studios were content to confine his range to playing different sides of essentially the same debonair character. Along the way, he single-handedly lifted the male movie dancer from lower-class billing to marquee prominence. Like Byron's idealized woman, who "walks in beauty like the night of cloudless climes and starry skies," rhythm escorted Astaire gracefully, carrying him from ballroom to park to photographer's studio. In Berlin's "Happy Easter," the opening number in *Easter Parade*, he sings the lyric while cantering along a New York street into a toy shop. There was no need for him to tap out the beat; his lithe body movements, evident even in his career-long jogs across living rooms to answer knocks at the front door and tingles of telephones, were sufficient to undergird his jaunty enthusiasm.

But it was when he activated his dancing shoes, as he does in the film's followup solo, "Drum Crazy," that Astaire displayed the incomparable wizardry that mesmerized audiences for decades. Certainly, no male dancer in movie history was more inventive or quite so popular for as long a period of time. When he announced his decision to retire after *Blue Skies* in 1946, Paramount was deluged with so many letters of protest that he changed his mind. Within two years he was back on the screen in *Easter Parade* in the part originally intended for Gene Kelly, who was too ill at the time to take it on.

Incomparable Teamwork. Like Astaire, Ginger Rogers (née Virginia Katherine Mc-Math) was similarly stage-trained and, like Joan Crawford, a dance wizard, becoming a champion Charleston dancer in Texas at the age of 15. She joined Astaire's stable of dancing ladies for *Flying Down to Rio* in 1933, even if she had to share the glory with Dolores Del Rio, the feminine lead. Ginger and Fred ranked only fourth and fifth in the list of cast members, behind Miss Del Rio, Gene Raymond, and Raul Roulien. Ginger had appeared in 20 films before joining Astaire, most of them, like *Carnival Boat* and *Hat Check Girl*, undistinguished melodramas that quickly dug their own graves in the commodious cemetery of forgotten films.

But even as early as 1932 her aptitude for both comedy and drama was apparent, leading in time to numerous estrangements from Astaire to appear in lighthearted comedy roles in *Stage Door* (1937), *Vivacious Lady* (1938), *Fifth Avenue Girl* (1939), *Lucky Partners* (1940), and finally as the heroine in the melodramatic *Kitty Foyle*, for which she won the 1940 Academy Award as best actress. Her triumph that year was all the more noteworthy considering the luster of competitors Bette Davis, Joan Fontaine, Katharine Hepburn, and Martha Scott. It was not until her second musical picture, *Gold Diggers of 1933*, released only a few months before *Flying Down to Rio*, that she was given the opportunity to sing and dance, but for only one song, "We're in the Money." Although she predominates in this sequence, about 30 other chorus girls join her in putting on a happy face while singing their Depression worries away.

The pairing of Fred and Ginger stands even today as a monument to the powerful role that personality and chemistry play in creating stars of the first magnitude, uniquely adept at plastering over the cracks in the plots, patter, and occasional palaver of their movies. To mention the name of one is to couple it automatically with the other, like those of Abbott and Costello, Crosby and Hope, Martin and Lewis, and of Spencer Tracy and Katharine Hepburn, William Powell and Myrna Loy, Walter Pidgeon and Greer Garson.

The artistic compatibility those stars brought to comedy and drama matched that of Astaire and Rogers in musicals. The man was perfectly attuned to complementing the talents of the woman, and *vice-versa*, each intuitively sensing when to praise and when to scold, when to speak and when to remain silent, when to extend the helping hand and when to withhold it. Matched in temperament and style, they anticipated how each would react to events, subtly playing off each other's strengths for the ultimate benefit of both.

Add musical talent to Astaire and Rogers' congeniality under the most troubling of scripted circumstances, and one discovers the reason that their picture-after-picture immersion in basically repetitive tales of the devil-may-care male pursuer *vs.* his ingenuous female target appeared fresh each time around. All their vehicles were romantic and lightweight and therefore easily digestible by fans of all ages. Tracy and Hepburn and the other non-musical couples cited above were usually married to each other when their pictures opened; Fred and Ginger were not, except for *The Barkleys of Broadway*, in which they play a bickering husband and wife musical-comedy writing team.

Fred's only ambition in their earlier pictures was to win Ginger in marriage, hers to keep him at bay till she had satisfied herself that his love was as sincere as he constantly contended it was. Other musical team mates, like Gaynor and Farrell, Powell and Keeler, MacDonald and Eddy, and, at the adolescent level, Rooney and Garland, were involved in similar screen romances, but none of them surpassed the popularity or longevity of the Astaire-Rogers partnership. It is highly unlikely that any pair ever will. Except for a brief tap routine with Ann Miller in *Stage Door* and a mild ballroom dance with David Niven in *Bachelor Mother* (1939), Ginger never danced on screen with anyone else after *Flying Down to Rio*.

Although not powerfully evident in *Flying Down to Rio*, largely because the screenplay was not centered on their relationship, the coupling of Fred with Ginger proved to be a master stroke of casting in their second film, *The Gay Divorcee*. Her musical talents matched Astaire's far more fully than in *Rio*, while the script-written personality flaws of each found compensation in the virtues of the other. Ginger was indecisive, Fred aggressive. She was practical, he was carefree, often careless, sometimes seemingly duplicitous while chasing after his lady love. She could be flirtatious, always innocent of the consequences;

playful Fred would have settled for an affair, but was easy prey to matrimony if that was what it would take to spend the rest of his life with Ginger.

It mattered little that these personality differences failed to add suspense to stories so predictable that audiences knew the outcome long before the ritualistic twists of the plot finally brought them together for good. But all flaws were happily disregarded whenever music swelled up from the sound track. The two were merged into one, coalescing in perfect harmony. Their cheek-to-cheek and tap dancing was sufficient to fill movie houses, because that was basically the only thing their fans had come to see.

As was typical of all of Astaire's films, save for *Carefree*, in which he plays a psychiatrist, and *The Sky's the Limit*, where he is a World War II Air Force pilot, he enters *The Gay Divorcee* not as a dancing hopeful, but as an established entertainer. Mature in years, he is still very much the schoolboy in affairs of the heart. Despite his accumulation of worldly wisdom, he is in many ways equally naïve as Ginger. His sophistication is real, but so is his happy-go-lucky eagerness to rush into amorous dalliance of the latest young woman to stir his affection. His initial realization that his chances are slim fails to deter him from trying. For Ginger he will accept rebuff and still land on his feet. As he noted in almost all of their pictures together, she is "different" from every other woman he had ever met and definitely the "only one" for him. His challenge is always to prove that his motives are sincere, not expedient, that it is marriage he's after, not a fling between Broadway shows.

An Evening in Paris. The film opens in a Parisian nightclub, a sensible—but much overused—device used to begin a musical movie with a song before a single word of dialogue is spoken. The tune, Mack Gordon and Harry Revel's "Don't Let It Bother You," is performed by an all-girl chorus severely restricted in size by the budgetary constraints imposed on musical films by the Great Depression. Attached to their hands are fluffy tiny cloth dolls, with the chorus girls' forefingers and middle fingers serving as legs for the toys. (A similar 1934 sequence, with slightly larger dolls attached to the chorines' ankles, served as the backdrop for the "Baby, Take a Bow" number in *Stand Up and Cheer!*, the highlight of that Fox film.)

Watching the show are vacationing bachelor buddies Astaire, as Guy Holden, dapper in his trademark tuxedo, and Edward Everett Horton, as Egbert Fitzgerald, a British barrister with little interest in, and even less aptitude for, the law. Neither is able to pay the check, having left their wallets in other suits, and so Fred promises to mail the money upon their return to their hotel. Surely the dubious head-waiter (Paul Porcasi) has heard of his friend, the renowned musical comedy star, Horton insists when their promise to live up to their financial obligation is greeted with suspicion. To prove he is who Horton says he is, Astaire hops on the bistro stage and taps out a chorus of the song. His routine convinces Porcasi that he is indeed in the presence of the foremost musical entertainer of the time, and out of respect he tears up the check.

The two friends' next destination is London, where we are introduced to Ginger (Mimi Glossop) and her dizzy, aristocratic Aunt Hortense (Alice Brady), whose erratic behavior is aptly suggested by her surname, Ditherwell. One of the screen's most adroit character actresses, Miss Brady plays the mindless matron to perfection, as she would for years until her death at 47 in 1939. When given the rare chance to portray a lower-class heroine, like the stubborn and resourceful mother of two fightin' Irish sons (Tyrone Power and Don Ameche) in *In Old Chicago*, however, she proved her versatility by being nominated for the Oscar for best supporting actress. Miss Brady, in fact, was a celebrated stage and silent screen actress before going Hollywood in 1933, having scored a huge personal triumph as Livinia in Eugene O'Neill's trilogy *Mourning Becomes Electra* on Broadway in 1931.

Trying to help her aunt deal with customs officials at a London dock, Ginger inadvertently slams the lid of a steamer trunk on her dress, rendering her immobile. Help is quickly proffered by Astaire, whose offer to extricate dress from trunk rips it instead. He then graciously lends Ginger his raincoat to cover her embarrassment, as well as to ingratiate himself with a young woman who had instantly piqued his interest. Ignoring his obvious enchantment with her, Ginger accepts the coat but refuses to give her name or hotel address. She later returns it to him as promised, sending it via messenger to Fred at his hotel. No note or other communication accompanies the parcel, leaving Fred in the dark on how to chase after a phantom.

Invoking his customary stubbornness to succeed where lesser men would falter, Fred swears to find her even "if it takes from now on." He fully expects to marry the girl, he confides to an astounded Horton. Overriding the barrister's objections that (1) it's apparent that the young lady wants nothing to do with him, and (2) finding her in a city with three million women is well nigh impossible, Astaire vows to persevere no matter what in the lyric of "Needle in a Haystack," the first of the two Herb Magidson–Con Conrad tunes written for the film. Yes, he concedes while tapping on the floor and over the furniture, the task will be difficult but love will steer him back into her presence.

As moviegoers of the time were aware, no matter how ego-bruising the lovers' introductory meeting, and regardless of the hero's dim prospects, Cupid had a long-established Hollywood habit of shooting his arrows straight into the coldest of hearts. Stymied in his search to find the lady on London streets and suburban crossroads, Astaire proves to be Fortune's favorite when the automobile he is driving hits the rear end of hers. He is enthralled at the sight of her, but Ginger is upset. Her goal is not romance but escape from her stalking lover. She abruptly drives off, Fred close behind her. Yet, as the gleam in Ginger's eyes and smiling lips imply, she's beginning to enjoy the pursuit almost as much as Fred does.

Unable to catch up to his prey, Astaire swerves onto a shortcut to head her off. Luckily—and inexplicably—he finds a collapsible "Road Closed" sign in the back seat of his rented automobile, and he places it smack in the middle of the country road along which Ginger is speeding. The sign forces her to halt in her getaway and gives him the opportunity to approach her and engage in badinage. Despite her coolness, more pretense than actual, Astaire proposes to her in one of the movies' quickest pleas for marriage-type love by one stranger to another. The film was only about ten minutes old. Although inwardly pleased by his amorous attentiveness, Ginger again drives away in a huff—but not before calling out her telephone number.

She is next seen in the company of Aunt Alice in Horton's London law office. There we learn that Ginger has been married for the past two years to a wandering geologist who prefers expeditions to far-flung places to settling down at home with Ginger. We also learn that Alice had once been engaged to Horton, who fled from her clutches by embarking on an elephant hunt in India. Ginger tells the barrister that her wish to divorce her husband has been stalled by his absolute refusal to discuss the matter. According to English law at the time, Horton points out, divorce is prohibited unless the husband agrees to it. In order to coerce the man into court, he suggests that client Ginger involve herself in a harmless but potentially damaging "love affair" that Horton will photograph. The pictures, in turn, will be handed over to hubby, Cyril, who Horton assumes will file for divorce the minute the shock wears off.

Although Ginger does not favor the scheme, her aunt treats it as a stroke of legalistic genius. With her long and wide-ranging experience in divorce—she's already gone through three of them—Alice's authoritative reasoning finally convinces her niece to follow Horton's advice. He welcomes Ginger's acceptance effusively, in no small part because he himself will handle all the details of the "case." His success should invalidate the opinion of his Doubting Thomas of a father that Horton is an oaf whose gross inadequacies as a barrister have splashed disgrace over the family's escutcheon.

The finalized plan requires Ginger and her aunt to go to the Bella Vista Hotel in Brighton (renamed Brightbourne in the film), then one of England's fanciest seaside resorts. Meanwhile, Horton will engage the services of a professional gigolo who will identify himself to Ginger by reciting the quotation, "Chance is the fool's word for fate." The quotation, incidentally, also happens to be a line spoken by Astaire in his most recent musical comedy.

At the Beach. At Brighbourne, Horton and other guests in a cocktail lounge are entertained by Betty Grable, as yet unfamiliar to moviegoers despite her underappreciated momentary appearances in 17 films over the previous five years. She lures the stodgy barrister into singing and dancing "Let's K-nock K-nees," another lively but undistinguished Gordon and Revel novelty, staged by Hermes Pan. Also bumping kneecaps were members of a chorus of bathing beauties, inserted into the number more for cheesecake than for any discernible dancing ability. No singer—or dancer either, for that matter—Horton merely speaks the words in rhythm, much as Rex Harrison would much later in *My Fair Lady*, but with far less polish and effectiveness. Horton, however, was especially gifted at comedy, having established himself as a master of it in a series of farces co-starring Patsy Ruth Miller beginning in 1928. In 1935, in *In Caliente*, he would spoof up another dance number. The song was Mort Dixon and Allie Wrubel's more substantial "The Lady in Red," and his partner was the equally playful Judy Canova.

Into the merry throng ambles Erik Rhodes, who as Rodolfo Tonetti is the male half of the prearranged clandestine love affair. He is met and briefed by Horton. Rhodes is to "seduce" Ginger and serve as hired co-respondent when her enraged hubby files for divorce. Warming to the plot, and particularly to the fee he expects to earn, Rhodes pledges to regard the bogus love affair as "strictly business." Horton gives him the identifying quotation, which Rhodes predictably mixes up into unintelligibility—"Give me a name for a chance and I'm a fool"—adding to the screenplay's humor while eclipsing the suspense. Particularly gifted at spouting hilarious malapropisms at a time when Hollywood screenwriters reveled in them, *farceur* Rhodes excelled at portrayals of the easily confused, self-obsessed plastic Lothario. He, along with many other subsidiary cast members and director Sandrich, would join Fred and Ginger the next year in *Top Hat*, an even greater masterpiece of Art Deco chic than *The Gay Divorcee*.

Later that night doubtful coincidence reenters the script when Ginger glimpses Astaire looking over the resort grounds from the balcony of his suite. He is equally quick to catch sight of her dining in the downstairs restaurant with aunt Alice Brady. She quickly runs from his view, while frantic Fred races downstairs to the hotel's reception room to cut off her escape. After several futile attempts trying to talk his way into her heart, he leads her into their first dance. Although it is true that their balanced movements strike today's audiences as studied, more "stagy" than cinematic, and perhaps embellished with a bit too many flourishes, it was this number that more than any of their other early dancefloor duets established their reputation as the screen's foremost representatives of grace and precision. This well-deserved encomium was to remain in effect throughout the next five years, and seven more musicals, up to and including their final RKO picture, *The Story of Vernon and Irene Castle*, in 1939.

The background song, "Night and Day," choreographed by Astaire himself, was the only Cole Porter tune picked up from 1932's *The Gay Divorce*, on which the film was based. (Hollywood feminized *Divorce* to *Divorcee*, in effect glamorizing the title and elevating Ginger's marriage to the focal point of the plot. Another reason for the title switch was the Hays Office's contention that there is definitely nothing gay about a divorce.) Porter's nine other stage songs— "After You," "How's Your Romance?," "I Still Love the Red, White and Blue," "I've Got You on My Mind," "Mr. and Mrs. Fitch," "Salt Air," "What Will Become of Our England?," "Why Marry Them?" and "You're in Love"—were dropped, for once a judicious West Coast excision, since none of them is included on any list of the composer's best songs. Moreover, their inclusion very well might have led RKO executives to forgo insertion of "The Continental" so as not to extend the film beyond the normal 90-minute running time.

Regardless of the title adjustment, it was evident that revising *The Gay Divorce* plot moved the Hollywood musical into unfamiliar terrain. The movie colony's male and female musical stars were rarely ever married at the outset of a film. The fun-loving beau was depicted as nothing more devilish than a playboy seeking to set up housekeeping with an innocent coquette. It was this matchmaking of two unmarrieds that moved the plot forward to their eventual engagement or wedding, the culmination in all the screenplays and the chief

ingredient that made the happy ending possible.

As might be expected from duetting a song with the passionate, total-commitment lyric of "Night and Day," Ginger at the conclusion is as enamored of Fred as was Claire Luce, who danced it with him in the 1932 stage musical, and equally receptive to consigning their sparring days to history. Mesmerized by the electricity of their dance together, Fred attempts to melt the last vestiges of Ginger's reserve by resorting again to verbal love notes. She accepts them graciously, but caution prevents her from encouraging more than a few. Undeterred, the stout-hearted lover admits philosophically that though he may fail in his quest, he will continue to hope for success. "Chance is the fool's word for fate," he muses aloud. The phrase strikes a dissonant chord in Ginger, who overhears it and infers that Fred is the for-pay lover sent by Horton to cooperate in her feigned seduction.

Believing that his love chatter had been nothing more than a buildup to the prearranged encounter, Ginger flares up at what she considers his insincerity. Her reaction astounds Fred, who becomes even more confused when, living up to her role in the divorce plot, she gives him her room number (216), along with the command to visit her at midnight. Apparently, Fred assumes, his virgin princess is accustomed to arranging trysts with men strangers. His face reveals even deeper shock when Aunt Hortense, who also believes that he is working for Horton, meets Fred in the lobby and encourages him to show up in her niece's room at the appointed hour. Good God, the old woman is obviously a go-between for Ginger's nightly lovers, a sort of high-class pimp!

The story picks up steam once Fred joins Ginger for the rendezvous. Hoping for at least a smile to lend warmth to the assignation, Fred is baffled when the lady reverts to her earlier defensiveness. She had realized that Horton would select a competent actor to serve as counterfeit lover, but she had no idea it would be Fred, or that he would play the part so well. In an extended scene, the two exchange comments rich in dual misinterpretation. The most reliable of standard comic devices, it manages to amuse because of the witty dialogue, even though the couple's frequent pauses to allow the audiences' laughter to subside tends to date this exercise in parrying innocent questions with inapropos answers.

The "Experienced" Roue. In one of her most pointed questions, Ginger asks Fred how long he has been in "this business." Thinking she is referring to his stage career, he proudly replies that he entered it at the age of 10, and furthermore that since then he has "entertained thousands of people," a figure that the astonished Ginger assumes refers to female clients. Meanwhile, Horton meets Rhodes in the lobby, and finally remembers to give him Ginger's room number. Up to it rushes the gigolo, intent on doing his duty.

Instantly envious of Fred's charm and suspicious of him as a business competitor, Rhodes decides to wait till he leaves before servicing Ginger. That she and Fred are falling in love is quite apparent despite Ginger's anger at his alleged deception and unhappiness at her apparent moral laxity. Yet, true love is not to be thwarted for long, at least in a Hollywood musical, even if occasional signals of their growing affection are galling to Rhodes. Meanwhile, the downstairs hotel dance floor has become crowded with about 80 chorus boys and girls preparing to entertain the guests with "The Continental," songwriter Herb Magidson and Con Conrad's spectacular production number and winner of the first Academy Award for best song. When strains of the tune creep into Ginger's room, her and Fred's delight in each other is made all the more obvious to Rhodes, who is thrown into a dither trying to restrain them from exchanging those dreamy looks that signal romantic involvement.

Fred had sung "Night and Day" to her; she repays the favor by singing "The Continental" to him while both glance down at the dance floor from her balcony. It is also briefly sung by a waiter, played by Eric Blore, an extremely talented Britisher whose eccentricities unfailingly pepped up even the dullest of the many comedies he appeared in, usually as a butler, over his 30-year film career. Like Rhodes, who also sings the song, Blore had appeared in the original *The Gay Divorce*. The final solo singer is a hotel guest (Lillian Miles), and then the camera centers on the chorus.

Credit for the highly artistic multi-level setting for the song largely falls to Carroll Clark and especially Van Nest Polglase, one of the most influential of all of Hollywood's art directors, who also created the imaginative sets of the dancing twosome's earlier *Flying Down to Rio*, as well as for the later *Top Hat, Follow the Fleet, Shall We Dance*, and *Carefree*. Such dramatic classics as *The Informer* (1935), *Winterset* (1936), *Gunga Din* and *The Hunchback of Notre Dame* (both 1939), and *Citizen Kane* (1941) also bear Polglase's imprimatur.

Superbly complementing "The Continental's" festive sets were film editor William Hamilton's pace-quickening series of intercuts of the ensemble dancers in action. Equally meritorious was cinematographer David Abel's cutting-edge camera deployment that alternates among a wide range of focuses—short, medium, and long—while interspersing dissolves and flash-pans in order to vary the visual menu without compromising the continuity of the 17½-minute sequence, which remains fluid from the first to the last of the six reprises. The dancing, supervised by Dave Gould, who had also directed it in *Flying Down to Rio*, mixes tap with acrobatics and tempos ranging from swing to tango to waltz. The artistic and technological advances in moving making between "The Carioca" and "The Continental" are so stunning that it is difficult to accept the fact that only about one year had elapsed between the shooting of these two production numbers.

The beat of the melody urging Fred and Ginger to join the happy throng, it is left to him to provide the means of their escape from under the watchful eyes of Rhodes, who is determined to protect his role as co-respondent. The ruse Fred comes up with is actually so transparent that not even a child would be fooled by it, but no matter. Grabbing a magazine from a table while Rhodes plays solitaire in the next room, Fred cuts out paper doll replicas of Ginger and himself and affixes them to the phonograph. He spotlights them with a lamp, which silhouettes the figures on the wall as they revolve on the turntable. Rhodes is happy, assuming that the whirling couple is content to dance the tune in Ginger's room, while off they go to the dance floor. There they naturally manipulate their steps so masterfully that they sweep the assembled dancers off the floor, turning them from participants into admiring observers.

Forced the next morning by their chumminess and the refusal of Rhodes to leave, Ginger decides to reveal her past to Fred. She admits that she is married, explains Horton's plot, and confesses that she had mistaken Fred for Rhodes. The lovers' reconciliation is sundered, however, when husband Cyril, played by William Austin, unexpectedly shows up in the room. Fred's presence notwithstanding, Ginger and Rhodes play their prearranged parts in hopes of convincing Austin that they are having a torrid love affair by indulging in haphazard petting. But Ginger's hubby is forgiving: Nothing is Ginger's fault, and he refuses to grant her a divorce. "Pack up your things and come home at once," he commands.

The next visitor to the already crowded room is Blore, a waiter by occupation and geologist by avocation, who recognizes Austin as "Professor Brown," a scholar whom he had met once and greatly admires. Innocent of the consequences, he mentions that Brown has had a French wife for years. Exposed as a bigamist, Austin hurriedly backs away from concocting an alibi he knows no one will believe, and departs the room and Ginger's life. Passing him on the way out are Horton and Aunt Hortense, who proudly announce that at long last they have been married.

Thus does *The Gay Divorcee* wind up its interlocking affairs in a whirlwind. The neglectful husband has been disposed of, Rhodes has been exposed as an incompetent hired hand who now wants nothing more than to return to the safe haven of home, wife, and children, and the middle-age barrister and kooky aunt are wallowing in long-delayed happiness. All that is left is the uniting of Fred and Ginger, a promise that audiences always knew would be honored, regardless of the plot detours imperiling its fulfillment.

As was customary in musical films, Fred and Ginger's impending marriage is celebrated in song, this time with a rousing reprise of the hit song. Dancing again to the strains of "The Continental," they hand their luggage to the bellboys, tip them, tap dance arm in arm out of the room—and the film. Recalling how they had overcome all previous problems, viewers were certain that cocky Fred and ladylike Ginger would undoubtedly surmount whatever future troubles might arise with a song, perhaps a sly wink at fate, secure in the belief that their future together would be one of cloudless skies and laughter ever after.

About to reenter the cold world of Great Depression, moviegoers took pleasure in basking vicariously in the glow of the dancers' till-death happiness, if only temporarily. The picture was but a pause, although a satisfying one, in their daily routine of seeking shelter from hardship in make believe. Fortunately for all concerned, *The Gay Divorcee*, was among the best and most diverting of the goodies assembled on the production lines of Hollywood's dream factories.

In mid–1995, Ginger Rogers died at the age of 84, having outlived Astaire, who died on June 22, 1987, by eight years. Eleanor Powell was a better tap technician, as her unparalleled footwork in the "Begin the Beguine" number in *The Broadway Melody of 1940* clearly attests. Rita Hayworth's gracefulness on the ballroom floor, in such a number as "I'm Old Fashioned" in *You Were Never Lovelier*, was the equal of Ginger's at her best. But among all of Fred's many female co-stars, Ginger remains the sentimental favorite. She was an excellent dancer and actress, and always gave the vivid impression that she enjoyed working with Fred and felt at home in his arms. The miracle of their partnership had never been seen before on the screen, nor has any dance team managed to replace them. Better than anyone else, each embodied charm and gracefulness during the most golden of all of Hollywood's Golden Ages.

Some 60 years ago Astaire himself best summarized Ginger's unique ability to light up the screen and fulfill many a moviegoer's dream of the ideal female lover in the lyric of a Jerome Kern song interpolated into the film version of *Roberta*. She was, Fred acknowledged, delightful to know, perfect from head to toe, appealing, dignified.

And "Lovely to Look At."

One Night of Love (1934)

A Columbia Picture. DIRECTOR: Victor Schertzinger. PRODUCER: Sara Risher. SCREENWRITERS: S.K. Lauren,

James Gow, and Edmund North, based on a story by Dorothy Speare and Charles Beahan. CINEMATOGRAPHER: Joseph Walker; SPECIAL EFFECTS: John Hoffman. FILM EDITOR: Gene Milford. ART DIRECTOR: Stephen Goosson. SOUND: Paul Neal. COSTUMES: Robert Kalloch. MUSICAL DIRECTOR: Louis Silvers. ORIGINAL SONG: Lyric by Gus Kahn, music by Victor Schertzinger. RUNNING TIME: 1 hour, 35 minutes. *Principal Players*: Grace Moore (Mary Barrett). Tullio Carminati (Giulio Monteverdi). Lyle Talbot (Bill Houston). Mona Barrie (Lally). Luis Alberni (Giovanni). Jesse Ralph (Angelina). Nydia Westman (Muriel). *Major Academy Awards*: Best Sound; Scoring. *Nominations*: Best Picture; Director; Actress (*Grace Moore*); Film Editing.

The world of grand opera was rarely invaded by Hollywood, nor were its major figures very often rounded up to perform, and then usually in cameos. Opera, after all, was widely regarded by the moguls as an elitist pleasure far beyond the capacity of the moviegoing public to comprehend or enjoy. In 1930, Grace Moore had joined with fellow Metropolitan Opera star Lawrence Tibbett in the filmed version of Oscar Hammerstein II and Sigmund Romberg's *The New Moon*. But that was an operetta that had originated on the Broadway stage, not at the Met, in 1928, and was therefore considered a fail-safe movie property. Throughout the twenties, operettas carrying scores especially by either Romberg or Rudolf Friml were as profitable as musical comedies, though far fewer in number.

The New Moon songs were still fresh in the memory of 1930 Americans, led by such dazzlers as "Stout Hearted Men," "Softly as in a Morning Sunrise," "Lover, Come Back to Me," and "One Kiss," which is almost a note-for-note duplicate of Vincent Youmans's "No, No, Nanette" (1925), but in waltz tempo. Typically dignified and at times murderous to sing, operetta songs demanded trained voices, and so into the film version went the virile Tibbett, a 1930 best actor nominee as Yegor in *The Rogue Song*, and angelic Grace. Their reputations lent this first of two Hollywood renderings of *The New Moon* a degree of prestige that other celluloid musicals with less exalted cast members were unable to challenge. Still acclaimed by many as the greatest baritone America has produced, Tibbett became a brief bobby-sox favorite after he succeeded Frank Sinatra on *Your Hit Parade* in the late forties. Throughout the 1920s, Miss Moore had appeared in Broadway

musicals as well as operas, and had built up quite a fan club as the popularizer of such songs as Irving Berlin's "What'll I Do?," which she introduced with tenor John Steel in *The Music Box Revue of 1923*.

Unfortunately, the two opera stars never appeared together in another film, though Tibbett made a total of six for MGM and Fox, and Miss Moore appeared in eight, including *The King Steps Out* in 1936. It was in that musical that she sang her best-known song, "Stars in My Eyes," a slight revision by violin virtuoso Fritz Kreisler of a song he had written for *Apple Blossoms*, which had starred the Astaires in 1919, and was given a new lyric by Dorothy Fields. Miss Moore returned to the film capital in 1934 to play the lead in *One Night of Love*, a weak nominee for the best picture award, but still the best known of all the grand opera-based Hollywood movies.

The picture's box office success nudged most of the major studios into their only sustained flirtation with Metropolitan Opera stars. Between 1935 and 1939, diva Lily Pons made three musical pictures, all containing popular songs as well as selected arias from her operatic repertoire. Gladys Swarthout also appeared in three, as did Metropolitan tenors James Melton, who had the good luck of singing Harry Warren tunes in all of them, and Nino Martini. Marion Talley made one film, Helen Jepson made a cameo appearance singing Verdi's "Libiamo ne' lieti calici" in *The Goldwyn Follies*, and Kirstin Flagstad, in her brief stint in *The Big Broadcast of 1938*, overwhelmed audiences with her violent gesturing and shrieking reprise of Wagner's "Brunhilde's Battle Cry," from *Die Walküre*.

Alternating the classics with contemporary love ballads in the same film became a relatively extended habit with MGM. For the musical drama *San Francisco* (1936), non-opera star Jeanette MacDonald vocalized not only the new and quite popular title tune (by Gus Kahn, Bronislau Kaper, and Walter Jurmann) and Freed and Brown's "Would You," but also an aria from Gounod's *Faust*. In 1941, starlet Kathryn Grayson picked up the torch, balancing long hair with pop in *Andy Hardy's Private Secretary*. She continued the practice in many of her later films, particularly *It Happened in Brooklyn* (1947), in which she sings the Sammy

Opera hopeful Grace Moore is unable to conceal a snicker at the rivalry of her two lovers, Lyle Talbot, left, the boyfriend from back home, and Tullio Carminati, her Italian vocal teacher, in *One Night of Love.*

Cahn–Jule Styne hit "Time After Time." In company with Frank Sinatra, she also amusingly duets Mozart's "La ci darem la manno," from *Don Giovanni*, and solos Delibes's "Bell Song," from *Lakme.* Appropriately, Miss Grayson played the role of Grace Moore in the semi-autobiographical *So This Is Love* in 1953, six years after the latter's untimely death in an airplane crash at the age of 46.

From 1943 to 1953, the famous Wagnerian tenor Lawrence Melchior kept the operatic flame alive in five MGM films. In 1961, Helen Traubel good naturedly participated in a Jerry Lewis film, *The Ladies' Man*, failing to sing a single note, and in 1954 sang a few Romberg songs, including, oddly enough, "Stout Hearted Men," in *Deep in My Heart.* In 1947, United Artists assembled the largest-ever gathering of artists representing the opera, concert and dance hall, and Broadway for *Carnegie Hall.* Besides Leopold Stokowski, the cast included Lily Pons, Jascha Heifetz, Rïse Stevens,

Ezio Pinza, Jan Peerce, Artur Rubinstein, Bruno Walter, Fritz Reiner, and Walter Damrosch, along with Harry James's and Vaughn Monroe's orchestras and Sam Coslow's briefly popular ballad "Beware My Heart."

According to Julius Bloom, for many years the hall's executive director, the acoustics did not assume the glories for which the showplace became renowned until a hole about the size of the stage was cut in the ceiling above it during the filming of the picture. The hole, hidden from the audience by the curtain and baffles, exposed a huge area that acted as a giant chamber for sound to roll around in, blend, mix, and reenter the auditorium, much to the delight of post–1947 listeners.

Considering the limited enthusiasm for classical music, it was inevitable that Grace Moore would launch Hollywood's ephemeral interest in opera by being selected to play the leading lady in a picture as musically foreign to the majority of Americans as *One Night of Love.*

An accomplished lyrical soprano, she was also an attractive 32 year old with better-than-average acting ability and an engaging personality and trim figure, which had to be zealously guarded against the tendency to expand into plumpness. Not the typical Hollywood musical, replete with the customary three- to five-song original score, chorus line, and shy heroine panting to display her talents on a Broadway stage, it contains only one new song. Thus, the film could have emerged as a simple love story with more drama than comedy in which another ambitious young lady succeeds in love and her career.

Unlike stage musicals, which until recently rarely introduced hit title songs, Hollywood specialized in them from the earliest all-talking days, largely to help promote the films in which they appeared. "One Night of Love" is but one of dozens of examples. Five years earlier "Sunny Side Up" became the first in a 30-year-long outpouring of tremendously popular title tunes that included "Puttin' on the Ritz," "The Broadway Melody," "Cuban Love Song," "One Hour with You," "Forty-Second Street," "Flying Down to Rio," "Flirtation Walk," "Let's Fall in Love," "Paris in the Spring," "Thanks a Million," "Pennies from Heaven," "San Francisco," "One in a Million," "Rosalie," "You're a Sweetheart," "Shall We Dance," "You Can't Have Everything," "Wake Up and Live," "Blues in the Night," "Thank Your Lucky Stars," "Can't Help Singing," "Out of This World," "Give Me the Simple Life," "My Dream Is Yours," and "Gigi," among many others. So pervasive was the linking of song and film titles that radio listeners grew accustomed to announcements on such a variety show as *The Kraft Music Hall* that "Bing Crosby will now sing 'Going My Way,' from the new Paramount picture of the same name."

In addition to *One Night of Love*'s nomination as best picture, the soprano herself competed as best actress against heavyweights Claudette Colbert, Bette Davis, and Norma Shearer. Miss Colbert won for her role as Ellie Andrews in *It Happened One Night*, which was voted best picture of 1934, beating out 11 other entries. Both films were produced by Columbia Pictures, a relatively minor studio when compared with such powerhouses as MGM, Warner Bros., Fox, and Paramount. Together, these five studios produced 69 of the 102 contenders for best picture between 1929 and 1940. Columbia was nominated for eight, five of them directed by Frank Capra.

Despite her Oscar loss, Miss Moore had scored a personal triumph. She was one of the very few leading actresses in the 67-year history of the Academy Awards to be to be nominated for her role in a musical. Unfortunately, her lackluster co-star, Tullio Carminati, failed to add much of anything to the picture, despite his 22 years' experience as a film actor in Europe and the United States. Neither musical nor particularly handsome, he shouts his lines quite well, but he was hardly the ideal choice to play Grace's lover. The warmth generated by their few tender moments together is saved from satiric interpretation solely by the young lady's own respectable acting credentials.

In light of Columbia's spotty musical-production history, its decision to revive Miss Moore's career by starring her in a movie revolving around grand opera was nothing short of remarkable. With the dictatorial and allegedly tone-deaf Harry Cohn firmly ensconced as president, even more astounding was his expending a hefty bankroll to qualify the film as an Oscar nominee. Exposed early in his professional life to popular music as a vaudeville performer and song plugger, Cohn showed little interest in musical films throughout his 34 years with Columbia, although his fascination with Rita Hayworth led in the early 1940s to three melodious and thoroughly enjoyable song-and-dance pictures, *You'll Never Get Rich*, *You Were Never Lovelier*, and *Cover Girl*.

Victor Schertzinger, the composer of "One Night of Love," a lovely song in waltz tempo, which by 1934 had lost most of its once formidable influence on American popular music, also directed the film. In 1935 he would direct Miss Moore in *Love Me Forever*, again providing the singing star with a lilting title song. His lyricist for both songs was Gus Kahn, from whom came the lyrics of such 1920s non-production ballads as "It Had to Be You" and "I'll See You in My Dreams," with music by bandleader Isham Jones, and "My Buddy" in collaboration with Walter Donaldson. For other films, Kahn teamed with first-rate composers Vincent Youmans for "The Carioca" and Nacio Herb Brown for "You Stepped Out of a

Dream," the composer's final hit written for an MGM picture, *Ziegfeld Girl* (1941) among many others.

One Night of Love was the first movie to win the Academy Award for best scoring, which along with the best song category, was inaugurated in 1935. The Oscar went to the Columbia Studio Music Department, then headed by Louis Silvers, a composer ("April Showers") and later chief musical director for 20th Century–Fox. Max Steiner, as head of RKO Radio's music department, was also nominated that year for *The Gay Divorcee* and the John Ford drama *The Lost Patrol*. Through 1937 the award was considered a music department achievement, and the Oscars were presented to the department head rather than to the individual composers.

The Contestant. That Grace Moore (Mary Barrett) has hitched her ambition to musical stardom on a grand scale is evident at the outset of *One Night of Love*. She sings the title tune during the rolling of the credits and, with the arrival of the first scene, the audience learns why. She is in the throes of a radio audition, hoping to win the top prize of an expense-paid trip to Milan and full tuition to study under Tullio Carminati (Giulio Monteverdi), identified as the "greatest operatic maestro in Europe," who at the moment is lazily cruising the Mediterranean with his protégé, Mona Barrie (Lally). Enamored of her teacher, but suspicious that his intense pleasure at listening to Grace's voice over the short-wave radio is the prelude to dropping her as the latest in a succession of grateful paramours, she is beginning to bore Carminati by trying to distract his attention away from the unseen singer.

Although Grace does not win the contest, she has succeeded in exposing her right to enter it and prefiguring the twisty plot to follow. Despite singing a popular song, she has no designs on the Broadway stage, but rather on the Metropolitan Opera House, among the most venerable of New York institutions since 1883 and probably the most difficult "show business" venue to which any artist could aspire.

Mona's jealousy proves to be unfounded when Carminati dismisses Grace from his mind after the name of another young lady is announced as winner. Maestro and singer, how-

ever, are destined to meet as master and pupil; equally certain is that Mona's temper, as fiery and subject to instant eruption as Carminati's, will be aimed at any female who dares to rival her affection for the great vocal teacher. Also listening to Miss Moore is Lyle Talbot (Bill Houston), deeply but hopelessly in love with her and the strongest supporter of her career hopes. Filmgoers of the time instantly recognized that pallid Talbot, self-effacing and sincere as ever, was bound in time to lose out to another man with more personality and zest. In film after film (*Our Little Girl*, 1935, *Second Fiddle*, 1939), his lady co-stars politely brushed aside his admirable faithful-dog loyalty, which they hoped would be duplicated by the far more effervescent other fellow who walks into their lives to stay.

Back home and disillusioned, yet determined to prevail over disappointment, Grace tells her mother and father that, having saved up $500—a princely sum in 1934—she will pay her own way to Milan for further study and hope for the best, thereby emphasizing the truism that youthful dreams recognize no boundaries, national or artistic.

The plan disturbs her worried mother, sympathetically played by Jane Darwell, an extraordinary character actress who, after years of appearing in minor roles, would prove her worth with her Academy Award performance as strong-willed Ma Joad in director John Ford's *Grapes of Wrath* in 1940, and the next year as Marie Dressler's successor as "Tugboat Annie." To dispel the elder woman's fears that somehow she will suffer egregiously by comporting with Italians, Grace appeals to motherly pride to obtain permission to make the trip. "You don't want me to be a quitter!" she exclaims, defying her mother's objection to her leaving home.

Giving up one's dreams, it should be remembered, was a cardinal sin in thirties movies, and family and friends were duty-bound to convince the downhearted that such a decision was always premature as well as a sure sign of cowardice. Mother Jane follows along in this timeworn tradition by agreeing that Grace should try her luck and expressing confidence that her daughter's exposure to "opera culture" will result in rapid career advancement.

The scene shifts to Milan, where other youngsters are deeply engrossed in practicing the violin, flute, piano, harp, and voices. An impromptu orchestra strikes up an aria from *La Traviata*, giving Grace the cue to walk onto the balcony of her flat and, as if entertaining her first audience from an elevated stage, burst into song to the delight of the onlookers assembled in the courtyard to listen. Her vocalizing is rewarded with sustained applause and a bouquet not of flowers, but of vegetables, thrown up to the flattered singer by her adoring audience. True to the conventional theatrical, operatic, and film depictions of struggling artists as contentedly confined to homey garrets, stomachs empty but heads feasting on visions of eventual rewards, Grace proudly displays the shafts of protruding carrots and celery to her equally pauperized, morale-building roommate, Muriel, amicably played by Nydia Westman, a ringer for Una Merkel in looks and gestures.

Nydia belongs to same club in which most of Hollywood's stable of subsidiary characters claimed membership. The job of these unheralded performers, ranging from Helen Westley and George Barbier to Cora Witherspoon and Alan Dinehart, was to add humor and sometimes conflict to the often mindless plots of musical pictures by investing their personality quirks and unquestioned acting prowess in them. Although she dislikes music, Nydia is the first to assume—correctly, as things turn out—that Grace is fated for stardom, and she enthusiastically assists her in every way possible.

She reminds Grace that she had already received an offer to appear next season at the La Scala Opera House, no minor achievement for a neophyte. Grace, however, refused after a realistic self-appraisal convinced her that she was simply not prepared to join such a prestigious company even in a minor capacity. That both are broke and weeks behind in the rent is of no consequence, an attitude that only deepens Nydia's respect for and devotion to Grace. There is such a thing as artistic integrity, and Nydia appreciates her roomie's determination to acquire the mandatory skills before venturing into a world of which thus far she has been only an observer.

Into their midst comes Talbot, who had also traveled to the Old World specifically to woo Grace. His offer to pay the girls' rent is turned down by Grace, who prefers not to subsist on charity, even from an old friend. His response is to invite her landlady (Rosemary Glosz), a former opera singer, into the flat, where she and Grace duet the "Sextet" from *Lucia di Lammermoor*. Enchanted with the applause her vocalizing generates, the landlady forgets to ask for the overdue rent and departs in ecstasy. Immediately afterward, Nydia reminds Grace that the nearby Café Roma is in need of a waitress. The availability of such demeaning jobs was another musical-film tradition. Slinging hash or jerking sodas, already accepted as honorable means of staving off starvation among the struggling Broadway-bound, was equally applicable to opera hopefuls. As expected, Henry Armetta, the owner of the Roma and everybody's favorite Italian, hires her.

Professional Help. In Carminati's luxurious apartment, meanwhile, the maestro is reprimanding Mona for arriving late for her singing lesson. Her admiration of her teacher's genius having turned to infatuation, she has become unresponsive to the nuances of his coaching. She is a poor singer, and, even worse, shows little interest in improvement, Carminati hollers, displaying the first of his temper tantrums, which filmgoers nonchalantly assumed was normal behavior among artists in any field, especially if they happened to be Italian. He will continue to berate everybody to the end of the film, forever basking in the reverence to which he feels his reputation entitles him. But he can be quick to adjust his personality to satisfy immediate needs. Like John Barrymore, who plays an almost identical role—and far better—in *Maytime*, Carminati easily exchanges his normal outrage when his orders are disobeyed for insincere paternalistic concern when an unforeseen crisis threatens to disrupt his own career plans.

In exasperation he dismisses Mona as a pupil, and swears to his pianist Luis Alberni, (Giovanni), another master at blowing off pent-up steam at the slightest irritation, that henceforth he will never attempt to teach another female amateur anything. It simply isn't worth the effort, he wails, revealing his elephantine ego. Without exception, he adds, every one of them falls in love with him and out of love with music. To relax his nerves, Carminati suggests that the two men take a brief walk and then dine at the Café Roma. The plot, like a cauldron of minestrone under boil, suddenly bubbles up with tasty morsels to whet viewers' appetites for drama. The unrequited Mona will surely reappear with a vengeance, since an opera trainee scorned is a harridan indeed. Grace has no money, and Carminati no longer has any pupils to badger. The prospect that the three shall meet is ruled by inevitability.

At the café, Carminati's attention is transfixed on Grace, its newest singing waitress, who is entertaining the appreciative diners with Rudolf Thaler and Alberto Pestlozza's "Ciribiribin" while dextrously balancing huge trays laden with plates of pasta on the palms of both hands. Once again the reaction to her solo is resounding applause, which tweaks Carminati's artistic sensibilities. He follows her to her dressing room, which the management apparently provides to staff members who can dish out entertainment as well as food.

After declaring excitedly that she has been blessed with a "once in a lifetime voice," he tempers his effusive praise by informing Grace that her technique still leaves much to be desired. But fear not, he bellows, the great Carminati can remedy her shortcomings. Offended by his domineering presence, Grace is nonetheless pleased at learning that her admiring critic is none other than the teacher whose services represented first prize in the radio audition she had failed only weeks earlier.

She becomes receptive to his urging to be his pupil, despite his threat that opera is a jealous mistress that abides no outside interest. She will work, work, work, and when she tires, he will drive her all the harder. In other words, his regimen permits no relaxation, ever. But when he is done with her, as Broadway musical producer Warner Baxter informed beginner Ruby Keeler one year earlier in *42nd Street*, she will shine like a star in the operatic heavens.

Dubious yet inclined to believe that he can be the agent of her artistic salvation, Grace is all the more reluctant to sign on as pupil when Carminati suggests that she take up residence in his villa. In another example of the film-musical heroine's misjudging the hero's motives, she demurs. He makes it quite clear, however, that his sole interest is training her as only he can; he is not looking for an affair. Not only that, but should she fall in love with him—a distinct possibility that arises naturally from the maestro's extreme self-absorption—she will be thrown out, period. As he had once warned Mona, business and love do not mix. His insistence that Grace will wind up hating him convinces her of his integrity, and off she goes to the villa.

There she passes through a series of bootcamp indignities, from learning how to breathe to strengthening the muscles of the abdomen and diaphragm through endless exercises. Yet to come is the imposition of a strict diet limiting the pupil's food intake to melba toast and a side order of spinach. Grace, however, is willing to endure the physical and mental torture in order to fulfill her teacher's chief goal of again introducing an outstanding novice singer to the opera-loving public, an objective that conveniently matches her own. Along the way, the maestro lives up to his reputation as implacable taskmaster to such a degree that Grace begins to respond to his demands with her own frequent outbursts of temper. She is indeed learning to hate him.

To make certain that love—for anyone—does not intrude, Carminati orders Talbot, who visits Grace impromptu to propose marriage, to leave the villa forthwith. Hoping to compensate for his rudeness to her friend, he confides to Grace that he is pleased with her progress and promises to let her sing with a provincial opera company "in about a year." Overjoyed at receiving a rare compliment, Grace revives her commitment to continue the struggle, a wise decision that results in a montage of later appearances by her in a variety of minor roles in operas throughout Italy.

It is while awaiting the curtain to rise on one of them that the sympathetic side of Carminati's typically caustic nature briefly emerges. Like all dominating males in musical films, he is capable of displaying warmth, which is allowed to creep up occasionally from beneath a frigid exterior to forestall a crisis. In this instance, the propellant for his kindliness is Grace's extreme nervousness. She is, in her own words, "sick with fear," too overwrought by insecurity to perform that night. She is finally becalmed by Carminati, who comforts her into singing a song for him in order to rachet up her self-assurance. As he accompanies her on the piano, she sings the traditional "Last Rose of Summer," Richard Alfred Milliken's musical version of the famous poem by Thomas Moore. Her rendition is excellent, fully warranting her Svengali-like teacher's exultant praise. Entranced more with his own cleverness in dissolving a impending disaster than with her voice, he even permits friend Luis Alberni to send Grace a bouquet of roses—but to be delivered after her performance is over, not before, as the pianist had planned.

Triumph and Discord. Grace goes on as scheduled and scores an immense hit in the unnamed opera. She and Carminati promptly embark on a tour of European capitals that brings them to a first-class opera house in Vienna, where she is to sing the leading role in *Carmen*. Mona reenters the plot when she spots the couple in a restaurant. She dallies for several minutes at their table, ostensibly to share a few pleasantries. Instead, her dialogue consists of spilling memoirs of their former romantic interludes, infuriating Grace and prompting her to stalk out of the restaurant. Now the unwilling victim of a love-hate relationship involving a former and a current pupil, the embarrassed teacher also leaves.

Back in her room at the villa, Grace concocts a plan to thwart any renewal of the Carminati-Mona affair by forcing him to pay attention to her as a woman, not just another apprentice in residence. She pretends she has lost her voice, attempting to prove it to him by speaking hoarsely and gasping between syllables. The panicky maestro calls in a battery of doctors who, after examining the patient, conclude that there is absolutely nothing wrong with her, or her voice. Grace's maid Angelina, played by one of the decade's greatest character actresses, Jesse Ralph (unforgettable as Aunt Peggoty in *David Copperfield* and Mrs. Burley in *San Francisco*), confirms Carminati's suspicion that his pupil's "illness" is merely a ploy. She tells him she had overheard Grace's earlier threat to take some sort

of revenge on him if he dared to see Mona again.

Perturbed by Jesse's disclosure, he sanctimoniously adds to the sympathy he had earlier shown toward Grace's loss of vocal dexterity by confessing that "I simply must have worked her too hard." Then, reverting to his characteristic slyness, he jabs a pin into his pupil's posterior. As expected, Grace is in excellent voice, issuing a powerful soprano scream that reveals her deception. Carminati barges out of the room, locking the door behind him. Grace, however, trying her best to suppress with anger her growing love for her teacher, gains her freedom by climbing out of the window. It is time to renew acquaintances with an old friend—the untempestuous Talbot.

Talbot is not in his Vienna apartment to welcome Grace, but Carminati is luckier in his quest for relief from tension. Also eager to find refuge in the company of a long-term acquaintance, he finds Mona at home and receptive to any advances he might make toward her. None comes, however. The maestro is far too busy battling his own growing attraction toward Grace to pay heed to his one-time pupil's blatant attempts to revive their courtship. Unable to relax with a drink and small talk, he marches out of the apartment and into the nearby Hotel Bristol.

Greatly subdued after a night's rest, Grace apologizes early the next morning to Jesse over the telephone from Talbot's bedroom. Her frank admission that her illness was faked and her escape from the villa a rash act of insubordination endears Grace further to viewers, but she undergoes more emotional turmoil when the maid innocently mentions that Carminati is not at home. Wrongly inferring that he had spent the night with Mona, Grace spitefully declares that she will not sing *Carmen* but marry Talbot instead. Returning home during the conversation, Talbot is bowled over at hearing the news that he is to be betrothed to his beloved. But his glee quickly fades to disappointment when Grace confides that no, she does not really intend to marry him. They can still be pals, though, and to prove it, she suggests they go out on the town and have some fun for a change. They both deserve a little, if only to cheer him up for being rejected as a husband and her for all the sacrifice and hard work that have brought her nothing but misery.

After the two have made the rounds of Vienna carnivals and sidewalk cafés—punctuated every so often by Grace's vandalizing poster advertisements of her scheduled appearance at the opera house—Carminati rushes to Talbot's apartment after gossipy Jesse informs him of Grace's impending marriage. All three meet in the apartment, where Grace, still unwilling to forgive Carminati's alleged fickleness, repeats her vow to marry Talbot and drop out of the opera.

The usually belligerent teacher accepts the declaration without rancor, but only because he has already formulated a plot to undermine Grace's plans. He extends his congratulations to Talbot, who is now thoroughly confused at the off-again, on-again status of the marriage. He must now return to the opera house, Carminati tells them, insisting that the evening's performance will go on. "*Carmen* has been advertised, *Carmen* will be sung," he says in the firmest of tones. Mona will substitute for Grace.

Her aversion toward Carminati converted into proud defiance at the mention of her rival's name, Grace retreats into planning revenge upon his departure. The people have paid to hear her sing and they will hear her—not Mona's "broken-down foghorn voice." She races to the opera house and confronts Carminati, who confesses he never had any intention of asking Mona to sing the part. His revealed trick reinfuriates Grace, who again refuses to live up to the entertainment profession's long-standing dictum that the show must go on. Her unbenevolent despot of a teacher responds by declaring that her decision will ruin her career before it really gets started, as well as render all his coaching worthless. He then professes his love for her, while explaining that he had spent the previous night alone in a hotel, not in Mona's apartment. Grace accepts his explanation and love pronouncement. Yes, she will go on—and this time she means it.

Her rendition of the aria from *Carmen* is nothing less than superlative. Not only was Grace Moore the most screenworthy of Hollywood's 1930s grand opera imports, but few other voices surpassed hers on a sound track. Her delivery is more straightforward and less tantalizing than Risë Stevens's version in *Going My Way* 10 years later. Grace is the coquette, Risë the temptress; the former the innocent playing at love as if for the first time, the latter the experienced heartbreaker aware of the magnetism of her steamy sexuality.

Her *Carmen* performance a smashing success, Grace is introduced to an enthusiastic representative from the Metropolitan Opera House, who offers her the chance to appear at that prestigious auditorium. Both his and her own estimation that she is ready to take advantage of this magnificent opportunity meets with strong opposition from Carminati, who insists that Grace needs a minimum of one more year of practice to qualify. Curiously, she changes her mind and agreeably concurs—her teacher is the boss and is undoubtedly better qualified than either she or the man from the Met to judge such matters.

Most other love films of the time, musical or dramatic, would have been content to end then and there on a hopeful note. All the plot complexities had been smoothed over. Presumedly, Mona has been disposed of for good, and Grace's subscribing to Carminati's verdict on her talent would have satisfactorily solved both her career and her personal problems. Moviegoers would correctly infer that she would marry the maestro, continue to study under him, and in a year or so make a sensational debut in New York. Columbia Pictures, however, thought otherwise, and crammed still more complications into the film.

The first appears at the villa, where Carminati is waiting for Grace to arrive to share a candlelight dinner. But Mona shows up instead, eager to reprimand him for not even mentioning her name to the Metropolitan Opera talent scout. Furthermore, she will not leave the villa until he calls the gentleman and recommends her. But Carminati insists that she, like Grace, lacks the professionalism to sing at that landmark opera house. Were either to attempt to do so, his reputation as a master vocal coach would be ruined.

In the midst of the argument, Grace enters the room, leaving in a huff the instant she catches Mona practicing her wiles on the maestro in the hope of winning him over to her cause. Getting nowhere, Mona also flees, reminding her one-time teacher of his own adage that "it is always a mistake to mix lessons and love." Grace, angered that Martinelli had cozied up to her not out of love, but out of desperation for her to honor her *Carmen* contract, boldly accepts the offer to sing at the Metropolitan on her own.

The Debut. Back in Manhattan, Grace is again in turmoil. Rehearsing the role of Mimi in *Madama Butterfly*, she is unable to follow the tempo provided by the orchestra. Behind the scenes the entire Metropolitan music staff concurs that she is hopeless or, as Carminati had predicted, unready to undertake such a monumental challenge. Grace is fully aware of the undeniable need for her teacher but refuses to admit it. Even Jesse's assurance that he does love her and confirmation that he did indeed spend that night by himself in a hotel room fail to spur Grace into calling on him for help and encouragement. She is determined to make her debut under her own steam, and nobody or nothing is going to stand in her way.

Assembled in the opening night audience are most of the minor characters who had influenced Grace throughout the film. Pianist Alberni and maid Jesse are there, as are Grace's parents and Talbot, he who had wisely conceded in conventional gallant fashion that they would never make suitable marriage partners because of his inability ever to fit into grand opera society. Lumps in their throats and tears of pride welling in their eyes, all the spectators tensely await the raising of the curtain on what they pray will turn out to be a milestone in the budding career of their favorite young lady. As old as musicals pictures themselves, this ringalevio of subsidiary characters as witnesses to the star's first notable achievement held little in the way of suspense, but it did guarantee that the mandatory happy ending was in the offing. In *One Night of Love* the ritual is played out as impeccably as in any of its predecessors, or successors.

A smidgen of surprise, however, is provided in the final scene. The opera overture is struck up and the camera focuses on Grace, whose worried expression reflects her fear of performing before such a distinguished audience. She should have saved herself the bother. Bravely walking onto the stage, hoping for the best but fearing the worst, she sees Carminati in the prompter's box. From his presence she gains much-needed confidence, and there is an immediate, perceptible improvement in her movements and gestures.

Gradually, under the guidance of the master, her professionalism breaks through the barrier of stage fright to verify the fact that she has all the earmarks of a star. She sings two Puccini arias, including the intensely dramatic "Un Bel Di Vedremo," in a style that can be described only as beautiful, even inspired. The cries of "Bravo!" that echo throughout the hall attest to her victory. She has passed the most arduous of tests; she has made it at the Met!

Perhaps Grace's natural talent would have surmounted her initial nervousness and allowed her to reap the rewards that her vocal gymnastics deserved. But surely of equal importance in restoring her confidence was Carminati's delight in observing his blonde pupil breathe life into Mimi. In the next to last frame, as simple and moving as any to be found in musical films, his lips send her the most welcome of messages. The din of the ovation that greets Grace's solo is irrelevant. Head bowed toward the audience but her moist eyes focused on the maestro's own tearful, happy face, she smiles and nods at him after correctly reading his silent lip-synching of what his heart is saying: "I love you."

Undoubtedly, the greatest sentimental value of motion pictures is the visual preservation of the past. The leading players are permitted to live forever, their youth in full flower and their talent at its pinnacle, the mannerisms that marked them as special people ever available to future generations to study, admire, or simply enjoy over and over again. Although more than 60 years have elapsed since the premiere of *One Night of Love*, it is actually only as old as yesterday. The characters' love-in, love-out entanglements, harboring of emotions ranging from spite to hope, and perseverance at converting setbacks into triumphs are as valid in 1996 as they were in 1934.

The Broadway Melody of 1936 (1935)

A Metro-Goldwyn-Mayer picture. DIRECTOR: Roy Del Ruth. PRODUCER: John W. Considine, Jr. SCREEN-WRITERS: Jack McGowan and Sid Silvers, based on an original story by Moss Hart; ADDITIONAL DIALOGUE: Harry Conn. CINEMATOGRAPHER: Charles Rosher. FILM EDITOR: Blanche Sewell. CHOREOGRAPHER: Dave Gould; "Lucky Star" ballet staged by Albertine Rasch. ART DIRECTOR: Cedric Gibbons; ASSOCIATES: Merrill Pye and Edwin B. Willis. RECORDING DIRECTOR: Douglas Shearer. GOWNS: Adrian. MUSICAL DIRECTOR: Alfred Newman. ORCHESTRATOR: Edward B. Powell; ARRANGEMENTS: Roger Edens. PRODUCTION ASSISTANT: Alex Aarons. SONGS: Lyrics by Arthur Freed, music by Nacio Herb Brown. RUNNING TIME: 1 hour, 43 minutes. *Principal Players*: Jack Benny (Bert Keeler). Eleanor Powell (Irene Foster). Robert Taylor (Bob Gordon). Una Merkel (Kitty Corbett). Sid Silvers (Snoop). June Knight (Lillian Brent). Harry Stockwell (Himself). Frances Langford (Herself). Buddy Ebsen (Ted). Vilma Ebsen (Sally). Nick Long, Jr. (Basil). Paul Harvey (Managing Editor). Snorer (Robert Wildhack). *Major Academy Award*: Best Choreography. *Nominations*: Best Picture; Original Story.

The second of Metro's four-part Broadway Melody series, and the last to be nominated for the best picture award, *The Broadway Melody of 1936* ranks lower than the original 1929 film in plot inventiveness but far above it in technical proficiency, dancing, singing, spectacle, acting, and humor. The new sparkling Freed-Brown score surpassed their 1929 songs in the number of hits, although none of them has managed to outdistance "The Broadway Melody" and "You Were Meant for Me" in long-term popularity. On the other hand, not one of the five freshly minted tunes was so poorly conceived—or so amateurishly performed—as the earlier film's "The Boy Friend."

"You Are My Lucky Star" is one of the collaborators' best-ever ballads, and "Broadway Rhythm," which concludes the film, is pure gossamer, entitled to a place alongside the very best of Movieland's jumbo production numbers. Overall, the tunes are superior to the five *Broadway Melody of 1938* songs, also written by Freed and Brown, and almost on a par with the five new Cole Porter melodies in *The Broadway Melody of 1940*.

Again, the story centers on the struggles of a young innocent, this time from Albany, New York, who has set her sights on a Broadway career. Building on the movie musicals' conditioning of audiences into accepting the right of young women to move to the city, live on their own, and not be considered a prostitute, the heroine is a combination of Anita Page and Bessie Love. Like Anita she depends on an important theatrical contact for success, but remains vulnerable to disappointment; like Bessie she is equally determined to make the grade, overcoming frustration with refreshing cheerfulness. In a pinch, the two Mahoney sisters could always fall back on each other for solace and inspiration. The girl from Albany most closely resembles Ruby Keeler in *42nd Street*, who was also on her own in New York, largely dependent on newly found acquaintances for sustaining her positive outlook whenever Broadway's harsh realities intruded on her congenital optimism.

MGM's selection of Eleanor Powell as Irene Foster proved to be a boon for both studio and film-musical fans. At 22, she was pretty as the proverbial picture and undeniably the most technically adept female tap dancer in Hollywood history, blessed with a lovely soprano voice, slim and curvaceous figure, and a natural grace and charm best described as awesome. By the time she hit Hollywood, she had already gained insight into the hazards, and glories, of Broadway through her appearance in several stage shows, *George White's Music Hall Varieties* in 1932 and *At Home Abroad* in early 1935 among them. It was in the latter show that Howard Dietz and Arthur Schwartz provided her with the self-descriptive song, "The Lady with the Tap." She had effortlessly transferred her charismatic stage presence to the screen earlier in 1935, playing a dancer in *George White's 1935 Scandals* opposite Alice Faye and James Dunn. Among the most camera-friendly of all musical actresses, she was tapped twice again by MGM executives to appear in the final two Melody films, dancing with George Murphy and Buddy Ebsen in the 1938 edition and with Murphy and Fred Astaire in 1940.

The Broadway Melody of 1936 is fun, nothing more, nothing less. Most of the credit for the humor goes to the inimitable Jack Benny, off and on the MGM payroll since 1929. A top-ranking radio star, he had made his exceedingly brief legitimate stage debut in 1934 in George S. Kaufman and Morrie Ryskind's *Bring on the Girls*, an inept political satire on

Eleanor Powell, center, is flanked by Vilma Ebsen and brother Buddy Ebsen while performing Arthur Freed and Nacio Herb Brown's "Sing Before Breakfast" on a Manhattan rooftop in *The Broadway Melody of 1936.*

President Herbert Hoover's Reconstruction Finance Corporation. The play opened and promptly closed at Washington, D.C.'s, National Theatre. It never made it to Broadway.

In *Melody* Benny plays Bert Keeler, the domineering half of a radio gossip team. His partner, comedian Sid Silvers, was also a collaborator on the screenplay. There was little doubt that Benny's character was based on Walter Winchell, and the actor duplicates the famous, or infamous, newspaper columnist and radio commentator's delivery style to perfection while reporting tidbits of scandal involving the rich and famous. Benny sits with the microphone clutched tightly in his right hand, hat on his head and self-satisfied smirk on his face, while rattling off news flashes in slam-bang fashion redolent with slang.

To further identify him as Winchell, he depresses a small hand-held clicker to separate his items into vocal paragraphs. Except for Paramount's Big Broadcast serials, *The Broadway*

Melody of 1936 is one of the few expensive 1930s screen musicals to touch on the world of radio. But its main plot conforms with tradition by concentrating on fledgling Powell's woolly adventures to win the starring role in the new stage show to be produced by her one-time high school boyfriend, Robert Taylor (Bob Gordon). Clearly, her goal is Broadway, not broadcasting.

It is unfortunate that Moss Hart, who wrote the Oscar-nominated story on which the film is based, did not join forces with his sometimes playwriting collaborator and wittiest of writers, George S. Kaufman, for the screenplay. The dialogue would surely have been even sharper than it is. It is also possible that Kaufman in his usual infinite wisdom would have advised against disguising Miss Powell as a fake Parisian singer-dancer in an effort to convince Taylor that she is qualified to undertake the leading role in his show. Neither her absurd gown and heavily cosmetized face nor her fractured French accent would fool anybody, least of all Taylor, and the entire episode loosens what remains of plot believability.

Several stalwarts from the ranks of Hollywood's legion of character actors, however, compensate for that and other screenplay lapses by lending their invaluable services to the picture. Una Merkel is excellent as Taylor's heart-of-gold secretary, as are the gangly-brother and vivacious-sister dance team of Buddy and Vilma Ebsen. June Knight, who had appeared with Silvers on Broadway in *Take a Chance*, is effective as the back-stabbing backer and eventually discarded star of Taylor's show, and the always reliable Paul Harvey, once again given the opportunity to trumpet his booming voice while badgering underlings as the managing editor of the *New York World Tribune*.

Also of inestimable value to the film is the strikingly attractive Frances Langford, an extraordinary singer who in the early 1940s would succeed Gloria Jean, who had succeeded Judy Garland, as vocalist on Bob Hope's network radio program. Although she appeared in a number of other thirties films, Miss Langford would have to wait till the World War II years to gain major celebrity status by accompanying Hope on his frequent tours of military installations. It is Frances who opens *Melody* by singing "You Are My Lucky Star." The man who introduces her, incidentally, is Don Wilson, then and for many years afterward the announcer on Benny's radio show.

Scandal-Mongering. The picture opens in a studio of radio station WHN. Reporting to his audience of "scandal lovers," Jack Benny (Bert Keeler) is bringing them up to date on which notables are about to be married or expecting a baby. Listening with increasing exasperation is newspaper editor Paul Harvey, who after the broadcast reams Benny for indulging in "rotten" tidbits lacking both substance and interest. For months now, all the gossip pouring out of his radio shows and columns have dealt with "old stuff" that no one cares about, he complains. What he wants Benny to do is peek over transoms and through keyholes to dig up some real dirt on New York and Hollywood personalities. Harvey adds that he will

not be satisfied with Benny's work until his exposés of peccadillos committed by the high and mighty incite every one of them into punching him in the nose.

Chastened by the dressing down, Benny confers with assistant Sid Silvers, appropriately nicknamed "Snoop," to line up likely candidates for a new series of smear campaigns. Their office overlooks a penthouse where June Knight (Lillian Brent), a flirty Park Avenue type, is giving a party. Among the guests is Robert Taylor (Bob Gordon), who, like most other penurious producers in Depression musicals, is having trouble rounding up seed money to finance his next show.

Understandably infatuated with him—Taylor was one of Hollywood's handsomest leading men—June proposes to furnish the $60,000 he needs. But Taylor is cautious, preferring not to accept that kind of help from an old acquaintance unless she agrees to regard the money as an investment that he is honor-bound to repay. From the background arises the tantalizing melody of "I've Got a Feelin' You're Foolin'," sung by June, who also dances it nicely in company with a chorus of guests. Also vocalizing on the song is Taylor. No great shakes as a singer, he uses his own instead of a dubbed voice, neither tempting popular music fans into greater appreciation of the clever lyric nor necessarily alienating them against it. Taylor never sang again in the movies.

In a curious but welcome departure from the film-musical habit of inserting songs in haphazard fashion, the lyric of this one manages to add a touch of "suspense" to the plot. Who's foolin' whom is what it's all about. Is June funding the show to help a friend, or is her motive to influence his selecting her as leading lady? Is Taylor playing up to her not because he loves her, but to get his hands on her money? The audience would not be given the clues to piece these puzzles together for another 55 minutes, even though they might be deduced by referring to the huge backlog of previous musicals on Miss Moneybags–Mr. Producer relations.

Observing the festivities, Benny wonders aloud why June and Taylor are becoming so chummy. Maybe they are silent lovers; or maybe it's just another example of a wealthy socialite's paying off a producer in order to advance her own stage ambitions. Either way, Benny smells a rat and decides to probe the relationship and report his day-to-day findings in his column and over the air.

A few days later into Taylor's office walks the prim and proper Eleanor Powell (Irene Foster), nervously winding her fingers around the strap of her handbag, as newcomers to the razzle-dazzle of Manhattan were wont to do. "I'm from Albany, too!", she exults to secretary Una Merkel (Kitty Corbett) after learning that her boss also hails from that upstate city. She knows him! Taylor and she were high school sweethearts, Eleanor recalls, proving their former relationship by showing Una the fraternity pin he had given her. Surely, he will remember her! Benny interrupts her reminiscences by barging up to Una and demanding to see Taylor to confirm his suspicion that June is backing his show. Told that the producer is not there, Benny seats himself on a couch opposite a mild-mannered, professorial-looking middle-age gentleman with glasses and the perpetual urge to audition his act to anyone within hearing range.

It was fitting that, dull as Robert Wildhack's vaudeville routine is, MGM should include it in a film musical with a Broadway locale. New York was still the home of what was left of vaudeville in 1935, and Wildhack was among its practitioners. His act in the film consists of emitting a variety of ear-piercing snores and then evaluating their applicability to different kinds of sleepers. His resonant examples of nasal congestion prompt Benny to regard him as some kind of nut, and he sidles away from him in the same way that Wildhack's dissection of human sneezes later unnerved comedian Willie Howard in *The Broadway Melody of 1938*.

Benny is offended when Taylor refuses to talk with him, while Eleanor is crushed when he sweeps past her without so much as a glimmer of recognition. Each leaves the office, Benny eager to identify June as Taylor's financier, regardless of the lack of proof, and Eleanor hoping somehow to rejuvenate her fading hopes for stardom. A little later, after hearing the tapping of toes on the roof of her tenement, she observes Buddy and Vilma Ebsen's performance of "Sing Before Breakfast," a merry little divertissement that underscored the mid–1930s Hollywood axiom that a song in the heart is as nourishing to the morale as food is to the body. They invite their new neighbor to join in, giving Eleanor her first chance to strut her stuff, which she accomplishes with dispatch by accenting the bouncy rhythm through a series of rapid-fire taps that sound like a machine gun and pausing every so often to lift a leg as high as anyone else ever did in any movie musical.

Also angling for that precious first Big Break, Buddy and Vilma recognize her extraordinary vocal and hoofing talents and urge her to try again to see Taylor, who at the time is seeking to find the young lady who had given Una his fraternity pin, but forgotten to retrieve it before leaving the office. Of course he remembers Eleanor from the old days, he exclaims, and he would happily greet her with open arms if only his secretary had thought to ask for her address.

Dissension in the Ranks. Taylor encounters another problem when June appears, angrily thumping a forefinger on Benny's newspaper column and demanding to know why Taylor had told the columnist that the only reason she is backing his show is her love for him. Equally disturbed over the news item, and protesting that he was not the source of it, Taylor marches from his own office into Benny's and slugs him in the face when he refuses to print a retraction. This first of three such pummelings administered to Benny pleases rather than upsets the columnist, since it proves that he is following managing editor Harvey's order to the letter: he has become the punching bag for at least one of the irate celebrities mentioned in his column.

That noon, at a lunch counter in a doughnut shop, Silvers agrees to help Una square herself with her boss, as well as lend a helping hand to Eleanor, by finding out where she is living. He cajoles Benny into reporting in his next column that Taylor desperately wants to get in touch with Eleanor. Convinced that Taylor has written her off, however, Eleanor is reluctant to return to his office even after Buddy reads Benny's news item to her. Still, her aspiration lingers on, as she makes quite clear by reciting

Katharine Hepburn's well-known *Morning Glory* speech on how certain she is of reaching her career goals, come what may. Eleanor's impersonation of the one-of-a-kind Hepburn voice is surprisingly good. The lady had comedic as well as musical talent.

Her optimism renewed by the Ebsens' urging her onward, Eleanor braces her psyche to reenter the obstacle course. She visits Taylor in the empty auditorium of the theater where his play is in rehearsal, easily captivating him with her charm, earnestness, and reminder that back in Albany they had once shared, the goal of earning reputations on the Great White Way. He has made it, she points out, and so will she, provided that he hires her as at least a chorus girl. In his realistic survey of the New York theatrical scene, Taylor adopts an avuncular role similar to that of Uncle Jed Prouty in *The Broadway Melody*. In sober tones he tries to dissuade her by citing the numerous heartaches that "hard and cold" Broadway inflicts on all beginners. But his warnings are unable to persuade Eleanor to break her commitment to succeed.

After he leaves to answer June's curt summons to meet with her this instant, Eleanor becomes transfixed by a dream that transports her from her seat to the stage, where in her mind's eye she visualizes herself not as an anonymous member of a chorus, but as the star. She reprises "You Are My Lucky Star," and then dances to it in a scene that, like the "Pretty Girl" number in *The Great Ziegfeld*, sadly falls short of its extravaganza potential because of the absence of Technicolor.

Disappointment shatters her dream when Taylor returns and announces that because of an unexpected crisis (trying to pacify the increasingly irritable June), he is unable to take her home. Sensing that his brusqueness has ended the conviviality inspired by their reunion, Eleanor leaves the theater. Meanwhile, Taylor is becoming more deeply mired in his newest production problem. June wants to be the star of his show, period. Since it's her money that's subsidizing it, why shouldn't he acquiesce to her desire, she demands to know. In Taylor's view, what the show needs is a big star, something that June is definitely not. He proposes to make a two-week inspection tour of Hollywood, "where all the stars have gone."

If he is unable to coax a name performer back to New York, he promises to give June the part.

The deal is overheard by Silvers, who reports it to Benny. The news upsets his chief, alerted to the dismal prospect that if Taylor selects someone other than Eleanor as star, Benny will be exposed as incompetent for having written of Taylor's professional interest in Eleanor. The answer, according to Benny's fitful logic, is for him to scoop his rival scribes by promoting somebody else as the star in order to exact revenge on the producer for his belligerence in the newspaper office. He christens his phantom celebrity "Madamoiselle LaBelle Arlette," a name he had just picked up from a cigar wrapper. In his column and radio show he begins circulating the tale that she is a prominent member of the *Comédie Française*, thereby sending Taylor off on a fruitless search for a lady that Benny is certain he will never find. He smiles. Taylor will soon discover that he can hit back, not in face maybe, but in the wallet, where it really hurts.

The Deceptive Chanteuse. When Taylor returns without a star—"They're all making pictures," he tells Una—she arouses his interest by revealing the availability of the sensational Arlette, who, it appears, is now in New York. Acting on Taylor's order to find her, Una reports back that the lady in question is residing temporarily at the Carleton Hotel. Actually, as the following scene discloses, Benny has anticipated Taylor's attempt to get in touch with the bogus Arlette, and has stationed Silvers in the Carleton to fend off any contact. Dressed in drag, Silvers poses as Arlette's maid with strict orders to inform all callers that Arlette is rehearsing and unable to talk or meet with anyone. To make the ruse believable, Benny orders Silvers to spin a phonograph record of a French songstress every time he answers the telephone. The song the lady repeatedly sings is "All I Do Is Dream of You," a Freed-Brown tune written in 1934 for *Sadie McKee*.

Desperate to complete the casting of his show, Taylor hires Buddy and Vilma, who strongly recommend Eleanor for the lead. Never having seen her perform, Taylor is unwilling to take a chance on an unknown, and he asks them to advise Eleanor to go back to her up-state home rather than risk further disappointment. Buddy dutifully relays the message to Eleanor, who ponders over which road to travel—the rocky one to Broadway stardom or the even more dismal one back to Albany.

Since Taylor is unable to interview Arlette, who is always in the throes of rehearsing the same song, he dispatches Una to the Carleton to urge the singer to consider his offer for an audition. Receiving no answer to her knock, she enters the room. Silvers is on duty, but snoozing. She glances at his wig, print dress, and cigar dangling from his lower lip, and quickly realizes that Taylor is being duped for some indecipherable reason. She leaves Silvers a sarcastic note, now more intent than ever on formulating a plot of her own help Eleanor land the star part in Taylor's show.

The first step is for Eleanor to return to Albany, as Taylor had recommended. Oozing with sympathy and promising to write, Taylor kisses her goodbye at Grand Central Terminal. She gets off the train, however, at 125th Street, meets Una there, and they share a taxi back to midtown Manhattan. Meanwhile, Taylor is involved in the rehearsal of "On a Sunday Afternoon," a melodious though minor period song performed by Buddy and Vilma in the downtown square of an 1890s small town. After the number, June lodges another complaint to Taylor over Benny's referring to her as a "no talent" in his most recent column. Neither, of course, is aware that Benny's motive for downgrading the lady is the thoroughly duplicitous one of inducing Taylor into replacing her with the non-existent Arlette and finally with Eleanor.

Furious over Benny's criticism, June whips out a run-of-the-show contract, signs it, and shoves it into Taylor's hands, demanding that he add his own signature. Before he can, Una rushes to tell him that none other than Arlette herself is waiting in the wings to see him. Taylor excitedly greets the Frenchwoman—actually Eleanor in disguise—and gleefully accepts her suggestion that she audition for him. Her extraordinary solo tap dance to "You Are My Lucky Star" lifts Taylor to a show biz seventh heaven, and, ignoring June's contract, he signs Arlette as his star. Wounded beyond repair,

June bolts away from the stage like a cannonball. Playing the piano for Eleanor's solo was the highly competent Roger Edens, a new MGM employee who in time would become a first-rank composer, musical director and arranger, and associate producer of musical pictures.

The Taylor-Arlette agreement puts Benny in a seemingly irreversible quandary. How can Arlette appear on Broadway when there is no Arlette? Who, he demands of Silvers, is the woman who is posing as her? And how did Benny's carefully wrought scheme unravel? Silvers finally admits that Una was the spoiler. He must have been asleep when she crept into the hotel room, he confesses, because he had recognized her handwriting on the note he found pinned to his chest that read, "One more rehearsal and you can swallow your cigar."

As in most film musicals, the ingenue's climb up the success ladder is rarely achieved without inviting further complications. In this instance, danger erupts in faraway France, where the real Arlette, a *bona fide* Parisian singer, is threatening to sue whoever it is who is impersonating her. Shocked by still another unexpected crisis, Benny devises a top-of-the-head solution: he will kill off the fake Arlette that evening. He invites Eleanor to his office, vows to unmask her as a fraud, and asks how she could ever have expected to pull off such a gag? (How Benny learned that Eleanor was masquerading as Arlette is conveniently skipped over.)

Eleanor admits that she had embroiled herself in the plot after reading about Arlette in his column simply to snatch the leading role in Taylor's show away from her. And, she adds, she will not drop the curtain on that dream for anyone. Impressed by her spunk, which is a carbon copy of his own, Benny tells her of the existence of the litigious living Arlette, warning that he must expose Eleanor or face a libel suit. Eleanor is downcast, lamenting the fact that she will be unable to attend Taylor's pre-opening publicity party that evening. Growing fonder of her, Benny concocts another plan to cheer her up and verify his earlier column announcement that Taylor was scouring the city to find his one-time classmate. But the scene fades out before he is able to fill her in on the details.

The party is in full swing when Benny, Silvers, and Eleanor—as herself—enter the huge hotel ballroom. Her appearance astounds Taylor, who had assumed she was back in Albany. And where is Arlette, he asks Benny, who replies that she has checked out of the Carleton for parts unknown. Before Taylor can figure out what has happened, and why, the orchestra breaks into "Broadway Rhythm," the musical highlight of the picture, and 17 years later to be one of the most memorable of the *Singin' in the Rain* production numbers.

The vocalist for Freed and Brown's second-best salute to Broadway, is Frances Langford, clad in top hat and tux. It is next danced by the Ebsens and a chorus of about 75 boys and girls—and even June Knight, who apparently had patched up her broken relations with Taylor. All this activity, stunningly choreographed by Dave Gould, is only the prelude leading to the arrival of Eleanor on center stage, who proceeds to dazzle the partygoers by circling the huge banquet table, twisting and turning and whirling with the precision of a state-of-the-art robotic dance machine, the personification of perfection, in every way measuring up to the most intricate solo routine ever performed by Fred Astaire.

In the final scene, Benny is seen calling in the story of Taylor's hiring Eleanor as his new star, and of their forthcoming marriage. As he is talking with rewrite, Taylor sings of his enchantment with Eleanor in "You Are My Lucky Star," an all's well that ends well conclusion that is duplicated at the end of *Singin' in the Rain*, when Gene Kelly croons it to Debbie Reynolds, another plucky little girl who, according to the billboard that looms high above their heads, has won the co-starring role in her husband-to-be's new musical film.

Despite its obvious quality, "You Are My Lucky Star" was skipped over for Oscar contention for best song in 1936. Perhaps it would not have won anyway, what with "Lullaby of Broadway," "Cheek to Cheek," and "Lovely to Look At" as competitors. But as long as movie songs are played and sung, "You Are My Lucky Star" will continue to occupy an honored place on the list of the most cherished popular songs to emanate from a 1930s sound track. And it did play a unique role in the picture, bracketing the storyline by appearing in both the opening and the closing scenes of this lively and amiable film.

Naughty Marietta (1935)

A Metro-Goldwyn-Mayer picture. DIRECTOR: W.S. Van Dyke. PRODUCER: Hunt Stromberg. SCREENWRITERS: John Lee Mahin, Frances Goodrich, and Albert Hackett. CINEMATOGRAPHER: William Daniels. ART DIRECTOR: Cedric Gibbons. FILM EDITOR: Blanche Sewell. COSTUMES: Adrian. MUSICAL ADAPTATION: Herbert Stothart. SONGS: lyrics (and original book) by Rida Johnson Young, music by Victor Herbert; additional lyrics and incidental music by Gus Kahn and Herbert Stothart. RUNNING TIME: 1 hour, 46 minutes. *Principal Players*: Jeanette MacDonald (Princess Marie de Namours de la Bonfain and "Marietta Franini"). Nelson Eddy (Captain Richard Warrington). Frank Morgan (Governor Gaspard d'Annard). Elsa Lanchester (Madame d'Annard). Douglas Dumbrille (Prince de Namours de la Bonfain). Joseph Cawthorne (Herr Schumann). Cecilia Parker (Julie). Walter Kingsford (Don Carlos de Braganza). Akim Tamiroff (Rudolpho). Edward Brophy (Alie). Harold Huber (Zeke). *Major Academy Award*: Best Sound. *Nomination*: Best Picture.

Although this operetta was 25 years old when MGM turned it into a film, its plot, at least in outline, was still well known because of its periodic New York revivals, little theater presentations, and cross-country tours since 1910. So undoubtedly the studio took a chance when barely a few minutes into the screenplay, heroine Jeanette MacDonald is presented as a maiden in rebellion against her uncle's demand that she honor royal protocol by dutifully marrying a man of comparable social stature, in this instance a Spanish prince. Despite her independent spirit, it seemed possible that, like Princess Flavia (Madeleine Carroll) in *The Prisoner of Zenda*, Jeanette would be thrilled by her chosen betrothed and gladly follow instructions. But Jeanette's court-appointed groom was no Ronald Colman, but rather a swaggering bore, too old for her, sans charm, sans wit, sans anything that would appeal to an adventurous young woman of taste.

In the Herbert original, which carried the working title of *Little Paris*, Marietta is so unhappily married that she flees from her husband and Old World stuffiness to take up residence in Louisiana. There she is wooed by a

Nelson Eddy and Jeanette MacDonald as the mercenary soldier and aristocratic lady refugee from an undesirable marriage in Victor Herbert's *Naughty Marietta*.

pirate, Etienne Grandet, who never appears in the picture, as well as by Captain Richard Warrington, who divides his time between chasing Etienne and Marietta. In Hollywood's hands, Marietta is an unmarried young woman of noble descent desperate to escape the shackles of wedded life to a man she abhors. If some moviegoers were alarmed at the studio's switching its leading character from sullen, disenchanted wife to playful, amoral virgin, no one took the time to complain. The MGM operetta benefitted nicely by revising the character of Marietta, who falls under the protection of handsome Captain Dick.

Lacking none of the glitter, heroics, and romance that made operetta so vastly appealing throughout the first quarter of the 20th

century, the filmed *Naughty Marietta* is closer to perfection than any of its past or future competitors ever came. The songs, of course, are among the best in Herbert's extensive repertoire. The singing is superb. The backlot locales are picturesque and could pass for authentic. The acting is good, sometimes very good, particularly by the comedy duo of Edward Brophy and Harold Huber as the comic bumblers whose shenanigans unite the lovers at the last moment, insuring a happy ending. In later screen life, each would add welcome levity to numerous Warner Bros. gangster films. Director W.S. Van Dyke was an accomplished MGM stalwart who had worked with D.W. Griffith on *Intolerance* (1916). In the sound era he directed four of the Thin Man films and such later MacDonald-Eddy operettas as *Rose-Marie*, *Sweethearts*, Noel Coward's *Bitter Sweet*, which the British had also made into a movie in 1933 starring Anna Neagle and Fernand Gravet, and *I Married an Angel*.

In fact, all the picture needed to qualify as a marvel of splendiferousness was Technicolor, which in 1935 was far too expensive an indulgence, even for lavish-loving MGM. Proving that not even scores by the great Irish-born composer were immune from rewriting, the studio dropped most of Herbert's lyricless incidental music and six songs: "Naughty Marietta," "It Never, Never Can Be Love," "Live for Today," "All I Crave Is More of Life," "If I Were Anybody Else but Me," and "Sweet By and By." Substituting for the Herbert omissions were several interpolations with words by Gus Kahn and melodies by Herbert Stothart, among the finest of MGM's musical directors, who in the twenties had collaborated on Broadway show tunes with Vincent Youmans, Rudolf Friml, and George Gershwin. His most notable movie background scores were written for Garbo's *Anna Karenina* (1935) and *Camille* (1936). He won the Academy Award for scoring *The Wizard of Oz* and a nomination for *Mutiny on the Bounty* (1935).

The only old-fashioned Broadway-inspired operetta nominated for the Academy Award, *Naughty Marietta* holds special historical interest as the first motion picture to co-star Miss MacDonald and Nelson Eddy. (It was his fourth film and her thirteenth.) They would appear together seven more times, ending their dual visits to movie houses in 1942 with Richard Rodgers and Lorenz Hart's *I Married an Angel*. Also adapted from the stage, this weakest of all their films together was a box office failure despite its most respectable score, which included the melodic title tune and "Spring Is Here," lyricist Hart's most melancholy probing into the loneliness of the lovelorn. Curiously, the uniting of Jeanette and Nelson came about more by chance than by design. MGM sought Allan Jones for the Captain Warrington role. In December 1934 he was touring opposite Maria Jeritze in Rudolf Friml's operetta *Annina*, the roadshow name given to Broadway's *Music Hath Charms*. But MGM balked at paying the $50,000 the Shuberts wanted to let Jones out his contract, and so Eddy was hired as replacement.

MacDonald and Eddy's popularity as undeniably attractive singers of light opera made them two of the best-loved performers of the time. (Jeanette ranked fourth among Hollywood's biggest money makers in 1936.) Neither possessed the acting ability of Irene Dunne or John Boles, who likewise appeared in operettas as well as songless dramas that required more than a pleasing singing voice to maintain audience interest. The songs the two MGM lovers sang in *Marietta* as in all their other movies consistently rose above the screenplays, which were equally superficial as the Broadway librettos that inspired them.

Except for her forays into the Canadian and American frontiers in *Rose-Marie* (1936) and *The Girl of the Golden West* (1938), the shapely, red-headed Miss MacDonald was usually outfitted in regal costumes befitting a Central European princess. Eddy, often wearing the garb of a privateer, as in *Naughty Marietta* and the 1940 remake of *The New Moon*, alternated between the macho revolutionary and the tender, caring lover intent on conquering Miss MacDonald as his partner for life. Among the innumerable unanswered questions surrounding best picture selections is why *The New Moon* was denied nomination. Actually, this film was handled more professionally than any other operetta, and the Romberg score equaled even *Marietta*'s in the number of hit songs and in production values.

Inevitably coy or stubbornly standoffish, Jeanette was quick to reprimand or airily dismiss any suitor's love making till she was ready to reciprocate. Spicing up her basic virginal sweetness were occasional lapses into coquettishness, and at times outright flirtation, to sustain male interest without diluting her ladylike reserve. It was in their lighthearted skirmishes that the two stars most closely resembled Ginger Rogers and Fred Astaire, even if the costumes and settings of their films existed in a time warp that made them appear quaint to the generation brought up on such sophisticated movie musicals as *The Gay Divorcee*, *Roberta*, *Top Hat*, and *Swing Time*. Genteel Jeanette wore her gossamer gowns well, clearly indicating that their purpose was to enhance her figure while reflecting the dress codes imposed by the aristocratic society to which she belonged by birth or was foreordained to join through marriage.

Eddy, on the other hand, was emblematic of the rough-hewn masculine world. In both *Marietta* and *Moon*, which resemble each other in plot, he is the bold and fair-minded leader of renegade backwoodsmen crusading to overthrow the privileged, a goal that further endeared him to the lower-economic classes sitting in the audience. Yet, Eddy also revealed an innate nobility that surfaced whenever politeness rather than decisiveness was deemed to be the wiser course to win converts to his cause or a lady to his heart. As Sergeant Bruce in *Rose-Marie*, he is faithful to his oath of office as a Royal Mounted policeman as he tracks down outlaw James Stewart, knowing that his capture will grieve Jeanette, Eddy's heart throb and Stewart's sister.

Whatever duty called upon Eddy to do, he did. His no-nonsense baritone delivery of stirring songs was apparent in his second film, *Dancing Lady* (1933), in his rendition of Rodgers and Hart's exuberant "Rhythm of the Day." So it came as no surprise that he would be equally effective leading men into battle with such thumping marches as "Tramp, Tramp, Tramp," "Song of the Mounties," and "Stout Hearted Men."

Eddy the actor, however, was inferior to Eddy the singer, with the majority of critics describing his acting as wooden, which it usually was. But he compensated for this inadequacy by singing love notes to Jeanette in the tenderest of ballads written by the likes of Friml and Romberg as well as Herbert, rather than by reciting the usual stilted dialogue the scripts imposed on him. It was in fact solely through their duets that both stars crowned their platonic love affairs with artistry.

Together, the "Singing Sweethearts" revived filmed operettas as no one else before or since. The studio czars had begun producing them as early as 1929, when the new sound track and two-strip Technicolor combined to insure at least short-term popularity. By means of these apprentice movies, the thin line of demarcation that separated operetta

from musical comedy was drawn. Operettas were typically set in the past and revolved around the love affairs and political machinations of royal personages in lands not to be found on any map, like the tiny principality where Princess Eleanor Powell frolics under the disapproving eyes of King Frank Morgan and Queen Edna Mae Oliver in *Rosalie* (1937). Musical comedy took the present as its time frame and centered on the loves and travail of commoners. These people went to court only after being arrested by the local police for speeding.

Sometimes operettas reflected contemporary society by clothing the characters in modern dress, as occurred in MacDonald and Eddy's own *Sweethearts* (1938), based on another sensational Herbert musical, which had opened 25 years earlier, on September 8, 1913, at the Great Ziegfeld's New Amsterdam Theatre. Sometimes the story line was updated by including current events, such as Warner's 1943 remake of *The Desert Song*, which introduced Nazi soldiers as the enemies of the dashing Red Shadow, played that year by Dennis Morgan. No marriageable prince or princess enters *Rose-Marie* or *Bitter Sweet*, but the leading characters' motives and speech ring with nobility of purpose. Neither money nor acclaim, so consistently sought after in musical comedy, is their dream. Nor is it to produce, write, or star in a Broadway musical. Romantic love was the sole prod that motivated operetta leads into mending broken hearts with a concluding kiss in closeup.

Considered by music buffs as occupying a position midway between grand opera and musical comedy, operetta seemed to be a safe bet for transfer to movie houses. It had been appreciated by great numbers of theater devotees since before the turn of the century, and many of operetta's highly melodic songs were as well known as any of their musical comedy and non-production competitors. They were recorded by many popular artists and orchestras, usually under the RCA Victor Red Seal (or "Classical") label, and heard on such relatively high-brow network radio programs as *The Voice of Firestone*, which often featured MacDonald and Eddy. Commentators referred to the songs as "semi-classical," pigeon-holing them as far below operatic arias but higher than ballads played in fox trot tempo.

Moviegoers' initial delight in operettas is understandable. Talking pictures' professionalism was gaining momentum. Such 1929 operettas as *The Desert Song* and composer Harry Tierney's *Rio Rita* quickly became countrywide favorites. But the movie operetta's overweight reliance on huge casts and ornate sets and costumes—roughly equivalent to those that decorated the religious extravaganzas of Cecil B. DeMille—to satisfy viewers' frenzy for spectacle was doomed to be cut short by the Great Depression.

All the pre–1930 operettas on film, such as Friml's *The Vagabond King*, Romberg's *Bride of the Regiment*, and Franz Lehar and Stothart's *The Rogue Song*, required the services of expertly trained singers from New York capable of handling the challenging melodies. Although measuring up to the vocalizing demands, veteran East Coasters like Dennis King and Lawrence Tibbett quickly lost their footing in Hollywood. Their pictures now stand as the dustiest of monuments to a noble experiment that fizzled out in fewer than two years.

In 1934, however, the rumbling of a film-operetta revival could actually be heard. That was a rather remarkable development considering the steep costs involved and the aftertaste of disillusionment that most of the earlier examples had left with both public and critics. For example, the typical banalities worked into *Golden Dawn*, a catastrophic mid–1930 Technicolor rendering of the stage musical, with lyrics by Oscar Hammerstein II and Otto Harbach, and music by Emmerich Kallman and Herbert Stothart, was judged by the *New York Herald-Tribune* as a "definite catalogue of vulgarity, witlessness, and utterly pathetic and proposterous nonsense." That was hardly the kind of review to encourage more operetta production.

Miss MacDonald herself was a major participant in the 1934–early 1935 revival process by appearing in the updated version of Franz Lehar's 28-year-old *The Merry Widow*. Jerome Kern suddenly became a reliable Hollywood source, providing the studios with three high-toned thirties stage hits that could boast respectable runs, *The Cat and the Fid-*

dle (with 395 consecutive performances), *Music in the Air* (342), and *Roberta* (295). (Only two revue musicals, Ole Olsen and Chic Johnson's *Helzapoppin* and Harold Rome's *Pins and Needles*, ran more than 500 performances during the entire decade, with the first show tallying up 1,404 and the second 1,108.) Miss MacDonald was also the feminine lead in *The Cat and the Fiddle*, Gloria Swanson in *Music in the Air*, and Irene Dunne in *Roberta*. The latter also appeared in the tuneful *Sweet Adeline*, Hammerstein and Kern's first post–*Show Boat* teaming, which had closed almost immediately after it opened in late 1929, one of Broadway's first victims of the Depression. Set in the Gay '90s, it was written with Helen Morgan in mind, and the lady made a success of the part singing "Why Was I Born?"

Also released in 1934 was a rare Hollywood original operetta, *The Night Is Young*, with Evelyn Laye and Ramon Novarro and a new score by Hammerstein and Romberg. All the pictures unexpectedly caught the public's fancy, bringing into the fold even detractors who, much as they might not care for the music, found satisfaction in the genre's ability to provide escapism on demand.

Responsible for the demise of both stage and screen operettas in the mid-forties was their artificiality and plot similarities and music that was no longer in vogue. The last of them with an original but routine score (by Edward Heyman and Rudolf Friml) was *Northwest Outpost*, which cast Eddy opposite Ilona Massey in his own final film appearance and fared poorly at the 1947 box office. Six years elapsed before Warner Bros. released the third version of *The Desert Song*, with Kathryn Grayson and Gordon MacRae as the sand-swept lovers.

MGM followed the next year with its second *The Student Prince*, starring Edmund Purdon (using Mario Lanza's off-screen voice) and one-time child actress Ann Blythe, and in 1956 with a new *The Vagabond King*, again starring Miss Grayson. Since then, Hollywood has eschewed operetta, as well as its composers. The last film based on the career of one of them, Sigmund Romberg, was *Deep in My Heart*, which encountered mass apathy in its travels along the movie house circuit in 1954 despite a solid performance by José Ferrer in the leading role. Nowadays, viewing operettas and songwriter "biographies" are restricted to screenings at revival houses and museums and on videocassette.

Master of His Art. It was appropriate that *Naughty Marietta* should have been selected in 1935 to usher in the Golden Age of film operettas. Victor Herbert, dead since 1924, was correctly regarded as the foremost composer of them and had enjoyed worldwide reputation since the late 1890s. A further honor would be bestowed on the Irish-born melody-maker in 1939, when Paramount made *The Great Victor Herbert*, the first motion picture based on the life of an American songwriter. (Shortly afterward, Fox released *Swanee River*, starring Don Ameche as Stephen Foster.)

That Herbert's songs fail to appear in chronological order in the 1939 film, and that many important details of the composer's personal and professional lives are either omitted or revised, is neither surprising nor particularly disappointing. All of Hollywood's songwriter "biographies" share a similar fate. The picture is quite respectable, and together with the MacDonald-Eddy films introduced the new generation of jitterbugs to numerous Herbert melodies, including "Ah, Sweet Mystery of Life," and 15 others, which are performed well by such players as Mary Martin, Allan Jones, and 15-year-old soprano Susanna Foster.

Playing Herbert was Walter Connolly, for years one of the thoroughbred character actors in the MGM stable, known best for his many roles with all the major studios as the fastidious, grumpy executive who enlivened such Grade-A movies as *Libeled Lady* (1936), *Nothing Sacred* (1937), and *Too Hot to Handle* (1938). His short stature, rotund figure, and neatly cropped mustache closely resembled Herbert's, and he was an excellent choice.

It was also in 1939 that Herbert's formidable reputation as a supreme melody-maker was further enhanced by the unexpected popularity of the instrumental "Indian Summer," helped greatly by the addition of a lyric by Al Dubin. One of the composer's loveliest idylls,

it was written originally for *Natoma*, the first of Herbert's two grand operas. Only the second such work by an American to play the Metropolitan Opera House, it opened at that auditorium on February 25, 1911, with soprano Mary Garden as the Indian maiden and tenor John MacCormack as a U.S. Navy lieutenant. The melody was one of several themes to be heard in orchestrated format only.

An equally deserving reason for applauding MGM's reviving a Herbert operetta as the first MacDonald-Eddy exercise, and Paramount's choosing him as the subject of the first "biographical" treatment of a Broadway composer, was Herbert's close relationship with the film industry, which began in 1916 and continued almost up to his death. Although absent from *The Great Victor Herbert*, his scores and songs for silent pictures were far more numerous and more prestigious than those of any other American composer. His symphonic accompaniment for the ultra-patriotic *The Fall of a Nation*, which opened in New York in 1916, was praised by most critics. Unfortunately, most of the music and the entire film, written and produced by Thomas Dixon, whose *The Clansman* had been lifted to permanent significance by D.W. Griffith as *The Birth of a Nation* (1915), have been lost. He also wrote the overtures to such other silent films as *Yolanda* (1922) and *The Great White Way*, *Little Old New York*, and *Under the Red Robe* (all 1923). His "Marion Davies March" was named for the actress who starred in *When Knighthood Was in Flower* (1922), which also contained Herbert's waltz song of the same name.

Not many of the composer's best-loved operettas were made into films. His *Mlle. Modiste* (1905) was shot entirely in two-strip Technicolor in 1931 and released as *Kiss Me Again*, actually the name of the hit song from the show. The perennial Christmas favorite *Babes in Toyland* (1903) was finally made into a film (also known as *March of the Wooden Soldiers*) after several false starts in 1934 with Laurel and Hardy as Santa's helpmates. It is a very good version indeed, far superior to Walt Disney's anemic 1961 reprise with Ray Bolger, Tommy Sands, and Ed Wynn, and to the 1986 remake with Keanu Reeves and Drew Barrymore. Herbert's grand old "March of the Toys" was given its finest screen rendition, complete with the rarely heard verse, by Sonja Henie and a large company of ice dancers in the finale to *My Lucky Star* in 1937.

The original *Naughty Marietta* opened on October 24, 1910, for a brief tryout at the Wieting Opera House in Syracuse, N.Y., before being moved a week later to Rochester, then Buffalo. It was produced between the composer's far less known *Old Dutch*, which included in its cast dancer Vernon Castle and nine-year-old Helen Hayes, and *When Sweet Sixteen*. Unlike these two minor works, which accumulated only 12 and 88 performances, respectively, *Marietta* achieved instant hit status at its November 7 Broadway premiere at the New York Theatre. Unanimous friendly reviews resulted in a respectable showing of 136 performances and an average gross of $20,000 in each of its 17 weeks (of eight performances each) before departing Manhattan for an equally rousing tour of communities west of the Hudson.

The show was produced by Oscar Hammerstein, the grandfather of Oscar II. Rida Johnson Young, one of the first women to earn distinction as a Broadway lyricist, wrote the book and the lyrics. Starring in the title role was Emma Trentini, a celebrated soprano then under contract to Hammerstein's Manhattan Opera House. Her co-star as Captain Richard Warrington was tenor Orville Harrold, also of the Manhattan Opera House. The cast, almost as huge as the one MGM assembled 25 years later, included 20 speaking parts and a host of incidental flower girls, quadroons, dancers, adventurers, pirates, street sweepers, San Domingo girls, French girls, Mexicans, Spaniards, and Indians.

The film version greatly expanded the sites where the characters mingle. On Broadway they were confined to three—the Place d'Armes, a marionette theater, and a ballroom in the Jeunesse Dorée Club, all in New Orleans. The time of the screenplay is misdated as 1780, erroneously picked up by MGM from the New York Theatre program. The year 1750 would have been more accurate, since Louisiana was ruled by Spain, not France, 30 years later.

The Unfinished Song. The picture begins with Jeanette on a shopping spree, wending her way through throngs of admirers to sing scales with a bird and accept a puppy as a gift from the keeper of a pet shop. Befitting her exalted social status and freedom-loving spirit, she grasps each outstretched hand with aristocratic gracefulness while ambling along the street, her richly embroidered gown dusting the pavement and her hat worn at a rakish over-the-eye angle, while her royal coach trails close behind to be constantly at her beck and call.

It is while visiting her former music teacher, played by Joseph Cawthorne, once one of Broadway's major comedians, that her mood changes from spirited to downcast. "I haven't seen the man I could marry," she confesses, after explaining that she is being forced to wed the Spanish nobleman, Don Carlos de Braganza (Walter Kingsford). "But I'll find him someday," she avers, setting the stage for the most protracted struggle of any film-musical heroine to identify her hero through his collaboration on the love song that lies dormant in her heart.

The key to her future happiness is an unfinished tune that Cawthorne plays on the piano. Taken aback by the beauty and plaintiveness of the first few notes, she describes them as the beginning of the "melody of the universe," so called because in them she detects intimations of immortality. She decides to help the teacher by writing a lyric, but can get no further than the opening line, "Ah, sweet mystery of life at last I've found you." The song (also known as the "Dream Melody") must remain incomplete, she acknowledges with sadness, until the man fated to be her true love helps her to complete the melody and lyric.

After implying that the man is definitely not Kingsford, she gaily climbs the stairs to the top of the three-story studio building and joins a happy band of students in singing the film's first song, the lilting "Chansonette." By the time she reaches the ground floor, the song has been picked up by passersby, who are similarly equipped with golden throats and acquaintance with the words.

Enter Jeanette's uncle, Prince de Namours de la Bonfain, the villain of the piece played by Douglas Dumbrille, one of filmdom's most accomplished and active specialists in mean-spirited roles who over the years was to be outwitted by many of the industry's biggest stars, including the Marx Brothers (*The Big Store*, 1941) and Hope and Crosby (*The Road to Morocco*, 1942). A rising star in the court of King Louis XV, he is confronting Jeanette in a palace antechamber with the demand that she go through with the arranged marriage, which is scheduled for next week at Notre Dame Cathedral. Either she marry Kingsford or face exile, maybe even prison, he warns in his usual menacing "no fooling, I mean it" tone.

After Kingsford marches angrily out of the room, Jeanette is approached by a scullery maid named Nanette, who has come to bid her mistress goodbye. A casquette girl, the maid is soon to sail for French New Orleans to become the wife of one of the settlers sent there earlier by the French to marry the planters and "civilize" Louisiana. Resigned to taking the trip because "Paris is not for the poor," she realizes that she and her true love, one Giovanni, will never be able financially to wed. The maid regards the voyage with apprehension, fearful of marrying a man she does not know and possibly can never love.

Jeanette shakes her head in sympathy; she and the maid are soul mates in that regard if in no other. But an idea suddenly blossoms in Jeanette's head—she will bribe Nanette to take her name and place on the ship's passenger list. That way the real Nanette will be free to marry the impoverished Giovanni, and Jeanette can escape her own forced marriage, maybe even find the love of her life far away from home.

On the day the ship is to disembark to the rousing tune of "Antoinette and Anatole," sung by the ladies' dockside friends and relatives, the substitute Marietta is dressed not in her customary finery, but in a plain peasant dress, thick eye glasses effectively shielding her face from recognition, and chomping noisily on a roll. Even the platoon of French soldiers in the service of the king that boards the ship to inspect the papers of its human cargo is unable to recognize her as the princess she is.

Like her compatriots, Jeanette nervously stares into the receding shoreline of LeHavre as the ship sets sail. On behalf of herself and all the other ladies, she bids a solemn farewell to her native land while beseeching God to watch over them in Herbert's lovely "Prayer." A few days afterward, however, she inadvertently reveals her courtly breeding by furnishing a comforting shoulder and encouraging words to the other nervous young brides-to-be crowded together in a below-deck cabin.

Blending the concern and kindliness that heritage has trained her to bestow on her subjects, Jeanette shares their fear of the unknown, mostly the highly depressing one of marrying a stranger. Maybe she can avert that potential disaster, she hints, maintaining that she for one will not accept any man as husband unless he can help her complete the fragmentary little tune she had worked on at Cawthorne's music studio. All talk ceases abruptly when the ship is invaded by pirates, easily the most roguish of blackguards seen since MGM's own *Treasure Island* (1934), who capture the ship after a short skirmish. They loot the passengers' treasure while menacing the frightened ladies by looking them over carefully like meat packers at a cattle auction, ready to pounce on those whom the men regard as the choicest of the lot.

Suddenly the strains of the marching song "Tramp, Tramp, Tramp" are heard in the distance. Leading the chorus of rugged mercenary scouts stomping along behind him is Kentucky-born Captain Richard Warrington (Nelson Eddy), his rich baritone voice declaring that they love a fight and will engage in one whenever freedom is threatened. Eddy and his band have earned a reputation as formidable defenders of justice over the years, and they easily prevail over the pirates, retake the ship in the name of France, and steer it onto land. Although appreciative of being rescued, Jeanette shows scant interest in Eddy, labeling him a "rude, crude Colonial," and quite a self-centered one at that. She does indicate fleeting pleasure at listening to his singing of "The Owl and the Bob Cat," and learning that he is unmarried.

Her agreeing to stroll with him into the woods gives every indication that this is to be the beginning of a beautiful friendship, even if she is as yet unwilling to regard him as a potential husband.

There, in a clearing illuminated by a brilliant saucer-shaped MGM moon, Eddy launches into the film's first ballad, the ever-lovely "'Neath the Southern Moon," originally sung by a quadroon named Adah in the 1910 version. Eddy's excellent, straightforward rendition entrances Jeanette, who even goes as far as praising his voice, if not the singer himself. An amiable braggart as well as accomplished soldier, Eddy agrees wholeheartedly with her appraisal of his talent in a rare instance of the singer's measuring up to the demands of light comedy. Displeased at his apparent elephantine ego, Jeanette MacDonald abruptly hurries alone back to the ship.

The arrival of their potential wives is announced to the male residents of the community by a number of Paul Revere riders, resulting in a massive exodus from the town square and thatched huts—and even the postponement of one pair of lovers' duel—to the beach where the immigrants have been congregated.

Among the welcoming party of males is the philandering Governor Gaspard d'Annard, played to the hilt by Frank Morgan, whose *Dimples*-like portrayal of a garrulous and devious pretender to authority would reach its apogee four years later as the Wizard of Oz. Unlike the other men, Morgan is married, but hardly happily, to Elsa Lanchester, actually the real-life wife of Fredric March, whose constant henpecking of the governor provides the film with much of its comedy.

Recognizing Jeanette as superior in upbringing to the rest of the young women, Eddy protects her from the horde of wannabe husbands by secluding her in an attractive cottage on the community's convent grounds. Though appreciative of his solicitude, she treats him with a coolness that clearly implies disapproval of his autocratic manner. But Eddy, after the fashion of the ill-at-ease outdoorsman unfamiliar with social decorum, awkwardly blurts out his own proposal to the young lady he nicknames "Blue Eyes." Astounded at his forwardness, she naturally refuses with regal disdain.

She remains in an argumentative mood until a song from the street catches her attention as a happy reminder of the times she had spent in Naples.

Singing it are employees of the local marionette theater owned by Rudolpho, the owner of a marionette theater, played by Akim Tamiroff, another of those reliable 1930s chameleon character actors who could successfully assume any kind of role, comic or dramatic. Jeanette gloriously reprises the "Italian Street Song," among the most intricate and fastest-tempo tunes in the literature of American operetta. Even Eddy is suitably impressed, temporarily pushing aside his self-conceit to join in the overall praise of her voice. Jeanette is flattered but unwilling as yet to encourage his obvious interest in courting her.

Search and Discovery. Later, after Eddy is unable to find Jeanette, who had escaped from the cottage after several falsehoods regarding her background aroused the suspicion of Governor Morgan, he luckily finds her in the marionette theater, where she and two male puppeteers are merrily singing "Ship Ahoy," a brief tale of the love of a maiden for a wandering sailor boy, to an audience of appreciative children. He hurries backstage to talk with her, only to run into Jeanette's demand that he leave her alone.

Her command is appreciated by onlooker Tamiroff, who, after Eddy's departure, verifies Jeanette's impression that the aggressive soldier is a practiced heartbreaker and unworthy of her.

Operetta rituals, however, dictated the eventual reconciliation of warring lovers, and in *Marietta* the icy barrier that so far had prevented Jeanette from admitting her growing love for Eddy goes into its meltdown mode when they accidentally meet a few days later. Her anger toward him gradually subsides into harmless banter. A significant drop in the decibel level that marked their verbal exchange at the theater is evident, as are the furtive smiles that are beginning to steal over the face of one while the other's is turned away. Clearly, fate is taking a hand in bringing the obstinate young man and the evasive young woman nearer and nearer together.

Consternation preys upon their emerging

happiness, however, when word reaches Eddy that Morgan is offering a reward for the capture of the missing Jeanette. Enmity had always existed between Morgan and his regular army troops and Eddy and his mercenaries, with the latter charging that the government troops are incompetent, while the home guard remained jealous of what the members felt was the mercenaries' usurpation of their military duties.

Eddy leads Jeannette into the woods and to an abandoned canoe. Resolving while he paddles across a lake to learn why she is wanted by the government, Eddy parries Jeanette's refusal to explain with an offer to help her escape anyway.

Nor is she disposed to even disclosing her real name to a virtual stranger, identifying herself as only "someone from somewhere." Her companion then admits that he has a "strong feeling for someone," while the off-screen orchestra, alert to the song cue, provides the accompaniment to Eddy's masterful solo of "Falling in Love with Someone," one of the loveliest of all musical confessions of love. With the single exception of his rendition of Sigmund Romberg's "Will You Remember?" in *Maytime* (1937), Eddy never sang a better or more difficult song, or so well.

His smooth delivery impresses Jeanette to such a degree that she tells him that she, too, has a confession to make: that she has written part of a love song that she expects to complete and sing, but only at the "right time," and with the right man, which is not quite yet.

Jeanette returns voluntarily to Governor Morgan's quarters, where, after intense prodding, she relates the details of her fleeing France in order to avoid entering into a loveless marriage with a boor. Stunned at the news, Morgan responds that Uncle Dumbrille is scheduled to arrive at the palace the very next day, along with the irritating Kingsford.

What's more, a ball is to be held in their honor, and Morgan demands that Jeanette attend it in order not to further antagonize either of his titled guests of honor. Then, in a desperate attempt by an inept politician to survive in his sinecure, Morgan orders her to

occupy a bedroom in the palace so that she will be available when Dumbrille asks to speak with her. Suspicious that Eddy might somehow foil his plans by coming to her rescue, Morgan sends word to the mercenary leader that he is to undertake a new assignment in a distant outpost. Furthermore, Eddy is to leave immediately and stay away from the palace.

Liveries manned by uniformed coachmen pull up at the front of the governor's palace on the evening of the ball to discharge the sumptuously garmented guests. In Jeanette's upstairs prison, Dumbrille is excoriating her for humiliating France and Spain, Kingsford and himself by deserting her intended husband without notice. After she insists she still will not enter into a loathsome union, her uncle lowers the boom by commanding that she sail with him and the pitiable nobleman back to France the next evening.

The Song Is Ended. After curtly departing the room, quarrelsome Jeanette is visited by Julie, a domestic played by Cecilia Parker, who two years later would be reborn as Andy Hardy's older sister, Marian, and continue almost exclusively in that role up to the series' finale in 1958.

She offers to help Jeanette escape, but her scheme is interrupted by a reprise from afar of "Tramp, Tramp, Tramp," a signal that Eddy and his men, their latest mission apparently completed in record time, are marching back into town. At the palace door, the mercenary chieftain insists on attending the ball even though he has no invitation to present to the doorkeeper. He finally gains admittance shortly after Jeanette enters the gala, and as their eyes meet, it is quite clear that it is love and love alone that has drawn him there. Missing from the assemblage is Kingsford, whose bout with seasickness has confined him to bed.

Jeanette agreeably joins Eddy and happily accepts his invitation to dance, her affection for him clearly superceding the aloofness that had characterized previous meetings with him. Asked to sing a song, she chooses the familiar ditty of old that so far she has been unable to finish. Ascending the nearby spiral staircase, she pauses on the third step and places her hand on the railing. Bending slightly over it and addressing the song directly to Eddy, she begins to sing "Ah, Sweet Mystery of Life," easily Herbert's most enduring ballad. This time she is able to sing it all the way through, thanks to Eddy, whose protestation of love during their dance has made it possible for her to complete the song and accept him into her heart.

Only now does she concede that it is love that rules the world, now and forevermore. Everyone alive constantly seeks it, but it is only the fortunate few who find love, which has the power to unite two kindred spirits in everlasting bliss. Every person must be willing to replace self-centeredness with a firm commitment to share life's experiences with another human being, thereby endowing the partnership with the compassion and tenderness needed to guarantee a life of perfect harmony. That Eddy is to be her eternal love is verified the minute he reprises the lyric without coaching as he walks slowly toward her. He has unlocked for her the mystery of life. The song ends in a duet, with each firmly grasping the hand of the other to affirm the depth of the love they are now celebrating in song.

Why this sequence has been subjected to parody over the years is a mystery itself. Surely, it is not the melody, which ranks as one of the most beautiful ever composed by Herbert, nor is it the lyric, which is one of Mrs. Young's finest. Most likely it is due to the heavily stylized placement of the two stars, Jeanette standing taller than her partner and giving the impression of singing at rather than to Eddy, who remains on the floor, separated from his lady love by the bannister. Whatever the reason, and despite the artificiality that admittedly pervades the sequence, this particular MacDonald-Eddy duet easily transcends anything else they ever did together. *Naughty Marietta*, after all, is an operetta. Everything about it is unworldly, imaginatively harkening back to a time and place well beyond the acquaintance of any mid-thirties viewer. The real question is whether the duet with all its studied flourishes is effective at announcing the end of Eddy's unrequited love for Jeanette. It is.

The duet renders the ballroom onlookers silent, uncertain whether to applaud or condemn the singers for their open display of passion. Not the least speechless is Uncle Dumbrille, who orders Jeanette back to her room, follows her into it, and scolds her for consorting so publicly with a mere mercenary soldier and embarrassing Kingsford in absentia. The solution is obvious: instead of tomorrow evening, the ship carrying Jeanette back to France will sail tonight.

Shortly after he leaves, Jeanette admits Eddy into the room. She acknowledges her love for him, prompting Eddy to formulate a plan for their escape. Following operetta tradition, the feat is accomplished without difficulty with the help of conspiratorial friends. After Jeanette and Eddy climb out of her bedroom window, they are "arrested" by fellow mercenaries Brophy and Huber, who, disguised as palace guards, arrive in the nick of time to escort the "captives" to a waiting carriage and freedom instead of to the guardhouse.

In the final scene the two lovers are shown riding through the countryside miles away from Governor Morgan's palace. The scene is peaceful and pastoral, replete with mounds of hay stacked on fertile farmland. A mountain looms high in the distance, symbolically separating Jeanette and Eddy forever from the duplicity and intrigues of the false world peopled by insincere courtiers, on which both have turned their backs. As he had promised, Eddy has carried her into an idyllic wilderness, which side by side they will transform into a paradise for two. All their cares and woes behind them, and a bright future newly opened to them, they reprise "Ah, Sweet Mystery of Life."

No mortal from the real world, let us hope, will ever trespass on the dreams of the glamorous young lady who scorned a royal wedding and the gallant singing soldier whose sole wish was to live happily with her ever after.

Top Hat (1935)

An RKO Radio picture. DIRECTOR: Mark Sandrich. PRODUCER: Pandro S. Berman. SCREENWRITERS: Dwight Taylor and Allan Scott, based on a story by Taylor. CINEMATOGRAPHER: David Abel; SPECIAL EF-

FECTS: Vernon L. Walker. FILM EDITOR: William Hamilton. CHOREOGRAPHER: Hermes Pan. ART DIRECTOR: Van Nest Polglase; ASSOCIATE: Carroll Clark. SETS: Thomas K. Little. SOUND RECORDING: Hugh McDowell, Jr.; SOUND CUTTER: George Marsh; MUSIC RECORDING: P.J. Faulkner, Jr. GOWNS: Bernard Newman. MUSICAL DIRECTOR: Max Steiner. SONGS: Lyrics and music by Irving Berlin. RUNNING TIME: 1 hour, 41 minutes. *Principal Players*: Fred Astaire (Jerry Travers). Ginger Rogers (Dale Tremont). Edward Everett Horton (Horace Hardwick). Erik Rhodes (Alberto Beddini). Eric Blore (Bates). Helen Broderick (Madge Hardwick). *Major Academy Award Nominations*: Best Picture; Art Direction; Song ("Cheek to Cheek").

"He gave her class and she gave him sex," Katharine Hepburn said in the mid-thirties of the Astaire and Rogers partnership. That is probably as good a definition of their phenomenal popularity as any ever offered. Each of their celluloid adventures called for a successor, and RKO Radio was alert to that fact. Spurred on by the tremendous box office reception to *The Gay Divorcee*, studio executives rounded up Fred and Ginger and most of the same actors and craftsmen for a new project they expected would win equal amounts of praise and revenue. Back in harness were producer Berman, director Sandrich, screenwriter Taylor—even sound cutter George Marsh. Parts were written for Fred and Ginger, Edward Everett Horton and Erik Rhodes that in many ways are quite similar to those they had performed in the earlier film.

What emerged from this family reunion was *Top Hat*, one of the most amusing, well-plotted, and popular musicals of the decade, the Hope diamond of all the Astaire and Rogers romps. The dancers were at their peak, and the subsidiary characters are woven into a complicated, often illogical screenplay that never lapses into dullness, even though it revolves around a case of mistaken identity, surely one of the oldest plot stimulators in existence. So witty is much of the dialogue that the film could stand on its own as a bedroom farce without the need of songs to provide a running commentary on the progress of the romance between the two stars.

But let us be thankful that *Top Hat* came out as a musical, giving Irving Berlin the platform for neatly tying his songs together like sprays in an exquisitely assembled bouquet. In fact, the picture is the only one boasting the two dancers that measures up in plot to the magnificent music created for it. Released on August 16, 1935, it was the second highest grossing film of the year, after *Mutiny on the Bounty*, earning $3 million on a $620,000 investment. At the Radio City Music Hall, the picture proceeded to break all existing records by taking in $134,800 the first week, or $24,000 more than any other film over the same time period, and racking up slightly more than $350,000 during its three-week stopover there.

Fred is enamored of no one but Ginger throughout the film. Again, he faces no serious competitors to win her, nor is her eventual reciprocation ever in danger of being trumped by another woman. This concentration on a single love affair contributed mightily toward stripping the film down to the basics. No extraneous romances were permitted to intrude and divert attention from the two stars' courtship. The picture cuts to the chase at the beginning and stays with it to the end.

Good as they are, the later *Follow the Fleet* is burdened with the rather boring details of the love of Randolph Scott for Harriet Hilliard, *Swing Time* with the mild love affair between Fred and Betty Furness (later to be the chief television spokeswoman for Westinghouse and a consumer advocate), and *Shall We Dance* with Jerome Cowan's infatuation with Ginger and Kitti Gallian's for Fred. It is impossible to imagine that any one of these three musicals would have achieved widespread popularity without music. On the other hand, the *Top Hat* songs are really icing on a cake that would have been appetizing without them.

Top Hat was the first of dancers' pictures with a score by Berlin, who subsequently would furnish Fred with songs for *Follow the Fleet* ("Let's Face the Music and Dance"), *Carefree* (the Academy Award-nominated "Change Partners"), *Holiday Inn* ("Be Careful, It's My Heart" [with Bing Crosby]), *Blue Skies* (a reprise of "Puttin' on the Ritz," performed originally by Harry Richman in the 1929 film of the same name), and *Easter Parade* ("Steppin' Out with My Baby"). Either alone or in company with Ginger, Fred introduces the *Top Hat* songs in a hotel suite, in a gazebo in the park, on a theatrical stage, and on a ballroom floor. Included among the tunes is "Cheek to Cheek," one of Berlin's all-time best and one

Fred Astaire and Ginger Rogers performing Irving Berlin's sparkling "Isn't This a Lovely Day (to be Caught in the Rain)?" in a gazebo during a thunderstorm in *Top Hat*.

of 1935's three outstanding best song nominees. So choice were the tunes that RKO gave Berlin his own credit card, an honor never before bestowed on any writer of songs for an Oscar-nominated musical.

Berlin began contributing songs to Hollywood productions as early as 1928, when his "Marie" appeared in *The Awakening* in 1928. Between 1929 and 1930, he wrote the complete scores for *Hallelujah* and Al Jolson's *Mammy*.

Not even a songwriter with his powerhouse credentials, however, was exempted from the cost-cutting regimen instituted by the Hollywood studios at the outset of the Great Depression. In 1931 United Artists dropped 12 of the 13 tunes he had written for *Reaching for the Moon*. Only "When the Folks High-Up Do the Mean Low-Down," sung by Bebe Daniels and a very young Bing Crosby, survived the assault.

Top Hat, like *The Gay Divorcee*, depends for its glamor and sophistication on reconstituting the pre-Crash Prohibition era, when Coolidge presided over a country of merrymakers. The Dust Bowl Roosevelt years are ignored in both films, and along with them any hint that by the mid-thirties, America has changed drastically. In the movies, wealthy top-hatted playboys were still quite plentiful, as were ermine-clad ladies who seemed to have no other clothes but evening dresses.

Top Hat finds Edward Everett Horton befuddled as ever, along with Erik Rhodes, now an egoistical dress designer, still spouting malapropisms and falling ever more deeply in love with himself. In essence, they and most of the other cast members reappear pretty much as the camera left them in *The Gay Divorcee*, except that Horton is now a producer of stage musicals. Another significant *Divorcee* holdover is Eric Blore, this time as Horton's valet, an accustomed role at which he was surpassed only by the ubiquitous Arthur Treacher and equaled by Charles Coleman. All three men exemplified the traditional English "gentleman's gentleman." Inwardly proud but outwardly self-deprecatory and alert to their employer's slightest need, they were confident of their superiority both as human beings and as masters of their profession. The most inspired newcomer to the cast was Helen Broderick, the mother of Academy Award-winning actor Broderick Crawford, a front-rank comedienne who was already a stage star when she appeared in the first of Florenz Ziegfeld's Follies 28 years earlier, in 1907. She and Fred had appeared together in the 1931 Broadway production of *The Band Wagon*.

Top Hat was the first Oscar-nominated musical to superimpose images of the two leading players during the credits. All we see of Fred and Ginger are their feet, encased in dancing shoes and tripping a light fantastic to the jaunty beat of "The Piccolino" in the background. It is doubtful that anyone in the audience didn't know who owned the feet, or failed to greet their appearance as an invitation to settle back, tear the wrapper off a candy bar or dip their fingers into a bag of popcorn, and get ready for 90 or so minutes of uninterrupted pleasure, fantasy-style. And it was served on a gleaming silver platter that even after 60-plus years shows few smudges of tarnish.

Back in London Town. Once again playing an American musical comedy star, Astaire (Jerry Travers) is in London to appear in the new show to be produced by Edward Everett Horton (Horace Hardwick). Although certainly not averse to relaxing as his busy schedule permits, Fred displays only mild interest in accepting Horton's invitation to accompany him on a weekend trip to Venice right after his show opens. Horton's wife, Helen Broderick (Madge), is already there awaiting the arrival of a young woman acquaintance. Ever-cautious Fred's initial suspicion that his producer friend has a boy-meets-girl scheme up his sleeve to lure him out of his precious bachelorhood is confirmed when Horton offhandedly remarks that Helen, one of Cupid's most active helpmates, will undoubtedly try to work her "matchmaking proclivities" on him. Fred's response to Horton's observation that the time has come for him to settle down is to sing of his determination to sidestep romantic involvement in the exuberant confessional song, "No Strings (I'm Fancy Free)."

After reprising the cleverly wrought lyric in praise of the single life, Fred segues into a lively dance, sending the rat-tat-tat of his taps from the bare floor into the bedroom below. There, unable to doze off, is furious Ginger (Dale Tremont). Her telephone call to the hotel manager (Edgar Norton) to stop the racket is relayed to Horton, who predictably misconstrues the manager's message. Mumbling to Fred that apparently some young lady is waiting downstairs in the lobby to see him, he departs the suite while Fred innocently continues his extraordinary routine unaware that a complaint has been filed against him as noisemaker.

Miffed that the manager is apparently unconcerned whether or not she gets her beauty sleep, Ginger herself barges up to Horton's suite and demands that Fred call a halt to his dancing. He apologizes profusely, humorously attributing his uncontrollable urge to tap his toes every so often to an advanced case of St. Vitus Dance. The lady is not amused, and she refuses his plea to spend a little time with him until his alleged illness subsides.

Undaunted, he follows her into the corridor, only to be told that she needs rest far more than conversation. But the connection that will evolve into romance has been made. One of Astaire's most endearing screen characteristics was the tendency to fall in love at first sight, especially when it was Ginger who came into view. Few actors were as able to project instant enthrallment quite so adroitly as the debonair Nebraska native.

If it's sleep she wants, Fred muses on the way back to his suite, he'll make sure she gets it by acting as her "official sandman." Sprinkling sand taken from an elevator ashtray over the floor, he proceeds to treat Ginger to a soft-shoe version of the song that rivals his equally brilliant sand dance to Johnny Mercer and Harry Warren's "I'm a Dancing Man" 18 years later in *The Belle of New York*. Sleepyhead Ginger can barely hear his soothing slides, and she glances appreciatively at the ceiling, her frown of annoyance replaced by the dewy-eyed look of a woman on the verge of falling in love. Obviously, she has been victimized by the same first-sight affliction that has turned playboy Fred into a beau eager to settle down in marriage.

With Fred's anti-marriage philosophy on the wane, the next day he sends Ginger all the poesies in a florist shop, exercising his delight in playing the committed lover by signing the card with the tell-tale message, "From your silent admirer." Because he is not a guest at the hotel, he tells the shop manager (Leonard Mudie) to charge the flowers to Horton's suite, inadvertently opening up the plot to its first troubling complexity. The agent for introducing it is the manager, who on the sly informs his assistant, played by an unbilled Lucille Ball in a blonde wig, that Alberto Beddini (Erik Rhodes), Ginger's dress designer friend, obviously has a rival for the lady's affection. Their

relationship, as the screenplay is careful to emphasize several times, is strictly business. Rhodes is in love with her, but Ginger tolerates him only because she enjoys advertising his creations by wearing them to glitzy affairs attended by upper-crust clients. Obviously, they occupy separate hotel rooms.

Later that morning, Ginger is dressed in an equestrienne habit when she meets Fred in the hotel lobby. Not as yet willing to encourage his advances, she spurns his offer to escort her to the Baldwin Riding Academy. So he bribes a hansom driver to replace him atop the cab. Disguising his voice with a cockney accent to delude his passenger, he proceeds to drive Ginger to the stables. But his ploy boomerangs when he starts tapping his feet to speed the horse along the journey. Ginger recognizes the rhythmic taps from the previous evening and, though flattered, resolves not to fall prey to his cleverness.

After curtly dismissing him without a thank you or tip upon their arrival at the academy, she mounts for a romp in the park. A severe rainstorm cuts it short, forcing her to take refuge in a gazebo. Disregarding her recent brush off, Fred reappears with the hansom and a wide umbrella in hopes of urging her back into the carriage. Again, she rebuffs him, but quickly buries her head in his arms at the first clap of thunder, which she admits has frightened her since childhood. Rarely before or since has a musical number been introduced so cleverly, as Fred proceeds to sing and dance her into ecstasy.

The thunder appeals to Fred, who explains why in "Isn't This a Lovely Day (to Be Caught in the Rain)?", one of Berlin's catchiest love songs. The pelting of raindrops and the clatter of cloudbursts may have destabilized her, but all that Fred can see, he sings, are rainbows arising from her glorious presence. Ginger condescends to listen to the lyric, and her interest is piqued when Fred, expecting to impress her with a solo dance, ambles to the center of the gazebo. In one of the movies' most inventive dance duets, Ginger rises to join him, aping his steps behind his back and then executing a few creative taps of her own.

Surmising that the two are soul mates when it comes to dancing, Fred is convinced that they can coexist in equally perfect harmony as husband and wife. He exults in their compatibility at the end of the routine, and the partners exchange congratulations and a warm handshake. Initially, the gazebo song was to have been "Wild About You." It was dropped, however, and Berlin picked it up in 1939 for his stage musical *Louisiana Purchase*. Also dropped from the *Top Hat* score was "Get Thee Behind Me, Satan," which was given to Harriet Hilliard to sing the next year in *Follow the Fleet*.

Later, in Rhodes's hotel suite, the pompous designer, who always refers to himself in the third person, is urging Ginger to accept Helen Broderick's invitation to join her in Venice. He will accompany Ginger so as to be available to take orders from the hoy palloy, who he is certain will be mesmerized by the expensive gowns that Ginger will model while there. She, however, is not the least enthusiastic about making the trip. Not even a telegram from Helen informing her that husband Horton is stopping at the same London hotel and will gladly accompany Ginger on the trip is able to change her mind.

What she will do is meet Horton face to face and apologize for her inability to fly with him to Italy. Because she has never met him, Ginger asks a hotel clerk for Horton's suite number. Rather than giving it to her, he identifies a briefcase-bearing figure walking along the mezzanine as the gentleman she wishes to speak with. While Ginger turns her back to the mezzanine to thank the clerk, Fred rushes over to Horton and tells him that he should return quickly to his suite to answer a telephone call.

Horton nods and presses the briefcase in Fred's hand before racing away. Then Ginger turns and glances up at him. She is naturally aghast at discovering that her dancing suitor is the husband of close friend Helen. Once on the lobby level, Fred hurries to her side, only to retreat when Ginger repulses his pleasantries, slaps him, and angrily sweeps past him out the lobby door. Later, in Rhodes' suite, she agrees with the designer to go to Venice after all, if only to "face the musicians," in Rhodes's garbled phraseology, and warn friend Helen of her husband's philandering.

After Fred relates the face-slapping incident to Horton, the latter orders butler Bates (Eric Blore) to follow Ginger day and night and report to him on her every activity. Convinced that Ginger is a tricky gold digger who has her sights on Fred's money, Horton is desperate to protect his young friend—and his musical show—from the scandal that surely would arise should Ginger succeed at provoking Fred into an unseemly liaison. Probably nothing else dates *Top Hat*, released at a time when house detectives still roamed hotel corridors, more than Horton's consuming fear that publicity of impropriety on the part of his star would adversely affect ticket sales, rather than attract SRO crowds eager to see the latest celebrity to become enmeshed in scandalous conduct.

That night at the theater, Fred gives an outstanding performance in the finest "the show must go on" tradition. Disregarding Ginger's rejection and discovery that she has mysteriously checked out of the hotel—personal problems that well might cripple a less consummate artist—he opens the second act of Horton's musical by singing and dancing Berlin's matchless "Top Hat, White Tie and Tails," a brilliantly conceived syncopated shooting gallery in pantomime. Choreographed by Astaire himself, this number was based on a similar routine he had danced four years earlier in *Smiles* to the tune of "Say, Young Man of Manhattan," by Harold Adamson, Clifford Grey, and Vincent Youmans.

In a series of single taps that reverberate through the auditorium like rifle shots, he "kills off" the male choristers one by one until only eight remain standing. These he wipes out in one fell swoop, increasing the rapidity of his taps until they sound like a discharge from a machine gun. The entire number is confined to an authentic, somewhat cramped stage setting, clearly indicating why Fred was so popular on Broadway and validating Mikhail Baryshnikov's assessment of Fred as the best dancer the ballet master had ever seen.

An unusually effective change of scene from the London theater to Venice is provided by a reprise of "Top Hat, White Tie and Tails." Played a second time by the theater's pit orchestra, the song is repeated after a brief dissolve by a small orchestra entertaining guests at the Lido, the Venetian resort where the rest of the plot will unfold. Asked by Helen whether husband Horton had looked her up in London, Ginger uneasily admits that he had, and moreover that she found him to be fascinating. Helen is dumbfounded at hearing that one-word description of Horton, having for years regarded him as uncompromisingly dull. The one-liners exchanged between the two confused women while dissecting Horton's personality may not strike current viewers as uproarious, as they were in the mid-1930s. But as spoken by Helen Broderick, they retain much of their humor, thanks to her blank expression and emotionless voice. Only Aline MacMahon (in Gold Diggers of 1933) and Marie Dressler in practically every part she played were equally capable of projecting understated perplexity at events they were unable to decipher.

Ginger's discomfort at learning that Horton and a friend will be joining them that afternoon leads Helen to suspect that Horton had been flirting with her in London. Ginger admits the truth, adding that he had sent her a roomful of flowers and even chased her in the park. Curiously, Helen is not the least perturbed, even expressing admiration that her middle-age husband is still so fleet of foot. She shrugs off the affair and informs the nonplused Ginger that his flirtations have been plentiful over the years but are harmless and "mean nothing." Besides, she adds, "When you're as old as I am, you take your men as you find them—*if* you can find them."

Ginger flees when Horton and Fred appear on the scene, but Helen welcomes them. She is as gratified to learn that Fred has already met Ginger as he is to find that the girl of his dreams is back within wooing range. To Helen, he is the ideal candidate on whom to practice her "matchmaking proclivities," and Ginger the perfect target for his affection. Because all the resort rooms are occupied, the management settles Fred and Horton in the bridal suite, which as created by the art-directing genius Van Nest Polglase ranks as one of the most sumptuous living quarters on film, an Art Deco masterpiece. Despite Horton's insistence that Ginger must not visit smitten Fred in the suite, she does just that in a desperate attempt to dampen his ardor with unladylike aggressiveness.

Out of the Past. In a highly amusing sequence reminiscent of Fred and Ginger's hotel room rendezvous in *The Gay Divorcee*, the couple engages in inappropriate responses to innocent questions, all the time running along different tracks of innuendo. Ginger just had to see him again, she says after a kiss. Fred is stunned by her unsuspected passion for him, recalling the slaps she had earlier administered to his ego. Unaware of his earlier remark to Horton that he had visited Paris only once— when he was 10 years of age—Ginger launches into a fictional tale of her and Fred's recent rendezvous in the City of Light. Finally realizing that Ginger is merely toying with him for some unaccountable purpose, he decides to out-fantasize her fantasy.

Of course he remembers her—but didn't she go by the name of Madeleine during their Paris affair? Well, it doesn't matter; it's quite apparent that she still loves him, and that's all that matters, Fred oozes with delight. His unexpected participation in her little game frightens Ginger, who exits the room to elude further manifestations of the rise in Fred's adrenaline. But later, when talking things over with Helen, she admits that she is growing quite fond of her husband, despite his outrageous conduct. This time Helen fails to react casually to Ginger's confession, vowing to herself to abort an affair that seems to be growing serious in order to keep Horton to herself.

At the resort nightclub, Ginger is quick to resent Fred's presence at her and Helen's table. But undeterred as ever by the lady's cold, cold heart, he succeeds in tempting her to dance with him. Ginger's reluctant acquiescence is helped along by Helen, now trying harder than ever to bring the couple together, not to hone her matchmaking talent but to get Ginger's mind off of Horton. "Go ahead, dance," Helen pleads to Ginger, who correctly senses that Helen no longer loves her "husband," if indeed she ever did. Muttering to herself that if his wife "doesn't mind, I'm sure I don't," Ginger strolls with Fred on to the dance floor.

The ballroom duet that follows, danced to the sweeping melody of "Cheek to Cheek," closely approximates the lyrical quality of the partners' earlier "Night and Day." As in their *The Gay Divorcee* dance, Fred croons the superlative lyric before leading Ginger into another expertly crafted dance routine that has taken its place among the screen's classics of choreography. A long song consisting of 72 measures, the number represents the most romantic pairing of the two stars ever directed by Hermes Pan. In *Second Fiddle* four years later, Berlin would reverse the position of the dancing couples in the song "Back to Back."

At the end, Ginger's face glows with unmistakable love of her partner, an emotional reaction that she finds unable to conceal, even from Helen. Correctly surmising that the time is ripe for him to pop the question, Fred follows her to an alcove, where his nervous schoolboy routine prevents him from proposing. She backslides into anger when he admits that he would happily demonstrate his love by asking for her hand in marriage, were it not for a "foolish promise" he had once made. Assuming he is referring to the marriage vow he exchanged with Helen, and not to his promise to Horton to stay away from Ginger, she gives him another slap—the third—and runs away.

Fred, Horton, and Helen are astounded a little later when Ginger telephones Helen to tell her that she has just married Rhodes. So that's why the management had asked Fred and Horton to vacate the bridal suite. Helen senses that Ginger and the dress designer are the "newly married couple" that the resort's gossip mongers are finding so entrancing. As Fred dimly reviews his attempts at winning Ginger's hand, Helen suddenly realizes why Ginger had found her "husband" so attractive: Ginger had confused Fred with Horton!

Facing the next night without sleeping quarters, Fred confronts Rhodes in an effort to argue him out of the bridal suite, but the stubborn groom refuses to leave. The hotel manager (Gino Corrado) sides with Rhodes, and Fred finally surrenders it to the newlyweds. Panting to consummate the marriage, Rhodes is frustrated by Ginger's unresponsiveness. He does manage to plant a kiss on her lips, however, only to have Ginger whisk her face away at the sound of Fred's taps again emanating from the room above. Brave Rhodes follows her instructions to stop the noise, waving a drawn sword and threatening to plunge it into the dancing man's belly as he ascends the stairs. Fred eludes death by retreating one flight down and reentering the bridal suite, where he attempts to placate Ginger by straightening out the not inconsiderable matter of who is actually who and which one is married to Helen.

In an obvious effort to provide a quick windup of affairs, the film falls back on age-old silliness, most of it, however, so professionally handled that the lapses in logic and pileup of absurd incidents fail to detract very much from the adroit plotting that preceded them. *Top Hat*'s final ten minutes are amusing, but more to the point, they are memorable as well, mainly because of the inclusion of one of the greatest dance finales to be seen in any film.

Joyful at Fred's clarification of the identity mixup and the chance to escape from Rhodes's clutches, Ginger happily joins him for a cruise in a gondola under the watchful eyes of gondolier Blore, still faithfully executing his role as Horton's private detective until, that is, he inadvertently falls overboard after breaking his oar. Once on land, he scurries back to the resort to announce that Fred and Ginger are drifting out to sea in an unmanned gondola. Rhodes, his honor insulted and nervous about Ginger's safety, jumps into a motor boat with Helen and Horton to find the stranded lovers before disaster strikes. Because Blore had previously siphoned off most of the gasoline to prevent Fred's commandeering the motor boat to speed away with Ginger, it is the trio of rescuers that becomes stranded at sea. Blore receives still another blow when he is arrested by the Venetian police for impersonating a gondolier.

The final scene returns Fred and Ginger to a table in the resort nightclub. In the background the orchestra is playing the opening strains of "The Piccolino" one of Berlin's preeminent production numbers and a fit successor to the dancers' "The Carioca" and "The Continental." Composed originally as an instrumental for the 1921 *Music Box Revue*, the song now sported a new and quite witty Berlin lyric. Ginger sings it, describing how the captivating Latin-based melody, written by a guy from Brooklyn, has thrown Venetians into a dance frenzy. After the chorus taps it out in spectacular Hermes Pan choreographic fashion, the camera presents a visual echo of the steps the two stars performed during the rolling of the credits by again focusing on Fred and Ginger's feet as they tap their way from their table to the center of the dance floor and reprise the tune.

At its completion, Horton races over to

them to report that Rhodes had fallen into the canal, caught cold, and is now on his way to settle affairs with Fred. This time, Fred is prepared to out-bravado Rhodes once and for all. Blore then steps into the scene to explain that Fred need not fear Rhodes's anger: he and Ginger are not married.

Winking slyly, the butler reverses the collar of his white shirt, indicating, as he proudly informs everybody, that he "very cleverly became a clergyman" at a most appropriate time. It was he who had performed the ceremony that supposedly united Ginger and Rhodes as man and wife. In Blore's on-the-spot judgment, marrying the two was the only way to satisfy's Horton's insistence that gold-digging Ginger's plot to tantalize Fred into a liaison be stopped. With Ginger now free to wed Fred, the happy couple, arm in arm, merrily share a few more "Piccolino" steps on their way out of the nightclub and onward onto the road to eternal happiness.

A perfect ending and fit tribute to the dancing man whom Rudolf Nureyev once characterized as "music in motion. He invented his own rhythm, he imposed his own musicality, as if he wrote another instrument into orchestration."

The Great Ziegfeld (1936)

A Metro-Goldwyn-Mayer picture. DIRECTOR: Robert Z. Leonard. PRODUCER: Hunt Stromberg. SCREENWRITER: William Anthony McGuire. CINEMATOGRAPHER: Oliver T. Marsh; "Two [New Amsterdam Theatre] Roof Numbers" photographed by George Folsey and Karl Freund; "Melody" Number by Ray June; and the "Hoctor Ballet" by Merritt B. Gerstad. FILM EDITOR: William S. Gray. ART DIRECTOR: Cedric Gibbons; ASSOCIATES: Merrill Pye, Eddie Imazu, John Harkrider, and Edwin B. Willis. RECORDING DIRECTOR: Douglas Shearer. CHOREOGRAPHER: Seymour Felix. GOWNS: Adrian. MUSICAL DIRECTOR: Arthur Lange; ARRANGEMENTS: Frank Skinner. ORIGINAL SONGS: Lyrics by Harold Adamson, music by Walter Donaldson; Hoctor Ballet lyrics by Herb Magidson, music by Con Conrad. RUNNING TIME: 2 hours, 59 minutes. *Principal Players*: William Powell (Florenz Ziegfeld, Jr.) Myrna Loy (Billie Burke). Luise Rainer (Anna Held). Frank Morgan (Billings). Fannie [Fanny] Brice (Herself). Virginia Bruce (Audrey Dane). Reginald Owen (Samston). Ray Bolger (Himself). Ernest Cossart (Sidney). Joseph Cawthorne (Dr. Ziegfeld). Nat Pendleton (Sandau). Harriet Hoctor (Herself). *Major Academy Awards*: Best Picture; Actress (*Luise Rainer*); Choreography. *Nominations*: Best Director; Screenplay; Film Editing; Art Direction.

Like so many MGM and other studios' pictures of the distant past, *The Great Ziegfeld* is too long, even considering the powerful influence exerted by its major character on pioneering the American musical revue. Competent at highlighting both true and false events in the life of America's legendary producer, it dwells far too extensively on incidents that fail to provide unique insight into the master showman's motivations. Nor does the film probe very deeply into the psychological reasons for Ziegfeld's unique ability, up to the very end of his life, to snap back from financial ruin, only to teeter again on the rim of insolvency with utter disregard for the consequences. Only 41 minutes shorter than *Gone with the Wind*, the picture is weighted down with insignificant details that are often duplicated or belabored.

"Ziegfeldian" was indeed synonymous with spectacle at any price, and with all his faults Ziegfeld could never be called cheap. The film surely provides enough eye-popping sets, costumes, and dance ensembles to satisfy anyone hankering after them. So numerous are the production numbers that five cinematographers were hired to shoot them. One's appetite for opulence is sated by the time the Harriet Hoctor segment, replete with her entourage of 25 chorus girls and six dogs, comes along. Its deletion would not have been missed. Miss Hoctor was more of an accomplished acrobat than ballet dancer—she also appeared in the finale of Astaire and Rogers' *Shall We Dance*—and few moviegoers were enamored of her specialty, or of the Magidson-Conrad tune "A Circus Must Be Different in a Ziegfeld Show." Her sprightly performance merely embellishes a film that should have been wound up by the time she arrives.

The film moves slowly, its noble attempt to place dual emphasis on drama and music forcing each to compete with the other for attention. Handled more artistically, the story and the songs would have complemented each other. Far too frequently the characters are boxed in by a single, claustrophobic set. Rarely does the camera venture beyond the four walls of a dressing room or apartment, a surprisingly late carryover from the Stone Age of talking pictures, when the industry for prestige purposes picked up Broadway dramas rich in dialogue but static in action, rarely expanding the number of settings beyond two or three.

Part of the mammoth "A Pretty Girl Is Like a Melody" set designed for *The Great Ziegfeld*. Perched atop the birthday cake centerpiece is Virginia Bruce.

The film deals seriously with the rises and falls of Ziegfeld at the expense of comedy, which is almost entirely absent save for the brief appearance of singer-comedienne Fanny (spelled "Fannie" in the cast credits) Brice. The ceaseless bickering between Ziegfeld and Billings (Frank Morgan), who serves as an amalgam of the former's numerous cutthroat competitors rolled into one, fast becomes monotonous through repetition. The acting, however, is superlative throughout, especially by William Powell, an established suave leading man with a largely unappreciated flair for comedy, best known at the time for introducing detective Nick Charles to the screen in the first of the Thin Man series in 1934.

He won an Oscar nomination as best actor for that role, and twice more as Godfrey Parks in *My Man Godfrey* (1936) and Clarence Day in *Life with Father* (1947). Powell still personifies Ziegfeld in the minds of most movie fans. The day after the real Ziegfeld's death,

Will Rogers eulogized him in *The New York Times*, ending his column with the words: "Goodbye, Flo, save a spot for me. You will put on a show up there someday that will knock their eye out."

Accordingly, Powell again played him in *Ziegfeld Follies* (1946), but as a dead man still insistent on pulling all the production strings from heaven. Unfortunately, the film knocked out few eyes. Fanny Brice rejoined Powell in the cast to appear in what must be the unfunniest skit of her career. Paul Henreid played Ziegfeld in *Deep in My Heart* (1954) and Walter Pidgeon in *Funny Girl* (1968). Curiously, no character named Ziegfeld shows up in person in *Ziegfeld Girl* (1941) or *Look for the Silver Lining* (1949), which revolves around Marilyn Miller, one of his most glamorous stars.

Equally effective in the acting department is Austrian-born Luise Rainer as Anna Held, whose insecurity as performer and lover often bordered on the neurotic. The first to win the best actress award in two successive years (Katharine Hepburn duplicated the feat in 1967 and 1968), Miss Rainer took home her second Oscar for her role as O-lan in *The Good Earth* (1937). She had made her American film debut two years earlier when she appeared with Powell in *Escapade*. Had film editor Gray applied his shears more generously to the final print, *The Great Ziegfeld* well might have become the classic the studio envisioned. Were it filmed a decade later, it most likely would have been split into two parts, like the Jolson and Brice "biographies" and *Three Smart Girls*, with "The Great Ziegfeld II" continuing the story from the point where he and his first wife separate. Possibly Gray's judiciousness would have impelled him to allow Miss Brice to sing all of her most famous song, "My Man," which she had achieved eight years earlier in the film of the same name. For some unaccountable reason, she disappears from both song and *The Great Ziegfeld* after reaching the halfway point of the chorus. (Moviegoers would have to wait till 1939 to hear it sung in entirety—by Alice Faye in *Rose of Washington Square*.)

Except for his final-reel conversion from addlepated business rival to sympathetic friend, Frank Morgan's role could certainly have been excised to about half its length. The film, incidentally, is the only Academy Award nominee on which three composers of popular World War I songs participated: Con Conrad ("Oh! Frenchy"), Walter Donaldson ("How 'Ya Gonna Keep 'Em Down on the Farm [After They've Seen Paree?])," and Arthur Lange ("A Mother's Prayer for Her Boy Out There")

Song Revivals and Newcomers. Besides such evergreens as Irving Berlin's "A Pretty Girl Is Like a Melody" and Buddy DeSylva and Joseph Meyer's "If You Knew Susie," the picture includes four new songs written by lyricist Harold Adamson and composer Walter Donaldson, the first three reprised in MGM's *Ziegfeld Girl*. The still-familiar "You," one of the finest production tunes ever to appear in a musical picture, is sung and danced by 20 flimsily dressed girls dancing atop their beds, which jut into the audience. "You Never Looked So Beautiful (Before)," with the chorus girls wearing towering peacock headdresses during their studied struts across the stage, is a pretty addition to the score, as is "You Gotta Pull Strings," with the ladies frolicking as puppets. "She's a Follies Girl," sung and splendidly danced by elastic-leg Ray Bolger, is a bubbly tribute to the beauties that peopled Ziegfeld's chorus lines. After the number is finished, one is struck by Bolger's foreshadowing the eccentric tap dancing he would perform three years later as the Scarecrow in *The Wizard of Oz*. A fifth song, the ballad "It's Been So Long," was dropped from the picture but ironically became the most popular of all the Adamson-Donaldson songs written for it.

Having accumulated a great number of gigantic hits over the years, from "Carolina in the Morning," one of Broadway's truly great novelty show tunes, in 1922 to "My Blue Heaven" in 1927, Donaldson was entitled by reputation and many years of laboring in the Hollywood vineyards, mostly MGM's, to write the original *Ziegfeld* songs. One of the first emigrants in the diaspora of tunesmiths who decamped from the East to the West Coast after the advent of talking pictures, he contributed songs to such pre-1936 films as *Cameo Kirby*, which introduced the lovely "Romance," *Hollywood Party*, *Operator Thirteen*, and *Kid Millions*. His and Adamson's lyrical "Did I Remember," from *Suzy*, was nominated for best song in 1936. The next year, Adamson entered into a long-term professional relationship with James McHugh and earned five more Academy Award nominations.

Brooklynite Donaldson was one of the few screen songwriters who had written tunes for Ziegfeld productions, including several Follies and one Midnight Frolic. He supplied the entire score for the producer's highly successful mid-twenties stage shows *Kid Boots* and *Whoopee*, which opened in 1928 with Eddie Cantor and Ruth Etting as the stars. When it was filmed in 1930, Donaldson's newly inserted "My Baby Just Cares for Me" became an overnight sensation. He also contributed songs to *Glorifying the American Girl* (1929), the only movie Ziegfeld, known as "Flo" or "Ziggie" to intimates, produced or appeared in.

The Follies quickly became a monument to the great producer, who despite his P.T. Barnum showmanship, was an obsessive craftsman in his own right, and the only one of the numerous stage revues that strikes the chord of recognition even among the latest generation of adults. Like Valentino and Houdini, whose surnames conjure up visions of the archetypal Latin lover and peerless illusionist, Ziegfeld's surname has become synonymous with entertainment on the grandest scale. No expense was too extreme to prohibit footlight appearances by the most gifted of professionals or the most garish of production numbers designed not to impress but to startle. Before turning to book shows in the early 1920s, Ziegfeld filled his musical extravaganzas with class-act performers from Broadway and vaudeville, even burlesque, whose polished routines abundantly reflected the love and care he took in achieving his production goals.

He built his Follies around beautiful girls, whose numbers exceeded 3,000 between his first in 1907 and his last in 1931. Some, like Paulette Goddard, who appeared in *No Foolin'* and *Rio Rita*, became show business icons; others married into money; while still others descended into poverty, scandal, or suicide. Probably all faced the temptations that consort with celebrity. As Paul Kelly, in the part of a Ziegfeld casting assistant in *Ziegfeld Girl*, warns a bevy of costumed young ladies before their first Ziegfeld show, it's up to each of them to decide whether to revel in or reject the myriad temptations that go with the job. Not every girl would be lucky enough to swap the chorus line of "A Pretty Girl Is Like a Melody" for a gentlemanly beau like Fred Astaire, as Joan Caulfield manages to do in *Blue Skies*. For a time a Ziegfeld Club, set up in the Presbyterian church on Park Avenue and East 65th Street, offered temporary refuge to one-time Follies girls stricken with the same periodic financial maladies as their boss.

Ziegfeld's greatest virtue was selecting the best available talent to create and oversee every element that made his shows the toasts of the town. Practically all the great comedians—Will Rogers, W.C. Fields, Leon Errol, Bert Williams, Eddie Cantor—appeared in his Follies, as did comedienne-singers Sophie Tucker and Fanny Brice. The only superstar never to appear in a Ziegfeld production was Al Jolson, who worked almost exclusively for the rival Shubert brothers. But even Al did his bit for Flo by entertaining the audiences that had paid their way into his *Show Girl*. Strolling every night down the main aisle to his seat, he sang the Gershwins' "Liza" while wife-to-be Ruby Keeler tap danced to the tune on stage.

The leading set designers, from Joseph Urban, the Viennese-born painter, sculptor, and architect, to Ben Ali Haggin, who specialized in grouping chorus girls into tableaux, worked regularly for Ziegfeld, even though neither is mentioned in the film. For the songs, he called on such stellar melody makers as Victor Herbert, Irving Berlin, Jerome Kern, and George Gershwin. A notorious spendthrift, Ziegfeld nonetheless was not above operating on the cheap when he felt occasional pressure to trim the budget. Composer J. Fred Coots once told this author of the many tremors of Ziegfeld's irritation that periodically shook his bones when he pled for payment for the songs he had written for him. "The usual response was that I wouldn't be getting all those ASCAP royalties if he hadn't put my songs into his shows," Coots said. "To Ziegfeld, his shows made the songs, not the other way around."

The producer was also given to frequent flings of invective to pep up a sagging cast, but the members still respected him. They knew he was not attacking them personally, but professionally, and that his bawlings out, like Warner Baxter's in *42nd Street*, were always for the good of the show, and furthermore that a good show meant long-term jobs. So much for William Powell's depiction of Flo as the unflappable diplomat whose overflowing kindness toward his underlings grew in direct proportion with the number of silver threads sprouting above his ears.

Fact vs. Fiction. The caveat in the credits that describes the film as "suggested by romances and incidents in the life of America's greatest showman, Florenz Ziegfeld, Jr." serves as ample warning that the biographical tidbits about to unfold are highly selective. It also suggests that viewers will be treated to a great deal of fiction underneath all the high Hollywood gloss. Accordingly, *The Great Ziegfeld* rearranges some incidents and both creates and excludes others, all in the sacred name of entertainment. Some pre-finale clouds are admitted into the screenplay, but for the most part MGM's Ziegfeld walks in sunshine, bouncing back from disaster with the ease of an experienced vaudeville tumbler.

Anything but rare until quite recently, such liberties were accepted by viewers who wanted their real-life heroes and heroines to reflect the highest standards of professional and private conduct. Far from showing zero toleration toward inventing fables to add drama to the lives of celebrities, regardless of their fields of endeavor, movie makers demonstrated little compunction about sweetening facts by distorting character and chronology, consequences and causes. Never pretending to be historians or journalists, they eschewed the factual for heartwarming confections. They were uniformly uninterested in creating controversy, the public unwilling to have it thrust upon them. Nowadays such "biographies" and stories based on fact are typically labeled "docudramas," a synonym for "history" that is not to be mistaken for literal reality. The movie house is not to be confused with the library.

Such was true of dramas as well as musical films. A spectacular example of art's preempting fact was *Inherit the Wind* (1960), undeniably arresting as theater but about as historically inaccurate as a film—or play—can get. The Scopes trial that forms the nucleus of the plot originated not in Dayton, Tenn., but in the New York office of the American Civil Liberties Union. John T. Scopes was never jailed, nor did he take the witness stand. He volunteered to test the law even though he could not remember ever teaching evolution, and probably never did, since he was also an athletic coach and only briefly substituted in biology. William Jennings Bryan's wife was not hale and hearty, but an invalid who definitely did not admire Clarence Darrow. The topic of sex and sin never came up at the trial, nor did Bryan believe that the world was created at 9 a.m. in 4004 B.C. And Bryan did not have a fit while delivering his last speech and die in the courtroom.

Similarly, many "facts" in Ziegfeld's life were mangled or based on falsehood. His first wife, Anna Held, was not single but married to a South American tobacco planter when Ziegfeld first met her, and it was she, not him,

who came up with the idea of producing the Follies, according to his second wife, actress Billie Burke. And no mention is made of Ziegfeld's daughter by Anna, only the one he sired with Billie.

Miss Burke not only turned down a marriage proposal from Enrico Caruso, whose name is never uttered in the film, but she was also introduced to Ziegfeld through the good graces of author Somerset Maugham, not at a ball in a Manhattan hotel. Unlike Myrna Loy's laid-back portrayal, Billie was quite uneven-tempered, flying into fits over Ziegfeld's suspected dalliances with other women, particularly Marilyn Miller, whose name is never spoken in the film. The producer's bravado boast to four detractors in a tonsorial parlor that Broadway one day will play host to the identical number of Ziegfeld hit shows, all running at the same time, is false. So is the subsequent roundup of the barbershop quartet by New York policemen so that he can have the pleasure of embarrassing them by giving each two tickets to the four shows. *Whoopee, The Three Musketeers, Rio Rita,* and *Show Boat* were indeed mammoth hits, but *Whoopee* closed before the other three shows opened, and *Rio Rita* vacated the new Ziegfeld Theatre before *Show Boat* replaced it there.

Viewers are not informed that before, between, and after these shows he suffered a string of flops, including *No Foolin', Betsy,* despite its Rodgers and Hart score, *Smiles,* with the Astaires and Vincent Youmans's ever lovely "Time on My Hands," *Show Girl,* Ziegfeld Follies of 1931, and *Hot Cha!* He was about $500,000 in the hole, some of it representing gambling debts, when he died at age 63 in 1932. He had always regarded movies as his most formidable competitors. Nonetheless, during the Depression year of 1931, he served as adviser to mogul Sam Goldwyn, who also became noted for assembling beautiful females under the umbrella title of the "Goldwyn Girls." Indeed, it was only through the generosity of close friend Will Rogers that Ziegfeld was able to pay his medical bills. Although quite moving, his death scene is fiction. Instead of expiring in a armchair in his New York apartment overlooking his Joseph Urban-designed Ziegfeld Theatre on Sixth Avenue, he died in a hospital bed in Santa Monica, California. He never would know that his New Amsterdam theater, the pride and joy of his artistic life, would be converted in 1933 to a motion picture house.

A ravishing red-haired beauty in her early Broadway career, Billie outlived her husband by 38 years, dying at 84 on May 14, 1970. Her most familiar screen role was that of Glinda, the "Good Witch of the North," in *The Wizard of Oz*. But her forte was portraying wealthy, slightly neurotic hostesses who turned fluttery, and then fell apart, when her party plans went askew because of some minor mishap. She had made her stage debut in 1902, when Ziegfeld was a nobody with big plans, as John Drew's leading lady in London's Pavillion Music Hall presentation of *My Wife*. And she married Ziegfeld in 1914, not the mid-1920s, as the film implies.

Even with these shortcomings, the film is a good one and has worn rather well over the years. Ziegfeld himself would surely have reveled in the music, highly decorative sets, fluffy costumes, and leggy chorus girls, around which MGM constructed a tale of a Broadway legend whose unique use of lushness, pageantry, and spectacle thrilled America for two decades. It was the second Hollywood musical to win the best picture award, and Miss Rainer was the first leading lady in a musical to be voted best actress. The only other musical she appeared in during her too brief Hollywood career was *The Great Waltz* (1938), which was based on Moss Hart's 1934 engaging stage libretto set to the music of the Strausses, Junior and Senior, of her homeland.

A Career Is Born. The first 30 minutes of the three-hour film could easily have been condensed into a mere five or ten minutes without compromising its artistry. In fact, omitting altogether the scenes where William Powell, as the young Ziegfeld, refuses to help his father, Joseph Cawthorne (Dr. Florenz Ziegfeld), operate his Chicago Musical College would have improved the pace of the picture immeasurably. So would thinning out his feeble attempt to make a quick mark on the carnival business by promoting muscleman Eugene Sandow (Nat Pendleton) at the 1893 Chicago World's Fair, while dreaming of spending his life in glorification of female splendor.

Also tiring are his duplicitous dealings with Frank Morgan (Billings), through which he grabs up the most sparkling of talents from under his competitor's nose. It is when Powell beats Morgan to the punch in hiring Luise Rainer (Anna Held) that the film takes hold of the audience. Widely known abroad for the song "I Just Can't Make My Eyes Behave," Luise impresses Powell with her rendition of "Won't You Come and Play with Me?" in a Paris theater. Although insolvent, he succeeds through disingenuousness to coax her into signing on the dotted line with vague promises of making her a superstar on the other side of the Atlantic.

In 1896 he works her into *The Parlor Match* at New York's Herald Square Theatre, the money for which he had borrowed from financier Diamond Jim Brady, a fellow bon vivant renowned for his gargantuan appetite and highly publicized love affair with the chubby actress Lillian Russell, portrayed fleetingly in the film by Ruth Gillette. The tune inserted into the show, actually the signature song of the real-life Anna Held, is "It's Delightful to Be Married," with words by Anna and music by Vincent Scotto. Even that melodious little cream puff is unable to sell enough tickets, resulting in the first of bookkeeper Samston's (Reginald Owen) perennial warnings that his pound-foolish employer is doomed to outspend himself into oblivion.

Ziegfeld promptly changes course from worrying about ticket sales to selling his star to the public. Henceforth, she will bear his imprint, succumbing to his every alteration of her personality to conform to American tastes. In effect, the domineering producer is out to turn a sparrow into an eagle, a kitten into a lioness. Elocution coaches are hired to improve her diction, so that her frequent mispronunciations are intelligible to English-speaking audiences; other specialists concentrate on her wispy singing voice. Ziegfeld himself instructs her on how to win the support of reporters by ingratiating herself with the press.

Under his guidance, Luise becomes a much-admired beauty and fashion plate, conscripting ordinary women into immersing themselves in milk baths and wearing copycat dresses and hats. Her coiffeurs become as widely imitated as those of contemporary dancer Irene Castle, her only rival as a trendsetter. All the while, Ziegfeld appeases her discomfiture by showering her with orchids, jewels, and glowing compliments on the success of her makeover, which he alone had engineered. The spotlight becomes her constant companion, off-stage as well as on, and her every public appearance worthy of unprecedented adulation, which this basically shy young lady with meager talent abhors with such intensity that she eventually falls victim to emotional instability. Despite intuitive and external warnings that Powell is an unrepentant ladies' man, Luise marries him. Their years together were not always delightful, but she remained deeply in love with him, even after he excludes her from his first showgirl-jammed production—the 1907 Follies. Although the screenplay hints that their wedding occurred about that year, it actually took place some 10 years earlier, in 1897. The union of the producer and his star performer naturally prompts visions by his chorus girls of similar matchmaking possibilities between themselves and other notable theatrical personages. Among the beauties is Virginia Bruce (Audrey Dane), a bit player in *The Love Parade* and possessor of filmdom's most seductive eyes, who in time would be the chief cause of the breakup of her employer's marriage. Playing a part similar to that of Lana Turner in *Ziegfeld Girl*, Virginia is the perfect recreation of the Ziegfeld girl gone wrong, impatiently awaiting opportunities to be wined, dined, and lavished with enough diamonds, for which she admits she would sell her soul, to insure a lifetime of financial security.

Having again depleted his funds through profligate personal and professional spending, Ziegfeld appeals to Morgan, now associated with the successful producing firm of [Marc] Klaw & [Abraham Lincoln] Erlanger, to lend him the money needed to launch his Follies. Morgan encourages Paul Irving (Erlanger) to ante it up, and Powell quickly drains it like water through a sieve to pay the inordinate expenses of outfitting the show with the finest of costumes, sets, and personnel. He opens the show on schedule at his New Amsterdam The-

atre, where he also maintained his office and produced his Midnight Frolics and Nine O'-Clock revues on the roof garden. Appearing in his 1907 Follies, which actually opened at the New York Theatre, are Eddie Cantor and Will Rogers, each nicely impersonated by Buddy Doyle and A.A. Trimble, respectively, even though neither star actually appeared in a Follies till 1917.

The continual specter of bankruptcy hovering over his head is unable to dissuade Ziegfeld from producing still bigger annual editions of his Follies, finally culminating in 1919. Intent on celebrating in his own unique way the end of World War I, he poured all his cash and headiest talent into the show. Stupendous was the word for it. The Irving Berlin songs included "A Pretty Girl Is Like a Melody," "Mandy" (dropped in 1918 from the songwriter's wartime revue, *Yip, Yip, Yaphank*), "You'd Be Surprised," and "I've Got My Captain Working for Me Now." Among the stars were Cantor, Eddie Dowling, Marilyn Miller, [Gus] Van & [Joe] Schenck, and Bert Williams.

In 1919 "Pretty Girl" was sung by John Steel. In MGM's recreation, it is performed on one of the largest sets ever built for a musical movie. So spectacular is it that it fairly boggles the mind and overwhelms the eye. In the center is a bulging cone-shaped edifice that resembles a birthday cake baked for a giant that revolves against a black backdrop seeded with stars. Atop it all stands Miss Bruce, gowned in a white formal dress that shimmers in the gentle fan-blown breeze, looking all the world like a fairy princess peering down majestically from Mount Olympus.

About 150 singers, dancers, and instrumentalists gorgeously costumed in tux and top hat and Marie Antoinette ballroom dresses take turns descending the long circular staircase while performing snippets from Puccini, Mendelssohn, Johann Strauss, and Leoncavallo, as well as a portion of Gershwin's *Rhapsody in Blue*. The handsome and unknown Stanley Morner mouths the "Pretty Girl" lyric, although the tenor voice singing it belonged to Allan Jones. Then a recent addition to the MGM roster, Jones in 1936 would star as Ravenal in *Show Boat* for Universal, and the next year with Jeanette MacDonald in MGM's own *The Firefly*. The wavy-haired Mr. Morner in

1939 would change his name to Dennis Morgan for his first Warner Bros. film, *Waterfront*. The entire "Melody" production is unquestionably overcooked. Still, it serves as an unsurpassed example of Hollywood glitz and ingenuity at their high-water marks. It was clear that MGM had accepted the crown as Ziegfeld's successor, even though the master himself would have been incapable of duplicating this production number on stage.

When Luise visits Virginia backstage to applaud her performance in the "You Never Looked So Beautiful (Before)" beauty parade, she finds sufficient evidence to regard the calculating chorine as her most serious rival yet for Powell's love. The dressing room is filled with flowers, and on Virginia's arm is a diamond bracelet that closely resembles the one Powell had given Luise during their courtship days. Both gifts, Virginia asserts a little too defensively, were given to her by an "old friend." As far as Luise is concerned, there is no need to identify the friend. But she is too timid to retaliate against either mistress or husband. Rather, her response is philosophical: how could Powell possibly remain faithful when he's surrounded day-in, night-out by successive bevies of the most beautiful girls in America?

Unfortunately for Virginia, she is as attracted to booze as to diamonds. She is obviously drunk when she makes her curtain speech after a New Amsterdam roof show. Appalled that anyone would insult him and his show with such "disgusting" conduct, Powell promptly fires her. He then rushes headlong into signing up new acts to add still more sparkle to his Follies. Among his first recruits is Sally Manners, an unbilled knockout blonde whom he hires on the spot. A ringer for Marilyn Miller, who made her Broadway debut in *The Passing Show of 1914* and in 1920 played the title role in *Sally*, she disappears quickly from the script without singing the song most closely identified with her. That pleasant task, performed by Miss Miller herself in the filmed *Sally* in 1929, would be postponed until 1946, when Judy Garland sang Jerome Kern's "Look for the Silver Lining" in her cameo role as Miss Miller in *Till the Clouds Roll By*. Three years later, June Haver, as Miss Miller, would reprise it with Gordon MacRae in the "autobiographical" *Look for the Silver Lining*.

Also signed up is the incomparable Fanny Brice, whose career highlights would be anthologized 40 years later by Barbra Streisand in *Funny Girl* and *Funny Lady*. Impressed with Fanny's on-stage rendition of Irving Berlin's "Yiddle on Your Fiddle, Play Some Ragtime," Powell presents her with a $2,700 mink coat, first to prove that he is indeed the big shot he says he is, and second to coerce her into joining his troupe. Questioned by an associate on the wisdom of signing up a performer from burlesque, Powell settles the matter by correctly observing that "some of the greatest stars came from there."

A mile-wide sentimental streak creeps into the script that, although entirely appropriate in 1936, tends to date the film even more than the wardrobe and songs. It appears in the person of Jean Chatburn (Mary Lou), who as a child, played by Ann Gillis, had been a frequent visitor to Dr. Ziegfeld's music studio and had offered to marry Powell once she grows up. Now, as a highly attractive adult and theater junkie, she is instantly taken under his protective wing, and he adopts a fatherly hands-off policy while planning a dancing career for her.

Enter Billie Burke. In the early twenties, Powell decides to begin producing shows with story lines in addition to his Follies. His treasury again depleted, he luckily receives a fresh infusion of funds from Morgan, again via the good graces of Erlanger. Shortly afterward, at a formal dance at the Astor Hotel, he meets Billie Burke, portrayed by Myrna Loy in the landmark role of a screen actress playing a living celebrity. Although she had never met him, she is aware of the producer's skirt-chasing exploits, from which she had deduced that he was "bald and pudgy." Powell pours on his indisputable charm that evening and steals her away from her escort, Morgan, who had plans of his own to steal her away from producer Charles Frohman (who actually died in the sinking of the *Lusitania* in 1915), with whom she was under exclusive contact. After several clandestine meetings, Myrna accepts Powell's proposal, and they are married across the Hudson in Hoboken, New Jersey.

Luise is devastated when she learns of the wedding in the newspapers. Her professional as well as personal life had disintegrated into stupefying purposelessness without the guiding hand of her estranged lover and mentor. Even after their divorce, Luise had kept alive the furtive hope that somehow, someday, he would return to her as the dutiful husband she still wants him to be. Nonetheless, she forces herself to telephone Powell and congratulate him. Only a closeup of her face is seen throughout the brief conversation scene, so perfect in mingling sorrow and bewilderment that it succeeds in erasing all the film's deficiencies and more than anything else insured Miss Ranier's winning the best actress Oscar.

Anguished as she is, she manages to convey her best wishes to him without the slightest hint of resentment. Her tearful eyes reflecting desperation, she controls her expectation of lifelong loneliness by engaging in a happy-talk résumé of the joyful existence she is about to enter. She's going back to Paris, she tells Powell. Yes, she'll be appearing in new shows over there. And yes, yes, she's divinely happy, too. "Goodbye, Flo," she whispers into the receiver and then falls sobbing onto her bed. Thus ends the single greatest piece of acting by any performer in any individual scene in the history of the film musical. Actually, Anna Held died in 1918, five years after divorcing Ziegfeld. She telephoned him on her deathbed, but he arrived at her side shortly after she died.

According to the screenplay, Powell, Myrna, and their daughter, Patricia, lived together in unalloyed happiness throughout most of the twenties. Most of his shows were hits, and he accumulated another fortune, only to fritter it away on countless gifts to wife and child that only a man with a sultan's wealth could possibly afford for very long. When his theatrical largess disappears in the stock market crash of 1929, Myrna hands back the jewels he had given her over the years to pawn and subsidize his plan to produce bigger and better shows. But the heavy toll of aging and worry has immobilized him. Luckily, her acting career earns enough to keep the family together, even if not in the luxury to which they had become accustomed.

The master showman's final film visitor is Morgan, no longer his rival, but softened into a reliable old friend on a visit to reminisce about the good old days, contentious as most of them were. Although also wiped out on Wall Street—a fact that Powell realizes but never mentions—Morgan continues to prop up his friend's nebulous hopes by offering to form a new 50-50 production partnership. Unlike other speculators, he assures Powell, he was smart enough to get out of the market "right in time." Oh sure, he lost a little money—didn't everybody?—but Morgan still has plenty left to finance their future. Then, strengthening the ties binding them together, they exchange memories—of Powell's Sandow *vs.* Morgan's "Little Egypt" carnival days, of Luise, of so many highs and lows on bygone Broadway that must forever live only in memory.

Just get well, Morgan pleads before he departs, and together they'll stage all those shows that each knows full well will never be brought to life. While Powell remains slumped in his chair, valet Ernest Cossart (Sidney) regales him with recollections of his past triumphs, which Cossart describes as the "finest things ever done on the stage," while major songs from many of them are played in the background. Cossart briefly leaves his side to answer the telephone and assure Myrna that her husband "seems to be resting comfortably." But his cheery evaluation is merely wishful thinking. Powell's right hand falls limp from the arm of the chair. Seconds later, the orchid he had pressed between his fingers slips to the floor. The Great Ziegfeld is dead.

The tragedy, however, is not limited to that one man. Only minutes earlier he had defined the word in larger terms when he posed a question to Morgan that applies to every living person, whether dreamer or doer, whose life is cut short while it still bristles with ambition: "Why," Powell had asked wistfully, "in a world so old, must life be so short?"

Three Smart Girls (1936)

A Universal picture. DIRECTOR: Henry Koster; ASSISTANT: Frank Shaw. EXECUTIVE PRODUCER: Charles R. Rogers; ASSOCIATE: Joe Pasternak. ORIGINAL STORY AND SCREENPLAY: Adele Commandini. CINEMATOGRAPHER: Joseph Valentine; SPECIAL EFFECTS: John P. Fulton. FILM EDITOR: Ted Kent. ART SUPERVISOR: John Harkrider; ASSOCIATES: Jack O. Hearson and Albert

Deanna Durbin tries to win father Charles Winninger's attention by serenading him with the song "Someone to Care for Me" in *Three Smart Girls.*

Nickels (gowns). SOUND SUPERVISOR: Homer Tasker. MUSICAL DIRECTOR: Charles Previn. ORIGINAL SONGS: Lyrics by Gus Kahn, music by Bronislau Kaper and Walter Jurmann. *Principal Players*: Deanna Durbin (Penny). Binnie Barnes (Donna "Precious" Lyons). Charles Winninger (Judson Craig). Alice Brady (Mrs. Lyons). Ray Milland (Lord Michael Stuart). Mischa Auer (Count Arisztid). Ernest Cossart (Binns). Nan Grey (Joan). Barbara Read (Kay). Lucile Watson (Martha). Nella Walker (Mrs. [Dorothy] Judson Craig). John King (Bill Evans). *Major Academy Award Nominations*: Best Picture; Original Story.

The 1930s introduced more gifted youngsters who dominated their films than any other decade before or since. They were irresistible as catnip, combining precociousness with endearing young charms, yet none of them came close to racking up the 150-plus appearances of Baby Peggy (Montgomery) in silent two-reelers and feature films. But a respectable number of them saw service in an array of popular, and sometimes prestigious, dramas of the Depression era, as well as in an astonishing number of frothy albeit pleasurable musicals. Standing tall in the crowd of talented youngsters was Canadian-born Edna Mae Durbin, who, thanks to frequent appearances on Eddie Cantor's weekly radio program, was summoned to Culver City, California, by MGM bigwigs to appear with another early adolescent newcomer, Judy Garland, in the 1936 featurette *Every Sunday.*

Born Frances Ethel Gumm and pushed into a musical career beginning at age three by a stage-obsessed mother, Judy and her two older sisters were groomed from babyhood for vaudeville. By 1929 Judy had appeared in at least one filmed short feature. Acting on George Jessel's suggestion, the child's surname had been changed by then to Garland, and she herself had altered her first name to the far more euphonious Judy. Perhaps because of her almost total unfamiliarity with the carefree joys of childhood, she projected a genuine and unaffected wistfulness for those missed years that only grew more intense as she grew into adulthood.

The wafer-thin plot of *Every Sunday* foreshadowed Deanna's later *One Hundred Men and a Girl* by presenting both youngsters as singing advocates of restoring the popularity of band concerts in a local park. Hopping uninvited onto the orchestra's gazebo platform, the girls vocalize several selections that unsurprisingly click with the meager audience, which the next time out swells to SRO size and rescues the instrumentalists from the threat of joblessness. Deanna concentrates on the classics, Judy tantalizes the jitterbug set by adding pep to the proceedings with swing tunes.

The result of the short bill-filler was the birth of two new stars whose youthful energy, charm, and extraordinarily effective performances in featherweight roles recruited vast numbers of admiring fans who kept the girls in business well into adulthood. Universal signed Deanna to a long-term contract, while MGM retained Judy. The prototype of the adolescent swinger, Judy helped to keep bouncy rhythms very much alive in her younger days, as, for example, with her late-thirties rendition of "Swing Mr. Mendelssohn," Gus Kahn, Bronislau Kaper, and Walter Jurmann's rug-cutter that so alienated her anti-hep cat middle-age teacher in *Everybody Sing*. Deanna remained sedate, so much so that she was considered to supply the off-screen speaking and singing voice of Snow White, which went instead to the totally unknown Adriana Caselotti, who later played a bit part in *The Wizard of Oz*.

Profitable as her earliest feature films were, Deanna never appeared on the honor roll of Hollywood's Top Ten moneymakers, although Judy made it twice, ranking tenth in 1940 and eighth in 1945. Following Deanna's screen outing in the anemic *For the Love of Mary* in 1948, she unexpectedly retired, even though at the time she was among Hollywood's highest-salaried actresses. Like Grace Moore, Deanna was beset with weight problems, which undoubtedly contributed to her decision to quit, as it did to MGM's forcing Judy into temporary retirement after *Summer Stock*—and 14 years' solid service with the studio—in 1950. Judy's temper tantrums, which plagued her throughout most of her adult life and often disrupted shooting schedules, also influenced her eventual dismissal.

Deanna was quite capable of handling operatic arias, a talent that Judy never displayed, as well as romantic ballads. The former's remarkable soprano voice complimented the essential sweetness of her characterizations, although the finest of her sorties into light classics would not occur until 1943, when she revived Victor Herbert's "When You're Away," complete with the rarely heard verse and coda, written in 1914 for the operetta *The Only Girl*, in splendid fashion in *His Butler's Sister*.

Over the course of their film careers, Deanna and Judy introduced 10 Academy Award nominations for best song. Six were by Judy ("Over the Rainbow," "Our Love Affair" [with Mickey Rooney], "How About You?" [also with Rooney], "The Trolley Song," "On the Atchison, Topeka and Santa Fe," and "The Man That Got Away." Deanna's were "My Own," "Waltzing in the Clouds," "Say a Pray'r for the Boys Over There," and "More and More." As their titles indicate, both girls' songs centered almost exclusively on young love, which Deanna approached with eagerness, Judy with anxiety. In 1938 Deanna shared a Special Academy Award with Mickey Rooney for "Personifying the Spirit of Youth"; in 1940 Judy won hers as the Best Juvenile Performer of 1939.

Sadly, the grown-up Deanna was heiress to the same misfortune that has afflicted other one-time child stars: she was cast in a string of mostly second-rate films that dampened enthusiasm for more and brought her career to an undistinguished end. But Deanna's singing voice suffered no diminution over the years, and it continued to enchant audiences in such later musical pictures as *Can't Help Singing* (1944), featuring a sprightly score by E.Y. Harburg and Jerome Kern, *Something in the Wind* (1945), which debuted Johnny Green's melodic title song, and *Up in Central Park*, the disappointing black-and-white 1948 film version of the 1945 Broadway hit operetta, with lyrics by Dorothy Fields and music by Sigmund Romberg.

Like the fan battles over who was the better singer, Crosby or Sinatra, or the better dancer, Astaire or Gene Kelly, the frequent Durbin *vs.* Garland comparisons are rendered null and void when each is observed closely in her respective films. Both were equally adept at comedy and portraying unsophisticated ingenues with hearts more seeing than eyes. It was at that point, however, that their careers took off in different directions. Deanna fairly twinkled as the ebullient teenager, only briefly dismayed by a reversal of fortune. Cheerfulness marked the true north of her Depression courage, an incalculable asset in keeping other people's hopelessness in remission. Judy's most endearing quality was her lack of experience in coping with problems too complex for her teenage characters to untangle. Deanna was exuberant and robust; Judy was fragile, her wistfulness reflecting the turmoil of the girl child wandering adrift on the threshold of adulthood, unprepared and thus apprehensive of entering life's unchartered territory.

When it came to devising plots to rescue family and friends, Deanna was the instigator, Judy the chin-up follower. It was no accident that Judy's tears were self-centered, springing from the pain of disillusionment. Deanna's, on the other hand, were typically tears of joy, shed in gleeful reaction to the successful conclusion of her latest crusade to lead her elders onto the path of enlightened conduct. Unlike Deanna, Judy was a gifted toe dancer, partnering with such terpsichorean wonders as Astaire (once), George Murphy (twice), and Gene Kelly (thrice).

Unquestionably one of the screen's all-time most compelling performers, Judy blossomed into a far superior dramatic actress, easily verifiable by her appearance at the age of 23 as a lonely New York working girl in *The Clock* (1945), as Mrs. Norman Maine in Warner Bros.' 1954 musical remake of *A Star Is Born*, and as Irene Hoffman in *Judgment at Nuremberg* in 1962, for which she earned a best supporting actress nomination. Deanna was simply unable to measure up to any significant degree, despite a valiant attempt as the lover of murderer Gene Kelly in *Christmas Holiday*. An ill-conceived 1945 melodrama, the film further alienated fans who were offended by listening to their darling's renditions of blues songs in a seedy nightclub.

Adolescents rather than child stars—each was 13 when *Every Sunday* was made—both girls qualified as majorettes in Hollywood's immense parade of doll-like princes and princesses who marched through the thirties with engaging bravado and style. Their presence multiplied quickly with the frequency of films dealing with the ravaging effects of the economic turmoil on families unable to provide a safety net for their children, the most vulnerable of Depression victims. Few stars of the time surpassed Deanna in projecting boundless enthusiasm to set things right. Addicted to adopting a chipper outlook even when her well-laid plans went awry, she ran rather than walked through her earliest parts, especially when propelled by a scheme to resuscitate hope in persons who had placed their trust in her ingenuity to bail them out of their latest predicament.

Movieland's Junior Set. From Jackie Coogan, who became an instant box office powerhouse with his appearance at age seven opposite Charlie Chaplin in *The Kid*, in 1921, to the studiously adorable Margaret O'Brien in the 1940s and Macaulay Culkin in more recent years, Hollywood's pre-pubescent performers have long occupied a special niche in the history of motion pictures, at times surpassing the popularity of even the most prominent adult stars. On the dramatic front, the precociousness of Jackie Cooper became evident when he was teamed with the formidable Wallace Beery in such early-1930s tearjerkers as *The Champ*, hoping against hope to light the fire of redemption in a burned-out has-been, and *Treasure Island*, struggling to reform a gruff but soft-hearted career pirate.

Freddie Bartholomew, born in Ireland and reared in England, scored a personal triumph at age 11 in *David Copperfield* (1935), especially in his encounters with the cruel Mr. Murdstone (Basil Rathbone) and the impoverished but undauntedly optimistic Mr. Micawber (W.C. Fields). Mickey Rooney, whose Hollywood days began when he was seven with an inconsequential appearance in the 1927 silent film *Orchids and Ermine*, displayed a talent that approached genius in *Slave Ship* (1936), *Captains Courageous* (1937), and *Boys Town*, the latter two in company with Spencer Tracy, who took home successive Oscars for his performances. Indicating a natural bent for comedy, Rooney was as perfectly cast as the tribulation-prone son of Judge and Mrs. James Hardy in the long-running Andy Hardy series as Gable was for the part of Rhett Butler in *Gone with the Wind*.

Anne Shirley, born Dawn Evelynee Paris and billed as Dawn O'Day in silent pictures, proved her worth as an actress in *Anne of Green Gables* in 1934. She received nomination as best supporting actress of 1937 for her role as Barbara Stanwyck's young daughter, Laurel, in *Stella Dallas*. Lifted intact from Broadway were the street-smart Dead End Kids, whose rambunctious presence in the 1937 film version of *Dead End* identified the slums, in particular those bordering the East River in midtown Manhattan, as fertile breeding grounds for criminals. Some of the Kids, notably Leo Gorcey and Huntz Hall, Bobby Jordan and Gabriel Dell, grew up into the Little Tough Guys, East Side Kids, and finally Bowery Boys. Fifteen-year-old Bonita Granville in 1938 took obvious delight in solving mysteries as the girl detective Nancy Drew, while Marcia Mae Jones (*These Three*, *Heidi*) and Sybil Jason (*Little Big Shot*, *The Little Princess*) each exhibited acting skill that belied their tender years. Then there was little Bobs Watson—Mickey Rooney's pint-size pal in *Boys Town*—actually an excellent child actor whose perennially tearful face made him the decade's most consistent, and outstanding, weeper.

Similarly appealing to 1930s audiences were gradeschoolers Spanky McFarland and his *Our Gang* cohorts and Dickie Moore, who played alongside such top-ranking stars as Greta Garbo and Paul Muni; and such nestlings as Davey Lee, Al Jolson's "Sonny Boy," the Dionne Quintuplets, Baby Leroy (Overacker), the pint-size nemesis of W.C. Fields, and Baby Sandy (Sandra Lea Henville), whom Bing Crosby lullabied to sleep in 1939 with Johnny Burke and James V. Monaco's "That Sly Old Gentleman (from Featherbed Lane)" in *East Side of Heaven*.

Mitzi Green retired from the screen at age 14, but not before entertaining audiences in *Tom Sawyer* (1930) and *Little Orphan Annie* (1932). In 1937, reversing the usual Broadway-to-Hollywood route to name recognition, Mitzi won a prominent part in the Rodgers and Hart stage show *Babes in Arms*, and it was she who first sang two of its biggest song hits, "Where or When" and "The Lady Is a Tramp."

Before entering into a brief career as a teenage singer in 1942, Ann Gillis replayed Mitzi's roles as Becky Thatcher and Little Orphan Annie in the 1938 remakes of both films, and played Deanna's kid sister in *Nice Girl?* (1941). In 1936 Edith Fellows, who was equally gifted in brat and wallflower roles in both musicals and dramas, was on the receiving end of another Crosby song, Burke and Arthur Johnston's priceless "Pennies from Heaven."

Musicals especially provided abundant employment opportunities for such juveniles as boy soprano Bobby Breen. Like Deanna, he was born in Canada and attracted nationwide attention through regular appearances on Eddie Cantor's radio program in 1936. (Cantor later ignited the careers of singers Dinah Shore and Eddie Fisher.) Bobby quickly became to RKO what Deanna was to Universal and Judy to MGM. Tomboy Jane Withers co-starred in a dozen minor but enjoyable Fox musicals up to 1940, gaining admission to the bottom half of the Top Ten list in 1937 and 1938.

Gloria Jean and Virginia Weidler neatly balanced each other's strong points, with Gloria excelling as singer but not actress, and Virginia honing her undisputed acting prowess in numerous dramas while never making the grade as singer or dancer. Discovered by producer Joe Pasternak, Gloria in fact was signed in 1938 by Universal as a replacement for Deanna, who was getting a bit too old for juvenile parts.

None of these gifted pre-teens and adolescents, or any male or female adult star for that matter, was able throughout the latter half of the decade to overcome the stiff competition generated by Shirley Temple, Fox's triple-threat youngster with the killer dimples and genuinely unique talent for acting as well as singing and dancing. Beginning her career at 3½ in a series of "Baby Burlesk" satirical shorts, she shot up in the popularity polls beginning in 1934, and the next year became the youngest performer ever to win an Oscar, the Honorary Juvenile Award, voted by the Academy's board of governors. Testifying to her immense world-wide popularity was her six-time appearance on the Top Ten list, including four consecutive years as filmdom's number one attraction, a distinction never duplicated by any other performer under the age of 21, and rarely ever by anyone older than that. (Only Bing Crosby and

Burt Reynolds have topped her successive top-of-the-list rankings with five each.)

She was the curly-headed moppet who confined the great Gable to second-place rank in the polls from 1936 through 1938, and the only Hollywood star to have her most popular films released on videocassette in both black-and-white and colorized versions. Still the most popular child star of all time, Shirley, like Deanna and Judy, continued in later years to share the limelight with many of Hollywood's top-ranking adult stars, from Joseph Cotten and Cary Grant to Ronald Reagan and John Wayne, until her voluntary retirement at age 21 in 1949.

Three Smart Girls Grow Up, the equally diverting Henry Koster-directed 1939 sequel to *Three Smart Girls*, is unique in that Universal dropped Barbara Read in favor of former *Our Gang* actress Helen Parrish in the role of sister Kay. Deanna and Nan Grey repeat their roles as the other two daughters of Nella Walker and Charles Winninger, who has become even more the absent-minded tycoon during the three-year lapse between films. The family's living quarters is an estate worthy of a Vanderbilt or Rockefeller.

Deanna's quest consists of conspiring with her father to make certain that her older sisters' love affairs result in selecting the proper mates to insulate their lifelong happiness. In *It Happened One Night* fashion, Nan deserts William Lundigan at the altar to marry Robert Cummings, her true love, while Helen picks up from where Nan left off, continuing the march down the aisle arm in arm with Lundigan. Former sister Barbara's romance with Ray Milland in *Three Smart Girls*, which bore strong traces of culminating in the exchange of marriage vows, is conveniently overlooked in the sequel by dropping both from the cast. Universal probably assumed that no one would notice or, if so, care. Without any new songs at her disposal, Deanna sings von Weber's "Invitation to the Dance," the traditional "Last Rose of Summer," and Edward Teschemacher-Guy d'Hardelot's "Because," from 1902.

In 1948, under the title *Three Daring Daughters*, the story of the *Three Smart Girls* was remade by MGM. It was Jeanette MacDonald's next to last film. Playing Deanna's role in her fourth film was Jane Powell, then 19 and also an excellent light music singer. Appropriately, the producer of the remake was Joe Pasternak, the associate producer of the Durbin vehicle.

Wealthy but Troubled. It is clear at the outset of *Three Smart Girls* that the film is going to concern itself with the travails of the moneyed class. They, too, the screenplay indicates, were faced with their own particular set of Depression-bred problems, quite different from those confronting the low- and no-income groups lodged in the economic cellar, to be sure, but nonetheless worthy of investigation, even sympathy. According to the movies, the primary problem of the destitute was how best to defer their dreams without discarding them while awaiting the return of prosperity; the primary preoccupation of the well-to-do in 1936 was holding on to their assets in a country that was barely holding its head above economic stagnation, had borne witness to a rash of corporate receiverships and bankruptcies, and had fixed the top federal income tax rate at 70 percent.

The difficulties the richest Americans faced in escaping financial ruin was made even more precarious by the oversupply of clever schemers intent on looting their treasuries through either fraud (à la Mischa Auer) or loveless marriage (à la Binnie Barnes and Alice Brady). *Three Smart Girls* concentrates on the wiles of these three characters, and by upsetting their applecarts, upholds such I-beams of traditional family life as compassion and solidarity.

That Deanna and her older sisters, Nan Grey (Joan) and Barbara Read (Kay), are children of privilege is apparent in the first scene. On vacation in Switzerland, Nan and Barbara are lazily cruising a scenic lake while Deanna entertains by serenading them with the melodious "My Heart Is Singing," the first of the two newly written songs composed by Bronislau Kaper and Walter Jurmann, who specialized in Durbin songs throughout much of their film tenure. Two very competent but unprolific composers, they were charter members of Deanna's Universal film family, along with director Koster, producers Rogers and Pasternak, Frank Shaw, and Charles Previn, who participated in many of the young lady's films into the early forties.

After swimming to shore, the happy threesome are distressed to learn from their nanny (Lucile Watson) that their father, Charles Winninger, the original Cap'n Andy in the 1927 *Show Boat*, is planning to remarry. The girls are not exactly devastated by the news, since mother Nella Walker, as regal and handsome a mature woman as ever appeared on the screen, has been divorced from Winninger for the past 10 years. Later, however, when Nella succumbs to tears while confirming their father's intention to remarry, her daughters realize that her love for him has not dimmed over the years of separation. Under the spell of Deanna's immense powers of persuasion, Lucile agrees to pay their fares to New York and chaperon them while they embark on their intrigue to break up Winninger's engagement to Binnie Barnes (Donna Lyons) and return him to their mother's arms.

Contrasting starkly with the dismal living quarters seen in many thirties musicals and dramas, Winninger's apartment on Park Avenue and East 60th Street is so posh that it houses a private gymnasium, pointing up the fact that not all families of the time were confined to decaying *Grapes of Wrath* hovels or *Mannequin* tenements. Perhaps because of Deanna's aristocratic looks and bearing, most of her early pictures included at least one luxurious backdrop, none of them more imposing than the family mansion in *That Certain Age* (1938) and the one inhabited by Charles Laughton in *It Started with Eve* (1941). Like Jeanette MacDonald, she gave the impression that, although not always to the manor born, she belonged in palatial surroundings, if only as a visitor. A major challenge of *Three Smart Girls* was to make the economic royalists who occupied the castles and duplexes on the Hudson fit candidates for the sympathy of audiences that, except for their movie house visits, had never seen the interior of an upper-class home.

That objective is achieved by Winninger's natural gift for blending comedy with the authoritarianism of a well-heeled but hazy business executive unable to remember without prodding anything that had occurred before yesterday. When told by his butler, Binns, played by the excellent character actor Ernest

Cossart, that his daughters had telephoned to say they were on their way over to his apartment, Winninger is uncertain of the exact number of daughters he sired, their names, why they want to see him, or where they have been for such a long time. True to his penchant for retreating into business or love affairs to escape personal crises, he rushes out of the apartment to keep a luncheon date with Binnie. But his disappearing act proves to be futile when Cossart tells the girls of their father's whereabouts. He also signs on as faithful ally after they explain the reason for their visit and assures them that he will help however he can to bring their parents back together.

The following scene focuses on a nervous Winninger and an impatient Binnie chatting at a restaurant table. He has something to tell her but at the moment is unable to find the right words. Finally, he blurts them out: he has not one, not two, but three children, and they're all girls. Anticipating trouble, Binnie is started by the revelation, and her tight-lipped displeasure is compounded when the three daughters rush over to the table, erupting into squeals of joy at the sight of their long-absent father. Binnie's usual façade of reserve crumbles in the excitement of the family reunion, only to be further ground into dust when the young ladies dominate the conversation by referring constantly to their mother.

Pouting with exasperation, she becomes a party pooper by stalking out of the restaurant and leaving Winninger to his annoying offspring. Barbara, meanwhile, had excused herself to send a telegram to mother Nella telling of her daughters' safe arrival in New York. At the Western Union office, she meets a very young Ray Milland, one of filmdom's handsomest leading players, whose overtures to her are repulsed not from lack of interest on Barbara's part, but from her inexperience at engaging in the rituals of flirtation.

Eager to get their hands on a bundle of money and fulfill their social-climbing ambitions, Binnie and mother Alice Brady agree to placate Winninger by playing up to his daughters at dinner the next evening. "Girls mean trouble," Alice had warned Binnie that afternoon, advising that every effort must be made to defang them by winning their affection, no matter how distasteful the process. Deanna, however, keeps punctuating the dinner conversation with reminiscences of the girls' mother in far-off Switzerland, adding an embarrassing coda to her running commentary by purposely spilling a glass of wine over Alice's evening gown. The result is Winninger's sending her off to bed like the naughty child Alice and Binnie are convinced she is.

Upstairs, Deanna decides to change bedrooms to escape Lucile's snoring. Instead of crawling beneath the blankets of her substitute bed—a Louis XV antique, no less— Deanna proceeds to take it apart, slamming the boards on the floor in a deliberate attempt to drown out Binnie's singing voice. Reacting to Binnie's complaint, Winninger hurries up to Deanna, who escapes a bawling out by enlisting his help in putting the bed back together again. The ensuing commotion, coupled with Deanna's soprano shrieks at her father's inability to fathom the complexities of the task, brings smiles to Alice's and Binnie's faces. They wrongly interpret the clatter as evidence that Winninger is administering a well-deserved spanking to his attention-craving daughter.

Seeking Fatherly Comfort. After the bed is finally assembled, Winninger sits on it while Deanna sings the melodious "Someone to Care for Me." Hers is an excellent version, far superior to Binnie's, which, according to the youngster's insightful diagnosis, was strictly below par. The tender Gus Kahn lyric is among his best, even though the song failed to register very high on popularity charts, largely because of the intense competition from about 200 other notable songs written for the screen and stage or independently throughout 1936.

The words are actually a subtle cry from an early teenager for guidance in matters of the heart, with which she is totally unfamiliar. One parent alone cannot steer any young girl in the right direction by providing all the advice she needs to contend with the hazards of falling in love either too early or with the wrong suitor. The song is, in effect, an appeal for family togetherness, complete with a caring father and mother who are always available to offer counseling based on their individual experiences.

Winninger is touched by Deanna's message, but too deeply involved in financial and Binnie matters to recognize it as an appeal to conscience.

Meanwhile, a handsome young male named Bill Evans, played poorly by John King, who manages Winninger's investments, visits the apartment and strikes up an acquaintance with sisters Nan and Barbara. They tell him of their disenchantment with their father's impending marriage, quickly winning him to their side in the crusade to thwart it. In Barbara's view, Binnie has been coached by Alice on how to inveigle Winninger into marriage not out of love, but in order to get their sticky hands on his money. The solution, King maintains, is to find another man even wealthier than their father to whom the two money-mad ladies can shift their attention. Luckily, he knows just the man to play the part—Mischa Auer. True, he "drinks like a sponge" and is almost penniless, but he's a certified Hungarian count who has retained enough of his aristocratic heritage to impress anybody. King promises to follow through with the scheme.

Formerly chained to small, insignificant parts as the Sad Russian in a host of mostly second-rate movie dramas, the tremendously versatile Auer was tapped by director Gregory La-Cava in 1936 to play the part of a high-society leech who impersonates a gorilla in *My Man Godfrey*. His standout work earned him an Academy Award nomination as best male supporting actor and a raft of plum roles as a comedian rather than the heavy.

A few days later, while horseback riding in Central Park, Alice and Binnie confront Winninger with still more complaints against his irksome daughters. Unwilling and unable to condone Deanna's recent conduct, he promises to send all three back to Europe the next day. As a farewell party, he suggests that he and the two ladies and his two older daughters go to the Jungle Club that evening. Meanwhile, Auer has agreed to play the part of gigolo in King's anti-Binnie ploy, hungrily accepting the first of his periodic installments of money as payment for his services. Auer is instructed to charm himself into Binnie's confidence and then heart at the nightclub as the first step in tempting her away from Winninger. King gives him a magazine so that Nan and Barbara will recognize him as the newly appointed rival for Binnie's affection.

Not very much intuition was required of audiences to assume that a case of mistaken identity, already as old as the Hollywood Hills, was in the offing. It arises at the Jungle Club bar when a slightly tipsy Auer leaves his seat to go elsewhere else for drinks with an old acquaintance. Unknowingly, he accidentally drops the magazine to the floor, where it is picked up by Milland, who had been chatting with Auer. Barbara catches sight of Milland, magazine in hand, and bolts over to him to explain exactly what he is to do to lure Binnie away from her father. Recognizing her from their brief meeting in the telegraph office, Milland is overjoyed at his recruitment to help her out, although he has not the vaguest idea why he should pretend to be an aristocrat that Barbara and her sisters had met on the Riviera. She admits that she hopes he's up to the challenge, what with his alleged drinking problem and lack of walking-around money.

Actually a rich banker from Australia with only a casual acquaintance with John Barleycorn, Milland cheerfully replies that he'll do his best. He looks upon the plot as a lark and enthusiastically follows orders to the letter. He makes the desired favorable impression on Alice and Binnie, particularly after Winninger confirms the fact that Milland's family not only operates the largest bank in Australia, but also owns practically the whole continent. With that knowledge bubbling in her mind, Binnie coyly responds to Milland's amorous entreaties by giving him her telephone number.

In his hotel suite the next day, Milland receives a call from Barbara, who has become the true object of his affection, not Binnie. She lambastes him for sending both her and Binnie a bouquet of flowers, exclaiming that she does not welcome such deviations from policy, particularly when it is she who is subsidizing the bogus love affair with her own limited funds. While walking with her in Central Park, contrite Milland vows to live up to his part of the bargain by asking Binnie to marry him when they meet that noon for lunch. Instead of rejoicing at the news, Barbara falls into a quandary: she is pleased at his dedication to

the cause, but even her valiant attempt at controlling her emotions cannot disguise a tinge of jealousy. Binnie has unwittingly become her rival.

Rescue and Reconciliation. Also jealous is Winninger, whose fear that Binnie is trending toward an assignation with Milland is compounded when he telephones her and learns from Alice that she is ill. He visits the apartment and, not finding Binnie in bed, becomes alarmed at spying Milland's bouquet of flowers bunched in a vase. Hoping to force Winninger into a quick marriage before playboy Milland, at best a doubtful candidate for marriage, gains the upper hand in what is developing into a three-cornered love affair, Alice intensifies his concern by declaring that most men find her daughter quite desirable. Her plan works. When Binnie enters the apartment, Winninger offers to marry her the next day in Atlantic City, but Binnie puts her enthusiasm on hold. What her mother had interpreted as fondness for Milland is fast developing into passion. Nettled by Binnie's hesitation, Alice agrees to the wedding on her daughter's behalf and telephones the story to a newspaper.

Auer is suffering the pangs of the previous evening's alcoholic interlude with his friend when King arrives to congratulate him on his Jungle Club performance. He is unaware that it is Milland and not Auer who deserves his plaudits. Auer is uncertain of where he was last night and what he had done. But he is pleased that Bill is pleased, regardless of the reason, and he requests and receives $500 more to carry on the game. Later, however, when King learns from Barbara that she also has been subsidizing the fake paramour's activities, he returns to Auer's flat and beats the "chiseler" up.

Depressed at hearing King relate the details of the fisticuffs, Barbara rushes to Milland's apartment to comfort him. She is astounded to find him in good health and spirits, without so much as a scratch on his face. Milland confesses that he does not know King and discloses his true identity. Any hope he had that spilling the beans would bring them closer together backfires when Barbara angrily stalks out of his apartment, trailing a laundry list of epithets, from "liar" to "fraud," in her wake.

Hoping to square things with her and her

sisters, Milland makes a last-ditch attempt to fulfill his obligation to circumvent Winninger's forthcoming marriage. He meets Binnie and gives her three steamship tickets, presumably for a honeymoon trip in Europe for her, him, and Alice. When Binnie tells her mother that Milland had just "more or less" proposed and produces the tickets as evidence, Alice is angry over the switch in marriage plans. "Ten million in the hand is worth $20 million in the bush," she cries, referring obliquely to Winninger, Milland, and Australia, respectively. Besides, in her view, Winninger's advanced age makes him far more likely to die before Milland, opening up a vast inheritance to Binnie before she herself gets much older.

Back at Winninger's apartment, Deanna is in the throes of misery. She is upset over her sisters' rivalry for Milland, which she considers a side issue, as well as over the newspaper story on her father's marriage, now only a day away. She steals into his bedroom and, after hearing that he does love Binnie, stonily refuses to attend the ceremony. She is going away, she tells him, without disclosing where. She simply cannot even imagine how sad her mother's face will be when she reads the wedding announcement. For the second time in the film, Winninger displays fatherly concern for his troubled daughter, this time patently aware that she does need someone to care for her. Tucking her under the covers of a spare cot in the room, he promises that they will have a "nice talk in the morning."

She is not there, however, when Winninger wakes up. Unable to find her in the apartment or building, the frenzied father orders his household staff to search the neighborhood. Deanna is next seen in a police station. Picked up as a runaway, she is posing as an opera singer from Paris newly arrived in New York to sing at the Metropolitan. To convince the gaggle of police officers in the station house, she gives them a sample of her talent by singing a Verdi aria. As her fans fully expected, she sings it extremely well for a 13-year-old. Her uniformed listeners also knew they were in for a musical treat, since they had instantly recognized her as one of Winninger's daughters—the one who's been taking all those singing lessons.

Back in his apartment, Winninger is being upbraided by Alice and Binnie for not sending the sisters back to Switzerland as he had promised, and for not recognizing Deanna's disappearance as just another "trick" to refocus his attention on her. Finally exercising parental protectiveness, Winninger reams both women for their indifference to Deanna's whereabouts and refuses to marry Binnie today or any other day. After they storm out, several police officers enter the apartment with Deanna in tow, and insist that unless Winninger begins to act more like a father than a distant relative, the lawmen will take her back to the station house. He gladly agrees, and father and daughter embrace.

There is a huge bouquet of flowers in Alice and Binnie's steamship cabin, but neither of the highly agitated ladies is the least interested in the posies. What counts is the message on the accompanying card. It expresses Milland's profound regret for not being able to take the voyage with them. He is booked for passage all right, but it is on the next *Queen Elizabeth* trip, not this one. Distraught at losing out on not one but two fortunes, Alice races out of the cabin in hopes of stopping the ship and salvaging Binnie's relationship with Winninger.

In the corridor she bumps into Auer, bandages on his face and one arm in a sling attesting to the beating King had inflicted on him. His conviviality and charm are unscathed, however, and he introduces himself as an unmarried count. That brief autobiographical note is all Alice needs to usher him warmly into her cabin. Eyes aglitter with visions of stacks of greenbacks, she guides him over to Binnie, who is equally enthralled at meeting the newest, and quite possibly the wealthiest, of all the men who have stepped into her life. Poetic justice has won the day. The fraud and the gold diggers are back in business, each competing to grab hold of a fortune that does not exist.

Meanwhile, true love, in the figure of Milland, is the latest visitor to the Winninger apartment. On his way to making amends to Barbara for his duplicity, he catches her in his arms as she runs out the front door, her sadness at supposedly losing the only man she has ever loved to Binnie changing instantly to joy in his warm embrace.

A few days later, as a steamship pulls into a New York dock, Winninger and daughters scour the faces of the passengers about to disembark. They quickly catch sight of Mother

Nella, whose enthusiastic waves provoke cheers of greeting from her family below. Once in their presence, she nervously approaches her former husband, who is equally unsuccessful at tamping down the happiness swelling up inside him at seeing her after a decade of absence. Between them stands Deanna, looking anxiously from one to the other. "Dad," she says, as if introducing the pair for the first time, "I'd like you to meet my mother." The camera then dollies into a closeup of Deanna's angelic face turning from one to the other, tears of happiness streaming down her cheeks like sprinkles of sunlight. Her family is together again, this time for keeps.

One Hundred Men and a Girl (1937)

A Universal picture. DIRECTOR: Henry Koster; ASSISTANT: Frank Shaw. EXECUTIVE PRODUCER: Charles R. Rogers; ASSISTANT: Joe Pasternak. SCREENWRITERS: Bruce Manning, Charles Kenyon, and James Mulhauser, based on a story by Hans Kraly. CINEMATOGRAPHER: Joseph Valentine. FILM EDITOR: Bernard W. Burton. ASSOCIATE MUSICAL DIRECTOR: Charles Previn. VOCAL INSTRUCTOR: Andrés deSegurola. PRODUCTION DESIGNER: John Harkrider. SETS: Jack Martin Smith. SOUND: Homer Tasker. GOWNS: Vera West. ORIGINAL SONG: Lyric by Sam Coslow, music by Frederick Hollander. RUNNING TIME: 1 hour, 24 minutes. *Principal Players*: Deanna Durbin (Patricia Caldwell). Leopold Stokowski (Himself). Adolphe Menjou (John Caldwell). Alice Brady (Mrs. John R. Frost). Eugene Pallette (John R. Frost). Mischa Auer (Michael Borodoff). Billy Gilbert (Garage Owner). Jack Smart (Stage Doorman). Bitters (Jed Prouty). Taxi Driver (Frank Jenks). *Major Academy Award*: Best Scoring. *Nominations*: Best Picture; Original Story; Film Editing; Sound.

Flighty and riddled with sentimental hokum, this film is nonetheless fully deserving of its Academy Award nomination. The economic problems it reflected were certainly serious enough to warrant commentary, and the film fulfilled the obligation to do so by massaging the social consciousness with an appealing light touch. Unlike *Our Daily Bread*, *My Man Godfrey*, or *Dead End*, it was never intended to troll the lower depths of deprivation and worry. But it still stands as one of the best of Hollywood's antidotes against the toxic effects of the Depression, which formed the meat and marrow of numerous pictures of the era. The implausible plot is predictable and thoroughly enjoyable at the same time, the characters are likable and sympathetic, and the cheerfulness its twinkling star exudes is downright infectious.

The nation had found a new girlfriend in Deanna Durbin, and audiences responded to a second helping of her effervescence and problem-solving ingenuity with enthusiasm. Seemingly never emotionally bent under the tonnage of adversity, but rather strengthened by it, she consistently held to her core belief that one should never seek comfortable retreat from hardship. Rather, everybody should face up to reality and strive to overcome the arrows of misfortune. Although only one of the tunes is new in her second feature, the young star was given even more opportunities to sing than in *Three Smart Girls*, calling on three classical composers for most of her material. For the second year in a row, one of her films was nominated as best picture, only the fourth from Universal among the 82 nominees between 1927-28 and 1937, inclusive. It did set a rather unique record, however, by representing the only time in Academy Award history that two musicals with the same female star were nominated for best picture in consecutive years.

The film's message is simplicity itself: retaining one's optimism is the surest way to overcome hardship, or in a Social Darwinism context, only the psychologically fit will survive fortune's disfavor. Even people at the absolute bottom of the economic totem pole were assured that no matter how dark the night, the sun was bound to break through the morning sky—provided that they never cease trying to activate their dreams. It was a popular film theme of the time, so much so that the Hollywood studios formulated it into a thriving cottage industry, blanketing the nation with happy-tale adventures of impecunious folks whose unbridled faith in the future helped them surmount the miseries of the present.

Unquestionably, no musical film preached this sermon better than *Babes in Arms*, based on Rodgers and Hart's 1938 stage musical, which opened on Broadway when the Depression was showing signs of ebbing. But *One Hundred Men and a Girl* comes as close as any other film to challenging it for top honors. Just as Mickey Rooney and Judy Garland resisted backsliding

With Leopold Stokowski conducting an "Orchestra of the Unemployed," Deanna Durbin thrills the Manhattan Concert Hall audience at the end of *One Hundred Men and a Girl* with a Verdi aria.

into pessimism, so does Deanna refuse to cite a succession of setbacks as an excuse for relinquishing hope and joining her elders in desperation.

Rather, she fights to be heard, and it is she who knocks the inhospitable forces leagued against her father to the floor with a metaphorical uppercut to the jaw. As in *Curly Top*, which in 1935 ushered in the cycle of "let's put on a charity show" Depression musicals, *One Hundred Men and a Girl* furthered the tradition by allowing Deanna to win the cooperation of Leopold Stokowski, then conductor of the celebrated Philadelphia Symphony Orchestra, in arranging a show of her own. Even an initially unsupportive artist of that stature finds himself unable for long to resist the pleadings of an undeniable young charmer for help. Although he battles against her persuasiveness longer than most, Deanna floors him in roughly the eighth round.

The bright-eyed ingenue's big problem was a familiar one, played in many different keys by all the studios—how to help her unemployed father, a classical trombonist, regain self-respect by earning enough money to raise his little family above their meager existence. The father is played by Adolphe Menjou, an excellent actor who had been in the movies since 1913. No longer the arrogant executive that made him such a commanding figure as editor Walter Burns in *The Front Page* (1931), the Damon Runyan bookie in *Little Miss Marker* (1934), and an abrasive producer in *One in a Million*, *A Star Is Born*, and *Stage Door* (all 1937), Menjou is in a state of emotional paralysis throughout practically all of the picture's 107 minutes, desperately trying to hold on to his evaporating hope for a rosy future. Nor does his wardrobe square with his annual accolade as one of the world's best-dressed men. Throughout most of the film he wears the same dark, crumpled suit, a testament to his descent into poverty.

No Unemployed Need Apply. We first meet Menjou (John Caldwell) while he nervously awaits an unscheduled meeting with Stokowski, who is rehearsing his orchestra on stage in Tschaikovsky's *Fifth Symphony*, which begins during the credits. Standing in the wings, cradling his trombone case like a baby, he is hoping to be hired by the great conductor, who brushes past him on the way to his dressing room, pausing only to autograph programs and accept the praise of adoring fans. Following closely behind is Menjou, who explains that he is in danger of being evicted from his flat for nonpayment of rent. The conductor's agent (Jameson Thomas, the fellow that

Claudette Colbert rejected at the altar in *It Happened One Night*) replies that the orchestra has no openings and calls for doorman Jack Smart, who brusquely escorts the desperate musician out of the concert hall and warns him never to return again. While trudging past the main entrance to the auditorium, Menjou catches sight of a lady's purse lying on the sidewalk. Willing to return it to its owner, he is shrugged off by one bejeweled socialite, who says the purse is not hers only moments before he is once again shoved away by the burly Smart.

On his way to his walkup flat on East 87th Street, Menjou is approached by his gimlet-eyed landlady, who reminds him that his rent is overdue. Offended by her superciliousness, Menjou rashly withdraws a handful of bills from a pocket and pays the $52 debit in full. As surprised as she is pleased, the landlady suggests that Menjou's trip to Stokowski must have resulted in a full-time job. Overhearing their conversation from the top of the stairs is daughter Deanna (Patricia), the prototype of unquenchable enthusiasm and amiability, who is delighted to hear her father's false reply that he is indeed the newest addition to Stokowski's renowned team of instrumentalists.

Unwilling to destroy Deanna's happiness, Menjou limply joins her in a brief celebration of his ability to finally "pay off everybody" by virtue of a steady paycheck. Later, however, he confesses to his flute-playing neighbor and fellow job seeker, Mischa Auer (Michael), that he was not even permitted to audition, but lacks the nerve to admit the truth to his daughter.

Meanwhile, downstairs in the landlady's apartment, Deanna is entertaining a gathering of tenants with her first song, the effervescent "It's Raining Sunbeams," which, like all good anti-Depression tunes, couples the change for the better in one family's fortunes with the assurance of near-term prosperity for everybody else. Following tradition, the upbeat Sam Coslow lyric announces the forthcoming restoration of financial security to the masses in symbolic terms. What appear to be raindrops in her elders' eyes are heaven-sent tiny shafts of sunlight in Deanna's. An even more poetic use of the weather metaphor would appear early the next year when Judy Garland also proceeds in "April Showers" fashion to brighten up the bleak American landscape. Singing Joseph McCarthy's words to the Milton Ager tune, she explains to her younger brother (Scotty Beckett) in *Listen, Darling* that the thunder should not frighten him. The claps are merely echoes of a kindly Nature playfully bowling "Ten Pins in the Sky" to awaken the sun into shining and the flowers into blooming.

The next day, after sprucing up her father's appearance with a homemade haircut, Deanna insists on accompanying him to his first rehearsal with his new "employer." Menjou balks, however, protesting that her presence would make him nervous. She decides to go anyway, and unknown to her father, saunters proudly past Smart, who stops her before she can enter the auditorium. Indignant, Deanna insists that she has a perfect right to be there. In case the dullard doorman has not heard, her father is Stokowski's new trombonist. The mere mention of the instrument conjuring up visions of Menjou, Smart orders her to leave and to remind her father that his presence at the concert hall will not be tolerated.

Unaware that his lie has been detected, Menjou returns home that night, happily relating the kudos his playing had prompted from Stokowski himself. Deanna's response is to break into tears, causing her father to admit his deception and explain that yesterday's windfall was found in a lady's purse. Deanna insists that he give it to her to return to its owner. Inside a change pocket is the name and address of the aristocratic Mrs. John R. Frost, who lives in a marble mansion on, presumably, Fifth or Park Avenue.

Urchin in High Society. A formal party is underway when Deanna arrives, purse in hand, and asks to see hostess Alice Brady (Mrs. Frost), again typecast as the dim-bulb socialite oblivious of everything except the perquisites to which she feels her station in life entitles her. With the exception of *My Man Godfrey*, which also teamed wife Alice with grouchy husband Eugene Pallette, no other Depression comedy, musical or straight, treated the wealthy with more disrespect than *One Hundred Men and a Girl*. As for overweight veteran Pallette, whose screen career extended as far back as *The Birth of a Nation*, he was as well known in the thirties for his bowling pin figure as for his never meeting a film family he didn't dislike and disparage. All in all, a tremendously accomplished character actor.

Alice's tuxedoed and expensively gowned guests have apparently been untouched by the economic disaster, and their scatterings of conversation fail even to mention the hardships that have befallen those whom it has practically devastated. Deanna's unexpected appearance is tolerated because her plain dress, childlike sincerity, and awkwardness are deemed quaint by the wallet-heavy spectators. In short, the misfit young girl has become the center of amusement.

Because Alice has so many purses to fit a variety of occasions, she is unable to identify the one that Deanna holds out for inspection as her own. Nor does she know or care what is inside the purse, whether it be a diamond ring or a huge sum of cash. Both her and her guests' frivolity is heightened even further when Deanna refuses Alice's offer of a $200 reward, preferring instead only $52.10, the exact amount that Menjou had taken to pay the rent plus Deanna's carfare to and from Alice's home. Disbelieving that anyone would settle for only one-fourth of the money offered to her, Alice gives the girl what she had asked for with the condescending manner of a wealthy diner tipping a waitress whose service had been deplorable.

Looking upon Deanna as a novelty, Alice parades her from guest to guest, most of whom regard her as more to be pitied than rejected out of hand. They pile her plate with hors d'oeuvres from the elegant buffet table, some even condescending to listen while she praises the undiscovered talent of her unemployed father. When she mentions that she has taken singing lessons, Alice requests a song, fully anticipating an incredibly poor performance by a rank amateur whose ambition far exceeds her training. But, who knows, maybe even that embarrassing interlude will prove to be a laughable incident that her guests can recite over and over again at later soirees.

Deanna, however, surprises everybody with Thomas T. Railey and Alfred G. Robyn's lovely and familiar "A Heart That's Free," display-ing a rare singing talent that takes her audi-ence of idlers utterly by surprise. Buoyed by the overall approval, Alice casually suggests she would like to hear her father play. Deanna, unaccustomed to separating the wheat of sincerity from the chaff of ridicule, accepts the offer seriously, but inadvertently creates more laughter by explaining that her father and his 100 out-of-work musician friends have no orchestra with which to au-dition their talents.

Acting on Alice's jocular comment that what the country needs right now is more or-chestras, Deanna proposes to start one. If she is successful, she asks, will Alice ask her vaca-tioning husband (Eugene Pallette), whose com-pany sponsors a radio program, to introduce it over the air? Eager to play along with the youngster, Alice agrees without actually com-mitting herself. "Let me know" when the or-chestra is ready to perform, she replies with a vacuous smile.

Back on East 87th Street, Deanna en-counters trouble convincing her incredulous father that none other than business magnate Pallette will feature his 100-man orchestra on one of his future radio shows. But Menjou prepares to swing into action after Deanna telephones Alice to verify the statement. With Mischa Auer listening in, Alice repeats her hope that Deanna will "let me know" when the orchestra is operational. Like Deanna, her father and friend also misinterpret her vague wording as a promise. What none of the elated trio heard was Alice's denunciation of her young caller as a "nuisance" when her butler had informed her that Deanna was on the phone. Obviously, Alice had never ex-pected the youngster to follow through with the orchestra plan; undoubtedly, she will con-tinue to be a pest, making more calls and re-quests. The previous evening's fun has come to an end: Alice is already tired of Deanna and uninterested in her dream.

Menjou forms his orchestra within a few days by recruiting fellow musicians from the neighborhood bar and grille where they con-gregate to sympathize with one another while seeking employment. Their practice hall is a garage on First Avenue, rented by the usually dour Billy Gilbert, who, like Mischa Auer, was

one of filmdom's greatest character actors, dis-tinguished mostly by his frequent Greek-tinged mispronunciations of even the simplest English words and, later in his career, by issuing the loudest sneezes ever recorded. (His was the voice and sneezes of "Sneezy" in *Snow White and the Seven Dwarfs*.) Also in the cast was the virtually unsung but ever-reliable Frank Jenks, rough of exterior but warm of heart, as a cab-bie with operatic ambitions of his own who shuttles Deanna from warehouse to the digs of her supposed elitist supporters.

While the men practice and Gilbert impa-tiently awaits his rent money, Deanna decides to report on their progress to Alice. Disappointed to learn that her supposed benefactress has left for Europe, she learns that Pallette has stayed in New York and is presently relaxing at the Merchants Club. A short-tempered practical jokester, Pal-lette spends much of his time trying to outfox fel-low club member Jed Prouty (Bitters), who is equally gifted at playing tricks. The upshot of the rivalry is Pallette's regarding Deanna's dec-laration that the orchestra is all set to audition for him as another Prouty ruse designed to fool him into taking a meaningless trip under false pre-tenses. But he agrees to go with Deanna to the garage and judge the musicians' qualifications for himself—all the while devising a scheme to re-spond in kind to Prouty's latest joke.

Pallette is stunned to find that what Deanna had told him is true. Inside the garage are 100 men holding their instruments and hoping to pass musical muster to make their debut on his radio program. Using his unique foghorn voice to advantage, he abruptly dis-misses the whole "crazy idea," maintaining that his wife had never told him of any such arrangement. Moreover, he insists that no as-tute businessman would ever invest in anything that offered absolutely no profit potential. In Pallette's view, what the orchestra needs to at-tract a sponsor is a "name" conductor, some-one with enough musical clout to command attention. His suggestion quickly dispatches Deanna on another journey to the Manhattan Concert Hall, where she hopes to enroll just the right person to lend prestige to her orches-tra of nobodies.

The Aloof Conductor. This time she is successful in stealing past the watchful doorman into the auditorium to listen to the Stokowski orchestra practice the Overture to Wagner's *Lohengrin*. Unwisely, she applauds at the finish, causing Stokowski to order his manager to eject her. He does, but Deanna sneaks back in, goes directly to Stokowski's empty office, and prepares to plead that he serve as guest conductor for her father's orchestra.

While there she answers a telephone call from the music editor of "The Daily Express." Innocent of the consequences of her answers to the man's questions, she says that contrary to rumors, Stokowski is not about to leave for Europe. Rather, he is going to conduct an orchestra of 100 jobless musicians on Pallette's radio show in the near future. The editor, excited over receiving an exclusive news story with such a built-in curiosity factor, replies that a feature article will appear in tomorrow's edition. He has incorrectly assumed that the authoritative, in-the-know voice he has been listening to belongs to agent Thomas's personal secretary.

Deanna returns covertly to the auditorium, where to the accompaniment of maestro Stokowski's orchestra, she sings Mozart's beautiful and intricate "Hallelujah in F-Major." Startled by her reappearance but visibly impressed with her voice, which he describes accurately as "remarkable," he asks the youngster who had taught her to sing. Deanna gives all the credit to her father, adding that he has an excellent symphony orchestra that is even better than Stokowski's. She implores him to conduct it "just for one night" to help it gain recognition. Stokowski is attentive, but when she mentions that it is currently practicing in a garage, the laughter erupting from his musicians mocks her sincerity. Stokowski's response is brief and apologetic: he would like to grant her request, of course, but he and his orchestra are soon to embark on a six-month European tour.

Crushed by the rejection, Deanna that night breaks into tears while relating her Stokowski encounter to Menjou, who does his best to comfort her by urging that she give up the radio show idea. "But it would have made so many people happy," she cries, referring not only to Menjou's musicians, but also to thousands of Depression-weary viewers desperately seeking diversion. "Fairy tales never come

true," her father counsels, unaware of the miracle about to be wrought by his inventive daughter.

A montage of newspaper headlines discloses the fact that her dream, shattered only yesterday, is beginning to piece itself together again. The restoration begins with the morning's "Express" headline announcing that "Stokowski to Conduct Orchestra of Unemployed Musicians." Particularly interested in the news are several of Pallette's aristocratic Merchant Club associates, including the fun-loving Prouty, who want to sponsor the orchestra not for altruistic reasons but, as one man explains, to burnish his company's image in the marketplace.

The film's two major plots—Deanna's ambitious plans for the orchestra and Stokowski's refusal to become enmeshed in them—now converge on their way to a combined climax. Perplexed as Stokowski by the news story, Deanna is at a loss to explain how such inaccurate information had been leaked to the newspaper. She telephones the "Express" music editor to ask where he got his story. His response that Thomas' secretary was the source startles Deanna into realizing that the editor must have mistaken her for the secretary when he called.

Meantime, hoping to pin down sponsorship of the orchestra before his business rivals beat him to the punch, Pallette visits Menjou in the garage and gives him a $1,000 check to secure the deal, which Pallette promises to honor provided that Menjou keeps his "pesky" daughter at bay. Menjou and his men are jubilant, but Deanna is depressed. She knows something that Pallette and her father do not: the news story is a fake. Obviously, she must make amends for the mixup by trying once again to coax Stokowski into conducting the orchestra, even at the peril of interrupting the temperamental artist's rigid work schedule.

She surprises the maestro by visiting him during piano practice in his luxurious three-level apartment. She admits her culpability in the newspaper scoop, hoping to calm Stokowski's rising irritation by adding that she had no idea that the telephone caller was a music editor. Besides, she continues, she had 100 good reasons for creating the fiction—the members of her father's orchestra, who as she speaks are tiptoeing into the lower level of the apartment, instruments at the ready. How they got in and why no servant alerted Stokowski to their presence are ignored. As Deanna and the maestro continue their discussion, Menjou strikes up his musicians in a rousing rendition of Lizst's "Hungarian Rhapsody."

At first alarmed, and then intrigued, by the music, Stokowski strolls onto the balcony to observe the performers in action. About midway through the "audition," he recognizes their musicianship and gradually begins to conduct them, first only mechanically with his right hand, then enthusiastically with both. As serenely happy as the players, he obviously is enjoying the audible proof that what Deanna had told him was entirely correct: these men are unquestionably professional in every sense of the word. The result of the unscheduled concert is spelled out in a followup "Express" story: Stokowski has postponed his European tour and will definitely conduct the "Orchestra of the Unemployed." And this time readers can bet the farm on the accuracy of the news. Stokowski himself is the source.

A short time later, after Menjou's orchestra has concluded the "Hungarian Rhapsody," which is carried over musically from Stokowski's apartment to the stage of the Manhattan Concert Hall, the great conductor addresses the audience. He wishes to thank the person who is chiefly responsible for the success of the concert, he says, nodding at Deanna. The camera focuses on her, immaculately groomed, white ribbon in her hair, her expressive eyes glowing in the warmth of the sunbeams she alone saw falling to earth in the darker days of the recent past, as she walks to center stage.

After casting a loving glance at her proud father, she sings an aria from *La Traviata*. The applause is deafening, and the picture ends in smiles of triumph exchanged by a down-but-never-out little girl of an era long passed, her grateful father, who was finally given the opportunity to exhibit his talent, and a world-class conductor, whose heady reputation has been enhanced by taking a chance on a group of unknown musicians.

That such happy endings rarely ever occur outside the movie house failed to diminish the impact of the film. Moviegoers sensed that things would turn out well in all Deanna Durbin movies, but the happy ending was only one of the many attractions of *One Hundred Men and a Girl*. The young lady herself was a treat to watch and listen to, and the compassion her occasional stumbles inspired among her fans was quite sincere, for her downs and ups pretty much paralleled their own in the real world. In the father-and-daughter bedroom scene, for example, after Stokowski had refused to conduct Menjou's orchestra, downhearted Deanna aptly summarized the usual reaction of her Depression-wounded viewers when their own optimistic expectations collided with reality. "Well, it was good while it lasted," she said, referring to her initial confidence that Stokowski would accede to her wish. "We were happy for a few minutes."

In those bleak times of yesteryear, even the briefest interlude of happiness was sufficient unto the day.

Alexander's Ragtime Band (1938)

A 20th Century–Fox picture. DIRECTOR: Henry King. PRODUCER: Darryl F. Zanuck; ASSOCIATE: Harry Joe Brown. SCREENWRITER: Kathryn Scola and Lamar Trotti; ADAPTION: Richard Sherman. CINEMATOGRAPHER: Peverall Marley. FILM EDITOR: Barbara McLean. CHOREOGRAPHER: Seymour Felix. ART DIRECTOR: Bernard Herzbrun and Boris Leven. SET DECORATOR: Thomas Little. COSTUMES: Gwen Wakeling. MUSICAL DIRECTOR: Alfred Newman. SONGS: Lyrics and music (and original story) by Irving Berlin. RUNNING TIME: 1 hour, 46 minutes. *Principal Players*: Tyrone Power (Roger "Alexander"). Alice Faye (Stella Kirby). Don Ameche (Charlie Dwyer). Ethel Merman (Jerry Allen). Jack Haley (Davey Lane). John Carradine (Taxi Driver). Paul Hurst (Bill Mulligan). Wally Vernon (Himself). Joe King (Charles B. Dillingham). *Major Academy Awards*: Best Scoring. *Nominations*: Best Picture; Original Story; Film Editing; Art Direction; Song ("Now It Can Be Told").

According to 1938 press releases from Fox's publicity department, *Alexander's Ragtime Band* took two years to complete and cost about $2 million, or roughly $45 million in 1998 dollars. If these time and budgetary totals are factual, and not just examples of Hollywood puffery, they are indeed impressive. *Gone with the Wind*, which was premiered in Atlanta about 18 months later on December 15, 1939, ran slightly more than twice as long as the black-and-white Fox production. Only the thirteenth

Alice Faye introduces a new Irving Berlin melody, "Alexander's Ragtime Band," in a San Francisco saloon in *Alexander's Ragtime Band*. Playing the violin is bandleader Tyrone Power. Don Ameche is at the piano and Jack Haley on drums.

movie filmed in three-strip Technicolor, it took one month short of a full year to complete at a cost of $4.25 million.

What is undeniable is that Fox regarded this all-star song-and-dance vehicle as a major production worthy of heavy investments in time, talent, and money. And the studio's optimistic assessment of the quality of the finished production was correct. *Alexander's Ragtime Band* was one of the most delightful and professionally mounted musicals of the 1930s, even if its plot added little to the old story of the disintegration, and finally restoration, of the friendship between two men. *Halliwell's Film Guide*, never noted for randomly dispensing accolades, awards it a rare three-star rating in the 1995 edition.

The stars who head the cast are superb, particularly Don Ameche, one of the best and least appreciated singers of the period, who strengthened his growing reputation as a first-class actor

equally at home in drama (*In Old Chicago*, 1937) and comedy (*Midnight*, 1939) as in musicals. The brother of Jim Ameche, the radio voice of Jack Armstrong from 1933 to 1938, Don finally achieved official Hollywood recognition of his acting talent in 1985, when he won the Academy Award for best supporting actor for his role as Art Selwyn in *Cocoon*, appropriately produced by 20th Century–Fox, where he had spent most of his early career. As *Alexander's Ragtime Band* shows, Ameche was a first-rate pop singer, displaying a purity of tone and harmony, clarity of diction, and highly refined sense of rhythm when called on to croon a tune.

Equally proficient was 25-year-old Tyrone Power as the aspiring bandleader who adopts "Alexander" as his professional name. The latest celebrity in a family of actors, Power could trace his professional roots to his great-grandfather, the Irish stage actor Tyrone Power, who appeared in numerous plays in the early 19th century. The Hollywood star's father, Tyrone Power, Sr., was active on the American stage and screen, appearing in dozens of silent films and one talkie, director Raoul Walsh's *The Big Trail* (1930), which also featured John Wayne.

The younger Power has been credited with a brief appearance, probably as a West Point cadet, in *Flirtation Walk*, but his face is difficult to recognize among the scores of other young men in uniform. His first triumph came with *Lloyds of London* in 1937, and within the next three years he was co-starring with such luminaries as Sonja Henie, Alice Faye, and Myrna Loy. Miss Faye, who never looked or sang better, carries off her transformation from bitchy unknown to ladylike Broadway star who marries the wrong man with grace and charm.

As the low-key "other woman," Ethel Merman was finally given the chance to display her own potent acting ability. Discovered by producer Vinton Freedley while she was appearing at the Brooklyn Paramount, she was one of Broadway's most electric musical comedy performers since the Gershwins' *Girl Crazy* in 1930. Hollywood, however, consistently shortchanged her abilities by confining her to subsidiary parts as the brassy, usually vindictive man-chaser (as in *Kid Millions* and *We're Not Dressing*, both 1934, and *Happy Landing*, 1937), scornful of her lost lovers and the girls who took them away, a sort of female Dead End Kid unwilling to forgive or forget even the slightest bruise to her ego. As the undisputed queen of the Broadway musical theater, her talents outshone the usually idiotic librettos. In all, she appeared in 13 Broadway shows up to 1970, not counting the 1966 revival of *Annie Get Your Gun* and her 1970 stint as the eighth star to play Dolly Levi in *Hello, Dolly!* on Broadway.

As Cole Porter's favorite singer, she appeared in five of his musical comedies, beginning with *Anything Goes* in 1934, followed by *Red, Hot and Blue* (1936) and *DuBarry Was a Lady* (1939). In *Panama Hattie* (1940) she stopped the Nazis from blowing up the Panama Canal; in *Something for the Boys* (1943) she again displayed patriotic fervor by piloting an endangered aircraft to safety and winning the Congressional Medal of Honor, thanks to her supersensitive teeth that could pick up radio signals. And so much for the theory that the typical Broadway musical comedy libretto was superior to the often silly film-musical screenplay. It was only after Broadway musicals began showing marked improvement in story line and treatment in the 1950s that the Hollywood musicals based on them also grew in artistic stature.

But God knows the lady could sing with the best of them, and Miss Merman does just that to perfection in *Alexander's Ragtime Band*. Renowned for her energetic deliveries in a ringing voice that never slurred as much as a single syllable of the lyrics, she was given both romantic ballads and show-stopping production songs in the 1938 film, singing the former with unusual sweetness, while belting out the latter with all the considerable verve at her command.

Expert Song Placements. The sets, particularly those decorating the nightclub floor shows, are uniformly excellent, as are the costumes by Gwen Wakeling, best known at the time as the designer of most of the authentic period and contemporary dresses worn by Shirley Temple since 1935. Similarly outstanding is veteran Seymour Felix's choreography, modest compared with his dance numbers in *The Great Ziegfeld* and other extravaganzas, but entirely appropriate to the small-scale dance floors and stages on which the songs are performed.

The picture marked the first time that older, established Irving Berlin songs vied for attention with his new ones, like "Now It Can Be Told," the third of his seven Oscar-nominated tunes from 1935 to 1954. Altogether, 26 older Berlin tunes are heard, some only momentarily in the background. Delving into both the recent and the distant past, the songs ranged from "Everybody's Doin' It," performed by vaudevillian Wally Vernon and Dixie Dunbar, and "Ragtime Violin," from 1911; "Say It with Music" and "Remember," from the twenties; to "Heat Wave," "Easter Parade," and "Cheek to Cheek" from the early thirties. Each song is deftly integrated into the plot with unusual devotion to chronological accuracy, earning Alfred Newman an Oscar for his musical direction. A second Academy Award nomination went to Berlin for best story, making him the only songwriter ever to be considered for such an honor.

He also remains the only major American songwriter never to have been subjected to a film biography, although *Alexander's Ragtime Band* brushes against several factual episodes in his long and distinguished career, and hints at others. Berlin, like Tyrone Power's character, worked his way up from seedy saloons to the big time, first as a singing waiter on Coney Island to Mike Salter's, better known as "Nigger Mike's," in Chinatown and then to Jimmy Kelly's on 14th Street on his artistic progression from southern Brooklyn to Broadway. Again like Power, Berlin joined the Army in World War I and wrote a show with an all-Army cast named *Yip, Yip, Yaphank* in 1918.

In many ways the omission of a full-fledged Berlin biomusical is unfortunate, since his life story is a colorful and inspirational testament to the genius of a young man born Israel Baline in Temun, Russia, and reared on Manhattan's Lower East Side who rose to the top of his profession. (He became known as Irving Berlin in 1908 after the printer misspelled his original name on the sheet music of his first published song, "Marie from Sunny Italy," for which he wrote the lyrics only.)

In 1921, together with Sam H. Harris, he built the Music Box Theatre, soon to be dubbed the "House of Hits," which still stands on West 44th Street and continues to book mostly successful shows. But judging from other "biographies," Berlin's disinterest in cooperating with Hollywood to musicalize his life story was prudent. The studios usually managed to handle the musical sequences very well, like the *Show Boat* portions of *Till the Clouds Roll By*, but the biographical details are usually out of sync with reality and the songs are inserted haphazardly, entirely ignoring the original date of their composition.

George and Ira Gershwin's climb to international acclaim was pretty much mangled in the otherwise musically appealing *Rhapsody in Blue* in 1945. Cole Porter suffered an identical fate in 1946 in *Night and Day*'s misguided congeries of falsehoods, along with Jerome Kern in *Till the Clouds Roll By* (also 1946), Bert Kalmar and Harry Ruby in *Three Little Words* (1950), lyricist Gus Kahn in *It Had to Be You* (1951), and Buddy DeSylva, Lew Brown, and Ray

Henderson in *The Best Things in Life Are Free* (1956). Curiously, the best and least fictive of all the songwriter biomusicals, MGM's *Deep in My Heart*, bombed at the box office. Operetta composer Romberg's music had simply lost its appeal, and his was no longer a hallowed name by the mid-fifties. *Words and Music*, MGM's lackluster 1949 tribute to Rodgers and Hart, surprised many viewers by including a reference to Rodgers's early ambition to be a salesman for children's underwear. Most people dismissed the idea as preposterous for a composer of genius, but the incident was based on fact.

In the view of Ira Gershwin, "When Berlin was at the top of his form…, there was no one greater." Although the statement is accurate, even Berlin was not immune from the Great Depression blues. Of the 13 songs he wrote for *Reaching for the Moon* in 1931, United Artists dropped 12. He remained in Hollywood throughout the mid-thirties, however, causing some of his admirers to wonder whether his skill at crafting songs for live performers in a Broadway musical had been seriously compromised. Not to worry. When his *Louisiana Purchase* opened on May 28, 1940, it marked Berlin's first Broadway show in seven years and the first to run more than a year there since the Gershwin brothers' *Of Thee I Sing* in 1931. Obviously, Hollywood had not adversely affected Berlin's artistry.

"Alexander's Ragtime Band" vied with "A Pretty Girl Is Like a Melody," "Always," and "Easter Parade" as the most familiar Berlin song in early 1938. "God Bless America," though written but not copyrighted in 1918, would not add to Berlin's glory till after Kate Smith debuted it on Armistice Day, 1938. "White Christmas" would not appear until 1942.

Written in 1910, praised by the perceptive George M. Cohan at first hearing, and interpolated the next year into the Broadway show *The Merry Whirl*, "Alexander's Ragtime Band" is one of the handful of American popular songs that have avoided obscurity for more than eight decades. Prestige was added to its popularity when Canadian soprano Eva Gauthier sang it at a recital at New York's prestigious Aeolian Hall on November 1, 1923. Also included in the program were songs by such classical writers as Henry Purcell, Bela Bartok, Paul Hindemith, Arnold Schoenberg, and Darius Milhaud.

Three months later, "Alexander's Ragtime Band" reappeared at the hall, along with Berlin's "A Pretty Girl Is Like a Melody" and "Orange Blossoms in California," as part of Paul Whiteman's innovative "Experiment in Modern Music" concert, which also introduced *Rhapsody in Blue*. (Because of the bandleader's four-year-long stint at the Palais Royal, a large dance emporium at Broadway and West 48th Street, the orchestra was officially billed as Paul Whiteman's Palais Royal Orchestra.)

Berlin himself once commented that "Alexander's Ragtime Band" was a song about ragtime, not a ragtime song. Nonetheless, composer Eubie Blake, no mean ragtimer himself, once described the song to this author as the "finest rag ever written," combining a march-like beat and a slightly syncopated melody line. Of its numerous recordings, perhaps the best was made by Bessie Smith (with Coleman Hawkins on clarinet and Fletcher Henderson on piano) on March 2, 1927, for Columbia Records. Like Blake's own "I'm Just Wild About Harry," which served as the themesong for Harry Truman's 1948 Presidential campaign, the Berlin tune eventually found its way into national politics, but less successfully.

Beginning in the fall of 1995, Lamar Alexander, then a contender for the Republican nomination for President, pounded out a foot-stomping rendition of "Alexander's Ragtime Band" on a piano at the end of stump appearances before dropping out of the race months before the 1996 GOP national convention. In a tie-in effort to enroll supporters in his campaign, Alexander often invoked the opening lines after shaking a hand and slipping a piece of promotional literature into it. "Come on along!", he would urge, "Come on along!" (Sammy Cahn, in 1960, rewrote his lyric to the Oscar-winning "High Hopes" as a campaign song for candidate John F. Kennedy.)

On the Glory Road. *Alexander's Ragtime Band* opens at a concert at the Fairmont Hotel in San Francisco about 1910 or so. The camera is centered on violin virtuoso Tyrone Power, who is playing to the delight of a full house that includes his music teacher, Professor Heinrich (Jean Hersholt), and aristocratic Aunt Sophie (Helen Westley). Power is bored; despite his intimacy with classical music, he prefers pop songs in much the same way that *The Jazz Singer*, a cantor's son, eagerly looked forward to escaping from the temple onto a Broadway stage. Power at this point in the screenplay is one step ahead of Jolson: he and fellow musicians have already been promised an audition to play regularly at a somewhat disreputable Barbary Coast bistro operated by Dirty Eddie (Robert Gleckler) specifically for devotees of hard liquor and fast music.

Excusing himself from attending a post-concert high-society gala by telling his aunt he has to hurry to a fictitious job at the Excelsior Bakery, Power rushes to Eddie's. Alice Faye (Stella Kirby), looking every inch the blowsy moll, complete with tight-fitting black dress and blonde wig, is already there when Power, pianist Don Ameche (Charley Dwyer), and drummer Jack Haley (Davey Lane) march to the bandstand. Alice has been trying to inveigle bartender Paul Hurst (Bill Mulligan) into giving her a singing job, assuring him of her ability to wow the customers with a song recently imported from New York.

Hurst for a change is cast as a good-natured, faithful helpmate, a role that contrasted starkly with his typical role as a crude, frequently sniveling, coward or heavy. Usually excelling in his brief screen stints, Hurst would gain some renown as the Union Army deserter whom Scarlett O'Hara shoots in the face in *Gone with the Wind*, and later as the pugnacious instigator of the lynching of three innocent men charged with cattle rustling in *The Ox-Bow Incident* in 1942.

Dirty Eddie dismisses Hurst's appeal to give a hearing to Alice in favor of listening to Power and his band. When the leader discovers that his musicians are unable to play anything because Ameche has misplaced the sheet music, Hurst comes to their rescue by passing Alice's song to Power, but without her permission. Under the spell of his baton, the band launches into a slow, entirely inappropriate version of "Alexander's Ragtime Band." After examining the sheet music closely, Power recognizes that the rhythm is different from that of any other song he had ever heard, and vastly more ingenious. He peps up the tempo, and the band's revised version scores a big hit with the customers.

It fails, however, to please Alice, who demands that Power explain why he "swiped" the song behind her back. In a placating mood, he parries her anger with an invitation to sing it. She does so, and extremely well, but absolutely refuses to join the band, which Dirty Harry has just enthusiastically hired on a full-time basis. But peacemaker Ameche intervenes, urging Alice into accepting the job as featured vocalist. With the invaluable help of his new songbird, Power and his boys soon graduate from the depths of Dirty Eddie's to the ultra-posh Roccoco Room of the Cliff House.

When Power condescendingly demands that Alice tone down her coarseness and dispense with her wig and florid costumes, the lady rebels against his Pygmalion-like attempt to make her over into something she neither is nor wishes to be. Power replies that his is a "class act" that will not tolerate the presence of a "comic valentine," meaning Alice, who quits on the spot. She soon reverses her decision, however, again under the soothing influence of Ameche, whose insistence that she cater to Power's advice springs as much from his own affection for her as from his desire to keep her with the band. Alice agrees to go on with the evening show, entertaining the audience with a perfectly splendid performance of "That International Rag," the second of Berlin's immensely popular hits from the distant past.

Change of Heart. Several days later, while Alice and Ameche are alone in the Cliff House, he plays and sings "Now It Can Be Told," a brand new song he had written expressly for her. The tender lyric and look in his eyes clearly announce the fact that his affection has gently turned to thoughts of love, undoubtedly urged on by her freshened-up appearance. Obedient to Power's demands, she has metamorphosed herself into a truly lovely young lady, her hair now revealing its natural light brown shade and her dress far more conservative than any of the bizarre creations she was accustomed to wearing.

As with all film-musical heroines entranced

while listening to a musicalized love confession addressed to her, Alice repeats the lyric then and there, as well as during her evening performance. Ameche's pleasure at her approval of his love song, however, fades to disappointment when she aims the lyric, along with loving glances, at bandleader Power, not at the pianist-composer. Incited to action by her overt love signals, Power chases after her when she leaves the bandstand. On a balcony they kiss in the shadows, their burgeoning romance witnessed only by a bright moon that spills its beams over the calm Pacific Ocean while strains of the love song written by Power's rival continue in the background.

Faithful to his imperturbable nature, Ameche accepts his defeat at romancing Alice with gentlemanly finesse, indicating not the slightest jealousy when all three dine the next day at a fancy restaurant. A newspaper report that Charles B. Dillingham, the preeminent Broadway producer, played by Joe King, is in San Francisco ignites the spark of excitement in the trio. The trick, of course, is how to tempt the showman into listening to the band. Certain that it has all the credentials necessary to qualify as pit orchestra for a Dillingham show, Power optimistically telephones the producer's hotel room, only to backtrack into depression when an associate informs him that Dillingham is far too busy to grant any interviews.

Stubborn Power calls the room again and, disguising his voice, mentions that he shares Dillingham's admiration for the culinary artistry of one Henri, the chef at the "Astor House." (The renowned producer for years lived at New York's Astor Hotel.) Power adds that Henri now cooks at the Cliff House and if the producer thinks his pompano is the be-all, end-all of gourmet delights, that's only because he hasn't tasted the chef's baby lobsters. The associate passes the message on to Dillingham, who happily directs him to reserve a table for him at the Cliff House that very evening.

Thrilled by Alice's rendition of "When That Midnight Choo-Choo Leaves for Alabam'"—and the baby lobsters—Dillingham invites her to his table and makes an offer he hopes she will not refuse. Minutes afterward, she breathlessly tells Power and Ameche of the producer's promise to star her in an upcoming Broadway musical, adding that the band will be joining her later in the Big Town—maybe. Ameche encourages her to snap up the opportunity while Power insists that she remain loyal to the band that gave her a career. Preferring Ameche's recommendation, she charges out of her dressing room when Power explodes and orders her to get out of his sight forthwith. Awash in anger, he then decides to break up the band.

A much larger and potentially lethal crisis hits Power on April 6, 1917, when the United States declares war on Germany. He and Haley enlist in the army and are next seen in their barracks at Camp Upton—renamed "Camp Yaphank" in the movie—on Long Island. Power's request to put on a show that will "beat the pants off" the Navy's popular stage revue, "Boom! Boom!"—presumably referring to the actual wartime Broadway show *Leave It to the Sailors*—is approved by the brass. Accordingly, the show goes on at the camp theater, with Power conducting the orchestra as his fellow soldiers harmonize on "I Can Always Find a Home at the YMCA" and Haley sings "Oh! How I Hate to Get Up in the Morning," originally introduced by Berlin himself in *Yip, Yip, Yaphank*. The show is such a success that, like *Yaphank*, it is transferred to Broadway.

Alice, by then a musical comedy star in Dillingham's "Come One, Come All," attends a performance of the Army show. Hoping to renew acquaintances with Power after a year's absence, she is instead rebuffed by his refusal to see her. To offset the possibility of her scheming to visit him anyway, as well as to prevent falling in love with her all over again, Power alters the choreography of the closing production number, as had Berlin at *Yaphank*'s final Broadway performance.

Instead of allowing the performers to make their customary bows to the audience after the finale, Power arranges them into two columns and marches them up the main aisle from the stage to the front door to the beat of "We're on Our Way to France." Outside the theater, they climb into trucks that will carry them to troop-transport ships awaiting them at a dock on the Hudson River. The soldiers' departure from the theater is rewarded with a hearty burst of patriotic applause from everyone in the audience, except

Alice. She watches their exit with eyes filled with tears.

The End of the Affair. After the Armistice is signed, civilian Power, appearing humbled after his battlefield experiences, visits Alice at the theater where her Dillingham show is in its 53rd week. Her warm greeting compels him to apologize for his former brusqueness and admit that only her love can rid him of the "horrible and useless" feeling that has crept over him. Alice, however, pulls away from his embrace, deepening his agony by revealing that she has been married for a year to Ameche, who had received his draft notice the day before the war ended. Now a successful composer as well as pianist, Ameche joins the couple. Jovial as ever, he welcomes congratulations and best wishes from Power, the latest in Hollywood's long lineup of heartsick though honorable losers.

It is a thoroughly forlorn Power who expresses bitter resentment over how much things have changed in the music world since he and Haley went off to the French battlefields to make "the world safe for democracy." He has lost all ambition and quickly dismisses his drummer friend's suggestion that he rebuild the band. Hoping to prod him into action, Haley introduces Power to his new discovery, Jerry Allen, a girl singer played by Ethel Merman, whose personality and talent regenerate Power's enthusiasm to the point that he decides to reenter the musical arena.

One of the film's most precious assets was musical director Alfred Newman's positioning the Berlin songs at various stages of the plot where the lyrics underscore the emotional impact of specific incidents on the various characters. Ethel's restrained delivery of "A Pretty Girl Is Like a Melody," sung with Power's newly reconstructed orchestra, for instance, gratifyingly foreshadows the bandleader's eventual reconciliation with Alice in the well-known couplet, "She will leave you and then / Come back again." Later, when Alice's search for Power proves to be fruitless, the words of "All Alone" are heard in the background. Similarly, the lyric of "Remember" is interpolated at just the right moment to highlight Alice's nostalgic recollections of the good old days in San Francisco upon learning that Ethel is a hit as band vocalist.

It soon becomes evident that Alice is looking upon her marriage as exciting as yesterday's mashed potatoes, as Dorothy Fields once described a hot romance grown cold. When Ameche suggests they go to the small Greenwich Village speakeasy where Power and Ethel headline the entertainment, Alice soulfully declines. Ameche's response is to mention that lately he's been doing a "lot of thinking," and if his impression that she still loves Power is correct, he is willing to call off the marriage, chalking it up to "experience, a grand adventure while it lasted." When Alice admits that she "most likely" does love Power, Ameche nods knowingly, and the scene ends with his amiable wish that the "two hotheads can pick up where they left off."

Alice later goes to the speakeasy on her own and learns from Ethel that the band and she are about to leave to play a gig in Paris. Alice also infers that Ethel and Power are in love. More or less discounting her chance of ever attracting him back to her, Alice joins Ethel in "Blue Skies," proving that she, like estranged husband Ameche, can accept defeat with nobility. She even sees the troupe off on their voyage to France.

There, at the Café de Paris, Ethel and the band and a 12-member chorus perform tremendously effective versions of two Berlin songs, one old, the other new. The first, with Ethel and choristers dressed in black "devil" costumes, is "Pack Up Your Sins and Go to the Devil," a big Berlin hit written originally for The Music Box Revue of 1923. The second is "My Walking Stick," vaguely reminiscent of "Top Hat, White Tie and Tails," with Ethel decked out in traditional black hat and tails, but wearing a polka-dot tie. Alice, meanwhile, has quit the Dillingham show during its road tour in Chicago. Bereft of both Ameche and Power, she no longer cares about the show or the fact that her abrupt resignation has automatically consigned her to the no-hire list of Dillingham and every other New York producer.

Together Again. Back in America, Ethel wisely turns down Power's marriage proposal, explaining that he is not, nor will he ever be, in love with her. Disappointed but not crushed by the rejection, Power later bumps into Ameche in a producer's office.

Certain that his friend still holds the torch for Alice, but is unwilling to admit it, Ameche launches into a bitter denunciation of his former wife's alleged character flaws. His criticism provokes Power into trying to silence him with a punch to the mouth. His sprightly friend escapes pummeling by correctly interpreting Power's manly defense of Alice as proof positive that the angry bandleader loves her still. Ameche agrees to help him search the city for her.

Now singing under the name of "Lily Lamont" in a tacky Village cabaret named Scarbi's Restaurant, Alice is now working for owner Paul Hurst, her old San Francisco supporter, who had emigrated to New York and amassed a fortune in bootlegging. Convinced that Alice still loves Power, he tries to argue her into attending a "Swing Concert" that Power is giving that evening at Carnegie Hall. Not only will she not attend the concert, but she is also resolved to quit this job, too, and leave town. No eyebrows would have been raised at the revelation that a non-classical orchestra had been booked to play in that esteemed concert hall. The Benny Goodman Orchestra created a sensation by playing a groundbreaking jazz concert there a few months before the film was released, on January 16, 1938.

Power's enlarged orchestra consists of about 75 musicians, including old pals Ameche on piano and Haley on drums. Sitting contentedly in the audience are Aunt Helen Westley and Professor Hersholt, each converted under Power's influence to viewing popular music as an art form with its own peculiar charm. The only person missing from the roundup of familiar faces is Alice, who has hailed a taxi to take her away from the cabaret. "Just drive around," the disconsolate young lady tells cabbie John Carradine when he asks for her destination.

As distinctive and memorable an actor as ever appeared on the screen, Carradine had a deep, resonant voice fit for high tragedy, but his hollow cheeks and tall, gaunt figure combined to win him mostly villainous roles in numerous B features that provided little opportunity for him to display his talent at full range. He is perhaps best remembered as the cowardly Jack Ford, the man who in 1939 shoots Tyrone Power in the back at the end of *Jesse James*.

This time out, Carradine, like Hurst, assumes the role of the good guy. Driving around Central Park, he turns on the cab radio, which is broadcasting Power's concert. Instead of complying with Alice's demand that he shut it off or switch to another station, he pulls up to the curb in front of Carnegie Hall. Reluctantly, his passenger obeys an inner urge to see the orchestra in action, only to find that all the seats and standing room have been sold out. Carradine follows her in the cab as she saunters along West 57th Street until she finally agrees to get back in it. Again slouched in the back seat, she is surprised when Carradine turns off the motor, lights a cigarette, and settles back to enjoy the concert.

As the program nears its conclusion, Alice urges him to drive away, but pauses when Power's voice is heard. He is telling the audience that he wants to play a song that means more to him than any other, and is dedicating it to the "one person with whom I associate it." Carradine steps out, opens the rear door, and points Alice toward the concert hall entrance, urging her to go inside, ticket or not. He had recognized her from the very beginning, he says, and was aware that she had once been in love with Power, and most likely still is.

Slowly, she walks backstage, where she is glimpsed standing in the wings by Ameche and then Power. Waving their arms, they call on her to join them on the stage and sing "Alexander's Ragtime Band," the song that had brought them all together many years ago, when success was only a wisp of a dream and Alice and Power's strained relationship had yet to ripen into love everlasting. Nothing, the screenplay implies, will ever separate them again.

All in all, quite a lovely film that, like a sturdy, well-maintained old brownstone, has aged gracefully. It is sentimental, but not excessively so. Expertly crafted it surely is, from acting and singing to dialogue and props. It unsurprisingly caught the fancy of *Variety*, which in 1938 described the picture as a "grand film musical which stirs and thrills." It still does.

The Wizard of Oz (1939)

A Metro-Goldwyn-Mayer picture. DIRECTOR: Victor Fleming. PRODUCER: Mervyn LeRoy. SCREENPLAY: Noel Langley, Florence Ryerson, and Edgar Allan Woolf, from the book by L. Frank Baum, adapted by Noel Langley. CINEMATOGRAPHER: Harold Rossen; ASSISTANT: Allen Davey; VISUAL EFFECTS: A. Arnold Gillespie. FILM EDITOR: Blanche Sewell. CHOREOGRAPHER: Bobby Connolly. ART DIRECTOR: Cedric Gibbons; ASSISTANT: William A. Horning. SET DECORATION: Edwin B. Willis. COSTUMES: Adrian. MAKEUP: Jack Dawn. SCORING: Herbert Stothart. ASSISTANT CONDUCTOR: Georgie Stoll. ORCHESTRAL AND VOCAL ARRANGEMENTS: George Bassman, Murray Cutter, Paul Marquardt, and Ken Darby. SONGS: Lyrics by E.Y. Harburg, music by Harold Arlen. RUNNING TIME: 1 hour and 59 minutes. *Principal Players*: Judy Garland (Dorothy [Gale]). Frank Morgan (Professor Marvel and "The Wizard"). Ray Bolger (Hunk and "The Scarecrow"). Bert Lahr (Zeke and "The Cowardly Lion"). Jack Haley (Hickory and "The Tin Man"). Billie Burke (Glinda, "the Good Witch of the North.") Margaret Hamilton (Mrs. Almira Gulch and "The Wicked Witch of the West"). Charley Grapewin (Uncle Henry). Clara Blandick (Auntie Em[ily]). "Terry" ("Toto.") And the Munchkins. *Major Academy Awards*: Best Scoring; Song ("Over the Rainbow"). *Nominations*: Best Picture; Art Direction; Visual [Special] Effects.

Believed to be the most watched movie in history, as well as the most written about, it has been seen in theaters and on television by more than one billion people. It took 22 weeks to film, involved 65 sets and 600 performers, and cost an astounding $2.77 million, equal to about $60 million today. A 160-piece orchestra played Herbert Stothart's Oscar-winning adaptation of Harold Arlen's music. Its special effects, ranging from the realistic backlot-whipped tornado to the cartoonish trees with gnarled human faces that toss apples at intruders, are mesmerizing. So is the dispatch of a squadron of actors, dressed as winged monkeys and propped up by piano wire, to capture the heroine, and the meltdown of the Wicked Witch of the West into a puddle of water.

Nominated for five Academy Awards, *The Wizard of Oz* won two of them on February 29, 1940. The film well might have been voted best picture, except for the misfortune of being released in Hollywood's golden year of 1939 and forced to compete with nine other excellent productions, including MGM's own *Gone with the Wind*, *Goodbye, Mr. Chips*, and *Ninotchka*. Fifty-six years later, however, during the 100th anniversary of the birth of the cinema in 1995, it was honored by Pope John Paul II's Vatican

Translating her dream of escaping from the hum-drum of Kansas farm life into a song, Judy Garland sings the Academy Award-winning "Over the Rainbow" in *The Wizard of Oz*. Looking on is her dog, Toto.

Pontifical Council for Social Communication as one of the 45 best films ever made. Cited for possessing "special artistic or religious merit," *The Wizard of Oz* was the only musical to appear on the list and one of only a dozen American films. (The other Hollywood-made movies were *Ben-Hur, Citizen Kane, Fantasia, Intolerance, It's a Wonderful Life, Little Women* (1933), *A Man for All Seasons, Modern Times, On the Waterfront, Schindler's List*, and *Stagecoach* (1939).

MGM purchased the rights to *The Wizard of Oz* in 1938 from Samuel Goldwyn, who had planned to turn it into a Technicolor musical with Eddie Cantor as the Scarecrow. Over subsequent months, the studio considered W.C. Fields and Ed Wynn among at least six other actors for the part of the Wizard, while Fanny Brice and Beatrice Lillie vied with Billie Burke to play the sweetly helpful Glinda, the Good Witch of the North. Potential directors with

imposing MGM credits included Norman Taurog (*Boys Town*) and Richard Thorpe (*Night Must Fall*), who were dropped, and George Cukor (*Camille*), who refused the assignment.

The directorial job was finally given to Victor Fleming, also credited with the direction of *Gone with the Wind*. He received valuable and unbilled assistance from King Vidor (*The Citadel*), whose footage comprised most of the Kansas sequences, including star Judy Garland's plaintive singing of "Over the Rainbow." Also lacking credit for lending their expertise to the film were Arthur Freed, the associate producer who later that year produced *Babes in Arms*, the first in his long list of MGM musicals, and Roger Edens, who arranged the musical background. Buddy Ebsen, who had danced briefly with Judy in Freed and Brown's "Your Broadway and My Broadway" in *The Broadway Melody of 1938*, was picked to play the Tin Woodman (usually referred to simply as the Tin Man), but an allergy to the heavy silver makeup required for the role forced him out of it.

The musical fantasy was previewed for the press in Los Angeles on August 9, 1939, less than one month before the outbreak of World War II. The Hollywood premiere was held six days later at Grauman's Chinese Theatre, and on August 17 it began its three-week engagement before stupendous crowds and to rave reviews at Broadway's Capitol Theatre.

Several MGM executives, including producer Mervyn LeRoy and Louis B. Mayer himself, had hoped to star Shirley Temple in the role of Dorothy. (Deanna Durbin was also briefly under consideration.) Shirley was far more popular than Judy, and in early 1939 she was closer in age (10) than Judy (16) to the original book character. Only recently, Shirley had scored a huge dramatic and box office success as Sara Crewe in *The Little Princess*. Negotiations broke down, however, when Darryl F. Zanuck refused to accede to LeRoy's request for the loanout of Fox's, and the nation's, number one box office attraction.

The six-year age difference that separated the two girls was significant, as anyone who has ever been subjected to the wailing of a high school junior ordered to consort with a fifth-grader for longer than five minutes is painfully aware. Wide-eyed Judy's immense skill as an actress, evident as early as 1937, however, made her the ideal choice for the part, despite her height and maturing voice and body. It is impossible today to picture any other earthling traipsing along the route from Munchkinland to the Emerald City.

In 1940 Shirley appeared in *The Blue Bird*, a dramatic fantasy based on Maurice Maeterlinck's 1908 six-act play that tells a story not too different from *Oz*'s. Beautifully—and expensively—filmed, *The Blue Bird* suffered alongside the Garland film, which could still be seen in some neighborhood houses, and it was Shirley's first commercial failure. Carrying the identical theme that true happiness is found at home in company with family and friends, and not externally in an imaginary land, the film nudged viewers into further unfavorable comparisons with *Oz* by similarly switching early on from sepia tone to Technicolor. Ironically, among its cast members was Gale Sondergaard

as Tylette the cat, who accompanies Shirley on her travels back to the past and ahead to the future. Before the filming of *Oz* got under way, Miss Sondergaard had turned down the part of the Wicked Witch of the West. Not the least comparable with the 1940 *Blue Bird*, which was given a rare 3-star rating by *Halliwell's*, was the lackluster 1976 Soviet-American remake that cast a roster of acknowledged stars, among them Elizabeth Taylor, Ava Gardner, and Henry Fonda, in totally unsuitable roles.

Oz marked the beginning of the long-term professional coupling of composer Harold Arlen and Judy, even though the songs were stylistically quite different from the bluesy melodies on which his reputation rested. He would supply her with both old and new tunes for almost three more decades. His first hit song, the rousing "Get Happy," sung by Ruth Etting in the 1930 stage production *The Nine-Fifteen Revue*, was reintroduced by Judy in standout fashion at the conclusion of *Summer Stock* in 1950. Four years later he and Ira Gershwin collaborated on the first-rate score for Judy's version of *A Star Is Born*. Arlen's final movie song for Judy was "Paris Is a Lonely Town," which the star sings off-screen for the animated cat character Mewsette in *Gay Purree* (1962).

A highly gifted composer, Arlen had written "Stormy Weather," "I Gotta Right to Sing the Blues," "I've Got the World on a String," "Ill Wind," and "Between the Devil and the Deep Blue Sea" for such early 1930s stage annuals as the Earl Carroll Vanities and the Cotton Club Parade. His pre-1939 Hollywood outings resulted in songs for Eddie Cantor in *Strike Me Pink*, Al Jolson in *The Singing Kid*, and Dick Powell in *Stage Struck* (all 1936). He also composed "Let's Fall in Love" for Ann Southern, "It's Only a Paper Moon" for Cliff Edwards, June Knight, and Charles ("Buddy") Rogers, and "Let's Put Our Heads Together," another Powell song, from *Gold Diggers of 1937*.

One of his and lyricist E[dgar] Y[ipsel] Harburg's best screen songs, "Last Night When We Were Young," written for Lawrence Tibbett to sing in Fox's *Metropolitan* (1935), wound up instead as an instrumental heard only in the background. In later years it was dropped from both Garland and Sinatra movies on the ground that the lyric was simply too sad in its melancholy references to the rapid decline of youth into middle age.

Arlen and Harburg were united again in 1939 for the Marx Brothers' *At the Races* ("Lydia, the Tattooed Lady"), and in 1944 for Broadway's *Bloomer Girl* and in 1957 for *Jamaica*. Despite his relatively small number of film songs, Arlen received five best song nominations, three of them in the single year of 1943. The exceptionally gifted Harburg, the author of two books of verse whose lyrics appeared in 29 Broadway shows and 52 films, received one. Of the team's proposed 13 *Oz* songs, three were dropped before they were completed, while a fourth was cut before the film was released. Of the remaining nine, seven are introduced within the first 40 minutes of the almost two-hour-long picture.

King of Ozophiles. Author Lyman Frank Baum, nicknamed the "Royal Historian of Oz," was born on May 15, 1856, in the village of Chittenango, near Syracuse, New York. The husband of Maud Gage, the youngest daughter of the noted women's rights campaigner Matilda Joslyn Gage, he tried his hand at many careers—actor, playwright, newspaper editor (in Aberdeen, S.D.), shop owner, and traveling salesman—before finally achieving renown as the author of fairy tales. He was 44 when the Chicago firm of George M. Hill Company published his first full-length Oz book, *The Wonderful Wizard of Oz*, in September 1900. Bobbs-Merrill published the second edition, renamed *The New Wizard of Oz*, in 1903. Each time, the book was an instant success, helped along by William Wallace Denslow's illustrations, which included 24 color plates and more than 100 textual drawings. It created a nationwide Ozmania that Baum kept alive by publishing 13 more book-length Oz tales. He died of complications after a gall bladder operation, aggravated by chronic heart trouble, on May 6, 1919.

The Magic of Oz was published the year of his death, and the last in the series, *Glinda of Oz*, found its way into print in 1920. An amazingly prolific writer of children's books under a variety of pseudonyms, he also wrote a series of "Little Wizard" stories and "Snug-gle Tales." Under the pseudonym of Floyd Akers, he wrote six "Boy Fortune Hunters" books, as Laura Bancroft seven "Twinkle Tales," as Edith Van Dyne 10 "Aunt Jane's Nieces" stories, and as Captain Hugh Fitzgerald two books on the adventures of Sam Steele.

Like Ziegfeld, Baum led a boom and bust life. More artist than businessman, he declared bankruptcy in 1911, eight years before his death at age 62. His Oz stories were his Follies, and the high regard in which he was held by readers was his greatest consolation as his life neared its end. His first book for children, *Mother Goose in Prose*, published in 1897, sold reasonably well, quite possibly because of the Maxfield Parrish illustrations. Writing an inscription in the copy he presented to his sister as a gift, he suggested why his Oz tales, yet to come, would captivate so many youngsters for generations to come. He loved children and wanted to entertain them with amusing stories. "I have learned," he wrote in part, "to regard fame as a will-o'-the-wisp which, when caught, is not worth the possession, but to please a child is a sweet and lovely thing that warms one's heart and brings its own reward."

Like the 1939 movie, Baum's Oz stories were quite traditional in approach, filled with such familiar fairy tale trappings as witches, wizards, and magic while preaching that good motives, ingenuity, and trust in oneself will always win, even though the way to victory is often rough. Baum's tales soon found their way onto the stage and then into films between 1903 and 1925. *The Wizard of Oz*, with music by Paul Tietjens, a St. Louis-born pianist-composer, opened on Broadway in 1903. A sequoia-size hit starring vaudevillian Fred Stone as the Scarecrow and partner David Montgomery as the Tin Woodman, it ran for an astounding 293 performances. Next came *The Woggle-Bug*, based on *The Marvelous Land of Oz*, Baum's second Oz book, with music by Frederick Chapin, which opened in Chicago in 1905. In 1913 the famous producer Oliver Morosco brought *Tik-Tok Man of Oz* from Los Angeles to Broadway, with music by Louis F. Gottschalk and book and lyrics by Baum. The eight short-lived songs, all published by Jerome H. Remick & Company, were "The Magnet of Love," "When in Trouble Come to Papa,"

"The Waltz Scream," "Dear Old Hank," "So Do I," "The Clockwork Man," "Oh, My Bow," and "Ask the Flowers to Tell You." None of them appears in the 1939 film.

Beginning in 1908 with *Fairylogue and Radio Plays*, which combined slides and moving pictures, Baum's Oz adventures could be seen on the silent screen. The author moved to Hollywood in 1910 and formed the Oz Film Manufacturing Company specifically to produce films based on Oz and other of his books. All told, four movies—the first three directed by Baum himself—were based on Oz. The company failed in 1915, but other studios fulfilled his wish to dramatize his characters for the masses.

Paramount released *The Magic Clock of Oz*, loosely based on Baum's *Queen Zixi of Ix*, in 1914; Alliance Film Company turned his book *His Majesty, the Scarecrow of Oz* into *The New Wizard of Oz* in 1915. *The Wizard of Oz* of 1925, produced by Chadwick Pictures Corporation, bears only the slightest relation to the 1939 film, almost completely abandoning Baum's original story. It remains notable for the appearance of Oliver Hardy, who the next year would team up permanently with Stan Laurel, as a Kansas prairie farmhand who disguises himself as the Tin Woodman. Eight years later, the National Broadcasting Company aired a *Wizard of Oz* radio series from September 1933 to April 1934.

A Most-Favored Property. Numerous post-1939 visits to the merry old land of Oz achieved little beyond strengthening the Garland film's reputation as Hollywood's preeminent children's classic. If anything, seeing them only increases one's delight in and reverence for the original. The Australian *20th Century Oz*, produced by Court Features and released in the United States in 1977, offered no serious competition, nor did the Royal Shakespearean Company when it staged an *Oz* celebration in London in 1987.

Between those years came *The Shirley Temple Show*'s September 18, 1960, adaptation of *The Land of Oz* on NBC television. In 1964 the same network televised Videocraft's hour-long *Return to Oz*, the first animated cartoon to travel over the rainbow. A second animated feature, the 90-minute *Journey Back to Oz*, was completed in 1964 but withheld from theatrical distribution till 1974. Rambling on about how Dorothy and her friends go back to Oz to defeat the Wicked Witch of the West's equally venomous sister, it featured voiceovers by Judy's daughter, Liza Minnelli, as Dorothy, Milton Berle, Ethel Merman, Mickey Rooney, Danny Thomas, and Margaret Hamilton, the only member of the original 1939 cast, as Auntie Em. By the time the telecast was released, Margaret had foresworn her wicked ways to earn widespread recognition as the unthreatening spokeswoman for Maxwell House Coffee in television commercials.

In 1978, Universal/Motown picked up the Tony-winning *The Wiz* from Broadway, and director Sidney Lumet filmed it with the original musical score by Quincy Jones and an all-black cast headed by Diana Ross (Dorothy), Michael Jackson (the Scarecrow), Nipsey Russell (the Tin Man), Ted Ross (the Cowardly Lion), and Richard Pryor (the Wizard). In 1981 along came *Under the Rainbow*, a certified exercise in futility starring Chevy Chase that centered uneasily on the mishaps committed by a band of pre–World War II Nazi spies and midgets while the original *The Wizard of Oz* is being filmed. An even worse rendering of the Oz legend appeared, courtesy of Walt Disney and the Silver Screen Partners, in 1985. Called *Return to Oz*, the picture was based ever so loosely on Baum's *The Marvelous Land of Oz* and *Ozma of Oz*. Staffed by a coterie of unknown players, it attacked the old story with something resembling purposeless vengeance by presenting Dorothy as a neurotic suffering delayed traumas from her earlier Oz wanderings. If not the worst film ever made, it surely deserves ranking somewhere on everybody's Top Ten list of Hollywood's biggest disasters.

As recently as 1996, Channel TNT telecast a concert version of the music from the 1939 film. Taped in New York at Lincoln Center's Avery Fisher Hall, the program starred Jewel as Dorothy, Natalie Cole as Glinda, Debra Winger as the Wicked Witch of the West, and Joel Grey as the Wizard. The show was notable only for restoring Harburg and Arlen's "The Jitterbug," a song-and-dance tune performed in the Haunted Forest by the Scarecrow, Tin

Man (played by Buddy Ebsen before he left the cast), Cowardly Lion, and Dorothy. Shot at a cost of $80,000, the number was wisely deleted from the final print in order to cut the film's running time. Substantially trimmed down was much of Ray Bolger's lengthy dance solo that follows his singing of "If I Only Had a Brain." Fans were already familiar with his nimbleness by virtue of his *The Great Ziegfeld* solo and *Sweethearts* duet with Jeanette MacDonald on "Jeanette and Her Little Wooden Shoes" in 1938. And, of course, like numerous Disney feature films, *The Wizard of Oz* has become a perennially popular ice show.

A number of allegedly hidden symbols with mystical meanings have been attached to various elements in the Oz story over the years. The most common concerns the author's alleged opposition to the monetary theories of William Jennings Bryan, a Baum contemporary who was opposed to what in later years would be termed the absolute rule of big business. Basing much of his economic philosophy on writer Henry George's "Single Tax" plan of the 1880s and the "Free Silver" crusade of 1896, Bryan was a vociferous advocate of the free and unlimited coinage of silver, which he believed would remedy the economic ills confronting U.S. farmers and industrial workers. George, who had been disturbed by the poverty that mocked California's gold rush glitter during the great crash of 1877, had proposed enactment of a single tax on profits from the unearned appreciation of land values in his impassioned 1879 book *Progress and Poverty*.

Nominated in 1896 to run for President by both the Democratic and the Populist parties, Bryan made history with one sentence in his acceptance speech: "You shall not press down on the brow of labor this crown of thorns; you shall not crucify mankind on a cross of gold." Bryan badly lost the election, but his central point was scarcely nonsensical. Rising gold prices had cruelly penalized debtors, an unfairness that was ameliorated only when gold was discovered in South Africa. To some interpreters of the Baum work, the Yellow Brick Road that leads directly to the lush green (as in "greenbacks") of the Emerald City is a signal that the author was a willing, if rather subtle, propagandist for the conservative Democrats, who preferred gold over silver to back the nation's currency.

Although it is true that many children's books can be classified as parables designed to spread the authors' philosophy of life on several levels—Swift's *Gulliver's Travels* is but one notable example—definitive proof that Baum's most famous work flirted even tangentially with such an esoteric subject as economics is inconclusive. Nor has the controversy surrounding his allegiance, if any, to one or the other wing of the Democratic Party been settled. Carrying absolutely no symbolism whatever was Baum's coinage of the word Oz. According to his own admission, he picked it up from the bottom drawer of his file cabinet, which was labeled O–Z.

A good-size collection of *Oz* memorabilia is on permanent display in "Dorothy's House," one of the nation's most unusual museums, which was built in 1907 in Liberal, Kansas—at what is now 567 Yellow Brick Road, to be exact. Thanks to extensive restorations made to the structure over the years since the MGM film, its exterior and interior now mirror Dorothy's home, down to the placement and style of the period furniture. After its occupants donated the house to the Seward County Historical Society in 1981, volunteers moved it from the countryside to the grounds of the Coronado Museum, where much of the refurbishing took place. On June 11 of that year, Kansas Governor John Carlin issued a proclamation officially identifying the house as the "Gateway to the Land of Oz [pronounced 'Oh's'] and Ah's." Further evidence of the abiding interest in Baum and his Oz books was the 1957 formation of the International Wizard of Oz Club.

As sentimental as any film ever made, *The Wizard of Oz* is one of those cinematic masterpieces that age cannot wither nor custom stale. If anything, it seems to improve with successive viewings. A veritable monument to its creators, it never allows massiveness of concept and execution to overpower what is basically a simple little allegory of a young girl who had to endure loneliness and uncommon dangers in a strange land before learning the simple truth that there's no place like home. Fittingly, it was left to MGM, then America's most successful and calculating purveyor of family values, to film the landmark version. The studio dedicated it to the "Young in Heart" who had been faithful to a story that "time has been powerless to put its kindly philosophy out of fashion."

Little Girl Lost. Why is it, pig-tailed Judy Garland (Dorothy) sings while resting her back against a tall stack of hay and gazing languidly into the sky, that she is denied entry into that wondrous land inhabited by bluebirds of happiness. That's where she longs to go, far away from the petty annoyances of life on earth. But exactly where is that tranquil realm? Maybe it exists only in the imagination, or maybe it lies too close to heaven to welcome a mere mortal. Perhaps it is heaven, and she is far too young to even consider going there anytime soon. Or could it be that she already resides in her dream world, right here on a farm in the Kansas flatlands, along with Clara Blandick (Auntie Em) and Charley Grapewin (Uncle Henry) and the trio of farmhands who have loved her ever since she can remember?

Her song, of course, is "Over the Rainbow," a gem of melodic pensiveness and the auditory equivalent of a rainbow itself, and still the film song most immediately identified with the singer who introduced it. Curiously, the song was thought to be too slow, and would have been excised had not Freed insisted on its retention. The words flow naturally from Judy's lips without a trace of bitterness. She's had a rough day, that's for sure, but she really doesn't want to escape from life, just daydream for a while until she can regain her composure. She's already suffered plenty of traumas for one day, and it's only mid-afternoon.

First of all, there was that dreadful old maid, Miss Gulch, superbly played by Margaret Hamilton, along with Eily Malyon, the cross cook in *The Little Princess*, the screen's most convincing harridan. As the youngster had explained earlier to her aunt and uncle, Margaret had hit her dog, Toto, with a rake, charging that he had chased her cat, an accusation that Dorothy vehemently denies. Toto never chases the cat, at least not often, nor does he ravage her garden, well, not usually, in the pursuit. And he definitely did not bite her, as the mirthless woman alleged, and it was only in the nick of time that Judy had rescued him from her clutches. But her guardians had been far too bogged down in domestic chores to sympathize with their excitable niece. Auntie Clara even expressed the hope that someday Judy would find a place where she won't be able to get into more trouble.

Then there are those three farmhands whom Judy had always regarded as friends. Hoping to get her out of their way, Ray Bolger (Hunk) had proffered only the foolish advice to use some brainpower and simply arrange to keep Toto away from Margaret's property. Bert Lahr (Zeke) told her to stiffen up her backbone and spit in the old lady's eye at their next encounter. Jack Haley (Hickory) didn't even open up his ears and heart long enough to console her with a single piece of advice. Little wonder Judy wants to escape from family, farm, and farmhands.

Her song finished, Judy's metal is tested further by another confrontation with Margaret, her lips still pursed, as if she had just tasted something sour. This time she has a sheriff's order permitting her to have Toto destroyed, she announces in the farmhouse living room. Furthermore, she has filed a damage suit to take away the farm if Judy's uncle and aunt refuse to surrender the animal. Despite Judy's tearful appeal to them, they stand aside while the menacing "old witch," as Judy calls her, imprisons Toto in a basket, stashes it at the rear of her bicycle, and pedals along the dirt road to the animal pound, revenge on her mind and grim determination etched on her face.

Toto, however, escapes from the basket and races back into Judy's arms. But surely his return doesn't mean that Judy has seen the last of trouble. What Toto's reappearance invites is a potential second visit from Margaret, probably more determined than before to see that he is put to sleep. Judy's solution to the problem is to pack a suitcase and hit the road with her dog. Once in the countryside, she comes across Frank Morgan (Professor Marvel), a fraudulent forecaster of the future whose alleged mystical powers impress no one but himself. His suspicion that Judy has run away from home is confirmed when she confides that her disenchantment with home life stems from her family's inability to understand or appreciate her. What she wants Morgan to do is take her along on his travels to distant parts of the world, even though it is doubtful that this tall-tale teller has ever ventured farther than the Kansas-Nebraska border. Maybe together they can find a Promised Land where all their troubles will melt away.

A genuinely kindly con man, Morgan delays approving her request by focusing his eyes on what appears to be his magical crystal ball. He had spied a photograph of Auntie Clara in Judy's basket, and hopes to use it to coax the runaway into returning home. What he sees in the ball, he tells her, is an elderly woman with a careworn face—her aunt, maybe?—who is crying her heart out. She has obviously been hurt by someone she loves very much, been kind to, and nursed in sickness. But now look! She has fallen into a swoon onto her bed! Worried Judy asks for more information, but the crystal ball inexplicably goes dark. No information on the fate of the woman is available. That's enough to send Judy scurrying off to retrace her steps back to the farm.

On the way, she is met by a rampaging twister that sends its midnight-black funnel of sucked-up earth on a zig-zag course across the land. Unable to find Judy, her fearful family and friends had secluded themselves in the storm cellar and locked it behind them. Judy's frantic kicks at the door and pulls on the handle are fruitless, and her screams are suffocated by the wailing of the wind.

With Toto in her arms, she races into her bedroom, where she is hit by a window frame the tornado had unhinged, and knocked to the floor. The house itself is then uprooted and sent swirling into the clouds. From the window, Judy gapes at reflections of neighbors also flying through the atmosphere. One of them is Margaret, who has been turned into a witch, a pointed hat perched atop her head and her black cape flapping against the broomstick that has replaced her bicycle, all the while rending the air with shrill cackles of laughter worthy of comparison with the howls of monsters on Hallowe'en night itself.

Into the Merry Old Land. The house abruptly falls with a thump. Startled, Judy opens the door and peers into a strange but beautiful land sparkling with beds of rainbow-hued flowers and a clear blue brook surrounded by tiny thatched huts, made all the more appealing by the switch in film from sepia to Technicolor. Judy's plea has been answered. Even without Professor Morgan's help, she has managed to travel beyond the moon and the rain to somewhere over the rainbow where dreams really do come true.

Thrilled but nervous, she summarizes her reaction to the breathtaking view in one of the screen's most familiar lines, "Toto, I've got the feeling we're not in Kansas anymore." Exactly where she is must await the appearance of Billie Burke, who alights from a huge bubble in a flowing dress and tiara and holding a wand, appropriate to her royal status as Glinda, the Good Witch of the North. She is in Munchkinland, Glinda explains to the amazed youngster, and has performed an invaluable service for the residents. Her farmhouse has fallen on the Wicked Witch of the East, killing her instantly. Only her feet, encased in ruby slippers, are visible under the wreckage.

Judy must be a living symbol of goodness to have brought such great happiness to the land, Glinda continues, and must be accorded all the ceremonial trappings suitable to welcome a national heroine. Turning to acknowledge the sounds of muffled giggling, she urges the little residents to come out of their hiding places beneath the flowers in the two-part song "Munchkinland." Come out, come out, Glinda the Good sings to the deliriously happy "Sleepyheads," shyly emerging from the flowers and tiptoeing over to Judy, who picks up the melody to set the record straight. She is not a good witch brought to them by a miracle from a star named Kansas, as Glinda had reported, but just a visitor dropped in their midst by a ferocious wind that tore her house from its foundation.

Notwithstanding her denial of magical powers, the little people give vent to their joy by singing "Ding-Dong! The Witch Is Dead," a spirited anthem to their freedom from the Wicked Witch of the East. A royal coach escorted by Munchkin soldiers drives up to the tune of "The Merry Old Land of Oz" and carries Judy to the mayor of "Munchkin City in the County of Oz." When the Munchkin Coroner (Meinhardt Raabe) unscrolls an official certificate attesting that the witch is not merely dead, but "most sincerely dead," the whole town repeats the lively dirge, and the mayor orders the beginning of "Independence Day" festivities. Honoring Judy for ending the reign of terror are two welcoming committees consisting of three girl ballerinas from the "Lullaby League" and a trio of tough boys representing the "Lollipop Guild," whose salutations provoke all the other Munchkins into praising the youngster as savior.

Their and Judy's happiness, however, is quickly dissipated by an explosive noise followed by billows of red smoke that usher in Margaret Hamilton (the Wicked Witch of the West), her ugly blue-green face snarling at the frightened celebrants from above her coalblack, ankle-length dress. She demands to know who is responsible for killing her equally fearsome sister. Receiving no answer, she reaches her hand to reclaim the precious ruby slippers, only to see them disappear before her eyes. Thanks to Billie's magic wand, they have been transferred to Judy's feet. Without recourse to her own substantial magical powers while in Munchkinland, Margaret is unable to remove them by force or trickery. There is little else for her to do but flee the scene, which she does after warning Judy that she will bide her time till she is able to "get you, my pretty, and your little dog, too!"

Depressed that trouble has tagged along after her even in this land of milk and honey, Judy expresses the wish to return to her Kansas homestead. Though difficult, such a trip can be arranged by a wonderful Wizard, a "very good but very mysterious" man who lives in faraway Emerald City, Billie assures her. But the journey is a long one fraught with difficulties, she warns, and the girl must walk the entire distance, never once removing the ruby slippers, lest she fall under the spell of evil Margaret.

Billie leads her to a circular path paved with yellow bricks that extends from the center of the community through the valleys and over the mountain tops as far as the eye can see. "Follow the yellow brick road," Billie sings, along with the Munchkins, before disappearing in her bubble. Judy steps gingerly on the road while the Munchkins switch songs to cheer her onward to the tune of "We're [You're] Off to See the Wizard (the Wonderful Wizard of Oz)."

Thus begins Judy and Toto's turbulent exodus from the placid land of harmless tiny people to the fabled but mysterious Emerald City, the equivalent of John Bunyan's Celestial City, by now surely one of the most familiar journeys in the whole of American literature. Skipping along the bricks at first, she soon slows down to a cautious gait, proceeding with the nervous agitation of a girl of eight on her way to the principal's office. But throughout the journey she will remain the sweet adolescent continually under siege by adult forces inimical to her well-being, the personification of good eventually triumphing over evil in true storybook fashion. No longer interested in settling down in a fantasy land, she stubbornly pursues her goal of resuming normal life far beneath the rainbow in Kansas. There she has family and friends, perhaps too busy at times to pay heed to her complaints, but essentially sincere helpmates in times of crisis. Now she has only the amorphous Billie on her side—but where is she? Why couldn't she lead the way to the Wizard? Is she her guardian angel or only an apparition that urges strangers to embark on difficult travels and then dismisses them from mind? Or must Judy learn through surmounting hardship that it is only in her earthly home that she will find true happiness?

This stranger in paradise, however, is destined to encounter several escorts on the mineladen trail to the home of the Wizard. The first is Ray Bolger (the Scarecrow), hanging from a big nail on a wooden pole in a cornfield. Like farmhand Hunk, he is indecisive and more than just a little confused—and confusing. When Judy asks which fork in the yellow brick road to take, the fellow points in both directions. Noting Judy's bewilderment, he confesses that he is unable to make up his mind, if in fact he has one. All he does is fritter away his time devoid of any usefulness, he tells the youngster.

He really doesn't perform even his menial job very well. He's unable to scare off the crows, which fly right over to him as to an old friend and rebegin pecking him apart, straw by straw. And he lives in constant fear of catching fire, knowing full well that he could never figure out how to extinguish the flames. What he needs, he confesses in the first chorus of a catchy three-part song with exceptional lyrics by Harburg, who rhymes "riddle" with "individdle" [individual] and "presumin'" with "human," is a brain. With one, he is thinking he could well be another Lincoln. The boundless enthusiasm born of hope catches hold of him when she suggests that the helpful Wizard is sure to give him one, and he happily joins her on the trek along the yellow brick road.

The second character Judy meets is a Jack Haley lookalike trapped inside a suit of tin and standing still as a smoke stack while mumbling a few words apparently in desperation. Judy finally interprets his incoherent muttering as a plea to lubricate his joints with the help of a small oil can that he is unable to reach. Following instructions, she loosens his lips and finally opens his mouth. Now able to speak clearly, Haley relates the sad tale of how, about a year ago, he rusted solid in a rain storm while chopping trees. Although delighted that he now can move about freely, he remains pestered by another, far more serious infirmity. The tinsmith that put him together, he explains in the second chorus of the song, forgot to give him a heart. "If I Only Had a Heart," he sings, he would be friendly toward everybody, even to the point of learning how to love them. Struck by Judy's assurance that the Wizard could very well furnish him with what he lacks, Haley joins her and Bolger. The twosome has become a threesome.

Later that night, Judy's final companion is found in the darkest part of a forest. It is a Cowardly Lion, who frightens the travelers by showing up unexpectedly and growling his intention to beat them to a pulp, one at a time or, if they prefer, all three at once. Bearing a remarkable resemblance to Bert Lahr, the monster becomes all the more assertive when nobody volunteers to answer his challenge. So fearful is Haley that his metal parts begin to clatter and clank, resulting in Lahr's dubbing him a "shivering junkyard." At a loss for a gladiator, he suddenly attacks Toto.

When Judy slaps him while defending the dog, Lahr breaks into tears, wiping them away with his tail. The truth is out: he's really all roar and no guts. The only creature his bluster and bluff frighten is himself, he admits between sobs, and he's been unable to sleep for weeks because he's too afraid of sheep to count them. In his musical lamentation on his lack of nerve—or "noive" in Lahr's telltale New York accent—he relates some of the marvels of strength he might achieve if only someone would give him the gift of courage. Judy and her two friends reach instant agreement: the Wizard is the fellow to see about that.

Tracking Judy and companions every step of the way by means of her crystal ball, angry Margaret has been trying to impede their progress by turning the journey into an obstacle course. What she had not anticipated was the creativeness of the youngster's allies in frustrating her malevolence. Instead of frightening Judy and Bolger, the fireball the wicked witch had thrown at them only stiffened his determination to squire his young companion along the route to Emerald City. Later, as Margaret gleefully watched a hoary old apple tree slap its fruit from Judy's hand after she had plucked it from a branch, the witch was again doomed to disappointment by the supposedly brainless Bolger. Quick as a wink he hatched a plan to antagonize the tree and its orchard cohorts into pulling their own apples from themselves and throwing them at the two hungry interlopers in retaliation.

Finally, Margaret's scheme to thwart Judy's reaching her goal by covering a huge field with sleep-inducing poppies had backfired when protectress Billie Burke produced a blizzard of snowflakes that awakened all four travelers from what was meant to be their final resting place. Clearly, Margaret needs even more devilish ploys to snatch those magical ruby slippers from Judy's feet. Few were the doubters that she was eminently capable of devising them.

Reaching Their Goal. Once beyond the haunted forest, which the travelers happily depart to the tune of "Optimistic Voices" (with Herbert Stothart as co-collaborator on the music), they enter the Emerald City and approach the imposing and colorful Palace of Oz. Somewhere inside that triple-tiered building crowned with tall steeples that seem to touch the doorstep of heaven itself is the miracle man who is to fulfill their dreams, Judy muses as she knocks on the enormous green door. A head pokes its way through a peephole, and the authoritative voice of a gruff old man demands to know who the callers are and what they want.

Judy replies that they have come to see the Wizard, only to be brusquely informed that no one has ever seen him and presumably no one ever will. Peeved at being disturbed, the doorkeeper, who, along with all the other major palace personnel, is played by Frank Morgan, finally admits Judy and her companions after she tells him that she has been sent by the benevolent Witch of the North and points to the ruby slippers as proof.

Quaking with fear, Lahr nonetheless anticipates the courage about to be bestowed on him by bursting into the song "If I Were King of the Forest." The sole unnecessary sequence in an otherwise tightly constructed screenplay, the song neither advances the plot nor adds very much in the way of amusement. Lahr's paean to courage is far too long, and he had already condensed the message in his earlier "If I Only Had the Nerve." Actually, his antics, facial contortions, and string of boasts dilute much of the carefully built-up suspense surrounding Judy's forthcoming meeting with the Wizard by postponing it for far too long a time.

She and her companions are then driven by carriage to the accompaniment of loud trumpet blasts and drum rolls into a huge room, where a volcano of fire and brimstone gives a pretty good indication of what hell must be like. There they confront a huge photographic image of the Wizard that suddenly appears on a wall above what appears to be an enormous bare stage. To its right is an ante room shielded from view by a curtain. A thunderous voice from an unseen man instantly numbs the visitors into silence. It is apparent that he is not interested in their wishes, nor is he the least willing to grant them any favors—for good reason, as the screenplay will later disclose. Hoping to get rid of them, the man demands that if they expect any help at all from him, they must bring back Margaret's broomstick as proof that she is no longer a threat to Oz. The challenge is indeed tremendously difficult, as the Wizard is fully aware, and one that he is certain will remove the petitioners from his presence once and for all.

Intent on obeying orders, the four leave the room posthaste and go deep into the Haunted Forest, in the middle of which stands the Wicked Witch's castle. Forewarned of their mission from her crystal ball, Margaret calls on her army of sky monkeys to capture the intruders. No match for the flying brigade, Judy is forcibly airlifted to the castle and terrified by mean Margaret. Like Miss Gulch before her,

she imprisons Toto in a basket and threatens to drown him unless Judy surrenders the ruby slippers. Judy reluctantly agrees, but Margaret is unable to remove them because, as she quickly realizes, they cannot be lifted from anyone's feet until the person wearing them is dead. Judy is promptly locked in a cell to await certain death, but Toto again escapes confinement and races through the forest until he finally meets up with Bolger, Haley, and Lahr. From the animals's anguished whines, they infer that the girl is in trouble, and they follow him back to the castle.

The three men succeed in overthrowing the marching "Winkie Guard" soldiers assigned to fend off enemies, and dress themselves in their uniforms. With Toto in the lead, they reenter the castle, where Haley chops through the dungeon door with his ax. Her allies free Judy and prepare to whisk her away with them. They are stalled in their tracks, however, when Margaret blocks their exit. Her revenge no longer centered solely on Judy, the witch prepares to kill all four, as well as Toto. Her first target is Bolger, whom she promptly sets on fire. Terrified of the fate of her highly combustible friend, Judy empties a pail of water over him. A few drops splash on Margaret, who bewails the end of what she terms her "beautiful wickedness" as she dissolves from sight until only her empty black costume and pointed hat, resting atop a pool of water, remain.

True to her nature as a thoroughly good person, Judy did not murder the Wicked Witch of the West any more than she was responsible for the death of her sister. Each was done away with accidentally, the former crushed in the fall of Judy's farmhouse, the latter liquidated by trickles of the water thrown to save the life of another person. Margaret's guards, equally happy over the demise of their cruel ruler, present Judy with the gift of her broomstick.

Clutching it in her hands, Judy leads her allies back to the Wizard's palace, all of them gleefully expecting fulfillment of their individual requests. But the devious Wizard again refuses to answer their pleas, even after Judy sobs that she has traveled a long and difficult distance expressly to beg him to let her return to Kansas and Auntie Clara, whose kindliness she has only recently begun to appreciate. Expressing canine fidelity to his suffering mistress,

Toto suddenly races up to the ante room hoping to attack the voice by grabbing the curtain in his teeth and pulling it asunder. Now standing unconcealed is a normal human being operating a battery of pulleys and levers and barking into a microphone to impress his visitors by means of mechanical rather than magical means.

Embarrassed at being discovered as the humbug he is, Morgan agrees to grant their individual requests, although not exactly in the formats they had anticipated. What he offers are substitute gifts, which he assures are quite satisfactory. Hoping to impress each recipient with pre-presentation speeches declaring the worth of the trinkets, Morgan gives a university degree in "thinkology" to Bolger, a heart-shaped clock to Haley (its ticking meant to substitute for heart beats), and a medal for exceptional bravery to Lahr. Everybody is satisfied but Judy, who sorrowfully reminds Morgan that he has not granted her wish to return to Kansas.

He complies with her request by announcing that he has been hired to serve as Wizard at the Omaha State Fair, and that she and Toto can accompany him on his balloon trip to Nebraska. Morgan then reveals how he had arrived in Oz years ago. A carnival balloonist on earth, he had risen one day into the sky, only to be blown by the wind into Munchkinland. Impressed with his height and gift of gab, the residents offered him the post of Wizard. Tempted by the prerogatives that go with the office, Morgan gladly accepted.

Later, as he, Judy, and Toto prepare to ride the balloon back to earth, Morgan addresses her three dismal comrades one by one, revealing that their recent activities on behalf of Judy have instilled in them the attributes they so devoutly sought. Having proved that his head contains a *bona fide* brain, Bolger is appointed to succeed Morgan as the Wizard of Oz. He will be assisted by Haley and Lahr, whose faithfulness and courage under the most trying of circumstances qualify them to undertake the duties of their new exalted positions.

Judy's goodbye and well wishes to her friends prove to be premature when Toto jumps out of the balloon to chase a Siamese cat. She runs after him, the balloon takes off, and the Wizard, unable to control it, waves farewell to all on his solo flight to Omaha. Judy's fear that she has lost her only chance to return home is dispelled by the reappearance of Billie Burke. Judy doesn't need her help, Billie tells the girl. She's always had the power to go back to Kansas, but first she had to learn something very important—namely, that she who hopes to find her heart's desire need not venture beyond her own backyard. For if she can't find happiness there, she won't find it anywhere.

That lesson having been learned, Billie continues, all that Judy has to do to leave Oz is to tap the heels of the ruby slippers together three times and say, "There's no place like home." In the film's most touching sequence, July bids a tearful goodbye to her three forlorn friends. "I know I have a heart," Tin Man Haley acknowledges as Judy kisses him, "because now it's breaking."

As Billie had promised, the taps carry Judy through the barriers of time and space, and she awakens back in her Kansas bedroom. The Technicolor land of Oz has been replaced by sepia, emblematic of the brown earth that seems to stretch into eternity from her window, and verifies the fact that she has voluntarily left a fairy land for reality land. Around her are grouped her worried uncle and aunt, Bolger, Haley, and Lahr. Even Frank Morgan is standing at her bedside. The Professor had heard about her accident and is there to offer his help in reviving her.

After studying her startled face and listening to her jumbled words, they all quickly dismiss as merely a dream her insistence that she has just returned from somewhere over the rainbow. A fascinating place it was, that's for sure, but one she admits she never wants to see again. But she admits that the invaluable lesson she learned there made the trip worthwhile. The youngster now wholeheartedly subscribes to the truth of the old saying that be it ever so humble, home is where the heart is, where the Christmas spirit of love and good cheer is present every day of the year.

Yankee Doodle Dandy (1942)

A Warner Bros. First National picture. DIRECTOR: Michael Curtiz. EXECUTIVE PRODUCER: Hal B. Wallis;

ASSOCIATE: William Cagney. SCREENPLAY: Robert Buckner and Edmund Joseph, from an original story by Robert Buckner. CINEMATOGRAPHER: James Wong Howe; MONTAGES: Don Siegel. DIALOGUE DIRECTOR: Hugh MacMullan. FILM EDITOR: George Amy. ART DIRECTOR: Carl Jules Weyl. CHOREOGRAPHERS: LeRoy Prinz and Seymour Felix; JAMES CAGNEY DANCE ROUTINES: John Boyle. TECHNICAL ADVISER: William Collier, Sr. SOUND: Everett A. Brown. MAKEUP: Perc Westmore. GOWNS: Milo Anderson. MUSICAL DIRECTOR: Leo F. Forbstein. MUSICAL ADAPTER: Heinz Roemheld. ORCHESTRAL ARRANGEMENTS: Ray Heindorf. SONGS: Music and lyrics by George M. Cohan. RUNNING TIME: 2 hours, 6 minutes. *Principal Players*: James Cagney (George M. Cohan). Walter Huston (Jerry Cohan). Joan Leslie (Mary). Rosemary DeCamp (Nellie Cohan). Richard Whorf (Sam H. Harris). Irene Manning (Fay Templeton). George Tobias (Dietz). Jeanne Cagney (Josie Cohan). Frances Langford (Nora Bayes). George Barbier (Sam Erlanger). S.Z. Sakall (Schwab). Eddie Foy, Jr. (Eddie Foy, Sr.) Minor Watson (Edward Albee). Douglas Croft (Cohan as a child). Patsy Lee Parsons (Josie Cohan at age 12). Captain Jack Young (Franklin Delano Roosevelt). *Major Academy Awards*: Best Actor (*James Cagney*); Scoring; Sound. *Nominations*: Best Picture; Director; Original Story; Supporting Actor (*Walter Huston*); Film Editing.

From both artistic and technical standpoints, *Yankee Doodle Dandy* is easily the finest of all of Hollywood's biomusicals as well as one of its great films. Flavored with patriotic overtones, it was nominated for the 1942 best picture Academy Award, and star James Cagney walked away with the justly deserved Oscar for best actor. *Life* magazine had predicted that his performance would win him the award, while *Time* called it "remarkable." *The New York Times'* Bosley Crowther termed it "as bold and ecstatically respectable a piece of acting as anyone could wish for." To the *New York Herald-Tribune's* Howard Barnes, it was the "consummate Cagney portrayal." Rose Pelswick commented in the *New York Journal-American* that "Cagney's Cohan was the actor's most brilliant bit of make-believe."

Michael Curtiz, whose next directorial assignment would be *Casablanca*, kept the film moving at a crisp pace, while James Wong Howe, one of Hollywood's best-ever cinematographers, turned in his usual professional job, as did dance directors LeRoy Prinz and Seymour Felix. The vibrant Cagney tap-dance routines staged by John Boyle were similarly outstanding. Adding substantially to audience enjoyment were the half-dozen veterans of the Warner Bros. stock company, whose flawless

appearances in bit but often pivotal roles gave the picture the aura of a Hollywood homecoming. As usual, George Tobias, George Barbier, S.Z. Sakall, and Minor Watson played their parts to perfection. Cagney's brother, William, became an associate producer at Warners with the film, later serving as full-fledged producer for the actor's *Johnny Come Lately* (1943), *Blood on the Sun* (1945), and *The Time of Your Life* (1948).

Despite all the talent surrounding him, Cagney was solely responsible for lifting the film from very good to classic. So well does he mirror Cohan's likeable conceit and performing skills that it is inconceivable to picture anybody else in the part. He *was* Cohan, and after a while one actually begins to believe that Cagney wrote all those 500-plus songs and appeared in all those plays. In short, "Jimmy the Gent" dominated the film as much as Cohan himself had dominated the Broadway of his time. Released in May of 1942, the movie was still making the rounds of neighborhood houses when Cohan died on November 7.

Cohan had sold the rights to his life story to Warners for $50,000, but retained the authority to approve both the casting and the screenplay. Genuinely pleased with Cagney's performance, Cohan more or less agreed with other observers that it was largely because of the actor that the film became practically an overnight classic. The first-night audience at the Broadway opening paid $25 per person not for a ticket, but for war bonds. The 88 best seats were priced at $25,000 each. The total evening's take of $5,750,000 was donated to the U.S. Treasury Department.

Although some persons may have been surprised that Cagney would assume such a musically demanding role, few doubted that he would master the challenge. Like Cohan, he had learned well the harsh lessons of the mean streets of New York, and over the years developed a brashness that, coupled with natural cockiness, made him one of the screen's finest actors. Unable, it seems, to turn in a second-rate performance even in second-rate gangland pictures, he personified the born leader, the little tough take-charge guy who never flinched from a confrontation, a man's man who placed loyalty above every other personality asset, and refused to cave in to the forces leagued against

James Cagney, as George M. Cohan in *Yankee Doodle Dandy*, entertains a theater audience with the patriotic "You're a Grand Old Flag."

him to the very end. The actor's turning down in 1956 the role of Alfred P. Doolittle in *My Fair Lady* deprived Broadway of what might have been a once-in-a-lifetime performance.

Yankee Doodle Dandy was Cagney's 39th film, but he had carved an indelible niche for himself as far back as his fifth screen appearance, in *Public Enemy* (1931), still one of the best in Hollywood's vast gallery of crime films. Like the other four major Warner Bros. gangsters of the tommy gun-toting thirties, all of them born or reared from early childhood in New York, Cagney was overpowering in all of his roles, similar as practically all of them were. Edward G. Robinson was equally hazardous to public safety, but his lawlessness was congenital. He never allowed conscience to dilute his supreme enjoyment of the wealth and notoriety he accrued from illicit activities. Like Paul Muni, Cagney was frequently driven into a life of crime to escape the endless struggles of living in a tenement environment, which their studio assiduously condemned as the root cause of all evil.

Humphrey Bogart was nothing if not mean to the core, unable to display any compensating virtues, while Cagney often revealed a soft spot that led to his downfall, as in *Angels with Dirty Faces* (1938). Even in such a later film as *White Heat* (1949), the blistering saga of Cody Jarrett, a cooly detached, nearly insane murderer, his excessive devotion to his mother managed to win Cagney a modicum of audience sympathy. The actor's closest rival as the criminal who would have preferred the straight life to the crooked, was George Raft, far more suave than the belligerent Cagney, handsomer in a Valentino context, and always faithful in his fashion to a rigid code of conduct that disallowed "ratting" on a pal under any circumstances. Along with Cagney a talented dancer, Raft was usually too much the gentleman to squeeze half a grapefruit in actress Mae Clarke's face, no matter how much she irritated him.

Along with Robinson the most versatile and volatile of the lot, Cagney was equally at home playing men of action, whether a car racer (*The Crowd Roars*, 1932), tabloid photographer (*Picture Snatcher*, 1933), lawman (*G-Men*, 1935), airline pilot (*Ceiling Zero*, 1936), crusading reporter framed for murder (*Each Dawn I Die*, 1939), prizefighter (*City for Conquest*, 1940), or comedian (*Boy Meets Girl*, 1938, and *The Bride Came C.O.D.*, 1941). That he could dance most respectably first became evident in *Taxi!* (1932), in which he and Loretta Young enter a dance contest. But it was in *Footlight Parade*, a 1933 Warner's musical blockbuster, that he really proved the point.

Substituting for a stage-frightened actor hired to duet Dubin and Warren's "Shanghai Lil," Cagney dons a sailor suit and joins Ruby Keeler in performing the number under Busby Berkeley's supervision, and it was one of the film's highlights. Atop a long bar, he displayed his Cohan-like suppleness, which combined rat-a-tat taps and the shuffle, his shoulders hunched and his legs pulled taut whenever they seemed about to buckle. John Garfield, incidentally, was among the chorus boy sailors.

First appearing on Broadway on September 29, 1920, when he began his theatrical career as a hoofer in *Pitter Patter*, Cagney himself had moved up the ranks from chorus boy to featured dancer in such topical revues as *The Grand Street Follies of 1928* and *1929*. He also curried favor with audiences and critics with his dramatic acting ability. He succeeded Lee Tracy as Roy Lane in Philip Dunning and George Abbott's *Broadway* in mid-1927, and in 1929 joined Joan Blondell in playwright George Kelly's *Maggie the Magnificent*, earning more praise in the role of Elwood.

Cagney never completely surrendered his fondness for involving himself in song-and-dance routines. As bandleader Terry Rooney in *Something to Sing About* (1937), he sang and danced one of Victor Schertzinger's five songs—"Any Old Love"; in *Boy Meets Girl* he limbers up his legs in a few dance turns, but without musical accompaniment. *The Oklahoma Kid* (1939) heard him warble two evergreens, "Rockabye Baby," in both English and Spanish, and "I Don't Want to Play in Your Yard." Eight years after *Yankee Doodle Dandy*, he appeared in his final musical picture, *The West Point Story*, singing three Sammy Cahn and Jule Styne tunes, "It Could Only Happen in Brooklyn," "Brooklyn," and, with Doris Day, Virginia Mayo, and Gordon MacRae, "The Military Polka."

It was Cagney's skillful handling of dramatic and occasional musical parts—a rare talent—that qualified him to play Cohan. Both men were short but commanding of presence, feisty, and dynamic. Like the "Yankee Doodle Boy," jut-jawed Cagney was always quick to deliver a quip or trade an insult, and as apt to throw a punch as to tender a compliment to his *vis-à-vis*. So well did Cagney embody Cohan's most enduring and endearing traits that songwriter Irving Caesar, who knew both men, once volunteered the opinion that while watching the film, "I thought I was watching Cohan playing himself."

"**Mr. Broadway.**" As if to emulate the proud protagonist in the Alexander Selkirk poem, Cohan was indisputably the "monarch of all I survey, / My right there is none to dispute." The land that Cohan ruled was the tiny but tremendously influential principality of Times Square. No one, not even Ziegfeld, dominated the Great White Way more than Cohan. Not only did the upstart from Providence, Rhode Island, produce plays, but he also wrote both dramatic and musical scripts, lyrics as well as music, sang as well as danced, and was one of the most popular actors ever to appear on the vaudeville and legitimate stage. Although not autobiographical, his play, *The Man Who Owned Broadway*, cogently summed up his career. Broadway had never played host to the likes of such a multi-talented person before—or since—he strode Broadway like the Colossus he was.

With his thick part-chutzpah, part-blarney streak, Cohan could sway doubters into believing that he was capable of handling any theatrical chore, a rather common boast that his participation at any level in a show upheld. A sincere superpatriot, he was never shy about proclaiming his love of country. He best expressed his devotion in song, proclaiming himself to be the "Yankee Doodle Boy" proud to live under the Stars and Stripes, which he serenaded with "You're a Grand Old Flag." His assertion of being born on the Fourth of July, however, is most likely false. His birth certificate clearly states that his birth date was July 3. His mother, however, maintained that he came into the world on that holiday, and he was only too happy to take her word for it.

His "Over There," completed the day after America entered World War I in April 1917 but not published till that June, remains the best and best-known battle song written by an American. And he honored his beloved Broadway with what is the champion of all anthems to that renowned street, "Give My Regards to Broadway." Other of his hits that have resisted oblivion include "Mary's a Grand Old Name," "Forty-Five Minutes from Broadway" (referring to the New York suburb of New Rochelle), and "Harrigan," the "name that no shame ever has been connected with." All these tunes, and more than a dozen others, appear in the film.

Unquestionably, Cohan did more than most of his contemporaries to put America on the musical map in the early years of the 20th century. Victor Herbert had already achieved that distinction, although the treasured songs he gave to the American musical theater were more Viennese-sounding than American, as were the plots and dialogue of his operettas. Cohan never succeeded in totally displacing operetta in favor of native working-class themes, but his plays and tunes were decidedly all–American and particularly popular with commoners who cared little for Old World aristocracy. He was one of them, and they appreciated his recreations of their life situations.

In his later years Cohan occupied decidedly second-place rank alongside his one-time partner, Sam H. Harris. He died on July 2, 1941, or about 16 months before Cohan, but not before producing a number of outstanding plays and musicals that surpassed anything on which he had collaborated with George M. Among them were the Marx Brothers' *Cocoanuts* (1925), 218 performances, and *Animal Crackers* (1928), 191 performances; *June Moon* (1929), 273 performances; *Once in a Lifetime* (1930), 305 performances; the Pulitzer Prize–winning *Of Thee I Sing* (1931), 441 performances; *Dinner at Eight* (1932), 232 performances; *Stage Door* (1936), 169 performances; *You Can't Take It with You* (1936), 837 performances; *The Man Who Came to Dinner* (1939), 739 performances; and *George Washington Slept Here* (1940), 173 performances. The run of each of these productions was highly respectable, based on the 527- performance total of the 1927 *Show Boat*. Almost all of them were made into equally successful motion pictures.

With all its glories, *Yankee Doodle Dandy* hews to the Hollywood tradition of fictionalizing or omitting incidents in the lives of the celebrities played out on the screen. For example, Cohan was awarded a Special Congressional Medal of Honor in 1936, and he opened in the stage musical *I'd Rather Be Right* in 1937. According to the screenplay, both events occurred in 1942.

The film lapses into silence over Cohan's controversial and eventually embarrassing siding with the Broadway producers during the Actors' Strike of 1919. It was called on August 7 of that year to protest the producers' refusal to recognize the Actors' Equity Association as bargaining representative for the performers in their plays. By the time it ended on September 6, 12 plays had closed and 23 others had been adversely affected at the box office by the absence of name actors and stage hands to move scenery, raise and pull curtains, and the like. The strike put Cohan in a quandary, since he was both a producer and a performer as well as owner of a Times Square theater named after him at Broadway and 43rd Street.

Despite the adulation in which he was held by actors, and the generosity he unfailingly displayed toward the down and out among them, Cohan joined the producer ranks. He quit the Lambs and Frairs clubs, and infuriated many old performer friends by adamantly refusing to buckle under to frequent appeals to listen to their side of the controversy. He and his fellow producers lost the battle, however, finally granting the strikers the eight-performance week, limitation of free rehearsal time, and wardrobe and baggage concessions.

Many actors never forgave Cohan for throwing his lot with their opponents, and their caustic comments and irreverent treatment forged a bitterness that remained with him throughout the rest of his life. Although he continued to produce shows into the early thirties, Cohan never again wrote a smash musical or, for that matter, another highly successful song. He scored a personal triumph in 1933 in *Ah, Wilderness*, but the playwright was Eugene O'Neill, not Cohan. Four years later he scored a minor one as President Franklin Delano Roosevelt in *I'd Rather Be Right*. This time the libretto was by George Kaufman and Moss Hart and the songs by Rodgers and Lorenz Hart.

An inferior political satire, particularly when compared with the Gershwins' *Of Thee I Sing* (1931), *I'd Rather Be Right* (originally carrying the title of "Hold Your Hats, Boys") unfolds the tribulations of a young couple whose wedding depends on the boy's getting a raise in salary. His prospects will remain slim, however, until and unless the President balances the federal budget, which he fails to do. Following FDR's advice, he marries his girlfriend anyway at the end. Produced by

Sam H. Harris, it opened on November 2, 1937, and ran for a respectable 266 performances. Sadly enough, Cohan returned to the Broadway stage for the last time in 1940 to appear in *The Royal Vagabond*, which closed after only seven performances. As the film points out, his career was over before his life ended.

Except for *Seven Keys to Baldpate*, a perennial stock company favorite that was made into a movie in 1929, 1935, 1947, and in 1983 under the title *House of the Long Shadows*, few of Cohan's stage presentations were of interest to Hollywood. Only two musicals were filmed. Mervyn LeRoy directed *Little Johnny Jones* in 1930, with Eddie Buzzell repeating the part of the jockey originally played by Cohan himself on the stage. Two years later, Buzzell became a director, with two Marx Brothers' films (*At the Circus* and *Go West*, 1940) and two Esther Williams' musicals (*Easy to Wed*, 1946, and *Neptune's Daughter*, 1949) among his credits.

In 1940, Norman Taurog brought another Cohan musical, *Little Nellie Kelly*, to the screen. The star was Judy Garland, who appeared as both daughter and wife of New York policemen, played by Charles Winninger and George Murphy, respectively. Only one Cohan song from the stage play appears in the film, the charming "Nellie Kelly, I Love You," which Frances Langford reprises in *Yankee Doodle Dandy*. Cohan failed to fare well as a movie actor. The first of his two non-hit sound films, *The Phantom President*, a political satire costarring Claudette Colbert and Jimmy Durante, featured an uncharacteristically unpopular score by Rodgers and Hart, which Cohan made abundantly clear he disliked from the start. (He didn't care for their *I'd Rather Be Right* score either.)

Cast of Heavyweights. Superb as Cagney is in *Yankee Doodle Dandy*, he faced formidable competition for acting laurels from as able a cast as Hollywood ever assembled. Playing his father, Jeremiah, was Walter Huston, for years before and after ranked high among the industry's outstanding character actors and himself the father of a real-life celebrity, John Huston, who in 1941 had made his directorial debut with the Bogart thriller *The Maltese Falcon*. Unforgettable as the stubborn old gold prospector in his son's *The Treasure of the Sierra Madre* in 1948, Walter also excelled as Samuel Dodsworth in *Dodsworth* in 1936 and as "Scratch," or Lucifer, in *All That Money Can Buy* in 1941. No better at singing than Cagney, Huston in 1938 had introduced one of America's greatest love songs, Maxwell Anderson and Kurt Weill's "September Song," in the stage musical *Knickerbocker Holiday*.

Rosemary DeCamp, whose speaking voice was familiar to radio fans of the *Dr. Christian* series and other airwaves dramas, is ideal in the sympathetic role of Mother Nellie Cohan. Playing George's wife, Mary, was Joan Leslie, one of the few film ladies equally capable as a dramatic and musical actress. Helped along by a pretty face and engaging personality, Miss Leslie's proficiency in singing and dancing earned her co-star billing the next year with Fred Astaire in *The Sky's the Limit*. Her musical talents went on further display in *Thank Your Lucky Stars* (also 1943), *Hollywood Canteen* (1944), *Rhapsody in Blue*, and *Two Guys from Milwaukee* (1946).

A one-time child actress billed under her birth name of Jane Brodel, she had appeared momentarily in such dramas as *Camille* (1937) and Alfred Hitchcock's *Foreign Correspondent* (1940); as Joan Leslie she made her dramatic debut as the crippled girl who turned down Humphrey Bogart's marriage proposal in *High Sierra*, followed by her portrayal of Gary Cooper's backwoods girlfriend in *Sergeant York* (both 1941).

Still another cast notable was Eddie Foy, Jr., as his one-of-a-kind vaudevillian father. Although the younger Foy's mugging with Cagney is brief, it is superb, faithfully distilling the feyness that distinguished his father's comic artistry, which the son had earlier displayed in *Frontier Marshal* in 1939 and *Lillian Russell* in 1940. He would again mimic the elder Foy in *Wilson* in 1944. In 1958, when Bob Hope played father Foy in *The Seven Little Foys*, the comedian was joined in a banquet table softshoe dance by a familiar figure appearing in a rare cameo role. The fellow was Cagney, back again as George M. Cohan, and the song was "Mary's a Grand Old Name."

Then there is Douglas Croft as the teenage Cohan. Genuinely effective as a pint-

size monster—the kind of child that adults never know whether to slap on the rump for brazenness or pat on the back for spunkiness—Douglas in 1942 also disrupted the lives of Jack Benny and Charles Coburn in the filmed *George Washington Slept Here*. From all accounts, the boy's precocious talent for alienating everybody with whom he comes into contact in *Yankee Doodle Dandy* accurately reflected the frequent tantrums thrown by the young "Georgie" Cohan in real life. Playing Cohan at age seven is Henry Blair; sister Josie is portrayed by two girls—Jo Ann Marlow (age six) and Patsy Lee Parsons (age 12).

Summons from the White House. The year is 1942. James Cagney (George M. Cohan) has just completed his opening night performance in the show *I'd Rather Be Right* at Broadway's Alvin (now the Neil Simon) Theatre. Nearing his 65th birthday, his hair threaded with silver but his step sprightly as ever, he is informed while backstage that the President of the United States wishes to see him. Worried that Franklin D. Roosevelt is angry at his daring to impersonate him in a musical comedy, and a satirical one at that, Cagney a few days later ascends the White House staircase to the Oval Office, where he meets not a sullen but a friendly Chief Executive whose admiration for the entertainer is boundless and sincere.

Roosevelt, played by Captain Jack Young, is seen only from the back or in profile as he praises Cagney for his long-standing overt expressions of patriotism and long service as one of the nation's preeminent entertainers. Asked who and what had influenced him to become a "symbol of the American spirit," his guest volunteers to chronicle some of the major events in his often hectic life. With the President settled back in his chair, Cagney enters with enthusiasm into an extended autobiographical sketch, which unfolds chronologically in a long flashback that continues up to the final few minutes of the picture.

It is clear from the outset of his story that this only son of vaudevillians Jerry and Nellie Cohan (Walter Huston and Rosemary DeCamp), billed at the time of his birth in 1878 as "The Irish Darlings," was destined to follow in their footsteps onto the stage. When he joins his parents at the age of four, the name of the act is changed to "The Cohan Mirth Makers." A few years later, when sister Josie, played by the actor's own sister, Jeanne Cagney, is added, the name is changed again, and the troupe becomes renowned as "The Four Cohans," one of the best-known acts in the history of vaudeville. George is billed as the "boy comedian, violinist, and dancer," his little sister as the "child actress, danseuse, and songstress."

The young Cohan (Douglas Croft) gains much valuable experience from his cross-country tours in sketches and melodramas. But the more professional he becomes, the more flagrant is his disregard for what he considers to be the inadequacies of other performers sharing the same bill. A veritable Peck's bad boy, he is combative, obstinate, and conceited—in short, a bona-fide brat without a single virtue, except a devout love of show business and a soaring aspiration to head its list of immortals. He is also a constant embarrassment to his conservative father and protective mother, and it is not long before their and everybody else's toleration of his irksome behavior sinks to zero.

The apogee of the lad's swelled-head syndrome is his dictating employment terms to none other than producer Edward Albee (Minor Watson), who responds to his demands by canceling his offer to feature the act at his newly opened Bijou Theatre in Philadelphia. The youngster's churlishness only proves that he is "not quite ready for the big time yet," the irate producer tells him on his way out the dressing room door. His father also weighs in to deflate his ego by spread-eagling his son on his knees and giving him a hearty spanking. Much as viewers might agree with Mother Rosemary's sympathetic but accurate verdict that the boy's offensiveness springs from high anxiety to make good, it is safe to assume that most of them nodded in approval of his father's action.

A decade or so later, love finds the adult George M. Cohan in the person of Mary (Joan Leslie), a stage-struck young fan who shuffles into his life while the family is performing in Buffalo. She visits him in his dressing room before he has time to remove the "old man" makeup he had worn while portraying his mother's on-stage father. Effusive with praise

for his acting, Joan is shocked, albeit pleased, to discover that her idol is not only a young man, but a charming one as well. An able comedian, Cagney is uproarious as he peels off his false white whiskers and wig and limbers up his creaky joints to expose his true age.

Displaying sincere appreciation of her singing and dancing talent in an on-the-spot audition, he takes the star-struck youngster under his wing, easily convincing her to follow the family to New York, where, as the "Dixie Nightingale," she appears on the same bill at a prominent vaudeville theater. Never shy at self-promotion, Cagney lands them both in trouble by switching the song she is scheduled to sing to one of his own compositions, "The Warmest Baby in the Bunch." Annoyed, theater manager Walter Catlett lowers the curtain before she finishes her stint. Charging that no one has the right to "bring down the curtain on a Cohan song," Cagney kicks Catlett so hard that he crashes headlong into the backstage sets, knocking them into pieces.

There in Manhattan, Cagney devotes most of his time to making the usual rounds of music publishers and theatrical producers in the hope of interesting at least one of them in his new song, "Harrigan." Performing the song with appropriate gusto and brogue are Cagney and Joan, his Irishness at such a fever pitch that one can almost see shamrocks sprouting from the floor. And heaven forbid that anyone take lightly his provocative jabbing the air with his right forefinger while brazenly defying anybody to say a "divil of a word agin' me." Although their two-man audience, publishers Dietz (George Tobias) and Goff (Chester Clute), are notorious for never reaching a consensus when assessing song quality, this time their verdict is unanimous: "Harrigan" is not for them. Neither is the latest play of another hopeful, Sam H. Harris, played by Richard Whorf, a competent but minor actor and later the director of such films as *Till the Clouds Roll By* and *Champagne for Caesar* (1950).

Whorf is also given short shrift by the argumentative producers, but he would return intermittently throughout *Yankee Doodle Dandy* as partner in the fabulously successful Broadway team of Cohan & Harris, which produced 50 plays between *Little Johnny Jones* in 1904 and the dissolution of the partnership in

1919. As the film points out, their partnership was so blissful and profitable that neither man ever felt the need to sign any sort of contractual agreement.

Cagney and Joan are not alone in failing to conquer Broadway at their first attempt. Also rejected are his parents and sister, now reduced to living mostly on the cuff and in complete boredom at a boarding house operated by Madame Bartholdi (Odette Myrtil) while awaiting the son to make his show business breakthrough. Never above telling a white lie, Cagney reports one evening that the Dietz and Goff firm had accepted his musical play *Little Johnny Jones*. What that means, he says, is that the three can resume their vaudeville circuit tours while he remains in New York to add the finishing touches to the play. They happily agree to his plan despite the sour note injected by sister Jeanne, who muses that the absence of her brother will turn the family act into something resembling a "carriage with three wheels."

It is in Jack's Grill that Cagney's glibness and Whorf's expertise at playing the straight man finally hit pay dirt by inveigling a chubby, derby-hatted gentleman into investing in *Little Johnny Jones*. Playing the role is S.Z. ("Cuddles") Sakall, whose static mannerisms helped to make him entertaining in brief roles but tiresome in longer stints. He is best remembered today as the manager of Humphrey Bogart's Café Amercaine in *Casablanca*, Barbara Stanwyck's gourmet cook-in-residence in *Christmas in Connecticut* (1945), and Doris Day's Depression-seared uncle in *Tea for Two*, the 1950 remake of *No, No, Nanette*.

Unique among Hollywood character actors for his thick Hungarian accent and bulging jowls, which he accommodatingly permitted servicemen to pinch at will in his *Hollywood Canteen* cameo, Sakall was a master at crumbling into incoherence when complex matters invaded his normal routine. In *Yankee Doodle Dandy*, he remains faithful to form by falling prey to one of the oldest ploys ever invented to sell an untested product to a reluctant buyer. Cagney is willing to let him produce his new play, he says, even though Dietz and Goff have already made him a good offer for it. Sakall falls for the ruse, egged on by

Cagney's lively sampling of one of the hits he had written for it, "Yankee Doodle Boy." (Actually, the real Sam Harris called on a gambler to provide the $25,000 seed money for the show.)

Into the Big Time. As with most stage musicals of the first decade of the 20th century—and for years afterward—the plot of *Little Johnny Jones* serves merely as a three-act peg on which to hang the songs. Johnny is an American jockey who has traveled to England to ride his horse, Yankee Doodle, to victory in the English Derby. Homesick for his native land, he is the darling of a group of American visitors who are awaiting the race to begin. Johnny loses, however, and officials charge him with throwing the race. Disgraced and forced to stay behind to clear his name, he waits till the chorus of departing Americans finishes their farewell song, "All Aboard for Old Broadway" (an excellent song interpolation by Jack Scholl and M.K. Jerome) before singing a farewell song of his own. "Give my regards to Broadway," he sings, "remember me to Herald Square." Then, glancing into the sky above the ship, he sees a rocket, which a friend had shot off to verify Johnny's innocence in the racetrack scandal. His dream of rejoining the gang on 42nd Street ere long is about to come true!

Beaming with the hoydenish grin of a leprechaun, Cagney turns, faces the audience, and reprises the song in an absolutely superlative dance solo on the pier. His jubilation is apparent in every tap of his drumbeat of ecstacy. His timing is impeccable, his pirouettes, mid-air clicks of heels, and twisting torso never endangering the gracefulness of his footwork. Whether his solo dance is the finest to be seen in any Hollywood musical is debatable; that it is astonishing is unquestioned. Except for Fred Astaire, in such a number as "Bojangles of Harlem" in *Swing Time*, no other male dancer tapped to any melody with greater exuberance or precision. It is safe to say that Cagney's nimbleness will survive in memory long after his shootouts with policemen and rival mobsters have been forgotten.

The show is a hit, but only the first in a steady succession of triumphs that soon turns its author and star into Broadway's first citizen. He calls his family back from the road and establishes the veteran vaudevillians as legitimate stage stars. For Joan Leslie he writes the namesake song, "Mary's a Grand Old Name," which under Whorf's prodding he talks Fay Templeton, then one of musical New York's favorite leading ladies, played engagingly by Irene Manning, into introducing it in a play as yet unwritten.

Accustomed to operettas, the star is not at all interested in participating in what she describes as the "loud, vulgar, and flag-waving" antics that distinguish the typical Cohan musical. Nor is she impressed by her visitor's typical tactless assertion that she should be thrilled at receiving an invitation to star in an all-Cohan show. Supported by Irene's producer, Abe Erlanger (George Barbier), Cagney wins her over to his side not by talking, but by singing the "Mary" song, which he avers will make her the toast of the town.

Forgetting for the moment the other young lady to whom he had already dedicated the song, Cagney tells Irene that it is hers for the asking, as is another tune he writes on the spot entitled "Forty-Five Minutes from Broadway," where the suburban "rubens have whiskers of hay / And Broadway only 45 minutes away!" Fortunately for Cagney, Joan proves to be a first-rate trouper by calmly accepting Cagney's permitting Irene to introduce "our song" to the world. As a consolation prize, he proposes marriage. Joan readily accepts, indicating from the outset of their life together the same self-sacrificing, sympathetic traits that made Myrna Loy and June Allyson such perfect screen wives.

Taking its name from the song title, *Forty-Five Minutes from Broadway* opens to the wild applause of critics and audience alike. Equipped with a pleasing if not outstanding soprano voice, Irene sings both songs, as well as the third hit, "So Long, Mary (Don't forget to come back home)," as she boards a New Rochelle-bound train.

An even bigger success is *George Washington, Jr.*, which is highlighted by the film's second impressive production number in which Cagney, dressed in the uniform of a Union soldier, sings and dances to "You're a Grand Old Flag," the songwriter's most stirring salutation to the "land I love." There is little doubt that this patriotic demonstration struck a much stronger patriotic chord with 1942 audiences than it would today. In May of that year, when the film was released, the United States was five months into World War II. Cagney's energetic delivery could easily be interpreted as less of an appeal to regard the flag as the emblem of liberty than a plea to his listeners to look upon that "high-flying flag" as the emblem of eventual victory.

The next 40 minutes of the film expertly encapsulates the few high points of the great showman's declining years. First comes the brilliant Don Siegel-directed montage of the numerous stage plays on which Cohan served as star or collaborator. With their titles—*The Honeymooners*; *The American Idea*; *Hello, Broadway*; *The Little Millionaire*; *The Yankee Prince*—spelled out in a blaze of white bulbs on Times Square marquees, and snatches of their chief songs heard in the background, the sequence is even more artistically handled than the similar survey of hit shows in *The Great Ziegfeld*. Practically all of the Cohan shows were forgotten by 1942, but his frequent short-lived successes verified the entertainer's claim to be only an "ordinary guy who knows what ordinary guys want to see." With the retirement of Father Huston and Mother DeCamp in 1912, followed by Sister Jeanne's marriage to their stage manager, Cagney becomes the last family member still in show business. He is now the Four Cohans rolled into one.

Onward to Victory! His grip on Broadway, however, is fast becoming more and more tenuous, eventually loosening altogether with the unqualified failure of his non-musical *Popularity*. Then, on April 6, 1917, America enters the war against Germany, and his career is revived in spectacular fashion. At 39, eight years above the age limit for recruits, he is unable to enlist in the Army. Yet he performs a vital patriotic service by tinkling a tune on a piano on the stage of a deserted theater that within a few hours would emerge first as simply an "American Victory March." More than any other song in his extensive repertoire, it was responsible for his winning international and everlasting fame.

Lustily sung by both Cagney and Frances Langford in a cameo as Nora Bayes, the popular singer who originally introduced it when the first contingent of Yanks were boarding the ships that would carry them to the battlefields of France, the renamed "Over There" quickly became the premier battle anthem of the war. No other war tune surpassed its bravado denunciation of Kaiser Wilhelm II and his "Hun" troops, or expressed more firmer faith in their defeat.

In one of the most genuinely tender scenes in a Hollywood musical, Cagney bids his dying father goodbye while thanking him for his lifetime help in grooming him to become what the elder man correctly describes as "an American institution." He does so by echoing the familiar phrase that he had spoken once upon a time at the conclusion of every Four Cohans vaudeville appearance: "My mother thanks you, my father thanks you, my sister thanks you, and I thank you." At the end of the recitation, Huston is dead. Within a few years, his mother and sister would also die. Without children or a future in the theater, the restless Cagney embarks with his wife on extended and largely unsatisfactory vacations in Europe. Not only were his producing days presumably at an end, but also those as an actor.

Miscast in the role of a retiree, Cagney in his graying years resembles a fire horse awaiting the call to action far more than an aging entertainer content to rest on his laurels. More than a little resentful at being shunted aside by his beloved Broadway, he is all the more disillusioned when four teenagers, including the vivacious Joyce Reynolds in her first screen appearance, rouse him from uninterrupted leisure on his farm to ask for water for the carburetor of their stalled jalopy. Engaging them briefly in small talk, Cagney is astounded to learn that none of them recognizes his name, his shows, even "Give My Regards to Broadway." Flustered by what he senses is his total anonymity among the jitterbug crowd, he later admits to Joan that he indeed misses the smell of greasepaint. But the bell in the firehouse has been rung: he has accepted the leading part in a new musical to be produced by none other than former partner Whorf.

The film then switches to Cagney back on stage in *I'd Rather Be Right*, singing Lorenz Hart's witty lyric to Rodgers's "Off the Record." In it, he discloses many of Roosevelt's so-called secret White House dislikes followed by the three-word warning to the note-taking press corps surrounding him that they must not print a single word. That Cagney, like the real Cohan, would portray the crippled President as capable of dancing in front of and atop a conference table was utterly disregarded by both the press and viewers. Many had longed to see the old master back in harness, and his nostalgic presence turned what was basically a second-rate musical comedy—and score, except for "Have You Met Miss Jones?"—into a modest hit.

The flashback ended, Roosevelt reappears and hands the Special Medal of Honor to the stunned but deeply honored Cagney. As the inscription reads, it is being awarded to him for writing "You're a Grand Old Flag" and "Over There," songs that the President says symbolize the American spirit as much as the songwriter's own life. Cagney acknowledges his pride of accomplishment by tapping to the tune of "Yankee Doodle Boy" down the White House staircase. Once outside he pauses to watch a parade of passing soldiers singing "Over There." Cagney joins the marchers and, after being urged by a soldier to sing along with them, adds his voice to the chorus.

The ending of the film is sheer perfection. The camera closes in on Cagney's face. Rather than expressing pleasure at the comeback of his greatest song after a quarter-century hiatus, his face is clouded over with deep concern bordering on sadness. He had probably never expected to hear American soldiers reprise it after 1918. But here they are again, columns of young Americans on the march back to war, swearing once more not to come back "till it's over, over there!" When that day would come was unknown. What Cagney's face clearly shows is realization that the new war will be far more devastating than its predecessor, and that many of the troops singing alongside him will never return from it. Looking closely into his face, one notices the glistening of tears about to fall from his eyes.

Going My Way (1944)

A Paramount picture. DIRECTOR AND PRODUCER: Leo McCarey. SCREENWRITER: Frank Butler and Frank

Cavett, based on a story by Leo McCarey. CINE-MATOGRAPHER: Lionel Lindon; SPECIAL EFFECTS: Gordon Jennings. FILM EDITOR: LeRoy Stone. ART DIRECTOR: Hans Dreier and William Flannery. SOUND RECORDERS: Gene Merritt and John Cape. SET DECORATOR: Steve Seymour. COSTUMES: Edith Head. MAKEUP: Wally Westmore. MUSICAL DIRECTOR: Robert Emmett Dolan; ASSOCIATE: Troy Sanders. VOCAL ARRANGER: Joseph J. Lilley. ORIGINAL SONGS: Lyrics by Johnny Burke; music by James Van Heusen. RUNNING TIME: 2 hours, 10 minutes. *Principal Players*: Bing Crosby (Father O'Malley). Barry Fitzgerald (Father Fitzgibbon). Risë Stevens (Genevieve Linden). Frank McHugh (Father Timothy O'Dowd). Gene Lockhart (Ted Haines, Sr.) James Brown (Ted Haines, Jr.) William Frawley (Max Dolan). Jean Heather (Carol James). Porter Hall (Mr. Belknap). *Major Academy Awards*: Best Picture; Director; Actor (*Bing Crosby*); Supporting Actor (*Barry Fitzgerald*); Original Story; Screenplay; Song ("Swingin' on a Star"). *Nominations*: Best Actor (*Barry Fitzgerald*); Cinematography; Film Editing.

Accustomed to choosing their favorites from a large assortment of male vocalists, contemporary popular music fans are incapable of even imagining a time when a single singer commanded the attention of practically all Americans. His name was Bing [Harry Lillis] Crosby. For the first 12 years of his illustrious career he faced only insignificant competition for the title of the nation's foremost troubadour. From 1933 to 1945 he was as big a star in the movies as he was on the radio. His combined sales of phonograph records reached well into the multi-millions.

His was the singing voice that most every American recognized instantly, and many of the film songs he introduced ranked among the best known of the period—"Love in Bloom," "Pennies from Heaven," "Sweet Leilani," "Only Forever," "White Christmas," "Swingin' on a Star," "Aren't You Glad You're You," "You Keep Coming Back Like a Song," "In the Cool, Cool, Cool of the Evening, "Zing a Little Zong," "Count Your Blessings Instead of Sheep," "True Love," "The Second Time Around," "Please," "Temptation," "Love Thy Neighbor," "It's Easy to Remember," "Empty Saddles," "Blue Hawaii," "I've Got a Pocketful of Dreams," "You're a Sweet Little Headache," "An Apple for the Teacher," "It's Always You," "Moonlight Becomes You," "Sunday, Monday or Always," "Ac-Cent-Tchu-Ate the Positive," and dozens of others. The first 13 songs were nominated for the Oscar between 1935 and 1961, earning Crosby number one rank as in-troducer of Hollywood's best song candidates. Writers of non-production and stage songs were equally delighted when Crosby recorded their tunes, since they were well aware that his recordings had a habit of outselling those made by anyone else, even the stars for whom the songs were written. He was, as the title of his 1950 movie proclaimed, the "Mr. Music" of America, and much of the rest of the world.

Beginning with the original Big Broadcast in 1932, Crosby's star power eclipsed that of every other male singer, and he would remain a formidable force in popular music for most of the next 30 years. Even those two gigantically popular crooners of the late twenties, Gene Austin and Rudy Vallee, were unable to withstand the musical assault launched by the one-time band vocalist from Spokane, Washington. Although Austin practically disappeared from sight, Vallee did manage to sing his way through most of the decade. As late as 1939 he introduced the pretty Irving Berlin nominated song, "I Poured My Heart into a Song" in *Second Fiddle*.

Al Jolson's star had dimmed perceptibly by 1932, and despite his appearance in several later movies, it would not glitter again till *The Jolson Story* returned him to celebrity status in 1946. Morton Downey and balladeer Arthur ("Street Singer") Tracey went into similar eclipse in the early 1930s, and Eddie Cantor's vaudeville-style singing rarely appealed to record buyers. Throughout the decade and beyond, Louis Armstrong appealed mostly to jazz aficionados, a far smaller audience than Crosby's, and Gene Autry's fans consisted almost exclusively of devotees of "Western" ballads. Compared with "Der Bingle," as Crosby was dubbed early in the World War II years, Nelson Eddy, James Melton, and Allan Jones were minor singers.

Kenny Baker won relatively few adherents as a regular vocalist on Jack Benny's weekly radio show or as introducer of such blue-chip film hits as Dubin and Warren's "Remember Me?" and the Gershwins' "Love Walked In" and "Love Is Here to Stay." Lanny Ross won only fleeting popularity in the movies, where in 1934 he introduced Gordon and Revel's "Stay as Sweet as You Are," and on several radio programs, including *Your Hit Parade* beginning in 1938. One of America's few successful Jewish

Bing Crosby, left, brings back memories of Ireland and his mother to Barry Fitzgerald by crooning the Irish lullaby "Too-Ra-Loo-Ra-Loo-Ral" in *Going My Way.*

popular singers, Buddy Clark (born Samuel Goldberg), was also helped by regular appearances on *Your Hit Parade* in 1936-38, although he would not reach his pinnacle until the late 1940s. Tenor Phil Regan, a one-time detective with the New York Police Department, was confined to intermittent popularity following stints in *Sweet Adeline* and with Frances Langford in *The Hit Parade* (1937).

Only Dick Powell and Fred Astaire qualified as bona fide rivals to Crosby's domination of the musical marketplace. But Astaire's dancing genius overpowered his vocalizing gifts, and by the late 1930s Powell's appearance in musicals had been reduced to an insignificant few, while Crosby's continued unabated. His greatest and earliest competitor was Russ Columbo, but that young man's career was cut short when he accidentally shot himself to death in 1934 at the age of 26. By 1938, Tony Martin had grown artistically into a respectable rival by virtue of

a rich baritone and straightforward delivery of Gordon and Revel love songs in a series of highly popular Fox musicals. By the time he came along, however, Crosby was far too deeply entrenched in the Number One position to be toppled by an interloper, even one with Martin's indisputable charm and masculine attractiveness. And from 1939 onward, Martin's movie career was subjected to lengthy lapses of inactivity, like the 1941 to 1946 period, part of which he spent in the U.S. Army Air Force, winning the Bronze Star.

The Kid from Hoboken. Not until 1942 would Crosby encounter a worthy challenger whose popularity would eventually surpass and long outlive his own. But not even Francis Albert Sinatra was able to usurp Crosby's firm grasp on the public during the early years of his meteoric rise. Crosby had ranked seventh and fourth among Hollywood's Top Ten moneymakers in 1934 and 1937, and fourth again in 1940. He reappeared on the list as number one in 1944 and remained there until 1949, when he fell to second, indicating that music buffs still preferred the "Old Groaner" to "The Voice," at least insofar as the movies were concerned. Crosby was named to the Top Ten list five more times in the early fifties to set the all-time record among musical stars of 15 total appearances. Sinatra first made the list in 1956, after Crosby's vocal magnetism had lost much of its allure, and paid five more visits to it, never ranking higher than fifth place, in 1957.

By the end of the 1940s, many other newcomers—Perry Como, Tony Bennett, Dick Haymes, Mel Torme, Frankie Laine, Nat King Cole, Andy Russell, Billy Eckstein, and Dean Martin—had arrived on the scene, each in his own way siphoning off members of the Crosby admiration society. As strongly as Astaire influenced an entire generation of movie dancers, Crosby's relaxed singing style was reflected by all of his 1940s and 50s competitors, like Como and especially Dean Martin, who up to his death on Christmas Day, 1995, freely admitted that he had slavishly imitated Crosby in developing his own crooning technique.

Many of Crosby's singing competitors bridged the gap from obscurity to recognition by appearing in movies, like Johnny Johnston, who introduced Mercer and Arlen's "That Old Black Magic" while Vera Zorina danced to it in *Star Spangled Rhythm* (1941). But save for Sinatra and Martin, much of whose initial film popularity was generated by teaming with his slapstick partner, Jerry Lewis, none of them developed into Hollywood heavyweights.

Not counting his early-career appearances in Mack Sennett shorts and cameos in such major Hollywood musicals as *The King of Jazz* in 1930, Crosby had made 30 feature films before *Going My Way*. A one-time law student at Gonzaga College, he formed a band with classmate Al Rinker, brother of singer Mildred Bailey, in the late twenties. In 1926 the two young men were hired by "King of Jazz" Paul Whiteman, who a little later added Harry Barris to the group, which became a fixture with the Whiteman orchestra as the "Rhythm Boys" for

three years. Crosby went solo in 1931, building such a sturdy reputation on the radio program *Fifteen Minutes with Bing Crosby* and through numerous recordings that in 1933 he began his 10-year stint as host of the weekly *Kraft Music Hall*. Barris followed his singing pal into the movies, usually playing bit roles as a musician in such Crosby pictures as *Rhythm on the River* (1940) and *The Birth of the Blues* in 1941.

Deft from the outset at comedy and wooing pretty ladies, Crosby actually had little experience acting out dramatic roles before 1944. That he was capable of making his mark as a serious actor was apparent not so much in *Going My Way* as in *Little Boy Lost* (1953) and particularly as the alcoholic has-been in Clifford Odets's *The Country Girl* the next year. *Going My Way* required little in the way of acting brilliance on Crosby's part, but he made the most of the few flashes of dramatics the part called for. On the whole, he ambles through the picture with his usual easy gait, repeating with seeming artlessness his accustomed role as the nonchalant outsider whose unruffled good humor conceals his deep-seated concern for securing the happiness of the people around him.

This first of his three outings wearing the garb of a Catholic priest—repeated in *Bells of St. Mary's* in 1945 and in the disastrous *Say One for Me* in 1959—paved the way for Crosby's becoming the second male lead in a musical to win the Academy Award for best actor. Few would deny that he did a respectable job in an undemanding part, but in no way was it superior to the complex role played by Alexander Knox in *Wilson* or Charles Boyer in *Gaslight*, two of the other 1944 nominees for the honor.

The film's grandest acting achievement was made by Barry Fitzgerald, who, like his actor-brother Arthur Shields, was a graduate of Dublin's prestigious Abbey Players, and Frank McHugh, a highly competent and largely unheralded former member of the Warner Bros. stock company who in the thirties appeared in no fewer than 69 Warner films. There is little doubt that Fitzgerald's congenital tendency to lapse too often into Emerald Isle coyness robs his performance of a measure of authenticity. But it surely adds charm to and arouses audience sympathy for the frail elderly pastor, whose stubbornness would otherwise be attributed to mistrust of Crosby's motives, the urge to protect the prerogatives of his high priestly office—or maybe hardening of the arteries.

So professional was Fitzgerald's performance that he was nominated for two Oscars, one for best actor, the other for best supporting actor, the only time any performer has been nominated for two Academy Awards for his work in the same film. He walked away with the best supporting actor statuette, while Crosby won for best actor, *Going My Way* for best picture, and Leo McCarey for best director and original story. Unfortunately, director Elliott Nugent, who should have known better, tried vainly to cash in on the popularity of the film by co-starring Crosby and Fitzgerald again as old *vs.* young doctors in *Welcome, Stranger* in 1947, a weak-sister followup with an unusually lackluster score by Burke and Van Heusen.

One of Hollywood's most versatile directors, McCarey piloted such comedy masterpieces as Eddie Cantor's *The Kid from Spain* (1932), the Marx Brothers' classic *Duck Soup* (1933), and Katharine Hepburn and Cary Grant's *The Awful Truth* (1938), in addition to *Love Affair* (1939) and its 1957 remake, *An Affair to Remember*. He also directed what must rank as the most heart-rending film in Hollywood history—*Make Way for Tomorrow* (1937)—with Victor Moore and Beulah Bondi as an elderly couple forced to live their final years apart from each other.

Going My Way is equally sentimental and rather often in danger of losing audience attentiveness by proceeding at a snail's pace, which accounts for its rather extensive running time. But under McCarey's stewardship the final scene, even if it does wring audiences dry of all emotion, actually lifts their spirits by reuniting mother and son after long years of separation. Few other directors, with the possible exception of Frank Capra, could have turned the ornery Barry Fitzgerald into such a thoroughly likable character, or have escaped critical censure for affixing such a tearful ending to a 1944 picture.

The writers of the three new *Going My Way* songs were Johnny Burke and James Van Heusen, among the best and most prolific of all of Hollywood's songwriting partnerships, who collaborated on movie tunes for 15 years. Nom-

inated 14 times for the best song Oscar, Van Heusen won it four times; of Burke's five nominations, one was a winner. A facile lyricist almost on a par with Johnny Mercer, Burke had written the words to most of Crosby's screen songs beginning in 1936 with "Pennies from Heaven." Joining with melody-master Van Heusen in 1939 for the non-production "Oh, You Crazy Moon," the twosome created the songs for 22 films, 16 starring Crosby. Burke went into virtual retirement in 1957, shortly after contributing the lyric to Errol Gardner's "Misty," one of truly great melancholy love songs. Van Heusen carried on, mostly with Sammy Cahn, to provide both Crosby and Sinatra with a stunning array of movie and independent hits for five more years. Curiously, *Going My Way* is the only nominated musical not to include a single note during the running of the credits of the songs to follow.

Crosby reached the age of 40 while *Going My Way* was being filmed. By then his voice had perceptibly deepened, like Al Jolson's, giving it a mature mellowness and warmth that were largely absent from the emotionally charged throatiness that distinguished such early recordings as "If I Had You" (1929), "Out of Nowhere" and "I'm Through with Love" (both 1931), and the great Great Depression anthem "Brother, Can You Spare a Dime" (1932). No singer was more casual, while remaining attentive to the interpretative and rhythmic subtleties of words and music than the mid-life Crosby. Como came close, as did Dean Martin, who all too often gave the impression that the ballad he was singing was actually a lullaby to put himself to sleep. Crosby's voice had never sounded better, nor would it ever again be quite so warm and sensitive, than in his *Going My Way* singing of "Silent Night" and Schubert's "Ave Maria," now classified as the finest selections in his Christmas and religious Decca Records portfolios.

In the 1962-63 season, *Going My Way* reappeared as a weekly television series, with Gene Kelly in the role of Father O'Malley. Even more recently, in *Sister Act 2: Back in the Habit* (1993), the plot was again revised, and poorly, as a starring vehicle for Whoopi Goldberg to resume the charade she had played as a bogus nun with charitable inclinations in *Sister Act*. In the second film the setting was transferred to San Francisco and the goal altered into preserving St. Francis High School, which was in danger of being razed and replaced by a parking lot, the same dilemma facing the Church of Saint Dominick in the Crosby film. The high school is saved from the wrecker's ball in the same way that St. Dominick's is restored—through the musical talents of the leading players, Crosby by writing hit songs, Whoopi by assembling a successful singing group from among her students.

The Unwelcome Newcomer. Father Charles Francis Patrick O'Malley (Bing Crosby) is not your ordinary Catholic priest. No less moral than his starched-collar brethren, he is fun-loving, abnormally casual in his relations with his fellow clergymen and parishioners, and a first-rate singer of popular songs who prefers to answer to the name "Chuck." A non-conformist peacemaker, he appears too relaxed to take seriously his new duties at St. Dominick's, the sole oasis of help and hope among mostly Irish-Catholic families in what in more recent years would be described as an inner-city slum.

On his way to the church, he joins a group of the boys playing baseball, only to watch helplessly as one of them bats a ball through a first-floor apartment window. He manages to calm down the angry resident, Mr. Belknap, played with customary vengeance by the always adversarial Porter Hall, by offering to pledge his mother-of-pearl rosary beads as collateral until he can get enough money together to pay for a replacement. Confirmed atheist Hall rebuffs him, however, citing the well-known fact that "priests never have any money." Obviously, the good Father is a born diplomat, but his skill at appeasing detractors will be put to even more severe tests as he tries to fulfill the unpleasant troubleshooting mission on which he has been sent by the bishop.

Meanwhile, in his office at the church rectory, Father Fitzgibbon (Barry Fitzgerald) is attempting to extricate the church from its latest crisis. Banker Gene Lockhart (Ted Haines, Sr.), head of the Knickerbocker Savings & Loan Company, has turned down his request for a $632.50 loan to purchase a new furnace. The church is already five months behind in its mortgage payments, and Lockhart warns that either the arrearage is paid in full or the church will face foreclosure. He then departs with his handsome, idealistic young son, James Brown, (Ted, Jr.), whose plea that his father recant the threat is parried by Lockhart's off-hand admission that only a fool would lend money to a church, but that he who even considers foreclosing on a church is a certified heel.

Fitzgerald pauses in his nervous contemplation of the chaos about to befall him to glance up in amazement at the sudden appearance of Crosby, who bounces into the room like a college freshman hoping to impress the football coach. Having been drenched by a passing street cleaning machine while rescuing the street kids' baseball from under a parked hardware truck, Crosby has redressed himself in slacks and sporty sweater. If first appearances predict the regard in which a newcomer will be held, Crosby has plunged to the top of Fitzgerald's least-likely-to-succeed list. Crosby, however, prefers to overlook the curate's obvious but unspoken displeasure. Part of his plan of action at St. Dominick's is to break down by example Fitzgerald's priestly reserve, but without offending him or his largely conservative congregation, in another screen exercise on the age-old psychological barriers that separate the undisciplined young man from the oldster held hostage to tradition.

That Father O'Malley is quite proud to display the name of the St. Louis Browns on his sweater fortifies the initial impression that he is an incorrigible optimist as well as an unconventional sort of fellow. Then the most unsuccessful team in baseball history, the Browns up to 1944 had never won the American League championship, and only rarely had been a strong contender for it. That year, in their only World Series, the Brownies lost to the St. Louis Cardinals, proving that O'Malley had pledged allegiance to the lesser of the city's two professional baseball clubs.

Fitzgerald is also proud. He built the church and had been serving its parishioners for more than 45 years, as well as friendly flocks of birds by providing them with a tree-filled garden sanctuary, which he continues to cultivate with loving care. Thus his questioning Crosby on what made him decide to become a priest arises from genuine belief that his new assistant has chosen the wrong profession. Additional mortification is piled on Fitzgerald when Crosby receives a call from an old boyhood chum, Father "Chuck" O'Dowd (Frank McHugh), another apparent clerical misfit who puts whatever decorum he possesses on hold to harmonize with Crosby on their East St. Louis high school anthem. Moreover, it seems that both take abnormal delight in such secular pleasures as golf, which Fitzgerald, an uncompromising devotee of the work ethic, regards as a "dereliction of duty." The two men are, as Fitzgerald's shakes of his head signify, hopeless birds of a feather.

Once the personality of the two leading characters has been established, McCarey conveniently, and expertly, divides the rest of the screenplay into three parts of equal significance. One-third involves the humorous, often touching, evolution of the Crosby-Fitzgerald relationship from prickly to harmonious; another traces the progress of two unrelated love affairs, one from the past, the other in the present; and the final third credits two ancient antagonists, religion and Mammon, for the eventual surmounting of seemingly insoluble problems affecting neighborhood youths and Fitzgerald's church.

In each of the three segments Crosby serves as counselor or mediator, unifying the overall plot and sustaining interest. Both he and Fitzgerald also provide viewers with abundant opportunities to smile, intensify their concern for the necessity of the older man's facing up to reality, and finally develop a lump in the throat when their ordeals are resolved. Blending these three audience reactions had never been achieved so skillfully in any previous Oscar-nominated musical. What emerges is as neat a cinematic package as Hollywood has ever put together. Only *Fiddler on the Roof*, released almost three decades later, would balance such disparate audience reactions with comparable adroitness.

The purpose of dispatching Crosby to St. Dominick's is not clarified until McHugh meets with him and Fitzgerald a few days later for a golf outing. Equally easy-going as Crosby, McHugh is subjected to Fitzgerald's disfavor as to exactly why he also decided to become a priest. After he leaves, Crosby confirms McHugh's suspicion that his assignment is to succeed Fitzgerald as curate, adding, however, that the old man as yet has no clue that his forced retirement has been foreordained.

Resentful Subservience. Crosby is proved wrong, however, when Fitzgerald, in a fit of petulance caused by his assistant's "progressive" Catholicism, disappears one rainy night from the rectory. Where he went is disclosed a few hours later when Fitzgerald, soaking wet and staring sheepishly into Crosby's anxious eyes, admits that he had visited the bishop in hopes of enticing the prelate into transferring Crosby to another parish. Instead, Fitzgerald continues, he learned the real reason why Crosby had been sent to St. Dominick's. Painful as the truth is, Fitzgerald cleverly switches roles from overseer of church affairs to Crosby's humble servant. He volunteers to vacate the master bedroom for a downstairs couch and henceforth eat all his meals in a restaurant. Naturally, Crosby refuses to accept these gestures of surrender and urges Fitzgerald to get into bed before he catches cold.

After contentedly devouring a substantial meal while ensconced in his regular bed, Fitzgerald pours them each a nip o' Irish whisky, one bottle of which his 90-year-old mother sends him every Christmas. He has not seen her since he left Ireland for America some 45 years ago. For the longest time, he confides to Crosby, he has planned to return for a brief visit, but somehow was never able to save enough money to pay the fare. The container holding the bottle is a music box, which when opened plays "(Too-Ra-Loo-Ra-Loo-Ral) That's an Irish Lullaby." Crosby croons the song, written in 1913 by J.R. Shannon, with appropriate tenderness that achieves the twin purpose of prompting Fitzgerald to relax in nostalgic reflections on the Emerald Isle and no longer look upon him as a rival, but as a friend. Crosby's contemporaneous recording of the 30-year-old song became a 1944 bestseller, attesting to the emotional power that the simplest of words when attached to an uncomplicated melody can convey.

Particularly amusing is a followup scene

where Fitzgerald agrees to accompany Crosby and McHugh to the golf course. Inevitably, the curate's opinion of the playing field as a "pool room moved outdoors" is modified into rapidly climbing enjoyment of the game, helped immeasurably by Crosby's and McHugh's explaining some of its rules. Elated when he hits a ball out of a sand trap onto the green and directly into the cup, Fitzgerald proudly attributes his success to his quick grasp of golfing fundamentals, even though today was the "first time I've ever had a caddy in me hand." What he will never know is that McHugh had picked up the ball, which landed at the far end of the green, and dropped it into the cup.

Also inevitable was tragedy's cruel visit to St. Dominick's, which is announced by the ringing of fire bells. The church is burned practically to the ground from a cause that is never disclosed. Surveying the charred beams and blackened stone with the somnambulant stare of the deeply afflicted, Fitzgerald is shocked by the devastation. Indentations of pain furrow his brow, and he looks every inch the frail old man he has suddenly become. Burned out of their leafy homes, even the birds have deserted the property, along with his long-standing dream of adding architectural improvements to his house of God that now lies in ruins.

Love Interest I. Romantic love is introduced with the appearance of Carol James, portrayed by Jean Heather, a pretty youngster confined in her brief film career to playing distressed teenagers. In *Double Indemnity*, her other major 1944 movie, she loses her father to murderers Fred MacMurray and Barbara Stanwyck; in *Going My Way* she runs away from home to escape the constant carping of mistrustful parents who she insists are conspiring to rob her of her individuality. She is introduced to Crosby by a policeman, who brings her to the rectory after picking her up for loitering on street corners. Her ambition is to be a nightclub singer, she tells Crosby, and to prove her qualifications she sings "The Day After Forever" to his piano accompaniment.

Yes, he nods, she's really pretty good at vocalizing, but are all those hand flourishes and facial contortions necessary? Offering to show her how to emphasize the lyric rather than herself, he launches into his own typical straightforward, gestureless rendition of one of Burke and Van Heusen's most charming sentimental love songs after "It's Always You," "Moonlight Becomes You," "Constantly," and "If You Please." Certain that she has learned from that single example the correct way to sing a ballad, Jean reaffirms her intention to traipse her way up the stairway to stardom. Almost penniless, she accepts a $10 "loan" from Crosby, whose worry that she will be victimized by an uncaring world is compounded by her Micawberesque declaration that things are bound to turn out just fine. "I'll get by," the young innocent assures him while flashing a confident smile as she hurries away from the rectory.

Jean is not seen again till the film nears its end. Unable to find her cherished singing job, she has moved into a vacant apartment owned by Gene Lockhart's savings and loan institution. When Crosby hears the news, he pays her a visit, mostly to learn how a girl with no job and presumably no money can afford the rent. At the apartment he makes a discovery that most likely sent shivers of disapproval down the spines of many 1944 viewers. Although implied rather than stated, Jean is being subsidized by Lockhart's son, James Brown, who has even purchased a piano for her.

Crosby's facial expression throughout the scene reflects his strong disapproval of her living arrangement, but he wisely refrains from railing against it. Instead, he sings a song designed to nudge the young couple into marrying. The right road is the one he himself has traveled, and the song helps him to recommend it as the only sure path to happiness. One of the very few musicalized sermons in a Hollywood musical, "Going My Way" is a little gem, the lyric uplifting rather than preaching. That the youngsters have received the message is indicated by their exchange of embarrassing glances as he sings it.

A few days later, after Lockhart has learned via neighborhood gossip of his son's tryst, the angry banker goes to the apartment with the express purpose of bringing it to an end. He is startled to find Brown there, dressed in pajamas and openly displaying his love of Jean. But following Crosby's musical advice, they have become man and wife. When the young man redresses himself in a U.S. Army Air Corps uniform and announces that he must leave immediately for military service, Lockhart is transformed into a mellow father-in-law who welcomes Jean into the family.

Love Interest II. The second interlude involving an unmarried man and woman is not nearly so romantic as the Brown-Heather coupling, but very well might have developed into a charming love affair if conditions had been different. What it does is serve as the hinge on which the screenplay swings toward its denouement. Crosby's accidental meeting with Rise Stevens (Genevieve Linden) proves to be disappointing for her but fortunate for him. Now a contralto with the Metropolitan Opera—which Miss Stevens was in real life—she exhibits unmistakable signs of having retained her long-ago fondness for him over their long years of separation. A most attractive young lady, Miss Stevens had made her Met debut in the title role in *Mignon* on November 2, 1938. Another highly competent performer who failed to recognize at least one rare career opportunity, she would refuse the offer to play Anna in *The King and I* on Broadway in 1951.

When Crosby removes his overcoat in her dressing room, the sight of his clerical collar and black priestly garment stuns her out of expecting a renewal their former relationship. But she recovers quickly and invites him to watch her rehearse for that evening's performance of *Carmen*. Her rendition of "Habanera" is superb, posing the inexplicable question why she appeared in so few films. She had brightened the screen in 1939 opposite Nelson Eddy in *The Chocolate Soldier*, revealing both singing and acting ability that exceeded Jeanette MacDonald's. But not even those talents, combined with a glamorous face and figure, tempted the moguls to groom her into a permanent Hollywood star.

The fortunate side of the Crosby-Stevens equation is her helping him, and in turn St. Dominick's, to shepherd one of his songs into print. She fails to impress hard-nosed music publisher Max Dolan, played by William Frawley, the veteran vaudevillian and character actor later to appear as Fred Merz in the *I Love Lucy*

television series, with "Going My Way," despite its being performed by her and Crosby's boy chorus on the Metropolitan Opera stage. But Frawley's chance hearing of the Oscar-winning "Swingin' on a Star," sung by Crosby and chorus after the publisher had presumably left the premises, saves the day.

Frawley buys the song, a lively tune with a message, on the spot, and from his advance payment and royalties the song later earns, Crosby is able to fund startup construction on Fitzgerald's new church. In order not to embarrass him by accepting such a large gift from a fellow priest, Crosby arranges to have $3,500 deposited by Frawley and associates in the hand-passed basket during the offertory of the next Mass. Happy in the false belief that it was his pulpit oratory that was solely responsible for the unexpected windfall, Fitzgerald reverts to his old self again, bubbling over with good cheer and confidence in his ability to continue to perform his duties with customary vigor.

Together Again. In spite of Crosby's participation in all the subplots, the screenplay is attentive to his primary role as guidance counselor for St. Dominick's parishioners, especially a gang of about 30 juvenile mischiefmakers dangerously veering toward lawlessness as a career. The one "crime" they commit in the picture—stealing a turkey from an unguarded poultry truck—would doubtless rank as little more than a childish prank to 1990s audiences, well indoctrinated in accepting violence as all-too-common behavior among teenagers and even younger children.

Going My Way's mea culpa ruffians seem almost too good to be true, utterly incapable of inflicting serious pain on anyone and amenable to reformation. The tough gang leader, Tony (Stanley Clements), for example, readily succumbs to Crosby's suggestion that the boys participate not in a practical workshop course, but in a boys' chorus under Crosby's direction. So enthusiastically does Clements react to the proposal that he bullies all his buddies, including the recalcitrant Herman, played by Carl Switzer, the former Alfalfa in the *Our Gang* comedies of the early '30s, and an uncredited "token" black youngster, into also joining the chorus. Dubbing all the group's songs was the excellent Robert Mitchell Boychoir.

Under Crosby's tutelage, the lads evolve into a most creditable singing ensemble, harmonizing on tunes ranging from "Three Blind Mice" to the aforementioned "Swingin' on a Star." Unlike the sedate "Going My Way," the bouncy "Star" song could easily qualify as a hand-clapping, foot-tapping tune written for a tent-sheltered revivalist meeting. The lesson it teaches dwells on the importance of staying in school up to graduation day as a means of escaping the drudgery of the menial jobs parceled out to uneducated adults. Without book learning, Crosby warns, even the street-wisest boy will grow up stupid as a mule, as illiterate as a fish.

All three plots converge minutes before the end of the picture. Christmas is approaching, and in accordance with that sentimental holiday, an emotionally charged parting vies with a welcoming to provide the picture with one of the most effective endings in the history of the film musical. Thanks to McCarey's impeccable timing, the final scene is not a single second overlong. Not a word is spoken, except by the chorus, which softly reprises the "Too-Ra-Loo-Ra-Loo-Ral" lullaby in the background.

The young choristers, like mentor Crosby, are all firmly committed now to helping others. Shedding their delinquent ways, they were instrumental in clearing the church of the debris that had littered the scorched main floor. Lockhart, learning from personal experience the value of St. Dominick's in propounding morality, has agreed to lend Fitzgerald the rest of the money required to rebuild his church. Fitzgerald has acknowledged the correctness of Crosby's unorthodox approaches to religion, a wise decision considering that McHugh has been appointed to fill the shoes of Crosby, who is leaving on a new assignment to another troubled parish. Jean Heather and husband Brown, whose life so far the war has spared, are in the church basement to bid Crosby farewell and hear Fitzgerald's sorrowful words of goodbye to his former helpmate. The departing Crosby has passed his mantle as chorus director to proud Clements, and the bishop has permitted Fitzgerald to remain as curate of the new St. Dominick's.

Before leaving to assume his new post, Crosby leads Fitzgerald into a hallway where, standing next to Risë Stevens, is his aged mother, whom Crosby had brought to America as his Christmas present to his former superior. Mother and son walk hesitatingly toward each other. They embrace in silence, the mother caressing his face, the son resting his head on her breast. The camera switches to Crosby, standing alone in the outside garden, dressed in hat and overcoat and holding a suitcase. Nodding his head in satisfaction while observing the long-delayed reunion of priest and parent, he slowly walks away from the little slum church and the admirable, reinvigorated old man who has learned in spite of himself to adjust with the times while continuing to devote his life to God and his parishoners.

Mission accomplished.

Anchors Aweigh (1945)

A Metro-Goldwyn-Mayer picture. DIRECTOR: George Sidney. PRODUCER: Joe Pasternak. SCREENWRITER: Isobel Lennart, suggested by a story by Natalie Marcin. CINEMATOGRAPHERS: Robert Planck and Charles Boyle. FILM EDITOR: Adrienne Fazan. CHOREOGRAPHER: Gene Kelly. RECORDING DIRECTOR: Douglas Shearer. ART DIRECTION: Cedric Gibbons and Randall Duell. SET DECORATIONS: Edwin B. Willis; ASSOCIATE: Richard Pefferle. COSTUMES: Irene; ASSOCIATE: Kay Dean. MAKEUP: Jack Dawn. KATHRYN GRAYSON'S VOCAL ARRANGER: Earl Brent. ORCHESTRATOR: Axel Stordahl. MUSICAL DIRECTOR: Georgie Stoll. SONGS: Lyrics by Sammy Cahn and Harold Rome, music by Jule Styne and Harold Rome. RUNNING TIME: 2 hours, 19 minutes. *Principal Players*: Frank Sinatra (Clarence Doolittle). Kathryn Grayson (Susan Abbott). Gene Kelly (Joseph Brady). José Iturbi (Himself). Dean Stockwell (Donald Martin). Pamela Britton (Girl from Brooklyn). Grady Sutton (Bertram Kraler). *Major Academy Award*: Best Musical Direction. *Nominations Only*: Best Picture; Actor (*Gene Kelly*); Cinematography; Song ("I Fall in Love Too Easily").

If the sole objective of film musicals is to provide audiences with temporary relief from worldly woes, *Anchors Aweigh* can be considered a roaring success. Revolving mostly around the off-duty rivalry of two American sailors to take sole possession of the love of a ravishing Los Angeles beauty, it omits any reference to the ferocious battles being fought in Europe and Asia during its filming. It is, in fact, a wartime movie that ignores war altogether. No one is shipped abroad to fight any enemy or is even wounded except by love arrows. No anxious parents are immobilized by fear at the arrival of a telegram, nor does any sailor boy nostalgically recall the happier days of the peaceful past, or dream of a postwar future crowned with personal and professional success, all clichés of the movie war dramas of the time.

Visits to the Stage Door or Hollywood canteens are rendered unnecessary by turning the deck of a Navy ship into a dance hall, and it is the beat of a peppy tune rather than the shrill whine of a bugle that spurs the uniformed lads into action. In effect, *Anchors Aweigh* is a direct descendant of such thirties Navy musicals as *Hit the Deck*, *Shipmates Forever*, *Follow the Fleet*, and *Born to Dance*. Its two intertwining, unsuspenseful plots are equally convoluted, especially during the final half-hour of running time. And, as usual, the attractiveness of the performers and the songs are the movie's chief assets.

Pleasant as it is, the film is overshadowed in plot and music by Fox's far more sedate and homespun *State Fair*, which was also produced while World War II was raging and eschews references to the conflict. For instance, not one uniformed man or woman can be spotted among the multitudes ambling along the midway at the 1945 Iowa State Fair. Whether inadvertently or by design, both escapist films reflected the nationwide optimism that the Allied victory was so close at hand that the time was ripe for Americans to turn away from the battles between nations back to battles between the sexes.

Anchors Aweigh's featured players are particularly ingratiating and largely responsible for the musical's immense popularity. Kathryn Grayson, then 23, had made her film debut in 1941 as a high school girl in *Andy Hardy's Private Secretary*, exhibiting a pleasing soprano voice by delving into the classics to sing Strauss' "Voices of Spring" and Donizetti's "Mad Scene" ("Ardon gl'incensi") from *Lucia di Lammermoor*. Pretty and always ladylike, the young woman with the Judy Garland upturned nose and Cupid's bow lips built a sturdy foundation for stardom over the next four years, be-

ginning with the 1942 remake of *Rio Rita*, and then in *Seven Sweethearts* and *Thousands Cheer*, the 1943 Army musical highlighted by her splendid vocalizing of Ferde Grofe's plaintive "Daybreak." Her equally talented sailor competitors, Frank Sinatra and Gene Kelly, by 1945 were at the cusp of their own outstanding careers.

The original Pal Joey in Rodgers and Hart's uniquely realistic 1940 portrayal of a crude gigolo, Kelly entered films in 1943 as the equally dislikable cad opposite Judy Garland and George Murphy in *For Me and My Gal*, an Arthur Freed–produced saga of the fortunes of three vaudevillians during World War I. An extraordinary dancer and choreographer, the multi-talented Kelly was a competent director and singer as well as actor, especially when portraying the smart-alecky type intent on pushing himself into the upper echelon of show business and winning the leading lady regardless of the trickery required to achieve both goals. His dance with a broomstick in *Thousands Cheer* was spectacular, as was his dance with his "alter ego," or conscience, in *Cover Girl* in 1944, and by war's end he was a fit contender for the throne occupied by King Fred Astaire on the MGM lot.

Kelly was unlike Astaire, yet of equal stature. Astaire preferred the tuxedo and a partner, Kelly the sweatshirt, loafers, and loose-fitting slacks, and he performed more solos than duets. Astaire felt at home entertaining the caviar crowd in Art Deco nightclubs; Kelly was most comfortable in the company of commoners eating blue plate specials in a diner. In their movies Astaire was an established professional at the outset; Kelly was always on the threshold of career success, usually not obtaining it till the end. Both were consummate perfectionists, each able to break into their routines with what seemed to be unrehearsed spontaneity that belied their mastery of technique and timing. Astaire was the more reserved of the two and the better singer. Only Kelly was able to blend the vitality of the streets with the decorum of the hotel ballroom, his impish grin and twinkling eyes inviting onlookers to settle back and relax while he entertained them. Astaire danced exclusively with professionals; the more democratic Kelly was never averse to traipsing the light fantastic with

Vying for the hand of Kathryn Grayson in *Anchors Aweigh* are Frank Sinatra, center, and Gene Kelly.

anyone who happened to be handy, like the little beggar girl (Sharon McManus) in *Anchors Aweigh* and the elderly lady florist in *An American in Paris.*

The Singing Sailor. Sinatra, whose name led the cast, was already the most popular performer in the picture, having succeeded in building a gigantic fan base from on-tour appearances with Tommy Dorsey's dance band, including the notable one at New York's Paramount Theatre in 1942. His movie career had begun to pick up speed by virtue of cameos in *Las Vegas Nights* (1941), crooning Louis Alter's Oscar-nominated "Dolores" in company with Dorsey's Pied Pipers quartet, and *Ship Ahoy* (1942), singing Burton Lane's "Last Call for Love" and "Poor You." The next year he appeared as solo vocalist on "Night and Day" in *Reveille with Beverly.* In his first combination singing-acting role, in the film version of Rodgers and Hart's *Higher and Higher* (1944),

which also featured boyish-looking Mel Tormé and witty concert pianist Victor Borge in minor parts, Sinatra introduced three lasting Harold Adamson–James McHugh hits, "I Couldn't Sleep a Wink Last Night," "A Lovely Way to Spend an Evening," and "The Music Stopped."

Also representative of his girl-shy, pre–Angelo Maggio film days was *Step Lively*, an inconsequential 1944 remake of the Broadway comedy *Room Service*, which in 1938 had been filmed starring the Marx Brothers. Although unable to match the acting of Frank Albertson in the part of the unsophisticated country-boy playwright, Sinatra again excelled as a singer of ballads, much to the delight of leading lady Gloria DeHaven, not to mention the legions of schoolgirl swooners who adored his naïvely seductive style that gave every one of them the impression he was singing the songs to her alone. That film marked the debut of Sammy Cahn and Jule [Julius] Styne as his film songwriters, a productive and profitable association for all three that began with "As Long as There's Music" and continued well into the next decade. Early in 1945 came the crooner's stirring rendition of Lewis Allan and Earl Robinson's "The House I Live In (That's America to Me)" in Mervyn LeRoy's award-winning, anti-discrimination short feature of the same name.

As MGM's proposed answer to Paramount's *Road to* teaming of Bing Crosby and Bob Hope, Sinatra and Kelly were reunited in two 1949 MGM musicals, *Take Me Out to the Ball Game* and their second Navy-based romp, *On the Town*, Kelly's own favorite and the first film musical filmed partially on locale, in Manhattan. Sinatra would also star opposite Miss Grayson in *It Happened in Brooklyn* (1947), in many ways a reworking of the *Anchors Aweigh* plot. In it, Sinatra plays a recently discharged soldier who sings new Cahn-Styne songs to Miss Grayson, but at the end leaves her to rival Peter Lawford and settles for a Brooklyn girl (Gloria Graehme), whose accent and background more closely resembled his own.

The *Anchors Aweigh* songs are for the most part exceptional. Sinatra's rendition of "I Fall in Love Too Easily" helped greatly to qualify it as a best song contender. An inestimable and breathtakingly fast versifyer, Cahn would write the lyrics of 21 more Academy Award–nominated songs, six of them introduced by Sinatra, including "Three Coins in the Fountain," "All the Way," "High Hopes," and "My Kind of Town (Chicago Is)."

London-born Styne's first song success, "Sunday," composed in 1926, reappeared in the early forties as the theme song of the Phil Harris and Alice Faye half-hour radio program, officially known as "*The Fitch Bandwagon*," which followed Jack Benny's show on Sunday evenings. Like Kern, Porter, Berlin, Rodgers, Arlen, and the Gershwins, Styne alternated in later years between East and West coasts, writing the scores for Broadway's *Gentleman Prefer Blondes* and *The Bells Are Ringing*, both subsequently made into films, and *Gypsy*. Many of his original screen songs—"I'll Walk Alone," "It's Magic," "It's a Great Feeling"— were nominees for the best song Oscar between 1944 and 1949.

Going on the Town. *Anchors Aweigh* is a perfect example of how the professionalism for which MGM had long been noted can support a movie musical without a single dramatic underpinning to tempt viewer interest throughout its overlong running time—two hours and 21 minutes.

Expertise exists at every level, from the Technicolor cinematography to the Academy Award–winning background musical score to the breakthrough half-cartoon, half-human dance skit between Kelly and a mouse. The catchy throwaway opener, "We Hate to Leave," whimsically addressed by Sinatra and Kelly to their buddies ineligible to join them on their four-day holiday from shipboard chores, presages the fun-loving fellowship that motivates the two male stars from start to finish and turns the film into one of the most enjoyable of the decade.

With the exception of "We're in the Money" (*The Gold Diggers of 1933*) and "Oh, What a Beautiful Mornin'" (*Oklahoma!*) the so-called "curtain-raising" song is usually expendable, dropped into a show as a sort of bonus for persons who get to the theater on time. "We Hate to Leave" probably is, too, but it does have an attractive lilt and rhyme to it, and it surely gives a pretty good indication of the girl-craziness to come.

The proficiency of the MGM masters and mistresses of illusion assigned to make much ado about essentially nothing generously compensates for the picture's lack of originality. There was absolutely nothing fresh about tracing the activities of two seagoing young men on shore leave, or the inevitability that both would fall in love with the same girl. Like Dick Powell and Pat O'Brien in *Flirtation Walk*, Kelly and Sinatra differ vastly in personality. The only things they have in common are the ship they serve on and the uniforms they wear.

Kelly is the jaunty, aggressive ladies' man programmed to beam his tantalizing smile while pursuing unescorted females who happen to drift into view. Sinatra, in the film a one-time assistant choirmaster and dedicated sipper of milkshakes who usually spends his furloughs in the local library, is woefully inadequate at chasing girls despite his upbringing in Brooklyn, which screenplays typically credited with producing brash types fearful of nothing, least of all women. Their friendship is rooted, however, in mutual bravery under fire (not depicted in the film), rather than on chance acquaintance, and is therefore credible. Recent recipients of the Silver Star, both had remained at their stations while their cruiser, *Knoxville*, was under attack, and Kelly had saved Sinatra's life by jumping overboard to rescue him from a watery grave. Neither, least of all the single-minded Kelly, is burdened with character complexities.

If Kelly (Joseph Brady) is regarded by his shipmates as the "biggest wolf in the Navy," Sinatra (Clarence Doolittle) wins hands down its saddest sack. Little wonder he looks upon Kelly with puppy dog affection. Maybe that happy-go-lucky heartbreaker can teach him a few tricks of the girl trade. In Hollywood on his way to meet Lola, his latest flame, Kelly is surprised to bump into Sinatra, on his way to nowhere in particular, who asks for assistance in becoming a ladies' man. "What's the sense of having your life saved if you can't have any fun with it?" he asks his heroic friend, hoping to wring a love lesson out of him.

Kelly's brief tutoring of Sinatra on how best to pick up women—a sort of elementary course for would-be Valentinos—is interrupted by the appearance of a policeman who insists that the sailors accompany him to the station house. There the shipmates meet 10-year-old Donald Martin, clothed in pajamas, bathrobe, and sailor's cap, whom the police had apprehended from a Los Angeles street. The son of a deceased Naval officer, the youngster had struck out on his own that evening to join the service. Unable to learn his name or address, Police Sergeant Edgar Kennedy had become convinced that only a sailor can coax the lad into revealing the information. Unfortunately, Kennedy's legendary slow-burn reaction to frustration is omitted in his brief appearance. The veteran character actor was approaching the end of his long movie career. In the meantime, Hollywood had trained a worthy successor in Donald McBride, whose Vesuvian eruptions when crossed terrified everyone within hearing range, particularly early 1940s bootcamp recruits.

Kelly accomplishes the feat in a matter of seconds by rashly promising the boy to use his influence to convince his Aunt Susie (Kathryn Grayson) to permit him to enlist in the Navy. Donald is played by Dean Stockwell, a strikingly attractive child with highly developed acting ability that would keep him on the screen into the present. As recently as 1988, he was nominated for best supporting actor for his role as "Tony the Tiger" Russo in *Married to the Mob*.

Prowling for a Career. Dean's aunt is not at home to welcome him and his sailor friends, an unexpected predicament that raises Kelly's temper to the boiling point. She should never have left her little nephew alone in the house, he complains to Sinatra; no wonder he had escaped so easily. What's more, her adult delinquency has already cost him two hours' mooching time with Lola. What Kelly does not know is that Kathryn, a movie extra, had left the boy in the care of a sitter, who went home after she assumed he had gone to sleep, and that the missing guardian is now enjoying a José Iturbi–conducted concert on one of MGM's scoring stages.

A dignified classical pianist with a knack for playing solid boogie-woogie for the edification of younger fans, the polished and personable Spanish-born Iturbi injected just the right amount of elitism into seven other 1940s musical films. It was he who played the masterful version of "Polonaise in A Flat" for Cornel Wilde, as Chopin, in *A Song to Remember* in 1944, which resulted in the sale of more than a million phonograph records. That same year Iturbi duetted his most famous piece, DeFalla's "Fire Dance," with his sister and piano partner, Imelda, in *Two Girls and a Sailor*. His selections in *Anchors Aweigh* range from Tchaikovsky to an intricate reprise of Friml's "The Donkey Serenade," first heard eight years earlier in the film, *The Firefly*.

Miss Grayson's ambition is to audition before Iturbi in hopes of putting her singing career on the fast track. She has been unable to meet him, however, which is all to the good. If she had, the film would contain no subplot whatever involving the three leads. When she returns home later that evening, she introduces romance, soon to be triangularized under the spell of musical comedy tradition. Sinatra is obviously smitten with her, while Kelly still regards her with hostility for leaving little Dean home alone. All he wants is to desert the house for Lola's arms, but he stays long enough to hear Sinatra serenade the boy with Brahms' "Lullaby," which succeeds in putting Kelly as well as Dean to sleep. Too late to keep his date with Lola after he awakens, hot-tempered Kelly barges out of the house. Sinatra follows closely behind, apologizing to Kathryn for their rapid departure.

Good sailors that they are, the pair puts on a bravado song-and-dance routine for fellow servicemen lodged for the night at a local U.S.O. Yes, the two agree, much to the chagrin of their envious listeners, their first night ashore was a spectacular success. Young women were plentiful, eager to be pursued in hopes of being caught. Serving as the vehicle for expressing their false boasts is the clever "I Begged Her." Kelly explains how he had lured one shy young lady into kissing him, and Sinatra, lying in his teeth, relates how another girl, after drawing him out of his reticence, was the recipient of his kiss. Sinatra's dancing naturally pales in comparison with Kelly's surefootedness, but the deficiencies are easily overlooked by the happy face he wears while tapping in unison with his formidable partner.

As the two had promised, they pay another visit to Dean, this time laden with toys. Sinatra has high hopes of romancing Kathryn, and Kelly vows to help his buddy win her affection. Each is astounded when they catch sight of another suitor, Bertram Kraler, played by Grady Sutton, among Hollywood's most recognizable but unidentifiable bit players, who entered films in 1925 with *The Mad Whirl*. Usually the polite luckless lover, the timid, priggish, chubby, and slightly effeminate Southern dullard was one of W.C. Fields's favorite foils. He is best remembered as Og Oggilby, the great comedian's prospective son-in-law, in *The Bank Dick* (1939), even then easily miffed when developments deviate from expectations.

With Sinatra at the piano and old tunes like "If You Knew Susie" assaulting Sutton's ears, the Navy pals enter into an amusing scheme to get rid of him pronto. Their plan is to convince Sutton that Kathryn, far from being the innocent he had assumed, is actually the "sweetheart of the boys at sea," widely

sought for her "lovin' ways." Shocked at the news, Sutton leaves the house in a huff. The sailors' happiness at dispensing so quickly with him turns to shame when Kathryn laments his loss. She actually cares little for him, but his mother is a member of the local Philharmonic Society and friend of numerous musical celebrities to whom she might very well have introduced Kathryn.

As compensation, Kelly dredges up from the inner resources of his fertile imagination what he believes is a foolproof plan to assuage her hurt and Sinatra's guilt feelings. Much to his buddy's astonishment, Kelly casually refers to Sinatra's long friendship with Iturbi, adding that only today Sinatra had persuaded the pianist to grant Kathryn an audition this coming Saturday—at 11:15 a.m., to be exact. Her hopes taking wing, she gratefully joins them in a celebratory dinner at a nearby Mexican restaurant, where, invited to sing for their suppers by owner Billy Gilbert, the young lady displays a soprano voice entirely capable of captivating even a connoisseur like Iturbi. Kathryn is definitely no amateur, even if she has yet to make her professional debut.

Her interpolated song is Vera Bloom and Jacob Gade's lovely "Jalousie," written in 1925. Miss Grayson handles the best song in the film nicely, accenting the tango beat while moving gracefully from table to table to address the lyric to attentive diners. The quality of her voice impresses Kelly—this is the first time he has heard her sing—and he happily escorts her onto the dance floor after Sinatra declines her invitation for a rhumba. (Faithful to his sheltered existence, the only music Sinatra can dance to is the waltz.)

Somewhat uneasy in Kelly's arms, Kathryn implies that she could easily fall for him were he to drop what she perceives as his tendency to regard women as playthings. Rather than angering him, her recital of his romantic shortcomings strikes Kelly as accurate to the point of embarrassment. He would be entirely open to reforming his "sea wolf" ways and compete for her love except for the fact that buddy Sinatra already has his heart set on her. Presumably, Kelly is chaste Kathryn's first heart throb, and he is unwilling to add her name to his little black book of "love 'em and leave 'em" prospects—for the sake of all three.

Alone at the table, Sinatra sings introspectively of his growing love for Kathryn in the very pretty ballad "What Makes the Sunset?" The answer, of course, is love, which not only makes the world go 'round, but also accounts for mankind's susceptibility to the beauties of Nature, including, unsurprisingly, those of the opposite sex. Listening to him is waitress Pamela Britton, almost a dead ringer in looks and voice for Betty Garrett.

That she is entranced with song and singer is obvious from her riveting attention while he massages the lyric. That she also began life in Brooklyn is made clear, as it was in so many Hollywood films, the second she opens her mouth to compliment Sinatra. She hails from "Greenpernt," she informs him, trying her best to inaugurate a courtship based on mutual fondness for their home borough. Far more down to earth than the ethereal Kathryn, Pamela's presence is the most "dramatically" rewarding in the film, even if her role is more of a reprise of earlier street-smart girls than a novelty.

Shy with Kathryn, Sinatra is free and easy with Pamela while exchanging back-home reminiscences in a free flow of conversation. No intuitive insight into film-musical screenplays was required for audiences to surmise that their compatibility will clear the path for Kelly to pursue Kathryn without fear of two-timing his friend. Given time, each of the couples would be suitably matched, thereby shuffling aside any pretense of suspense, slight as it was to begin with, revolving around which sailor would wind up in which lady's arms. The only problem facing the sailors was how to coerce the unapproachable Iturbi into auditioning the unknown Kathryn.

Later that night, she also sings of her love—for Kelly—in "All of a Sudden (My Heart Sings)," written by "Jamblan" [Henri Herpin] and Harold Rome, who throughout his career overwhelmingly preferred Broadway to Hollywood. She sings the words almost at the level of a whisper while her face appears in one of the longest closeups ever seen in a Hollywood musical. Her sincerity, combined with demureness and emotional control, softens the tremendously passionate lyric into a restrained yet heartfelt expression of the love of a maiden for a worldly lady

killer on the verge of redemption, surely one of most satisfying of love affairs to moviegoers of the time.

First Jerry, Then José. Kelly's determination to arrange the interview with Iturbi suddenly takes on a new urgency for three reasons: he is convinced that Kathryn's voice, as well as the lady herself, will impress Iturbi; his silent love for her demands that he do all he can to advance her career; and, above all, it was he who had lied about Sinatra's friendship with the maestro. At MGM's Culver City headquarters, Kelly wanders into the Hollywood Day School, attended by child stars and the offspring of studio employees. Totally unrelated to the plot, the visit provides the musical with its most visually arresting sequence. Asked how he won his medal, Kelly tells the children, who include Dean Stockwell, an imaginative tale of his adventures in a strange land. His animated dancing partner is Jerry, the clever little mouse who had already earned the affection of fans of MGM's contemporary Tom and Jerry cartoon series by always outwitting Tom the cat's every ploy to capture him. Kelly's and Jerry's parts in the sequence were filmed separately and then joined together on the final print.

Passing himself off as a sailor in the Pomeranian Navy, Kelly finds himself in a storybook, Oz-like country populated by tiny sad-faced animals and birds who refuse to join him in his hornpipe dance. They are not allowed by law to engage in such frivolities, they explain. Angry over such a wicked law, Kelly barges into the hilltop castle of the ruler to reverse it. There he meets Jerry, sitting on his throne and looking as glum as his subjects. He admits that he has forbidden all merriment throughout his kingdom because he himself is unable to sing or dance.

Kelly is adamant in proclaiming, in "The Worry Song," a Ralph Freed and Sammy Fain interpolation, that these talents are available to anyone whose heart is warm and happy. He then dances a few steps, and the two strike up an energetic tap duologue that is brilliant in both concept and execution and ranks as one of the most innovative on film. "Look at me, I'm dancin'!" Jerry cries out between titters of astonishment at his rapid progress at aping Kelly's movements. The result of his pride of accomplishment is lifting the entertainment ban and awarding Kelly a medal for helping him to win back the love of his subjects. And that, Kelly explains to his young audience, is how he got his Silver Star.

The first thing Sinatra learns on the crusade to entice Iturbi into holding the elusive audition is that entering a Hollywood studio is fraught with difficulties. With the help of Kelly's bravado, Sinatra manages to finagle a pass and stumbles across Iturbi practicing on the piano. He misses his chance to plead Kathryn's case, however, by mistaking Iturbi for a piano tuner. Later, thrown into a panic by the fast-approaching Saturday morning deadline, both sailors intensify their efforts, only to arrive minutes too late to meet with the maestro at the Hollywood Bowl and then at his residence, despite spending Friday night camped on his doorstep.

Interwoven with the poor prospects of arranging for the audition is the slow but steady progression of the love affair between Sinatra and Pamela, which is revealed primarily through the lyrics of two exceptional Cahn-Styne ballads. The first, "The Charm of You," sung by Sinatra ostensibly to express his deep feeling for Kathryn, instead turns into a paean of praise for Pamela, whose starry-eyed response is that he "sings like a boid."

A short time later, however, he acknowledges the inner turmoil that his lingering fondness for Kathryn *vs.* his developing love for Pamela has inflicted on him in the poetic lyric of "I Fall in Love Too Easily." The film's most substantial ballad in terms of furthering the screenplay, it reveals the crisis faced by an unsophisticated young man so desperate for a mate that he is willing to accept a mere smile as an invitation to romance, a malady common to the loneliest of hearts whose love expressions are more often unrequited than shared.

Meanwhile Kelly, the professional lover, is experiencing his own girl trouble. Lola has fled from his mind in favor of Kathryn, whom he regards as not a handy someone to woo on leave, but rather as the type of girl "you come home to" and marry. When he finally learns that Sinatra's big love is Pamela and not Kathryn, his spirits soar. But there is always

that nagging problem to tamp them down. How is he going to straighten out that damn Iturbi thing? To solve it, the film relies heavily on role reversal, and the scenes that follow bear witness to Sinatra's gradual emergence from his cocoon while his glib, fast-talking shipmate crawls into one of his own making.

Kelly admits to Kathryn that he is tongue-tied in her presence, which to him is incontestible proof that he is indeed in love with her. Unable to speak the words of love simmering in his heart, he proposes to act them out for her benefit in another imaginary tale in which he masquerades as a dancing Mexican bandit who steals into the palace hideaway of Princess Kathryn in hopes of absconding with her. As expected, his vigorous dance to a medley of traditional Mexican songs is superb, but the entire sequence is unnecessary and so overwrought that it intrudes rather than amplifies.

As the thrilled observer, Kathryn scarcely moves, appearing content to be romanced by her dashing suitor, whose Douglas Fairbanks acrobatics carry him up the castle wall and along turret tops to the balcony on which she stands are more appropriate to a pirate than a lover. As in the ballet finale to *An American in Paris*, a rose is used as the emblem of Kelly's love for the young damsel. Kathryn catches it in her hand at the beginning, then drops it to the ground at the conclusion, symbolizing her surrender to Kelly, who rewards her with a kiss.

Kathryn finally meets Iturbi, not in his office but in the MGM commissary on the morning of the supposed audition. Expecting momentarily to perform for him, she expresses delight in his interest in her. Nonplused, Iturbi disavows any knowledge of Sinatra's existence or of the alleged commitment to listen to her sing, causing Kathryn to retreat from him in tears. But thanks to the film musical's firm policy of permitting every struggling youngster to win professional recognition, Iturbi comforts her by lauding her friend's show of helpfulness, even if misguided, and offers to judge her talent after all. Kathryn's subsequent A-plus performance of the Tchaikovsky-based "Waltz Serenade" (with words by Earl K. Brent) not only impresses Iturbi, but also serves as a screen test that commands the attention of several studio executive spectators. It will not be long, one assumes, before she becomes one of

MGM's top musical stars, a pretty convincing example of how accurately art can imitate life.

Their leaves over and back on the ship, Sinatra and Kelly are downcast. Neither gloomy Gus is aware of Kathryn's success until Iturbi himself appears and tells them the news and invites them to join him and his orchestra on the main deck. Addressing the assembled crowd of sailors and officers, he praises Kathryn as a major talent who was "discovered by the United States Navy." The orchestra strikes up "Anchors Aweigh," the same military anthem it had played in the very first scene. In separate cutouts to the left and right of the screen are Sinatra and Pamela and Kelly and Kathryn, gazing into each other's eyes, then locked in an embrace, and finally sharing the kiss demanded at the conclusion of all musical pictures, even as late as 1945.

An American in Paris (1951)

A Metro-Goldwyn-Mayer picture. DIRECTOR: Vincente Minnelli. PRODUCER: Arthur Freed. STORY AND SCREENPLAY: Alan Jay Lerner. CINEMATOGRAPHER: Alfred Gilks; BALLET PHOTOGRAPHER: John Allen; MONTAGE SEQUENCES: Peter Bailbrisch; SPECIAL EFFECTS: Warren Newcombe and Irving G. Ries. FILM EDITOR: Adrienne Fazan. ART DIRECTORS: Cedric Gibbons and Preston Ames. SET DECORATIONS: Edwin B. Willis; ASSOCIATE: Keogh Gleason. CHOREOGRAPHER: Gene Kelly. RECORDING SUPERVISOR: Douglas Shearer. ORCHESTRATOR: Conrad Salinger. COSTUMES: Orry Kelly; BEAUX ARTS BALL COSTUMES: Walter Plunkett; BALLET COSTUMES: Irene Sharaff. HAIR STYLES: Sydney Guilaroff. MAKEUP: William Tuttle. MUSICAL DIRECTORS: Johnny Green and Saul Chaplin. SONGS: Lyrics by Ira Gershwin, music by George Gershwin. RUNNING TIME: 1 hour, 53 minutes. *Principal Players*: Gene Kelly (Jerry Mulligan). Leslie Caron (Lise Bouvier). Oscar Levant (Adam Cook). Georges Guetary (Henri Baurel). Nina Foch (Milo Roberts). *Major Academy Awards*: Best Picture; Screenplay; Cinematography; Musical Direction; Art Direction; Costumes, including Beaux Arts Ball and ballet. *Nominations*: Best Director; Film Editing.

Six years had elapsed since the previous musical best picture nominee, and once again the new contender starred Gene Kelly, this time singing and dancing stage and movie songs composed by George Gershwin (*né* Jacob Gershwine, a misspelling of Gershvin). Like Richard Rodgers, Gershwin wrote songs for only a handful of screen musicals even though his reputation during the first 10 years of talk-ing pictures exceeded that of any other popular composer with the exception of Irving Berlin. He was, in fact, a major celebrity both at home and abroad, admired by fellow composers and worshiped by fans, particularly in Europe.

His death of a malignant brain tumor on July 11, 1937, two months short of his 39th birthday, cut short by decades the Hollywood career on which he had only recently begun to concentrate his efforts. Based on the quality of his songs for *Shall We Dance, A Damsel in Distress,* and *The Goldwyn Follies,* the first two released in 1937 and the third in 1938, his composing genius showed no sign of diminution in the last year of his life. There can be no doubt that these picture scores would have earned him carte blanche entry into any studio any time he wanted to enter it, or that he would have continued to enrich many later musicals with his contributions.

For *Shall We Dance* he wrote the catchy title song and "(I've Got) Beginner's Luck," "Let's Call the Whole Thing Off," "Slap That Bass," "They All Laughed," the Oscar-nominated "They Can't Take That Away from Me," and the instrumental "Walking the Dog," later retitled "Promenade." According to Library of Congress records, "King of Swing" was copyrighted in 1936. With a lyric by Al Stillman instead of brother Ira, the song later that year found its way into *Swing Is King,* a Radio City Music Hall revue. A marvelous and intricate production number, the song is on a par with the composer's "When Do We Dance," from *Tip Toes,* which opened in New York on December 28, 1925, and included a very young Jeanette MacDonald as Sylvia.

A Damsel in Distress featured "A Foggy Day," "Nice Work If You Can Get It," "I Can't Be Bothered Now," "Stiff Upper Lip," "Things Are Looking Up," and two madrigal-sounding novelties, "The Jolly Tar and the Milkmaid" and "Sing of Spring." The score of *The Goldwyn Follies* consisted of "I Love to Rhyme," "I Was Doing All Right," "Love Is Here to Stay," and "Love Walked In." Omitted was "Dawn of a New Day," which was later revised by composer Kay Swift and used as the official march of the 1939 New York World's Fair.

Actually, Gershwin was one of the first major stage composers to contribute a song to

Leslie Caron, as the French perfume salesgirl, and Gene Kelly as the ex–G.I. with artistic aspirations in a scene from *An American in Paris*.

a motion picture. Entitled "The Sunshine Trail," it served as theme song for director Thomas H. Ince's 1923 silent epic of the same name. He returned to film composing eight years later with the seven-song score for *Delicious*, a charming romantic fable co-starring Janet Gaynor and Charles Farrell. "Delishious" was the hit, a mild one that lay dormant until Joan Leslie reprised it in *Rhapsody in Blue*. The other songs, "Blah, Blah, Blah," "Katinkitschka," "Somebody from Somewhere," "You Started It," and two brief background instrumentals, including an excerpt from his as-yet uncompleted *Second Rhapsody*, filled out the score. In 1946, ten of his songs, with "For You, for Me, Forevermore" leading the pack, were revived posthumously for the Betty Grable–Dick Haymes period musical, *The Shocking Miss Pilgrim*, and three more for Billy Wilder's *Kiss Me, Stupid* in 1964.

In all, at least one original Gershwin song appeared in 49 stage shows between 1916 and 1936, including *Half Past Eight*, which died a quick death in 1918 in Syracuse, New York, and never reached Broadway. *Girl Crazy*, which ran at the Alvin Theatre for 272 performances, a successful showing in 1930, was remade three times into a movie, in 1932 and 1943 under the original title, and in 1965 as *Where the Boys Meet the Girls*. (Among the instrumentalists in the pit orchestra for the 1930 *Girl Crazy* were such future stars as Benny Goodman, Glenn Miller, Jimmy Dorsey, Gene Krupa, Jack Teagarden, and Red Nichols.)

Gershwin's *Strike Up the Band* was filmed in 1940 and *Lady Be Good* the next year. Neither bore the slightest resemblance to the stage pieces, except for using two of the Broadway songs as title tunes, while *Funny Face* in 1957 and *Porgy and Bess* in 1959 by and large remained faithful to the 1927 and 1935 original scores. Of all the films featuring Gershwin songs, the "biographical" *Rhapsody in Blue* contains the most—27—some of them played only partially or consigned to the background, but thankfully showcasing Anne Brown's superb rendition of "Summertime."

The only musical best picture winner without a single new tune written expressly for it, *An American in Paris* repeats a half-dozen *Rhapsody in Blue* songs, in every instance bettering their exposure. Back in harness, and at his best, is Gene Kelly in his oft-repeated role as the charismatic hothead, whose utterly enchanting performance was largely responsible for the classic film's winning the best picture award. Kelly himself was presented with a Special Academy Award for his "brilliant achievement" as actor, singer, director, dancer, and cinematic choreographer.

As conscientiously as *Singin' in the Rain* preserved the integrity of the Freed-Brown songs, *An American in Paris* treats the Gershwin songs with respect bordering on reverence. Kelly and Oscar Levant's duet of the lighthearted "Tra-La-La," for instance, displays a comic inventiveness equaled only by the "Good Morning" romp in *Singin' in the Rain*. Similarly, the twosome's reprise of "By Strauss" adds to its melodious appeal by Kelly's invitation to an elderly woman florist (Mary Young) to dance it with him, inserting a touch of tenderness to a rare Gershwin waltz that in reality was a satire on pop songs and their writers, including George and Ira themselves.

In the finest example of remaining true to the spirit of the original song, Kelly gives a sing-along English lesson to a cluster of little French children using one of the composer's liveliest tunes as his text. "I Got...," one child after another calls out as he points a finger at them, signaling Kelly to complete the phrase with the proper response, "...Rhythm." Their teacher then launches into bubbly tap dances made even more delightful by his imitations of a cowboy, chugging locomotive, and Charlie Chaplin. It is with such little touches as these that the old songs are given new life without in any way compromising their swing and sway.

Others besides Kelly contributed mightily to the film's glory, from Alan Jay Lerner, of the Lerner and (Frederick) Loewe partnership, for his excellent story and screenplay, the most literate of all pre–*Gigi* musicals; Vincente Minnelli for his sturdy direction; Johnny Green and Saul Chaplin for their award-winning scoring.

Cedric Gibbons and Preston Ames's art direction perfectly complements Edwin B. Willis and Keogh Gleason's decorative sets to a degree unmatched by any previous Technicolor musical.

Essentially the film is a magnificent, highly entertaining hybrid, about four-fifths incorporating tried and true elements of the old-fashioned movie musical, and the other fifth breaking ground by devoting 17 of its final 20 minutes to an immensely complex and cacophonous tour de force danced almost totally in ballet format. Its length and seemingly endless stream of characters tend to nudge the sequence onto the debit side of the artistic ledger, but the film is so asset rich that it is able to overcome even this sometimes heavy handed exercise. Not the least of the virtues is the Technicolor photography, which had rarely been used to greater advantage. From *Anchors Aweigh* on, all the Oscar-contending musicals were shot in color, although not always in Technicolor, the brightest, clearest—and most expensive—of all the color processes.

Kelly's supporting players were ideally cast. As the struggling artist too proud to accept charity to survive, the dancer turns in the finest performance of his career except for his Don Lockwood role in *Singin' in the Rain*, which is quite similar in content and character development. As the little French gamine who pouts and dances her way into Kelly's heart, 20-year-old ballerina Leslie Caron was a most attractive newcomer to the ranks of Hollywood's sweetly innocent heroines, evincing solid dramatic as well as musical skill as the coy maiden forced to confront marriage problems at far too early an age.

Although in a few instances her French accent is difficult to decipher—and the same can be said of Georges Guetary—not even the most anti–Gallic of fans could deny that her reference to Kelly as "Meestaire Mooleegon" is as charming a mispronunciation as one could wish for. One of very few actresses to dance with both Kelly and Fred Astaire, she would reappear in such musicals as *Daddy Long Legs* (1955) and, of course, *Gigi*. The versatile actress, whom Kelly himself discovered, is also remembered as the beguiling 16-year-old orphan in *Lili* (1953) and as co-star of the bleak drama *The L-Shaped Room* (1962) and the comedy *Father Goose* (1964).

Oscar Levant's appearance as Adam Cook, an unemployed concert pianist on his eighth fellowship, was his ninth since *The Dance of Life* in 1929, and his trademark mock sarcasm and self-effacement provide *An American in Paris* with most of its humor. His role as a grumpy, egotistical pianist most likely would have won him few admirers were it not for the affability he wove into the characterization and the fact that his piano playing fully justified his high self-regard. According to literary agent Scott Meredith, Levant and Gershwin's lifelong friendship began in 1930, when they frequently ran into each other while Gershwin's *Strike Up the Band* was playing at the Times Square Theatre and Levant's *Ripples* directly across the street at the New Amsterdam.

Especially noteworthy in the film is Levant's superior rendition of the third (Allegro agitato) movement of Gershwin's *Concerto in F [Major]* while lying in bed puffing on the ubiquitous cigarette and day dreaming of his debut with a symphony orchestra. Given the chance to do so in a soliloquy, he plays violin and kettle drums as well as piano, serves as conductor, and awards himself the wildest of applause, save for one loud dissenter—also played by Levant. Composed in 1925, the concerto, originally entitled "New York Concerto," was orchestrated by Gershwin himself, unlike *Rhapsody in Blue*, which was twice orchestrated by Ferde Grofé, once for its Paul Whiteman debut, and later for the standard symphony orchestra. It is the latter version that has been played ever since.

A minor composer of film scores himself, as well as a chief interpreter of his friend's concert hall works, Levant lends his piano virtuosity to four of Gershwin's songs. He sings along with Kelly on all of them, and even though his frog-like voice does little to enhance their romanticism, his exhilaration at helping to resurrect the old songs is obvious.

Georges Guetary was an accomplished French cabaret singer virtually unknown to Americans despite his having earned a solid reputation in Europe. His role as a musical comedy star came naturally to him, and he is quite likable as the faithful friend of Kelly and Levant, whom he serves as bon vivant builder-upper and dependable soft touch for an occasional franc or two. His combination fatherly and romantic love of Leslie is often touching,

even if the dilemma of which emotion to pursue is so typical of musical comedy that any onlooker could anticipate the decision long before he makes it. His ringing tenor voice does justice to several Gershwin ditties, above all "I'll Build a Stairway to Paradise" (on which Buddy DeSylva served as lyric collaborator), the film's only other full production song-and-dance number, which he performs while ascending an illuminated staircase supporting glamorously gowned chorus girls every step of the way.

Released on November 9, 1951, *An American in Paris* marvelously depicts the kind of life any aspiring painter would love to live. The setting is Paris, one of the world's great art and love centers, its charming Left Bank side streets crammed with equally charming mom-and-pop shops and cafés, where a smile is as welcome as a sou. Flowers sprouting from little table-top vases and on sale in stalls sprinkle rainbows of colors over interiors and exteriors. Residents and visitors are all friendly, the streets are spotless, and not a cloud is permitted to blot out the pervasive sunlight.

Frolicsome street gangs consist of lovable lower-economic-class urchins on eternal recess from school and worry, deliciously happy in their environment, which in most other cities would be classified as a once-reputable neighborhood in decline. Music floats on the air, sending young and old into dance or vocal spasms of sheer delirium. Kelly's tiny garret may be congested with fire-sale furniture and art supplies, but from his window he can feast his eyes on quaint little chimney pipes twisting their way up to and along the roofs of centuries-old tenements and, far in the distance, the majestic Eiffel Tower. Who, Ira Gershwin might well ask, could ask for anything more?

Ex-G.I. Kelly is comfortable and eternally hopeful there, declaring in his voiceover introductory narrative that "if you can't paint in Paris, you better give up and marry the boss's daughter." Besides, the man is as stubborn as he is ambitious and, as he soon demonstrates, willing to subsist in poverty and suffer art critics' inattentiveness rather than surrender his precious independence.

The Artist at Work. It is early in the morning, and Kelly, as Jerry Mulligan, is once again carrying his stock-in-trade—easel, brushes, and canvas—on his way to Montmartre, that haven where amateurs without a sale to their name converge with moneyed tourists hoping to purchase samples of works from the early green period of undiscovered masters. In an amusing brief scene, Kelly walks past an unbilled actor playing Winston Churchill, who is as doggedly devoted as his fellow artists to committing the landscape to canvas. Undaunted by months of watching people pass by after casting indifferent glances at his merchandise, Kelly cheerfully spreads several of his land and seascapes on the sidewalk and from nails in a stone wall.

Moments later, a young woman pauses longer than usual to inspect several of his works. She introduces herself as Milo Roberts (Nina Foch), a rabid fan of all the arts, painting in particular. Self-assured, elegant, and patronizing, she offers to buy two of his originals for an astonishing 15,000 francs—or about 50 American dollars—each. Immensely pleased as he is over this unexpected windfall, Kelly is unable to complete the transaction when Nina tells him that he must accompany her to the Ritz Hotel in her chauffeur-driven limousene, explaining that she never carries that much cash with her. Her request sounds logical to Kelly, and he enters behind her into the limo despite slight misgivings that this obviously cultured woman has more on her mind than acquiring paintings by an unknown.

Later, after effusively praising his talent in her Ritz suite, Nina invites him to a party she is giving that evening "for a few friends." His suspicion has been confirmed: the lady is nothing more than a dilettante more interested in showing off her artist friends than purchasing their *objets d'art*. But she is pretty, and 30,000 francs is a hefty fee merely to show up at a soiree.

Their relations take a decided turn for the worse when Kelly is chagrined that evening to learn that he and Nina are the sole partygoers. Feeling victimized, he denounces her for the ruse, scoops up his two paintings, and, calling his highest moral principles into play, informs her that he will not be her paid lover, regardless of the size of her bankroll. In short, while his paintings are for sale, he is not. Nina manages to pacify him by explaining that her interest in him is genuine, proving it by proposing to advance his career by sponsoring a one-man show in the near future. Kelly calms down. Protégé is far more respectable than gigolo. Nina invites him to co-celebrate their business arrangement by squiring her to a small, crowded, and smoke-filled cabaret.

Sitting at a table opposite them is Leslie Caron (Lisa Bouvier), a petite amalgam of sweetness and shyness that contrasts starkly with Nina's shallow ultra-sophistication. It soon becomes clear to the audience, not to mention Nina, that once Kelly's rambling gaze focuses on Leslie, any hope Nina may entertain of redirecting his attention back to her has dissipated. To make matters worse, he asks Leslie for a dance, during which he sings "Love Is Here to Stay."

His romantic crooning produces two results, one expected, the other not. Irritated by his affront, Leslie answers his request for her office telephone number by transposing two of the digits, which are innocently corrected by one of her friends at the table. Now consumed with jealousy, Nina barges out of the cabaret, followed by Kelly, whom she lambasts for indulging in what she believes is his penchant for picking up "stray women." His anger rising proportionately with hers, Kelly departs the cab in a huff, further destabilizing their relationship, which at this point seems headed for permanent dissolution.

He calls Leslie the next day at the perfume shop where she works as a salesgirl, only to encounter a frigid reception. His flirtation, which last night was a "small annoyance," is now a "large nuisance," she tells him before slamming the receiver. Like all persistent movie lovers, Kelly regards the rebuff as a challenge, and he follows up the phone call with a visit to the shop. Exuding wit and charm, he manages to strike a truce with Leslie largely by convincing a finicky elderly tourist from Wisconsin (Florence Bates) that only the most expensive fragrance on display can attract a swarm of suitors. She buys a bottle and Leslie rings up a hefty sale.

Ambition-oriented Nina is not about to see her plans unravel because of a grudge, and when she next meets Kelly in the neighborhood's cozy Café Bel Ami, she implores him to let her make arrangements for the promised one-man exhibition. All he need do is spend three months practicing his art in the airy and commodious skylighted studio she has just rented for him. Concerned that the lady may very well be out to exploit him, but aware that offers like that do not come along every day, Kelly consents to the deal.

As soon as she drives off, he returns to the café to keep a dinner date he had made with Leslie, and from there they stroll to a moonlit patch of greenery bordering the Seine, where Kelly leads her into an exquisite reprise of "Love Is Here to Stay." Containing one of the loveliest of Gershwin's melodies, the song is significant for another reason besides welding the two dancers' hearts together. It was the last song the composer worked on before his death, and the words are in reality a love poem dedicated to him by his lyricist brother. Although they will never collaborate again, Ira insists that his love for George will always remain with him, eternal as the Rock of Gibraltar. Using George's music sheet notations, Ira, composer Kay ("Fine and Dandy") Swift, and Levant completed the song a few weeks before *The Goldwyn Follies* was released on February 23, 1938.

Faithful to his word, Kelly throws himself into his work, whipping out a stunning assortment of landscapes, façades, and portraits—all of them painted expressly for the film by Gene Grant. Most of his time in the studio, however, is spent on preserving the image of beauteous Leslie, shown seated on a handsome chair and holding a rose, on a canvas that he is careful to conceal whenever Nina drops up for a visit. Both patron and painter are pleased with his progress, but Kelly's normal exuberance is descending into inertia, partly to protest Nina's intensive work schedule, but mostly because Leslie had run away from him a few days earlier without cause or explanation.

Fortunately, the often acerbic Levant is also a valuable friend in need onto whose perpetually slumped shoulders Kelly feels free to unload his burden. Levant is aware of the reason for Leslie's absence, but is unwilling to divulge the love of Georges Guetary (Henri Baurel) for her out of fear that the knowledge would inflict still more pain on his heartsick companion. So his advice to Kelly is to restore his congenital optimism by going full steam after the love of his life. "'S Wonderful" to be in love, Levant asserts, prompting Kelly into acquiescence by singing and dancing to the Gershwin brothers' merriest tribute to the happiness that arises from a compatible love affair.

Past-Present Conflict. Kelly and Leslie meet again in the little park, where he declares his undying love. His confession leads her to make one of her own. She was only a little girl during the Nazi occupation of France. Since both parents were members of the Resistance, Guetary took her into his own home and assumed responsibility for her protection and caring until the end of the war. The penalty for harboring enemies of the Nazis was death. But not once over the past six years had he asked anything of her in return, Leslie explains. Not until just the other day, this is, when he proposed marriage, which she feels obligated to accept. She admits she does not love him, but how could she possibly refuse to repay the many kindnesses of her selfless benefactor, who she has no doubt is deeply in love with her.

Stunned by the revelation, Kelly walks slowly away from her, determined to submerge his self-pity in the pursuit of Nina, who at least is handy and uncommitted. Pleased with his attentiveness, and uninterested in learning the reason for it, Nina invites him to the Art Students' Ball. It is there that the five major characters meet and point the plot to its inevitable conclusion. Leslie is driven to the ball by Guetary, Kelly and Nina arrive together, and Levant, dressed as a cowboy, contributes to the festivities by good naturedly pounding out Gershwin melodies to appreciative listeners grouped around the piano. Unwilling to submit to the seemingly irreconcilable loss of Leslie, Kelly escorts her onto a balcony terrace in order to make one last appeal for her love. His hope is dashed, however, when she tells him that she and Guetary are to be married tomorrow.

The camera then shifts to a closeup of Guetary's face, now clouded over with the consternation of a man who has just learned that his fiancée had accepted his proposal out of a sense of duty rather than love. He has overheard their conversation and is in a quandary over how to react to it. After exchanging dispirited looks and sad goodbyes, Leslie leaves Kelly to descend the steps leading to the street, where Guetary is awaiting her next to a parked taxicab. She pauses a few moments to cast a fleeting glance up at Kelly, then joins Guetary in the back seat, and the cab pulls away.

Kelly watches the cab until it disappears and then raises his head to stare vacantly into the Paris skyline, which he proceeds to sketch on the back of a discarded Beaux Art program. His jottings fade into the figure of a man—himself—who bends to pick up a rose from the sidewalk, a gesture with a significance yet to be explained, as the film enters its dream ballet finale. The musical accompaniment of the sequence is Gershwin's *An American in Paris*, which made its debut at Carnegie Hall on December 13, 1928. Along with Franck's *Symphony in D Minor* and Wagner's "Magic Fire Scene" from *Die Walküre*, the suite was performed by the New York Philharmonic Society Orchestra under the baton of Walter Damrosch.

The razzle-dazzle ballet, lasting almost one-third of an hour, is frequently overpowering, but nonetheless a miraculous coalescence of music, choreography, cinematography, lighting, costuming, and set design unparalleled in the annals of the Hollywood musical. Featuring a grand total of about 100 participants, the slight story centers on Kelly, breathless with excitement at his introduction to the fabled City of Light. He is eager to imbibe its splendors, become a willing captive to its influences, and perhaps find romance somewhere in the city's tangle of narrow side streets. He flirts with a young maiden—Leslie—but backtracks into casualness when his taps fail to arouse her interest.

With so many other sights and sounds assailing his senses, from military parades to a chorus of can-can girls, he expects that dismissing her from mind will come quickly. First, he dances with four other young men in an effort to forget her, and even performs an extraordinary apache dance symbolizing his acceptance of the life of a solo male, his only concern the constant search for pleasure, ever free to seek companionship wherever he can find it.

Yet, it is love—selfless and therefore true love—that inundates the entire sequence, and Leslie soon enters into a series of reappearances, each separated by a chorus line of French soldiers on parade. She ignores Kelly at first, at one point walking out of view with the wiggle and bounce of an inexperienced young girl trying so hard to play the part of a temptress that her exaggerated gestures arouse ridicule rather than passion.

Unable to stay away from each other, they finally share the depth of their mutual affection in a short subsidiary ballet on a massive marble fountain in Place de la Concorde. The swirl of colors that distinguishes all other portions of the sequence is here narrowed down to only pale blue shafts of light that play upon the surrounding heroic statuary, then deepen in tone to silhouette the two dancers against a background of midnight black. This remarkable scene was the most provocative display of seductiveness to be seen on the screen until *All That Jazz* carried the passionate mating of dancing lovers to its extreme in 1979.

Merging the ballet into the plot of the picture is accomplished by the parting of the lovers, signified by Leslie's spurning of Kelly's advances. Devastated, he is no longer interested in maintaining his independence of spirit and action, or even seeking acclaim as a painter. He had found the only girl who could make his life complete, and he has lost her. Along with Leslie, the soldiers, gendarmes, pedestrians, school children, and shopkeepers have deserted him. Now he is alone, with only the rose, held tightly in his hand, to remind him of a lovely love affair that has slipped from his grasp.

Comparisons between this film's insertion of a story line into Gershwin's concert piece and the one in *Rhapsody in Blue* are inescapable. In the 1945 black-and-white movie, the protagonist is Gershwin himself, played by Robert Alda, who arrives in Paris, checks into a hotel, and walks the streets to gather inspiration to complete his great orchestral work. Some five minutes shorter than the *An American in Paris* ballet, it is equally effective, although far less incandescent. Each revolves around the craving of a young man for fulfillment, Alda by incorporating Parisian impressions and sounds into his music, Kelly in the love of a woman. The *Rhapsody in Blue* sequence, highlighted by the familiar "homesickness" section, one of the greatest blues melody ever written, is far superior to its reprise in the later film, which submerges much of the emotional content of the music under a frenzy of choreographic excesses.

Back on the balcony, Kelly stares aimlessly into space, more tortured than previously by the realization that his fantasy was nothing more than a mirror reflection of the end of his romance with Leslie. Suddenly his eyes are illuminated by a spark of hope. The taxi has returned, and Leslie steps out of it while breathing a sigh of relief at seeing Kelly still there. She races up the stairs while he rushes down toward her. Watching them is the gentlemanly Guetary, a wan smile testifying to his sadness at breaking off his engagement to a woman in love with another man. He then signals to the cabbie to drive away as the American painter and the little Parisian salesgirl meet midway in a rapturous embrace.

Although Kelly appeared in 20 more pictures, both musicals and dramas, none of them was nominated for the Academy Award, not even *Singin' in the Rain*. It was in that masterpiece that the love-happy, waterlogged star performed his greatest dance, splashing through puddles and twirling his umbrella in an ecstasy of delight while reviving the 1929 title tune. Referring to this number when told of Kelly's death at age 83 on February 2, 1996, Liza Minnelli appropriately summed up her and the public's fondness for the man in a short sentence worthy to be his epitaph: "Whenever it rains, I'll think of him and smile."

Seven Brides for Seven Brothers (1954)

A Metro-Goldwyn-Mayer picture. DIRECTOR: Stanley Donen; ASSISTANT: Ridgeway Callow. PRODUCER: Jack Cummings. SCREENPLAY: Albert Hackett, Frances Goodrich, and Dorothy Kingsley, based on the story "The Sobbin' Women," by Stephen Vincent Benét. CINEMATOGRAPHER: George Folsey; SPECIAL EFFECTS: A. Arnold Gillespie and Warren Newcombe; FILM EDITOR: Ralph E. Winters. CHOREOGRAPHER: Michael Kidd. ART DIRECTOR: Cedric Gibbons. RECORDING SUPERVISOR: Douglas Shearer. SET DECORATORS: Edwin B. Willis and Hugh Hunt. COSTUMES: Walter Plunkett. HAIRSTYLES: Sydney Guilaroff. MAKEUP: William Tuttle. MUSIC SUPERVISOR: Saul Chaplin; MUSIC DIRECTOR: Adolph Deutsch. ORCHESTRATORS: Alexander Courage, Conrad Salinger, and Leo Arnaud. SONGS: Lyrics by Johnny Mercer, music by Gene dePaul. RUNNING TIME: 1 hour and 42 minutes. *Principal Cast Members*: Jane Powell (Milly). Howard Keel (Adam [Pontabee]). Jeff Richards (Benjamin). Russ Tamblyn (Gideon). Tommy Rall (Frank). Howard Petrie (Pete Perkins). Marc Platt (Daniel). Matt Mattox (Caleb). Jacques d'Amboise (Ephriam). *Major Academy Award*: Best Scoring. *Nominations*: Best Picture; Screenplay; Cinematography; Film Editing.

If charming is the word to describe *An American in Paris*, delightful is the word for *Seven Brides for Seven Brothers*, the first musical nominee in Cinemascope. Howard Keel and the six other members of his Pontabee clan exemplify the three Bs of authentic masculinity—beefy, burly, and boisterous. Even the most boyish brother, Russ Tamblyn, could very well measure up to the family's standards of manhood, given time to add more meat to his bones and lower his voice from tenor to bass.

The site and time frame—the Oregon Territory in the 1850s—also bespeak the ruggedness of the untamed wilds where only the most adventurous of pioneers would dare to tread. There are no polished Fred Astaires among the townsfolk who drift in and out of the picture, nor do they live in marble mansions or congregate in private clubs or white tablecloth restaurants that serve brandy alexanders and French cuisine. To the contrary, these adult males are rough-hewn frontiersmen who slurp their beverages, eat with their fingers, and engage in fisticuffs at the drop of an implied insult.

In short, the film is as refreshing as a breeze that filters through pine needles to cool the withering heat of a summer's day. It is also like no other musical that came before it, although its influence on later song-and-dance shows was negligible. Except for *Li'l Abner* (1959), which was based on composer dePaul's only stage musical, which was based on Al Capp's popular cartoon strip, the moguls made no further safaris to the nation's Dogpatches for inspiration. Perhaps not too surprisingly, both films provided employment for the same lyricist, composer, and choreographer.

Like *The Sound of Music*, *Seven Brides for Seven Brothers* was filmed mostly alfresco, permitting audiences to view the green hills and flower-dotted landscapes in all their pristine loveliness. Although some of the action takes place in shops and log cabins, the picture was

Newly married Howard Keel and Jane Powell celebrate their wedding day by dueting "Wonderful, Wonderful Day" in director Stanley Donen's *Seven Brides for Seven Brothers.*

the first Oscar-nominated musical to partially desert the back lot for the great outdoors. Stephen Vincent Benét, whose original story provided the framework for the screenplay, had earlier supplied Hollywood with the plot for *All*

That Money Can Buy. A reworking of his short story "The Devil and Daniel Webster," the picture is a virtual compendium of superlatives, ranging from the extraordinary acting (by Edward Arnold as Webster, and Walter Huston as the Devil) to the background music supplied by Bernard Herrmann, reputed to have regarded his Hollywood work as "extremely distasteful." He apparently made few friends among his associates, many of them describing him as gruff and difficult. But his music for the classic RKO Radio film won the 1941 Academy Award for scoring of a dramatic picture in a field of 20 competitors, one of them Herrmann's own nominated score for *Citizen Kane*.

Stanley Donen's name has been most prominently linked to that of Gene Kelly, whom he met in 1940 while both were dancing in the chorus of *Pal Joey*. The two worked together on *On the Town*, *Singin' in the Rain*, and *It's Always Fair Weather*. *Royal Wedding* and *Seven Brides*, however, proved that Donen was entirely capable of piloting a musical on his own and investing it with quality, style, and wit. Among his post–*Seven Brides* musicals was the trio of Broadway-based properties, *Funny Face*, *The Pajama Game*, and *Damn Yankees*, each a memorable hit. Equally gifted at mystery yarns and romantic comedy, he also directed Audrey Hepburn, the co-star of *Funny Face*, in *Two for the Road* (1967), and four with Cary Grant, one very good (*Charade*, also with Miss Hepburn, 1963) and three so-so's, *Kiss Them for Me* (1957), *Indiscreet* (1978), and *The Grass Is Greener* (1960). Donen later directed Liza Minnelli in *Lucky Lady* (1975) and George C. Scott in *Movie Movie* (1978), a harmless and hilarious satire on 1930s gangster and musical films that spoofs *Kid Galahad* and *42nd Street*.

The *Seven Brides* cast is excellent and the songs superb, even if not exactly electrifying. The possessor of a strong baritone voice, Keel was capable of crooning a soft and low ballad whenever called on to do so. By 1954 the commanding, self-assured actor was already a veteran of musical films, having sung Berlin songs in *Annie Get Your Gun* (1950); Kern songs in the 1951 *Show Boat* and *Lovely to Look At*, the 1952 remake of *Roberta*; Porter songs in *Kiss Me Kate* (1953); and Friml songs in MGM's 1954 repeat of *Rose-Marie*.

His *Seven Brides* co-star, Jane Powell, was likewise an accomplished musical comedy performer. In her 1944 screen debut at age 15 in *Song of the Open Road*, she helped to cheer up the work-a-day world set by assuring that even though today is Monday, the only thing blue

is the sky. As gifted at singing as the very young Deanna Durbin, but without the latter's repertoire of classical airs, she proceeded to captivate audiences with her lovely soprano voice into the late 1950s. Bearing her name as co-lead were such MGM musicals as *Three Daring Daughters*, *A Date with Judy* (both 1948), *Two Weeks with Love* (1950), *Rich, Young and Pretty* (1951), and the 1955 reprise of *Hit the Deck*. For her cameo in *Deep in My Heart*, she duetted Romberg's "Will You Remember?" with Vic Damone, whose voice was simply not up to the challenge of singing operetta-style. In *Royal Wedding* (1951) she added dancing to her résumé as Fred Astaire's much younger sister and partner in several dance duets in addition to singing Alan Jay Lerner and Burton Lane's beautiful Oscar nominee, "Too Late Now," to Peter Lawford.

None of the other cast members, with the exception of Russ Tamblyn, achieved stardom, good as each of them is. By the end of 1954, musical pictures were so few that singing and dancing youngsters were denied a sufficient number of outlets to exhibit their talents. Like Miss Powell, Tamblyn appeared in his first movie, the non-musical *The Boy with the Green Hair* (1948), as an early teenager. For the next six years he was cast in mostly insignificant parts in a half-dozen dramas and comedies. *Seven Brides* was his entree into musical pictures, which would include the fantasy *Tom Thumb* (1958) and reach its peak with *West Side Story*. A nimble dancer with a flair for acrobatics, Tamblyn in 1957 became one of the very few musical comedy personalities to be nominated for the Oscar as best supporting actor, but it was for his performance as Norman Page in *Peyton Place*, a drama.

MGM took no chances when it commissioned Johnny Mercer to write the *Seven Brides* lyrics. One of the most respected of all Hollywood wordsmiths, he had already been nominated for nine Academy Awards, including three winners, and had appended his name to a host of other movie and stage song hits. If the studio heads were concerned about handing the music assignment to Gene dePaul, their decision turned out to be a good one. Despite his skimpy credentials, which consisted primarily of song contributions to 14 motion pictures, including such 1940s film novelties as "Pig Foot

Pete," "Mister Five by Five," "Cow-Cow Boogie," and "Milkman, Keep Those Bottles Quiet," he had a sentimental side that produced such tender ballads as "Star Eyes," one of the last screen songs sung by Dick Powell (in *In the Navy*, 1941), the ultra-lovely "I'll Remember April," and "Irresistible You," all quite popular at the time. Each of his eight tunes for *Seven Brides* is most professionally crafted and, whether jivey or lyrical, fits the character who sings it. Mercer's lyrics carry the appropriateness still further. Far from the Valentine doggerel that plagued many film songs of the early 1950s, and made them susceptible of being randomly dropped in or dropped out of the script, Mercer's creative lyrics elaborate on the dialogue that precedes every song to an astonishingly high degree, particularly for a film musical.

Goin' to Town. Howard Keel (Adam Pontabee) is in town to shop at Fred Bixby's General Store, but not only for victuals to appease his own and his six brothers' voracious appetites. He is also there to get himself hitched to the "gal for me," who must be both beautiful and a rare jewel of a workhorse willing to cater to the family's multitudinous needs. His bride will be expected to coddle and feed them like a mother, discipline them like a father, and clean the house, farm the land, fetch the well water, and, in her spare time, be their laundress, tailor, nurse, adviser, schoolmarm, and referee. The marriage would in fact be one of convenience—Keel's—and his pride compels him into believing that his proposal will be snapped up, even though he and his brothers are known far and wide as the "seven scroungey backwoodsmen," and there are 10 men for every woman in the community.

As he explains in the opening song, "Bless Yore Beautiful Hide," which he sings while sauntering along the main street to inspect likely candidates among the passersby, so important to him is a healthy helpmate that he will go as far as swapping a mule for her, even paying her way through cooking school, if necessary. His roving eyes, however, fail to detect a suitable partner until they catch sight of Jane Powell (Milly), busily chopping wood with the verve and stamina of a miniature lumberjack.

Could it be that she's the one for him, he wonders. Pretty she is and obviously a hard worker, thus definitely worth closer inspection. To check further into her wifely qualifications, he seats himself at a family-style table in the town restaurant, beaming upon learning that the young lady also cooks and dishes out as sublime a beef stew as he has ever tasted. Minutes later he approaches her at the back of the restaurant, where he is pleased to observe her milking a cow without raising a bead of perspiration.

In what is most likely the screen's most whirlwind courtship, he proposes marriage, which Jane accepts after barely a moment's hesitation. She admits that what she most desires is to cook and care for a man of her own, not the scores of male diners required by her waitress job. Besides, she has no reason to disbelieve Keel's picturesque description of his ranch as homey and bountiful. Although his proposal was indeed abrupt, she agrees that such is the price one pays for living in a land regulated by a strict agricultural timetable that permits little in the way of social niceties between planting and harvesting. To prove his love, Keel shaves off his Lincolnesque beard, revealing a youthful, handsome countenance below a shock of shaggy light brown hair.

Later that day they are married by the Rev. Elcott (Ian Wolfe), who suspends his reluctance to do so after Jane convinces him that Keel is just the fellow she has been looking for lo, these many years. Without any mention of a honeymoon, or of her workload, for that matter, the couple hits the 12-mile trail to Keel's mountain home on a rattling buckboard. On the way, during a pause while he waters the horse, Jane sings of her happiness in the bridal waltz "Wonderful, Wonderful Day," the film's prettiest song. Sung as she runs over a plush Currier and Ives open field festooned with flowers grouped into colorful wedding bouquets, the song serves as lyrical testament to her happiness at becoming his wife and expectation of sharing a grand and glorious future together. But, like Snow White when she first enters the forest home of the seven dwarfs, Jane is due to encounter a few surprises that will test her stamina.

The first is being introduced to Keel's

hulking brothers, all but Russ Tamblyn (Gideon) towering over her like mighty oak trees, and all but Tommy Rall (Frank) bearing impressive Biblical-sounding first names. The second is viewing the unkempt interior of the farmhouse, which appears never to have been disturbed by broom, dustrag, or mop. Her third shocker—the discovery that rather than cooking and caring for one man, she is expected to tend to the needs of six more—is alleviated somewhat by the sincerity of the brothers' welcome.

Instantly warming up to her physical assets and slave potential, they appreciate all the more Keel's good luck in procuring her so fast. Apart from adding much-needed beauty to the household, she seems most willing and able to assert the necessary authority to instill a sense of order and decorum to its accustomed chaos. Not every woman would have the temerity to leave what they assume was a great job in town for a totally unrewarding life in the desolate suburbs. She is indeed something special.

Jane adapts quickly to her new routine. The boys help her gather firewood, and then group themselves at the table while awaiting the results of any housewife's severest test: the tastiness of her first meal. From the lip-smacking aroma wafting from pots to nostrils, it promises to be sheer manna, and the men attack their plates with a ferocity that appalls their ladylike cook, who immediately takes them to task. They eat like hogs, she scolds, commanding each to sit quietly and await his turn at plucking morsels from the food tray, and to precede the attack by saying grace.

The young homemaker is even more disenchanted, however, at the way the sedentary boys while away their evening hours. Apparently, their zest for life and rowdiness sink with the setting sun, leaving them trapped in idleness with nothing to do but wander purposelessly from room to room or lean against a wall in perpetual boredom. This evening, however, they finally have something to pique their imagination. In an amusing scene, they keep urging Keel to join Jane in the upstairs bedroom, to which she has retreated in disgust, and do what comes naturally. He finally manages to evade their ubiquitous presence, but is perplexed when his newly betrothed refuses to bed down with him. What he really wants, she complains, is a "handy girl," not a wife, and therefore she is under no obligation to consummate the marriage. He protests that he does want a wife, but one who will gladly work alongside him to transform his eyesore of a hut into a home.

His plea fails to placate Jane, and so Keel decides to sleep in a tree just outside the bedroom window. Jane then provides insight into what she views as the ideal, storybook marriage in the ear-pleasing "When You're in Love." Realizing at the conclusion that perhaps her major chore is to do all she can to make the marriage work, she invites Keel to crawl into bed with her, where the head of the house is convinced he belongs on his wedding night or otherwise lose face with his brothers. Reminiscent of the uproarious John Wayne–Maureen O'Hara wedding night, bed-smashing episode in John Ford's *The Quiet Man* (1952), the couple's bed also breaks under their combined weight. This time the noise is greeted not with the look of amazement of a lone witness, Barry Fitzgerald, but with the satisfied nods and smiles of Keel's six attentive brothers grouped together downstairs.

Etiquette Lessons. Now officially installed as the woman of the house, Jane the next morning adopts a take-charge stance, demanding that her brothers-in-law shave and hand over their underwear for washing. Their initial rebelliousness at being bossed about by a woman is quickly superseded by willingness to conform when Jane offers to introduce them to all the unattached ladies in town. Although they regard her plan as a gesture of friendliness, in reality her goal is to get the whole pile of them married and out of the house. From her lessons in etiquette, they learn the importance of removing their hat and "saying something nice" when in the presence of a woman, and above all never to "grab her like she was a flapjack." Other rudiments of how best to "spark a lady" are delivered by Jane in the congenial yet eminently practicable "Goin' Co'tin'," a sprightly advice-to-the-lovelorn song.

Certain that following her rules will give them a competitive edge over their prospective rivals, the boys prepare to attend the forth-coming barn-raising and picnic extravaganza. They already know how to barn dance, and that skill, coupled with grooming themselves into display window mannequins, persuades them that they will carry home their own brides once the festivities are over.

The barn-raising dance is easily the most energetic, muscular, and yet perfectly synchro-nized on film. Involving Keel's brothers as well as dozens of other young men and a score of girls, who gyrate into spectacular jumps, leaps, deep-knee bends, and mid-air somersaults, the dancing emerges as a brilliant combination of virility and unexpected gracefulness. The choreography remains a monument to the tal-ent of Michael Kidd, whose pre–Hollywood career on Broadway had earned him five Tony Awards. Even his excellent dance routines for the movie versions of *The Band Wagon*, *Guys and Dolls* (1955), and *Hello, Dolly!* pale in com-parison with this part-tap, part-ballet *Seven Brides* athletic exercise. Like choreographer Bob Fosse an excellent dancer in his own right, Kidd in 1955 would team up with Gene Kelly and Dan Dailey as one of the three dancing former Army buddies in *It's Always Fair Weather*.

The song accompanying the dance is "Bless Yore Beautiful Hide" sung this time as a question rather than a declaration, indicat-ing each brother's indecision over which charmer he should take with him to the preacher. Unfortunately, the barn raising erupts into a free for all when the other young males sabotage the brothers' attempt to win the contest by lifting and nailing all four walls into place in one fell swoop. Not only are the wooden walls smashed to pieces; so is the brothers' reputation. Far from being the po-lite dandies they pretend to be, they show by their aggressive response that they are still the social misfits they always were.

Their dancing partners are wounded to the heart by the boys' obvious fondness for brawling, as is Jane. But the young men, es-pecially Tamblyn, who has a crush on Alice (Nancy Kilgas), the daughter of Preacher Wolfe, long to settle down with the maidens of their choice, but are unable to gauge the depth of their feelings. When Tamblyn asks Keel whether his attraction toward Alice is actually love, the big brother replies with a

reprise of "When You're in Love," using a new lyric to explain how to recognize true love, and why once it is found it should never be suppressed. Now Tamblyn shifts his chief worry to the fear that his and his brothers' belligerency very well may have turned the girls' parents against them, a logical progno-sis that proves to be accurate. The broken-hearted sextet are forced to leave for home without so much as a fiancée, much less a wife.

Back in their humble abode, the brothers bewail their lack of female companionship in "Lonesome Polecat," a most humorous song of despair highlighted by Mercer's clever internal rhyming and mock mournfulness. Their deso-lation is compounded by the impending arrival of winter, which will close off further trips to town, effectively putting the self-described "lovesick bull calves" in cold storage till spring.

As the days drag on, Keel devises a scheme to revive their spirits. Jane's dowry consisted of two items, the Bible and Plutarch's "History," or *Lives of the Noble Grecians and Romans*. The latter book has had a profound effect on Keel, especially the tale of the Sabine Women. Ac-cording to the ancient historian, Keel tells his brothers, the Roman soldiers who had con-quered the Sabines became so enamored of the women folk that they went into town one night and carried them off. Why, Keel suggests, don't the brothers do as the Romans did, thereby ex-hibiting their manhood and bringing happi-ness to their girlfriends.

The song outlining his strategy is "Sobbin' Women," a delectable battle anthem that im-presses his listeners with its call to action while making the most of his mispronunciation of the word Sabine. In Keel's usage, "Sobbin'" im-plies that the girls are equally desolate as the boys, spending their time shedding tears and pining for their return. With Keel gleefully in the lead, the brothers jump into the buckboard for their last pre-winter excursion into town.

Attacking the Citadel. Risking parental furor because of their nocturnal spree, the six emotionally charged brothers depart on indi-vidual surreptitious forays from house to house to capture their prey. Tamblyn gets his Alice by invading her bedroom and carrying her away. Another frightened lass is snatched up as she leaves a party, another from her own front porch, and a fourth whisked away by a cover over the head, a grab at the waist, and a sling over the shoulder before being deposited alongside the other conquered wives-to-be at the back of the buckboard. The merry girlnapers then take off with their sullen cargo, with a wagon full of outraged fathers and other townspeople in hot pursuit. Flush with victory, none of the brothers notices that not a single girl is the least appreciative of her captor's clumsy display of passion.

High on a mountain ridge, one of the girls lets loose with a piercing scream that causes an avalanche. Keel escapes it by only a few feet, but the avengers are stopped in their tracks by the cascading snow that buries the path in a mound of white. Unable to continue, the would-be rescuers retreat back to town, lamenting the sad fact that they will not be able to venture up to Keel's ranch before the spring meltdown. Even more troubling is their sudden realization that their daughters are facing a fate worse than death: six unmarried pairs of boys and girls in the same house, and not a preacher in sight!

Irritated by the girls' lack of enthusiasm for their lovers' daring escapade, Keel orders them to set up housekeeping in the barn, along "with the rest of the livestock," in his indelicate phraseology. Jane also pounces angrily on the men, Keel in particular, for pulling a stunt she describes as revolting. To get away from her and the sobbin' women's nagging, Keel departs the house to hibernate in his trapping cabin even farther up the mountain. While he is there, relations between Jane and his brothers begin to thaw when Tamblyn apologizes for the kidnaping and recommends that the victims be returned to their homes once the weather permits, and they all begin to treat her with the kindness of the truly concerned after learning that she is expecting a baby.

The warm thoughts generated by the expectation of seeing the new arrival early in the spring provide the girls with enough incentive to withstand the lingering winter, and they soon entertain visions of starting families of their own in their song-and-dance rendition of the lilting "June Bride," another likable ballad that refers to the forthcoming April showers, May flowers, and June weddings. In due course,

the flowers do come along, as does Jane's baby girl, Hannah, inspiring the kidnapees to regale the glories of the new season with "Spring, Spring, Spring." Like Jane's earlier wedding day song, it is sung while the girls cavort on a grassy knoll richly decorated with a rainbow of Technicolored hues.

When Tamblyn visits Keel in his cabin to tell him of the birth of Hannah, he is astounded to find that the news only deepens his big brother's anger, which has barely subsided over the intervening months. Disappointed that the baby is a girl, Keel refuses to go back home, even knocking Tamblyn unconscious when he stubbornly tries to force the new father into making the trip. With the mountain pass again open, the militant fathers once more are speeding along the road to Keel's ranch, their eyes flaring with anger and their hands clutching rifles.

Keel is there, but "only for a short time" to visit his wife and child. The sight of little Hannah miraculously displaces his former contempt for her with an intuitive desire to protect the infant from danger. He repents his part in the kidnaping, admitting that he now understands the agony that the girls' fathers must have suffered during the long months of separation from their own children. He welcomes Hannah into the family, embraces Jane, and prepares to transport the young women back to their homes. When his brothers revolt, Keel threatens to fight them all, individually or together, if they persist in opposing him. The frightened girls run away, but return as the wagon load of fathers pulls onto the property.

Expecting to be met with open arms by their daughters, the men are disappointed to find that not a single one wishes to return to town. Instead, they all want to remain in the mountains with the brother of her choice. The fathers are adamant, however, demanding that their offspring board the wagon while they shoot the brothers like the dogs they assert they are. Suddenly, a cry from baby Hannah rents the air, silencing men, brothers, and girls. Whose baby is that, one father asks, fearing the worst while glancing from one girl to the other. "Mine!" they all reply in unison.

Later that afternoon, with the fathers' shotguns aimed at the back of each unwed Pontabee brother, the six young men and their girlfriends are married by the Reverend Wolfe. Happiness abounds—Keel will remain with Jane, this time forever, his brothers have their brides, and the fathers have been spared from being "scandalized" by their own kin. All in all, a delightful film, as tuneful, imaginative, and witty as a musical can be.

The King and I (1956)

A 20th Century–Fox picture. DIRECTOR: Walter Lang; ASSISTANT: Eli Dunn. PRODUCER: Charles Brackett. SCREENWRITER: Ernest Lehman, based on the novel *Anna and the King of Siam*, by Margaret Landon. CINEMATOGRAPHER: Leon Shamroy; SPECIAL EFFECTS: Ray Kellogg. FILM EDITOR: Robert Simpson. CHOREOGRAPHER: Jerome Robbins. ART DIRECTORS: Lyle Wheeler and John DeCuir. SET DECORATORS: Walter M. Scott and Paul S. Fox. SOUND: Carl Faulkner, E. Clayton Ward, and Warren Delaplain. COSTUMES: Irene Sharaff. MAKEUP: Ben Nye. ORCHESTRATORS: Edward B. Powell, Gus Levene, Bernard Meyers, and Robert Russell Bennett. BALLET ARRANGEMENTS: Trude Rittman. MUSIC SUPERVISOR AND CONDUCTOR: Alfred Newman; ASSOCIATE: Ken Darby. SONGS: Lyrics by Oscar Hammerstein II, music by Richard Rodgers. RUNNING TIME: 2 hours and 13 minutes. *Principal Players*: Deborah Kerr (Anna [Leonowens]). Yul Brynner (King [Mongkut]). Rita Moreno (Tuptim). Martin Benson (Kralahome). Terry Saunders (Lady Thiang). Rex Thompson (Louis [Leonowens]). Carlos Rivas (Lun Tha). Patrick Adiarte (Crown Prince Chulalongkom). Alan Mobray (Sir John Haig). Geoffrey Toone (Edward Ramsay). *Major Academy Awards*: Best Actor (*Yul Brynner*); Art Direction; Costumes; Scoring; Sound. *Nominations*: Best Picture; Director; Actress (*Deborah Kerr*); Cinematography.

He amassed such an extensive catalogue of exceptionally beautiful melodies that Richard Rodgers always gave the impression, authenticated over his five-decade-long career, of being incapable of composing a poor song. Whether collaborating with Lorenz Hart (from 1918 to 1943) or Oscar Hammerstein II (1943–1959), he flooded Broadway with songs that have passed the severest test of time with flying colors. Especially in collaboration with Hammerstein, he set the standard for precisely interpreting character personality and motivation in song.

A master of the waltz, he successfully carried on the sweeping melodic style of operetta's Big Three—Herbert, Friml, and Romberg. But he was equally facile in deviating from the norm when the libretto called for love songs cast in a satiric mode ("Thou Swell," "The Lady Is a Tramp," "Zip") or for *Your Hit Parade*–caliber tunes ("Poor Johnny One Note," "This Can't Be Love," "I Wish I Were in Love Again"). "Bewitched" tells the tale of an aging lady overjoyed that her steamy sexuality has not abandoned her; the even wittier "To Keep My Love Alive," the last Rodgers show tune to carry a Hart lyric, centers on a much-married lady who kills her husbands when she tires of them.

But it was at the sweetly sentimental but saccharine-free love song that Rodgers excelled to a degree unmatched by any other American songwriter. "There's a Small Hotel" is a classic ballad, and not only among honeymooners, and so are "My Romance" and "Little Girl Blue" (both from the same 1935 show, *Jumbo*); "My Funny Valentine" (referring to a young man named Valentine, not to February 14); "It Never Entered My Mind" (the beautiful Shirley Ross–introduced song that RKO unforgivably dropped from its remake of *Higher and Higher*); and "I Could Write a Book," People Will Say We're in Love," "If I Loved You," "You'll Never Walk Alone," "Some Enchanted Evening," "This Nearly Was Mine," and enough others to fill several pages of this book.

A few composers, like Jerome Kern, Romberg, and Frederick Loewe, have now and then ascended to Rodgers's lyrical heights, but none displayed such consistent creativity over as long a period of time. Still another imposing testament to Rodgers's genius was his maintaining unparalleled composition artistry over his long partnership with lyricists as vastly different in their approach to writing love lyrics as the down-to-earth realist Hart, who ranks with Cole Porter as Broadway's wittiest lyricist, and the arch romanticist Hammerstein, for whom the kindlier side of nature was a boundless source of simile and metaphor. Apparently unfazed by songwriting technicalities, Rodgers wrote his melodies before Hart gave them lyrics; with Hammerstein, the words came first.

Steeped as he was in the tradition of the musical theater, Rodgers, like Gershwin, was often motivated by an innovative streak that, for example, led him in 1936 to indite the dramatic ballet "Slaughter on Tenth Avenue" as part of his score for *On Your Toes*, a satire involving a European ballet company patterned

Deborah Kerr attempts to teach Siamese King Mongkut (Yul Brynner) the polka with Rodgers and Hammerstein's "Shall We Dance" in *The King and I*.

after the Ballet Russe de Monte Carlo, one of the world's foremost dancing companies. (The piece was danced by Tamara Geva, Ray Bolger, and George Church in the stage show, and 12 years later by Gene Kelly and Vera-Ellen in MGM's *Words and Music*.) Apparently unoffended by the show's barbs, the Ballet Russe commissioned Rodgers to write the music for *Ghost Town*, the troupe's first work with an American theme created by an American choreographer (Marc Platt) and an American composer.

Rodgers himself conducted the favorable opening-night performance on November 12, 1939, at the Metropolitan Opera House. Walter Terry, music critic of the New York Herald-Tribune termed it a "grand success," noting that the composer was at his "melodic and rhythmic best." The company presented *Ghost Town* for five performances during its 1939 season in New York, included it in the repertory for its subsequent tour (Rodgers conducted it again in Chicago), and then brought it back to New York in the spring of 1940. Curiously, the score thereafter languished in obscurity, and not a note was heard from then until 1978, when DRG Records, Inc., recorded it along with Harold Arlen's *Civil War Ballet* and Cole Porter's *Within the Quota*, two other orchestral pieces, on a single long-playing disk. Set in the Sierras, the Rodgers work centers on the downfall of a once-thriving mining community turned into a ghost town when the mountains ran out of iron ore.

Victory at Sea, the monumental Emmy and Peabody Award-winning television documentary on American and Allied naval operations during World War II, began its television life on October 26, 1952, while *The King and I* was still running on Broadway, and continued in half-hour installments for the next 25 consecutive Sundays. Highlighting the telecast was Rodgers' superlative 13-hour background musical score, which was orchestrated and recorded by Robert Russell Bennett, one of the theater's great musical arrangers, and the NBC Orchestra. From it emerged two popular songs, "The Guadalcanal March" and what became known as "No Other Love" after Hammerstein added a lyric and inserted it into *Me and Juliet*, which opened in New York on May 28, 1953.

Rodgers's collaboration with Hart supplied the songs for 29 stage shows (he wrote eight more with Hammerstein). *Spring Is Here*, *Evergreen*, *The Boys from Syracuse* (based on Shakespeare's *A Comedy of Errors*), *Babes in Arms*, and *Too Many Girls*, were subsequently made into movie musicals. Although the twosome's Hollywood assignments were unfortunately rare, no better movie musical exists than *Love Me Tonight*, which debuted their "Lover," "Isn't It Romantic," "Mimi," and the rousing title tune. Introduced by Al Jolson in *Hallelujah, I'm a Bum* (1933) was their ever-lovely "You Are Too Beautiful," while Bing Crosby popularized "It's Easy to Remember," "Soon," and "Down by the River" two years later in *Mississippi*.

Like Gershwin, Rodgers copyrighted his first song as a teenager. He was 14 when he wrote the words and music of "Campfire Days" in 1914; Gershwin was the same age when he wrote "Since I Found You," with words by Leonard Praskins, in early 1913. Rodgers first met Hart in 1918, when they were 16 and 23, respectively, and later that year their first collaboration, "Any Old Place with You," was introduced by singer Eve Lynn and actor Alan Hale in the Broadway show *A Lonely Romeo*. The next year Rodgers matriculated at Columbia University, where in 1920 he became the first freshman to write the music for one of the school's annual varsity shows, *Fly with Me*, with lyrics by alumnus Hart. Although classified as amateur productions, the shows were presented at the Hotel Astor in Times Square, giving the participants the feeling that they were operating not at the collegiate level but in the big leagues.

The songs were so liked by vaudevillian and producer Lew Fields that he transferred all of them, plus eight new ones, including Hart's devilishly clever "Love's Intense in Tents," into *The Poor Little Ritz Girl*. The show tallied a respectable run of 119 performances, no doubt helped by the eight additional tunes contributed by the far better-known Sigmund Romberg. Rodgers and Hart's second varsity show, *You'll Never Know*, appeared in 1921, when Rodgers left Columbia to study at the Institute of Musical Art, now the Juilliard School of Music.

After five lean years, the partners finally hit pay dirt with "Sentimental Me and Romantic You" and especially "Manhattan," still a favorite with die-hard New Yorkers. Written for the 1925 edition of The Garrick Gaieties, the first of the intimate fund-raising revues staged on behalf of the Theater Guild, "Manhattan" was introduced by Sterling Holloway, who by the mid–30s had become familiar to moviegoers for his vacant facial expression and high-pitched voice in frequent bit parts as a somewhat dim-witted juvenile. The 1926 edition of the same serial musical introduced Rodgers and Hart's "Mountain Greenery."

Rodgers joined Hammerstein in *Oklahoma!*, only weeks before Hart, too ill to participate in that Pulitzer Prize–winning theatrical landmark, died at 48 on November 22, 1943. The new team, the most prolific and prestigious in Broadway history, rose to even higher acclaim with *Carousel* (1945), which also won the Pulitzer, and *South Pacific* (1949), with *The King and I, Flower Drum Song,* and *The Sound of Music* serving as their crowning achievements in the 1950s. In a way, their partnership was a reunion of two one-time Columbia students. Hammerstein, a fraternity brother of Rodgers's, had himself participated in a Columbia varsity show, and was on the school's committee of judges that had approved the *Fly with Me* libretto and songs.

Another highly acclaimed Broadwayite, lyricist-librettist Hammerstein had kept himself brilliantly occupied from 1920 to 1943 by collaborating with many other major composers of the era: Jerome Kern (*Sunny, Show Boat, Sweet Adeline, Music in the Air, Very Warm for May*); Sigmund Romberg (*The Desert Song, The New Moon*); Rudolf Friml (*Rose-Marie*); George Gershwin (*The Song of the Flame*); Vincent Youmans (*Wildflower, The Rainbow*), appending his name to dozens of stage-based hit songs from "Who?" and "Ol' Man River" to "One Alone" and "All the Things You Are."

Part poet and part commercial lyricist, Hammerstein was nominated five times for the Oscar for best song—an honor bestowed only once on Rodgers and not at all on Hart—and he toted the statuette home with him for "The Last Time I Saw Paris" (written with Kern in 1941) and "It Might as Well Be Spring" (with Rodgers in 1945). Despite the writing team's awesome credentials, Hollywood tapped Rodgers and Hammerstein for only a few songs, an irredeemable loss for the movie musical. One of them, "Boys and Girls Like You and Me," had earlier been cut from *Oklahoma!*, and was dropped as well from MGM's *Meet Me in St. Louis* in 1944. The other, "There's Music in You," showed up in 1953 in *Main Street to Broadway*, noted not for its plot or music, but for cameos of such celebrities as Ethel and Lionel Barrymore, Shirley Booth, Rex Harrison, Helen Hayes, Tallulah Bankhead, and Mary Martin.

However infrequently the moguls called on Rodger and Hammerstein for original scores, they were anything but shy about adapting many of their fail-safe stage pieces to celluloid. The first two Technicolor pickups, *Oklahoma!* (1955) and *Carousel* (1956), co-starred Gordon MacRae and Shirley Jones. Like Howard Keel, MacRae was a prototype of barrel-chested masculinity with a rich baritone to match. He was an ideal choice for the male lead in both musicals, having performed many such theatrical parts while hosting network radio's *The Railroad Hour* in the late forties.

In the filmed *The King and I*, Deborah Kerr substituted for Gertrude Lawrence, who had died of cancer midway through the Broadway run on September 7, 1952, as the teacher. Yul Brynner repeated his stage role as the King of Siam, as Thailand was known in English-speaking nations until 1949, when Thailand was recognized everywhere as the official name. Based on real people in real-life situations, both the stage and the film versions took a number of liberties that added significantly to the original story's emotional impact. Even after fifty years the film has yet to be shown in Thailand, which does not take kindly to criticism of its rulers. Movie audiences had been introduced in 1946 to the proper English governess who in 1862 traveled to Bangkok to teach the king's 67 children in *Anna and the King of Siam*. That black-and-white film was based on Margaret Landon's half-fact, half-fantasy 1943 novel of the same name, a bestseller that relied heavily on Anna Leonowens's own two books of memoirs, *The English Governess at the Siamese Court* (1870) and *The Romance of the Harem* (1873). The movie was not among the best films of the year, nor were Irene Dunne and Rex Harrison, excellent as they usually were, particularly winning in the leading roles. The picture, however, won an Academy Award for cinematographer Arthur Miller and nominations for Talbot Jennings and Sally Benson for the screenplay, Bernard Herrmann for scoring, and Gale Sondergaard for best supporting actress. Harrison was sought to play the king again in the musical stage version, but declined in order to appear in T.S. Eliot's *The Cocktail Hour*. Incidentally, the king, at the opening of the musical version, has already sired 106 children; at the end he has added five more.

Sited in an enchanted land where very few 1950s Americans had set foot, the musical demanded the infusion of spectacle—in costumes, in sets, in production dancing—to make it effective theater. The producers were alert to that requirement and fulfilled it to perfection. Attesting to the musical's enduring popularity was its visually and audibly arresting return to Broadway on March 15, 1996, almost exactly 40 years after the release of the motion picture. It opened to almost unanimous rave reviews, except for *The New York Times*' critic, Vincent Canby, who found little to commend, and won four Tony Awards, including best revival of a musical.

The drama tells the story of a Welsh lady, born Ann Edwards, who upon the death of her British Army clerk husband, Thomas Leonowens, altered her name and became a schoolteacher in Singapore's British community. Later she was hired by the egomaniacal King Mongkut, or Rama IV, a realist who sensed that he had to modernize his kingdom lest it fall victim to colonialism or disintegrate on its own. Although the musical suggests that Anna served the king for only a few months, she actually spent about five years in Siam.

Her kindly references to her husband, Tom, who died about a year before she left for the kingdom, as a captain in the British Army were false. He was never appointed to that high a rank, and her life with him was one of deprivation and insecurity caused by his frequent spates of unemployment. Mongkut reigned for 17 years, dying in 1868. His son and successor, Chulalongkom, or Rama V, continued his father's Westernization policies throughout his reign, which ended with his death in 1910. Meanwhile, Anna had settled in America, while her son, Louie, went back to England, later returning on his own to Siam and becoming a solid supporter of the new king, his boyhood friend.

Far better as a work of art was the Rodgers and Hammerstein deluxe color version of the Siam story, obviously because of the music, which assuredly measured up to the high standards the two songmen strove to maintain with each passing show. Five of the songs became perennials—"I Whistle a Happy Tune," "Getting to Know You," "We Kiss in a Shadow," "Shall We Dance?," and, above all, the ultra-dramatic "Hello, Young Lovers," which was outfitted with one of the composer's all-time best melodies, written as a waltz but almost never performed as one. Excluded from the film were "Western People Funny," "My Lord and Master," "Shall I Tell You What I Think of You?," and the irresistible "I Have Dreamed." *The King and I* won the best picture Oscar, and Brynner became the third actor in a musical to win the best actor award. Miss Kerr lost out on the top female acting accolade to Ingrid Bergman's *Anastasia*.

In some ways *The King and I* qualifies as an operetta. The songs are as lilting, and at times almost as difficult to sing, as any written by Herbert. It is set in the past, as well as in an exotic foreign land assumed to be neck deep in quaint Oriental customs, revolves around a monarch and his courtiers, and contains its share of luckless lovers. But the deaths of both the king and another male lover violated the operetta dictum that the libretto be basically frothy and all affairs ended happily. Dorothy Donnelly and Romberg's *The Student Prince* also concludes on a downbeat note, but neither the young prince nor the peasant girl he is duty-bound to renounce in favor of a royal marriage dies, despite the breaking of their hearts.

Besides being among the first of the collaborators' rather shallow probes into distinctly foreign cultures virtually unknown to most Americans, *The King and I* bears Hammerstein's inimitable stamp of making absolutely sure that his lyrics are inseparable from the story. Similarly, Rodgers wove his music smoothly into the plot in much the same way that composers integrate their background scores into films. The conductor of a musical play gives the orchestra a music cue every time he raises his baton and leads the orchestra into playing a show theme. From *Oklahoma!* on, the typical Rodgers stage score called for many such cues. *The King and I*, for example, with only 16 musical numbers, contained 46 cues. Even when no singing was taking place on stage, the orchestra provided a continuous murmur of music, sometimes under the dialogue, other times used to illustrate a scene in pantomime. The ability of this technique to add to the plausibility of the action and, above all, to ease the transition from speech to song is invaluable.

The King and I, which opened on March 29, 1951, at the St. James Theatre, represented another landmark but superficial Hammerstein probe into the harmful effects of prejudice and racial discord—indeed, the struggle between freedom and tyranny—which he had actually begun as far back as 1927 with the miscegenation theme in *Show Boat*. He continued his crusade in *Carousel* by dealing with the enmity and bitterness caused by class conflicts involving selfish Maine employers and exploited workers, which the movie version elected to mute to a whisper. In *The King and I* the democratic schoolteacher who wants to change certain Siamese customs stands on one side of the cultural abyss; on the other are leagued the king, courtiers, and many commoners who want to keep them.

Unlike many directors of musicals who only rarely had been exposed to the genre in their apprentice days in Hollywood, Oscar nominee Walter Lang had earned a reputation as a most successful purveyor of Fox's musical comedies long before *The King and I* even appeared on the stage. He was particularly proficient in displaying Betty Grable to best advantage in such forties films as *Tin Pan Alley, Moon Over Miami, Song of the Islands, Coney Island, Mother Wore Tights*, and *When My Baby Smiles at Me* (a remake of *Coney Island*). Later vehicles for other stars included the 1945 *State Fair, Call Me Madam* (1953), *There's No Business Like Show Business* (1954), and *With a Song in My Heart* (1952), with Susan Hayward in the role of singer Jane Frohman.

Exemplary is the best word to describe the performances of the two leading players in *The King and I*. Always ladylike, but never hesitant to protest any infringement on what she regards as basic moral principles, Miss Kerr's Anna is far more typical of the heroines for which she became respected— like Sister Angela in *Heaven Knows, Mr. Allison* (1957), for example—than as the passionate Karen Holmes in *From Here to Eternity* (1953). Like Irene Dunne, she received six Academy Award nominations for best actress but failed to win a single one. Perhaps, if her singing voice had been her own, she might have fared better at the 1957 awards ceremonies, since her acting in *The King and I* is nothing short of superlative.

Brynner is likewise exceptional as King Mongkut, helped immeasurably by his having appeared in the role some 1,246 times during the musical play's original Broadway run. Actually, the actor turned the role into a multiple-year annuity, as Carol Channing has with Dolly Levi, appearing as the king some 4,625 times in New York and on the road up to a few months before his death in 1985. About half the king's age—the real Mongkut was in his 60s in 1862—he is entirely plausible as the arrogant, domineering autocrat, defying contradiction by standing erect with his hands on his hips when issuing orders and arms folded on his chest when propounding his views. His voice is deep and resonant, and combined with his steely glare, it easily subdues opposition to his latest edict or opinion.

But the strongman king is not cruel. He does have a sense of humor as well as the potential to adapt to reality, two admirable traits that he exhibits in his soul-searching songs, which, like Shakespeare's asides, are addressed to the audience as much as to himself. Unlike all other stars in musicals, Brynner not once sings a ballad even to one of his assembly of wives, as he did, for example, to Mary Martin in his earlier Oriental musical, *Lute Song*, in 1946. He had made only one film, *Port of New York* (1949), before *The King and I*, giving no indication of either his acting or his singing talent in that potboiler crime melodrama.

Miss Kerr's singing voice was supplied by Marni Nixon, who like Debbie Reynolds in *Singin' in the Rain*, dubbed all of the star's vocals while concealed from the sight of the audience. The totally unknown but versatile, and always unbilled, Miss Nixon sang for a host of unmusical female performers, including Natalie Wood (*West Side Story*) and Audrey Hepburn (*My Fair Lady*), who were admitted into pictures solely for their looks, acting ability, audience appeal, and sometimes availability. Finally, in 1965, Miss Nixon was given a brief on-screen character role as Sister Sophia in *The Sound of Music*.

Off to the Orient. A sailing ship is stalled in Bangkok harbor awaiting the incoming tide to carry it to its appointed pier. Aboard is Deborah Kerr (Anna), who is advising her son, Rex

Thompson (Louie), to surmount his fear at their setting up housekeeping in a strange land by doing what she does when faced with a frightening situation over which she has no control. Her response at such times is a typical Hammerstein palliative. "I Whistle a Happy Tune," she tells the lad, much as Maria, the heroine of *The Sound of Music*, concentrates on pleasant mental pictures till thunderstorms and other troubling occurrences pass away. That Deborah will soon need all the cheerfulness she can muster to ease her distress becomes apparent when Martin Benson (Kralahome), the king's faithful and powerful prime minister and right-hand man, boards the ship to escort the pair to the palace.

Curt, bossy, and officious, Benson further displeases Miss Kerr by appearing in a topless costume, hardly a common sight in the 1860s, even at England's Brighton Beach seaside resort. She begins to wonder whether making that long voyage from England to Siam was a wise decision. Already, the two cultures seem so incompatible that she very well may find it impossible to slough off the former and adapt to the latter. But she is a teacher by profession, loves children, and can use the 20 English pounds a month her new job will pay. Besides, she can shield herself and her son from offensive Siamese behavior by taking refuge in the brick house—"outside palace walls"—that she had been guaranteed as part of her employment contract.

Upon arriving at the palace, however, she worries whether a jaunty tune will again be sufficient to perk up her morale. Entering the royal chamber of the king. Yul Brynner (Mongkut), she is devastated at his rudeness toward his subjects, who bow before him, their foreheads touching the floor as if in prayer, while he surveys them from his elevated throne with seeming contempt. Functioning at his usual hubristic high, the ruler seems to revel in adulation, which he expects to receive from everyone who enters his exalted presence. To Deborah, his arrogance indicates that the king is basically insecure. But whether her opinion is right or wrong, she has no intention of buckling under to his every whim. Polite, yes, but subservient—never!

Most shocking of all to Deborah is Bryn-

ner's acceptance of the gift of the Burmese slave girl Tuptim, played by Rita Moreno, from a prince of Burma as a token of that country's desire to smooth relations with Siam, its most implacable enemy. Grudgingly presented by her secret Burmese lover, Lun Tha (Carlos Rivas), the girl is most assuredly unwilling to serve Brynner as another vassal for his monumental passion, but realizes that she is in no position to protest her fate. Though not disposed to speak with Deborah at the moment, the King tolerates her intrusion while he busies himself with matters of state. With accustomed curtness he explains that he expects Deborah to indoctrinate his children, and those of his stylishly saronged wives who "have sense enough for learning," in Western culture as a means of reshaping Siam into a "modern, scientific country" and bringing "truth and justice" to his people. His proudest achievement to date was installing Siam's first printing press, indicating to Deborah that his motive for sending for her is sincere. But, she infers, she is not to interfere with his keeping alive those customs of which he approves.

His imperiousness slowly begins to soften into friendliness when he senses that, unlike his docile wives and children, Deborah is neither impressed with his title nor fearful of his temper. He rather admires her spunk in declaring, contrary to his royal opinion, that English women do not rank "lowly" compared with men. He even refuses to take umbrage at her threat to go back to England that very day unless he lives up to his commitment to provide her with a house, which he promptly dismisses, arguing that the palace is to be her home. After all, he is the boss, and she must toe the mark along with everybody else.

Deborah is constrained from departing in outrage by Brynner's invitation to meet with a scattering of his wives and children. Delighted as she is with his "head wife," Terry Saunders (Lady Thiang), and the other young kept women, she is convinced that the king, despite his grandiose plans to improve the lot of his subjects, is so deeply involved in self-admiration that he is unable to spare any for his spouses. A similar lack of affection applies to his relationship with his progeny, about 15 of whom are presented to Deborah while the off-screen orchestra plays the "March of the

Siamese Children," as stately a melody as Rodgers ever wrote.

The little royal princes and princesses have been groomed as automatons, much like the von Trapp children in *The Sound of Music*, ever careful not to offend their father by deviating by word or gesture from the regimen he has imposed on them from birth. Even Patrick Adiarte (Crown Prince Chulalongkom), Brynner's son by Terry Saunders and the apple of his eye, has been starched into submissiveness, and he greets Deborah with the cold formality of a child ambassador summoned to court.

Despite her misgivings, Deborah decides to remain in the palace "for a while." She strikes up an acquaintance with some of the ladies of the court, particularly Rita, who admits that she is in love with the Burmese boy who had unwillingly delivered her to Brynner earlier that day. Deborah understands the girl's sorrow. She, too, knows from experience that no woman can stop loving the man to whom she has given her heart.

Glancing at a picture of her deceased Tom, she tries to comfort Rita by singing a love song to lovers everywhere, reliving her own former happiness by recalling her marriage to Tom and inspiring her listeners to remain faithful to the men of their dreams. As sublime a piece of lingering nostalgia as Broadway has ever heard, "Hello, Young Lovers" is among the songwriting team's loveliest and most perceptive ballads. Miss Nixon's warm and sincere reading of the lyric makes it an unforgettable experience.

Like Maria von Trapp, Deborah easily wins the affection of the children, and they establish a rapport that far transcends the usual pupil-teacher relationship. She hopes she has done as much for them as they have for her, she tells them one day as a prelude to singing the biggest hit of the show. As she explains in the genial "Getting to Know You," children often teach their teachers quite a bit, too, and the insight into Siamese culture they have given her has proved invaluable to her own learning process. She now better understands why they act and react the way they do, and loves them all the more for being themselves. If they had always thought that Siam was one of the largest countries on earth, it was because they had never seen a map that accurately displayed the world of nations according to scale; but then, she informs the temporarily disillusioned class, England is pretty small, too.

King Brynner is also learning a few things, and it is no easy task for him to accommodate change in what he is discovering is a constantly changing world. Everything is "A Puzzlement," he concedes in a musical monologue that casts him as a forward-thinking but perplexed ruler trying to defend his belief in numerous falsehoods. How could he be so wrong about so many things, he wonders, and what is it that makes him so adamant in resisting the truth in matters he really knows so little about? Clearly, Deborah's teachings are having an influence beyond the classroom into the throne room. His difficulty in subscribing to many strange theories is definitely long range; toward the end of the picture he is still lamenting more puzzlements in another soliloquy, "Song of the King."

Brynner finally takes her word for it that the world is round, and not supported on the back of a big turtle, as he had assumed. He has heard about the American Civil War, which in the time frame of the musical was still going on, admires Lincoln, and is amazed to find that a woman wrote *Uncle Tom's Cabin*. Temporarily oblivious of the fact that keeping his wives in bondage qualifies him as a slave master, he offers to compensate by sending Lincoln several pairs of elephants for breeding purposes, even though both animals are male. It is the king's hope that in time the American President will see to it that the animals are tamed and used as "beasts of burden" to transport arms and other materiel in his war to end the enslavement of an entire race of people. He is dissuaded from following through with his gesture of friendship after Deborah explains that the Union Army does not need to climb mountains to attack the enemy or, presumably, a Hannibal to lead it.

Frequently suspicious of Deborah's reliability as a historian, Brynner alternates between childlike amazement and obstinate denial when confronted with certain facts that run counter to long-held beliefs. What he wants is confirmation not confusion. Fascinated by Deborah's use of the word "etcetera" as verbal shorthand for listing related items, he adopts it as a means of reducing his own verbiage when issuing proclamations. Enforcing the custom that disallows the head of anyone else to rise above his own while in his company, he demands that Deborah spread-eagle herself on the floor while he lies in a semi-prone position to fathom the complexities of the Bible, which he defines as a "think book."

Forbidden Love. One night, Deborah reluctantly answers Carlos Rivas's appeal to arrange a meeting between him and slave girl Rita, even though the penalty for all three would be death if caught. As the lovers rendezvous, Rivas complains bitterly at the restrictions imposed by Brynner on fraternization between his subjects and anyone with a drop of hated Burmese blood. He no longer wants to meet Rita in secret and speak in whispers. Elaborating on his disenchantment, they duet the splendid ballad "We Kiss in a Shadow," in which both express the hope that someday they will be free to announce their love to the world and marry. (Rivas's vocalizing was dubbed by Reuben Fuentes.)

Rivas's fear that such a happy ending is beyond their grasp spurs him into planning a bold move to escape from Siam. Giving Rita a white chala flower, he tells her that when she receives another flower just like it, he will be close by, ready to carry her off by boat to a new life of happiness in another country.

As if Brynner's internal struggle to discard centuries-old Siamese customs were not sufficient to pester him, Deborah adds to the king's troubles by again vowing to return to England unless she is given the promised separate residence. He refuses, chiding her for expecting to be treated differently from the way his "other servants" are. Reminding him that she is not a member of his harum, she angrily stalks away, determined to pack her things and leave Siam forever.

Not even pleas from her royal pupils to rethink her decision are able to change her mind, but she does listen closely while Terry dissects the king's personality. He surely has his faults, she admits, but he is basically a caring, if sometimes thoughtless, man genuinely disposed to learning all he can. He often stumbles and falls but has devoted his life to improving the lives of his people. Just as surely, he needs help but is far too proud to humble himself to request it. Her petition

that Deborah proffer it voluntarily, delivered in the lovely ballad "Something Wonderful," wins the day. Deborah will visit the king and help him however she can.

Although pleased at her reappearance and promise to continue in her teaching post, Brynner is quick to unload one of his most pressing problems on her. The news from abroad is that the British regard him as a barbarian. What hurts even more is his feeling that he is unable to dispute the charge. Sympathetic Deborah counsels him into furnishing proof to the contrary by inviting the British ambassador, Sir John Haig, and his friends and associates to a huge banquet to be followed by some sort of entertainment. Playing the ambassador is Alan Mobray, whose almost 200 screen roles as manservant, butler, diplomat, and stuffy confrere of leading men made his face one of Hollywood's most recognizable.

Brynner applauds the suggestion, for which he takes all the credit, certain that the affair will show Western representatives how very civilized both king and court actually are. All his wives will be gowned in European-style dresses, even given shoes to wear. The finest cigars will be available, the napkins will be silk, and, since Europeans are unable to manipulate chopsticks, silverware will be provided, "etcetera, etcetera, etcetera." Deborah is to arrange the banquet, and if all goes well, she will be rewarded with that much sought-after house of her own.

Selected for the guests' postprandial amusement is an Oriental version of *Uncle Tom's Cabin*, rewritten as "The Small House of Uncle Thomas" by Rita, who also acts as narrator. Like no other production number on film, it is uniquely charming in a pseudo-exotic sort of way. The sequence is made visually and audibly arresting by combining formalized group dancing and a highly lyrical instrumental accompaniment, simple movable props, and stunning yellow and orange costumes that sparkle all the more when set against a black background.

The players act out several incidents from Harriet Beecher Stowe's famous anti-slavery work, which was serialized in the periodical *National Era* between 1851 and 1852, when it was published as a book. Like the finale of *An*

American in Paris, the 15-minute ballet is too long, and it also refers tangentially to the love problem that is disrupting the lives of two of the film's major characters—Rivas and Rita, who in her spoken prologue indirectly castigates Brynner for prohibiting the couple's romance. Although she never mentions the king by name, he is well aware that he is the object of her scorn, and he orders her to omit the rest of her speech and get on with the play.

Not above inserting autobiographical liberties into the Stowe plot, Rita's rewrite allows Buddha to help Eliza rejoin her lover, "George," by freezing the ice on the river to permit her escape. He then calls on the sun to melt it when the dastardly Simon Legree, a not very subtle personification of Brynner, steps on the ice in pursuit. His death by drowning obviously pleases Rita, who looks upon Legree as an evil tyrant dedicated to wreaking havoc on little Eliza for no other reason than revenge. The king is not amused.

The gala is a huge success, prompting Ambassador Mobray's promise to present Queen Victoria with a glowing report on both the banquet and Brynner. It is also responsible for integrating two sets of love affairs, the newly developing one between Deborah and Brynner and an older one that Deborah had dismissed from mind. Among the guests that evening was Edward Ramsey (Geoffrey Toone), a friend of Deborah's who had once proposed to her and loves her still. As they dance, he urges her to reconsider his offer, reminding her that Tom is dead and that she is "much too young to bury your heart in a grave." Brynner instantly recognizes that they make an attractive couple, and he is not above trying to write finis to their relationship.

Deborah responds to the king's obvious delight in European-style dancing by offering to teach him the polka to the merry melody of "Shall We Dance?" Displeased at being taught the steps while merely holding hands, he soon demands that they dance arm in arm, just as all the other partygoers had. Accordingly, the king and the hoop-skirted commoner swirl majestically over the floor in an extraordinarily rousing dance duet that is worthy of comparison with the waltz danced by Louis Jourdan and Jennifer Jones in Vincente Minnelli's *Madame Bovary* (1949), still the most dazzling ballroom dance on film.

That the relationship between Brynner and Deborah is mellowing into something deeper than mutual respect between master and schoolmistress is made quite apparent by their exchanging looks of love at the conclusion of the number. In a symbolic gesture attesting his affection, Brynner removes a ring from his finger and gives it to his thrilled dancing partner. Seconds afterward, the peaceful scene is disrupted by the appearance of Rita, who has been captured by palace guards while trying to flee into the arms of Rivas. Posing as a rickshaw driver, he had entered the building and given her a chala as a signal that their escape was imminent.

Enraged at learning that any member of his household would even consider cuckolding him, Brynner reverts to his more normal role as unforgiving disciplinarian by preparing to whip Rita as punishment. He brushes aside Deborah's plea for leniency, only to discover that her impact on him is far stronger than he would have believed possible. No longer hostage to obstinacy, he is unable to administer the beating, and angrily tosses the whip on the floor. After hearing one of the guard's report that the girl's lover has been found dead in the river, Rita is dragged screaming from the room. Deborah, charging that the British were correct in labeling him a barbarian, returns Brynner's ring and marches away, more intent than ever on leaving Siam on the next ship.

Ashamed at his inability to defend his honor by meting out "justice" to Rita, and conscious of his loss of esteem among the guards who witnessed his role reversal, Brynner remains in seclusion for the next several weeks. Gradually growing weaker and weaker, no longer interested in living, and upset at Deborah's refusal to speak with him or cancel her homeward trip, he spends his days lying on a cot while awaiting death. His condition seems to verify Prime Minister Benson's earlier warning to Deborah. Her efforts to reform the king by replacing his absolute authoritarianism with Western humaneness will destroy him, he told her; "he will tear himself in two trying to be something he can never be."

Faithful to her conviction that forgiveness is a cardinal virtue, Deborah visits the dying king an hour before her ship is to sail. That she does love him is apparent from the tears that well up in her eyes at the sight of the enfeebled condition into which this once-dynamic man has fallen. He unquestionably deserves praise for doing his best to modernize his nation despite his initial distrust of much of Western ideology. His final act is to install his crown prince son as his successor. It with pride that she listens to young Patrick's first proclamation that henceforth no one will ever again be forced to bow in the presence of a Siamese monarch. It may be only a baby step in introducing democracy to the kingdom, but to Deborah it is proof that her teachings have had a beneficial impact on the youngster as well as on his father, who agrees that the proclamation is wise.

Brynner is also pleased when Deborah accedes to the new ruler's appeal that she stay at her post, and Brynner offers to give her back the ring, which she willingly accepts in grateful silence. His final gesture of forgiveness completed, Brynner dies. His left hand falls over the side of the cot. Deborah kneels, and then kisses and buries her face in the hand. It is the king who has left Siam, and Anna who will stay. It was she who had wielded the stronger influence of the two, this pretty but "difficult woman" whose charm, spirituality, and tenacity of purpose won the hearts and minds of the people.

Gigi (1958)

A Metro-Goldwyn-Mayer picture. DIRECTOR: Vincente Minnelli; ASSISTANTS: William McGarry and William Shanks. PRODUCER: Arthur Freed. SCREENWRITER: Alan Jay Lerner, based on the novel by Colette. CINEMATOGRAPHER: Joseph Ruttenberg. FILM EDITOR: Adrienne Fazan. COSTUMES, SCENERY, AND PRODUCTION DESIGNER: Cecil Beaton. ART DIRECTOR: William A. Horning and Preston Ames. SET DECORATORS: Henry Grace and Keogh Gleason. MAKEUP: William Tuttle and Charles Parker. HAIRSTYLES: Guillaume and Sydney Guilaroff. ORCHESTRATORS: Conrad Salinger. VOCAL SUPERVISOR: Robert Tucker. FILM SUPERVISOR: Dr. Wesley C. Miller. MUSIC SUPERVISOR AND CONDUCTOR: André Previn. SONGS: lyrics by Alan Jay Lerner, music by Frederick Loewe. RUNNING TIME: 1 hour, 56 minutes. *Principal Players*: Leslie Caron (Gigi). Maurice Chevalier (Honore Lachailles). Louis Jourdan (Gaston Lachailles). Hermione Gingold (Inez Alvarez [Mamita]). Eva Gabor (Liane d'Exelmans). Isabel Jeans (Aunt Alicia). Jacques Bergerac (Sandomir). *Major Academy Awards*: Best Picture; Director; Adapted Screenplay; Cinematographer; Film Editor; Art Direction; Set Decoration; Costumes; Scoring; Song ("Gigi").

Sidonie-Gabrielle Colette's best-known work in America in 1958, and since, is a meant-for-the-movies story about youth, happiness, and love. MGM fortunately custom-tailored *Gigi* for the screen without sacrificing any of the novella's overall charm, and outfitted the movie with songs that match the sparkle and wit of the screenplay. Included among them are two classic pitter-patter novelties, "It's a Bore!," with sardonic Louis Jourdan belittling every one of sybarite Maurice Chevalier's pleasures in life, and "I Remember It Well," a humorous yet tender exchange of reminiscences of things past between Chevalier and Hermione Gingold.

The result was a masterpiece that lifted the film musical to its zenith at the same time that the genre was free-falling into its four-decades-long decline into near oblivion. The most original adult-oriented film musical, *Gigi* was indeed made at a perilous time when just about everyone in Hollywood thought it would be sheer folly for any studio, even MGM, to gear up to produce another musical.

Unfortunately, Colette died four years before the picture was released. The only musical to win an Academy Award in every category in which it was entered, *Gigi* benefitted greatly from the staff of professionals who guided it through the production process. Among them was the almost totally unknown Joseph Ruttenberg, the extraordinarily gifted Russian-born cinematographer with three Academy Awards to his credit and the equal in many respects of Gregg Toland and James Wong Howe. Although he had photographed one earlier MGM musical, *The Great Waltz*, in 1938, he was most highly regarded for dramas, among them *The Women* (1939), *Waterloo Bridge* (1940), *Mrs. Miniver* (1942), *Gaslight* (1944), and *Somebody Up There Likes Me* (1956).

The few non-stage–based Hollywood musicals between *Seven Brides for Seven Brothers* in 1954 and *Gigi* in 1958 were for the most part depressingly commonplace, a circumstance that did little to tempt moviegoers into clamoring for more. The settings for most of them finally deserted Broadway for other venues; *White Christmas*, for example, was played out mostly in Vermont, and *High Society*, an excellent remake of the stage and film comedy *The Philadelphia Story*, in the environs of that

Now grown up and ready for love, Leslie Caron dances with Louis Jourdan at Maxim's, the famous Paris restaurant, in *Gigi*.

Pennsylvania metropolis. But the plots were anything but new. They still centered on untangling misunderstandings that endangered the bliss of the two central characters. Like the show that always went on, the screenplays also saw to it that all impediments to happiness were removed.

In the absence of story originality, pickups from Broadway vastly increased in number. They failed to inspire confidence that Hollywood could prosper without calling on established musicals for material, but at least the high-production values the studios lavished on their warmed-over stage librettos proved that they were still capable of turning out quality musicals, even if the sources were primarily imported from New York. Similarly, the songs for the few original musical films were inferior compared with those introduced on the screen over the previous 30 years. Throughout the 1950s, many of the melodies that people hummed, on their way into as well as out of the movie house, had already become standards from their earlier stage exposure.

By 1958, the ranks of the legendary word and melody masters responsible for the success of the film musical had been thinned out by decades of retirement and death. Such esteemed melodists as Harry Warren, Harry Revel, James McHugh, and Nacio Herb Brown were in virtual retirement; George Gershwin, Jerome Kern, Sigmund Romberg, Richard A. Whiting, Ralph Rainger, Walter Donaldson, and Victor Schertzinger were dead. James Van Heusen began concentrating on occasional theme songs for dramas and comedies. Irving Berlin, Harold Arlen, and Arthur Schwartz confined themselves largely to Broadway, as did Cole Porter, whose final original film score, for *Les Girls* in 1957, was the least successful in his 21-year movie career.

Widely Experienced Author. The foremost French woman author of her day, Colette was elected to the Royal Academy of Language and Literature of Belgium in 1936. She was a grand officer of the Legion of Honor as well as the first woman member, and later president, of the prestigious Goncourt Academy. America's National Institute of Arts and Letters honored her with a diploma. She began her writing career in 1895, when as the wife of publisher Henri Gauthier-Villars, she created a semi-autobiographical heroine named Claudine and wrote about her libertine adventures as a schoolgirl in *Claudine at School*, a sort of spicy prelude to *Gigi*. She added three more novels to her Claudine collection, all of them developing into bestsellers. After separating from her husband in 1905, Colette spent the next eight years as a music hall dancer, mime,

transvestite, and singer. Basing the bulk of her characters on show business acquaintances, she became noted for creating women who were able to grow and survive in the soil of adversity.

During World War I, Colette worked the battlefields of France as a reporter for the newspaper *Le Matin*, and after the Armistice became its literary editor. Other successful novels followed—*Cherie* in 1920 and *Break of Day* in 1928. The latter work established her reputation as an introspective writer who shunned tortured self-analysis for simple self-discoveries based in nature, or, as with Gigi, in the purity of lower-economic-class girlhood.

Published in 1942, *Gigi* was the source of a 1950 French nonmusical film, qualifying the 1958 film as the first remake of a movie to win the Oscar as best picture. The story was then adapted for Broadway in 1951 by Anita Loos, the most successful female screenwriter in Hollywood history and author of the 1925 novel *Gentlemen Prefer Blondes*, later made into a play and then a movie. While *Gigi* was still in the casting stage, Colette was on vacation in Monte Carlo, where she spotted a delicate English actress with no stage experience performing a bit role in *Monte Carlo Baby*, which was being filmed in the foyer of the hotel. Colette turned to her third husband, Maurice Goudeket, advising him that the search for the right young woman to inhabit the leading part was over.

"This is our Gigi in America," she exclaimed, pointing to the totally unknown Audrey Hepburn, born Audrey Kathleen van Heemstra Hepburn-Ruston. She got the part, toured the United States with the show, and seemed a shoo-in to repeat it in the film. But Miss Hepburn ruled otherwise, expressing no interest in the screen version. The role was given instead to Leslie Caron, not because she had played *Gigi* in the London production of the Loos play, which was a disaster, but based on her winsome performance in *An American in Paris* seven years earlier. Her ability to project the look and verve of an innocent and sometimes awkward teenager only marginally interested in learning the facts of life was still potent, and she became the first of only two female performers to star in two best picture musicals. Her singing voice, however, was not her own, but dubbed prettily by Betty Wand.

Despite its overtones of *My Fair Lady*, in many ways Gigi is an extension of Miss Caron's role in *An American in Paris*. She is afflicted by love troubles in both films, flattered first by Kelly's charisma as a flirt and then by Louis Jourdan's good-humored attentiveness as a stand-in older brother. Not until both men become serious lovers with marriage on their minds does she permit herself to welcome them into her virginal heart. For most of the film, Gigi is a fun-loving adolescent, while Lise Bouvier in *An American in Paris* is drained of much of her youthful vigor by the dismal prospect of marrying a man she respects but does not love. That girl could never have abandoned her film-long seriousness to join in singing such a merry song as "The Night They Invented Champagne."

In a rare example of reprising a film musical on the stage, Edwin Lester and Arnold Saint-Subber in late 1973 presented the Los Angeles and San Francisco Light Opera's production of *Gigi* at the Uris Theatre (now the Gershwin) in New York. Heading the cast were Alfred Drake (who two years earlier had been considered for the Yul Brynner part in the filmed *The King and I*) in Chevalier's role as Honore Lachailles, and Agnes Moorehead as the imperious Aunt Alicia. Gigi was played by Karen Wolfe, and the dashing Gaston Lachailles by Daniel Massey. Most of the film score was retained, to which Lerner and Loewe added four new songs, "The Earth and Other Minor Things," "Paris Is Paris Again," "In This Wide, Wide World," and "I Never Want to Go Home Again." Despite its meager run of 103 performances, the revival won the Tony Award for best score in a year noted for both lackluster musicals and songs.

End of an Era. The last of Hollywood's truly inspired home-grown musical pictures, *Gigi* was the flagship production of the "Freed Unit," the nickname of MGM's so-called "Royal Family" of multi-talented men and women who worked on song-and-dance spectacles under the supervision of producer Arthur Freed. It premiered in New York on May 15, 1958, at the Royale, a legitimate theater rather than a movie house. Alan Jay Lerner, the son of the founder and president of Lerner Stores, a women's clothing chain, earned his second

Academy Award for the screenplay. Equally romantically inclined when writing lyrics as Frederick Loewe was when composing music, Lerner first joined Loewe for the 1943 stage revue *What's Up?* Their next work together, *The Day Before Spring* (1945), which won a New York Drama Critics Award, was a musical of undeniable attractiveness in both story and score that somehow never clicked with the public.

And then, on March 13, 1947, came their whimsical *Brigadoon*, which ran more than a year, toured extensively, and in 1954 was made into a motion picture starring Gene Kelly and Cyd Charisse. Set in a small Scottish village unlisted on any map, the musical gave birth to such hit songs as "Almost Like Being in Love" and "The Heather on the Hill." The pair then collaborated on *Paint Your Wagon* in 1951, *My Fair Lady* in 1956, and *Camelot* in 1960. These three musical plays were also given the Hollywood treatment, the first, with Clint Eastwood and Jean Seberg, in 1969, the second, with Rex Harrison and Audrey Hepburn, in 1964, and the third, starring Richard Harris and Vanessa Redgrave, in 1967. Berlin-born Loewe had made his Broadway debut, sans Lerner, in 1938 with *The Great Lady*.

Unlike *An American in Paris* the exterior and some interior scenes in *Gigi* were shot on location, with the picture's biggest banquet for the eyes consisting of the plush interiors of Aunt Alicia's home and the famous Parisian restaurant Maxim's, where the film's only production number, and a weak one at that, is performed to the sweeping melody of "She's Not Thinking of Me." Cecil Beaton's costume, scenery, and overall production design are praiseworthy in recreating the period frills and frocks, as well as the graciousness and glory, of turn-of-the-century Paris. His creativity, surpassed only by his design work on *My Fair Lady*, was ably abetted by Henry Grace and Keough Gleason's extraordinary set decorations. The gifted Beaton, who would be knighted in 1972, won Academy Awards for his artistry for both MGM films.

The picture represents the finest work by Vincente Minnelli (who also directed *An American in Paris*), even though he was not totally responsible for its outstanding success. He was called back to Paris to begin shooting *The Re-*

luctant Debutante before the final revisions to *Gigi* were completed in Hollywood. Hired in his stead to supervise the refilming of the "I Remember It Well," "She's Not Thinking of Me," and "Soliloquy" sequences was Charles Walters, an experienced MGM film-musical director (*Good News*, 1947, *Easter Parade*, and *High Society*) whose name is omitted from the opening credit cards.

Along with Miss Caron, every other principal member of the *Gigi* cast turns in a career-high performance. Appearing in his fourth Oscar-nominated musical, the most of any leading player, 72-year-old Maurice Chevalier is exemplary as the dapper aristocrat roué—a character absent from Colette's book—who also serves as narrator and unifier of the plot. No longer the middle-age man who first romanced Jeanette MacDonald as long ago as 1929, he had obviously lost none of his Gallic charisma or playfulness over the years.

His white hair gave him the look of a distinguished elderly boulevardier, which was exactly the part he was assigned to play. His eyes by then were bracketed by wrinkles, but they still emitted that familiar old sparkle, and his smile was as magnetic as ever. Chevalier in fact steals the picture like a second-story man who carries away the family jewels from a safe while a party is going on downstairs. His presence enriches the film to a degree that no other performer, not even that British geriatric marvel, Hermione Gingold, is able to match.

Chevalier's—and the film's—opening and closing song, "Thank Heaven for Little Girls," is an aging man's tribute to the opposite sex. His puckish grandfatherly glee in glimpsing a bevy of girl children playing in a Parisian park is tempered, however, by the sobering awareness that he most likely will not be alive by the time these gamines grow into adulthood. But he accepts that inevitability with a "that's life" shrug of the shoulders. Generations come and go; theirs is beginning to peek over the mountain tops while his is descending.

If, as he suspects, his trysting days are over, well, he can find at least partial gratification by living vicariously while advising his nephew on the subtleties of love-making. Later, in "I'm Glad I'm Not Young Anymore," Chevalier finally admits that he is no longer constitutionally fit to undergo any more of the emotional wear and tear typically inflicted on lovers.

After World War II, Chevalier appeared mostly in French films until 1957, when he returned to the United States for *Love in the Afternoon* opposite Gary Cooper and Audrey Hepburn, his first American movie since *Folies-Bergère* in 1935. The major reason for his 12-year postwar absence was due to the rather substantial anti–Chevalier sentiment stirred up by allegations, never proved, that he had voluntarily entertained German troops during the war. The actor would appear in 16 more minor films after *Gigi*, two of them in cameo, without adding very much burnish to his once-formidable reputation.

So it is fitting that in "I'm Glad I'm Not Young Anymore" he briefly reverts to the Chevalier of old by tipping his straw hat over his eyes and shuffling off screen with the sly little soft-shoe routine that had helped to make him an international favorite. The year *Gigi* was released, the Academy of Motion Picture Arts and Sciences acknowledged his "contributions to the world of entertainment for more than half a century" with a Special Oscar.

The selection of Louis Jourdan as Chevalier's nephew was both curious and felicitous. Curious because although born, like Chevalier, in France—he in Marseille, Chevalier in Paris—Jourdan had lost practically all vestiges of a French accent by the time Gigi came along. Audiences seemed not to notice this lapse in authenticity, but, then, they never cared that they never saw Howard Keel's or Russ Tamblyn's breath while they argued high in the Oregon mountains in the middle of winter either. Both of Gigi's aunts speak in cultured British accents, and Eva Gabor in her own special aromatic blend of American English flavored with the patois of a Hungarian refugee. Nor had Jourdan any experience in musical films, having been cast as a leading man in dramas and comedies in seven French motion pictures from 1939 to 1945, and in similar roles in his 11 pre–Gigi American movies, which included Alfred Hitchcock's *The Paradine Case* in 1948 and *Three Coins in the Fountain* in 1954.

But the choice was a happy one in that Jourdan was handsome, convincing as a suave man about town, and a competent actor. If his character change from a bored, stuffy, intensely self-centered upper-class idler to the sincere lover humbled by Gigi's naïvety and desire for respectability comes as a pleasant surprise, it is because he handles his reformation so adroitly. His singing of the Academy Award–winning "Gigi," which, like no other ballad in any film musical, reveals the hero's sudden realization that the immature youngster he had known has somehow been recreated into an alluring goddess almost overnight is commendable.

In one of the screen's greatest love lyrics, inseparable from the plot, he admits that he had not observed the change in her, or in his regard for her, till that very moment. Perhaps he had been standing too far away from her, or maybe up too close, while the youngster imperceptibly blossomed into womanhood. But whatever the reason, his relationship with Gigi will never again be the same as it was only a short time earlier. What was then companionship has evolved into passion.

Although the theme of Gigi is adult, particularly when compared with previous musical pictures, it is developed tastefully throughout. The girl's duty in life is to become a courtesan, nothing more, nothing less. Aunt Alicia, whose grandiose lifestyle attests to the spoils a dedicated mistress can accrue over the years, is decidedly in favor of such a career. Marriage is okay, she tells Gigi at one point, but only late in life, after both bride and groom have tired of playing the field. So she fills her usually vacant hours grooming Gigi in the social graces that will guarantee success as a paramour, and, not incidentally, enhance the uppity aunt's own standing in Jourdan's exclusive social circle. Even Hermione Gingold briefly tolerates her granddaughter's apprenticeship as a hired lover under the lure of finally obtaining enough of Jourdan's apparently endless funds to rise above her hand-to-mouth existence.

Luckily for all concerned, especially the Hollywood censors, the story was set over there in Paris, where such affairs were assumed to be as old as the city itself, not over here in the United States, where they were also practiced, but rarely within view of a Hollywood camera. By the late 1950s, Americans had surely become immune to taking offense at the wealthy European male's infidelity, having been conditioned to the custom through novels, plays, and foreign films. Besides, Jourdan was cultured and impeccable in dress and manners, not the crass *Broadway Melody* type of playboy producer settling amenable ingenues in penthouses within commuting distance of his own apartment.

Gigi, however, is one of the most obstinate, yet lovable, heroines ever to appear in an American film musical. She sticks nobly to her guns, wielding a powerful influence to which even Jourdan is susceptible. His acquiescence to reformation makes him equally appealing as her future mate for life at the conclusion of this tale of the revolt of sweet maidenhood against upper-class victimization, of middle-class morality *vs.* aristocratic prerogative.

Eyeing the Ladies. Among the frolicky schoolgirls being serenaded by Maurice Chevalier (Honore Lachailles), one stands above the rest. By no means the prettiest of the lot, Leslie Caron (Gigi) is the personification of carefree youth, her straight brown hair bouncing against the back of her colorful print dress as she scampers merrily on the green carpet that covers the Bois de Boulogne, one hand pressed against the top of her white wide-brimmed hat to hold it in place. Chevalier pays little attention to her, unaware that within a short time the youngster will play a decisive role in his nephew's life— and in his own by testing his perspicacity as a counselor-at-love.

Of supreme importance to him at the moment is tipping his own hat in appreciation of the passing procession of fashionable ladies, some on foot, others in gilded carriages. Such an activity is to be expected, of course, of a man who describes himself as a lover by profession and life-long collector of beautiful things, with women at the top of the list. True, they can be a source of irritation, he tells the audience, by forever insisting that marriage follow courtship as night follows day. Naturally, men are not nearly so wedlock-prone, he continues, vaguely echoing Yul Brynner's pronouncement in *The King and I* that women are like blossoms, men like bees. Women are put on earth mainly to satisfy the desires of the opposite sex while searching for their ideal mates, to whom they must remain forever faithful. Men, on the other hand, must be free to fly from flower to flower, sampling their loveliness without any compulsion to remain true to any one of them. Or so the potentate with the biggest harem in Siam believed.

Later that morning Chevalier is joined by his bachelor nephew, Louis Jourdan (Gaston Lachailles), whom Chevalier had invited to lunch with him and an old friend. The elder Lachailles enjoys the young man's company, even though he regards him as a thirtyish spoiled brat, so rich that he gets a manicure every morning and cannot remember the name of a railroad he just bought. But being in his presence helps to keep Chevalier young, if only in spirit.

How Jourdan manages to accomplish this transfer of youthfulness is a mystery. Rather than deriving happiness from life, he is indifferent to its pleasures. "It's a Bore!," Jourdan confides during the carriage ride to the luncheon site, renouncing his uncle's praise of everything from the beauties of nature to the thrill of horse racing. He even identifies Parisian girls as bores, including those who respond to his romantic overtures with a yes instead of a no. He finally becomes bored with his uncle, too, and abruptly departs the carriage to visit Hermione Gingold (Mme. Alvarez, known familiarly as "Mamita"), in her modest second-floor flat, where she lives with granddaughter Gigi. Although she is never seen, the third resident is Gigi's mother, a one-time minor opera soprano who spends her days closeted inside her bedroom practicing scales.

Jourdan is disappointed when Hermione reminds him that today is Tuesday. Gigi is having her usual luncheon date with her Aunt Alicia (actually her great-aunt), a reclusive lady with a shady past living in luxury, thanks to a series of affairs with noblemen of various rank and nationality. Splendidly played by Isabel Jeans, a veteran stage and screen specialist at portraying cool and detached aristocratic ladies, the 67-year-old glamour girl gives Chevalier a close race for acting laurels, balancing her haughtiness with congeniality while patiently awaiting the time that her tutelage succeeds in transforming Gigi from gangly, giggling girl to worldly-wise young woman.

There is, she insists to her cavalier pupil, a proper way to walk into a room, to sit down, and to eat that instantly separates patrician from plebeian. Of equal importance to acquiring the graces practiced so assiduously by the ruling classes is the ability to judge the quality of jewelry at first glance and of cigars by sniff and feel. Irritated by Gigi's lack of interest in her etiquette lessons, Isabel nonetheless perseveres. The girl is not altogether hopeless. She does have eyes, lashes, teeth, and hair good enough to compensate for her "impossible" nose, "nondescript" mouth, and "too-high" cheekbones, comparisons that are of no concern whatever to Gigi.

After her aunt leaves the room in disgust, Gigi voices her displeasure with what she terms her country's besottedness with love in the spirited soliloquy "(I Don't Understand) the Parisians." Love is all they think about, she complains; even worse, the women are inclined to equate sincerity by the number and price of the gifts their men bestow on them. Gigi vows to have none of it as she skips along the street back to the Bois de Boulogne, where she meets Jourdan and accompanies him to the Ice Palace. It is clear that he is very fond of her. He admires, perhaps envies, her vitality and childlike enthusiasm for the simplest of pleasures. Her outlook on life is always upbeat, while his is one of anticipating a future as suffocatingly dull as the past.

It is while at the skating rink that Gigi is alarmed to discover that Jourdan, like everyone else in Paris, lives and breathes love. Upset at seeing his current mistress, Eva Gabor (Liane d'Exelmans), in the arms of her skating instructor, Sandomir (Jacques Bergerac), he invites her to share a night on the town with him. The major event of the evening's activities is dinner at Maxim's, to which Lerner and Loewe add merriment tinged with satiric overtones by blending three melodies that expose the futility of the life he is leading.

Jourdan's assertion that Parisians never engage in blackening one another's reputation is given the lie when the excitable diners erupt into whispered character analyses to the tune of "Gossip" upon the arrival of each pair of lovers. Meanwhile Miss Gabor, in a brief but engaging performance as a younger version of Aunt Alicia, occupies her time ignoring Jourdan to flirt with other men, gushing with delight at the attention they give her, and finally dancing the instrumental "A Toujours" with a distinguished gentleman she has just met. "She's Not Thinking of Me," Jourdan sneers to himself in the conversational lyric of the third song, the very pretty waltz of the same name. As might be expected, he soon reverts to his normal behavior when events do not turn out as planned. Bored stiff with the restaurant, the chatter, and especially Eva, he leaves the restaurant in a miff.

The next day, Chevalier comes to the rescue of his nephew's ennui by persuading him that he should see Eva once more, not to revive a relationship in which neither is interested, but so that he can be the one to break it off. It's all a matter of "male patriotism," Chevalier insists: "the woman must not have the last word!" Aware that his uncle speaks from long experience sweeping away the embers of burned-out love affairs, he accompanies him to a restaurant on the outskirts of Paris.

There Jourdan is displeased to find Eva embracing and kissing Bergerac at a table. On the sly, he offers to pay him 1,000 francs for the promise never to see Eva again, an offer that the handsome gigolo finds impossible to refuse. Jourdan then curtly informs Eva that their romance is over. Later that day, unable to contend with the loss of two lovers in one fell swoop, Eva commits "suicide." If nothing else, her death will appear in the morning newspapers, elevate her to celebrity du jour, and win the sympathy of gossip-loving readers. The afternoon papers, however, report that she has recovered nicely, as usual having swallowed "insufficient poison" to end her life, as Isabel acidly comments to Hermione.

The incidents of the past few days, however, have taken a heavy toll on Jourdan's mental health. Although the loss of his latest mistress is of no consequence, he at last is becoming bored with the rituals of romance—squiring devious young women to countless soirees and deceiving them with promises he has little intention of keeping, only to suffer more dagger stabs when love turns to hate. The best times of his life are spent with Gigi, too young to have mastered the art of dissembling and too innocent to recognize it in others, always sincere and unimpressed with false sophistication.

Wishing to capitalize on her ebullient good humor, he invites her, Hermione, and Chevalier to a weekend at a seaside resort. Gigi celebrates the forthcoming vacation by singing "The Night They Invented Champagne," a rollicking testimonial to her happiness at deserting the sweltering streets of Paris for the smell of sea air and the feel of warm sand while gamboling barefoot on sunny beaches. What she does not know, but moviegoers instinctively surmised, is that the seashore will be the scene where Jourdan's appreciation of Gigi's girlish charms lightly turns his mind to thoughts of love.

Love also pays a visit to Chevalier and Hermione, but it springs from the vault of memory rather than from the chance meeting of two elderly strangers. They once were lovers but separated when Hermione learned that Chevalier had temporarily switched his affection to another young lady. Seated opposite her at a table overlooking the beach, Chevalier tries to impress by recalling details of their last date, as if it ranked as one of the most delightful romantic interludes of his life.

"I Remember It Well," he sings to her after erroneously identifying the day and hour of the date, what she was wearing, where they went, and what they did. The month was June, not April; Hermione's gown was blue, not gold. Infallible in correcting him ever so politely throughout the song, Hermione unintentionally reinforces Chevalier's gnawing fear that his memory lapses are proof that he is indeed getting old. In one of the most touching lines in popular music, she is quick to assure her still-debonaire singing partner that though other men do age, he never will, oh no, oh no. The most heartfelt duet in any film musical, the song is nothing short of a masterpiece of restrained sentiment shared by a long-estranged couple well past their prime, painfully aware that the only thing they now have in common is loneliness.

From Caterpillar into Butterfly. Exercising her acute insight into developing love affairs, Grandmother Hermione detects Jourdan's desire to claim Gigi as his own. The news so excites Aunt Isabel that she enrolls Gigi in a graduate course in programming a young virgin into a polished woman of the world. Her earlier lessons were designed merely to teach Gigi how to pander to the privileged class; the advanced studies will admit her immediately into it by training her to be a fit mistress for Jourdan. Although still indifferent toward Isabel's teaching, Gigi receives passing grades in the art of seduction by recognizing the nuances that separate the dignified lady courtesan from the woman of the pavements.

How expert she has become is made quite apparent to Jourdan on the first of his six subsequent visits to Gigi. No longer clumsy or disheveled, she is clad in a stunning, close-fitting white gown that announces her evolution into a breathtaking, lovely temptress. Unwilling as yet to accept his chipper playmate as a desirable young woman, Jourdan ridicules her dress, protesting that it makes her look like an "organ grinder's monkey." He barges out of the flat, leaving Gigi in tears.

Almost immediately, however, he returns, apologizes for his rudeness, and asks Gigi for a date. Hermione, perhaps recalling her own short-circuited love affair with his Uncle Chevalier, objects, citing Jourdan's "scandalous reputation" and her own fear that he will compromise Gigi. What Hermione wants and Gigi deserves, she maintains, is the companionship of a gentleman who will "answer for her future," or in crasser terms, be willing to pay for her companionship by providing the girl with life's necessities and at least some of its luxuries. Again Jordan explodes, reprimanding Hermione for angling to marry Gigi off to the first man who shows interest in her, whether he be only an underpaid bank clerk or plumber, have his children, and exist in perpetual squalor.

Angrily pacing the street, he tries hard to convince himself in a "soliloquy" that Gigi is not worth enduring any more emotional torture. What is she really but a foolish little girl, too infantile to bother with, a snip best forgotten as quickly as possible. And yet, he confesses while seguing into "Gigi," her surprising emergence from the cocoon of childhood as a completely ravishing creature has captured his heart. Actually, she is a sheer delight and, paying her the highest of compliments, he concedes that she has never once been a bore. Back he goes to the flat, this time to make arrangements with Hermione for Gigi's

becoming his mistress, vowing to care for her "beautifully." Pleased at the offer, she calls Gigi into the room to discuss the details with him.

Businesslike Jourdan eagerly explains the material benefits to be expected from such an official liaison, which will include a house, servants, and automobile as starters. Gigi, however, is the marrying kind who prefers a church wedding to a string of "one-night stands" with a man with a distaste for life-long commitment. Her goal is to be a marriage partner rather than the possession of someone who will drop her at will when he tires of her. Jourdan's inevitable response is to beat a hasty retreat from the flat and appeal for advice from Chevalier.

Appalled to hear that his nephew's proposed sponsorship of Gigi has been "refused, rejected, rebuffed, and reputed," the elder man predictably recommends that Jourdan drop Gigi from mind and enter into another round of nocturnal carryings-on with other girls who will appreciate his many assets, physical as well as financial. Jourdan agrees but unenthusiastically. His comment that such a cure is often worse than the illness indicates to Chevalier that he is more than casually interested in Gigi, and moreover that his love for her might very well result in surrendering his bachelorhood. After the distraught young man leaves, Chevalier heaves a sight of relief, thankful that his age prevents his becoming embroiled ever again with the temperamental Gigis of Paris, who typically wound rather than exhilarate, torment rather than please. "I'm Glad I'm Not Young Anymore," he sings with the contented air of a man who welcomes his new role as observer instead of participant in affairs of the heart.

Meanwhile, Chevalier's prognosis of Jourdan's heart tremors is proved accurate when the young man again ascends the stairs to Gigi's flat. Whether he goes there to rescind or repeat his offer is not entirely clear, but her conciliatory opening sentence pleases him. She would "rather be miserable with you than without you," she admits, thereby cementing the deal. To celebrate, Jourdan suggests an evening at Maxim's. Later, alone in her bedroom, Gigi sings of her uncertainty as to whether she has made the right decision in "Say a Prayer for Me Tonight," which had been dropped two years earlier from *My Fair Lady*. A much-too-somber appeal for divine guidance and protection, it is not one of the songwriters' better efforts, and tends to overdramatize Gigi's quandary while adding little of melodic value to the score.

Prepared to play the part of kept woman with aplomb, Gigi is the essence of refinement and gaiety at Maxim's, happily displaying all the tricks of the trade drummed into her by Aunt Isabel. Curiously, her hearty laughter at Jourdan's every comment and quickness to attend to his every need—even subjecting a cigar to feel and smell tests before handing it over to him—offends rather than pleases Jourdan. She is certainly not the winsome child in whose company he once reveled. She has turned into a silly, immature, Eva Gabor type of young woman, indistinguishable from all the other females he has known and veering perilously close to boring him. Grabbing her by the hand, he pulls her from the restaurant back to her flat, where he deposits the hugely disappointed apprentice mistress and leaves without uttering a word. Oblivious of which specific social amenities she had broken, Leslie again breaks into tears of despondency, a Cinderella returned to her home well before midnight.

Jourdan scarcely reaches the pavement when "Gigi" swells up in the background. In a rare but wise departure from the typical musical comedy format, the lyric is omitted. The melody itself suggests the words; there is no need to reprise them. That Jourdan is deeply in love with Gigi is made obvious by his pondering, alone and in silence, whether to revisit her and accede to her fondest wish. He does, reentering the flat for the sixth time to ask the amazed yet gratified Hermione to give him the "infinite joy" of bestowing Gigi's hand on him in marriage. Her immediate compliance with his request is greeted with the lovers' broad smiles and concluding kiss. All has ended so well that even the prospect of stuffy old Aunt Isabel's attending the wedding is not beyond the range of possibility.

West Side Story (1961)

A Mirisch Pictures-Seven Arts Enterprises/United Artists picture. DIRECTORS: Robert Wise and Jerome Robbins; ASSISTANTS: Robert E. Relyan and Jerome M. Siegel. PRODUCER: Robert Wise; ASSOCIATE: Saul Chaplin. SCREENWRITER: Ernest Lehman. CHOREOG-RAPHER: Jerome Robbins. PRODUCTION DESIGNER: Boris Leven. CINEMATOGRAPHER: Daniel L. Fapp; PHOTOGRAPHIC EFFECTS: Linwood Dunn. FILM EDITOR: Thomas Stanford. SET DECORATOR: Victor Gangelin. SOUND: Murray Spivak, Fred Lau, and Vinton Vernon. SOUND EDITOR: Gilbert O. Marchant; ASSOCIATE: Marshall M. Borden. COSTUMES: Irene Sharaff. HAIRDRESSER: Alice Monte. MUSIC EDITOR: Richard Carruth. MUSICAL SUPERVISORS: Saul Chaplin, Johnny Green, Sid Ramin, and Irwin Kostal. MUSIC CONDUCTOR: Johnny Green. ORCHESTRATORS: Sid Ramin and Irwin Kostal. MUSICAL ASSISTANT: Betty Walberg. VOCAL COACH: Bobby Tucker. DANCE ASSISTANTS: Tommy Abbott, Margaret Banks, Howard Jeffrey, and Tony Mordente. MUSIC: Lyrics by Stephen Sondheim, music by Leonard Bernstein. RUNNING TIME: 2 hours and 33 minutes. *Principal Players*: Natalie Wood (Maria). Richard Beymer (Tony). Russ Tamblyn (Riff). Rita Moreno (Anita). George Chakiris (Bernardo). Simon Oakland (Lt. Schrank). Ned Glass (Doc). William Bramley (Officer Krupke). Tucker Smith (Ice). José DeVega (Chino). *Major Academy Awards*: Best Picture; Director(s); Cinematography; Supporting Actress (*Rita Moreno*); Supporting Actor (*George Chakiris*); Film Editing; Costume Design; Art Direction; Scoring; Sound. *Nomination*: Best Adapted Screenplay.

The road to the Broadway debut of *West Side Story* was a long and circuitous one. According to Leonard Bernstein, Jerome Robbins telephoned him shortly after New Years's Day 1949 and proposed the idea of collaborating on a musical based on the Romeo and Juliet story, but set in an American slum. Bernstein liked the idea, as did playwright-screenwriter Arthur Laurents, who eventually wrote the book, his first for a musical. But none of the three took further action until 1955, when Laurents and Bernstein met—accidentally—in Beverly Hills.

Taking a cue from news stories on gang rumbles mostly involving Mexicans living in Los Angeles, Laurents suggested that the nationalities of the dormant musical be switched. Instead of Italian Catholics *vs.* Jews, as Robbins had initially proposed, Laurents recommended that the two opposing gangs consist of whites *vs.* Puerto Ricans, and that the site of their widening polarization be a wild and woolly slice of Upper Manhattan in transition, where clashes between the two groups were mushrooming by the mid–1950s. Thus did *West Side Story* evolve into a rare Broadway example of artistry feeding on history as it was being enacted on the streets.

Finally, in September of 1957, the show opened on Broadway with the largely unknown Carol Lawrence as Maria, Larry Kert as Tony,

Natalie Wood and George Chakiris as the Upper Manhattan Puerto Rican sister and brother in Stephen Sondheim and Leonard Bernstein's *West Side Story*.

and Chita Rivera as Anita. It remained there for two years, but failed in its bid for the best musical Tony. In 1961 it was released as a film of all substance and no reminders of the musical comedy drivel of the past. As regards its ending, unquestionably the most melodramatic in movie-musical history, all that can be said in its defense is that it works. Thirty-five years later, *West Side Story* is still one of the most relevant of all movie musicals, collecting 11 Academy Award nominations and winning first place in ten of the categories. The first musical of its kind—and thus far the last as well—the film created a sensation in New York that was duplicated many times over in communities large and small, even those without intimate knowledge of the disintegration of neighborhoods where youthful rebels of different cultures fought for what they believed to be righteous causes for control of the streets.

The film is conventional only in the most restricted sense of the word. Its central plot is a love story, but it ends in tragedy, as does the Shakespearean model, pulling the typical "and they lived happily forever after" appendage up by the roots. True to the work's sustained injection of the adrenaline of resentment from beginning to end, several of the characters are unappealing, in no way related to their likable Broadway and Hollywood musical comedy predecessors who faced the sole challenges of excelling in show business and winning the mate of their dreams.

The high school-age gang members, whether Jets (all white and mostly of Anglo-Saxon heritage) or Sharks (exclusively Puerto Rican), are in constant turmoil throughout the film. No Jet has made a noticeable mark on society, save for earning a reputation as a neighborhood troublemaker. Nor has any Shark, whose future has been foreclosed by opposition to his presence. Their enmity results in ritualistic outbursts of bravado to conceal the fact that the boys' lives are essentially barren of everything but hate.

Both groups' contempt for authority beyond that exercised by their leaders is similar to the anti-social behavior of the youths in *The Blackboard Jungle* (1955). In *West Side Story* the hostility spills from classroom into the streets, and there is no sympathetic teacher around to nudge them into conformity with the rules of acceptable conduct. In fact, the sole authority figure who takes a professional interest in the gang members' activities is Police Lieutenant Shrank, a foe of all immigrants whose chief concern is maintaining order throughout his beat. To achieve that goal, he is careful not to favor either gang, a seemingly diplomatic maneuver that results in his being regarded as the oppressor of both.

Descended from the street-smart Dead End Kids of the 1930s, the Jets are equally determined to fight poachers on their domain,

the single common goal that unites them in fellowship and represents their sole purpose for being. Better to unite in a crusade for neighborhood superiority, and first crack at the few available good jobs, than to blandly accept day-labor drudgery that pays wages so low that the people in them can be assured of a lifelong sentence to poverty, with little expectation of parole for good behavior. Besides, gang membership cultivates a sense of belonging to something bigger than oneself. Intent on observing their gang's rituals to the letter, the boys swagger instead of walk when traveling in a group, even if their closeness results in being treated like outcasts by their elders, who increasingly regard them as miscreants on their way to becoming full-fledged criminals. Unflinching loyalty, the ultimate test of maleness, finally leads to hubris and from there to both gang leaders' downfall.

The youngsters' parents are never seen and rarely heard, clearly indicating that the story is about the younger generation, the future, if you will. It is similarly clear that the parents, having lost all hope of changing the world, are content merely to survive in it. *West Side Story*'s adult family members are well versed in the struggle to make ends meet, fully aware that their livelihood, maybe even their lives, depends on non-involvement in the hostility that accompanies the decay of a once vibrant neighborhood.

Victor Gangelin's sets perfectly project the woeful downfall of the territory. Lining each side of the streets, pock-marked with cracks and crevices, are columns of graffiti-laden tenements hooked together like unsold cookie boxes deteriorating on grocery store shelves, not a daylight of difference identifying one block from the other. Security for the Jets is found in an isolated playground with a concrete floor and topped by a high wire fence. There the air crackles with the snapping of the boys' fingers in unison with a rhythmic beat expressing their solidarity and defiance, their endless search for self-esteem invigorated by collaborating on the latest plot to whip their rivals in open warfare.

The dialogue of necessity is only semi-realistic; tight censorship permitted no obscenities, unquestionably in vogue, then as now, when two sets of angry young men square off.

Like the 75 rough-and-ready American prisoners of war crammed into the seedy *Stalag 17* (1953), who express their animosity only through facial contortions and macho jaw-to-jaw confrontations, no one utters the four-letter words so common to later screenplays. A certain shock value is derived from the boys' milder streetspeak expletives, since at the time such terms of nonendearment as "spic," "wop," and "polock" carried almost as much force as any curse word in the language. The argot, however, does date the picture by the frequent use of such dead-language words as "chicks" for female groupies and "Daddy-O" for the allegedly glamorous take-charge gang leader.

Bitterness and Tragedy Unrelieved. Like no other Hollywood musical, *West Side Story* succeeds in projecting the starkest picture of slum life. Its overriding depiction of futility is unrelieved by any Panglossian sheen suggesting that, given time, relations between the two gangs will improve. Only the filmed *Cabaret* rivals it in closing all exits of escape from despair. Exemplary in their roles are Russ Tamblyn as Riff, the leader of the Jets, George Chakiris as Bernardo, his counterpart in the Sharks organization, Richard Beymer as Tony, and, above all the others, Rita Moreno as Anita. The film is one of the very few in which three of the leading characters depend on outside singers to dub their voices: the ever-reliable Marni Nixon (for Natalie Wood), Jimmy Bryant (for Richard Beymer), and Betty Wand (for Rita Moreno).

The thundering ensemble dancing, ranging in popular tempos from be-bop to mambo, is the most virile seen on the screen since the "June Is Busting Out All Over" routine in *Carousel*. It is executed with all the panache and excitement that signaled Jerome Robbins's mastery at transferring the rhythm of the streets to the eyes as well as to the ears, a choreographic wonder that never fails to add to the impact of the music rather than detract from it. In many ways, the dancers of both sexes serve as a Greek chorus, with their gyrations commenting on the unstable relationship between the two gangs. Two of Leonard Bernstein's instrumentals are particularly effective as metaphors for New York while interpreting each gang's inner rage at its

rivals: "The Dance at the Gym," which appears as a violent prelude to the high school dance, and "The Rumble," during which the Jets exhibit their martial arts powers on their way to the fatal gang war under a highway bridge.

Natalie Wood, who began her film career at the age of five in *Happy Land* in 1943, is successful in the role of the pretty and ever-hopeful Maria. Fondly remembered at the time as the little girl in the Christmas classic *Miracle on 34th Street* (1947), she surprised critics of her supposed lack of emotional maturity in dramatic parts. Nominated twice for the Academy Award for best actress (for *Rebel Without a Cause*, 1955, and *Splendor in the Grass*, 1961), and again in the post–*West Side Story* year of 1963 for *Love with the Proper Stranger*, she nonetheless saw her reputation sullied by the Harvard Lampoon's instituting the annual "Natalie Wood Award," an unwarranted and egregiously insulting "honor" that the publication bestowed for a short time on the actress who, according to its editors, turned in the worst screen performance of the year.

Maria was her most illuminating role, forceful in recounting the life of a young maiden—a reincarnation of Shakespeare's Juliet Montague—who, as the sister of a Shark, has the misfortune of falling in love with a Jet bearing a strong identity with Romeo Capulet. At 23, she had enough of the "little girl" left in her to captivate practically any male at first sight, especially with her rendition of such songs as the lilting "I Feel Pretty."

Miss Wood (dead at the age of 43 in 1981) displays adequate virtuosity as actress and dancer in *West Side Story*. Her mother was a ballet dancer, and the child began taking lessons when she was little more than two years old. In *West Side Story* her sedate dancing is far more ornamental than frenzied, differing greatly from the boys' fiercely aggressive movements that symbolize their release from tension that is stifling their individuality. Miss Nixon's dubbing blends seamlessly into the persona of Maria. Hers is a sweet voice, clear as a bell and perfectly cadenced whether the song is lilting or dramatic.

West Side Story has been termed an American opera by, among others, New York critics

Will Crutchfield and Clive Barnes. There is little doubt that the stage and film versions conform to a quasi-operatic format, even if the descriptive adjective "popular" usually precedes the word. As much as any other American work, including Maxwell Anderson and Kurt Weill's 1949 masterpiece, *Lost in the Stars*, based on Alan Paton's insightful novel of South African life in the apartheid era, *Cry the Beloved Country*, and Gershwin's *Porgy and Bess*, *West Side Story* represented another attempt at writing opera American-style. Based on the 1927 play by DeBose and Dorothy Heyward, the all-black Gershwin "folk" opera is set in another slum called Catfish Row. Also an innovative work, it was far less commercially successful in 1935 than Bernstein's was in 1957. The latter's score emulates Gershwin's by alternating passionate and lyrical romantic ballads, and in the minds of some persons surpasses it. Many of both composers' songs, appropriate to be designated arias, developed into hits. Bernstein's in particular sound all the more beautiful by being performed against a background of environmental chaos with the potential of destroying the residents of a besieged Manhattan community. Indeed, the greatest achievement of the Bernstein work is how aptly the music acts as tender counterpoint to the ugly and brutal scenes that surround the songs.

Composer Bernstein, a man of wide-ranging and inestimable musical skills who was convinced that American opera would one day emerge from the Broadway musical theater, had planned to write the lyrics as well as the music. When it became apparent that the combined task would prove to be formidable, Stephen Sondheim was hired to supply the words. Selecting Sondheim as collaborator was an extraordinarily lucky break, for the young man—he was then 27, Bernstein 39—had already acquired what amounted to genius at fitting superb lyrics to music. Although he had written music for several minor Broadway productions before 1957, it was with lyrics that he excelled, earning the still-valid reputation as one of the best wordsmiths in the business. He subsequently provided the lyrics for Jule Styne's *Gypsy* and Richard Rodgers's *Do I Hear a Waltz?* (1965).

Like Frank Loesser, an earlier lyricist (mostly with Paramount Pictures) who during World War II took on the added burden of writing music as well, Sondheim successfully tackled both assignments after his final collaborative venture, the forgettable *Mad Show* (1966), with music by Mary Rodgers, daughter of composer Richard. His new show, the perennial favorite *A Funny Thing Happened on the Way to the Forum*, opened in 1962. This most progressive of Broadway's post-modern composers went on to lay claim to Tony awards for *Pacific Overtures* (1967); *A Little Night Music* (1973), made into a film in 1977; *Sweeney Todd* (1979); the Pulitzer Prize-winning *Sunday in the Park with George* (1984); *Into the Woods* (1987); and *Passion* (1994). *Company* (1970), his most engaging musical comedy of manners, points up the emptiness of the lives of the affluent, while *Follies* (1971) which contains the least typical but most delightful of his songs, revived the Ziegfeld tradition for contemporary audiences by centering on the reunion of three veteran chorus girls who had first met while dancing in the "Weismann Follies," produced on Broadway by the fictitious Dimitri Weismann.

Like most of his contemporaries, Sondheim has only infrequently written songs for the movies, among them the background score for *Stavisky* and *Reds*. His "Sooner or Later (I Always Get My Man)," from *Dick Tracy*, was voted best screen song of 1990. Bernstein, a one-time professor of music at Brandeis University and Charles Elliot Norton professor of poetry at Harvard, his alma mater, amassed a résumé of musical activities rivaling those of composing great Victor Herbert. He was regular or guest conductor of numerous concert orchestras, including the New York Philharmonic, which he also served as its first American-born musical director beginning in 1958, conductor of the Metropolitan, LaScala, and Vienna State opera orchestras, and composer of a lengthy series of instrumental works, including a sonata for clarinet and one-act opera, symphonies, song cycles, chamber music, a ballet (*Dybbuk*), and a mass.

In 1944 he wrote the music for Jerome Robbins's ballet *Fancy Free*, which later that year evolved into the wartime musical hit *On the Town*, which was made into a film in 1949. Bernstein's next scores were for Broadway's *Wonderful Town* (1953), better known under its source title of *My Sister Eileen*, and then Lillian Hellman's dramatization of Voltaire's *Candide* (1956), recently revived to great acclaim in New York. Three years prior to the Broadway opening of *West Side Story*, Bernstein provided Hollywood with the background score for *On the Waterfront*. Dissonant to the extreme for a mid–1950s movie, the electrifying music wielded a powerful influence on other composers of background scores, as well as on his own *West Side Story*. Dispensing with the traditional lyrical and romantic style, Bernstein opted for the sometimes harmonic complexities of contemporary concert hall music to undergird the discordant labor union-management relations that form the backbone of the text. The result was a seminal, if underappreciated, musical achievement.

One of only three nominated musical film with its credits appearing at the end rather than the beginning, *West Side Story* is especially noted for its prelude, which consists of a high-level overview of New York, swooping north from the Battery at the foot of Manhattan until it zooms onto an Upper West Side playground and its congregation of Jets. Apparently, little attention was paid to logical progression; the Empire State Building, for example, appears twice, in one instance before the Equitable Life Building at 120 Broadway, fully 60 blocks to the south. The sequence was created by Saul Bass, a graphic designer much respected for creating visceral, iconic images that enlivened the rolling of 42 sets of credits, beginning with the grotesquely deconstructed arm that identified *The Man with the Golden Arm* in 1955. Unfortunately, Bass' style was carried to excess by such a "title decorator" as Maurice Binder, whose artwork introducing *Charade* was a jumble of color streaks and letters signifying little.

On the Verge of Chaos. Considering all the simmering hatred over territorial poaching that inevitably erupts into violence, threats of revenge, and clandestine meetings between the lovers, *West Side Story* continues to impress as a marvel of compression. Only about 30 hours elapse between the first and the final scenes. But within that short period, the lives of the central characters are irrevocably changed for the worse, and the strife that had divided the neighborhood gangs into armed camps, far from being settled amicably, gives every indication of continuing well into the future.

The Jets' inflexible determination to retain oversight of their little strip of urban decay despite the aggressiveness of the newcomer Sharks to gain a foothold comes into sharp focus in the opening scene. Led by Russ Tamblyn (Riff), the jaunty, fair-skinned Jets delight in menacing the outnumbered Sharks, chasing even their swarthy leader, George Chakiris (Bernardo), from their domain. The boys' raucousness is quickly quieted by the appearance of Simon Oakland (Lt. Shrank) and William Bramley (Officer Krupke), ever on the lookout to quell the one incendiary incident that will act as the fuse for igniting widespread juvenile mayhem.

More tolerant of the Jets than the Sharks, whom Oakland consistently derogates by referring to them as "you people," both lawmen abandon pleading for the suspension of hostilities by demanding it. After asserting their congenital dislike of all restraints on independence of movement, Tamblyn and his buddies adopt the code of silence regarding their plans while feigning compliance. The lawmen's departure fails to pacify the Jets, however, and Tamblyn resorts to typical braggadocio by proposing that he confront Shark leader Chakiris, the brother of Natalie Wood (Maria), that night during a "get-together" dance in the high school gymnasium and schedule an "all-out rumble" to settle once and for all the question of which gang will rule as king of the hill.

Although Tamblyn prefers slugging it out with fists rather than with knives and guns, he bows to the insistence of his more lethal-minded associates by agreeing to leave the choice of weapons up to the Sharks. He and his gang then celebrate with mass exhilaration what they believe is their cultural and battlefield superiority by dancing and singing their ferocious anthem, "Jet Song," in the playground before sauntering unopposed into the streets, every boy eagerly pledging fidelity to the group's sense of superiority.

Tamblyn first visits his best friend, Richard Beymer (Tony), a handsome and sensitive young man who has quit the Jets but retains his reputation as the supreme neighborhood toughie. Tamblyn hopes to enlist him in the cause, but Beymer has reformed to such an extent that he now works at Doc's soda and candy shop. But his fondness for Tamblyn, who lives with his family, clouds his better judgment, resulting in his reluctant acceptance of the latter's invitation to attend the dance that night and participate in what Tamblyn terms a "war council." Although his job is menial, Tony looks upon it as an entry-level position that could very well lead to advancement and eventual passport out of the neighborhood. In fact, as he discloses in the forceful soliloquy "Something's Coming," he anticipates a miracle, of something truly great, coming his way as compensation for deciding to better himself through respectable means instead of bashing Puerto Ricans.

At the dance, chaperoned by Officer Bramley, Beymer meets Natalie, looking prim and proper in a spotless white dress, whom he instantly regards as a vision of sweetly innocent loveliness. She is similarly spellbound by the young man, so much so that brother Chakiris takes offense at the couple's obvious mutual attraction and orders her date, José DeVega (Chino), to take her home. Eager to set a time and place to hold the war council, Tamblyn and his Jets once again snap their fingers as a prelude to their provocative and vigorous anti-Shark dance, which is answered in kind, signaling each gang's contempt for the other. The result is the forging of an agreement to meet later that night at Doc's to set the time and place for the rumble.

Beymer, meanwhile, has left the gym to follow Natalie home at a safe distance. As he walks along, he sings of his love for her in "Maria," one of the most beautiful songs ever sung from a sound track. To him the name sounds like a word in a prayer, and he speaks it with reverence. He is happy to affirm that the undefined miracle he had forecast in "Something's Coming" really has arrived, not in the guise of a promotion or unexpected offer for a white-collar position, but in meeting Natalie. She is now as vital to his happiness as life itself, the only sight he sees, or cares to see, wherever he goes, even when they are apart. The ballad has yet to be surpassed as a declaration of love immediate and everlasting, sacred rather than profane, so all-consuming as to defy any im-

pediment to its fulfillment short of death itself. The dark of the late evening sky, however, suggests not only that their love is imperiled, but also that any lessening of the mutual antagonism between Jets and Sharks is similarly a lost cause.

It is left to Rita Moreno (Anita), the girlfriend of Chakiris and co-worker of Natalie's in Madam Lucia's dress shop, to sing rooftop praises to her adopted country from the perspective of a Puerto Rican whose parents had emigrated to the mainland hoping to find opportunity and security. That is all Anita wants, too, and despite the disappointments she has encountered, she regards the United States as a multistranded tapestry of various nationalities rather than a synthetic carpet of whites only. She prefers the Island of Manhattan to the Island of Puerto Rico, she insists to Chakiris and his Shark supporters, describing her native land as an ugly place plagued with disease and hurricanes and flying bullets.

The song strongly implies that Anita's good humor and unassailable confidence will in time combine to move her into a higher echelon of society. Even now, her optimism likens her to the hardy Allanthus altissma, the "tree of heaven" that made its film debut in *A Tree Grows in Brooklyn* (1945). Typically crammed into small patches of dirt dug at the edges of sidewalks throughout much of the five boroughs, the wiry tree stubbornly lives a desperate life as a symbol of big-city survival, capable of blooming even though rooted in cement and weathering all sorts of disabuse while hectically hanging on to life.

The exceptional Sondheim lyric Anita sings in the lively Latin-tinged "America" clearly identifies the United States as the true Miss America, a strikingly attractive land willing to bestow comfort, hope, and material possessions on all enterprising newcomers to its shores. In short, she maintains, despite its flaws, which can be overcome, America is okay with her. And wouldn't it be nice if everyone else, above all the Sharks and Jets, strove to achieve more than just control of the turf they are forced to share. They will not, however, and one Shark after the other demeans her assessment of America as a magnificent country with denigrations designed to deflate her patriotism. The country is indeed a land of freedom and opportunity, two boys interject, but only if you happen to have been born white. Those who were not are indeed free, but only to work at dead-end jobs at substandard wages and seek opportunities where none exists.

Tony and Natalie's next meeting, held later that night in seclusion in the alley behind her flat, brings the film's analogy to Shakespeare's *Romeo and Juliet* to its most recognizable point. A masterpiece of irony, the gracefully stylized scene emerges as a testament to the powerful love the two youngsters now share. Centuries earlier, Shakespeare had immortalized the "sweet sorrow" of his lovers' parting in the moonlight with some of the most compellingly romantic lines ever written. The *West Side Story* lovers' goodnight is commemorated in their duet of "Tonight," another superlative song, actually a Valentine in which each affirms undying devotion to the other from that night forward. Performed near the fire escape of the dingy tenement instead of on the balcony of a princely mansion, the lyrical yet dramatic song aptly compensates for the film's overall lack of Shakespearean gentility in the same way that Robbins's explosive ballet sequences are used to contrast with the pomp and ceremoniousness of the Shakespearean drama.

Into the Fray. Congregated near Doc's, the agitated Jets await the arrival of their enemies and confirmation of the time and site of the rumble. Instead of the Sharks, however, it is the familiar police lieutenant and patrolman who show up to order the boys to call off the forthcoming battle and go home. The youngsters' response is to nod in agreement and then, once the adults leave the scene, to ridicule the law in the outrageously satirical "Gee, Officer Krupke." Embellished with a sharp twin-edged lyric, the mock-heroic song belittles the typical "tough cop" who spends his time pushing kids around instead of putting his life on the line by tracking down career criminals.

Cleverly invoking victimization as the source of their delinquency, the boys poke unbridled fun at the same social doctrine seriously espoused in the thirties by Warner Bros. and, to a lesser degree, other Hollywood studios in such films as *Dead End*, *Angels with*

Dirty Faces, and *Dust Be My Destiny*—namely, that it is the environment rather than their heritage that is to blame for the infractions committed by impoverished juveniles. They are really good boys, the Jets protest with sarcasm. They exist at the bottom rung of the social ladder, and that is where they are expected to remain. Good intentions are meaningless in an indifferent society that has even deprived them of parental love and guidance. Misunderstood and therefore misjudged, they have developed into misfits in need of psychoanalysis and consequently in no way responsible for their corrosive behavior.

When the Sharks appear, Tamblyn issues the challenge for a rumble, which Chakiris promptly accepts. The lone dissenter is Beymer, who is further anguished when the combatants choose rocks, rather than just fists, as the chief weapons. The rumble is scheduled for after dark the next day under a nearby highway bridge. Before the gang members disassemble, Lt. Oakland returns alone in hopes of diffusing the anger he knows will lead to open combat. Announcing that he is tired of keeping "hooligans in line," he insists that someone tell him where the rumored rumble is to take place. He is ignored, however, as is Ned Glass (Doc), who displays more reason than spleen while advising the boys that their so-called final all-out rumble will not result in permanent victory, but rather invite later challenges to dethrone the winner.

The suspense generated by the impending brawl is temporarily suspended by the reappearance of Natalie, who is primping and preening in front of a full-figure mirror in the dress shop in anticipation of her date with Beymer. "I Feel Pretty," she sings delightedly to Rita, who agrees with her assessment, although her nervousness over the forthcoming rumble tempers her enthusiasm. When Beymer arrives, Rita implores him to stop the fight before it starts in only a few hours. Not in favor with the Jets because of his recent absences from their meetings, he nonetheless promises to do what he can.

Now alone in the shop, Natalie and Beymer in effect marry themselves by reciting the traditional marriage vow, promising to take each other as partners for life. Their spoken words culminate in the beautiful wedding song,

"One Hand, One Heart," which each pledges to the other till death do them part.

The scene shifts to the site of the rumble, where the showdown is preceded by the appearance of peacemaker Beymer, hoping to forestall the fight before it starts. But he is too late, and his argument too weak; neither gang is willing to forfeit what it believes will be a clear-cut victory. Tamblyn nominates Tucker Smith (Ice) to engage in hand-to-hand combat with Shark Chakiris. When it seems that he is gaining the upper hand, Tamblyn boldly enters the combat, only to be stabbed to death by Chakiris. Distraught by the death of his close friend, and tormented by Chakiris's taunting him for alleged cowardliness, Beymer picks up the discarded knife and kills him in the free-for-all that suddenly breaks out. Members of both gangs finally flee the scene at the sound of a police siren in the distance.

While awaiting Beymer's arrival, Natalie is joined on her tenement roof by DeVega, her one-time boyfriend, who tells her that Beymer has killed her brother. She refuses to believe him, but later, when Beymer appears on the roof, he admits the killing and begs her forgiveness. In desperation to retain her love, which Natalie is actually unwilling to withhold, he vows to take her away from the "lousy world" of their neighborhood.

Exactly where they will go is uncertain, just "Somewhere," far away in some dream world that Beymer believes does exist. Another four-star love song, "Somewhere" is a worthy rival to "Over the Rainbow" as a wishful appeal for escape into new surroundings free from the troubles of the present. In it the lovers cast aside the glum and forbidding world they have known. It is time for a change of site to a peaceful place where they can live and love together, a brave new world of endless light, shining like a star that not even clouds are allowed to dim. Their vow to find such a paradise, however, does not guarantee the absence of further trouble from upsetting their plan. For now they must part, Beymer to borrow money from Doc to pay the expenses of their escape to "somewhere," Natalie to await the appointed time to meet him at Doc's and accompany him to the bus terminal and freedom.

Reassembled in a parking lot to consider how to respond to Tamblyn's murder, the Jets vote to resume the rumble. They are deterred, however, by Tucker Smith, who, in "Cool," wisely counsels against stirring up more trouble by looking for it. The time has come to conclude an armistice, not to resume the warfare, he argues. Since Smith is evidently the dominant Jet since the death of Tamblyn, the other gang members are willing to accept his advice, and they trudge disconsolately back to Doc's.

While Natalie prepares to join Beymer, Rita angrily expresses her contempt for him by singing the diatribe "A Boy Like That." She questions how her friend Natalie could possibly love Beymer, her brother's killer. Equally destructive of continuing their courtship, she adds, is the fact that he is neither a Puerto Rican nor a Shark. Forget him, she urges, and find another lover of her "own kind." Natalie refuses, maintaining in the second half of the two-part song that "I Have a Love" whom she will never desert, regardless of his nationality or the pain he has inflicted on her. And his name is Tony.

Seeking refuge from Shark marauders and the police, Beymer hides in Doc's cellar. Rita, sent by Natalie to tell Beymer that she is on her way to meet him, instead delivers a message of her own. Still incensed at Chakiris's murder, and disgusted at the verbal and physical abuse meted out to her by a small band of Jets in the store, this normally cheerful young woman concocts a falsehood as her revenge. DeVega, she tells the boys, had become jealous after learning of Natalie's love for Beymer and killed her. Then Rita, having proved that even she is susceptible of contracting the virus of hate, leaves the store in disgust.

Dazed at overhearing the news, Beymer emerges from Doc's, determined to avenge his sweetheart's death. Rushing along back alleys and shouting out DeVega's name, he runs into Natalie, then on her way to Doc's. Relieved of despair over her rumored death, and no longer interested in finding DeVega, Beymer embraces her in a paroxysm of happiness. They are spotted by DeVega, who shoots Beymer in the back. He dies in Natalie's arms.

Grabbing the gun from DeVega, the usually mild-mannered girl appears ready and willing to shoot him or anyone else who interferes with her farewell to her lover. Holding the weapon firmly with both hands, she turns from DeVega to a scattering of sullen members of both gangs who have been silently observing the drama. Unable to pull the trigger, she drops the gun to the pavement. Tears falling from her face as a signal of her desperation to comprehend the reason for the loss of both brother and sweetheart, she slumps to the side of the dead young man who never again will speak another word of love to her. Unlike the Shakespeare play, this Juliet does not also die. There is no reason for her suicide. Beymer's death has drained all the life out of her, leaving her dead emotionally, wedded only to memories of the unrecoverable past.

Slowly, the gang members file out of the parking lot. No pedestrians are walking the streets, no noise disturbs the ominous quiet. The Jets' and Sharks' turbulent little corner of the world is temporarily at rest.

The Music Man (1962)

A Warner Bros. picture. DIRECTOR: Morton Da Costa; ASSISTANT: Russell Llewellen. PRODUCER: Morton Da Costa. PRODUCTION SUPERVISOR: Joel Freeman. SCREENWRITER: Marion Hargrove. CINEMATOGRAPHER: Robert Burks. FILM EDITOR: William Ziegler. CHOREOGRAPHER: Onna White; ASSISTANT: Tom Panko. ART DIRECTOR: Paul Groesse. SET DECORATOR: George James Hopkins. SOUND: M.A. Merrick and Dolph Thomas. COSTUMES: Dorothy Jeakins. MAKEUP: Gordon Bau. HAIR STYLIST: Jean Burt Reilly; MISS JONES'S HAIRSTYLES: Myri Stoltz. MUSIC SUPERVISOR AND CONDUCTOR: Ray Heindorf. ORCHESTRATORS: Ray Heindorf, Frank Comstock, and Gus Levene. VOCAL ARRANGEMENTS: Charles Henderson. RUNNING TIME: 2 hours, 31 minutes. *Principal Players*: Robert Preston (Harold Hill). Shirley Jones (Marian Paroo). Buddy Hackett (Marcellus Washburn). Hermione Gingold (Eulalie MacKechnie Shinn). Paul Ford (Mayor Shinn). Pert Kelton (Mrs. Paroo). Ronnie Howard (Winthrop Paroo). The "Buffalo Bills" (Olin Britt, Ewart Dunlop, Oliver Hix, and Jacey Squires). *Major Academy Award*: Best Scoring. *Nominations*: Best Picture; Film Editing; Art Direction; Costumes; Sound.

The disreputable character that actor James Woods plays in *Diggstown* (1992) most likely never heard of "Professor" Harold (*né* Gregory) Hill, but he makes a valid distinction between a con man and a hustler. According to Woods, a hustler is a loner who bamboozles a trusting soul and quickly leaves town. The con artist is the gregarious type who bilks a whole community of innocents and then sets up housekeeping there, sometimes becoming one of its most respected residents. The former has little personality; the latter is so engaging that his charm easily conceals his total lack of scruples, permitting him to project absolute sincerity while pilfering whatever it is he is after.

The extroverted, people-friendly Mr. Hill, the non-professorial protagonist in Meredith Willson's Tony Award-winning *The Music Man*, remains the best-known and cleverest confidence man ever to practice his wiles on the screen after perfecting them on the Broadway stage, where the musical ran for 1,375 exuberant performances. The holder of an advance degree in film-flamnery. He is smooth as silk, slippery as an eel, and glib as a carnival barker. So adept is he at his nefarious calling that he most likely could sell the Brooklyn Bridge to the mayor of New York in the morning and a case of snake oil to a physician that evening.

Like *Hello, Dolly!*, *The Music Man* is a rather late celluloid reminder that once upon a time both stage and screen musicals existed solely to amuse. The plots and dialogue were silly, all but the leading characters forgettable, the incidents predictable. The difference between the failures and successes depended almost wholly on the stars, acting, and songs.

Turned down by both Danny Kaye and Gene Kelly, the part of the Music Man was handed over to Robert Preston, a highly talented substitute who had portrayed the trickster to perfection 883 times and won his own Tony in the process. It is doubtful that without Preston, *The Music Man* would have achieved distinction on either coast, and certainly no best picture nomination, for the goings-on are definitely too slight to sustain its length. Not even W.C. Fields, a master manipulator of people and events, as in *You Can't Cheat an Honest Man* (1939) and *Never Give a Sucker an Even Break* (1941), could have been more convincing as the fast-talking, larcenous scalawag hoping to win converts to his get-rich-quick scheme by preaching bogus moral sermons.

With Preston hopping about the stage, the corny as Kansas in August plot created a major stir on Broadway by recreating the ambience of hinterland America in 1912. Woven into its

Leading the band from the high school to the main street of River City, Iowa, to the foot-thumping beat of "Seventy-Six Trombones," is Robert Preston, the sly salesman in *The Music Man*.

fabric were several very good songs in a variety of rhythms, including interludes of novelty barbershop quartet numbers, sung by the "Buffalo Bills" (who appeared in both stage and screen versions) to an unseen lady named "Lida Rose." The star's poignant rendition of the ballad "Till There Was You" is excellent; his zippy rendition of the lively "Seventy Six Trombones," a throwback, perhaps, to Willson's early years with John Philip Sousa's U.S. Marine Band, is made even more joyous by Preston's nimbleness at prancing in march tempo. Only two songs were cut from the Broadway score: "My White Knight" and the very pretty "It's You."

Like Edward G. Robinson as Little Caesar, Errol Flynn as Robin Hood, and James Cagney as George M. Cohan, Preston was born to play the personable fraud who takes advantage of the gullible people of River City, Iowa, including the mayor's wife. As rugged and wavy-haired a scoundrel as Howard Keel, Preston

had the benefit of a well-rounded movie career long before taking on the part of Hill on Broadway in 1957.

He had become a film favorite in 1939, and for the next 18 years played a wide variety of he-man roles mostly for Paramount. Best remembered as the self-sacrificing bugler brother in *Beau Geste* and Brian Donlevy's fellow conspirator in *Union Pacific*, he was also a lawman (*North West Mounted Police*), adventurer (*Reap the Wild Wind*), soldier (*Wake Island*), and cowboy (*Tulsa*). He was never given the opportunity to sing a single song, nor did he ever rise above second- or third-place billing—until *The Music Man*. Preston sings six of the show's songs in a voice best described as adequate but marvelously effective, earning him another singing role on Broadway opposite Mary Martin in *I Do! I Do!* in 1966. At 64 in 1982, he clearly proved that age had not diminished his talent by taking on the role of Toddy in Leslie

Bricusse and Henry Mancini's *Victor/Victoria* with customary gusto.

Set in the kind of pretty, leafy small midwestern town that Booth Tarkington wrote about and 1930s movie comedies like *Theodora Goes Wild* (1936) took place in, *The Music Man* is light as air and bright as sunshine. It also contains most of the standard characters that had peopled Hollywood's bucolic musical comedies for decades. The outgoing outsider is there, as are the gossipy women, the fatuous politician, the shy girl and effervescent boy lover, and the "I'm from Missouri," show-me townsfolk wary of cottoning up to strangers. Also typical is the on-and-off love affair between the crafty outsider and the girl next door, who must patch up their differences just in time for everything to wind up on a happy note.

Shirley Jones is appealing as Preston's librarian lover, played by Barbara Cook on Broadway, proving that her Academy Award-winning performance as a prostitute, of all things, in *Elmer Gantry* (1960) had not affected her prowess at projecting the unassailable wholesomeness that had catapulted her to stardom as Laurie in *Oklahoma!* and Julie in *Carousel*. Appearing in his third film was eight-year-old Ron(ny) Howard, and a fine job he does, lisp and all, as Shirley Jones's younger brother, Winthrop, and with Preston the co-singer of "Gary, Indiana." He is best remembered, of course, as Opie on television's *The Andy Griffith Show* and as Richie in *Happy Days*, and currently as an accomplished film director. Performing their usual subsidiary roles in competent fashion are Charles Lane as the sheriff and Mary Wickes as a society matron. The bearers of two of the screen's most familiar faces, each appeared in scores of films, Lane most notably as the confused federal income tax agent in *You Can't Take It with You* (1938), and Miss Wickes as Monte Woolley's harried nurse in *The Man Who Came to Dinner* (1941).

The rest of the cast caricatures are similarly rooted in tradition, although not so humorous as they undoubtedly were meant to be. Hermione Gingold as the mayor's foppish wife fails to measure up in any way to her role as Leslie Caron's grandmother in *Gigi*. Paul Ford, whose raspy voice and W.C. Fields–like demeanor seemed to make him the ideal choice

to play the blustery mayor of River City, becomes tiresome by constantly falling into memory and speech lapses after being hoodwinked. He descends into a prime example of precocious senility rather than domineer as the bemused champion of moral integrity. Buddy Hackett, as Preston's long-time confidant, likewise fails to amuse, and his singing and dancing to "Shipoopi" are so poorly executed that he appears more foolish than funny.

The picture itself is much too long (except when Preston appears in the scenes), and many of the incidents could have been excised without detriment. For all of its movement, *The Music Man* fails to progress very far very fast. Repetitions of incident are plentiful, and much of the dialogue is little more than unnecessary and unrevealing padding. But yes, the film does have an infectious cakes and ale flavoring that can easily lull the defenseless viewer into disregarding every single one of its faults.

If ever the packaging of a Broadway—and Hollywood—musical depended almost exclusively on the talents of but two persons, it was *The Music Man*. The lion's share of the creative credit belongs of course to Preston, and to Meredith Willson, a native of Mason City, Iowa, who wrote the script from a story he had co-authored with Franklin Lacey, as well as the lyrics and music. An accomplished instrumentalist and songwriter, he played first flute with the Sousa band in 1921–23 and then with the New York Philharmonic from 1924 to 1929. Composer of two symphonies and other instrumental works, he also wrote three big independent song hits—"You and I," "Two in Love," and "May the Good Lord Bless and Keep You"— as well as six World War II songs, including "And Still the Volga Flows," adapted from Rachmaninoff's *Second Piano Concerto*.

In the late–thirties, Willson served as musical director for *Maxwell House Coffee Time* (You and I" was its themesong), and his orchestra also appeared on *The Big Show*, one of radio's last variety programs. A noted wit like bandleader Ray Noble, the composer of "The Very Thought of You" and supplier of the music for the *Burns and Allen* and *Edgar Bergen and Charlie McCarthy* radio shows, Willson frequently added a touch of humor by delivering wisecracks in a soft, nonchalant Dennis Day tone, wrongly suggesting that the irony lying below the surface of his remarks was unintentional. Beginning his movie career about the same time as Preston, he was twice nominated for the Academy Award for his background scores for Chaplin's *The Great Dictator* (1940) and *The Little Foxes* (1941). His second big stage musical, *The Unsinkable Molly Brown* (1959), was also made into a film five years after its Broadway debut and starred Debbie Reynolds, who received an Oscar nomination for her performance in the title role.

When Willson teamed up with Robert Preston for *The Music Man*, its success was as certain as the fact that it was God who made all those little green apples, as Preston himself verifies in a line from "Seventy Six Trombones." Why he did not receive an Academy Award nomination as best actor is, as Yul Brynner might have phrased it, "a puzzlement."

Fox in the Chicken Coop. Asked by a fellow traveling salesman on the train pulling into River City, Iowa, where he is going, Robert Preston (Harold Hill) replies, "Wherever the people are as green as the money." Successfully concealing his identity while the rest of the men denounce his unsavory activities in a patter song, the "Professor" gets off the train in the hope that picturesque but sleepy-time River City, population 4,412, fits the bill as a community of unsophisticated, uncomplicated folks who prefer to pay cash on the barrel head for whatever goods they can be talked into buying. Preston has an intense dislike of extending credit. Installment payments stretch out the time needed for him to collect the money for his services and equipment, delaying his typical hasty exit.

Undoubtedly, Preston is a top-drawer salesman, but one who relies on deceit and counterfeit sincerity to sway doubters into customers. His specialty is setting up boys' bands, which has afforded him a comfortable living by promising to supply the kiddies with brass instruments, instruction books, and uniforms. The only problem arising from his efforts is his inability to read a single note of music—and his custom of skipping town before the goods arrive with pockets bulging with unearned coin of the realm. The victims of his thievery are the

parents and later salesmen, who are automatically placed on the hit list of every town they follow him into. But then, none of them matches Preston's charm, enthusiasm, or proficiency at distinguishing the sucker from the suspicious, and so they probably deserved expulsion.

Eager to peddle his wares in River City, Preston is snubbed by everyone he meets, an unexpected occurrence that the folks themselves try to ameliorate by bursting into the welcoming but warning song "Iowa Stubborn." They are that, they aver, as well as curt, but they are also generous to a fault when it comes to extending hospitality to strangers who pose no threat to their placid existence. Pleased at hearing their self-analysis, Preston fortifies his decision to remain in town when he runs into Buddy Hackett (Marcellus Washburn), a slicker from Brooklyn who used to shill with him in bygone days. Now an assistant in the town's livery stable, Hackett has presumably "gone legitimate" and settled down in River City. But he remains ever on the lookout for easy money, and one surmises that he can be enticed into reviving the partnership at the drop of a foolproof caper.

Later that night, Preston greets the news that the town's only billiard parlor has installed a pool table as the perfect excuse to launch his campaign for a boys' band. Circulating among the crowd in the town square, he vilifies both parlor and pool table while promoting the band as the only means of upholding the after-school morality of River City children. Without such a beneficent outlet for youthful enthusiasm, they very well might fall victim to the corrupting influence of the Pleeze-All billiard emporium, he sings. And everyone knows what that can lead to: reading dime novels, smoking cigarettes, carousing with "libertine men and scarlet women," even uttering such curse words as "swell"—each of them representing giant steps "on the road to degradation." The letter P, as in pool, Preston cautions with the fervor of a singing evangelist, rhymes with T, and what that means is "(Ya Got) Trouble."

The song over, and his listeners in a frenzy over how to protect their children, Preston spies the "maiden lady" librarian and part-time piano teacher, Shirley Jones (Marian Paroo), walking through the square on her way home.

She has had a tough day at the job, spending much of it defending such books and authors as *The Rubaiyat of Omar Khayyam* and Rabelais, Chaucer, and Balzac to Hermione Gingold (Eulalie MacKechnie Shinn), who regards their works as pure smut that should not be allowed shelf space in the library. That her husband, Mayor Shinn, played by Paul Ford, owns the billiard parlor, which Preston had earlier defined as the "devil's playground," is of no interest to Hermione. Far more important to her is her role as the town's first lady and avocation as its morality weathervane, ever alert to judging which way the winds of misconduct are blowing.

Although initially tough nuts to crack, the Shinns will eventually succumb to Preston's offer to provide the town with its most "desperate need"—a band. Hermione is victimized by his flattery when he appoints her chairwoman of the Ladies Auxiliary for the Classical Dance, a post that allows her to perform the lead in several terpsichorean endeavors best described as fatuous. In time, the mayor also will look kindly upon the roguish salesman, even though contrary to Ford's wishes, he abets the courtship of his daughter, Susan Luckey (Zaneeta), and Timmy Everett (Tommy Djilas), the town's chief mischief-maker.

Naturally, Shirley rejects Preston's lighthearted but irksome overtures of friendship, and dismisses him with the hauteur of a queen. She would be regarded as quite a catch by any male, but her standoffishness, usually misinterpreted as indifference, tends to scare away any would-be suitors. Such formality may be appreciated in a librarian, complains her widowed mother, played by Pert Kelton, another carryover from the Broadway production, who encourages her, in "The Piano Lesson," to defrost herself and lower her standards a bit when it comes to accepting beaus. She is, after all, well on the road to spinsterhood, Pert warns, and tempest fugit. Why not strike up a friendship with this Preston fellow, she urges; maybe he is the one for her.

Shirley is indeed very much concerned about finding a lover, as she asserts in the self-revelatory "Goodnight, My Someone," a lovely lullaby in waltz time, which she sings as a sort of appeal to the Evening Star for assistance. The die has been cast. The "someone" will undoubtedly turn out to be Preston, but how can such a prim and proper young lady ever become enamored of such an unrepentant scoundrel?

Preston becomes the beneficiary of an unexpected bonanza when he discovers that both adults and children are to participate in a patriotic show in the high school gymnasium as a prelude to celebrating the July 4 holiday. He attends the function, happily learning that a major part of it consists of quarrels among the adults over the introduction of the pool table, a controversy that Preston had already incited and instantly prods him into deepening the people's anxiety. Jumping on the makeshift stage, he sides with the protesters and repeats his assertion that a band will serve better than anything else to dispel fears that their youngsters will take the immoral road to adulthood.

Invoking the honored name of Sousa, whose long-ago appearance in River City recalls fond memories among the townsfolk, Preston segues into "Seventy Six Trombones," the biggest hit of *The Music Man* and just about the peppiest march to emanate from the Broadway stage. Dressed to the nines in a spiffy bright red bandmaster's uniform, he performs the number in outstanding fashion, so much so that the assemblage follows him out of the gymnasium onto the main street, where they gleefully march behind him. His superb salesmanship seems ready to pay off.

Shirley, however, is appalled at the carefree abandon he has injected into her usually staid neighbors. When Mayor Ford seems to favor approving Preston's band project, she expresses her disgust with anyone who would fall for such a scheme proposed by a "fly-by-night salesman." Her strong opposition finally pushes the mayor into demanding to see Preston's credentials and references to prove that he is qualified to carry the title of "professor." Rarely thrown off course by a challenge, Preston promises to acquire them from the Gary (Indiana) Conservatory of Music. Gary is his birthplace, he asserts, and he received his degree from its music college in '05.

He has still not provided his scholastic record by the time of the July Fourth festivities in Madison Park a few days later. When approached by members of the school board, played by the "Buffalo Bills," who demand to see his credentials, he again vows that they'll get them as soon as he gets them, and then cunningly avoids further discussion of the matter by chasing after Shirley. She again rebuffs him, strongly implying that she will have nothing to do with him until he provides certified proof of his musicianship.

Victory Is Nigh. Through tact, perseverance, and exaggeration, Preston wins over the rest of the townspeople, who believe his contention that any child can easily be taught to play any musical instrument. What does the trick, he tells them, is his unique "Think System." Deceptively simple, it involves acquiring the skill not through study but osmosis, something like whistling. A tune comes into the head, Preston explains, and then burrows through the lips and comes out as a whistle. No practice is needed, nor is the ability to read music. Plans for organizing the band will go ahead, he assures the impressed parents. It will take about four weeks to receive the shipments of trombones, tubas, cornets, clarinets, and piccolos, music books, and uniforms, he adds while collecting advance payments for the goods and making arrangements with Hackett for a quick getaway well before deadline time.

Only one other obstacle seems beyond solution. Preston would love to take Shirley along with him on his exit from River City, but she still regards him and his band proposal with disdain. Hackett, too, is becoming upset with him, but for a far different reason. Preston's fondness for the young librarian is quite apparent, leading Hackett to worry that he may scuttle the con game to win her love. There is no chance that will happen, Preston confides in "The Sadder-But-Wiser Girl," professing his distaste for the demure innocent. As always, the kind of girl he prefers is the worldly type with plenty of love-making experience behind her.

But his analysis of Shirley's character changes upon hearing rumors of her alleged shady past as consort to wealthy "Old Man" Madison, who upon his death had donated the library to the town and the librarian's job to Shirley, presumably in perpetuity. River City's cadre of elderly society ladies jealously condemn Shirley's trysting in "Pick-a-Little,

Talk-a-Little," in which their clacking is emulated by a cluster of hens wallowing in the dirt they scratch up from the soil beneath them.

Convinced that the ladies' scandalous comments are true, Preston redoubles his pursuit of Shirley in the library, dallying long enough one evening to woo her into falling under his spell with the catchy "Marian, the Librarian." The springboard for a dazzling full-chorus whirl-a-gig production number, the routine is the best in the film, understandably nudging Shirley into gradually reassessing her opinion of him. Preston's case is further enhanced when Mother Kelton weighs in with another appeal for Shirley to put aside her juvenile dream of finding a Prince Charming, least of all in River City, and accept him as husband. Second-best is better than nothing, she counsels, prompting her daughter to define her idea of the ideal husband in "Being in Love." He will be quiet, honest, and gentle, she points out, skipping over the fact that Preston shows none of these qualities. And, she readily admits, she has long been dreaming of such a man, and will continue to seek him out.

A few days later into River City comes the Wells Fargo Wagon, welcomed by the song of the same name, sung cheerfully by the residents in anticipation of receiving the goodies they had purchased through retailers' catalogues months earlier. Among the packages are several containing the first meager parcels of band instruments, which excites the elated spectators into believing that the band project is about to become reality. And so, it seems, is Preston and Shirley's love affair, which decidedly shows signs of blossoming after her display of warmth toward him while they share strawberry phosphates in the local soda shop.

A fly in the ointment appears that night, however, with the arrival of an anvil salesman, Harry Hickox (Charles Cowell), one of Preston's detractors in the opening train scene, who bumps into Shirley. Hearing that Preston is also in town, he proceeds to describe him as a "flim-flammer" and, even worse, a notorious ladies' man, with a girl in every port in his territory. What Harry intends to do is report Preston's presence to the mayor and have him ejected from the town forthwith. He must hurry away, he tells Shirley, because he has to catch the next train, due to depart in a matter of minutes.

Curiously, Shirley is not horrified at the salesman's defamations, but actually begins flirting with him to keep him from visiting the mayor. Harry is so encouraged by her playfulness that it is not until only moments before the train is to leave that he realizes he cannot spare the time to meet with the mayor. He races toward the station, and temporarily out of the lovers' lives. Relieved of his presence, Shirley joins the "Buffalo Bills" in addressing her infatuation with Preston in the melodious ballad "Will I Ever Tell You?" But the question is left unanswered. The time is not yet ripe for opening her heart to the brash newcomer.

Later, keeping their prearranged date on a foot bridge, River City's version of lovers' lane, Shirley and Preston duet the finest ballad in the score, the ever-beautiful "Till There Was You." It was a long wait to hear the song—two hours and seven minutes. Its bracing melody, together with Shirley's obviously enthrallment of the romance that Preston has introduced into her life, prompts him to imperil their love by exposing his true identity.

But before he can find the right words, she shushes him. She knows all about him, having discovered from checking the 1890–1910 volume of the *Indiana State Educational Journal* that Gary had not been built until '06, one year after he allegedly was graduated from its music conservatory, which did not exist in '05. As for her "liaison" with benefactor Madison, she clears the air on that one by telling Preston that he had been a close friend of her deceased father and appointed her librarian so that she could earn enough money to support her family.

Meanwhile, Hackett has been scouring the town for Preston to tell him that the good people of River City are up in arms. Salesman Harry Hickox, still in town and stubbornly vindictive, had disclosed Preston's long history of engaging in fraudulent activities, and the men have formed a posse to hunt him down. Shirley urges him to flee, which he refuses to do. A group of men catch up to the immobile Preston and demand the return of their money. Despite Shirley's spirited defense of the beleaguered love of her life, the men persist in lead-

ing him to a high school classroom, where a "trial" is to be held.

Knowing that he is guilty of all the charges lodged against him, Preston stands motionless and silent while the "jury" ponders the accusations of the duped. Suddenly, Shirley addresses the crowd. Yes, he most likely is guilty as sin, but despite, or rather because of, his chicanery he actually did a great deal of good for River City, adults and children alike. He instilled a powerful sense of pride as well as joy in them, in addition to increasing the town's "spirit and neighborliness." Why even the children's practice exercise on Beethoven's "Melody in G," about as poor a rendition as was ever played anywhere at any time, strikes the mothers and fathers as the height of professionalism. As for the kids, how proud they felt of themselves for pleasing their parents by exhibiting their musical talent. In essence, Preston gave the town something to live for, to look forward to, to cooperate in—developing a band—*their* band!

Her plea works. His vilifiers are willing to forgive, if not forget. True, Preston did furnish the children with the promised instruments, even if he did fail to provide the training to play them. A brief time passes, and Preston reappears on the outdoor steps of the school. Behind him are the band members in full uniform, instruments at the ready, alert to every wave of his baton. Having renounced his wicked ways, he is aware that only Shirley's and his own faith in his abilities will permit him to pull off his final trick. For here stands a bandleader unable to read music or conduct a bunch of musically illiterate offspring who must depend on an untested "Think System" to regale their parents and friends with a harmony of notes blown out of unfamiliar instruments.

The song they play, "Seventy-Six Trombones," not so surprisingly turns out to be a treat for the ears. Jauntily, leader and band traipse merrily down the main street to the applause of onlookers. The band project was not a swindle after all; the tune is played with remarkable precision. Over to Preston's side hurries Shirley, who holds out her hand to him. He grasps it firmly. A reformed con man he may be, but no one would be surprised if he marched again with her down the aisle of a church as a respected River City dignitary gone legitimate. James Woods was right.

Mary Poppins (1964)

A Walt Disney picture. DIRECTOR: Robert Stevenson; ASSISTANTS: Joseph L. McEveety and Paul Feiner; ANIMATION DIRECTOR: Hamilton S. Luske. CO-PRODUCER: Bill Walsh. SCREENWRITERS: Bill Walsh and Don DaGradi, "based on [three] *Mary Poppins* books by P.L. Travers." CONSULTANT: P.L. Travers. CINEMATOGRAPHER: Edward Colman; SPECIAL EFFECTS: Peter Ellenshaw, Eustace Lycett, and Robert A. Mattey. FILM EDITOR: Cotton Warburton. CHOREOGRAPHERS: Marc Breaux and Dee Dee Wood. ART DIRECTORS: Carroll Clark and William H. Tuntke; ANIMATION ART DIRECTOR: McLaren Stewart; ANIMATORS: Hal Ambro, Oliver M. Johnston, Jr., Milt Kahl, Ward Kimball, Eric Larson, John Lounsbery, Hamilton Luske, Cliff Nordberg, and Franklin Thomas. SETS: Emile Kuri and Hal Gausman; NURSERY SEQUENCE DESIGNERS: Bill Justice and Xavier Atencio. COSTUMES AND DESIGN CONSULTANT: Tony Walton. COSTUMES: Bill Thomas. COSTUMERS: Chuck Keehne and Gertrude Casey. MAKEUP: Pat McNalley. HAIR STYLIST: La Rue Matheron. SOUND SUPERVISOR: Robert O. Cook. SOUND MIXER: Dean Thomas. MUSIC SUPERVISOR, ARRANGER, AND CONDUCTOR: Irwin Kostal; ASSISTANT TO CONDUCTOR: James Macdonald. MUSIC EDITOR: Evelyn Kennedy. DANCE ACCOMPANIST: Nat Farber. SONGS: Lyrics and music by Richard M. and Robert B. Sherman. RUNNING TIME: 2 hours, 19 minutes. *Principal Players*: Julie Andrews (Mary Poppins). Dick Van Dyke (Bert and Mr. Dawes, Sr.). David Tomlinson (George W. Banks). Glynis Johns (Mrs. [Winifred] Banks). Matthew Garber (Michael). Karen Dotrice (Jane). *Major Academy Awards*: Best Actress (*Julie Andrews*); Film Editing; Visual Effects; Scoring (*Richard M. and Robert B. Sherman*) Song ("Chim Chim Cheree"). *Nominations*: Best Picture; Director; Adapted Screenplay; Cinematography; Art Direction; Costumes; Scoring (*Irwin Kostal*); Sound.

Not even the most observant Londoner strolling along Cherry Tree Lane in 1910 would suspect how truly strange are the happenings going on at number 17. A solid and charming residence at the bend in the street, the spotless white house with the picket fence and manicured lawn has quite a few secrets to reveal. Not the least of them is the presence of a buoyant young lady with magical powers and an important homily targeted at the owner, Mr. George W. Banks, his wife, and by extension all parents everywhere.

Anything but new, the lesson is dressed up in the technical wizardry that the Disney people had perfected over the years, and sermonized most engagingly by one of the studio's all-time favorite characters in the most satisfying of Disney's combination animated and live-action film. Her name, of course, is Mary Poppins, and it is she who bridges the generational gap between the imaginative world of children and the harsher one inhabited by adults. Except for the powerful anti-hunting message that pervades *Bambi* (1942), and opened a floodgate of tears among its youngest spectators, no other Disney film preaches quite so effectively.

Simply stated, the two Banks children living in the picturesque house are practically orphans even though their parents are very much alive. Convinced that they are regarded as vassals by the two persons from whom they most want love, the youngsters are left to amuse themselves as best they can by a curmudgeonly father whose waking hours revolve around the London bank in which he is a minor officer forever courting advancement. Only slightly less aloof is their disoriented mother, so engrossed in furthering the suffragette movement that she is unable to devote more than a few stray moments to guiding her son and daughter into adolescence and beyond.

Neither parent is tyrannical or cruel. They are simply indifferent to their children's most basic need—the companionship of adult members of the household, who instead pass their parental obligations on to surrogates in the form of governesses. Disgruntled with their living arrangement, the children retaliate in accordance with their tender years, not by directly confronting their parents with complaints, but by driving a succession of nannies wild and eventually out of a job.

Like the von Trapp youngsters, yet to be presented on the screen, Matthew and Jane Banks are rebels with a cause. Only after the beneficent influence of Mary Poppins has worked its wonders are both parents awakened to their proper roles in family life. The father learns that making money to pay expenses is indeed vital to the happiness of all, but also that it is not his sole responsibility. And the mother finally realizes that however valuable her contributions are to promoting equality of the sexes at polling places, which she advocates in the film's first song, "Sister Suffragette," it is the welfare of her children that should be her major concern.

The 73rd of the 86 feature films for which Walt Disney himself acted as producer or executive producer, *Mary Poppins* is laudable from start to finish. For its time, it was a marvel of special effects as well as a textbook example

Dick Van Dyke and Julie Andrews use the backs of turtles as stepping stones into a world of Disney animation in *Mary Poppins*.

of how to apply the light touch to a problem affecting many dysfunctional families without losing sight of its seriousness. This tale of the mirthful young lady who parachutes into the lives of the Banks family on an umbrella was the first musical fantasy to be nominated for best picture after *The Wizard of Oz*, as well as the first of Disney's movies to win the award, an extremely belated gesture on the part of the Academy of Motion Picture Arts and Sciences. Altogether, the film received 13 nominations, the most ever for a musical. Julie Andrews took home the Oscar for best actress in her first film, which in many ways served as a warmup exercise for the governess part she would play the next year in *The Sound of Music*.

Like most Disney productions, the Mary Poppins characters range from the silly and mystical to the autocratic and philosophical. One's own imagination and willing suspension of disbelief bring even the most clownish of them into high relief as integral to the plot and the family values the film is designed to convey. Dick Van Dyke, who plays both the impecunious idler Bert and the senile banker Mr. Dawes, Sr., a hilarious descendant of Ebenezer Scrooge, continued to display the energy and artistry that marked his appearance in both the Broadway and the Hollywood versions of *Bye Bye Birdie* (1963) and, beginning in 1964, as the husband (Rob Petrie) of Mary Tyler Moore (Laura) in the *Dick Van Dyke Show*, one of the most successful and genuinely amusing of television's sitcoms.

As with *Funny Girl* four years later, *Mary Poppins* is studded with representatives from 1930s Hollywood, all of them nearing or at the end of their long careers: Jane Darwell, as the Bird Lady; Ed Wynn, as Uncle Albert; Reginald Owen as Admiral Boom, a slightly demented combination weatherman and timekeeper who fires a cannon to announce the hours of the day; Hermione Baddeley, as the Banks' housemaid; Elsa Lanchester, as the children's pre–Mary Poppins governess; and Arthur Treacher as Constable Jones, who returns runaways Matthew and Jane to their home, even though his demeanor indicates that he really cannot blame their wanting to escape from the rigors of contending with indifferent parents.

Furnishing the 12 songs for the film were brothers Richard M. and Robert B. Sherman, whose lengthy service with the Disney organization resembled that of lyricist Ned Washington and composer Frank Churchill, its major songwriters during the late thirties and early forties, and of lyricist Howard Ashman and composer Alan Menken in more recent years. Collaborating on both words and music, the Shermans contributed songs to more than a dozen Disney movies beginning with *The Absent-Minded Professor* and *The Parent Trap* in 1961. Their *Mary Poppins* songs, which included the Oscar-winning "Chim Chim Cher-

ee," raised the musical level of the picture to a height surpassed only by Churchill's score for *Snow White and the Seven Dwarfs* 27 years earlier. The brothers' subsequent Academy Award-nominated songs were "Chitty Chitty Bang Bang," from the 1968 picture of the same name; "The Age of Not Believing," from *Bedknobs and Broomsticks* (1971); "The Slipper and the Rose Waltz (He Danced with Her, She Danced with Me)," from *The Slipper and the Rose* (1977); and "When You're Loved," from *The Magic of Lassie* (1978).

Particularly noteworthy in *Mary Poppins* were the Shermans' interpolation of four brief stream-of-consciousness songs as modified operatic recitatives, all chanted by Mr. Banks. In the first of them, "The Life I Lead," he attempts with scathing solemnity to justify his insular life as breadwinner and undisputed lord of the manor. He describes his professional life as rewarding as his home life, excusing his aloofness toward his children as vital to devoting his waking hours to worshiping his bank as a virtual temple of commerce. The other three untitled songs point up what he feels is the children's need to regard life with seriousness, not merely as a source of amusement; on the value of investing money rather than donating it to charitable causes; and on the importance of ridding the children of Mary Poppins's alleged harmful influence by firing her.

The songwriters' most amusing and inventive song, "Supercalifragilisticexpialidocious," is not quite so impossible to pronounce as it might seem at first glance, thanks to the perfect matching of syllables to notes. Mary Poppins, in fact, encounters no difficulty pronouncing it backward. To be found in some dictionaries, including *The Random House Dictionary of the English Language*, the 34-letter tongue-twister meaning all is fine replaced antidisestablishmentarianism, coined by the British prime minister William Gladstone, as the longest word in the English language if, that is, one ignores osseocarnisanguineoviscericartilaginonervomedullary, which Thomas Love Peacock created in the novel *Headlong Hall* to describe in 51 letters the structure of the human body. Even the *Oxford Universal Dictionary* omits that one from its pages.

P(amela) L(yndon) Travers, born Helen Lyndon Goff, the spinster author of the Mary

Poppins books, died in London on April 23, 1996, at the age of 96. A native of Maryborough, Queensland, Australia, the one-time dancer and Shakespearean actress vastly preferred anonymity to publicity and refused to disclose details of her personal life, going so far as to try to conceal even her sex by signing her works simply P.L. Travers. And she always insisted that she had never meant to write for children with her seven novels on the adventures of the magical nanny she created.

The first *Mary Poppins* book, published in 1934, quickly became a critical and popular success that sold in the millions and found its way into more than 20 foreign languages. Six sequels followed, ending with *Mary Poppins and the House Next Door* in 1988. Although all were set in 1930s England, the 1964 movie was transposed at P.L.'s suggestion to the earlier Edwardian Era, when authoritative fatherhood was in full flower. Despite her collaboration on the film as "consultant," she was dissatisfied with the finished product. "I think I was disturbed at seeing [the story] so externalized, so oversimplified, so generalized," she said in a 1967 interview.

Mary was a complex young lady whose unique gifts ranged far and wide beyond her capabilities as a nanny. The author allowed her book to be filmed largely because, in her words, "I do not want to see Mary Poppins tucked away in a closet." The movie was based on three of the novels, the original 1934 *Mary Poppins*; *Mary Poppins Comes Back* (1935); and *Mary Poppins Opens the Door* (1943). All were illustrated by Mary Shepard, whose drawings, especially of Mary's costumes, are duplicated with amazing accuracy in the film.

Miss Travers revised *Mary Poppins* in 1981 after the San Francisco Public Library banned it because of concern over its treatment of minorities. She rewrote the offending chapter, "Bad Tuesday," deleting references to a South Sea island black woman who holds a "pickaninny" on her lap, speaks in dialect, and offers watermelon slices to everybody she meets. In the new version, exotic animals substitute for human beings.

Governess for Hire. Matthew Garber and Karen Doltrice (Michael and Jane Banks)

are really not wicked children. Nor can their smug father, David Tomlinson (George Banks) or flighty mother, Glynis Johns (Mrs. Banks), a younger version of the Billie Burke stereotype, be classified as mean-spirited parents. They care deeply for their son and daughter, but heavy involvement in personal matters has forced them into relying on nannies to rear them. Actually, the children are willing to accept discipline as vital to their development; what they resent is their parents' delegating their own responsibilities to hired caretakers.

Already their nanny-bashing has cost the family the services of Elsa Lanchester (Katie Nanna), the second governess in a month to fly out of the house on wings of ruffled feathers after complaining about the "little beasts'" demonstrated rebelliousness against her authority. Once again, father Tomlinson is required to place a want ad in *The Times*. Irritated even further when the children give him their own handwritten version, and sing of the virtues of their idea of "The Perfect Nanny," he tears it up and throws the pieces into the fireplace. What Matthew and Karen want is a cheery and rosy-cheeked, kind and witty, sweet and pretty successor; their father wants the reverse, a no-nonsense, bossy matron.

The children's dream nanny arrives the next day in the person of a Glinda-like good witch, Julie Andrews (Mary Poppins), who has blown into town on the back of a powerful east wind. In her hand she is holding their ad, which she apparently had pieced together from the torn fragments the wind had sucked up the chimney flue. Tomlinson's bewildered look contrasts sharply with the gleeful smiles radiating from his children's faces. As far as they are concerned, the gracious, attractive young lady has all the earmarks of the ideal custodian.

Their father infers from the young woman's serenity and confidence that she is entirely capable of exacting obedience from his little son and daughter once she learns that persuasion will simply not work. He hires Julie, or, rather, she hires herself, accepting the job before it is offered on a one-week trial basis. If she likes it, she will remain; if not, he must look elsewhere. As for references, she has none, except an insightful ribbon that pronounces her to be "almost perfect in everything."

Not what one would call a severe disciplinarian, Julie nonetheless stresses the need for fastidiousness when its comes to tidying up the children's nursery. Her only other possession besides the umbrella with a talking-parrot handle is a carpetbag with an endless bottom. From it she extracts a bazaar's worth of items—a plant, a hat rack, a wall mirror, a floor lamp—which she uses to brighten up theirs and her own adjoining room. Within a few blinks of the eye, the nursery is whipped up into a cozy and sparkling retreat fit to be inhabited by children of modest wealth.

Matthew and Karen agree with her that there is indeed a place for everything, and that everything does indeed look better when in its rightful place. Julie also has the perfect answer to turning the drudgery of keeping the room clean into a joyful experience. What one should do, she explains in the tuneful "A Spoonful of Sugar," is to look upon the results as well worth the demands of the task, much like swallowing cold medicine after flavoring it with strawberry.

Later, during a walk in a nearby park, the three meet Dick Van Dyke (Bert), a street entertainer and old acquaintance of Julie's. Brimming with cheerfulness, he invites them on a voyage to whichever faraway land they select from a series of landscapes he had just chalked on the sidewalk. They choose the English countryside, where Julie and Van Dyke, along with hordes of the Disney studio's typical frisky, wide-eyed animated animals, who pop up from everywhere to titter and frolic in company with the four live performers, celebrate their freedom from life's burdens with the catchy theme song of the trip, "Jolly Holiday." Featuring the most felicitous union of animals and music since *Fantasia* in 1940, the scene is highlighted by a penguin dance equaled as an expression of carefree camaraderie only by the Gene Kelly and Jerry Mouse duet in *Anchors Aweigh*.

The imaginary trip takes Julie and Van Dyke for a ride on a carousel, where their wooden horses suddenly break away from the merry-go-round to join live horses in pursuit of a fox with a thick Irish brogue, and then race against a field of rivals in a steeplechase. Julie's horse wins, and she and Van Dyke summarize their delight in victory with the immensely clever "Supercalifragilisticexpialidocious," an expression of happiness called on when one does not know what else to say, and the movies' greatest nonsense song.

A rainstorm dampens their enthusiasm for traveling farther into Van Dyke's strange world. It also erases his sidewalk sketches, forcing the return of all four back to the park. The thrill of the day's adventures linger with Matthew and Karen, they are unable to fall asleep that night until Julie serenades them with a rare movie lullaby with the unusual title of "Stay Awake." Noted for her cleverness, their nanny guides them into sleep by playfully trying to dissuade them from slumberland—and from the pleasant dreams she insists all good children find there.

The next day finds David Tomlinson in a quandary. Under Julie's guidance, not only are the children much more cheerful, but so are the usually dour housemaid, Hermione Baddeley (Ellen), and cook, Reta Shaw (Mrs. Brill), who go about their duties with a song on their lips. Such displays of happiness without apparent reason are so rare in the house that the suspicious father assumes that the lapse in decorum is due to Julie's inability to subdue the children's unruliness. Yet, they seem to like her very much and most likely would revolt against her dismissal.

Tomlinson becomes even more unnerved a little later when the children relate the fun they had while accompanying Julie and Van Dyke on a visit to her Uncle Albert, played by Ed Wynn, a one-time vaudeville and legitimate stage and radio comedian with the appropriate nickname of "The Perfect Fool." The old man was an absolute riot, the children exclaim, when he sang the merry "I Love to Laugh," while proving the contention by falling into a laughing jag throughout the visit.

Indeed, the old fellow lives to laugh, he had told them, and even made it possible for them to float along next to him only inches below the ceiling of his room, where he held a tea party for his airborne guests. Naturally, Tomlinson regards the tale as sheer poppycock and refuses to believe a word of it. The many years he has spent in the cold world of business have dulled his imagination and killed all interest in laughing for laughter's sake. To him, nothing in life is to be taken lightly.

Hoping to stop Julie's apparent intention to fill his children's heads with fantasy rather than the virtues of upper-middle-class deportment, he upbraids her for introducing them to "worthless frivolities" and orders her to cease and desist. His house is to be run like a bank, with undivided attention paid to each task. Seriousness of mind, strict adherence to policy, and punctuality are to be the major assets of all family members. Rather than dismissing his complaint as a pitiful outcry from a totally humorless man, Julie suggests that he is committing a cardinal sin by trying to run his family like a business. She dares him to give the children an inside look at his bank's operations and then defend them as proper substitutes for the laughter of happy children.

Cold World of Commerce. Father Tomlinson's bank is situated in a Dickensian netherworld of gloom and darkness, where sitting on the stone steps of St. Paul's Cathedral is the kindly Bird Woman, played by 85-year-old Jane Darwell in her final screen appearance. Julie had already introduced the children to the old woman by proxy, singing of her love of birds, pigeons in particular, in "Feed the Birds (Tuppence a Bag)" the previous evening. And there she is, just as Julie had depicted her—a rare example of a caring person in a heartless world, sitting alone in her tattered clothing, her head capped with a dilapidated black hat, pleading with passers-by to buy a bag of crumbs for the ragamuffin birds swarming over to her looking for food.

Matthew Garber wants to contribute tuppence to the cause, but his father cajoles him into depositing it in a savings account at his bank. He is supported by the bank's chairman, Mr. Dawes, Jr. (played by Arthur Malet), a wheezy elderly executive with numerous infirmities and a history of pandering to greed rather than dispensing charity, also played with comical exaggeration by Van Dyke, who grabs the coins from Matthew's hands. Persisting in his desire to contribute the money to the welfare of the birds, the child demands the return of his enforced deposit, but the money-mad chairman refuses his request.

Matthew and his sister react by loudly pro-claiming that the bank will not return his tuppence. Mistaking the message as evidence that the institution either cannot or will not release any of the funds in its safekeeping, worried men wearing stovepipe hats and derbies bolt to the tellers' windows to withdraw their deposits, endangering the bank by threatening a brief run on it. David Tomlinson is humbled by the chairman's charge that he must bear all responsibility for his children's throwing the Fidelity Fiduciary Bank into chaos and damaging its proud reputation. He reminds him in the sternest of tones that it has not suffered such indignity since it was forced into temporary default 137 years earlier after depositors discovered it had financed a shipment of tea to Boston.

Fearing retribution, Matthew and Karen run into the street and along the grimy back alleys of London's financial district. There they come across Bert, now wearing the guise of a chimney sweeper while reprising "Chim Chim Cher-ee," which he had first sung, and with different words, at the beginning of the film while entertaining strollers as a one-man band. Julie happens along, and excited as the children over Van Dyke's invitation to get a 'sweep's bird's-eye view of London from rooftops, she joins them in zooming up the chimney to the top of a dingy building.

Along with a chorus of about 20 more 'sweeps, she and Van Dyke sing and dance to the melody of "Step in Time" in the film's only large-scale production number. As happens so often in movie musicals, the routine is much too long to sustain audience interest, even though the choreography is spirited and the participants animated by the desire to startle by engaging in calisthenics in march tempo. This part of the film could easily have been shortened by half; the chorus' leaping about is excessive, and the song is not among the best written for the picture.

Their happiness ends, however, when Tomlinson confronts Van Dyke in his house, where they join forces in singing a tribute to the "Fidelity Fiduciary Bank." His career has been ruined, he moans, blaming all his and his family's woes on Julie's negative influence. Van Dyke counters by praising her gift for bestowing happiness wherever she goes by furnishing living proof that joys, like childhood, are all too brief not to be grasped tightly while they are available.

Too disconsolate to accept Van Dyke's appraisal of Julie's worthiness without introspection, Tomlinson undergoes a personality analysis. Just how high on the scale of life's priorities should happiness rank, he asks himself, in effect questioning the marketplace values he has defended so staunchly for so long. Is he, as Julie had charged a few days earlier, just a short-sighted man unable to see past his nose? And what about his children? Will his bondage to the bank cause him to miss the precious sight of watching them grow into adulthood? His love for them becomes most pronounced when, under the spell of Van Dyke's efforts at bringing the family closer together, Matthew and Karen walk over to Tomlinson, apologize for their conduct at the bank, and Matthew gives him his tuppence to deposit for him.

Tomlinson is summoned back to the bank, where he hurries with his children to show up promptly at 9 p.m. Expecting to be fired, he withstands being drummed out of his job with grace, even disdaining the chance to appease his superiors' anger by apologizing on his son's behalf. In light of his recent soul searching, he seems relieved at the loss of his position, even indicating that he has at least a mild interest in witticisms by repeating one of Uncle Ed Wynn's corny little jokes that so convulses the feeble old chairman with laughter that he drops dead (off-screen) to the floor.

The ability to laugh at oneself, and occasionally at life itself, it would seem, can be enjoyed only by persons who take neither very seriously. That was the misguided bank chairman's fatal flaw: concentrating his life on credits and debits, profit and loss, deposits and withdrawals had robbed him of a sense of humor. Death was therefore a natural consequence of his having unexpectedly replaced his lifelong snarl with laughter.

The next day Tomlinson finds an old childhood kite and offers to fly it again with Matthew and Karen at a festival in the park. Mutual love and respect have returned to the solid and charming house at the bend of Cherry Tree Lane. From her bedroom window Julie watches the happy parents and youngsters scamper along the street while singing "Let's Go Fly a Kite," which happens to be the children's favorite pastime also.

It is clear to Julie that sharing one another's happiness now permeates the Banks household. Like the unworldly Cary Grant in *The Bishop's Wife* (1947), Gordon MacRae in *Carousel*, and above all Henry Travers, the apprentice angel Clarence in *It's a Wonderful Life* (1947), she realizes that her unique services are no longer required and that it is time for her to leave. The wind, now blowing favorably from the west, beckons her and she raises her umbrella and sails across the sky for an unknown destination. As she flies over the park, the camera picks up the Banks brood and the surviving bank executives, who have joined the gathering of parents and children in squealing with delight as they watch a battery of kites flapping in the breeze. Chances are good that Matthew and Karen will never again need another nanny.

P.S.: Tomlinson kept his job at the Fidelity Fiduciary Bank, and in addition was promoted to full partnership in the firm.

My Fair Lady (1964)

A Warner Bros. picture. DIRECTOR: George Cukor; ASSISTANT: David Hall. PRODUCER: Jack L. Warner. SCREENWRITER: Alan Jay Lerner, based on the play *Pygmalion* by George Bernard Shaw. CINEMATOGRAPHER: Harry Stradling. FILM EDITOR: William Ziegler. ART DIRECTOR: Gene Allen. COSTUME, SCENERY, AND PRODUCTION DESIGNER: Cecil Beaton. SET DECORATOR: George James Hopkins. CHOREOGRAPHER: Hermes Pan. SOUND: Francis T. Schied and Murray Spivak. MAKEUP SUPERVISOR: Gordon Bau. SUPERVISING HAIR STYLIST: Jean Burt Reilly. ORCHESTRATORS: Alexander Courage, Robert Franklyn, and Al Woodbury. VOCAL ARRANGEMENTS: Robert Tucker. MUSIC SUPERVISOR AND CONDUCTOR: André Previn. SONGS: lyrics by Alan Jay Lerner, music by Frederick Loewe. RUNNING TIME: 2 hours and 50 minutes. *Principal Players*: Audrey Hepburn (Eliza Doolittle). Rex Harrison (Professor Henry Higgins). Stanley Holloway (Alfred P. Doolittle). Wilfrid Hyde-White (Colonel Pickering). Gladys Cooper (Mrs. Higgins). Jeremy Brett (Freddy Eynsford-Hill). Theodore Bikel (Count Zoltan [Aristid] Karpathy). *Major Academy Awards*: Best Picture; Director; Cinematography; Actor (*Rex Harrison*); Art Direction; Costumes; Sound; Scoring. *Nominations*: Best Adapted Screenplay; Supporting Actor (*Stanley Holloway*); Supporting Actress (*Gladys Cooper*); Film Editing.

The usually astute Oscar Hammerstein II in the early 1950s maintained that a musical version of *Pygmalion* "can't be done." He and partner Richard Rodgers had already had a go

Jeremy Brett (Freddy Eynsford-Hill), Audrey Hepburn (Eliza Doolittle), and Rex Harrison (Professor Henry Higgins) at the Ascot racetrack in *My Fair Lady.*

at it, but given up. Lyricist E. Y. Harburg volunteered the opinion that the original play was such a perfect work of art that no other hands should tamper with it. Later Mary Martin, after hearing an early run-through of several of the proposed *My Fair Lady* songs, commented that lyricist Lerner and composer Loewe "have lost their talent." She also refused the offer to play Eliza, proving once again that even great actresses are susceptible to huge judgmental errors.

There was little doubt among the principals involved in revamping the Shaw play into a musical that inserting songs while preserving the Shavian wit would be a formidable challenge. With a stubbornness almost unmatched in theatrical circles, Lerner and Loewe persevered for three years and, as the old saying goes, the rest is history. *My Fair Lady* finally opened on Broadway at the Mark Hellinger Theatre on March 15, 1956, closing 2,717 performances

later on September 29, 1962. (In London it ran for 2,281 performances.)

With Julie Andrews and Rex Harrison as the Broadway leads, the literate verbal and musical sparring between Eliza Doolittle and 'Enry 'Iggins was transformed into a classic worthy of comparison with the George Bernard Shaw source. The trepidation that had plagued *My Fair Lady* every step of the drawn-out progression from conception to debut was missing when Hollywood undertook the screen version. The pitfalls had been ironed out, many of the songs were already the best known of the time, and Harrison had agreed to co-star in it. All that producer Jack L. Warner had to do was wait for the Broadway closing. Having secured a firm foothold on the stage with *The Boy Friend*, the 1954 English musical burlesque, Miss Andrews continued as Eliza in New York and London for three and one-half years.

A titan among the century's Irish men of

letters, Shaw himself had written the screenplay for producer Gabriel Pascal's *Pygmalion* in 1938, widely regarded then as now as one of the most tasteful and intelligent of 1930s movies. (A Shaw devotee, Pascal later produced and directed the films *Major Barbara* and *Caesar and Cleopatra*, and produced *Androcles and the Lion*.) Based on Shaw's five-act 1912 play of the same name, the 1938 best-film nominee brilliantly compressed the plot into a mere 96 minutes while remaining true to the sturdy characterizations and cultivated dialogue. Playing the misogynist professor of languages was scholarly-looking Leslie Howard, who also co-directed the picture with Anthony Asquith. Wendy Hiller, in what was only her second screen appearance, was equally flawless as Eliza. Wilfrid Lawson's portrayal of Alfred Doolittle as a cockney ruffian lacked the joviality of Stanley Holloway's in *My Fair Lady*; and although Scott Sunderland turned in a reputable job as Colonel Pickering, Wilfrid Hyde-White's depiction is far better, at once sympathetic (toward Eliza) and cynical (toward Higgins).

Adding to the 1938 British picture's prestige was the excellent background score by Arthur Honegger and editing by David Lean. The cinematography was by Harry Stradling who, in one of those odd happenings that fascinate movie fans, was called on 26 years later to photograph *My Fair Lady*. Both Howard and Miss Hiller contended for the best acting award. Other Academy Award nominations went to Cecil Lewis, Ian Dalrymple, and W. P. Lipscomb for their scenario; Shaw won the Oscar for his screenplay. In 1964, the renovated version became one of the best-loved musical films of all time. Notwithstanding its overt class consciousness and use of social experimentation as plot motivator, both antagonistic to the American spirit, the film collected 12 Academy Award nominations and won eight of them.

The original Shaw work achieved the nearly impossible goal of becoming a hit play by updating and adding humor to the time-worn Cinderella story, with which *Pygmalion* has more than just a nodding acquaintance. Some 19 centuries earlier, the Roman poet Ovid (Publius Ovidius Naso) had told the tale of Pygmalion, a mythological king of Cyprus and a sculptor. He became enamored of one of his creations, a beautiful statue he named Galatea, and in answer to his prayer, Aphrodite, the goddess of love and beauty, brought it to life. John Marston repeated the story in a 1598 poem, William Morris in one of 24 verse tales in *The Earthly Paradise,* about 1869, and W.S. Gilbert, of Gilbert and Sullivan fame, in his 1871 comedy *Pygmalion and Galatea*. The ageless plot has continued well into the late 20th century, with traces of it surfacing in such a recent film as *Pretty Woman* (1990).

Shaw had always insisted that *Pygmalion* was not a love story, a major frustration with Hammerstein in his aborted attempt to rewrite it as a musical comedy. *My Fair Lady*, however, treats it as one. In the original 1912 play, Eliza walks out on Higgins at the end. In an epilogue Shaw describes her subsequent marriage to her shabby genteel suitor, Freddy Hill, with whom she opens a florist shop. Shaw insisted on this unromantic ending and resisted efforts to impose a false sentimentality on it. Curiously, in light of Shaw's refusal to give his film rights for *Pygmalion* to any Hollywood mogul, he did try to append a Hollywood ending to the 1938 film. According to Pascal's widow, Valerie Pascal Delacorte, Shaw on February 24, 1938, wrote a letter to her producer husband in which he marries Eliza to Freddy and gives them co-ownership of a florist shop financed by Colonel Pickering. Pascal, however, ignored the letter. When the preview of the film was over, Shaw never referred to the omission.

Much earlier in his career, as if to verify his anti-sentimentalism reputation, Shaw had sent a critical zinger to Charles Dickens for writing an alternative happy ending to *Great Expectations*. Originally, Estella ignores Pip to marry another man, from whom she eventually separates because of cruelty. In the rewrite, suggested by Dickens's novelist friend Edward Bulwer-Lytton, Estella and Pip are united. Shaw dismissed the second version as preferable only to "sentimental readers who still like their stories to end at the altar."

Lerner's absolutely brilliant adaptation for both stage and screen follows Shaw's 1938 script closely, so much so that contemporary viewers of the old movie can practically hear music swelling up when Howard demands that Miss Hiller continue practicing "the rain in Spain stays mainly in the plain" until she can pronounce all the words to his satisfaction.

Finding an appropriate title for their musical forced Lerner and Loewe into coining and rejecting several candidates. According to Joshua Meltzer, son of screenwriter Lewis Meltzer (*The Man with the Golden Arm, Autumn Leaves,* 1956), his father wrote a play in the early fifties entitled "My Fair Lady." He received a telephone call from Lerner, who asked whether he could use it for the musical adaptation of Shaw's *Pygmalion.* "My father said, 'Sure,' and gave it to Lerner," Joshua said recently. "My father retitled his play *Come and Kiss Me.*"

Not inclined to delete very many of Professor Higgins's invectives against "guttersnipe" Eliza, Lerner inadvertently encountered the ire of 1960s feminists who found the dialogue frequently insulting and demeaning to women. In many respects their criticism was justified. Harrison is unquestionably a male chauvinist, indulging with abandon in allusions to women's alleged irrationality, which, when added to his frankly brutish ridicule of Audrey Hepburn's shortcomings, were practically predestined to offend.

But criticism was the price Lerner had to pay for keeping much of Shaw's dialogue intact. It also lends a great deal of poignancy to Harrison's pleasing discovery that he has "sculpted" a cultural goddess from the basest of materials in "I've Grown Accustomed to Her Face," one of the most engaging love ballads of the period. Like Pygmalion, Harrison's desire to breathe life into Miss Hepburn, an urchin rather than a gamine, is answered. But he achieves his goal his own way—not by appealing to a god for help, but by instilling into a living creature the gracefulness of speech and movement that makes her the equal of any other lady in the kingdom.

In many ways, the Svengali-Trilby relationship between the professor and Eliza is equivalent to the one involving Aunt Alicia and Gigi. Although differing from her Parisian counterpart in economic and therefore social status, Eliza is likewise subjected to what might be termed character upgrade by a strong-willed adult with definite ideas on how to mold her into the ideally cultivated icon. Like Aunt Alicia, Professor Higgins is independently wealthy and goaded into volunteering to teach his pupil how to polish her image primarily because the overwhelming challenge it presents intrigues

him. In the end, both young women are groomed to perfection with potentially disastrous results.

Were it not for Louis Jourdan's change of heart, Gigi would have spent the rest of her life freelancing her love to the highest bidders. Had Higgins not become enamored of his creation, Eliza would have faced a similar fate. Erased of all vestiges of her lower-depths upbringing, she would have become a woman without a country, unfit to resume her salesgirl career among former working-class friends with whom she no longer has anything in common, and yet unequipped by parentage and background to consort with the landed gentry on her own. As Eliza herself complains to her often contemptuous tutor, he has turned her from a seller of flowers into a fashionable young lady in danger of selling herself to survive.

The cast is excellent. Like Yul Brynner, Rex Harrison repeated his Broadway role. A first-rate stage and movie actor, he was accustomed to playing the lead in film versions of classic plays, including Sheridan's *School for Scandal* (1930) and Noel Coward's *Blithe Spirit* (1945), and best of all as Adolphus Cusins in Shaw's *Major Barbara* (1941). Actually, Warner Bros. wanted Cary Grant to play Higgins, but he bowed out on the basis that Harrison owned the part and deserved reprising it on the screen.

Curiously, Miss Hepburn and the featured player who reprises *My Fair Lady's* biggest song hit both depended on dubbing to "sing" their songs, while the male lead speaks rather than sings most of his lyrics. Never pretending to be a singer, Harrison nonetheless performs his musical numbers with remarkable skill, talking almost all of his lyrics, much like Louis Jourdan in *Gigi,* pausing at exactly the right moments and modulating his voice to accent his emotions, which range from disgust to astonishment to tenderness.

Audrey Hepburn is a scintillating Eliza, proving that her replacing Julie Andrews in the role was a stroke of inspired casting. Miss Hepburn could sing, but not all that well, and so once again Marni Nixon was recruited as off-screen vocalist. Perhaps, had Miss Hepburn sung all her tunes, instead of just "Wouldn't It Be Loverly?", she might have been nominated for best actress, although the Academy rarely awarded it to two leads in the same picture, and never in a musical. Singing for Jeremy Brett was tenor Bill Shirley, whose forthright version of "On the Street Where You Live" is superb. Director Cukor, who by 1964 had amassed one of Hollywood's most prestigious lists of film credits—from *Dinner at Eight* and *Little Women* (both 1933) to *Camille* (1936), *The Philadelphia Story* (1940), and *Pat and Mike*—egged his players into giving the finest performances of which they were capable. This time, and for the only time, Cukor won the Academy Award for his expert piloting.

Colette died a few years before Hollywood released *Gigi*, and Shaw died without seeing either Broadway's or Hollywood's *My Fair Lady*. The witty playwright with the twinkling eyes and Uncle Sam beard, however, put up a good fight, dying in 1950 at the patriarchal age of 94, six years before the musical opened in New York.

Bridging the Cultural Gap. It is about 11 o'clock on a rainy night in London. The Covent Garden theatergoers are queuing up for hansom and motor cabs to take them to restaurants for late-evening suppers or nightcaps or back to their homes. Suddenly, Audrey Hepburn (Eliza Doolittle) emerges from the neighboring market square, London's principal wholesale market for food and flowers, where small-time entrepreneurs sell their merchandise from individual stalls. Not your typical musical-comedy heroine in appearance or manner, she is boisterous, slovenly, poorly attired, and pounding the pavement like a longshoreman while hawking her bundles of flowers in a thick cockney accent. Listening carefully to her curbstone English while taking notes is Rex Harrison (Henry Higgins).

Fearing that he is a "copper" who is documenting her activities as a prelude to arresting her, Audrey protests his interest in her, pointing out that she is only a poor but good girl trying to eke out a modest living as best she can. Harrison assures her that his fascination is the result of accidentally hearing her dialect and speech pattern, from which he says he can peg the birthplace of any speaker within an accuracy range of two to six miles. He is a scholar in phonetics, or the "science of speech," he explains, and shows her his notes, which to Au-

drey are as impossible to decipher as a page full of hieroglyphics.

Among the spectators is Wilfrid Hyde-White (Colonel Pickering), a distinguished Sanskrit scholar recently embarked on a study of the estimated 147 dialects spoken in India. He has traveled to London expressly to meet Harrison, who himself had planned a trip to India to strike up an acquaintance with the Colonel. Harrison invites him to stay at his townhouse at 27-A Wimpole Street, where each will be readily available to analyze the other's pedanticism. Turning to Audrey, whose voice reminds him of "chickens cackling in a barn," Professor Harrison complains that she should be jailed for assassination—of the English language.

Every time she opens her mouth, she cheapens the language arts that Shakespeare, the Bible, and Milton had placed at the pinnacle of human communication, he laments before launching into his first musical diatribe, "Why Can't the English (Teach Their Children How to Speak)?" Nowadays, he maintains, speakers of correct English are regarded as freaks by people who do not realize that language proficiency is the surest way to personal and professional advancement. He adds that he could reincarnate even Audrey into a virtual Queen of Sheba fit to mingle with Buckingham Palace swells—or at least qualify her for employment in a respectable shop that caters to aristocratic ladies. Audrey, however, shrugs off the boast and warns him to stay away from her. Obviously, Harrison groans as he drops a pocketful of coins into her basket and walks away with Hyde-White, her only interest is money.

Thrilled with the unexpected largesse, Audrey breaks into the film's first hit. "Wouldn't It Be Lovely?", she sings to her fellow merchants, always to have this much cash in hand. With a steady supply she could easily rent comfortable living quarters and live in the lap of luxury, which to her means gorging herself with chocolates as desired. Shortly afterward, however, she learns that easy-come money has a way of going just as effortlessly.

Early next morning finds Audrey's tipsy father, Alfred P. Doolittle, played to the hilt by Stanley Holloway, a one-time London music hall comic and hilarious holdover from the stage musical, wandering through the market in search of her. A ne'er-do-well without a regular job or the will to acquire one, he wants to "borrow" half a crown in order to continue his binge, which bar owners have cut short by refusing to extend more credit to him. Basically a Dickensian character, as perennially impecunious yet lovable as Mr. Micawber, Holloway beams his widest grin when Audrey reluctantly gives him the half-crown, and off he goes to continue his pub crawl. (Holloway's son, Julian, played Doolittle in the latest New York revival, which opened December 9, 1993, and featured Richard Chamberlain as Professor Higgins.)

Determined to rise above her father's pathetic condition, Audrey pays a visit the next day to Harrison and insists that he teach her to speak properly. At first disinclined to accept her as a pupil, Harrison relents under the persuasion of Hyde-White. Bursting with excitement upon realizing that this "deliciously low" and "horribly dirty" flower girl will present him with the biggest challenge ever to his artistry, he proposes to give her lessons for free, as well as lodging and meals. But she must live in his house for six months, follow his every instruction precisely, and permit his housekeeper, Miss Pearce (Mona Washbourne), and staff to bathe her, burn her clothing, and outfit her in more appealing dresses. Audrey finally agrees, after branding the professor a "great bully" who obviously takes extreme pleasure in belittling his inferiors.

As for Mona and Hyde-White's concern over the possibility that Harrison may become romantically involved with the girl he sarcastically refers to as "that barbarous wretch," Harrison responds with "I'm an Ordinary Man," assuring them that he is wedded only to confirmed bachelorhood. He abhors women's tendency to disrupt men's precisely plotted daily routines, disturb their love of isolation and quiet, and bicker over the time they spend in intellectual pursuits. As regards the far more important question of what Harrison intends to do with Audrey once she completes his course, his reply is both curt and cruel. If she passes muster in the highest of societies, he will reward her with a gift of money and open up an exclusive ladies' shop for her to manage. If she fails, he will put her in jail, where he is still convinced she belongs.

The Smell of Money. When next seen, Father Holloway has imbibed a sufficient amount of spirits to feel compelled to celebrate what to him is the ideal life. Singing "With a Little Bit of Luck," he informs his envious marketplace listeners that anyone can escape the drudgery of work and confinement of marriage, and still live life to the fullest by succumbing to every temptation. The trick is to duck all responsibility whenever it rears its ugly head. At the end of the song, Holloway's intention to continue in his lackadaisical lifestyle is reinvigorated when a friend reveals that Audrey has moved from her basement apartment into the home of a Professor Higgins. All smiles, Holloway merrily contemplates the fortune to redound to him by virtue of his daughter's having made a satisfactory connection with an upper-class gentleman.

Like Grace Moore in *One Night of Love*, Audrey soon learns that her teacher is a taskmaster who firmly believes that sparing the rod of heavy workloads and constant carping inevitably spoil the child. Using a battery of recording gadgets that rivals the contraptions in Dr. Frankenstein's laboratory, Harrison forces Audrey into endless, painstakingly dull training sessions on how to breathe and correctly pronounce the letters of the alphabet, the vowels in particular. The penalty for non-cooperation is equally severe: no meals and, even more hurtful, no chocolates.

Visited one day by Holloway, who regards his daughter's presence in Harrison's household as the basis for a loan, the professor parries the man's blackmail attempt by suggesting that he take her back home with him that very day. He is tiring of her, he says, and would welcome her absence as a reprieve from the horrors of trying to educate her. Hoist on his own petard, Holloway quickly adopts a conciliatory stance. Born out of wedlock, Audrey has been a heavy burden to care for, especially for one of the "undeserving poor," as the derelict parent describes himself. Now he finds himself beset with a staggering number of needs that only money can satisfy. Devoid of any pretensions of morality, he is entirely willing to let her remain in the house, even as a live-in concubine, for the modest sum of five pounds. Eager to get Holloway off his hands and get back to work, Harrison gives him the money, sending him away with the broad but disbelieving smile of a man who had just won the Irish Sweepstakes.

Later, teetering on the brink of a nervous breakdown, Audrey gives vent to her hatred of Harrison in the revenge song "Just You Wait." Never, whether in sickness or in health, will he receive a word of sympathy from her, she vows, jumping for joy when in her mind she witnesses his execution by firing squad. Harrison's household staff, however, affirms their loyalty to their master in the followup "Servant's Chorus" by pitying him for having to contend with such a woebegone pupil who has yet to show the slightest promise of living up to his exacting standards.

But the professor's perseverance finally pays off. After he turns Audrey into a female Demosthenes by jamming her mouth with marbles, she surprises him, as well as herself, by perfectly enunciating exactly where it is that the rain in Spain mainly stays. Prompted by Harrison's smile, she merrily repeats the sentence in the celebratory song "The Rain in Spain." "By George, she's got it!" Harrison exults while dancing the tune with her.

He then announces that the time is here to test her progress in public. He will dress her to the nines and take her to the races at Ascot, where the equally thoroughbred spectators will give her either a failing or a passing grade in elocution and deportment. Her enthusiasm at attending the affair, however, is overshadowed by the unexpected switch in her regard for Harrison. "I Could Have Danced All Night," she later sings to herself, recalling how their brief dance together had awakened the latent sexual attraction she has developed for her torturer. Although his interest in her is linguistic rather than romantic, perhaps, as she continues to proceed rung by rung up the ladyhood ladder, he will come to look upon her as a woman, not just a pupil.

A Day at the Races. With the lovely "Ascot Gavotte" played instrumentally in the background, Harrison and Audrey wander with the other ladies and gentlemen, all wrapped in their Sunday finery, about the famous racing grounds. A far cry from the Covent Garden Eliza of the recent past, the Ascot Eliza is the equal of any of the other exquisite Cecil Beaton-garbed mannequins in elegance and propriety. She is the focus of all overt and covert glances, partly because of her hat, roughly the size of an eagle's nest and quite likely the most imposing chapeau ever seen on film.

Among her admirers is Jeremy Brett (Freddy Hill), a devoted but foppish social climber who falls immediately in love with her, and Grady Sutton, who appears only momentarily in one of his final screen roles. (Also cast in a bit part was Henry Daniell, of the velvet voice and cold heart. On a par with the early Basil Rathbone as a movie villain, he died several months before the picture was released.) Most impressed of all with Audrey is Harrison's handsome mother, played by the exceptional character actress Gladys Cooper, a three-time nominee for the Academy Award for best supporting actress and the British soldiers' favorite pinup girl in World War I.

Not as yet able to shed every shred of her waywardness, Audrey reverts to the slang of the streets while telling her admirers, as an increasingly agitated Harrison signals Hyde-White to step in and do something, of her aunt, who had died from drinking too much gin. An even bigger *faux pas* is her loudly cheering the horse "Dover" on to victory. Brett had placed a bet for her on it and, caught up in the excitement of the moment, she hollers to the faltering animal to "move your bloomin' arse!" (Lerner substituted bloomin' for bloody, a rather strong expletive in Victorian times, apparently feeling that using a word that had shocked earlier generations would have had the effect of anti-climax in 1956.)

One lady spectator faints at hearing Audrey's curse, causing Harrison to tremble with fear that Audrey has not only blown her cool, but also detonated the edifice of gentility he had so carefully constructed for her. Luckily, her other listeners accept her "small talk" with the same aristocratic toleration of Alice Brady toward Deanna Durbin in *One Hundred Men and a Girl*. They find her to be refreshingly outspoken, and that is enough to permit Audrey to figuratively cross her own finish line with a few lengths to spare.

If asked, Freddy would have given her an A-plus for her smashing debut. Enchanted with her looks and girlish enthusiasm, he brings her a bouquet of flowers the next day. Excited at walking along Wimpole Street, he sings of his delirium in being so near to her, in the ever-lovely "On the Street Where You Live"— where, incidentally, Elizabeth Barrett also resided before her marriage to Robert Browning—the biggest success in the entire Lerner and Loewe catalogue. Unable to see her, he leaves the bouquet with Mona, retreats to the opposite side of the street, and continues to stare ecstatically at her house.

Impressed with Audrey's Ascot triumph, Harrison prepares to give her the ultimate test. She is to accompany him and Wilfrid Hyde-White to the annual Embassy Ball. The latter is not so sure as Harrison that her conduct will pass muster with the attending dignitaries, among whom will be the queen and a prince of Transylvania and several other crown heads of Europe.

Beautifully outfitted in a shimmering white evening gown, her hair smartly coiffeured and her face impeccably glamorized, Audrey rewards Harrison's faith in her by starring as the major attraction of the evening. The ballroom sequence, steeped in the gracious formality that pervades a gathering of royalty out for a respite of relaxation and gossip, is enhanced by the instrumental "Embassy Waltz," which compares favorably with any song in the same tempo written by Richard Rodgers.

Further contributing to the sedateness of the Embassy Ball is the stylized choreography of Hermes Pan, whose earlier routines had added still more sparkle to numerous Astaire and Rogers dances throughout the thirties. His masterful direction is entirely in keeping with the stately music and movement of the dancing couples along the ballroom floor. Ever conscious of the dignity Harrison expects her to convey, Audrey winds her way from guest to guest with the unrufflable poise of a princess, winning encomia from everyone she meets. She also incites a great deal of discussion as a woman of mystery whom nobody remembers ever meeting before.

Among the party attendees is Theodore Bikel (Count Zoltan Karpathy), a Budapest native and one-time pupil of Harrison's who has become a master dialectician and fluent speaker of 32 languages. What's more, he boasts to the professor and Colonel Hyde-White, his ability

to pinpoint anyone's origin after the shortest of conversations has led to the exposure of more than one imposter hoping to crash into society by constructing a fraudulent background. Fearful of impending disaster, Harrison's and Hyde-White's normal imperturbability collapses when the hostess assigns Bikel to the task of satisfying her curiosity as to Audrey's lineage.

His asking Audrey for a dance throws the two men into near panic over the possibility she will make another "arse"-like slip and unmask their duplicity. But Audrey's speech is appropriate throughout the ordeal, and Bikel is pleased to report that she is a cultivated foreigner, most likely a Magyar princess. In Bikel's view, Audrey's meticulous enunciation stamps her as a product of Continental, and not British, upbringing, and since her beauty, charm, and speech have so easily captivated everybody, she must have been born in Hungary, too.

Back in the Wimpole Street house, Hyde-White is elated over Audrey's dignified debut. All the glory, he sings in the laudatory "You Did It," belongs to Harrison for engineering such a magnificent coup. Basking happily in the warmth of his friend's musical flattery, Harrison nobly shares congratulations with Hyde-White for his assistance. Standing alone and ignored in the room is Audrey, hoping but not exactly expecting to receive acknowledgment of her own part in the evening's victory. But Harrison gets most of the praise, Hyde-White some of it, and Audrey none of it. Her resentment reaching the boiling point, she later throws Harrison's bedroom slippers at him when he asks where they are. Alarmed at her unexpected tantrum, he attributes it to weariness caused by the long months of stressful training and testing.

But the experiment is over, he tells her, and she is now free to go where she wants and do what she wants. And just where is that, she hollers. She has indeed risen above her marketplace background, yet not high enough to be mistaken for a princess. Appalled when Harrison casually offers to talk the Colonel into opening up a florist shop for her, or to ask his mother's help in finding her a suitable husband, Audrey screams back that the only thing she wants is to move out of his house.

She does just that, bumping on the way out into faithful Freddy, who still spends most of his wide-awake hours camped across the street awaiting the chance to woo her. Desperate for proof that at least one man is fond of her, she reproaches him for his feeble attempts at love making. Her desire is for action, not words, she tells him in the lively and antagonistic "Show Me." Simple terms of endearment are no longer fit substitutes for a show of masculine assertiveness—like an unexpected embrace and a kiss, for example. But unlike Harrison, Freddy is not the dominant type, and he is ejected from Audrey's life and the film with the end of the scene.

Parental Reformation. Back in her familiar Covent Garden stamping grounds on a visit, Audrey is chagrined at the reception she receives from her envious old friends. Decidedly out of place, what with her fancy dress and dulcet tones, she strolls along rarely recognized or, when she is, unwelcomed. Her mood changes to wonderment when out of a pub stumbles her tuxedo-clad father, reeling in the afterglow of another bout with demon rum. He reports that he is to be married later that day—to her mother—and is now rolling in money and morality. Through the good graces of Harrison, who wanted to get the old fellow off his hands for good, Holloway struck up an acquaintance with a wealthy and charitable gentleman. The happy result of their camaraderie was Holloway's inheriting the princely sum of 4,000 pounds a year at the death of his benefactor.

The money is fine, he admits, but rather than subsidizing a life of endless pleasures, it has forced him into becoming a responsible member of the hated middle class. Thus the marriage, Holloway sighs. But he expects to make the most of his few remaining hours of freedom before the wedding. In "Get Me to the Church on Time" he demands of his many fellow celebrants who, between guzzles of booze straight from the bottle, join him in singing and dancing to that riotous mock elegy to lost bachelorhood. As show-stopping a production number as any other on film, it depends largely on Holloway for its orgiastic merriment. He is up to the challenge, polishing his superb performance with verve and vigor that surpass his antics in the stage version.

Difficult as that alcohol-inspired divertissement was to equal in lyric and melody, Lerner and Loewe managed to do so with the amusing song that highlights the meeting between Audrey and Harrison at his mother's house a short time later. It is obvious from his apologetic approach to Audrey that the professor's habitual iciness is on the thaw. Although unable to speak his mind, he admits he misses her beautiful presence and would assuredly welcome her back if she asked. But Audrey, supported by Mother Cooper, has no intention of ever again submitting to the rigors of co-existing with him. Just who does he think he is, she sings to him with a defiant glare and impudent shake of a finger. "Without You" the earth will still spin on its axis, rain will fall on the Spanish plain, spring will break out in blossoms, and the English will muddle through. The same applies to her: she doesn't need him either. Harrison, convinced that she will never derive happiness from his companionship, exits the house, mad as hell but with the cool courtesy expected of a gentleman scholar.

Though seething with anger at the arrows she had slung at him, Harrison talk-sings a love song on the way back to his Wimpole Street residence. Like Louis Jourdan's "Soliloquy" and "Gigi," Harrison's "A Hymn to Him" (subtitled "Why Can't a Woman Be More Like a Man?"), sung that morning when he discovers she's run away, has evolved into "I've Grown Accustomed to Her Face," which for the professor is just about the strongest declaration of love he is capable of making. The earlier song is devoted to a litany of complaints against all women's inability or refusal to react like a man to life's unending burdens. But he willingly acknowledges in the second song that he has become so fond of her that he would gladly overlook the feminine foibles he earlier enumerated.

Maybe she's just a habit he's finding hard to break. And yet, and yet, his life is emptier without her, like winter without sunlight. Could it be that their differences actually complement the individuality of each?

He enters the house and slumps into an armchair. Within seconds he is joined by Audrey, who stands speechless while looking down at him from the door of his study. He is pleased, but his reserve and male stubbornness prevent his rushing into her arms, even glancing at her. Instead, true to his inherent bossiness, he leans his head against the back of the chair, pulls his hat over his face, and pops the question: "Where the devil are my slippers?"

The ending of the 1938 filmed *Pygmalion* is virtually the same. Resisting any show of emotion except irritation to the end, Leslie Howard concedes that he has become accustomed to Wendy Hiller's "voice and appearance," rather than only her face, in a soliloquy. He, too, utters his last line while sitting down and wearing his hat, but with his head turned away from the camera. And he wants his slippers brought to him.

It is assumed that Audrey, like Wendy before her, will fetch them and this time hand rather than fling them at the professor. That may not represent what moviegoers would regard as a heartfelt version of a happy "Hollywood" ending, but it does conclude one of the greatest of all musical pictures on a cheerful note.

The Sound of Music (1965)

A 20th Century-Fox picture. DIRECTOR: Robert Wise; ASSISTANT: Ridgeway Callow. ASSOCIATE PRODUCER: Saul Chaplin. SCREENWRITER: Ernest Lehman, "with the partial use of ideas by Georg Hurdalek." CINEMATOGRAPHER: Ted McCord; ADDITIONAL PHOTOGRAPHY: Paul Beeson; SPECIAL PHOTOGRAPHIC EFFECTS: L.B. Abbott and Emil Kosa, Jr. FILM EDITOR: William Reynolds. PRODUCTION DESIGNER: Boris Leven. CHOREOGRAPHERS: Marc Breaux and Dee Dee Ward. SET DECORATORS: Walter M. Scott and Ruby Levitt. SOUND RECORDING SUPERVISORS: Fred Hynes and James Corcoran. SOUND: Murray Spivack and Bernard Freericks. DIALOGUE COACH: Pamela Danova. COSTUMES: Dorothy Jeakins. HAIRSTYLES: Margaret Donovan. MAKEUP: Ben Nye. PUPPETEERS: Bil Baird and Cora Baird. MUSIC EDITOR: Robert Mayer. VOCAL SUPERVISOR: Robert Tesher. MUSIC SUPERVISOR, ARRANGER, AND CONDUCTOR: Irwin Kostal. SONGS: Lyrics by Oscar Hammerstein II, music by Richard Rodgers; additional lyrics and music by Rodgers. RUNNING TIME: 2 hours, 52 minutes. *Principal Players*: Julie Andrews (Maria). Christopher Plummer (Captain von Trapp). Eleanor Parker (Baroness Elsa Schraeder). Richard Haydn (Max Detweiler). Peggy Wood (Mother Abbess). Anna Lee (Sister Margaretta). Daniel Truhitte (Rolfe Gruber). Ben Wright (Herr Zeller). The von Trapp Children: Charmian Carr (Liesl); Heather Menzies (Louisa); Nicholas Hammond (Friedrich). Duane Chase (Kurt). Angela Cartwright (Brigitta). Debbie Turner (Marta). Kym Kavath (Gretl). *Major*

Academy Awards: Best Picture; Direction; Film Editing; Scoring; Sound. *Nominations*: Best Cinematography; Actress (*Julie Andrews*); Supporting Actress (*Peggy Wood*); Art Direction; Costumes.

Notwithstanding its hefty number of musical sequences (12 songs and eight reprises), there was no doubt that *The Sound of Music* would be made into a movie. In fact, it was the sounds of Richard Rodgers's music that largely accounted for the immediate and perennial appeal of both the stage original, which opened on November 16, 1959, at New York's Lunt-Fontanne Theatre, and the 1965 film. Whether Fox executives suspected that the property would qualify as the most popular movie musical of all time is unknown. If so, their confidence was surely warranted; if not, the gold rush in ticket sales must have nudged them into contemplation of why they should have been so blessed by the gods who guide motion pictures through the marketplace.

A major contributor to the film's gigantic success was its heavy reliance on sentimentalism, or schmaltz in many critics' terminology, which wends its way through the screenplay like blood through the veins. Why its syrupy drippings should have been singled out as a major flaw is something of a mystery, since musical pictures from their inception depended to varying degrees on appealing to the heart rather than the intellect for success. *The Sound of Music*, of course, was a latecomer in this regard, and therefore liable to barbs from persons who had assumed that Hollywood's well of tears had finally run dry.

Speaking on behalf of the disenchanted were Judith Crist and Pauline Kael, in 1965 two of the severest of New York movie critics. To Miss Crist, *The Sound of Music* was the "least inspired, let alone sophisticated," of the Rodgers and Hammerstein musicals, "square and solid sugar." Referring to its remunerative box office take, Miss Kael complained that henceforth it would be "even more difficult for anyone to try to do anything worth doing, anything relevant to the modern world, anything inventive or expressive." Their brickbats, however, failed to deter the Academy of Motion Picture Arts and Sciences from voting the film the best picture of 1965 against some pretty stiff competition, most notably *Doctor Zhivago* and *Ship of Fools*. Altogether, *The Sound of Music*

The von Trapp family members blend their voices in "So Long, Farewell" at the Austrian Salzburg Folk Festival near the end of *The Sound of Music*. From left to right are Nicholas Hammond, Kym Kavath, Angela Cartwright, Julie Andrews, Christopher Plummer, Charmian Carr, Heather Menzies, Debbie Turner, and Duane Chase.

was nominated for nine other Oscars, or only three fewer than the number given to *Gone with the Wind*, ranking it among the most blessed of all film musicals.

More than its Broadway source, the film incorporates every single ingredient needed to captivate sentimental audiences of all ages and insure what *Variety* used to call "boffo box office." It is opulent with breathtaking panoramic views of the Austrian countryside and with inordinately attractive and likable characters, especially the von Trapp children, ranging in age from five to 16, and the singing nuns, who exude the wisdom, gentle humor, and refinement assumed to be perquisites to joining their model religious order. Even the German Nazis and their Austrian supporters who favor the *Anschluss*, or Germany's unlawful annexation of Austria, are depicted as more human than monster. Stern and unyielding as they are, these evildoers are presented as ordinary people caught up in the philosophical and political ranting of the Fuehrer,

who just happened to be one of history's most gifted demagogues.

Analogous to *The King and I*, but more contemporary and less restricted to the studio's sound stages, the film centers on the children's beloved governess (Julie Andrews), who, like Deborah Kerr before her, superbly fills the role of substitute mother, friend, and indeed playmate to them. Their father (Christopher Plummer) is as relentlessly strict as Yul Brynner, and like that potentate, must learn that a child's respect for his or her male parent does not necessarily translate into love. Essentially, both men are despots, even if enlightened ones, equally tight-fisted when it comes to dispensing fatherly affection. Thus, each in his own way has to learn through humility and a restructuring of values that love is earned, not demanded.

The captain's two handsome sons are well groomed and obedient, as are his five pretty daughters, all of them lineal descendants of the fresh-face moppets of the 1930s, equally cute (or "cutesy," if you will) and endowed with crowd-pleasing talent. According to the movies of that earlier decade, children were to be heard as well as seen, but never in conflict with the traditional rules of conduct laid down by responsible adults. If these paragons of youthful virtue were the cause of most of the scorn heaped on the Broadway play for violating the more liberating culture of the late 1950s, and then on the Hollywood film for running counter to the even greater permissiveness of the 1960s, both versions were at least faithful to the stated time frame, "the last Golden Age of the Thirties."

Hollywood strayed far and wide from the stage libretto, which was based on the true story of *The Trapp Family Singers*, written by the real Maria Augusta (von) Trapp, who along with her husband and children fled Austria in 1938 and took up permanent residence in the verdant hills of Stowe, Vermont. She outlived her husband by 40 years, dying in 1987.

Most of the plot deviations consist of fleshing out the libretto by permitting the extremely mobile camera to expand into on-location sites only mentioned in the stage text. The dialogue was adjusted or expanded accordingly, thereby vastly improving the original source, which too often crowded the limited stage space with too many people.

Several songs were deleted, including "How Can Love Survive," sung on Broadway by Marion Marlowe (as Baroness Elsa) and Kurt Kasznar (as Max Detweiler), and "No Way to Stop It," also sung by Miss Marlowe and Kasznar, along with Theodore Bikel (as Captain von Trapp). "My Favorite Things," originally sung by Mary Martin (as Maria) and Patricia Neway (as the Mother Abbess), is reprised in the film by Miss Andrews and the seven children, a creative rearrangement that provides the movie with one of its most charming sequences. "The Lonely Goatherd," the original thunderstorm song, is sung in the film by children and governess during a puppet show.

That the musical play took almost six years to travel from Broadway to Hollywood was due to its long-running presence in New York—which also prevented the stage children from repeating their roles in the film—and to the obvious lengthy and painstaking preproduction efforts that Fox devoted to making certain that the finished work would live up to expectations. The final collaboration between Rodgers and Hammerstein, who died on August 23, 1960, at the relatively young age of 65, *The Sound of Music* had success written all over it from the start. "A sensational musical is on its way to Broadway," *Variety* announced after reviewing the first pre-Broadway tryout at New Haven's Shubert Theatre on October 3, 1959. Unanimous critical accolades were issued following its opening at the Boston Shubert on October 13, and still more after its New York premiere six weeks later, when *Variety* praised in detail what it considered to be the show's strongest assets, which covered almost everything in it: "an absorbing book, outstanding score, splendid acting and singing, engaging personalities, and an overall blend of enchantment and drama."

Looking Backward. Unquestionably, the warm public reception given to the film was due at least in part to its reviving the "old-fashioned" musical. Only a precious few had been released between 1959 and 1965, and die-hard movie-musical patrons, only then beginning to recover from the gritty realism of *West Side Story*, welcomed it with proverbial open arms. There is little doubt that *The Sound of Music*'s story would have fitted neatly into any Hollywood studio's production schedule between 1929 and 1945, although the results would have been far less spectacular. The first three-fourths look back to earlier movie musicals rather than ahead for inspiration. The heroine overcomes all obstacles to marrying the man of her dreams, who stands far above her in accomplishment and social status, and the ready-made family she inherits quickly accepts her as mother because of her unflagging good spirits, which raise their own, and tenderness in soothing their cares away. Even the final fourth, where the villains are introduced, is not much different from the many wartime musicals that pitted the lovers against a historical backdrop seething with danger, from potential death or dismemberment on the battlefield to cracking under the strain of a long separation.

Typical of all Rodgers and Hammerstein musicals, even the comparatively minor *Allegro* and *Me and Juliet*, the music was superior to the libretto. From *Music* emerged seven hits, more than 50 percent of total songs, a remarkable achievement. Only *Carousel* and *South Pacific*, with eight each, top *Music*'s record. No other songwriting team in Broadway history filled their shows with a comparable number of standard tunes.

The partners co-produced the stage musical in company with Leland Hayward and Richard Halliday. The libretto was by Broadway veterans Howard Lindsay and Russel Crouse. Adapting it for the screen was the redoubtable Ernest Lehman, already highly esteemed for such outstanding screenplays as the two earlier best picture musicals *The King and I* and *West Side Story*, in addition to *Executive Suite* and *Sabrina* (both 1954) and *North by Northwest* (1959). The experienced and able director Robert Wise had been practicing his craft for two decades, with results ranging from the inconsequential (*Mademoiselle Fifi*, 1944; *Criminal Court*, 1946) to the substantial (*I Want to Live*, 1958; *Two for the Seesaw*, 1962; and, in collaboration with Jerome Robbins, *West Side Story*).

Miss Andrews succeeded Mary Martin to star in the film, marking the second time in eight years that the latter was denied access to a role the world was convinced she owned; she also lost out in 1958 on repeating the Nellie Forbush part in *South Pacific* to Mitzi Gaynor. Both cast switches were inevitable, despite Miss Martin's deserved reputation as a highly polished performer, beginning with her modest strip-tease to Cole Porter's "My Heart Belongs to Daddy" in *Leave It to Me* in 1938, which she repeated eight years later in *Night and Day*, and experience in 12 movies up to 1953. The sole reason for her suffering these two losses was her age. She was 51 when the filming of *Music* got under way, hardly youthful enough to portray Maria, the childlike postulant at the Nonnberg Abbey in Salzburg who becomes caretaker of the love-starved children of a retired Austrian naval officer. But Miss Andrews, herself a fine actress and singer imbued with gracefulness when she moved, spoke, or sang, had met with an identical rebuff in 1964, when the role of Eliza Doolittle, which she had made famous in *My Fair Lady*, was given to Audrey Hepburn.

Fox's choice of the typically competent Christopher Plummer as the patrician Captain von Trapp, the only two-dimensional character in the film, however, was a judgmental error, not serious enough to mortally wound the picture's overall effervescence, but tending to weigh it down with all too many reminders that this middle-age widower desperately needed the companionship of a woman. He does love his children but is unable to show it, giving the impression that the most they can expect from him is a tight-lipped smile of toleration toward their infrequent outbursts of childish delight. As a career military man, he was undoubtedly respected but not loved by his men. Years of maintaining ironclad control of his emotions, an asset for an officer but hardly for a father, have conditioned him to treating friends and family with a reserve that wrongly implies indifference, if not callousness.

He treats his daughters as well as his sons like enlistees. They snap to attention and line up in descending height immediately after he whistles them into his presence. They respond to every order with alacrity, and without dissent. They are, in fact, his troops, his home guard, living in a sort of boot camp environment that allows little wiggle room to act their ages. The only protocol Plummer does not force upon them is to shout "Yes, sir!" and salute.

Theodore Bikel, who originated the role on Broadway, was equally handsome and elegant as the captain, but he managed to exude more warmth than Plummer—in addition to looking quite comfortable while singing and strumming a guitar. (Plummer's vocalizing was dubbed by Bill Lee.) In Bikel's portrayal, the captain was admirable from beginning to end, a born aristocrat without a bone of pettiness in his body. Plummer, on the other hand, comes across as a sour martinet, equally dislikable as Louis Jourdan in *Gigi* until he, too, falls in love.

Bikel, too, may have failed early on to evince deep concern for his children's personality development, but he always wore his heart on his sleeve, treating them with sympathy even while pounding military decorum into them. Plummer's conversion from absolute ruler to loving father willing to sacrifice his substantial material possessions by pulling up his roots for the safety of his children is more pronounced than Bikel's. It is also far less convincing, since he had so successfully blocked out any indication that such a transition was even remotely possible.

Rounding out the cast of highly proficient actors are Richard Haydn, an excellent film comedian and director, whose role as the butler in *And Then There Were None*, the peerless film version of Agatha Christie's *Ten Little Indians*, was still familiar to many movie fans 20 years later. Competing in that 1945 film against such longtime scene-stealing personages as Walter Huston, Barry Fitzgerald, Mischa Auer, Judith Anderson, C. Aubrey Smith, and Roland Young, Haydn held his own remarkably well, thanks mostly to his stiff but humorous ultra-formal mannerism and nasal voice, neither of which is in evidence in *The Sound of Music*.

Unfortunately, the Haydn on exhibition in the film is only a pallid copy of the supreme realist depicted on the stage. He is given little to do, all of it insignificant and basically unfunny. In the Broadway version, Max is quite vociferously pro-Nazi and opposed to the marriage of the captain and the baroness, citing their lack of money and other problems as assurance that they cannot find happiness together, since both have been immersed in it most of their lives. In the film he looks forward to the marriage in the absurd belief that the consolidation of two fortunes will somehow redound to his benefit.

Also largely wasted is Eleanor Parker, a fine actress with 24 years of Hollywood experience and three best actress nominations behind her. Apart from looking fetching as ever as the mature, wealthy and widowed Baroness Elsa from Vienna, she was asked to do little more than walk and sit in almost complete boredom in the few scenes allotted to her. Unlike the stage musical, in which the baroness' approval of the *Anschluss* is a major contributor to the dissolution of her engagement to the captain, the film presents Eleanor as totally apolitical.

The grand old actress Peggy Wood, then 65, who had appeared as a chorus girl in the original *Naughty Marietta* in 1910, however, fares much better in her decisive role as the Mother Abbess, for which she received nomination for best supporting actress. Also in the

abbey is Anna Lee, marvelously acting out her brief role as a well-disciplined but pragmatic nun. Among the children, only Angela Cartwright (as Brigitta) achieved widespread recognition, primarily stemming from her playing Danny Thomas's daughter on sitcom television.

The most glorious feature of the film was the DeLuxe color photography, which gives the picture a pastoral splendor still unsurpassed by any other musical. Like *West Side Story*, it opens with a spectacular aerial view, moving from majestic, snow-capped hills across shimmering lakes and above a castle and woods just beyond the borders of Salzburg, a cinematic masterpiece creating the illusion that people sitting anywhere in the theater could actually breathe in the clear mountain air. Suddenly, Miss Andrews appears in her convent dress, running along a level patch of emerald-green grass, twirling in ecstatic response to the beauties of nature, her arms outstretched as if to embrace the landscape and shield its loveliness from desecration. As she declares in the opening and title song, echoes of "The Sound of Music" can be heard reverberating from the surrounding hills as their pines sway to the rhythm of the melody she sings. The film had no intention of duplicating the claustrophobic sets that restricted the action of the stage play to interior scenes and confined the scenery to mere conversational references that audiences could only imagine.

Mischievous but Harmless. Because the trip between the singing fields and the abbey is a long one, Julie Andrews (Maria) is unable to get there till after evening vespers. Not that this is the first example of her tardiness or flouting Abbey rules. But this time her conduct has imposed an unusually severe handicap on even her most ardent supporters, like Anna Lee (Sister Margaretha), as they once again try to counter their opponents' argument that Julie is temperamentally unfit to follow rules. Even the adversaries, however, concede that the lively young lady is a veritable bundle of cheerfulness with a gift for painting the convent with sunshine and their own faces with smiles.

And, they further admit, she has never been late for meals. But she is always getting into some sort of trouble, and so far has shown little promise of becoming an asset to the abbey. The nuns then proclaim her failings and virtues in the film's second song, "Maria," with both admirers and detractors agreeing that the little flibbertigibbet is both angel and headache, compelled to wander at will like a moonbeam. Stopping her from doing what comes naturally is as impossible as trying to hold a wave on the sand or halting the movement of a cloud. A decision on her future simply has to be made.

Penitent as always, Julie attempts with little success to beg forgiveness for what Peggy Wood (the Mother Abbess) is convinced is the girl's innate spirit of rebelliousness. She has heard all her excuses before, and Julie's maintaining that it was the hills themselves that had beckoned her to visit them fails to dissuade the aging nun from suggesting that the novice has undertaken the wrong career.

Her recommendation is that Julie leave the convent "for a time," assuring that she can serve God on the outside as well as on the inside, probably better. Luckily, there is a job open at the estate of Captain Georg von Trapp, who is in need of a governess for his seven children. Peggy urges her to apply, since the experience could very well help her to learn exactly what God expects of her. What the Mother Abbess skips over is that Julie will be the family's twelfth governess in fewer than two years, and that her immediate predecessor had lasted only two hours in the position.

Although disappointed, Julie is determined to get and excel at the job. Carrying a bag filled with clothing and other essentials in one hand, and a guitar in the other, off she goes to the von Trapps, certain that her temporary dismissal from the convent has a purpose. Mother Peggy had once told her that "When God closes a door, He always opens a window." And, as she sings "I Have Confidence in Me," a new Rodgers's interpolation into the score, she is satisfied for now to accept the window about to be opened up to her as one of opportunity.

Desperate for a governess, Christopher Plummer (Captain von Trapp) hires Julie on the spot, stressing that her major task will be constraining the youngsters' frequent impulses to act their age. She is to regard them in the same way he does—as potentially unruly children constantly in need of discipline. Appalled at the stifling military formality that characterizes relations between father and offspring, Julie correctly surmises that the captain's household has not been a happy one since the death of his wife. Though pleased at the chance to learn something useful on the job, she is pestered by the realization that she is perhaps the least qualified of applicants to impose orderliness on what appears to be a brood of resentful children.

Julie is quick to discover the pleasure the children derive from misbehaving when, during their introductions, she pulls an unwelcome frog from a pocket of her dress and later, at their first dinner together, she swats a pine cone from her chair after sitting on it. Apparently the children, aware that their father would never tolerate such displays of churlishness, have selected her as the target of their discontent. Yet, for all the von Trapps' lack of familial warmth, love is not entirely absent from the household. The eldest child, 16-year-old Charmian Carr (Liesel), is in the throes of first love with Daniel Truhitte (Rolf Gruber), a handsome blond boy who has called at the house to deliver a telegram to the captain. Upon his arrival, Charmian excuses herself from the table to meet and embrace him near the secluded lake on the estate grounds.

Feeling that her love for him is most likely adolescent infatuation, Daniel seeks to warn her of the perils facing innocent young girls on the verge of entering into the world of men by singing "Sixteen Going on Seventeen," a melodious peek into the heart of a young girl, neither a child nor yet a woman. What she needs is a mature counselor who will guard her against making mistakes of judgment or action. He, of course, is just the right person to act as guide. He is, after all, 17 going on 18, and therefore vastly more experienced and wiser than little Charmian. In her own chorus, she eagerly submits to his protection, promising to exercise caution in love matters in order to avoid the pitfalls that ensnare the immature.

Julie is settling herself in her bedroom when Charmian climbs through the window, and they strike up a friendly conversation once Julie vows not to reveal a word of her rendezvous. A succession of thunderclaps sends the other six frightened children into the room, the so-called "brave" boys as well as the girls, who join Julie on her bed, where she proceeds to calm their nerves by explaining in "My Favorite Things" how she manages to keep her cool under even the most trying circumstances.

What she does, she tells them, is fill her mind with pretty thoughts, like the gentle tapping of raindrops in springtime, the sight of kittens' whiskers and snowflakes, and the aroma of freshly baked apple strudel. Their reverie concludes on an unpleasant note, however, when the captain interrupts Julie's singing and demands that she never again allow the children to indulge in such foolishness. Discipline, he reminds her, is the first rule of the house, and he insists that she "acquire some of it" herself. He then storms out of the room after ordering the children back to theirs. Saddened at having irritated her employer, Julie intuitively senses that music and laughter offend him because they remind him of the happier days when his wife was alive to share them with him.

A few days later Plummer leaves on a trip to Vienna, where he will escort Eleanor Parker (Baroness Elsa Schraeder) back to the estate for an extended visit. Despite her desire to conduct herself according to the captain's no-nonsense regimen while he is away, Julie commits another infraction by supplying the children with new clothes, which, in Scarlett O'Hara fashion, she sews together from the green drapes hanging in her bedroom. If she no longer can perk up their lives with songs, at least she can supply them with colorful, youthful-looking clothing to play in. Then, in even further defiance of the captain's strictures, she takes the children on a bicycle trip into Salzburg and for a picnic on her beloved mountain retreat. Since she is at her happiest when singing, they persuade her to teach them the rudiments of music so that they might sing along with her.

In her first lesson, Julie explains that each note on a piece of sheet music has its own name—like "Do, Re, Mi," for example. And the eight of them are not the least difficult to memorize; all one has to do is link each note to a familiar object. "Do" (doe), for example, is the accepted name for a female deer, and "re" (ray) for a shaft of sunlight. Her happy pupils learn fast and they continue to practice the song

while bicycling over hill and dale, in effect giving birth to the soon to be world-renowned Trapp Family of Singers.

Upon their return home, they greet Eleanor and another guest, Richard Haydn (Max Detweiler), a minor Austrian impresario and social sponge eager to live in regal splendor at the expense of his wealthy friends. Far more preoccupied with self-preservation than with the growing danger to Austrian independence, Haydn offends host Plummer by insisting that Germany's inevitable annexation of Austria may not be quite so bad for the country as Plummer believes. Backing away when the captain castigates him for his apparent sympathy with the Nazi cause, Haydn insists that he has "no political convictions." Plummer sadly muses that he prefers to remain faithful to his homeland, even if the disappearing world he has known will most likely never return. Haydn is content to dismiss the altercation as inconsequential, not a test of his patriotism, and reconcentrates on his own goal of finding musical talent to perform in the forthcoming Salzburg Folk Festival.

Having fallen overboard in a rented canoe, Julie and the children had further rattled Plummer by returning home soaking wet. He vents his anger at Julie for dressing the children in play clothes and taking them on an excursion. When she protests that she only wanted to free the children from what she calls their customary strait-jackets, he fires her. When he hears the children singing "The Sound of Music" to welcome the baroness, however, he instantly recognizes their talent, even joining them in the song. Their harmonizing together prompts smiles and embraces by all the participants, the family's first overt expression of happiness that Julie has witnessed. The proud father even apologizes to Julie for his behavior and asks her to stay on as governess.

A Changing Household. To celebrate the defrosting relationship between father and family, and to please Eleanor and Haydn, Julie and the children stage a marionette show highlighted by their singing "The Lonely Goatherd," while pulling the strings to manipulate the puppets. Particularly attentive is Haydn, who at the end offers to enter the children in the festival, only to be informed by Plummer that he will never allow them to perform in public.

But that night he does respond to his children's pleading that he entertain them by accompanying himself on his long-unused guitar while he sings "Edelweiss," Rodgers's very simple and monumentally beautiful anthem to the little Alpine flower, or "snow blossom," as Plummer calls it, found almost everywhere in the Austrian and Swiss countryside. Actually a song of patriotism, and Hammerstein's last published lyric, it serves as the strongest indication thus far of Plummer's resolve never to accede to the Nazi takeover of his country.

Gradually emerging from his shell of unsociability, Plummer reopens the ballroom to hold a formal-dress party in Eleanor's honor. Unknown to him, the site is to serve as the focal point of a new love affair that will affect the lives of the three principals. Together, Plummer and Julie dance to the strains of "Laendler," a dignified and intricate folk dance performed in exquisite synchronization, only to have his partner desert him with unexpected suddenness. Thinking that Julie feels ill at ease in her peasant dress, Plummer invites her to the ball and suggests that she change into a more fashionable evening gown. Julie's obvious affection for the captain does not elude the watchful eyes of Eleanor, now unable to conceal her envy of her youthfulness, beauty, and abundance of charm. She offers to help the governess choose an appropriate party dress, and follows her to her bedroom.

There Eleanor insists that Julie is falling in love with Plummer, and that she had left him during the dance because she sensed the captain's mounting romantic interest in her. Fearful Julie recognizes the truth in the statement, and is determined to call an immediate halt to what she suspects is a budding love affair. Still officially an acolyte, Julie welcomes Eleanor's suggestion that, like Hamlet's Ophelia, she get herself to a nunnery before she falls victim to passion. Julie changes back into her usual peasant dress, leaves a note for the captain on a downstairs table, and flees the estate for the abbey, unnoticed by all the partygoers except Eleanor, no longer resentful but smiling in triumph.

Not a man to watch his theatrical plans dissolve before his eyes, Haydn connives to obtain Plummer's permission for the children to entertain the guests. The song they choose to sing is the lullaby "So Long, Farewell," during which each child bids the audience goodnight before departing the scene. All except little Kym Kavath (Gretl), that is, who is carried up the stairs by Charmian after the five-year-old falls asleep on the bottom step.

Expecting soon to become Plummer's wife, Eleanor fails miserably in her attempts to ingratiate herself with the children, who she is well aware are extremely saddened by Julie's departure, particularly without so much as a goodbye. She is simply too inflexible to play ball with them, too tired to engage in any other activity, and too bored to show any interest in their musical development. Eleanor is further dismayed when the youngsters' sole response to the news that she is to be their new mother takes the form of seven unemotional kisses on the cheek. Knowing that she will continue to suffer in comparison with Julie, Eleanor devises a protective scheme. She will pack all the children off to boarding school immediately after the wedding.

Refused entry to the convent on a trip to Salzburg, the children gradually reconcile themselves to the permanent loss of their vivacious young lady companion. Julie, too, is battling her own discontent by appealing to the Mother Abbess for advice on how to suppress the "new strange feeling" that came over her whenever she was in Plummer's presence. Sagely surmising that Julie regards the convent as a fortress to shield her from the challenges of the outside world, Peggy insists that the love between a man and a woman is every bit as sacred as that between a nun and God.

"You must live the life you were born to live," the older woman counsels. Julie must return to the estate and decide for herself whether she prefers to be a wife and mother or a nun. Either way, Peggy contends, she will be serving God. She counters Julie's protest with the words to the ever-lovely "Climb Every Mountain" (actually sung by Margery McKay), worthy of inclusion in a hymnal, urging Julie to follow a variety of roads until she finds her dream of a perfect life.

Acquiescing to her superior's recommendation, Julie returns to Plummer and children, only to learn that his impending marriage to Eleanor has closed off the first road she had intended to travel. She pleases him by apologizing for her abrupt departure, but then depresses him by agreeing to stay only until he can find a proper substitute. Later that afternoon, Plummer gives Eleanor an expensive gift, supposedly in honor of their forthcoming wedding. But both realize that the gift is really meant to atone for his unwillingness to marry her. Anticipating the loss of Plummer the moment Julie reentered the house, Eleanor trumps the captain by breaking off the engagement herself, asserting that he is too independent-minded to ever need her or her money. With her eyes reflecting the deep pain of rejection, but in a calm voice, Eleanor returns the gift and whispers a fond "Auf Wiedersehen" before disappearing in the shadows.

A short time later, Julie joins Plummer in the garden. When he reveals that the engagement has been called off, she feels free to indicate her love for him without in any way dishonoring either him or herself. Attesting to her love is "Something Good," a new and quite moving ballad that Rodgers wrote expressly for the film to replace the less effective "An Ordinary Couple," which in the stage version served to announce the couple's love for each other. In Julie's view, her newly found happiness can be attributed to her having done an unspecified something good somewhere to somebody sometime in the past. Plummer responds by confirming his undying love for her in the second chorus.

Their marriage, which took place in 1927, not 1938, is performed in the Abbey church and highlighted by the dignified "Processional," or "Preludium," that accompanies Julie, dressed in a stunning white bridal gown, as she begins her walk down the aisle. The stateliness of this splendid scene, however, is compromised by the inexplicable followup reprise of "Maria" as she approaches the altar. The lighthearted melody, as well as the woefully inappropriate lyric, sung by a chorus of nuns, detracts significantly from the solemnity of the occasion. In the stage version, the only music to be heard was the "Processional."

Cutting short the honeymoon when the *Anschluss* is completed, Plummer again rages at Haydn when he suggests that Plummer accept the annexation with silence, if not grace. Haydn himself is prepared to participate as required in the so-called "New Order," advising that "one must try to get along with everybody." Young Daniel Truhitte, now dressed in a Nazi uniform, enters the house to deliver a telegram from Berlin. Charmian, bewildered at the young man's aloofness toward her and "*Sieg Heil!*" salute, gives it to her father, who is instructed to report within two days to the naval base at Bremerhaven and accept a commission in the German Navy.

Plummer contemptuously regards the command as an insult to his and Austrian integrity. Realizing that escape to Switzerland is his only alternative to being arrested for insubordination, he subscribes to Julie's suggestion that it can be achieved by participating in the folk festival competition that evening. In a clever move designed to convince Austrians and the world at large that annexation will in no way disturb the enjoyment of traditional theatrical events, Ben Wright (Herr Zeller), a local Nazi official, has permitted the affair to go on as scheduled.

Wright attends the festival and warns Plummer that if he neglects to follow Berlin's orders, he will be removed to Bremerhaven by force. Plummer replies that he will surrender himself, but first he must join his family on stage. The suspicious Nazi approves and seats himself in the first row, the better to keep tabs on the singers' movements. Plummer reprises "Edelweiss," introducing it as every Austrian's personal "love song" to his native country and urging the audience never to allow that love to wither and die. The rest of the family join in singing "Do-Re-Mi," also new to the score, and the children reprise "So Long, Farewell." This time, however, instead of deserting the stage one by one for their bedrooms, they leave the theater.

Hoping to give the family time to put as much distance as possible between themselves and the theater, a sympathetic Haydn, his love of country revived by Plummer's performance, punctuates his reading of the names of the three winning contestants with verbiage and frequent pauses in his recitation. When he announces the von Trapps as first-place winner, the audience is astounded not to see them reappear to claim the prize. Particularly concerned are

Wright and several of his armed henchmen, who immediately make a spirited dash from the concert hall to their car.

With the assistance of Peggy Wood and other nuns, Plummer, Julie, and children take refuge in the Abbey cemetery. They elude detection by flashlight-carrying Nazi troops, who carefully inspect all the crypts. Satisfied that the escapees are elsewhere, they hurry away to continue their search on the church roof. But when Charmian spots Daniel among the soldiers, he hears her gasp of recognition, pulls a pistol from his holster, and orders the family to come out from behind a cluster of gravestones. Instead, Julie and the children scurry out of the cemetery while Plummer confronts the young soldier and invites him to join in their flight from Austria. "You'll never be one of them," he assures Daniel, referring to his fellow Nazis. For a moment, Daniel stands motionless, giving Plummer time to grab the pistol from his hand.

But his assessment of Daniel's character was mistaken. Faithful to his indoctrination, the one-time messenger and boyfriend of Charmian shouts to the others that he has found their prey.

Plummer races in his family's footsteps to their car, parked in front of the Abbey. Seconds after they drive away, the Nazis jump into their own car. But their plan to overtake them is foiled when they are unable to start the motor. As one of the nuns reports to the delighted Mother Abbess, she and a few of the others have committed a most "grievous sin." While the soldiers were busy in the cemetery, they lifted the hood of their 540K Mercedes Roadster and disabled the ignition system. The Nazis, however, have sealed all borders, causing the runaways finally to complete their escape by foot.

The final scene shows all nine von Trapps standing high above the floor of Austria, looking south to freedom. Under the leadership of the resilient father, the family has weathered the *Anschluss* and is now only a horizon away from realizing its fondest dream. They have climbed their last mountain and forded their last stream in their desperate effort to find a safe harbor in Switzerland. For the next seven years, the sounds of music heard in their homeland will be more martial than waltz, but the edelweiss will survive the frost that now grips the country. Together, the one-time stiff-necked naval captain, dejected children, and girl governess, whose example had turned them into a loving family again, nod a final so long and goodbye to Austria.

Doctor Doolittle (1967)

A 20th Century-Fox picture. DIRECTOR: Richard Fleischer. PRODUCER: Arthur P. Jacobs; ASSOCIATE: Mort Abrahams. SCREENWRITER: Leslie Bricusse, based on Doctor Doolittle stories by Hugh Lofting. CINEMATOGRAPHER: Robert Surtees; VISUAL EFFECTS: L.B. Abbott, Art Cruickshank, Emil Kosa, Jr., Howard Lydecker. FILM EDITORS: Samuel E. Beetley and Majorie Fowler. CHOREOGRAPHER: Herbert Ross. PRODUCTION DESIGNER: Mario Chiari. ART DIRECTORS: Jack Martin Smith, Ed Graves, Walter M. Scott, and Stuart A. Reiss. SOUND: 20th Century-Fox Studio Sound Department. COSTUMES: Ray Aghayan. SCORING: Lionel Newman and Alexander Courage. SONGS: Lyrics and music by Leslie Bricusse. RUNNING TIME: 2 hours, 25 minutes. *Principal Players*: Rex Harrison (Dr. John Doolittle). Samantha Eggar (Emma Fairfax). Anthony Newley (Matthew Mugg). Peter Bull (General Bellowes). William Dix (Tommy Stubbins). Richard Attenborough (Albert Blossom). Portia Nelson (Sarah Doolittle). Geoffrey Holder (William Shakespeare the 10th). *Major Academy Awards*: Visual Effects; Best Song ("Talk to the Animals"). *Nominations*: Best Picture; Cinematography; Film Editing; Art Direction; Sound; Scoring.

He tried hard, but after a year of struggling to write the screenplay and lyrics, Alan Jay Lerner came to the conclusion that he could do little with *Doctor Doolittle* and gave up. Star Rex Harrison threatened to pull out of the project after Lerner's departure, but he remained true to the famous live show business tradition by sticking with it even though his discerning eyes recognized that the film would never qualify as a classic, even a hit.

More than likely he long regretted his decision, especially in light of his earlier involvement in another stupendous Fox disaster, *Cleopatra* (1963), although Harrison was at least nominated as best actor of the year for that one. Perhaps his judgment was still clouded over in 1967, or perhaps he experienced a sudden surge of hope when Leslie Bricusse, a very fine lyricist and composer with a rare Lorenz Hart flair for concocting clever internal rhymes, was assigned to write the screenplay and put the words to his own music.

Rex Harrison and Anthony Newley admire the human characteristics embodies by the good doctor's parrot, Polynesia, in *Doctor Doolittle.*

Harrison was correct in judging Bricusse's talent, but not even the score, delightful as much of it is, could compensate for the lackluster results of producing the second and least attractive of the four Oscar-nominated musical fantasies since *The Wizard of Oz.*

The tale the picture tells was far too ambitious for Fox, which should have left the undertaking to the Disney folks. Had their studio been interested in it, the film might have developed into a highly successful property. As things turned out *Doctor Doolittle* was a critical and commercial dud, sporting one of the most absurd and convoluted stories ever filmed. Compounding the assault on the imagination are the frequent superfluous scenes that extend the picture far beyond the running time it deserves. The love story was unnecessary to begin with, poorly handled, and left hanging at the end. Likewise, the Sea Star Island natives' second threat to the freedom of Harrison and his shipwrecked friends is embarrassingly redundant. The title clearly indicates that the lead-

ing figure is an adult. The result was outfitting what should have been a children's tale in sheep's clothing that neither young nor old wanted to try on for size.

The child lead, William Dix (as Tommy Stubbins), is not only incidental to the plot, but also the poorest boy actor in a nominated musical since Rex Thompson appeared as Deborah Kerr's son in *The King and I.* He has little to do, and what he does do fails to add anything in the way of charm or suspense to a film that was aimed primarily at the children's market. All the plot elements are instigated by Harrison, and it is through his eyes alone, rather than Billy's, that the picture hoped to involve the audience in an oversupply of absurd adventures in which every other character is an inconsequential participant. At least the young Mr. Thompson's part was a small one. He was not expected to serve as catalyst for the change in relationship between king and parent, or as chronicler of the events leading up to it. Billy Dix, on the other hand, should have been central to the *Doctor Doolittle* plot, thereby unifying all the incidents rather than merely following along on the eccentric Harrison's globe-spanning voyage.

Also detrimental to this updated *Arabian Night*'s tale is its length, almost two and one-half hours. Hollywood already had proved it knew how to make highly enjoyable children's pictures, a lesson that the Fox executives had presumably forgotten. Jackie Cooper was co-star of *Treasure Island* (1934), Freddie Bartholomew of *Kidnapped* (1938) and *The Swiss Family Robinson* (1940), and Tommy Kelly of *The Adventures of Tom Sawyer* (1938), and all four movies thrived at the box office. These novel-based plots were brilliantly condensed so that the lads either motivated or reacted to every incident, and not one of the films exceeded one hour and 45 minutes in length, testifying to their directors' skill at stripping the stories down to the bare essentials.

Occasionally successful as a stage actor and sometimes a songwriting collaborator with Bricusse, Anthony Newley is horribly miscast as Harrison's wisecracking Irish helpmate, spouting unamusing one-liners that generally refer to his pride of heritage, which his gravy-thick brogue amply demonstrates, and periodic need of a liquid pick-me-up to settle his nerves. His acting reeks with insincerity, particularly when aping the shyness of a tongue-tied lover, giving the impression that he wanted to complete his chore and get away from the Fox lot as quickly as possible. Not that the apple of his eye is an expert at throwing off flirty-flirty looks here and there, only to back away when either Newley or Harrison interprets them as love calls. Notwithstanding her beaming prettiness, Samantha Eggar serves no purpose other than to decorate the film, consistently unable to enliven it, invest it with humor or tension, or compensate for its glaring inadequacies.

As for Newley's singing, an inharmonious blend of whines and whinnies, it manages to mangle every one of the six songs he is called upon to vocalize either alone or in concert with other cast members. Harrison's singing is not very much better, having changed very little since he first donned a musical cap on Broadway in 1956, but audiences had grown accustomed to his talking his lyrics, and rather admired his forthright style. Nonetheless, neither man does justice to two of Bricusse's prettier ballads, "Something in Your Smile" (Harrison) and "Where Are the Words?" (Newley) in the course of the *Doolittle* screenplay.

Like many other disappointing films, this one boasts several features deserving of critical praise, indicating quite clearly that technical proficiency was definitely present when the production was put together. The sets and art direction, sound and color are quite respectable. Indeed, the film garnered eight Academy Award nominations, winning the Oscar for visual effects, which are stunning from start to finish. The hundreds of on-screen animals are adequate to their assignments. Of them all, a chimpanzee and a parrot named Polynesia would rank up there with Rin Tin Tin and Lassie as scene-stealers while supplying the film with its few comic moments.

Harrison does a creditable acting job, worthy of some kind of honorary award considering the handicaps he had to overcome while dealing with the material handed to him. He is quite comfortable in his second screen outing as an independent scholar pursuing an esoteric linguistic discipline. None of Professor Higgins' intellectual superciliousness or impatience corrupts Harrison's even temperament, and he is as willing to learn as to teach. His early assertion that he has "nothing in common with the human race" smacks of Higgins's preference for isolation from fellow human beings, and the doctor also displays the capacity to love at least one of them. Like Higgins, Doolittle is not fated to die a bachelor. Doolittle is far more human than Higgins, even if less fascinating as a character.

Despite the film's box office drubbing, Fox can take some comfort from producing a musical that had not originated on Broadway, which by 1967 had been the chief source of movie musicals for a dozen years. Also worthy of compliments were the studio's frequent insertions of animal-rights appeals, most of them issued by Harrison at his most dramatic moments. There is no doubt whatever that John Doolittle loves animals. His establishment of the Anglo-American Fox Protection Society is greeted warmly by Samantha, even though her uncle is fanatically attached to the "sport" of fox hunting. And in his courtroom song, "Like Animals," he defends four-legged and winged creatures against the common perception that they are of value only as purveyors of meat for the human stomach and fur for protection against inclement weather with stinging persuasiveness. Definitely an asset to the film, Harrison's relationship to animals evokes the same awareness of mankind's cruelty toward them that had made such early Disney features as *Dumbo* (1941) and *Bambi* (1942) such all-time sentimental favorites.

After the fashion of *Seven Brides for Seven Brothers*, the 14 *Doctor Doolittle* songs display the craftsmanship of an excellent but largely unsung composer, even if none but "Talk to the Animals," the year's best song winner, made the grade as a resounding hit. For most of his career, Bricusse has alternated between the East and West coasts as often as any of his contemporaries. At times he has provided just the lyrics, like Fred Ebb and Sheldon Harnick, other times only the music, like Cy Coleman and Marvin Hamlisch, and sometimes both words and melody, like Stephen Sondheim and Jerry Herman. He earned success in both places, slightly more from his Hollywood visits than on Broadway.

Among Bricusse's stage song hits written with and for Anthony Newley are "Gonna Build a Mountain" and "What Kind of Fool Am I?", both from *Stop the World—I Want to Get Off* (1961), made into a movie (without Newley) five years later, and "Who Can I Turn To (When Nobody Needs Me)," from *The Roar of the Greasepaint, the Smell of the Crowd* (1964).

Briscusse's Hollywood tunes include four other Academy Award nominees, "Thank You Very Much," from *Scrooge* (1970), a musical version of *A Christmas Carol*, for which Harrison was unsuccessfully sought to play the title role; "Life in a Looking Glass," from *That's Life* (1986); "Somewhere in My Memory," from *Home Alone* (1990); and "When You're Alone," from *Hook* (1991). Other of his film lyrics appeared in *Goldfinger* (1964) and *You Only Live Twice* (1967), both with music by John Barry; *Goodbye, Mr. Chips* (1969), for which Bricusse wrote both lyrics and music; *Willy Wonka and the Chocolate Factory* (1971), lyrics only to Newley's music, which included "The Candy Man"; and *Victor/Victoria*, lyrics only to music by Henry

Mancini. Most recently, Bricusse completed the book and lyrics for Frank Wildhorn's music for *Jekyll & Hyde: The Musical*, based on the Stevenson novella, which opened on Broadway on April 29, 1997.

The Doctor and His Menagerie. The story opens amid the charming rusticity of the village of Puddleby-on-the-Marsh in the west of England in the year 1845. The winning personality and genius of Rex Harrison (Dr. John Doolittle) provide the theme for the opening song, "My Friend the Doctor," sung by Anthony Newley (Matthew Mugg), an Irish-born fish peddler, to a village boy, William Dix (Tommy Stubbins). The most noteworthy of the doctor's gifts, Newley sings in homage, is his uncommon ability to communicate with a wide assortment of animals. About 600 live in his house or elsewhere on his property, presenting him with plenty of opportunities to practice such diverse languages as horse, cow, sheep, donkey, pig, and mouse until he masters them.

Visiting Harrison, Newley and Billy are impressed to find that the doctor's project du jour is studying to speak goldfish as the first step in learning the whereabouts of the legendary and quite elusive Great Pink Sea Snail. Long the subject of sailors' chanties, the 2,000-year-old animal most assuredly exists, Harrison tells them, and, of even greater surprise, is related to an even better-known creature of mystery, the Loch Ness Monster.

Once he acquires enough money to fund an expedition, Harrison expects to seek out the snail in its watery home. Anything but shy about roaming the world, the good doctor has just returned from a trip to the Congo, where he cured a crocodile of a toothache by extracting the offending molar.

To facilitate the search, he has also undertaken the study of mackerel and halibut in order to make it easier for him to acquire intimacy with the ancient shellfish language, which Harrison describes as "extremely complicated." Once this linguistic feat has been achieved, he can take advantage of various deep-sea crustaceans as guides to finding his fabled quarry.

That Harrison is a true supporter as well as healer of animals is confirmed in his first solo,

"The Vegetarian," which he delivers while Newley and the boy prepare to eat a hearty meal of fried meat products. Yes, Harrison admits, he, too, fancies such dishes as roast beef and deviled ham, but considers it the height of meanness to eat one's friends, and therefore he has restricted his diet to flowering shrubs growing on his vast property. In a brief flashback, he also explains why some years earlier had he had switched his medical practice to treating animals rather than human beings. The major reason was to facilitate the exodus of his bossy sister, Portia Nelson (Sarah), from his house. No fan of the animal kingdom, she continuously disparaged his growing interest in them. As for his human patients, they seemed to the doctor to be little more than cry babies, wailing over imaginary illnesses and minor pains and aches, and much more devoted to gossiping than to preserving their health.

Everything worked out well for Harrison: his irate sister moved out and he, emboldened by the advice of his pet parrot, Polynesia, henceforth practiced only veterinarian medicine. The bird had complained that there was not one good animal doctor in the whole of western England, implying that the market potential of setting up such a practice would be vast. The parrot was also instrumental in urging him to learn animal languages, which in the film consist of unintelligible grunts accompanied by agitated bodily movements. Now 189 years old, she speaks about 2,000 of them herself, including such presumably extinct dialects as unicorn and dodo, and had promised to teach all of them to Harrison, who at the moment is fluent in only 498 of them.

Referring to animals as "so much more fun than people," Harrison is delighted to find that he can instruct his patients verbally on exactly how to cure themselves of disorders by following his directions. And, like the short-sighted horse that dutifully reads aloud the lines on an eye chart through a new pair of spectacles, all the animals obey instructions and never fail to reward their doctor with nose-to-nose verification of their fondness for him.

Also fascinated by Harrison's language proficiency and inherent kindness toward creatures both great and small is Samantha Eggar (Emma Fairfax), the niece of the blustery, aristocratic village magistrate, General Bellowes,

played by Peter Bull. Shunted aside for most of her life by the uncle who never recovered from her not being born a boy, she admires Harrison's independence of spirit. Wishing to incorporate some of it into her own life, she sings "At the Crossroads," a pretty but strangely incoherent exposé of her decision to achieve more in life than simply satisfying Bull's desire that she conduct herself in the traditional lay-back manner of wealthy young heiress-to-be.

Considering the huge gap in their ages, she has also unaccountably become enamored of Harrison. Uncertain of which of life's roads to take—the one that casts her as a model of feminine decorum, or the other one that encourages her to enter into unladylike adventures— she fails to resolve her dilemma in the song. What is certain is that she will return, thankfully only intermittently, to provide the film with the mildest of love interests.

The unexpected arrival of a "bi-cranium" llama, a gift from a friend in Tibet, excites Harrison into believing that he can raise the money to subsidize his sea snail search by exhibiting the unique "push-pull" creature in a circus. After all, he reasons, how many people have ever seen an animal of any species with two heads, one at the front, where it belongs, and the second at the other end, where it does not.

He gains a partner in the person of Richard Attenborough (Albert Blossom), in an all-too-brief appearance as the owner of the Mammoth Circus and the film's only human performer who manages to breathe life into the picture. His initial refusal of Harrison's offer to share the profits from featuring the freak animal on the runway is reversed when, as Attenborough lustily concedes, "I've Never Seen Anything Like It," the film's sole production number. Money quickly pours into each man's coffers from the llama's four-week engagement of three performances a day, four on Saturdays.

The show, however, offends Samantha, who bristles with contempt at Harrison for betraying the standards of the veterinarian profession by becoming, in essence, a common animal trainer in a cheap circus. Harrison acknowledges his guilt and compensates for his lapse into blatant commercialism and recoups Samantha's respect by comforting "Sophie," a circus seal. She misses her husband, the animal tells him, who remained at the North Pole after her capture. Harrison is determined to take her to Bristol Channel, from which she can swim north to freedom and reunion with her beloved.

Harrison succeeds in spiriting Sophie away from the circus in a baby carriage. Then, he cleverly disguises Sophie as his ill grandmother by stealing a bonnet and shawl from a sleeping old lady, and together doctor and seal board the stage for Bristol. Soldiers, however, halt the coach before it reaches its destination to search for Jack Fitch, a notorious highwayman. Unobserved, Harrison secludes Sophie and himself in a nearby hay wagon and issues an order to the horse to drive away. Shortly afterward, he bids goodbye to the forlorn animal in the film's most tender sequence, made all the more emotionally rewarding by his singing of the lovely "When I Look in Your Eyes," surely the only parting love song ever addressed to a seal, and most effective in portraying the extreme attachment, if not love, that had developed between two such dissimilar creatures. At the end of the song, he tosses Sophie into the channel, and she swims away toward her Polar destination.

Love at Another Level. Meanwhile, another love affair, this one between two mortals, is beginning to draw Newley close to Samantha. While not exactly bowled over by his attention, she reacts to his singing declaration that she is the most beautiful of all the "Beautiful Things" on earth with schoolgirl coyness that prompts him to finding beauty, formerly unrecognized, all around him. The landscape suddenly beams with reflections of the loveliness that her presence has opened up to him, and Newley is mesmerized by the glorious sights suddenly opened up to him through his association with her.

But his rhapsodizing is cut short when he learns that the police have arrested Harrison for stealing the garments in which he had clothed Sophie. Derided alike by Magistrate John Bull and observers at his trial for demonstrating his skill at conversing with animals, Harrison is sent to jail, where he will await transfer to an insane asylum, where Bull is convinced he belongs as a potential threat to society. Despite the doctor's having obtained the

money to take the voyage to find the sea snail, it now appears he will not be leaving England for a long, long time.

The authorities, however, had not anticipated being outfoxed by Harrison's comrades, Samantha, Newley, and Dix, who immediately get down to the business of freeing him. One plan involves tearing down the jail walls by an elephant, but that fantastic idea is quickly dropped when Polynesia assures the trio that she will engineer Harrison's escape all by herself. How she will achieve the goal is suspended temporarily by the reintroduction of Samantha and Newley's romance. Already progressing nicely, it is further enhanced by Newley's sly approval of Samantha's desire to participate in the forthcoming cruise, first as a stowaway, then as ship's cook. The appreciative kiss she gives him again sends him into ecstasy. "After Today," he sings to the tune of the mildly popular and sprightly song, he will no longer feel lonely, no longer despair of his future. A new life has dawned for him, and he revels in the expectation that he will encounter nothing but happiness every step of the way from this day forward.

An inspired strategist, Polynesia wins Harrison's freedom while he is being transported from jail to an asylum-bound stagecoach. Under her direction, her chimp buddy guides the doctor into a nearby riderless coach and sets it in motion. She then orders the policemen's horses and hounds not to chase after the coach. It and Harrison quickly disappear from sight.

Switching to the interior of the good ship *Flounder*, then on the high seas about 10 miles off the coast of northern France, the camera picks up Harrison, more than ever elated at the prospect of making the acquaintance of the sea snail. Even his discovery that Samantha is aboard ship fails to diminish his enthusiasm. Having no idea where he might find his prey, he listens while she calls off a number of exotic far-away places for his consideration. Why not go to Paris, Cairo, Capri, Vienna, Monte Carlo, or Barcelona, she suggests in "Fabulous Places."

But businesslike Harrison is not looking for a vacation site. Opening a map of the world in an atlas, he watches while Samantha randomly plunges a pin into it. It lands on Sea Star Island, a floating parcel of lush greenery and barren rock that was once a part of the African continent. They will head there, Harrison says, and he will interrogate various fishes for advice on where to proceed in his quest to find the sea monster.

Troubles, however, rear their ugly heads to frustrate Harrison's plans and, it is assumed, to inject a little excitement into the plot, which so far has been totally absent. First, the *Flounder* is torn apart by an avalanche of waves—the visual effects highlight of the film—and Harrison, Newley, and Dix are reduced to riding the bounding main on chunks of flotsam disgorged by the sinking ship.

Ahead of him, Harrison catches sight of Sea Star Island and steers toward it. There, much to his and the others' relief, he finds Samantha, whom they feared had drowned. Harrison's pleasure in finding her alive and well opens the script to the shiest of love songs, "I Think I Like You," which ever so slightly resembles the awakening of love Harrison had expressed so refreshingly in "I've Grown Accustomed to Her Face" years earlier. As expected, Samantha returns the compliment, laying the foundation for the least hotly contested winner-take-all triangularized love affair to be found in any film musical.

That the four are not alone on the island is evident by the sudden appearance of a band of spear-carrying natives, who seclude the intruders in a thatched-hut jail for safekeeping. How to free themselves and escape certain punishment is the question. The answer is supplied by Geoffrey Holder, the monarch of Sea Star, a true noble savage who calls himself William Shakespeare the 10th. The bearer of such a hallowed name is bound to be a cultivated man, which is exactly what Holder is. Averse to any vestiges of tribal cruelty, he frees the captives and escorts them on a tour of his kingdom. A sort of warm-weather Shangri-La, the island is home to a museum and a library, Holder notes with pride, adding that his guests are just in time to attend the island's annual Shakespeare festival.

Unfortunately, after drifting north into ever-colder climates for many years, most of the island's jungle animals have caught cold. Despite his chumminess with the potentate, Harrison is blamed for the illnesses, and he sets out to prove that he and his comrades had not infected the animals by curing them. His jungle travels on the back of a giraffe while searching for patients quickly became the most identifiable scene pick up by the film for publicity purposes. He also decides to counter the possibility of the victims' relapsing into even worse diseases by reattaching the island to the northern tip of climate-friendly Africa, which, according to Holder, have been separated for about 5,000 years. Harrison's helpmate in the project is a gigantic whale, which he instructs to push island and continent back together again, like two pieces of a puzzle, into a perfect fit.

Sadly, the vibrations caused by the whale's shoves send the towering "Great Rock" from its precarious perch atop a mountain down into a volcanic crater, a most serious offense that Holder declares is punishable by a "death of 10,000 horrible screams." Tied to stakes and awaiting what seems to be certain death by spears, Harrison and friends are saved just in the nick of time. Much to the delight of Holder and his soldiers, the natives discover that the fall of the Great Rock occurred at the instant the whale had finally managed to connect the two land masses. Instead of execution, the four adventurers are granted freedom, and Harrison is rewarded with the promise of living the rest of his life in the lap of luxury as thanks for his earth-moving engineering.

Harrison's adroitness at making friends with Holder, curing the animals' sniffles, and recruiting the whale to do his bidding naturally impress Newley. Once again he celebrates the doctor's genius by singing more praises to him in "Doctor Doolittle," a happy-talk tune shared by a group of native children.

A short time later, Harrison beholds the most glorious sight in his world. There, snoozing atop an inlet, is the Great Pink Sea Snail, an unfrightening monster about the size and roughly the shape of a mammoth gondola. Harrison plots to enlist its support to return Newley, Samantha, and Billy back to England, who are to take the trip after setting up housekeeping in its commodious belly. From England, the snail can make its way to Scotland and find companionship by joining its fearsome cousin deep in the bowels of Loch Ness. Harrison elects to stay behind rather than endure perhaps lifelong incarceration in the insane asylum.

Maybe, he suggests to disheartened Samantha, he will pass the time by riding—alone—to the moon on the back of a giant Lunar Moth, which strikes her as the most intriguing adventure yet to evolve from Harrison's unfettered imagination. His refusal to take her along leaves Samantha with no alternative to joining Newley and Billy inside the snail for the trip back to Puddleby-by-the-Marsh.

With the snail and cargo receding fast from gloomy Harrison's eyes, hope is given the necessary musical-comedy shot in the arm with the totally unexpected reappearance of Sophie, her happy seal hubby at her side. Sophie reports that every single animal in England is on strike and refuses to perform its customary farm and other chores till their favorite doctor is given a reprieve and permitted to practice his profession in his own country once again. Certain that the animals' nationwide work stoppage will overturn his sentence, Harrison climbs aboard the Lunar Moth and leaves the island for home, bringing to an end the most disappointing film ever to receive a best picture nomination since *She Done Him Wrong*.

But at least that film had Mae West in it.

Funny Girl (1968)

A Columbia picture. DIRECTOR: William Wyler; ASSISTANT: Jack Roe and Ray Gosnell. PRODUCER: Ray Stark; ASSISTANTS: David Dworski and Lorry McCauley. SCREENWRITER: Isobel Lennart. CINEMATOGRAPHER: Harry Stradling; SPECIAL EFFECTS EDITOR: Joe Henrie. SUPERVISING FILM EDITOR: Robert Swink. FILM EDITORS: Maury Winetrobe and William Sands. PRODUCTION DESIGNER: Gene Callahan. CHOREOGRAPHER: Herbert Ross. ART DIRECTOR: Robert Luthardt. SET DECORATOR: William Kiernan. SOUND SUPERVISOR: Charles T. Rice. SOUND: Arthur Piantadosi and Jack Solomon. MISS STREISAND'S COSTUMES: Irene Sharaff. MAKEUP SUPERVISOR: Ben Lane. MAKEUP: Frank McCoy. HAIRSTYLES: Virginia Darcy and Vivienne Walker. DIRECTOR OF MUSICAL NUMBERS: Herbert Ross. MUSICAL SUPERVISOR AND CONDUCTOR: Walter Scharf. MUSIC EDITOR: Ted Sebern. ORCHESTRATIONS: Jack Hayes, Walter Scharf, Leo Sauken, and Herbert Spencer. VOCAL DANCE ARRANGER: Betty Walberg. ORIGINAL SONGS: Lyrics by Bob Merrill; music by Jule Styne. RUNNING TIME: 2 hours, 31 minutes. *Principal Players*: Barbra Streisand (Fanny Brice). Omar Sharif (Nick Arnstein). Kay Medford (Rose [Mama] Brice). Anne Francis (Georgia

James). Walter Pidgeon (Florenz Ziegfeld, Jr.) Lee Allen (Eddie Ryan). Frank Faylen (Keeney). *Major Academy Awards*: Best Actress (*Barbra Streisand*). *Nominations*: Best Picture; Supporting Actress (*Kay Medford*; Cinematography; Film Editing; Scoring; Song ("Funny Girl"); Sound.

Fanny Brice was one of the lucky ones. No goddess in either looks or figure, she was admitted into the Ziegfeld Girls Club at age 19, and at her death 40 years later had lots of money and friends and was living in an 18-room Hollywood mansion with the mandatory swimming pool. Few of the other prominent club members ended their lives in comparable comfort, some dying penniless (Jessica Reed) or well before their time (Olive Thomas, at 22), others committing suicide (Bobbey Storey and Allyn King) or suffering through their final days in destitution and obscurity (most of them).

But bony-legged Fanny was different from the beginning of her career. Lacking any hint of shyness, she was cocky, assertive, and insistent. Her talent must have approached the genius level, or how else account for her making the grade with the Great Ziegfeld despite her plain vanilla appearance? Undoubtedly, her acceptance of that shortcoming proved to be a blessing in disguise. As *Funny Girl* shows in tracing the stages of her trajectory from Manhattan's Lower East Side to the swankiness of a Ziegfeld production, slapstick, not good looks, would have to be her passport to success.

So it was through sweat and tears, trial and error, and constantly snapping back from rejection that she perfected her singing and mugging until the world recognized what she had known from the start: she was the kind of performer that comes along once in a generation, if that often. To her, not only must the show go on, but she had to be in it. At her death at 59 in 1951, she was still remembered fondly as one of the brightest stars ever to send a glow over the orchestra right up to the second balcony. As Barbra Streisand cries out in near desperation in an opening scene of the film, "I gotta get on the stage somehow!" Any way at all would do, and if that meant constantly blowing her own horn, so be it. "That's when I live, on stage," she confesses.

Playing Fanny Brice in *Funny Girl*, Barbra Streisand hurries through the Baltimore railroad station on her way to rejoining Omar Sharif in New York while singing "Don't Rain on My Parade" as a warning to other Ziegfeld girls not to try to stop her.

According to songwriter Harold Rome, whose face brightened noticeably when he mentioned Miss Streisand during a 1981 interview, he sensed that the Brooklyn-born young lady with the clarion voice was a natural for stardom the first time he heard her sing during auditions for the revue *I Can Get It for You Wholesale*, which opened off Broadway in 1962 with her and Elliott Gould in leading roles. "She had that indefinable something that made me and everybody else in the theater feel we were witnessing the debut of a major talent," Rome said. "There was no need for any of us to bring out the best in her; she had it from the moment she walked on the stage to apply for the part of Yetta Tessye Marmelstein. Call it presence, call it driving ambition, call it inspiration. It was probably a combination of all three. She was perfect."

Neither the musical nor Rome's songs shook the theater world to its foundation. But Barbra did. Some 35 years later, people still look back upon her rendition of "Miss Marmelstein" as one of the comic highlights of the 1962-63 season. Probably no one would have enjoyed it more than Fanny Brice, who very well might have pictured Barbra playing her on stage and screen, just as Sophie Tucker was sure that Judy Garland was the only actress who could act out her life. Another of Barbra's early triumphs was her 1963 appearance on Judy's CBS television show, where she was every bit as accomplished at belting out songs as her hostess, who admitted as much during the course of the program.

Barbra got an even bigger break in 1964, when she was metamorphosed into Miss Brice in *Funny Girl* on Broadway. Four years later she repeated the role in the movies, becoming the second woman after Julie Andrews to win the best actress award in her debut performance on the screen. Other musical pictures followed, including *Hello, Dolly!* (1969) and *On a Clear Day You Can See Forever* (1970), as well as several nonmusicals that depended for success not so much on their screenplays as on her consummate artistry as a comedienne and dramatic actress, which she had skillfully combined in *Funny Girl*.

The only musical actress besides Julie Andrews to win the top acting Oscar in her film debut (she tied with Katharine Hepburn in 1968), Miss Streisand ranked among Hollywood's Top Ten attractions in 1969 (in 10th place) and 1970 (ninth) returned in 1972 (fifth), 1973 (sixth), 1974 (fourth), 1975 (second), 1977 (second), 1978 (10th), 1979 (fifth), and for the last time in 1980 (ninth place). As of 1997, she is the only movie actress to write the music for an Academy Award-winning best song ("Ever-green"), which she duetted in 1979 with Kris Kristofferson in *Evergreen*, the second musical remake of the 1937 Fredric March-Janet Gaynor drama, *A Star Is Born*.

One of the greatest of Broadway's female clowns and mimics, Fanny Brice (born Fannie Borach) entered motion pictures almost immediately after they began to talk. Like so many stage-reared musical stars, with the notable exception of Eddie Cantor, Fanny failed to live up to expectations in any one of them. Part of the reason was her total unfamiliarity with movie-making, which kept changing with a steady succession of innovations, and the fact that the technical aspects of recording sound was so rudimentary as to bring out the worst in any performer.

Fanny's long-forgotten 1928-30 films, *Night Club*, *My Man*, *Be Yourself!*, and *The Man from Blankley's*, were not exactly flops, but neither did they turn into the one-woman bonanzas the studios had anticipated. After a six-year absence, she returned to films in 1936 for a brief stint in *The Great Ziegfeld*. Two years later, MGM wrote her, to disadvantage, into *Everybody Sing*, in which she played a maid in the Bellaire household opposite Judy Garland and Allan Jones, and mugged her way through Bert Kalmar and Harry's Ruby's comical "Quainty, Dainty Me." Eight years passed before her next screen role, in *Ziegfeld Follies* (1946), where she was dropped with William Frawley and Hume Cronyn into the hopelessly unfunny skit "The Sweepstakes Ticket" that made younger spectators wonder what all the fuss over her had been about.

Neither Fanny nor Barbra pretended to be the Mary Pickford type, groomed into debutante perfection by makeup artists. Each, however, was quite an attractive young woman. Early stills of Fanny show her to have been far prettier than one might imagine, especially for a woman whom theatergoers knew best as a jokester who specialized in contorting her face while playing the adult fool or the awkward, nettlesome little child she immortalized as Baby Snooks. Barbra easily bested Fanny in every conceivable physical way, even when wearing her hair in the beehive style so fashionable in the early decades of the 20th century.

Mixing Fact with Fiction. The movie, like

the stage musical, takes the usual "biographical" liberties, by 1968 a tradition when treating
the lives of show people, or in fact anyone with
a readily recognizable name in any field of endeavor. She was discovered by Ziegfeld himself,
but not at Keeney's Theatre, as the film reports.
Rather, it was at Seamon's Transatlantic Burlesque Theatre, where he became so impressed
with her singing of Irving Berlin's "Sadie Sa-
lome" that he quickly signed her for his 1910
Follies. She did win an amateur night contest
at Keeney's, but she was only 13, and the film
ignores this minor triumph.

Fanny had wisely followed Berlin's advice
that she sing the song with a Yiddish dialect,
and forever after in both stage and film musicals delivered all her comic songs, and much of
her dialogue, in that manner. She became practically a *Follies* fixture, appearing in six more
editions up to and including 1923, as well as
several other Ziegfeld revues, sharing top
billing with the likes of Cantor, W.C. Fields,
Will Rogers, Bert Williams, the Dolly Sisters,
and vaudevillian headliners (Gus) Van and
(Joe) Schenck.

Fanny was brought up by her mother,
Rose, who ran the saloon that her husband,
Charles, had opened before their divorce.
Never losing sight of her burlesque background, Fanny was at her best when lampoon-
ing silent movie stars, evangelists, ballet and
fan dancers, and other celebrities, whom Barbra imitates outrageously in the riotous "The
Swan" number midway through the film.
Adept at projecting pathos, which served her
well in her occasional antic illuminations of the
forlorn life of the unbeautiful female, she made
theatrical history by switching from her usual
hoydenish delivery of comic songs to the dramatic with "My Man." One of the century's
great end-of-the-affair love songs, the English
words by Channing Pollock were substituted
for the original French lyric, written in ... by
... to Maurice Yvain's music for "Mon
Homme."

Although the film indicates that she introduced the song to American audiences in the
late twenties, she actually sang it in *The Ziegfeld
Follies of 1921* while carrying a torch for Jules
W. [Nick] Arnstein, born in Norway as Wil-
ford Arndt Stein, whom she had married in
1918. The next year, he was arrested for partic-

ipating in the pilfering of $5 million in bonds
from a bank messenger.

Fanny did remain true to her man while he
served his sentence, unable or unwilling to believe that he was capable of masterminding the
theft. "Why, he couldn't mastermind an electric bulb into a socket," Barbra jokes to reporters, repeating Fanny's exact words as they
appeared in 1919 newspapers. Omitted from
the film is Fanny's brief 1911 marriage to Frank
White, a barber from Springfield, Mass., which
lasted only a few days and was officially dissolved one year later, and her bearing Arnstein
a second child (only daughter Frances is mentioned). Arnstein repaid her fidelity by taking
up with another woman. It was that affair,
rather than his purported insistence on stepping voluntarily out of her life to protect her
career, that prodded her into divorcing him
after his release from prison in 1927.

Despite these factual failings, *Funny Girl* is
an excellent musical. Miss Streisand is the embodiment of Miss Brice, expertly distilling the
essence of the latter's personality and talents.
Fanny was a woman of overriding ambition
with strong family ties and unreserved loyalty
to those who had helped her along the way.
She maintained a realistic assessment of her
gawkiness, hoping to compensate for her glamour girl inadequacies by acknowledging them
with humor. (Barbra, too, aims some jokes at
herself. Her first words in the film, spoken as
she glances at herself in the mirror, are the self-
deprecatory, "Hello, Gorgeous!")

The acting is superb throughout, particularly by Kay Medford as the fatalistic but
chicken soup Jewish mother unable to contend
with her daughter's fierce ambition but supportive of it. Walter Pidgeon, whose Ziegfeld
never quite measures up to William Powell's,
manages in far fewer scenes to personify the
paternalistic nature of his relations with members of his casts. Also very good in her brief
role is Anne Francis as Georgia James, most
likely a stand-in for Vera Maxwell, Fanny's best
showgirl friend who, along with partner Wallace McCutcheon introduced the fox trot in
The Century Girl in 1914. Especially commendable is Egyptian-born Omar Sharif, still
dashing but far more subdued than he was in
Lawrence of Arabia (1962) and *Doctor Zhivago*,
whose daredevil fascination with gambling cou-

ples his character with Gaylord Ravenal in *Show Boat* and eventually ruptures his marriage to Fanny.

Equally deserving of high praise is director William Wyler, whom Lawrence Olivier once credited with teaching him how to act in films. One of Hollywood's superior craftsman, he had never before directed a musical picture, but he infused *Funny Girl* with the character development and tightly constructed narrative that distinguished such dramatic films as *Dead End*, *Jezebel* (1938), *Wuthering Heights* (1939), *Mrs. Miniver, Double Indemnity, The Best Years of Our Lives* (1946), and *The Heiress* (1949), all superior examples of his mastery of the film medium.

Of particular interest to character actor watchers are the brief appearances of two of Hollywood's one-time busiest bit players. Appearing as a bartender in Mama Medford's saloon is Frank Sully, while the slim, graying Billy Benedict, who began representing Western Union as far back as 1936 with *Captain January*, is the fellow who delivers Ziegfeld's telegram to the Brice household about 30 minutes into *Funny Girl*.

As with *Three Smart Girls*, the Fanny Brice saga is continued in a second part, which, thanks to the immensely gifted James Wong Howe, remains one of the finest photographed of all musical films. It is quite a different Fanny Brice that Miss Streisand portrays in the 1975 followup, *Funny Lady*, which carries the former funny girl through the Depression well into the 1940s. Wiser but sadder, Miss Streisand reappears without any vestiges of the playful sincerity of the clownish stage-struck youngster that viewers admired in *Funny Girl*. Instead, the new Fanny is a model of self-assurance and more than a little caustic toward almost everybody she meets, except for Roddy McDowall, who is wasted in the role of the typical faithful hanger-on, ever available to comfort the icon entertainer when personal problems threaten to aversely affect her performances. Even though she is on the downside of her once fabulous career at the beginning of the sequel, Fanny is determined to hold on to the celebrity status she had achieved while fighting for recognition during the teens and twenties.

Stage jobs are hard to find until she meets the brash Billy Rose, a one-time teenage Gregg shorthand speed king turned lyricist and shoe-

string producer. Under his sponsorship she stars in *Crazy Quilt*, which opened on Broadway in 1931, and sings the well-known tribute to the Woolworth chain, "I Found a Million Dollar Baby (in a Five and Ten Cent Store)," with a lyric by Rose and music by Harry Warren. The song, actually introduced by comedian Ted Healy in the original show, was only one of several big hits that Warren wrote for two Rose shows. Others include "Cheerful Little Earful" and "Would You Like to Take a Walk?," both from *Sweet and Low* (1930), originally entitled "Corned Beef and Roses," which starred Fanny and George Jessel. For some reason, this show and the songs are omitted from *Funny Lady*.

A proficient lyricist, Rose collaborated with many other first-rate composers, Vincent Youmans among them, for songs ranging from novelties ("Barney Google," "Don't Bring Lulu," "It's Only a Paper Moon," "That Old Gang of Mine") to ballads ("Me and My Shadow," "It Happened in Monterey," "Without a Song," "More Than You Know") to production numbers ("Great Day," "Back in Your Own Back Yard," "There's a Rainbow 'Round My Shoulder"). Most of these songs are absent from the picture. In their place were five new ones from John Kander and Fred Ebb, most notably the delightful Oscar-nominated "How Lucky Can You Get," and "Blind Date" and "Let's Hear It for Me."

Miss Streisand does very well indeed in the musical routines (all too few) and the dramatic sequences relating to her 1929 marriage to Rose and eventual divorce in 1938, when he became enamored of swimming star Eleanor Holm, played by Heidi O'Rourke, the star of his spectacular *Aquacade*, a part of the 1939 World's Fair. Omar Sharif reappears in a few brief scenes as former husband Nicky Arnstein, largely to stress the fact that their love for each other never really died in divorce court. Tying their relationship to *Funny Girl* are the background reprises of "People" whenever they meet.

Miscast in the Rose role, as he would be in 1991 in another musical, *For the Boys*, a copycat version of the World War II adventures of Kay Francis, Carole Landis, and Betty Grable in *Four Jills in a Jeep*, was James Caan. He is unable throughout *Funny Lady* to project the nervous energy of the over-ambitious showman who in time developed into a respectable producer of such bona fide stage hits as *Jumbo* (1935), *Carmen Jones* (1943), and Cole Porter's *The Seven Lively Arts* (1944). His Diamond Horseshoe nightclub on West 46th Street played host to numerous celebrities. He even bought the Ziegfeld Theatre, as well as the National, which he renamed the Billy Rose Theatre (now the Nederlander).

Oddly, the sequel makes no mention of Fanny's movies, nor does Miss Streisand appear as Baby Snooks even though references are made to the singer-comedienne's many appearances as that famous brat toddler, which she originated on the stage during her *Follies* days. It was the airwaves, however, that made Snooks one of America's best-known kiddies. She was heard first in the mid-thirties on *Ziegfeld Follies of the Air*, then on *Maxwell House Coffee Time*, which featured Frank Morgan as host, beginning in 1937. (*Music Man* Meredith Willson's orchestra provided the music.) Snooks moved to the *Palmolive Beauty Box Theater,* another comedy-variety show before finally becoming a first-rank star with the launching of *The Baby Snooks Show* in the early forties. The child's long-suffering father, Daddy Higgins, was Hanley Stafford, who had followed Jack Arthur and Alan Reed into the part on the Maxwell House program. Stafford also played detective Thatcher Colt, which for several seasons was broadcast on Sunday afternoons, after *The Shadow* had concluded his latest exposé on the "evil that lurks in the hearts of men."

Although *Funny Lady* won no Academy Awards, it was nominated for five. Besides best song and cinematography, it competed for best scoring, costumes, and sound.

Flashback to Meaner Times. About to relive her early grubbing-for-attention days in flashback format—one of the oldest but almost always successful movie-making techniques—Barbra Streisand (Fanny Brice) enters the film sitting alone in the empty auditorium of the New Amsterdam Theatre, where she is starring in the Follies. At the pinnacle of her career, she is also at the lowest point of her off-stage life. The undisclosed year is most likely 1927,

shortly after she ended her nine-year marriage to Omar Sharif (Nick Arnstein).

Her reflections carry her back to her late-teenage years on Henry Street, a major artery of New York's poverty row. An adventurous stage-struck young lady, Barbra has talked Keeney, played by another veteran character actor, Frank Faylen, into giving her a shot at replacing a chorus girl in his latest theatrical revue. No go. To Faylen, the kid simply doesn't have the glamour it takes to wow the mostly male audiences and, for all he knows, never will.

Hardly the type to let rejection scuttle her dreams, Barbra submerges her disappointment in song, conjuring up visions of the success to be hers in the soliloquy "I'm the Greatest Star." Overhearing her is Faylen's assistant, Lee Allen (Eddie Ryan), the prototypical Hollywood helpmate of the show biz amateur and eventually her career-long faithful confidant. Without the theater owner's approval, he permits Barbra to join the chorus in that evening's "Roller Skate Rag" production number. Unaccustomed to wearing wheels on her feet, Barbra disrupts the novelty dance routine by crashing into the other girls, falling three times to the floor, and once almost into the front row seats.

The audience, however, awards her performance with howls of laughter, thinking that her tumbling is a legitimate part of the choreography. Gratified by the response, she further entertains with the interpolated song "I'd Rather Be Blue Over You (Than Be Happy with Somebody Else)," also sung while roller skating, but minus the pratfalls. Not part of the original Merrill-Styne score, it was written in 1928 by her third husband, Billy Rose, and Fred Fisher for the motion picture *My Man* and is easily the best song in *Funny Girl*. Allen, carefully noting the audience's enthusiastic reaction, writes finis to her hopes of becoming a dancer. She is obviously a natural crowd-pleaser as a singer and comedienne.

Why, he asks her in the movie's most moving sequence, did she tell him she could dance on skates, when all the time she knew she was unable to. Tears in her eyes, Barbra replies that she'd have passed herself off as a juggler if that's what he'd wanted—and she can't juggle either. What she wants, she explains, is for people to laugh with her, not at her, as they did during her first skating routine. Then, in response to her question of why he had hired her, Allen provides unique insight into the major reason for the youngster's eventual success. "Because you wanted it so much," he confesses.

A second boost to her career arrives a few evenings later in the person of Sharif, who goes backstage expressly to congratulate Barbra on her performance. Equally convinced as she is of the towering talent she possesses, he further enchants her by predicting that she will be a "big star some day." He proceeds to bargain with Faylen, whom Allen had converted to her cause, over her salary, finally raising it from the theaterowner's initial $15 a week offer to $50. Barbra's stock in herself takes an astounding leap a few days later when she receives a telegram from Walter Pidgeon (Florenz Ziegfeld) inviting her to audition for a job in his next Follies. Both mother (Kay Medford) and daughter are jubilant, knowing full well that their meeting could result in Barbra's Broadway debut. It would also shut the mouths of Mama Medford's envious neighborhood friends who had ridiculed Barbra's slow progress toward stardom in the song "If a Girl Isn't Pretty," referring to their disbelief that she can succeed without a leading lady's looks.

For her audition solo before Ziegfeld, Barbra sings "Second Hand Rose," one of Fanny's all-time biggest signature songs, which was actually written for the *Ziegfeld Follies of 1921* by Grant Clarke and James F. Hanley. (Unfortunately, she never does sing another Hanley tune she made famous, "Rose of Washington Square," which developed into an equally immense hit.) Pidgeon hires her on the spot for the majestic salary of $75 a week, but runs into trouble when he insists that besides "Second Hand Rose" she also sing "His Love Makes Me Beautiful" in the "Most Beautiful Bride in the World" skit. Barbra objects, citing the lyric's describing her as beautiful as the reason. Her participation would just embarrass her, and possibly the show as well. Pidgeon's response is an either-or proposition: either she sing it or leave the Follies. Barbra chooses to comply with the order, but in her own inimitable way. She appears on stage amid a chorus of peacock-strutting ladies with a pillow tucked under her wedding dress to suggest that the bride-to-be is already pregnant by pointing a finger at her swollen stomach and joking that what lies inside is the "beautiful reflection" of a passionate courtship. Angered at her disobedience, Pidgeon nonetheless keeps her in the show. Always the savvy producer, he wisely bows to the verdict of the audience, whose wild applause turns the number into a show-stopper worth five curtain calls.

Again, Sharif proffers his congratulations at the conclusion of the skit, and happily escorts Barbra to a first-night celebration party at the family saloon. Displaying the innocent curiosity about men that finally converts the shy wallflower into a woman in love, Barbra tries to offset her growing affection for him by balancing his magnetism with doubts about his willingness to settle down with only one woman. Then there is the matter of his profession. Apparently content to live the hectic life of a gambler, Sharif seems to be flush with money one week, then without any at all the next. The plans he makes are always either indefinite or tentative, depending exclusively on which way his luck is blowing.

The man is lonely, probably just as much as she is, she sings to him in "People," a rare philosophical love song and the best remembered of all the *Funny Girl* standards. When it comes to love, she will accept only the real thing, not a fling. What she wants is one person, a very special person, who will make her life whole by devoting himself to her alone. Her plea sending offshoots of unease into his normal cool detachment, Sharif refrains from making any proposal, decent or otherwise, that might lead to a firm commitment. Instead, he tells her he must leave for Kentucky, where he operates a horse-breeding farm. Although disappointed, Barbra is not floored by the news. She still has career challenges to keep her mind active and away from reminders of the handsome fellow who, it would seem, has just stepped out of her life only days after entering it.

Love Finds a Way. By the time the two meet again, a year has passed. Now in Baltimore, Barbra is touring with the Follies and Sharif is there to race his horse, Elsie, at Pimlico. Glancing at the animal's spindly shanks,

Barbra compares them with her own shapeless legs, proving once more that she is still falling back on humor as a defense against her physical deficiencies as much as on a genuine desire to be liked. She reluctantly accepts the gambler's invitation to dinner that evening in a private dining room, where helped along with sips of vintage wine, Sharif arouses her interest with "You Are Woman, I Am Man." Barbra responds to his declaration of love by reversing the pronouns and verbs and expressing her own for him. In an unusual departure from tradition, all the lyrics are different from those sung in the stage original, but the effect is the same: he has swept her off her feet. Chopped liver he isn't, in Barbra's view. And since she doubts that a convent would admit an unmarried Jewish girl, she is only too happy to welcome him as lover, not just friend.

Business matters, however, again call him from her arms when Elsie loses the race and Sharif loses the horse, forcing him to travel by ship to Europe in hopes of recouping his fortune. Evincing the same determination that had made her the biggest star in Ziegfeld's crown, Barbra decides on her own to accompany him on the voyage. He is her man and her job is to help him in a crisis. Defending her right to happiness, she overrules the objections of the other members of the touring company with the defiant musical order, "Don't Rain on My Parade," as she marches with determined steps along the Baltimore railroad station to the track that will take her back to New York.

Surprised but pleased at her unexpected appearance aboard ship, Sharif proposes to marry her, but only if he is dealt the right cards in a series of ocean-going poker games. Luck proves to be a lady one night, and he wins a bundle big enough to choke Elsie. Barbra celebrates their impending shipboard wedding with the ethnic song "Sadie, Sadie," a Lower East Side synonym for a married woman, which she is elated to become soon afterward. A steward's slip-of-the-tongue reference to Sharif as "Mr. Brice," however, punctures his pride, which is destined to endure further wounds when he falls out of the chips and has to depend on his wife's money to support both of them. (Similar surname mixups, intentional rather than inadvertent, would also pester future hubby Billy Rose, although that "Mr. Brice" was far wealthier than husband number two.)

Back in America, the couple moves into a castle-like suburban estate with luxurious furnishings that rival the opulence of the jewels and other gifts Sharif continually bestows on Barbra. After the birth of Frances, he invests heavily in Oklahoma oil wells, only to lose everything when they spew out sand instead of black gold. The disaster compels him to downsize the family's living quarters to a Manhattan apartment, another blow that speeds up his creeping estrangement from Barbra, who he realizes has of necessity usurped his role as the family's meal ticket.

Acting on the advice of Mama Medford that her daughter should help her husband, not merely sympathize over his misfortunes, Barbra secretly arranges for a mutual friend, a gambling executive, to offer Sharif a full partnership in his enterprise as well as the job of manager of a new club he plans to open on the East Side. When Barbra admits under pressure that it was she who had arranged the meeting, and in addition agreed to put up the required $50,000 partnership fee, Sharif angrily turns both offers down. The breakdown of their marriage is now well on the way to a breakup.

Correctly surmising that a hefty infusion of funds would salvage what is left of his self-esteem, and marriage as well, Sharif badly mismanages what he believes is the solution to his problems. He joins another friend in an ill-fated scheme, a phony bond deal that results in their arrest for embezzlement. Rather than prolong the misery that he and Barbra would undergo from a drawn-out trial, Sharif pleads guilty without even informing his lawyer of his intention to do so.

His sentence is two years (of which he served only 18 months). Before leaving for Leavenworth, he pleads with Barbra to divorce him for her own and Frances's good. She refuses, maintaining that she will stick with him during incarceration and afterward. During their conversation, he had ironically called her "funny girl," and in the film's tenderest song after "People," she places his term of endearment in the context of her present circumstances. A "Funny Girl" in the eyes of theatergoers, she is actually a very sad girl, her personal life disintegrating at the same time that her hold on the public has lifted her to the top of her profession.

Only twice before had a new song inserted into a film remake of a Broadway musical received Oscar nomination for best song. The first, "Lovely to Look At," went into *Roberta* in 1935, the second, "Pass That Peace Pipe," into *Good News* in 1947. Merrill and Styne's "Funny Girl" was the third to achieve that distinction. All three of the songs lost.

The flashback over, the film reenters the New Amsterdam. Barbara is still in her seat, her reminiscing completed, her tearful eyes and trembling voice revealing her for what she is—an off-stage shadow of her theatrical self. No longer the clown, no longer the happy-go-lucky girl with the nimble wit, she cannot overcome the effects of a broken heart that she knows will never be completely mended. She is visited in her dressing room by Sharif, recently released from prison, and this time she agrees to the divorce he again urges upon her.

The final scene, a closeup of Barbra as she performs and pledges her eternal love to Sharif in "My Man," ranks high on the chart of the movies' most intense depictions of a sensitive woman pouring her heart into a song with biographical connotations. While it is true that her rendition is more typical of the Streisand of 1968 than the Brice of 1921, at least when compared with Fanny's own partial version in *The Great Ziegfeld*, Barbra's vocalizing is superb, only slightly less effective than Judy Garland's as-yet unsurpassed emotional delivery of Leonard Gershe's "Born in a Trunk" number in the 1954 *A Star Is Born*. There is little doubt that Barbra will always look upon Sharif with deep affection, maybe even love, for, as she had confided earlier, he did something for her that no one else had ever accomplished.

For a time, he made her feel beautiful.

Oliver! (1968)

A Columbia picture. DIRECTOR: Carol Reed; ASSISTANT: Colin Brewer. PRODUCER: John Woolf. PRODUCTION SUPERVISOR: Dennis Johnson. PRODUCTION DESIGNER: John Box. SCREENWRITER: Vernon Harris. CINEMATOGRAPHER: Oswald Morris; SPECIAL EFFECTS: Allan Bryce. FILM EDITOR: Ralph Kemplen; ASSISTANT: Marcel Durham. CHOREOGRAPHY AND MUSICAL SEQUENCES: Onna White; ASSOCIATE: Tom Panko; ASSISTANTS: Larry Oaks and George Baron. ART DIRECTOR: Terence Marsh; ASSISTANTS: Ray Walker and Bob Cartwright. SET DESIGNERS: Vernon Dixon and Ken Muggleston. SOUND SUPERVISOR: John Cox. SOUND EDITOR: Jim Groon. SOUND RECORDERS: Buster Ambler and Bob Jones. COSTUMES: Phyllis Dalton. MAKEUP: George Frost. CHIEF HAIRDRESSER: Bobbie Smith. MUSICAL SUPERVISOR, ARRANGER, AND CONDUCTOR: John[nie] Green; ASSOCIATE MUSIC SUPERVISOR: Eric Rogers. ORCHESTRATIONS AND CHORAL ARRANGEMENTS: John[nie] Green. ADDITIONAL ORCHESTRATIONS: Eric Rogers. CHOREOGRAPHIC MUSIC LAYOUTS: Ray Holder. MUSIC EDITOR: Kenneth Runyon; ASSOCIATE: Robert Hathaway. MUSIC COORDINATOR: Dusty Buck. SONGS: Lyrics and music by Lionel Bart. RUNNING TIME: 2 hours and 33 minutes. *Principal Players*: Ron Moody (Fagin). Shani Wallis (Nancy). Oliver Reed (Bill Sikes). Mark Lester (Oliver). Harry Secombe (Mr. Bumble). Jack Wild (The Artful Dodger). Hugh Griffith (The Magistrate). Joseph O'Conor (Mr. Brownlow). *Major Academy Awards*: Best Picture; Director; Art Director; Sound; Scoring. *Nominations*: Best Actor (*Ron Moody*); Supporting Actor (*Jack Wild*); Adapted Screenplay; Cinematography; Film Editing; Costumes.

With the exception of *David Copperfield*, released in 1935 by MGM with as perfect a cast as Hollywood ever assembled, only the British have done justice to Charles Dickens in adapting his novels to the screen. Not that Hollywood failed to put its best foot forward with each new project involving that eminent Victorian author, the equivalent of Chaucer in prose, whom the distinguished literary critic Edmund Wilson once called the "greatest dramatic writer the English had had since Shakespeare."

The Tale of Two Cities, another 1935 MGM release, was most respectable, as was the studio's *A Christmas Carol* (1938), with Reginald Owen as Scrooge, so much better than Hollywood's later two versions, the musicalized *Scrooge* of 1970 starring Albert Finney and the *Scrooged* of 1988, a modern-day update revolving around the hateful president of a New York television company. But even the 1938 film pales into near insignificance when compared with the 1951 British-made *Scrooge*, sometimes entitled *A Christmas Carol*, with Alistair Sim deporting himself in curmudgeonly fashion as the bitter old man who defined the Christmas spirit as "humbug." George C. Scott, who played Fagin in the 1982 television version of *Oliver Twist*, also portrayed Dickens's infamous miser on the television screen. Filmed in the historic town of Shrewsbury, England, it was the first *Carol* to be shot in color. In 1996, *A Christmas Carol* musical was presented live

Ron Moody urges his coterie of juvenile thieves to be sure to "Pick a Pocket or Two" in the Carol Reed-directed *Oliver!*, voted best picture of 1968.

for the third successive season in New York, with lyrics by Lynn Ahrens and music by Alan Menken. Tony Randall appeared as old Ebenezer.

The British have a special fondness for Dickens that exists only rarely between author and countrymen anywhere else in the world. Maybe it is their long-lived love affair with their "Father Christmas" that explains why they are so good at turning his books into films. Part-historian, part-crusader, part-humorist, part-dramatist, Dickens is English to the core, ever fascinated with the London of his era, intimate with the ways of its hard-nosed gentry, lower-class deprivation, and the nobility of which even the most destitute of its residents were capable. To tire of Dickens, with all his sentimentality and exaggerated characters, whether virtuous, evil, or comic, is, as Samuel Johnson once said of London, to tire of life itself.

On Stage, Screen, and Television. With the exception of Shakespeare and Sir Arthur Conan Doyle, no other English writer has supplied motion pictures with as many sources of inspiration. In the sound era alone, all but six of Dickens's 18 novels have been made into films, and increasingly in recent years, into television specials and miniseries, like the superior *Martin Chuzzlewit*, aired by the Public Broadcasting System in 1995 and repeated in 1996. Produced in England, that three-part program once again underscored the singular brilliance of the British in lifting Dickens's plots and characters from the printed page with the attentiveness to detail and respect they deserve. All of the master writer's novels need a great deal of culling before appearing in movie houses in typical 90-minute condensations. The best of them survive the sometimes drastic editing without damaging either content or continuity, or sacrificing very much of the humor.

The one notable exception to this rule was the Royal Shakespeare Company's 1981 production of *The Life and Adventures of Nicholas Nickleby* on Broadway. Divided into two parts, the dramatization lasted more than eight and one-half hours and tickets cost $100 for both halves, an alarmingly high price for the time. But people flocked to see the highly innovative stage piece, and it turned into a theatrical triumph.

Oliver Twist occupies an honored place in both American and British movie history. The first known film version, only recently discovered, was made in the United States and released in May of 1912, predating *Richard III* by five months. The oldest surviving complete feature film longer than one reel, *Richard III* is regarded as the first film adaptation of a Shakespearean play. Playing the doomed king was British-born Frederick Warde. In 1922,

Oliver Twist again went before the camera, this time co-starring Lon Chaney as Fagin and child star Jackie Coogan as Oliver. The *Oliver Twist* of 1934, actually too ambitious a project for the Hollywood of the Depression, is a minor work, despite Dickie Moore's appealing portrait of the tempest-tossed little orphan.

Unfortunately, the other Dickens works transcribed into American screenplays have foundered, often quite badly, in measuring up to their author's genius at constructing plots with as many turns and twists as a kite in the wind, and peopling them with scores of characters with funny names and idiosyncrasies. The majority of the revolving door men and women are able to renew their grasp on the reader's attention even after the lapse of several chapters between appearances. The *Great Expectations* of 1934 was not much better. *The Mystery of Edwin Drood*, which in 1935 supplied Dickens's unfinished novel with an ending almost as inept as the one the British gave it in the 1993 remake, was inglorious.

Of far more consequence as examples of cinematic art were the British versions of *The Old Curiosity Shop* (1934), *Nicholas Nickleby* (1947), *The Pickwick Papers* (1952), *Little Dorrit* (1987), and *Hard Times* (1988). Proving that the British did not always excel when dealing with the great storyteller and would-be playwright was the poor reupholstering of *The Tale of Two Cities* in 1958, which could boast only a sturdy musical score by Richard Addinsell. Similarly, the 1975 repeat of *The Old Curiosity Shop*, this time retitled *Mister Quilp* and featuring a few undistinguished songs by Anthony Newley, who also played Quilp, one of the most loathsome in Dickens's gallery of rogues, deserves little in the way of praise at any level.

No motion picture based on Dickens has surpassed David Lean's *Great Expectations*, the 1946 *suces d'estime*, which was remade into a respectable television movie in 1974 with an excellent cast that included James Mason, Margaret Leighton, and Robert Morley. In 1989 a three-part television miniseries once again retold the familiar story. Appearing with Anthony Hopkins was Jean Simmons, the Estella in Lean's 1946 film, who played the part of the bitter old-maid recluse, Miss Havisham.

If any Dickensian film adaptation rivals Lean's *Great Expectations*, it is the same director's flawless *Oliver Twist* of 1948, for which he also collaborated with Stanley Haines on the screenplay. Lean's final film, this *Oliver Twist* is Dickens at his best, uncompromisingly faithful to the novel, forbidding in its journey through London's seamiest side, and acted with uncommon skill by a celebrated cast.

Unlike Mark Lester in the musical, nine-year-old John Howard Davies is memorable as Lean's Oliver, as is Anthony Newley as The Artful Dodger. Robert Newton, that archvillain whose cruel, shifty eyes had made him an especially menacing Long John Silver, of *Treasure Island* fame, was a natural for the role of Bill Sikes. Also present was Alec Guinness in his most controversial role as Fagin, his face so unmistakably, and offensively, Semitic that the J. Arthur Rank Organization sought to counter the complaints by deleting a number of the closeups in some of the prints. Francis L. Sullivan, a Dickens specialist and always proficient heavy who had played the oily Mr. Jaggers in both the 1934 and the 1946 *Great Expectations* films, as well as The Rev. Crisparkle in Hollywood's *Edwin Drood*, was cast as Mr. Bumble, and Henry Stephenson, that grand old impersonator of British aristocrats in one of his last screen appearances, as the kindly Mr. Brownlow.

Published chapter-by-chapter in periodical format in 1837-38, *Oliver Twist* was the second of Dickens's great works. Completed when the author was 26, it followed closely on the heels of *The Pickwick Papers* (1836-37) and immediately preceded *Nicholas Nickleby* (1838-39). That the author was already at the plenitude of his powers as a novelist well before reaching the age of 30 was made abundantly clear in the story of the little foundling who, after escaping from a workhouse, falls among thieves in the urban nightmare that was 19th-century London. Still one of the best-known novels in English, *Oliver Twist* abounds with typical Dickensian ruffians, scoundrels, innocents, and heartwarming eccentrics.

Besides the music, the major glory of the film *Oliver!* is how cleverly the original stage librettist, songwriter Lionel Bart himself, turned what is essentially a tragic tale with a compensatory happy ending into a musical comedy.

Screenwriter Vernon Harris followed Bart's example throughout, tracing Oliver from the time he brazenly asks for a second helping of gruel through his apprenticeship as a pickpocket to his final welcome into the home of his elderly benefactor.

The bearer of the most powerful story ever to be made into a musical, *Oliver!* is undeniably a classic in its own right, qualified for comparison with David Lean's masterpiece. The sets, the costumes, the acting—from the lowliest bit player to the stars—is first-rate throughout. Greatly condensed to allow time for the songs and dances, *Oliver!* succeeds in evoking the hideousness of the slum where Fagin tutors his young pupils in the criminal arts, the impoverishment of the masses, and society's callous disregard of the very young. It also achieves the impossible task of reforming Fagin, played exceptionally well by Ron Moody, who had essayed the same part in the 1960 stage musical, into a humorous, almost lovable, villain without overlooking the evil he represents. Purists who complain of the musical's permitting Fagin to escape the gallows need only check the caveat in the film's credits, which states quite clearly that *Oliver!* was "freely adapted from the novel by Charles Dickens." Sadly, Moody's Oscar-winning performance failed to earn him additional classic roles, except as Uriah Heep in the 1970 television remake of *David Copperfield*.

Reduced to its essentials, the familiar plot tells the tale of a child of unknown parentage born in a workhouse and reared under the cruel conditions to which pauper children of the time were heir. The tyrant at whose hands Oliver Twist especially suffers is Mr. Bumble, the beadle, a minor parish officer appointed to keep order in public institutions. The boy runs away, reaches London, and is taken under the wing of a gang of thieves headed by an elderly Jew named Fagin. With the pluck and luck of a British-style Horatio Alger, however, he in time is rescued by a wealthy man who, like Nancy, recognizes the boy as worth saving from the miserable life that is certain to be his.

The other chief members of the enterprise are the detestable burglar Bill Sikes, his companion Nancy, and The Artful Dodger, an impudent, opportunistic young pickpocket. Every effort is made to convert Oliver into a skillful thief. But he is temporarily rescued by the rich Mr. Brownlow, who takes a fancy to the lad. Oliver, however, is kidnaped by the gang, whose interest in him has been intensified by a sinister person named Monks (deleted from the musical play and film), who displays an unaccountable interest in the boy.

Oliver is forced to accompany Bill Sikes on a burgling expedition, during which he receives a gunshot wound and comes into the hands of Mrs. Maylie and her protégée Rose (both deleted), by whom he is kindly treated and reared. After a time Nancy, who has developed some redeeming traits, reveals to Rose that Monks is aware of Oliver's parentage and wishes all proof of it destroyed, and also that there is a questionable link between the lad and Rose herself. In the course of an inquiry into the matter, Nancy's participation in Oliver's rehabilitation is discovered by the gang, and she is brutally murdered by Sikes. Trying to escape from the police, he accidentally hangs himself, and the rest of the gang are captured and Fagin executed. Monks, found and threatened with exposure, confesses what remains unknown of Oliver's heritage:

Monks himself is Oliver's half-brother and has pursued his ruin animated by hatred and the desire to retain the whole of his father's property. Rose is the sister of Oliver's unfortunate mother, who died in childbirth. The boy is adopted by Mr. Brownlow, Monks emigrates and dies in prison, and Bumble ends his career in the workhouse over which he had formerly ruled with total contempt for its inmates. It takes a great deal of faith in one's own literary gifts to rewrite Dickens, but Bart succeeded nobly at the task. His plot alterations were creative and, beyond that, supremely judicious.

The fifth consecutive Oscar-nominated musical to be based on a stage libretto, and the third to win as best picture, *Oliver!* was a tremendous hit in London before it duplicated its success on Broadway in 1960. As usual in the post–World War II years, the film version relies as much on the acting and direction as on the music for its high rank. Moody is entitled to a special salute for service beyond the call of duty, especially when, daintily holding a parasol, he dances merrily

with his young trainees to the tune of "Pick a Pocket or Two."

The direction, too, is expertly handled by Carol Reed, one of Britain's most stylish directors known for blending character with the appropriate atmospheric background. His only musical venture, *Oliver!* was preceded by such inspired dramatic works as *The Stars Look Down* (1939), *Odd Man Out* (1947), *The Fallen Idol* (1948), and, more than all the others combined, *The Third Man* (1949).

The Dickensian Touch. As in no other nominated musical film, every single major sequence in *Oliver!*, except those unfolded in the dramatic 20-minute plot windup, contains at least one song that illuminates the latest predicament confronting the character or characters who perform it. Bart's songs number 13, nine of which contain more than one verse or chorus. For "Pick a Pocket or Two," "I'd Do Anything," and "Reviewing the Situation" he wrote four choruses; for "It's a Fine Life" and "Oom-Pah-Pah" three each.

All the songs, whether of love, friendship, or loneliness, whether accompanying dancers in a tavern or sung as a soliloquy, are placed with such precision in the screenplay (as in the original libretto) that one can deduce the content of the first three-fourths of the story simply by citing their titles in chronological order. In the opening workhouse scene, for example, when Oliver and about 60 other young orphan paupers march barefoot into the dreary mess hall, the song they sing, "Food, Glorious Food," clearly expresses their dismal hope of receiving something better than the usual slop they are served day-in, day-out. Ironically, on one wall hangs a sign proclaiming that GOD IS LOVE.

But even the least tasteful breakfast is appreciated by the famished. So when Oliver, played by 10-year-old Mark Lester, dares to approach Harry Secombe (Mr. Bumble) and his equally obnoxious wife (Peggy Mount), extending his empty bowl in his hands and declaring, "I want some more," it seems like a reasonable request from a growing youngster. Bumble, however, is upset at this deviation in protocol, and proceeds in the song "Oliver!"— sung with disgust rather than as a term of endearment—to inform the boy that incarceration in a small cell and a beating will be inflicted on him if he ever again requests more than his usual ration of food.

The recalcitrant Oliver is eventually expelled by the well-fed governors of the institution as a troublemaker. "Boy for Sale," Bumble sings to passers-by and shopkeepers while trudging with the boy along the snowy streets in search of a buyer. Bumble wants seven guineas for the child, but willingly accepts the three guineas finally offered by Mr. and Mrs. Sowerberry (Leonard Rossiter and Hylda Baker), the two stern, Murdstonelike authority figures who operate a funeral home, then called "undertaking parlor." Assigned to lead processions of mourners from church to cemetery at children's funerals, and once again deprived of companionship in a drab setting, Oliver laments his poor fortune in the song "Where Is Love?" a touching testament to the loneliness of a boy who has never received any, not even from his father or mother, whom he never knew. To escape further demonizing by the Sowerberrys and their jealous assistant, Noah Claypole (Kenneth Cranham), Oliver escapes and embarks on the 42-mile trek to London, much as David Copperfield fled the grimy London bottle factory for Dover and his Aunt Betsy Trotwood.

The fourth song, "Consider Yourself," one of the show's biggest hits, is a change of pace tune that brings a smile to Oliver's lips and hope to his heart by notifying him that good luck has at last seemingly come his way. It is sung to him by The Artful Dodger, portrayed in extraordinary fashion by Jack Wild, also nominated for an Academy Award. He befriends Oliver in the expectation of recruiting him into the band of pickpockets overseen by "a respectable old gentleman" named Fagin. The song is reprised several times by a host of butchers and other laborers, newsboys, policemen, and street entertainers in a well-executed and lively production number that carries the viewer ever deeper into the pits of working-class London.

Starved for friendship as well as food, and dependent on the Dodger for both, Oliver follows him over crushed cobblestone alleys and past rotting brick buildings to Fagin's quarters. Quickly noting the boy's finely chiseled features and inherent politeness, the usual telltale signs of the born aristocrat, even when penniless and clad in tattered clothing, Fagin takes a shine to Oliver. He introduces him to his pupils, whom he regularly addresses as "my dears," and promises to help him every way he can. In repayment, he advises in "Pick a Pocket or Two," Oliver is to practice until he becomes as nimble fingered as his Dodger buddy.

The life the gang leads may not be to Oliver's, or even the other boys' liking, Fagin admits while he and they give the newcomer his first lesson on the finer points of pilfering in public. But unqualified to do anything else, they defend their occupation as necessary to their very survival. Besides, lifting a bankroll from a wealthy man's trousers gives them something else of benefit—peace of mind derived from the knowledge that they are capable of making their way in a heartless world while provoking their so-called "betters."

Among the denizens of Fagin's underworld is Shani Wallis (Nancy), the girlfriend of Oliver Reed (Bill Sikes), who abides his cruel jests and frequent abuse out of a love for him that none of her waitress friends at the neighborhood tavern is able to comprehend. Like Julie in *Show Boat*, she loves her Bill because, well, because he's her Bill. Indeed, despite the woeful existence she has lived throughout her young life, she affirms her contentment with her lot, provided that Sikes continue to single her out for relaxation, if nothing else. "It's a Fine Life," she sings to a torchy melody used to dispel any illusions that her man will ever marry her and settle down like an ordinary husband. He is what he is, she admits, and that is good enough for her. At least she has found someone to love.

In Thieves' Company. Nancy is next seen on her visit to Fagin, to whom she has been dispatched to collect the proceeds he has obtained from fencing the batch of ill-gotten goods that Sikes had brought to him after his latest nocturnal sortie into an upper-class house. A favorite with the gang, she takes an instant liking to Oliver, who strikes her as somehow to the manor born. As a sort of welcome to the lad, she and the other boys enter into the exuberant "I'd Do Anything," a gem of a production number, to express their fondness for one another and, incidentally, the youngsters' respect for the resourcefulness of their rap-scallion schoolmaster. According to the whiskerless thieves, there is nothing, absolutely nothing, that either she or Fagin could ask that they would not do, anytime, anywhere. As the plot progresses, it is Nancy who will have ample opportunity to prove her willingness to do anything to lend a helping hand to Oliver.

The camaraderie being shared by the members of this mutual admiration society reaches its climax when Fagin commissions the Dodger to accompany Oliver on his first pick-pocketing venture. He sends them off with the admonishment to "Be Back Soon," and with boodles of goods extracted from unguarded pockets. The Dodger manages to relieve the gentlemanly Joseph O'Conor (Mr. Brownlow) of his wallet, but in the ensuing ruckus it is Oliver who is wrongly arrested and brought before Hugh Griffith (The Magistrate), a classic British comic actor whose thick unruly eyebrows above a droopy face and bearded jowls present him as easily the most Dickensian, in looks and mannerisms, of all the actors in the film. The embodiment of alcoholic ineptitude, he is windy, obtuse, bumbling, and corrosive in his all-too-brief appearance. Dickens would have loved him.

The case is dismissed when an eyewitness protests that Oliver is not the culprit, and Mr. Browlow, alert to the lad's unusual sensitivity and affability, invites him home. His charming townhouse-on-the-square abuts a park that, the next day, becomes the stage where a huge congregation of shopgirls selling roses, milk, and other items, engages in a well-orchestrated production number, "Who Will Buy?" in which each girl tries to entice the homeowners into purchasing her wares. Watching the spectacle from his clean and comfortable bedroom is Oliver, happy for the first time in his life. What neither he nor his benefactor knows is that the boy has unwittingly become an enemy of Sikes, who fears that Oliver will report his and Fagin's activities to the police.

Despite Nancy's assurance that Oliver is no squealer, Sikes proposes that she cooperate in his campaign to kidnap the boy from under Brownlow's nose. Enraged when she refuses, he knocks her to the floor with a vicious slap across the face and warns her to reconsider. Left alone in pain, she realizes that she has no alternative to participating in the scheme. Her decision to remain faithful to Sikes to the bitter end, regardless of the consequences, is revealed in the lovely and quite dramatic "As Long as He Needs Me," Bart's finest ballad and one of the best stage songs of the early sixties. Departing from tradition, Nancy sings the song to herself instead of to Sikes, who had fled the scene, along with Fagin and his youthful associates.

Together, Nancy and Sikes abduct Oliver as he walks along the square on an errand and return him to Fagin's quarters. Sikes demands that the boy tell him whether he had informed on the gang or suffer a beating until he does confess. Nancy intercedes, warning that if Sikes touches Oliver, she will go to the police and "finger" Sykes and everybody else involved in illegal activities. His customary fear of Sikes compounded by Nancy's threat, Fagin later reconsiders his vocation in private in the self-revelatory "Reviewing the Situation," which is performed and played in the background in klezmer style.

Should he continue in his wicked ways or reform and find an honorable job somewhere in the outside world, Fagin ponders. Consumed by greed, he has been able over the years to build up a respectable cache of jewels, which he keeps concealed in a brick wall, that should be sufficient to support him in old age. And yet, he sings, he happens to like the thievery business, so much so that he decides to stay in it.

Hoping to rescue Oliver from Sikes's revenge for botching a burglary in which both were involved, Nancy escorts the lad to the tavern. To distract Sikes from attacking him, she entices her waitress friends and a band of drunken revelers to join her in "Oom-Pah-Pah," a tuneful and energetic song-and-dance number that sends the participants rotating over the floor and shielding her and Oliver's disappearing act from the bar into the night. When Sikes learns of her plan to deliver Oliver back to Mr. Brownlow at London Bridge, he beats her to death with his cane before the meeting takes place. Pursued by the police, he is shot dead atop a warehouse. Fagin, now in serious danger of arrest, rushes from his garret with his chest of jewels into the street. He slips, however, and inadvertently drops the chest to the ground, where it is swallowed up, as if by quicksand, in a patch of deep mud.

Mr. Brownlaw, having discovered that Oliver's mother, Emily, was his long-lost niece, welcomes the sobbing boy back into his home. As for Fagin, bereft of his retirement assets and his boys scattered hither and yon, he again reviews his situation, unable to determine whether to stay crooked or go straight. His decision is made easy by the reappearance of the Dodger, who smiles at the old man while proudly exhibiting a wallet he had just stolen from a spectator to Sikes's death.

Fagin sighs. Bless the boy, he is already a reputable master of the trade. Wrapping his arm around him, Fagin walks contentedly with his star pupil, like Charlie Chaplin leading Paulette Goddard at the end of *Modern Times*, into the bright new future promised by the rising sun.

Hello, Dolly! (1969)

A 20th Century–Fox picture. DIRECTOR: Gene Kelly; ASSISTANT: Paul Helmick. PRODUCER: Ernest Lehman; ASSOCIATE: Roger Edens. SCREENWRITER: Ernest Lehman. CINEMATOGRAPHER: Harry Stradling; SPECIAL EFFECTS: L.B. Abbott and Art Cruickshank. FILM EDITOR: William Reynolds. PRODUCTION DESIGNER: John DeCuir. ART DIRECTORS: Jack Martin Smith and Herman Blumenthal. CHOREOGRAPHER: Michael Kidd; ASSISTANT: Shelah Hackett; DANCE ARRANGEMENTS: Marvin Laird. SET DECORATORS: Walter M. Scott, George Hopkins, and Raphael Bretton. SOUND SUPERVISOR: James Corcoran. SOUND: Murray Spivak, Vinton Vernon, Jack Solomon, and Douglas Williams. COSTUME DESIGNER: Irene Sharaff. MAKEUP SUPERVISOR: Dan Striepeke. MAKEUP ARTISTS: Ed Butterworth and Richard Hamilton. HAIRSTYLING: Edith Linden. MUSIC EDITORS: Robert Mayer and Kenneth Wannberg. MUSIC SCORERS AND CONDUCTORS: Lennie Hayton and Lionel Newman. ORCHESTRATORS: Philip J. Lang, Lennie Hayton, Herbert Spencer, Alexander Courage, Don Costa, Warren Barker, Frank Comstock, and Joseph Lipman. CHORAL ARRANGEMENTS SUPERVISOR: Jack Latimer. SONGS: Lyrics and music by Jerry Herman. RUNNING TIME: 2 hours, 9 minutes. *Principal Players*: Barbra Streisand (Dolly Levi). Walter Matthau (Horace Vandergelder). Michael Crawford (Cornelius Hackl). Marianne McAndrew (Irene Molloy). Tommy Tune (Ambrose Kemper). Danny Lockin (Barnaby Tucker). E.J. Peaker (Minnie Fay). Joyce Ames (Ermengarde). Judy Knaiz (Gussie Granger [Ernestina Semple]). Louis Armstrong (Orchestra Leader [Louis]). *Major Academy Awards*: Best Art Direction; Scoring; Sound. *Nominations*: Best Picture; Cinematography; Film Editing; Costume Design.

A great deal of type has been set over the years lamenting this film version of the long-running Broadway musical, which won 10 Tony Awards, the most ever for a musical. It is too long, according to many critics, too trite, too splashy, too heavy handed in mounting the production numbers, too picture postcard in resurrecting the sidewalks of little old spic and span New York, too crammed with tintype characters, too laden with predictable plot twists and turns.

Guilty as the picture is on all these counts, it is saved from obsolescence by the quality of the music and the immensely likable cast. If the plot is lightweight, which it is, it is no more so than its sources. If the scene in the hat shop reminds one of similar episodes common to the English Restoration farces, it also differs from them in one important respect: the two young men in *Dolly* are trying to seclude themselves from the eyes of their boss, not from a husband they have turned into a cuckold. The dialogue is almost unanimously unfunny throughout, the characters artificial, and the awkwardness and naïvete of the boys from Yonkers so incredible that one wonders how they survived for 24 hours in the Big Town to the south.

Up to the present, *Hello, Dolly!* is the last in the long line of traditional Hollywood musicals that so enchanted audiences from the beginning of the sound era. Its plot could have been written by operetta librettist Henry Blossom, its music by Romberg or Herbert. The film is far closer in spirit to *Seven Brides for Seven Brothers* than to *Funny Girl* or *Gigi*. But, then, why look for profundity where it is not meant to exist. No one associated with the original Broadway comedy or its musical successor pretended that the production objective was to analyze the mysteries of life among the marriageable and suggest ways to solve them.

Dolly must be looked upon for what it is: a glossy divertissement, more professionally rendered than a great many of its predecessors. Delivering absolutely no message whatever, either political or cultural, it resembles the carefree movie musicals of the 1950s more than those of the 1930s, which by and large were never reluctant to offer suggestions on how to overcome hardship, if only by laughing at trouble while waiting for the economic winds to change. To its credit, *Dolly* was outfitted with

Back in Harmonia Gardens after a long absence, Barbra Streisand greets the restaurant staff with the title song from *Hello, Dolly!*

an outstanding score notable for its stylistic variations. Indeed, not since the early forties, when the rumba and other Latin American-leaning songs began vying for attention with the ballads, waltzes, swing tunes, and novelties written for the screen (many of them by Harry Warren, then working for Fox), had any musical film rewarded the faithful with more song hits with greater diversity of tempo than *Hello, Dolly!*

Today, the majority of this musical movie's off-camera artists share the anonymity of most of the cast members. Except for Gene Kelly, Barbra Streisand, Walter Matthau, and possibly Tommy Tune and the great "Satchmo," no one else's name is recognizable, gifted as each of them was at his and her specialty. Such is the penalty that all talented musical craftsmen and women and performers have paid since *Dolly* played the neighborhood houses. The movie musical has declined so drastically in number that even its top practitioners have been given precious little opportunity to revive it, or the new generation of talents to improve their skills through the trial and error of steady practice.

Twenty-eight years old in 1997, *Dolly* was the last Oscar nominee to recruit men and women who had helped to shape the movie musical comedy, ranging from Kelly and Harry Stradling to Lennie Hayton and Lionel Newman. As expected, the costumes designed by Irene Sharaff, who in 1933 began her costuming career on Broadway with Irving Berlin's *As Thousands Cheer*, are exceptional, as are the too-often overwrought six dances choreographed by Michael Kidd.

Then there is the matter of the songs. Jerry Herman need not take a back seat to any of his contemporaries when it comes to writing clever lyrics and memorable music. Fortunately, Fox included all but one of the songs—"Motherhood March"—he wrote for the Broadway original. The sweetness of his love songs are on a par with the best of earlier composers who filled their Hollywood scores with hits, and his lyrics are above par. Unlike most of his predecessors, Herman cast his *Hello, Dolly!* tunes in the widest array of rhythms. Besides fox-trot ballads, in which all the film composers specialized, the show includes two marches, two novelties, a waltz, three upbeat full-fledged production numbers, and another with ragtime overtones—and not a poor song among them.

An extraordinary craftsman, Herman is one of the very few songwriters in Broadway history to write both lyrics and music. His Great White Way songs are far fewer than those of the superactive Irving Berlin and Cole Porter, who also wrote their own words, but two of his 1960s title tunes, each named after leading female character in musicals, are today almost as well known as anything written by his two illustrious predecessors.

The more recent of the songs, "Mame," was the highlight of the 1966 musical comedy rewrite of Patrick Dennis's novel *Auntie Mame*. The other, "Hello, Dolly!," made an even cleaner sweep of the nation, thanks largely to the bestselling recording by Louis Armstrong, who also sings it in the film, and its service as President Lyndon B. Johnson's campaign theme in 1964 ("Hello, Lyndon, / Well, hello Lyndon!..."). So warmly was Armstrong's recording greeted that it managed to knock the Beatles off the top of the popularity charts in 1964, a feat that he termed his greatest triumph. Not since Hammerstein and Kern's "Sunny," produced in 1925, had Broadway given birth to a title song that matched the popularity of the show of the same name that introduced it.

The only lyricist-composer ever to have three musicals running simultaneously on Broadway—*Dear World*, *Hello, Dolly!*, and *Mame*—Herman began his career with the revue *Nightcap*, which was premiered in 1958 and ran for almost two years. It was followed shortly afterward with a second revue, *Parade*. His initial on–Broadway venture was *Milk and Honey* (1961), set in Israel and containing three songs of more than passing interest, "Shalom," "I Will Follow You," and "There's No Reason in the World." His latest musical comedy, *La Cage aux Folles*, based loosely on two French and Italian comedy films released in 1978 and 1980, began its respectable Broadway tenure in 1983. (A third film, *La Cage aux Folles III*, came out in 1985.)

In his recent autobiography, Herman frankly assesses his purpose for writing music. Decidedly a member of the "old school" of song writing, he describes himself as a "razzmatazz musical comedy writer, a cheerful man whose life is dedicated to making people smile and feel good and leave the theater humming a show tune." He certainly reached his objective with *Hello, Dolly!*, giving audiences plenty to hum about with a half-dozen melodies ranging from lighthearted to lighter than air.

One of Herman's most recent ventures, the songs for *Mrs. Santa Claus*, was telecast in December 1996, and billed as the first original musical written for television since Rodgers and Hammerstein's *Cinderella* in 1957. The star, Angela Lansbury, had starred in the original *Mame* and *Dear World*, winning two of her four Tony awards.

The source of *Hello, Dolly!* was the 1954 comedy *The Matchmaker*, which playwright Thornton Wilder based on the 1938 play *The Merchant of Yonkers*, which in turn had been based on an early 19th-century Viennese comedy by Johann Nestrox. Portraying the likable but conniving Dolly Levi was actress-playwright Ruth Gordon. In the 1958 film remake, the part was given to Shirley Booth, a superior stage actress and winner of the best actress Oscar for her role as Lola Delaney in *Come Back, Little Sheba* (1952), which she had also starred in on Broadway. A little on the dumpy side and bereft of glamor in face, figure, and voice, but an actress of rare virtuosity, the middle-age Miss Booth was Dolly incarnate.

It was Carol Channing, however, whose name was fated to be indelibly linked with the character after producer David Merrick signed Herman to add music to Thornton's play. Curiously, considering her initial—and perennial—success as Dolly, Miss Channing was not Merrick's first choice. That distinction went to Ethel Merman, then the undisputed queen of musical Broadway, who unwisely turned the part down, although she did appear briefly in the leading role in 1970. Perceived by some Broadwayites as rather a lame substitute, Miss Channing had not appeared in a smash show since Leo Robin and Jule Styne's *Gentleman Prefer Blondes* way back in 1949, when, as Lorelei Lee, she introduced the indestructible "Diamonds Are a Girl's Best Friend" to the world. She repaid Merrick's confidence with interest, however, taking complete charge of a part that seemed to have been written exclusively for her. In 1995, she was back on Broadway to reintroduce the aggressive businesswoman to a new generation of *Dolly* fans in a 14-week limited run. She was then 74 years old.

Hello, Dolly! opened at the St. James Theatre on January 16, 1964, and posted 2,844 consecutive performances, temporarily replacing *My Fair Lady* as Broadway's longest-running musical. A major reason for its staying power, apart from the contributions of Jerry and Carol, was Merrick's novel idea of replacing the leading lady every so often with big-name entertainers, including Pearl Bailey, who starred in an all-black version in 1967. Some of the other substitute stars, Ginger Rogers, Martha Raye, and Betty Grable, were well past their prime, but as an exercise in using the pull of nostalgia as a box office additive, the device helped greatly to extend the run of the show. Dorothy Lamour headed the national road show company in 1968.

Like the play, the film is set in the 1890s, providing still another example of the continuing fondness of stage and movie audiences for musicals that bore little or no relation to the era in which they were produced. Audiences of the 1960s especially enjoyed backward glances at the America of yesteryear, possibly hoping to avoid contact with that decade's troublesome occurrences by refusing the relive them inside a theater.

Starring as Dolly in her second film, Barbra Streisand is handicapped by her age, causing one to shudder the two times she refers to herself as this "old gal." She was 27 in 1969, while Miss Channing, who had appeared in several Hollywood musicals, was 48, clearly an age appropriate to a busy-body entrepreneur with vast experience in man-woman relationships that she manipulates to effect her own mercenary ends. But Barbra compensates for the lack of middle-age bulge and wrinkles with her expert vocalizing, which was as good as that of any other songstress of the late sixties, including the divine, rusty-throated Carol herself.

But *Dolly* is no *Funny Girl*. Its plot suffers in comparison with the insightful recording of the personal and professional problems that characterized the life of Fanny Brice and made her such an appealing heroine. Dolly is the same at the end of the picture as she was at the beginning; Fanny evolves from scheming and energetic stage-struck hopeful to mature exponent of her craft, achieving her goal by hopping from one stepping stone to the other like a surefooted lass determined to cross the River Jordan.

Dolly, on the other hand, is clearly an adept practitioner of her craft at the beginning, and as a result fails to give the audience any reason to cheer her on to career fulfillment.

Nor, unlike her Brice role, is Miss Streisand given much of a chance to engage in anything remotely resembling dramatic acting. The single exception is her self-assessment in the park that leads to the sudden awareness that, active as she is in the world of commerce, she is missing out on life's other opportunities, like becoming one of her own clients and forming a long-lasting attachment with a man of more than passing interest. Her conversations with men, as with women, are prompted by visions of earning substantial fees, and she tries to shield herself from emotional injury by indulging in wisecracks and self-promotional testimonials to her professional proficiency, often shashaying around like a young Mae West seeking harmonious relationships. Walter Matthau is, as usual, masterful in his portrait of the lumbering hulk, a small-town businessman fully aware of his skimpy qualifications as a lover, but so dependent on women for creature comforts that he tries to frustrate the marriage plans of his own niece to keep her cooking breakfast for him. Another able performer, for years now the daddy long legs of the Broadway stage, is Tommy Tune, who easily arouses admiration with what seems to be his effortless dancing, seemingly on stilts. Unfortunately, he appears only briefly, and never alone, in several of the dances, largely because Michael Kidd sought to out-spectacle the Broadway choreography of Gower Champion, who in his dual role as director wisely tamped down any tendency he might have had to engage in excess.

Love for Sale. Female entrepreneurs were not common in the America of 1890, but Barbra Streisand (Mrs. Dolly Levi) would have made her mark on the business world even if they were as numerous as they became a century later. She was industrious, discreet, persuasive, and supremely confident. Instead of selling commercial products, she derived her enviable reputation from the service sector, guaranteeing to provide clients with whatever it is they feel they need. Chief among them were the best available mates culled from her list of marriage-minded bachelors and spinsters. She even outdoes her Gay Nineties contemporary, the Mae West of *She Done Him Wrong*, in self-promotion and deal making. But Barbra was neither naughty nor notorious, or a confidante of the losers and nobodies who frequented Bowery saloons. She was an uptown

lady "who arranges things," a sort of go-between for matching seekers and fulfillers of dreams.

First seen jutting forward as prominently as a ship's prow, Barbra boards a motorcar in the seven-minute prologue to the film and enthusiastically passes out business cards to potential patrons while singing "Just Leave Everything to Me." She continues her self-promotion on the street, boasting that she can handle any assignment, whether it be boarding kittens, polishing toenails, teaching the mandolin or French, or rounding up members of the opposite sex to whisper sweet nothings in their ears. And all matchmaking negotiations, she stresses, are conducted "in an atmosphere of refinement and elegance" appropriate to the social status of both herself and her highly selective clients. Bringing potential lovers together is the one service that Barbra performs herself, for despite her myriad activities, she is primarily a marriage broker, the Americanized version of the yenta.

Today she is on her way to Yonkers, then a small and grassy-green suburb of The Bronx, not to furnish a paying customer with his or her ideal spouse, but to break up the engagement of two young lovers already committed to marrying. The young lady is Joyce Ames (Ermengarde), the niece of Walter Matthau (Horace Vandergelder), the bachelor owner of a gigantic hay and feed store in downtown Yonkers whose systemic truculence has left him "friendless and mean," in his own words.

Successful at concealing his standard musical comedy heart of gold behind a façade of gruffness, Matthau has hired Barbra to escort Joyce back to New York and keep her there until her passion for Tommy Tune (Ambrose Kemper) dies away or is superceded by another love affair, whichever comes first. Matthau dislikes Tommy because of his ambition to become a painter. To Matthau, any young man who plans to earn a living by other means than selling something "that everybody needs every single day" is unworthy of marrying anyone, especially his niece.

Matthau is picked up in his store reluctantly promoting two young clerks, Michael Crawford (Cornelius Hackl) and Danny Lockin (Barnaby Tucker). Although he classifies both as occupational misfits, he needs them to operate his store while he ventures to New York to visit Marianne McAndrew (Irene Molloy), whom he is "seriously considering" inviting into wedlock. He is fond of her, even if for the wrong reasons. Like Howard Keel in *Seven Brides for Seven Brothers*, what he really wants is a sweetheart of a bride with sturdy arms and legs to keep his house and store up to snuff.

Outlining his expectations in "It Takes a Woman," Matthau enumerates the duties that Marianne will handle all by her lonesome—from setting traps for mice, and presumably emptying them as needed, to cleaning the stables, taking out the garbage, and repairing leaks in the plumbing. A plot-oriented song, "It Takes a Woman" succeeds very well at providing insight into Matthau's miserliness and low regard for women. In addition, it is singularly melodic for a relatively minor show tune, at times foreshadowing the lilt that songwriter Herman later incorporated in "We Need a Little Christmas" for *Mame*.

Matthau's prospective marriage upsets Barbra, although she pretends to be happy at hearing the news. She has her own sights set on him—after all, he is "half a millionaire"—and begins to question the wisdom of having introduced him to Marianne. Not above angling to earn still another fee, which is never refundable no matter how things turn out, as well as to keep Matthau away from the altar, she tells him of an heiress, even wealthier than he is, whom she already has lined up for him to meet. But it's too late, Matthau informs her; his heart belongs to Marianne.

As he drives away to the Yonkers railroad station on the first leg of his trip to Manhattan, Barbra clearly evinces her feeling toward him by singing "It Takes a Woman" with a new set of lyrics. According to her version, the woman is the dominant marriage partner, capable of changing her man into the perfect husband she has been looking for her whole life. And the man for her is Matthau.

The snappish store owner is not the only person to leave Yonkers for New York. Barbra arranges for Tommy Tune to also go there in order to be near his beloved Joyce, and she invites both to join her that night at Harmonia Gardens, Barbra's favorite Manhattan dining

spot. Meanwhile, Matthau's two clerks renege on their promise to tend to business while the master is away by closing the store the moment he is out of sight. Hoping to at last taste the thrill of adventure, they vow not to return home till each has kissed at least one Big City girl. Helpful as ever, Barbra recommends Marianne's millinery shop as a likely place to find female companionship, a suggestion that sends shivers of excitement up and down the boys' spines. Never closing her eyes to developing new business, Barbra secretly hopes that this "arrangement" will result in Marianne's falling in love with one of them, stranding Matthau in bachelorhood by turning down his proposal.

Enthusiastic to make an impression on Manhattan ladies, the young men duet the finger-thumping "Put on Your Sunday Clothes," the film's first dazzling production number, stressing the importance of looking one's best when seeking female companionship. After they lock up the store, the scene switches to the Yonkers railroad station, where a crowd has assembled to send them and the other passengers off with a cheerful reprise of the boys' peppy salute to sartorial splendor. The scene in some ways reminds film buffs of the far superior railroad station scene in *The Harvey Girls*. In that 1945 MGM musical, however, the townspeople welcome the carloads of newcomers with Mercer and Warren's Oscar-winning "On the Atchison, Topeka and Santa Fe." *Hello, Dolly!* reverses the celebration, with the Yonkerites wishing their neighbors God speed on their journey out of town.

Believing that clothes make the woman as well as the man, Marianne is busily sprucing up her own appearance while singing the very pretty "Ribbons Down My Back," in her Manhattan shop. The typical musical comedy hybrid of sugar and spice, Marianne sings it to her assistant, pert, pretty, and scatterbrained E.J. Peaker (Minnie), a delightful, and traditional, blithe spirit who seems to be right at home singing and dancing, as well as at reinterring the childlike bliss of the boy-crazy, ready-for-love blonde pinhead. Marianne's purpose for decking herself out in her holiday finery is to impress Matthau, whom she admits she does not love but regards as her passport out of the millinery business, which she hates.

Michael and Danny follow Barbra's advice

by visiting the shop, only to learn rather quickly that their quest for kisses from the two young ladies will be frustrated by their shyness. Their pallid attempts at brushing aside this handicap are dropped, however, when they run for cover under a table and into a cupboard after catching sight of Barbra and Matthau approaching the shop entrance. Indicative of his pallid generosity and romantic inclinations, Matthau presents Marianne with a box of chocolate-covered peanuts, unshelled. The twosome's unamorous *tete-a-tete* abruptly ends when he senses from her nervousness that she is quite likely concealing a lover somewhere in the store.

Although unable to verify his suspicion, Matthau explodes into anger at her alleged deception and stalks toward the front door, swearing never again to "trouble" Marianne with his presence. He halts momentarily to demand the return of his peanuts and to announce that he will spend the rest of the afternoon marching in the patriotic 14th Street Parade.

Creeping out of their hiding places and still intent on sampling some of Manhattan's less fearsome adventures, the two clerks are forced to refuse Barbra's suggestion that they take Marianne and Minnie to Harmonia Gardens for dinner. They simply cannot afford such an expense, and, even worse, neither can dance. Eager to provide a service, Barbra proceeds to teach them a few fundamental steps with the lyrics of the sparkling waltz song, "Dancing," which could very well be the most tuneful stage song of the sixties. Her two pupils carry the song out of the dress shop onto neighboring streets and a park with a giant water fountain and an adjoining badminton court. Joining them in the film's production highlight are about 25 couples whose festive terpsichorean manipulations combine the overstated inventiveness of Busby Berkeley and the sprightliness of the dance routines in *The Great Ziegfeld* as well as any other post–1936 film-musical nominee. The immense assortment of highly competent chorus boys and girls are all excellent, particularly Danny Lockin, who executes several rare double-axle spins in midair.

At the conclusion of the number, Marianne's growing love for Michael leads her into assuring Barbra that the world is "full of won-

derful things." It is then that the audience sees the real matchmaker, the one nobody knows. Agreeing with a wan smile, Barbra is no longer able to conceal her lonesomeness after being on her own for so long. A fiercely independent widow, she now finds little reason to celebrate her personal July 4th. In a closeup, her face clearly reveals the wistful need of a special somebody to care for her, and she for him. She knows many people, but almost all of them are either clients or the specialists who perform the services she arranges. For far too long she has been little more than a wallflower in the dance of life.

Glancing into the sky to address a departed spirit, she issues an appeal to dear Ephron, her late husband. She wants to reenter society, to live life again to the fullest, as she did when he was alive to share its joys with her. Give me a sign, she urges him, a sign that he is prepared to release her from her prolonged mourning period. She will remain faithful to his memory, but she must rejoin the human race before time runs out on her, or, as she words it, "Before the Parade Passes By," leaving her stranded on the sidewalk, an observer rather than a participant in life. The festive sounds of the dancing merrymakers have receded, producing a silence much like the stillness that announces the end of a party after the final guest has left. Barbra begins walking, slowly at first, then gaining traction that moves her rapidly from her secluded bench in the park into the sunlight of rebirth.

She is next seen watching the columns of high-steppers nimbly marching to the tune, one of the all-time best Broadway marches, in the tumultuous 14th Street Parade. A member of Lodge 26 of the Knights of the Hudson, Matthau is there, along with war veterans, horse soldiers, floats, suffragettes, bagpipers, lady gymnasts, iron-jawed members of the Women's Christian Temperance Union, and a team of Kleisdales pulling a Budweiser Beer carriage. Thrilled at spotting an out-of- work actress friend, Gussie Granger, played with high hare-brained effectiveness by Judy Knaiz, Barbra scurries over to her float and hires her to play a role that night at Harmonia Gardens. A cash down payment seals the deal.

Barbra next sidles up to Matthau and she apologizes for the disappointing millinery shop incident. His self-esteem devalued, Matthau angrily discharges her, asserting that he no longer wants to be listed among her clients. Barbra, however, is made of sterner stuff, and she refuses to accept her dismissal without attempting to cater to his need (and hers) once more. She invites him to a private dinner that evening at 7:30 at Harmonia Gardens. There, she promises, he will meet a rich and beautiful heiress—"You know, the one I mentioned to you the other day in Yonkers"—by the name of "Ernestina Semple," an alias for Judy that she concocts on the spot. Like the spoiled child he essentially is, Matthau ignores the invitation. Once wounded, he shies away from the potential for additional injury to the heart.

Without missing a beat, he stomps away after branding her, in insulting Henry Higgins fashion, a "damn exasperating woman," to which he will later add such other encomia as bossy, scheming, meddling, inquisitive, and irritating. But the renewal of optimism that had just lifted Barbra from despondency has instilled in her a new optimism worthy of a warrior on the way to a battle he is certain his side will win. Weaving her way through the marchers, she reprises her confidence song, triumphantly embracing life and Matthau as just the man to take dead Ephron's place.

Hey, Fellas, It's Dolly!. It is evening in lower Manhattan. Michael and Danny greet their dates, Marianne and Minnie, outside the entrance to the sumptuous Fifth Avenue Hotel. With little less than one dollar between them, the young men are not at all eager to treat the ladies to a pre-dinner aperitif in the hotel's lounge or, for that matter, to spend it on carriage fare to take all four to Harmonia Gardens on East 14th Street, which at the time boasted such renowned gastronomical emporia as Lüchow's and Delmonico's. Instead, under Michael's prodding, they agree to walk the 25 blocks. None of them needs carriages or streetcars to project an aura of class, he insists. In short, Michael continues in the playful song "Elegance," all four could pass for Fifth Avenue swells, envied by the aristocratic likes of Commodore Vanderbilt, J.P. Morgan, and Diamond Jim Brady for their exquisite upperclass breeding.

Barbra, meantime, is singing a tune of equal importance to realizing her own vision of happiness. Although she has not received any sign that Ephron approves of her seeking romantic involvement, she confesses in the introspective ballad "Love Is Only Love" that she has chosen Matthau as her next husband. She will, however, keep her promise to introduce him to "Ernestina," who according to the conspiritorial ladies' prearranged plan, will dine with him at Harmonia Gardens. Love is not expected to appear on the menu, since Judy has already agreed with Barbra to reject Matthau as an "entirely unsuitable" husband, leaving Barbra free to chase after him once his ego has been crushed for a second time in the same day.

Featuring the most imposing interior set to be seen in any 1960s film musical, the restaurant is richly decorated in Gay Nineties gilt and grandeur, and dominated by a red-carpeted staircase that descends from the entrance to the main dining area, which surrounds a dance floor. Circling the perimeter are the cozy private dining rooms. Seated in one of them are Marianne and Minnie, along with their bankrupt male escorts, who raffishly order champagne and pheasant for four.

Assembled at the bottom of the staircase are the head waiter, played impeccably by Rudolph Reisenweber, who deploys his staff with the curtness of a Prussian field marshal. Standing next to him is his assistant, played by Fritz Feld, the 69-year-old veteran character actor who by then had been waiting on tables in innumerable movies in for about 30 years, and the restaurant's uniformed waiters. Abuzz with excitement upon learning from Tommy Tune that Barbra is on her way, they are unable to contain their glee at seeing her again after several years of absence, for no one else in the entire city of New York, Reisenweber insists, has a "happier smile, warmer heart, or larger appetite."

Barbra's scheme to become Matthau's betrothed shifts from neutral into first gear when Judy brusquely leaves him alone in their private dining room and races outside to report to Barbra, who is waiting in a parked hansom cab. She has followed instructions to the letter, the actress informs Barbra, and deflated Matthau's balloon by giving the clear impression that he is in no way worthy of her romantic interest, or, by implication, of any other woman's. Barbra's turn has come. In one of the grandest entrances in film history, she strides into the restaurant, then pauses to survey the diners and staff from atop the staircase before slinking her way, step by dainty step, to the bottom level, where the waiters rush to greet her.

"Hello, Dolly!" they shout in unison to the object of their affection, who returns the favor by singing as magnetic a tune as ever appeared in a Broadway musical. The *pièce de résistance* of the score, practically universal in appeal and recognition, it is reprised five times, never relinquishing its grip on the audience's attention, whether sung solo or by Barbra's adoring chorus of waiters, or danced. Throughout the lengthy production number, Barbra enthusiastically extends her greeting to the staff, each of whom—Harry, Manny, Danny, Hank, Stanley, et al.—she addresses individually in a gesture of unalloyed fondness. Among the greeters is jazz great Louis Armstrong, the restaurant's bandleader and owner of one of the most distinctive voices ever to be recorded on a sound track, then appearing in the last of his 23 movies (he would die two years later), which began with *Pennies from Heaven* in 1936.

Matthau's attempt to sneak unnoticed out of the restaurant is foiled when Barbra persuades him to join her in another dinner for two. Still angry over Judy's deserting him for no perceptible reason, Matthau is further antagonized when Barbra announces her own lack of interest in ever becoming his marriage partner. So when did he ask her to marry him, he replies defensively. Glancing at the couples on the dance floor, he is astounded to discover Tommy and his niece there, and he demands that they separate. A scuffle ensues, which ends in Matthau's expulsion, but not till he also peers unbelievingly into the faces of his two clerks, who are also expelled, with Marianne and Minnie, for nonpayment of their bill.

The musical comedy adage that true love eventually triumphs over adversity is verified in the little park near Harmonia Gardens. The smitten male is Michael, who proposes to Marianne with "It Only Takes a Moment," an immensely pretty ballad that his coyness and awkward delivery push practically to the brink of ruination. Supportive of his view that the few seconds it takes to ask the right woman for her

hand in marriage insures a lifetime of happiness for both bride and groom, she accepts him as her future husband, even after he admits he is not the rich fellow he has pretended to be.

No such meeting of hearts, however, graces the acrimonious exchange between Barbra and Matthau. Unable to win him over, she announces that she is through with him for good. Fire in her eyes and ice in her tone, she rebukes him for his ill-treatment in the raggy "So Long, Dearie," swearing to have nothing more to do with him, or with Yonkers either. Symbolic of her threat to step out of his life, she climbs into a hansom and disappears.

Back in his Yonkers store, Matthau is still distraught over the disappointing events of the previous evening. Luckily for him, all the principal players in the Harmonia Gardens drama are on hand to serve as targets for venting his anger. Reneging on her vow never to set another foot in Yonkers, Barbra arrives moments later to make a final effort at dredging a proposal out of him, difficult as she realizes that task undoubtedly will be.

Maybe, she muses, the man is simply too wealthy, too self-sufficient to need the love and companionship of a wife. And there is that other barrier to furthering her one-sided romance: Ephron has not as yet signaled his approval of her remarrying. She recalls her late husband's axiom about the relationship between love and wealth, to wit, "Money, if you'll pardon the expression, is like manure. It's not worth a thing unless it's spread around, encouraging young things to grow." Surely, Matthau will someday realize that he needs more than money to live the ideal life, or so she hopes.

What with Michael and Danny's threat to open a rival feed store directly across the street, niece Joyce's inflexible determination to marry Tommy Tune, and everybody's apparent deep dislike of him, Matthau descends into a shattering sense of loneliness. His unexpected admission that it is most likely time for him to get married, but only if Barbra is the bride, sends a momentary surge of delight into the lady's bloodstream. It would seem that she has served successfully as matchmaker for herself. Dutifully winding up her professional chores, she arranges for Matthau to give his blessing to the weddings of Tommy and his niece and Michael and Marianne, and then to accept Danny as a partner in the feed store. All that is needed now to guarantee everybody's happiness is that all-important signal from over the rainbow.

As for his consuming interest in accumulating riches, Matthau unexpectedly dismisses it as a foolish way to occupy one's time and efforts. "Money, if you'll pardon the expression, is like manure...," he suddenly recites to Barbra, transporting her into seventh heaven with words she is positive have been sent from Paradise. Ephron has come through! He has given his seal of approval to his widow's second marriage!

Matthau gets her to church on time, and the film ends with the betrothed and guests so awash in happiness that they sing most of the show's songs. He actually manages to smile as he kisses her, while Barbra, radiant in her hourglass bridal gown, glows in the realization that she is again a marcher in the parade of life. Marianne was right: life is filled with such wonderful things! And, as Barbra has proved, with a little bit o' luck and a touch of chutzpah, anyone can get her share of them.

Fiddler on the Roof (1971)

A Mirish-Cartier Productions/United Artists picture. DIRECTOR: Norman Jewison; ASSISTANTS: Terry Nelson, Paul Ibbetson, and Vladimir Spindler. PRODUCER: Norman Jewison; ASSOCIATE: Patrick Palmer. SCREENWRITER: Joseph Stein. CINEMATOGRAPHER: Oswald Morris. FILM EDITORS: Anthony Gibbs and Robert Lawrence; ASSISTANTS: Brian Mann and Wally Nelson. PRODUCTION SUPERVISOR: Larry DeWaay. PRODUCTION DESIGNER: Robert Boyle. PRODUCTION MANAGER: Robert Lloyd. CHOREOGRAPHER: Tom Abbott; ASSISTANT: Sammy Bayes. ART DIRECTOR: Michael Stringer. SET DECORATOR: Peter Lamont. SOUND: Gordon K. McCallum. SOUND EDITOR: Les Wiggins. SOUND MIXER: David Hildyard. COSTUME DESIGNERS: Elizabeth Haffenden and Joan Bridge. MAKEUP: Del Armstrong and Wally Schneiderman. HAIRDRESSER: Gordon Bond. MUSIC ADAPTER AND CONDUCTOR: John Williams. ORCHESTRATORS: John Williams and Alexander Courage. OFF-SCREEN VIOLIN SOLOIST: Isaac Stern. SONGS: Lyrics by Sheldon Harnick, music by Jerry Bock. RUNNING TIME: 3 hours, 1 minute. *Principal Players*: Topol (Tevye). Norma Crane (Golde). Leonard Frey (Motel). Molly Picon (Yente). Paul Mann (Lazar Wolf). Michael Glaser (Perchick). Raymond Lovelock (Fyedka). Louis Zorich (The Constable). Zvee Scooler (The Rabbi). Tutte Lemkow (The Fiddler). The Daughters: Rosalind Harris (Tzeitel). Michele Marsh (Hodel). Neva Small (Chava). Elaine Edwards (Shprintze). Candice Bonstein (Bielka). *Major*

Academy Awards: Best Cinematography; Scoring; Sound. *Nominations*: Best Picture; Direction; Actor (*Topol*); Supporting Actor (*Leonard Frey*); Art Direction.

"When Topol began playing Tevye in London for the first time, my wife and I flew over to see him. We were bowled over by both his charisma and his performance," *Fiddler on the Roof* lyricist Sheldon Harnick commented as this book was in progress. "While his performance was not as richly comic as Zero Mostel's—nor was any other actor's, for that matter—he brought other values that more than compensated for whatever comic values were lost. In my opinion, his stage performance carried over into the film. I thought he was wonderful in both. By the way, composer Jerry Bock and screenwriter Joe Stein were also surprised that director-producer Norman Jewison didn't use Zero in the film. My recollection is that he felt Zero was simply 'too big' for the screen."

Rarely ever has the musical theater introduced a character who dominates the production in which he or she appears to the extent that Yiddish author Sholom Aleichem's world-famous Tevye does in *Fiddler on the Roof.* Through sheer force of personality, the peasant dairy farmer is the cynosure of all eyes from beginning to end, the sun around which all the other players, and the plot itself, revolve. The finest of the actors selected to play him over the years have had to exhibit bigness in both talent and bulk in order to justify the commanding presence of this gentle giant of a troubled father reluctantly growing ever more accustomed to grief, but never wallowing in despair. Living in virtual serfdom, he is increasingly saddened over the loss of the cherished customs under which he grew into adulthood while acknowledging his inability, and apparently God's unwillingness, to prevent their further erosion. At the end they exist only in memory.

But his nobility and optimism remain constant, even after he and his family are expelled from their tiny Ukranian village, near Minsk, about 1910. Like the von Trapps almost three decades later, the family looks forward to resettlement in a new country with confidence. Highly principled but penniless, Tevye throughout the musical has to exhibit the mesmerizing

Topol, as Tevye the Jewish milkman, sings of the value of maintaining strict adherence to "Tradition" at the beginning of *Fiddler on the Roof*, the musicalized version of Sholom Aleichem's tale of *Tevye's Daughters*.

talent of an Al Jolson or Sophie Tucker, who so towered over their competitors that the luckless performers consigned to follow their acts on the vaudeville circuits in effect were forced to concede that their careers were at an end, or fast approaching it.

Mostel, whose starring role as the Roman slave Pseudolus in Stephen Sondheim's *A Funny Thing Happened on the Way to the Forum* deservedly enchanted audiences in 1962, was the ideal first Tevye when *Fiddler* opened on September 22, 1964, at the Imperial Theatre. Splendidly exhibiting the stubborn authoritarianism and occasional tenderness of the tortured middle-age milkman, Mostel for nine months imbued the role with unmatched gusto in gesture, dialogue, song, and dance. According to Stein, Mostel's Broadway performance was "quite wonderful," and he eagerly sought the opportunity to reprise it in the film. "But he made Tevye more comic than tragic. Both the libretto and the screenplay wanted Tevye to convey both."

The riveting musical play, like the man who came to dinner, stayed on and on in its Great White Way home for 3,242 performances, the most of any nominated Broadway-based musical film, with such accomplished actors as Paul Lipson, Luther Adler and Herschel Bernardi succeeding Mostel. Fyvush Finkle, later awarded an Emmy as best supporting actor in a dramatic series for his role as attorney Douglas Wambaugh in CBS' *Picket Fences*, appeared in *Fiddler* for 12 years in various locales, the capstone of his long career. The *New York Times'* Howard Taubman adequately summarized the unanimous verdict of his fellow opening-night critics when he wrote: "Compounded of the familiar materials of the musical theater—popular song, vivid dance movement, comedy and emotion—[*Fiddler on the Roof*] combines and transcends them to arrive at an integrated achievement of uncommon quality."

For several years the musical ranked as the second longest-running production in Broadway history, having tallied up only 92 fewer performances than the then leader, *Life with Father*. By late 1996, its number of consecutive performances placed it fifth among all musicals, exceeded only by *A Chorus Line* (with 6,104), *Oh! Calcutta!* (5,852), *42nd Street* (3,486) and *Grease* (3,384). Already surpassing *Fiddler's* total but still running on Broadway through the 1990s are *Cats*, which at the end of 1996 had completed 5,941 performances at the huge Winter Garden, *Les Miserables* (4,026), and *Phantom of the Opera* (3,726).

Certainly, translating *Fiddler* into a film, especially without Mostel in the cast, posed formidable challenges to its creators. With the possible exception of James Cagney's George M. Cohan in *Yankee Doodle Dandy*, no other Academy Award–nominated musical contains a character of such overpowering magnetism as Tevye, not even *The King and I*, not *West Side Story*, not *My Fair Lady*, *Oliver!*, *Hello, Dolly!*, or *Cabaret*. An unqualified success, the finished product was nominated for eight major Academy Awards and won three.

Fiddler failed in its bid for best picture, and Topol for best actor. The first award went instead to *The French Connection*, a *bona fide* but derivative thriller based on the true-life smashing of a heroin-smuggling ring by the New York detective Edward R. Egan, nicknamed "Popeye" Doyle, the second to its star, Gene Hackman. As a result of *Fiddler's* losing the Oscar, no musical picture has been able to claim that coveted award since *Oliver!* in 1968. The executive producer of *The French Connection*, incidentally, was G. David Schine, a partner in Schine-Moore Productions, better remembered for his involvement in the 1954 Army-McCarthy hearings, which also spotlighted attorney Joseph N. Welch, who five years later would play Judge Weaver in *Anatomy of a Murder*.

Lyricist Harnick was "more than personally satisfied with the film: I thought it was superb. In fact, every time I see it, I appreciate even more the thought, care, and artistry that Norman Jewison brought to it. I was and still am delighted with the camera work and the various cinematic devices that Jewison found to make this a genuine film experience rather than just a filmed stage play."

Harnick also regards the cast assembled by Jewison as excellent, with the single exception of Norma Crane, who essayed the role of Topol's wife, Golde. Not Jewison's first choice, she substituted for an Israeli actress who, on her way from Munich to London for a screen test, was injured when a terrorist's bomb exploded in the plane and injured her badly. "Norma Crane was quite a competent actress," Harnick observed, "but the quality she brought to the screen was too contemporary; there was not enough of the 'peasant' about her." And there is little doubt that the film-long bluntness and jaundiced view of life that her Golde displays are more appropriate to those of Kay Medford, as Barbra Streisand's mother in *Funny Girl*, than to what might be expected from the helpmate of a man unable to gain much traction in his struggle to move forward under the leaden weight of tradition.

In Harnick's view, Michael Glaser was "primarily an actor, not a singer, and so his Perchik lacked the rich singing voice that Bert Convy had brought to the role. And Michele Marsh, lovely as she was as Hodel, could not compare vocally with Julia Migenes, who went on to a successful career in opera." But he was "particularly pleased" with Rosalind Harris (Tzeitel), Leonard Frey (Motel), Molly Picon (Yente), Louis Zorich (the Constable), and Zvee Scooler, who played an innkeeper in the Broadway production, as the Rabbi. Despite his stellar performance, [Haym] Topol, then only 36, actually reached the pinnacle of his career with *Fiddler*, the second of his American-made films. His only other picture of merit, disappointing when compared with the musical, was *Galileo* (1975), in which he played the title role. On the stage, Yente was played by Beatrice Arthur, later to star in television roles as a domineering woman, like *Maud*, who rarely cracked a smile.

Harnick attributes much of the film's celebrity to the spirit of cooperation that existed between Stein, who had attracted attention in 1959 with his libretto for Marc Blitzstein's *Juno*, a musical rendering of Sean O'Casey's *Juno and the Paycock*, and Jewison, a nominee for best director for the 1967 Sidney Poitier-Rod Steiger classic, *In the Heat of the Night*, voted best picture of the year. Other of his films are *The Russians Are Coming, the Russians Are Coming* (1966), *The Thomas Crown*

Affair (1968), the Broadway-based musical *Jesus Christ Superstar* (1973), and *F.I.S.T.* (1978). Harnick applauded Stein's remaining faithful to his original libretto in constructing the screenplay without neglecting the camera's ability through frequent closeups to magnify the musical's impeccable stagecraft. Jewison's experience with the film medium was, of course, vital to injecting reality into the film without in any way compromising its folk-tale ambience.

Four Years of Preparation. As early as mid–1960, Harnick, Bock, and Stein began mulling over the idea of translating one of author Aleichem's tales into a musical. The first to be considered was the novel *Wandering Star*, which, however, Stein regarded as too vast a project, what with its huge number of characters, sprawling landscape, and generational-long time span, to be adaptable to stage presentation. Since Aleichem was so admired by all three, they agreed with Stein that other of his works were well worth mining for inspiration. The trio devoted the next several months to reading much of his material that had been translated from Yiddish into English.

Eventually, one of the men—or possibly all three simultaneously—proposed that *Tevye's Daughters* serve as the major source, and Stein began writing the libretto, which reduced the number of daughters from seven to five, and took about one year to complete. "Before we went into rehearsal," Harnick recalled, "Jerry Bock and I made a fairly long list of prospective titles. Included among them was 'Where Poppa Came From,' which we preferred, as well as *Fiddler on the Roof,* suggested by *The Green Violinist*, a painting by Marc Chagall showing a violinist hunched over the rooftops of a village. Hal Prince eventually approved of that title, feeling that it was the only title on the list that indicated a play with music."

Sholom Aleichem, translated from the Hebrew into "Peace be upon you!," was born in Russia in 1859 with the name Shalom [Solomon] Rabinowitz. An extremely prolific writer of novels, plays, and some 300 short stories, he settled, like Tevye, in New York in 1906 after fleeing the Kishinev pogrom, dying there

in 1916. His *Tevye's Daughters* was translated into English in 1949.

Fortunately for Stein, who, like many other Broadway craftsmen, expressed a dislike of working for the Hollywood studios, the screenplay was completed "very quickly." Remarkably for a Broadway-based film, no orders came to delete any scenes, although some were trimmed a bit and others played out in different settings. The four scenes and one expansion that were added enhanced the Hollywood version, in Harnick's view.

"There's a new scene in which a Czarist functionary orders the reluctant Constable to carry out the pogrom in Anatevka or regret the consequences," the lyricist noted. This made the Constable's dilemma more understandable as well as making him a slightly more sympathetic character. Another new scene shows Perchik exhorting a peaceful crowd in Kiev into trying to improve their lives by joining his anti-government protest movement. Then the Czarist cavalry soldiers charge into the crowd, swinging their sabers and disrupting the assembly. From a historical viewpoint, the scene was invaluable in showing the cruelty that was going on in Russia at the time.

"Having Golde go to the Russian Orthodox church to ask the priest about Chava brought a new locale and atmosphere into the film that illuminated both her character and the plot," he explained. "Then, toward the end there's a lovely, touching new scene in which Tevye says goodbye to his horse, his cows, and his goats. This scene makes his expulsion from Anatevka that much more real and moving. Also, the pogrom at Tzeitel's wedding was extended and, taking advantage of the great reality afforded by film, made even more violent and frightening."

Two stage songs, however, were deleted. The first, "Now I Have Everything," sung on the stage by Perchik after Hodel accepts his marriage proposal, was in Jewison's opinion too "middle class" and lacking sufficient revolutionary ardor. So Harnick and Bock wrote a substitution, "Any Day Now," which "sounded as though it might have been a traditional Red Cavalry song," Harnick said. It was orchestrated and Michael Glaser, the film's Perchik, recorded it for the sound track. But Jewison, later looking for material to excise in order to cut the running time, dropped the song, which Harnick still admires so much that he often performs it at benefits and other occasions. Also expendable was "I Just Heard," the gossip song originally sung in Act II of the Broadway production. "It works well on stage," Harnick noted, "but would probably have seemed too 'stagy' on the screen."

Apart from these two instances, every musical number from the stage play was used, uncut, in the film, a circumstance that Harnick termed "nothing short of amazing" considering Hollywood's long-established tradition of rewriting imported material. Such accurate rendering of a borrowed plot and characters would have been virtually impossible in the early history of the film musical, when Hollywood specialized in framing mildly interesting characters against the familiar backdrop of seemingly hopeless love affairs, interrupted every so often by pretty tunes performed by pretty people. By the time of the filmed *The King and I*, however, such piffle was out, strong story lines were in. Save for such rare exceptions as *The Music Man*, *Doctor Doolittle*, and *Hello, Dolly!*, only post–1958 musical films with plots of substance filled movie house seats and attracted Academy Award nominations for best picture.

Fiddler stands at the pinnacle of the musicalization of basically serious plots. Neither a king nor a star entertainer, a Cohan or a Ziegfeld, Tevye is the quintessential fellow at the bottom of the economic totem pole, the striver conditioned to plodding onward in the hope of rising above his threadbare existence, his life most closely paralleling Eliza Doolittle's in social status. Unlike *West Side Story*'s frustrated street gladiators, he does not rebel against society by fighting other peasants for village supremacy. Nor is he a polished lecher like Gaston Lachailles, abusive like King Mongkut, contemptuous like Henry Higgins, greedy like Fagin, vindictive like Bill Sykes, aloof toward his children like Father Banks and Captain von Trapp, or conspiratorial like Dolly Levi, who also sought Divine guidance in sorting out her life.

Rather, throughout the film Tevye is a strong family man, charitable neighbor, and deeply religious, though often frustrated by his own daughters in his goal of widening the territorial arc of his devotion to tradition. A believer in the adage live and let live, he himself is nonetheless a standard bearer of religious prejudice. Rather than turning him into a dislikable character, his inability to surmount his fierce opposition to daughter Chava's marrying a Gentile makes him all the more human.

Similarly of inestimable value was *Fiddler*'s purveying the essential optimism of the original story and musical play. That was no easy task considering that Tevye's options were circumscribed by certainties, none of them comforting. Despite the shocks that impinge on his pursuit of contentment, if not happiness, the movie underscores the triumph of hope over hardship, of character over circumstance, to a greater degree than even the Depression-era film musicals with their repetitious assurances that the tough times are bound to improve with the passing of time. Things get progressively worse, not better, with Tevye, and his poverty is permanent, not temporary. Rather than looking to the national government for assistance, he is put in the further precarious position of scratching out a living in a rural and remote ghettoized village that abuts a disapproving Russian Catholic Orthodox compound. Considering that the Constable's superior officer disparages their Jewish neighbors as "Christ-killers," the place hardly qualifies as solicitous to Tevye's need of generosity or sympathy.

The 1964 stage production was the first to retell the Tevye tale as a musical. The story, however, had earlier been filmed in part-comedy, part-drama versions. The gifted Maurice Schwartz, the Russian-born founder and chief actor and director of the Yiddish Art Theatre on New York's Second Avenue—where Fyvush Finkle also earned his acting credentials—played the leading role in the 1939 film *Tevye*. Theodore Bikel, before making his New York stage debut in 1955, acted the part in *Tevye the Milkman* at the Habimah Theatre in Tel Aviv, the birth city of Topol. Curiously, Joseph Green, a walk-on in 1927's *The Jazz Singer* and later producer of prestigious Yiddish films, passed up the opportunity in the late thirties to make a Tevye film from fear that the subject of intermarriage was too anti-clerical for his native Roman Catholic Poland. He was responsible, however, for furthering the career of Molly Picon—Yenta in the film version—by giving that marvelous Yiddish cinema actress her first starring screen role in the first of his four films, *Yidl mitn Fidl* (*Yiddle with His Fiddle*) in 1936. The story of a mischievous young woman who poses as a man in a troupe of wandering musicians in Depression-era Poland became a hit in New York, drawing large audiences to the Ambassador Theatre, a legitimate playhouse then showing films. Green and Miss Picon teamed up again for *Mamele* (*Little Mother*) in 1938.

Gathering Experience. *Fiddler on the Roof*'s lovely and often lively score represents the peak of the Harnick and Bock partnership, one of the few top-ranking teams of musical collaborators of Broadway's postwar years. Engagingly flavored at times with Eastern and Central European klezmer, the songs arise directly out of a plot or script situation, while a greater than usual number became popular favorites even with people who had not seen the stage or film versions.

Bock had made his composing debut on Broadway with three songs for the revue *Catch a Star* in 1955. Other of his songs subsequently appeared in Ziegfeld Follies, and his background score for *Windows of Manhattan* contributed to that short feature's winning a 1958 Academy Award for Columbia Pictures. In tandem with Larry Holofcener and George Weiss, Bock in 1956 furnished the lyrics and music for *Mr. Wonderful*, which boasted Sammy Davis, Jr., two memorable songs—the title tune and "Too Close for Comfort"—and a clever and literate book co-written by Stein and Will Glickman. The next year, *The Body Beautiful* ("Hidden in My Heart" and "Just My Luck") united Harnick, Bock, and Stein for the first time. Although not a great success, the show did indicate the unique compatibility of spirit among composer, lyricist, and librettist that seven years later would result in *Fiddler on the Roof*.

In 1959, Bock again joined with Harnick for the Pulitzer Prize–winning *Fiorello!*, which revolved around certain incidents in the life of Fiorello LaGuardia, New York's legendary "Little Flower" of a mayor, played by Tom Bosley. From the production came two delightful novelties, "Politics and Poker" and

"Little Tin Box," in addition to the pretty ballads "'Til Tomorrow" and "When Did I Fall in Love?" The show also marked the songwriters' initial effort under the aegis of Harold Prince, who tapped them shortly afterward to provide the score for *Tenderloin* ("My Miss Mary") and *She Loves Me*. Based on the Miklos Laszlo play and featuring Ludwig Donath, Larry Parks's memorable "Papa" in the 1946 and 1949 two-part "biography" of Al Jolson, *She Loves Me* added the catchy title song, "Days Gone By" and "Dear Friend" to Broadway's extensive catalogue of successful musical comedy songs. The 1963 production again delighted Broadway audiences when it was revived during the 1994-95 season.

Harnick became a writer and performer in USO shows while in the Army, which he entered in 1943. Following a brief postwar stint with Xavier Cugar's orchestra (Harnick plays the violin), he displayed his musical and versifying talents with the immensely witty novelty "The Boston Beguine," which appeared in New Faces of 1952. Between that year and 1957 he wrote lyrics for such stage shows as *Two's Company*, *Littlest Revue*, *Take Five*, *Kaleidoscope*, and John Murray Anderson's Almanac. His two post–*Fiddler* musicals were *The Apple Tree* ("Beautiful, Beautiful World") and *The Rothschilds* ("I'm in Love, I'm in Love!"), with music by Bock. To date, his last screen credit was the title song for *Blame It on Rio* (1984), with music by Cy Coleman. Meanwhile, Stein wrote the screenplay for *Enter Laughing* (1967), adapted from his play, based on Carl Reiner's novel about his early struggles to become an actor. Stein next wrote the book for Kander and Ebb's *Zorba* (1968), and then, in 1979, co-wrote with Alan Jay Lerner the libretto for Lerner and Burton Lane's *Carmelina*, inspired by the 1968 movie *Buona Sera, Mrs. Campbell*.

There is little doubt that *Fiddler on the Roof* would have succeeded nicely as a straight play. Comedy and tragedy course side by side through dialogue and incident in perfect balance. The leading characters are compelling, their worries and hopes universal, their motives clearly delineated. Tevye's equivocation over whether to adjust to the present by rejecting the past represents a dilemma still faced by many people the world over, while his frequent pleadings to God to provide solutions to his problems are often humorous and always touching. Adding music to the story, especially of the quality of the Harnick-Bock score, only increases its charm while expanding its relevancy by permitting Tevye, for example, to openly expose his troubled relations with his God through melodious soliloquys that brilliantly underscore his philosophical and religious ruminations.

How well Jewison mastered the complexities of turning *Fiddler* into a movie was summarized by Harnick: "He isn't Jewish, but he did so much research in preparation for the film that he became quite knowledgeable about things Jewish. As a result, either Topol or someone else suggested that he should be made an honorary Jew and renamed Norman Christianson!"

Morning in Anatevka. In a creative 10-minute pre-credits prelude, the camera pans the unattractive little village of Anatevka as a rooster announces the dawning of another day, most likely to be no different from any other in the lives of its residents, already inured to performing their daily rituals come rain or come shine in the same way that earlier generations did. Like automatons they undertake their labors in the fields, the kitchen, the shops, the Hebrew school, the temple. And suddenly there he is, rumbling slowly along a well-worn dirt road atop his horse-drawn milk-delivery cart, his white-flecked hair and beard making him appear years older than he actually is, Topol (Tevye), the devout Orthodox dairy farmer with the five daughters and irascible wife of 25 years, already weary as the day begins, expecting little from life other than to be permitted to live it with dignity in peace and harmony, a modern-day Job content to leave his fate in the hands of a benevolent if sometimes mysterious God.

Straddling himself on the two-sided sloping roof of a house, one leg firmly planted to the left of the peak, the other to the right to maintain his equilibrium, is a wiry man (Tutte Lemkow) dressed in black. He—or rather virtuoso violinist Isaac Stern—is playing variations on the jaunty title tune, which is never sung, on his fiddle, seemingly impervious to the events taking place beneath him, aware that every single action, good or bad, bears the stamp of inevitability that no one is capable of altering. He will reappear periodically throughout the film whenever a crisis of more than usual severity affects Topol, who, now looking directly at the audience, enters into his dual role as narrator of events and chief participant in them.

The man in black, he explains, is a symbol of himself and his fellow villagers. Every one of them is a fiddler on the roof, playing merry tunes while striving not to slip and break his or her neck by tumbling to the ground. What keeps the Fiddler from losing his balance is adherence to the traditions passed down by his forebears from time immemorial, those bedrock concepts on which the entire edifice of Anatevka stands. And, as Topol verifies while singing the vibrant opening song, it is "Tradition" that keeps the villagers on an even emotional keel, neither falling into despondency over their poverty nor foolishly anticipating the day when their miseries will miraculously vanish.

Luckily, Topol continues, their religion provides the people of Anatevka with a tradition for everything, from how to sleep and eat to how to wear clothes and work. The men have long acknowledged God's superiority by wearing a prayer shawl and keeping their heads covered, even when in bed. The village itself is firmly rooted in tradition, Topol happily acknowledges, making certain that among its population are the traditional beggar, peddler, and "beloved rabbi." What was long ago ordained, Topol is content to accept. At times he may question God's purposes, but peace prevails between them. The doubts that arise in Topol's mind never drive him into reneging on his obligation to observe the rules that were laid down in antiquity.

The questions he addresses to God, and sometimes to himself, never take the form of a gripe. In fact, more often than not he plays the part of a fair-minded judge, always willing to present both sides of a case by prefacing what he assumes is God's defense of the latest catastrophe with the words, "On the other hand...." Fortunately for Topol, tradition has taught him how to absorb difficulty without blasphemy. Far from whining when his horse goes lame, for example, he accommodatingly pulls the delivery wagon himself, allowing the animal to follow side by side at its own pace.

Excitement briefly enters Topol's farmhouse with the arrival of Molly Picon (Yente), the widowed and gossipy Dolly Levi of Anatevka, who is eager to impart what she terms "once in a lifetime news." Pleased at again fulfilling her traditional duty as matchmaker, she announces to Norma Crane (Golde) that she has found just the man to marry Rosalind Harris (Tzeitel), Topol's eldest daughter, who, according to another tradition, must take a husband before any of her four sisters can even think of becoming a bride. Mother Norma is delighted with Molly's candidate for husband, Paul Mann (Lazar Wolf). The village butcher and wealthiest man in town, Mann is regarded by both Norma and Molly as a good catch for any girl. True, the cranky old widower may be three times Rosalind's age, but, as all five daughters know only too well, they will be lucky to find any man to marry, considering the skimpiness of the dowries available to them.

After Molly leaves, Rosalind questions her mother on the purpose of her visit, more than slightly nervous over the distinct possibility that she herself was the topic of conversation. Unknown to both parents, Rosalind happens to be in love with Leonard Frey (Motel), an impoverished young tailor whose sole unsoaring ambition is to save up enough money to buy a sewing machine. Her chagrin at the prospect of marrying someone else—an old, unattractive fellow, for all she knows—is countered by her ever-realistic mother's appraisal of marriage. A husband is "not to look at, but to get," she informs her abject daughter. The butcher apparently has been casting his eyes on the 19-year-old for months now from behind his meat counter. Such continuing attention implies to Norma that Mann's regard for Rosalind has had sufficient time to ripen from infatuation into true affection, and has not arisen simply out of fear of spending his last years in solitude. That, however, is a fate that Rosalind foresees may very well befall her if she ever weds a man old enough to be her grandfather.

Still unaware that her fate has been sealed, Rosalind joins her sisters in satirically commenting on Molly's alleged professionalism while mimicking her actions and speech. Agreeing that she is a specialist in bringing couples together, for better or worse, are Michele Marsh (Hodel), the second-oldest and prettiest of the five daughters, and her equally romance-minded sister, Neva Small (Chava), each depressed at the prospect of winding up an old maid if Molly is unable to find Rosalind a suitable suitor pretty soon. Together, they address Molly in the show's first hit song, the spirited and wistful—and wishful—waltz, "Matchmaker."

What the girls want is a husband who is youthful, slender, handsome, and intellectual—in short, everything that senior citizen Mann is not—but wealthy, too. Holding little faith in Molly as Cupid, the sisters conclude the song by stating their preference for finding husbands on their own, without any help from the matchmaker. Ironically, three of the daughters will do exactly that. They will flout tradition by insisting on marrying for love, thereby pushing their father into acknowledging that he is not immune to the changes wrought by the maturation of adolescents.

Visions of Grandeur. Also oblivious of the deal struck by Molly and his wife, Topol enters into a period of meditation in his barn. Why, he asks while looking heavenward, has God decided to burden him with still another trouble by inflicting pain on his reliable horse? In fact, why has He made so many poor people when it is so evident that a pauper's life is miserable from start to finish. It is cures that Tevye seeks, not more sickness. He has plenty of that already.

Trying to put a happy face on his own existence, Topol cheerfully dreams of great wealth, momentarily dismissing the overwhelming odds against ever achieving the goal. The vehicle for his all-too-human display of vanity is "If I Were a Rich Man," one of the finest and best-remembered songs of the 1960s.

Merging a clever lyric with a foot-stomping beat, the tune opens the portals to the most engaging of all of Topol's individual scenes. Unlike many leading men—and sometimes women—in earlier Hollywood musicals, the stars of more recent times are required to sing and dance as well as act. Topol succeeds spectacularly at all three in this panegyric to the good life. His singing voice thunders with envy of the wealthy, then drops several decibels to serve as a poignant reminder that he will surely never reside in a large house and luxuriate in expensive comforts. Pounding his feet on the floor to accent the tempo, his eyes gleaming with visions of how he would live ostentatiously in order to publicize his wealth over the width and breadth of Anatevka, he instantly becomes the symbol of Everyman, folklore's ultimate survivor of hard times, stubbornly overcoming despair by assuming that one day fortune will smile on him as a reward for contending so dutifully for so long with his inherited misery.

In the center of the village, the virus of change is being spread by Michael Glaser (Perchick), a former university student from Kiev and aspiring revolutionary. Impressed with his education, the small and largely illiterate gathering listens attentively as he explains that newspaper stories of the forced eviction of Jews from their homes by the Czar's soldiers are true. No radicals themselves, his audience soon regards him as an agitator, the voice of the outside world in which they have no interest and from which they prefer to remain aloof. They ignore his caution to take action before the same disaster "infects" their own village. Glaser's earnestness, however, appeals to Topol, who strikes up a friendship with the young man and invites him to be a guest in his house for the summer and pay for his room and board by tutoring his daughters.

Later that night at the farmhouse, Glaser is invited to share the family's sabbath meal, which is preceded by the stately and lovely "Sabbath Prayer," sung by Norma and Topol, wearing the traditional skull cap and kaftan, as a plea to God to always bless and protect their children and shield them from the ways of strangers, one of whom, ironically, is now in their midst. Perhaps inspired by the solemnity of the occasion, Topol agrees to Norma's suggestion, originated by Molly, that he visit butcher Mann, whom he dislikes, to discuss a business matter.

Greeted warmly by Mann in his handsomely furnished living room, Topol happily permits the old man to constantly refill his glass with choice vodka throughout their humorous conversation scene. What his host is after,

Topol surmises, is one of his cows, and not until about three minutes into their bargaining does he realize that Mann's objective is to obtain his permission to marry Rosalind. The butcher's vow that she will "never know hunger" and that he will do his best "to try to make her happy" is sufficient to win over Topol. To celebrate their meeting of minds, the men salute each other with the bouncily optimistic "To Life (L'chaiim)," which they agree can indeed be joyful, at least at times like the present, as well as brutal. Life can never defeat those who are happy and healthy, they sing.

The two men then carry the song into a tavern, where they imbibe a few additional swallows of vodka and join with their fellow patrons in a boisterous dance in honor of the forthcoming nuptials. Also there are about a dozen young Russian males who both startle and please Topol. The tension that the meeting of representatives of two such disparate cultures in close quarters creates in him quickly disappears when the young men join the dance and then raise their glasses to toast Mann's happiness. Later, in a highly amusing coda to the sequence, Topol welcomes the butcher into the family. "I always wanted a son," he confesses while pressing his palms on the old man's shoulders. "But I hoped for one younger than the father!"

On his way back home, Topol meets Louis Zorich (the Constable), a minor Russian official and friend whom out of respect Topol always addresses as "Your Honor." The man's concern over the plight of the Jews suffering exile in outlying parts of the country is genuine, as is his aversion to the government's periodic purges, buttressed no doubt by his fondness for Topol. But he has neither the will nor the nerve to protest. Like other comparatively prosperous men in impoverished lands, the Constable has witnessed the horrors of peasant life, which he regards as a plague that he has no intention of catching. He will hold on to his job come what may, since the salary, perks, and pension are his guarantee of at least lower-middle-class existence in old age. Later, when the people of Anatevka are struck with the same calamity, he will excuse his unwillingness to object by repeating the age-old refrain of the faithful government minion that he has no other choice but to carry out orders, however unpalatable they may be.

With sincere reluctance he informs Topol that Anatevka has been designated as the site of a future army incursion—not exactly a pogrom, he assures his friend, just another in the current round of anti–Jewish "demonstrations." The news turns Topol's glow of intoxication into sober consideration of why the Russians are coming to his village. Typically, he poses the question to God. Jews, he concedes, have historically been His chosen people. "But," he asks in the tortured tone of a man who has been indicted for a crime he did not commit, "once in a while can't You choose someone else?" when considering candidates for upheaval. As usual receiving no signal that his words have been heard, he drinks a toast to God, turns, and dances a jig on the way home. Close at his heels is the Fiddler, hoping with his tune and antics to relieve Topol's distress and renew his traditional faith in God's reasonableness.

Shattering of Tradition. Although Mother Norma is elated to find that Topol approves of Mann as Rosalind's future groom, the bride-to-be is anything but. Admitting in the barn that she loves Frey the tailor, she appeals to her father to cancel the wedding, even tearfully throwing herself at his feet to change his mind. "Unthinkable!" he roars. Some traditions, like daughters marrying the men selected by matchmakers, are inalterable. Nonetheless, he finally relents, admitting that Frey, to whom Rosalind has confided she has been "unofficially engaged" for a year, is an "honest hard worker," while hoping to God that someday the young man will get that damn sewing machine and provide his daughter with the comforts of life to which he feels she is entitled. Also influencing his reversing his decision was Frey's unexpected, and admirable, show of manly courage by firmly asserting his love for Rosalind and their mutual right to happiness despite Topol's opposition.

Shortly afterward, Rosalind and Frey react to Topol's blessing by duetting "Miracle of Miracles," a pretty and sprightly love ballad steeped in merriment that refers not so much to Topol's approving their marriage as, in Frey's view, to God's giving Rosalind to him as wife, to love and cherish for a lifetime. Certainly, Frey sings, none of His other wonders, including even the parting of the Red Sea, surpasses the priceless gift He has bestowed on one impoverished little tailor in an insignificant little village.

Despite his occasional blustering and anguished insistence that he is master of the household, Topol has been cut to the quick so often by his sharp-tongued wife that he delays as long as he can calling her attention to bad news, particularly if it runs counter to her expectations. In bed that night, however, he disposes of Rosalind's switch of lifelong mate from Mann to Frey by explaining to Norma what he had seen and heard in a recent dream. The major players in it were Mann's dead wife, played by Patience Collier, and Norma's own beloved—and also dead—grandmother, who act out Topol's dream on sepia-tinted film that underscores the unearthly, and totally fictitious, nature of the sequence. In the background is heard composer Bock's instrumental "Teyve's Dream." According to Topol, Mann's widow threatened to strangle Rosalind if she marries him, while the grandmother advised Rosalind never to consider marrying the man. The tale frightens superstitious Mother Norma, who accepts the ghostly warning as an omen that Rosalind's scrapping of Mann is unquestionably a fortunate occurrence.

In the memorable scene that follows, a stately candlelight parade of villagers escorts Rosalind, dressed in her finest virginal white, and Frey, wearing a black suit and his prized top hat, to the open-air canopy where their marriage ceremony is to be performed. The subsequent wedding ceremony, quite possibly the most beautiful and reverential on film, evokes in Topol and Norma sentimental reminders of the past in "Sunrise, Sunset," an eloquent and melancholy epithalamion to the inexorable passing of time. The happy couple, only yesterday merely children, are now young adults, husband and wife, on their way to creating their own special memories, which all too quickly they will file away for future reference. As for Topol and Norma, they who such a short time ago were young parents are now in middle age, momentarily beaming with pride like the morning star before advancing even further into the evening of life.

The reception, with its exuberant dancing

to the tune of "Wedding Celebration," includes the exquisite "bottle dance" by four male villagers and the presentation of gifts to the newlyweds. In this superb sequence, as well as in the earlier tavern scene, choreographer Tom Abbott's adaptations of the original Jerome Robbins dances sparkle and light up the screen with their abounding good cheer and inventiveness. (*Fiddler* was Robbins's final Broadway triumph before returning in 1969 to the New York City Ballet.) The guests' delirium is so contagious that even butcher Mann joins in the festivities by giving the happy pair five chickens. Unlike the typical discarded lover in earlier film musicals, however, he turns out to be a poor loser, later engaging in a quarrel with Topol over who is to blame for his being shunted aside to drift alone through the rest of his life.

But that is only the first of three altercations that disrupt the affair. The second occurs when Glaser offends the most conservative of the guests by affirming Rosalind's right to decide for herself which man she wants as husband. The brazen young activist then asks Michele to dance with him, as they had earlier on an grassy field in celebration of their growing attraction for each other. That time, however, they were unobserved; this time Glaser publicly disregards the prohibition against such activity by mixed couples. Like the other villagers, Topol is stunned by Michele's audacity at accepting his invitation. For a second time, a growing anti-tradition sentiment has infected one of his daughters, and figuratively his feet are beginning to slip on the roof. He recovers, however, and in a gesture of support for Michele, motions to Norma to dance with him.

With the abrupt arrival of a band of Russian thugs, the festivity is purged of all hilarity, and the villagers' ideal of coexisting peaceably with their neighbors threatens to dissolve in a pitched battle. As Constable Zorich, who is in command of the troops, had warned, Anatevka's time has come to be subjected to a "demonstration," a long-established tradition of Russian origin that is revived every so often to remind Jewish populations that their livelihood, and lives, depends solely on the good will of the national government. Stunned into silence, the cele-brants watch the horses trample through the reception hall, overturning tables and smashing dishes, and then through fields and houses, several of which the men ransack and set afire.

After they leave, Topol's face, as stricken with disbelief as Barry Fitzgerald's while surveying the burned-out ruins of his parish church in *Going My Way*, again looks upward, appealing to God to explain the reason for the pillaging he has just witnessed. Surely, Topol surmises, His purpose must be a just one; otherwise why would He have permitted such an outrage. No excuse, no apology, however, is offered.

Stubbornly retaining his faith in God, Topol is picked up a few days later in the countryside singing again of the importance of respecting tradition's role in everyday activities. His confidence is further eroded, however, when Glaser announces his intention of leaving Anatevka for Kiev. "Tremendous changes are taking place in Russia," he tells Topol at their meeting on a bridge. Topol steels himself in the valid expectation that one of the changes is about to descend on him. He and Michele, Glaser continues, are engaged, and both would welcome Topol's blessing, although the young man makes it clear that their marriage will take place even if he withholds it. He has "important work to do" in Kiev, he says, and Michele would be the ideal helpmate.

The Flexible Father. Again Topol's initial reaction is resistance. His daughter, he insists, will follow long-established custom by staying in the village and awaiting Molly Picon's selection of a husband. But as had happened with Rosalind, Topol again surrenders precious tradition by tendering his approval. He attempts to console himself by recalling that, although he has lost two daughters to nonconformity, three still remain with him, and he is determined to see that they toe the traditional mark. Once more disconcerted over the need to inform Norma of this newest family crisis, Topol this time blurts it out, then tries to counter her disappointment by reverting to the playfulness that had characterized their courtship days by asking "Do You Love Me?"

The question is appropriate. He has now

inflicted the second emotional wound on her, each caused by collaborating with Rosalind and then Michele on repudiating his own traditionalist views. Maybe, he hopes, the lyrical ballad may tempt her into revealing her true feelings by evaluating him as husband over their quarter-century of marriage. Although his words are tender in meaning and delivery, Norma's are not. Her cantankerous responses to his questions turn the duet into less of a love song than a realistic appraisal of their years together, more troubled than triumphant, she reminds him. But they have survived, she notes, finally admitting that yes, she supposes she does love him. Topol had been wishing for a more enthusiastic reply, but he is content to discover that, as his mother and father had predicted years earlier, he and Norma would learn to love each other. Rationally, he can expect little more than that.

Later, on a wintry afternoon in Kiev, Glaser's open-air polemic exhorting his listeners to undertake the admittedly difficult task of freeing themselves from the bondage of Imperial Russia meets with disaster when cavalry troops, their rapiers drawn, charge into the crowd of men and scatter them. Subsequently captured and imprisoned in a Siberian "settlement," he writes to Michele asking her to join him there. Topol is firm, at first, in his refusal to let her desert his house to live in that "frozen wasteland," as Glazer himself had described it in his letter. But once again his innate compassion dictates that he accede to her wish.

Father and daughter's sad exchange of goodbyes at the village railroad station ranks as one of the most poignant albeit ironic scenes in the film. Michele's sorrow is the greater since, besides realizing that the two most likely will never meet again, she is aware that the village of her childhood is no longer her home. That a piece of her heart will always remain there is substantiated in her solemn farewell song, "Far from the Home I Love." In it she recalls the simple girlish joys of the irretrievable past, but insists that henceforth her home must be wherever Glazer is.

As she sings, the camera retreats from closeups of father and daughter to provide a wide-angle view of the station and the village beyond it. The charm in which her memories have wrapped Anatevka is entirely absent from the screen. What the audience sees is a flat and unprepossessing landscape, so isolated as to be forbidding, stretching in numbing silence to the point where the leaden sky meets the distant horizon. Twice earlier cinematographer Morris had used imaginative camera angles to induce subjective responses to individual *Fiddler* scenes. They appeared in closeups of Topol as he pondered whether to disallow the marriages of Rosalind and Michele. Although actually standing very near to him, each girl and prospective groom were photographed as if they were far beyond hearing range of his words. The clear implication was that the daughters and their mates preferred not to listen to his complaints, and furthermore that they and Topol will continue to drift even farther apart unless he grants their wishes.

Michele, however, will never forget the village, and recalling its sights and sounds over the years, she magnifies each into a fond vignette made all the more pleasurable by recalling only the good times. That Topol has accepted her unalterable decision to join Glazer and marry him is obvious when she boards the train. "Take care of her," he prays to God, as tears of loss well up in his eyes.

A very brief respite from Topol's mounting disappointments is provided at the house of Frey and Rosalind when the Rabbi (Zvee Scooler) blesses the sewing machine recently acquired by the tailor. Joyfully contemplating the surge in business that the mechanizing of his trade will bring—itself a break with tradition—Frey excites the approval of all the guests. But any hope Topol might have cultivated of finding long-term solace proves elusive when Neva Small (Chava), the third-eldest child, presents him with another crisis by seeking approval to marry Raymond Lovelock (Fyedka), a young Gentile she had met only recently while strolling in the countryside.

This time Topol remains adamant in his refusal to comply. He was able to overcome his other two daughters' dereliction of tradition by marrying men of their own choosing, but this love affair is different. That Neva spurned the services of the village matchmaker was bad enough; that Lovelock is a Christian is unforgivable. What she is requesting, Topol implies, is his permission to marry outside her faith. Unable to abide this sacrilege, he demands to an even harsher degree than Anita in *West Side Story* that the prospective bride choose one of her "own kind."

Equally upset is Mother Norma, who, upon finding Neva missing from the farmhouse a few days later, visits the Reverend Father, a Russian Orthodox Catholic priest (Vladimir Medar), who verifies that he had married the couple. Instead of rallying his forbearance at hearing the news, Topol is crushed by it. This time, against Norma's wish, he will withhold his blessing permanently. He prefers, as he discloses in the lament "Chava," to remember her as the pretty little girl, graceful and sweet, who loved to dance and overfilled his heart with joy, rather than as the young, independent woman who has broken one of the most restrictive of his religion's traditions.

His intransigence, however, forces him to face a Hobson's choice in his relations with her. Either he forgive and forget—an impossibility in his view—or turn his back forever on her and her husband, in effect disowning his daughter and refusing to acknowledge Lovelock as her betrothed. Topol chooses the latter course, but the agony it inflicts on him is soon submerged in an even greater tragedy. He and his neighbors have been ordered to evacuate Anatevka within three days. Confirming the new edict is the Constable, who, as expected, apologizes to Topol for its harshness and again pleads for his friend's understanding that he is powerless to prevent the exodus. Then, eclipsing any hope the angry villagers may have of thwarting the edict, the Constable declares that if they refuse to sell their property to the government, the army will drive them off of it.

Singing farewell to their homes in the dirgelike "Anatevka," the residents impassively scoop up their belongings while feigning relief at leaving a village that is rotting before their eyes. It never actually was a safe harbor from trouble, they agree, but rather a dismal place that worsened rather than improved their lives. Yet Norma sweeps the floors of her dwelling before closing the front door for the last time, careful not to leave a dirty house behind her.

Topol and Norma will emigrate to New York, where his brother-in-law lives. Mann the butcher, who parts from Topol in amity, will resettle in Chicago, and Molly Picon in Palestine. Rosalind, Frey, and their baby son will live temporarily in another Russian community until the tailor earns enough money for them to join her parents in the United States. Neva, still seeking to mend father-daughter relations, tells Topol that she and her husband plan to set up housekeeping in Cracow, Poland, as a mark of protest, since her marriage to a Christian qualifies her to remain in Russia.

Topol fails to respond to her peacemaking effort, even though it is quite evident that this is the last time he will set eyes on her. Desperately unhappy over his reaction, tearful Neva is cheered somewhat by hearing her father's softly uttered prayer, "God be with you." As she and her husband, who had remained silent throughout the parting, hurry away, Neva addresses her mother: "We will write to you in America, if you like." Topol turns away from the couple to walk into the barn to extend a special thanks to his animal friends for helping him to make a living over the years.

Though emotionally exhausted and physically depleted, the familiar Topol emerges briefly when, exercising his prerogative as the household's authority figure, he orders Rosalind to make sure she doesn't forget to take the baby along with her. Then, indicative of the humor that somehow manages to emerge whenever he is shortchanged by fate, he dryly observes to a neighbor that the ever-present threat of being forcibly removed from their homes is "maybe why we always wear our hats."

The path Topol had trod at the beginning of the film is the same that he and his neighbors take on their way to new lives in new environments. Like the von Trapp family atop a hill in southern Austria, looking toward freedom in Switzerland, the emigres' emotions range from sorrow to optimism as their village disappears behind them, but few take the time to cast a final glance at it. Better to look forward than back, especially when the past is unrecoverable.

Following a short distance behind Topol is his faithful companion in times of peril, the Fiddler, nonplused at being forced for good from his accustomed rooftop perch. He is playing his familiar melody with verve, tracing Topol's steps with long rhythmic strides that seem to reflect his delight in escorting his friend from the old world into the new. Ever resilient to changing conditions, this wry symbol of

Topol's and the other villagers' alter-egos personifies grace under pressure and the stoical determination to overcome adversity. And, he seems to imply, he and all the other Anatevka expatriates will do exactly that. Be adaptable or be extinct is his motto.

Created out of Jewish folklore, the noble peasant Tevye continues to serve as an inspiration for all people everywhere at any time who are confronted by crisis. Author Aleichem breathed life into him; *Fiddler on the Roof* immortalized him.

Cabaret (1972)

An ABC Pictures Production/Allied Artists picture. DIRECTOR: Bob Fosse; ASSISTANTS: Douglas Green and Wolfgang Glattes. PRODUCER: Cy Feuer; ASSOCIATE: Harold Nebenzal. SCREENWRITER: Jay Allen. RESEARCH CONSULTANT: Hugh Wheeler. CINEMATOGRAPHER: Geoffrey Unsworth. FILM EDITOR: David Bretherton. PRODUCTION DESIGNER: Rolf Zehetbauer. PRODUCTION MANAGER: Pia Arnold. ART DIRECTOR: Jurgen Kiebach. SOUND: David Hildyard; ASSISTANT: David Ramirez. CHOREOGRAPHER: Bob Fosse; ASSISTANT: John Sharpe; DANCE COORDINATOR: Jutta Deil. COSTUMES: Charlotte Flemming. MAKEUP AND HAIRSTYLING: Raimund Stangl and Susi Krause; MISS MINNELLI'S HAIRSTYLES: Gus Le Pre. WARDROBE: Ille Sievers. DIALOGUE COACH: Osman Raghed. MUSICAL SUPERVISOR, ARRANGER, AND CONDUCTOR: Ralph Burns. MUSIC COORDINATOR: Raoul Kraushaar. MUSIC EDITORS: Robert N. Tracy, Illo Endrulat, and Karola Storr. MUSIC ASSOCIATE: Fred Werner. SONGS: Lyrics by Fred Ebb, music by John Kander. RUNNING TIME: 2 hours and 3 minutes. *Principal Players*: Liza Minnelli (Sally Bowles). Joel Grey (Master of Ceremonies). Michael York (Brian Roberts). Helmut Griem (Maximillian von Heune). Marisa Berenson (Natalia Landauer). Fritz Wepper (Fritz Wendel). Elizabeth Neumann Viertel (Fraulein Schneider). *Major Academy Awards*: Best Director; Actress (*Liza Minnelli*); Supporting Actor (*Joel Grey*); Cinematography; Film Editing; Art Direction; Scoring; Sound. *Nominations*: Best Picture; Adapted Screenplay.

British-born Christopher William Bradshaw-Isherwood most likely never dreamed that his introspective "Berlin Stories" would provide the source of a hit Broadway play and an even more successful musical 15 years later. Consisting of two novels, *The Last of Mr. Norris* (1935) and *Goodbye to Berlin* (1939), the stories tread a fine line between comedy and tragedy in depicting the adventures of touchingly fragile human beings caught in the web of an incompetent national government soon to turn monstrously inhumane under its successor regime.

Wisely, playwright and screenwriter John van Druten's *I Am a Camera* in 1951 and John Kander and Fred Ebb's *Cabaret* in 1966 both retained the smooth, sometimes playful, and always nonjudgmental voice of Isherwood's alter-ego narrators. Otherwise, the play and the musical would have been handicapped by domesticating the two leading characters' personal histories, making them appear too grotesque and too burdened with symbolic messages to appeal to a wide spectrum of theatergoers. Even further redolent with intimations of the violence then on the rise and the chaos to follow, the film was not limited in scope to simply tracing the adventures of a rather puritanical young man observing a dissolute young woman marching to the drumbeat of negativism in a society undergoing massive changes.

A member of the so-called "Auden Gang," which included such angry and highly literate young poets as W.H. Auden and Stephen Spender among the rulers of English letters during the 1930s, Isherwood in the late 1920s had become attracted to literature as the proper vehicle for expressing his discontent with what he felt were traditional English hypocrisy and stodginess. He attacked both with vehemence in his first two published novels, *All the Conspirators* (1928) and *The Memorial* (1932). Moving in 1929 to Berlin, which inspired his most intriguing subject matter, Isherwood witnessed the German nation's political turmoil first-hand through acquaintances with Berliners of all social classes and philosophical persuasions. From them he constructed the unforgettable characters who people his "Berlin Stories," including Sally Bowles, to whom the author devoted an entire chapter.

The "photographic" style of the novels became an Isherwood trademark that made him uniquely able to communicate personal experiences while permitting readers to interpret their significance without benefit of his own beliefs as guideposts. In fact, in *Goodbye to Berlin*, the author describes himself as a "camera with its shutter open, quite passive, recording, not thinking." After Adolf Hitler's assumption of the chancellorship of Germany in 1933, Isherwood fled the country, eventually emigrating to the United States when the

Michael York and Liza Minnelli as the ill-starred lovers in *Cabaret*, which won Miss Minnelli the 1972 Academy Award as best actress.

Fuehrer invaded Poland six years later. He became a screenwriter for Metro-Goldwyn-Mayer and continued to write novels, among which *A Single Man* (1964) is considered his masterpiece.

Cabaret, which holds the rare distinction of winning the Tony, Drama Critics' Circle, and Grammy awards, opened in New York for a three-year run on November 20, 1966, at the Broadhurst Theatre. The stars were Jill Haworth as Sally Bowles; Tony-winning Joel Grey, whose Borscht-circuit father would star in the musical revue *Hello, Solly!* on Broadway in 1967, as the Kit Kat Club's vulgar master of ceremonies; and composer Kurt Weill's widow, Lotte Lenya, in the role of Fraulein Schneider. Weill, the son of a Dessau cantor, fled Germany, like Isherwood, in 1933. One of his most important works, *The Rise and Fall of the City of Mahagonny*, indicted the moral bankruptcy of the Weimar Republic, and caused a riot by Nazis at its opening in Frankfurt in 1930.

Cabaret was staged by Harold Prince, the most successful producer of theatrical musicals since Ziegfeld, who since the mid-1950s has been known to prefer untypical story lines, legitimately termed daring in subject matter and treatment. Sometimes his projects failed (*Merrily We Roll Along* and *Superman*), but more often than not they resembled *Cabaret* by becoming instant classics—*West Side Story, Fiddler on the Roof, Sweeney Todd.*

Unquestionably the best directed and photographed, and most contemporary in spirit of all the Oscar-nominated musicals, the 1972 film is also the most sardonic and sexually frank in dialogue, gesture, and facial expression. Its star, Liza Minnelli, with whom composer Kander and lyricist Ebb had already carried on an extensive professional relationship, appears as the luckless lady, Miss Bowles. Michael York plays her sometimes lover, and the inestimable Joel Grey, who suggested the title of the show, recreates his original stage role to chilling perfection. The film surpasses the Broadway musical as a somber study of the disillusionment of two mostly amiable characters unable to contend with the aimless drifting of the fragile German Weimar government then in power or to properly gauge the ripening appeal of Hitler, who was dedicated to overthrowing it and subsequently launching an international nightmare. Unlike the other twin tower of 1970s musical films, *Fiddler on the Roof*, *Cabaret* is not satisfied to combine melancholy disillusionment and unsanitized realism, which each does brilliantly. It also projects an almost hallucinogenic portrait of self-destruction on both an individual and a national scale.

From Republic to Dictatorship. The year is 1931, when the Weimar Republic, Germany's first noble experiment in democracy, was cracking under the fusillade of contempt and criticism leveled by the Nazis. The transformation of the country into a republic had been initiated immediately after Armistice Day, 1918, when Prince Max of Baden, the last Imperial chancellor, turned his authority over to Friedrich Ebert, a Socialist deputy in the Reichstag. The new chancellor's promise to institute popular elections for a national representative parliament was fulfilled on January 19, 1919, when the new National Assembly convened at Weimar and elected Ebert to the office of Provisional President of the Republic.

His government began life under a dark cloud that hovered over it for the next 14 years by signing the Versailles Treaty, which ended World War I, six months later. The action was ceaselessly castigated by right-wing extremists, who maintained that the peace was a sellout perpetuated by pacifists and cowards. When Ebert died in 1925, he was succeeded by an irresistible candidate, Paul von Hindenburg, then 78 years old. But not even that respected field marshal of the Great War was able to reverse the declining popularity of the government. It had been wracked first with crushing war-reparations payments; then with a staggering rate of inflation; then with a prolonged depression that consigned hordes of bitter unemployed young men, nicknamed "desperadoes," to suppressing their pride and living off the dole; and finally with frequent fights between Communists

and Adolf Hitler's National Socialists on the mean streets of Berlin. The collapse of the republic finally came in 1934, when Hitler, as gifted and seductive a demagogue as the world has ever seen, succeeded the senile von Hindenburg as the undisputed leader of Germany.

Curiously, the flowering of the German motion picture industry occurred during the Weimar years, thanks particularly to the Universum Film Aktien Gesellschaft, or UFA (1918–45), the prestigious film studio where Sally Bowles aspires to find employment. In 1930, its *The Blue Angel*, which drips with almost as much cynicism and despair as *Cabaret*, brought fame—and a Hollywood contract—to Marlene Dietrich, hired by director Josef von Sternberg after the far superior actress Brigette Helm refused the part of cabaret entertainer Lola Lola.

From UFA and other German studios emerged some of the greatest film classics— *The Cabinet of Dr. Caligari* (1919), which featured Conrad Veidt, later to appear as Colonel Strasser in *Casablanca*; *The Last Laugh* (1924), a rare full-length silent film without titles; and four gems directed by Fritz Lang. The first, *Dr. Mabuse* (1922), a pioneering gangster film, was followed two years later by *Die Nibelungen*, based on the 13th-century Siegfried legend that had so entranced Richard Wagner. *Metropolis* (1927) contemptuously paralleled ruling-class luxury with the hellish factory conditions borne by lower-echelon working slaves. *M* (1931), a harrowing treatise on mob violence, starred Peter Lorre, who, as the cowardly Ugarte, would steal the letters of transit so assiduously sought by Veidt in *Casablanca*.

The tenth of the 13 nominated film musicals from 1956 to 1991 to be derived from a Broadway original, *Cabaret* lost to *The Godfather* in the best picture sweepstakes, but its stars and creators fared nobly at the 1973 Academy Award festival. Liza Minnelli, already an Oscar nominee for her role as Pookie Adams in *The Sterile Cuckoo* (1969), was named best actress, while Joel Grey won as best supporting actor, Bob Fosse as best director, Geoffrey Unsworth as best cinematographer (and his camera work is an absolute marvel throughout), and Ralph Burns for his inspired musical background. The screenplay, based more weightily on the van Druten play than on the "Berlin Stories," placed Jay Allen in the running for an Oscar, but it eluded her.

In all, *Cabaret* garnered a grand total of 10 Academy Award nominations, the fifth highest total of all film musicals, tying it with *Going My Way* and *The Sound of Music*. Only *Mary Poppins* (with 13), *My Fair Lady* (with 12), and *West Side Story* and *Oliver!* with 11 each, received more nominations. As winner of eight awards, the film tied with *My Fair Lady*. Only *West Side Story* and *Gigi* won more Oscar statuettes, 10 and nine, respectively.

The Men Behind the Songs. Like Rodgers and Hart and Rodgers and Hammerstein, the show's composer-lyricist team is always referred to as Kander and Ebb, reversing the usual custom of placing the writer of the words before the name of the composer. Again like Rodgers's two musical partnerships, their collaboration has enjoyed a rare decades-long life span, and their names have been appended to both Broadway and Hollywood musicals as well as to television and cabaret shows, a singular accomplishment at any time, but especially in light of the virtual demise of the film musical since the late 1950s. Of all the comparatively recent Broadway-based songwriters, not even Lerner and Loewe or Sheldon Harnick and Jerry Bock have been coupled on playbills as frequently as Kander, who began his career as rehearsal pianist for *Gypsy* in 1959, and Ebb.

The pair first combined talents in the early 1960s to create the hit single "My Coloring Book" for Barbra Streisand. Their Broadway collaboration began with *Flora, the Red Menace* (1965), which made a star of Liza Minnelli, who at 19 became the youngest actress to win a Tony Award for a musical. Over the next 18 years they continued to furnish her with such substantial tunes as "Lucky Lady" and "While the Getting Is Good" for the 1975 film *Lucky Lady*, "City Lights" for *The Act* (1978), which won the star her second Tony, and several more for *The Rink* (1983). Their television special *Liza with a "Z,"* won an Emmy as the Most Outstanding Single Program of 1966 and introduced the catchy "Liza with a 'Z' (Say Liza)." For her performance, Miss Minnelli was named Female Star of the Year by the National Association of Theater Owners.

Kander and Ebb's *The Happy Time* was followed by *Zorba*, adapted from Nikos Kazantzakis's screenplay for *Zorba the Greek* (1964), with Herschel Bernardi playing the role originated in the film by Anthony Quinn, and *70, Girls, 70*. In 1981, their *Woman of the Year*, the musical adaptation of the classic 1942 Tracy and Hepburn film, won Lauren Bacall a Tony and gave her two sturdy song successes, "One of the Girls" and "Sometimes a Day Goes By." Their most recent stage success came in 1993 with *Kiss of the Spider Woman: The Musical*, based on the best picture-nominated 1985 film of the same name. The star was Chita Rivera (*née* Dolores Conchita del Rivero), winner of one of the seven Tonys awarded to the production, which was voted the year's best musical.

Along with helping Frank Sinatra celebrate his return to show business with material for the television special *Old Blue Eyes Is Back*, the partners wrote the music and lyrics for *Gypsy in My Soul*, with Liza Minnelli, Shirley Maclaine, and Goldie Hawn, and *Baryshnikov on Broadway*, which featured the international ballet star. For Chita Rivera, the original Anita in *West Side Story*, they created the nightclub act *Chita Plus Three*. Composer of the background score for *An Early Frost* (1985), the first television movie to center on the growing AIDS crisis, Kander in 1995 wrote the television scores for two Hallmark Hall of Fame television specials, *Breathing Lessons* and *The Boys Next Door*. Opening to generally favorable reviews on Broadway in April, 1997, was his and Ebb's newest musical, *Steel Pier*, revolving around a dance marathon in the Atlantic City of 1933.

In Movieland, to which few Broadway songwriters have been invited to furnish fresh material over the past four decades, Kander and Ebb contributed new song insertions for *Funny Lady* (1975), the second half of Barbra Streisand's Fanny Brice story. Among them was "How Lucky Can You Get," a best song contender that lost to actor-songwriter Keith Carradine's "I'm Easy," from *Nashville*. That same year Kander composed the background music for the Academy Award-winning short subject *Norman Rockwell*, and collaborated with Ebb on the title song. In the early eighties, they furnished a few songs to *Still of the Night* (1982) and *Places in the Heart* (1984). But it was in 1977 that the pair combined talents for one of the best-known songs ever written for a Hollywood musical.

Why it was ignored by the American Academy of Motion Picture Arts and Sciences remains a clueless mystery to Kander as to countless popular music buffs. Entitled "New York, New York," it appeared in the 1977 Martin Scorsese-directed picture of the same name, which revolved around the big-band era of the forties and starred Liza Minnelli, who introduced the song, as the career-oriented girlfriend of saxophonist Robert de Niro. Although the length of the film (2 hours and 33 minutes) diluted plot effectiveness, the song quickly gathered enough momentum via Miss Minnelli's and Frank Sinatra's frequent reprises to gain immediate and what promises to be permanent recognition.

A brilliant embodiment of the classic virtues of economy and directness, the song generated far more enthusiasm and attained far greater popularity than any of that year's best song nominees: "Candle on the Water," "Nobody Does It Better," "The Slipper and the Rose Waltz (He Danced with Her, She Danced with Me)," "Someone's Waiting for You," even the winning "You Light Up My Life." Thus did "New York, New York" join two other movie-based "location" songs, "San Francisco" and "Hooray for Hollywood," and such ballads as "I Only Have Eyes for You," "A Foggy Day," "September in the Rain," "In the Still of the Night," "Too Marvelous for Words," "There Will Never Be Another You," "Moonlight Becomes You," "Spring Will Be a Little Late This Year," and "Time After Time," in the pantheon of quite glorious songs ignored by the Oscar nominating committee.

Whether the lyric influenced the nation's largest bank, Citibank, to advertise its alertness to customer needs by declaring that "The Citi Never Sleeps," is unknown. What is fact is that then Mayor Edward I. Koch became so enamored of the song that in 1985 he adopted it as the city's official anthem. The designation was no mean honor considering all the praiseworthy New York and Broadway songs written over the past 100-plus years, ranging from James W. Blake and Charles B. Lawlor's "The Sidewalks of New York" ("East side, west side, all around the town") and Victor Herbert's "In Old New York" to Rodgers and Hart's "Manhattan" (which mentions sites in all five boroughs) and Bob Hilliard-Jule Styne's "Ev'ry Street's a Boulevard (in Old New York)," which made its debut in Dean Martin and Jerry Lewis's 1954 movie comedy *Living It Up*.

To this day, "New York, New York" serves as theme song for Koch's radio talk show, and via amplification of the Sinatra recording escorts New York Yankee fans out of the big Bronx ball park, even when the team loses the game. The Sinatra version, incidentally, was ranked sixth on the list of the "Top 40" jukebox singles of all time, compiled in 1996 by the Amusement & Music Operators Association, a Chicago-based entertainment and vending trade group. Its members own or service about one-half of the nation's 250,000 commercial CD and 45-rpm jukeboxes. On the previous 1992 list, Sinatra's "New York, New York" placed tenth. Ranking ahead of the song in 1996 were, from number one to number five, Patsy Cline's "Crazy"; Bob Seger's "Old Time Rock & Roll," Elvis Presley's double-sided "Hound Dog" and "Don't Be Cruel," Bobby Darin's "Mack the Knife," and Steppenwolf's "Born to Be Wild."

Reaching the Apex. Unquestionably the crowning glory in the career of both Kander and Ebb, *Cabaret* in some respects resembles their cold-blooded *Chicago* (1977), particularly in the overt cynicism of the lady protagonist and the rough-and-tumble atmosphere of its era, the "Roaring Twenties," when anything went, at least when accompanied by a jigger of bootleg booze and a pop tune with a Charleston, Black Bottom, or Varsity Drag beat to it. Ebb co-wrote the show with Bob Fosse, who also directed and choreographed it, basing the libretto on the play of the same name by Maurine Dallas Watkins, a *Chicago Tribune* reporter who covered the actual 1924 court case. Carrying on Broadway's recent inundation of mega-musical revivals, *Chicago* was returned to Broadway in November 1996, with tickets going on sale as early as mid-June. The star, Ann Reinking, also adapted Bob Fosse's original choreography.

The musical tells the story of the brainless libertine Roxie Hart, a married chorus girl who murders her unfaithful lover, avoids prison, and winds up a vaudeville headliner in company with another murderess. George Abbott directed it as a Broadway comedy in 1926 (it ran a respectable 172 performances), and the next year it became a silent film starring Phyllis Haver. *Chicago* was renamed *Roxie Hart* in 1942, and Ginger Rogers was assigned to essay the title role. As if to foreshadow the acerbic allusions to 1920s morality that course through the picture, the producers dedicated it to "all the beautiful women in the world who have shot their husbands full of holes out of pique." Besides the effervescent "Razzle Dazzle," the highlight of the Broadway show, the score includes another hit, "All That Jazz," which in 1979 would provide the title for choreographer Fosse's film "biography."

A big talent who, like Bette Midler and Barbra Streisand, has been denied access to movie musicals in later life, but only because of the paucity of such productions, Liza Minnelli made her first screen appearance in *In the Good Old Summertime* as the infant daughter of Van Johnson and Judy Garland, who happened to be her real-life mother as well. The 1949 musical was a remake of the Ernst Lubitsch classic *The Shop Around the Corner*, which featured James Stewart and Margaret Sullavan in their most charming-ever roles. The only woman to be named Las Vegas Entertainer of the Year three times, as well as Entertainer of the Year twice by the American Guild of Variety Artists, Miss Minnelli is extraordinary as *Cabaret*'s dedicated hedonite who succumbs to near despair only when her words or actions fail to shock. Rejected as Sally Bowles on the stage because of her lack of an authentic English accent, she was accorded lavish praise by composer Kander, who described her performance in the film as "quite wonderful" to this author. In the movie, of course, the redoubtable Sally is an American expatriate, not British, thereby disposing of the accent problem.

This nationality switch is only one of the modifications of character and incident that distinguish the film from the stage version. Indeed, so conceptual and pervasive are the dissimilarities that Kander regards them as "quite different" productions. "Fred Ebb and I were really not prepared for the changes worked into the screenplay," he said recently. "Seeing the finished product really required a great deal of adjustment on my part, but when the film was over, I had to admit that, with all its deviations from the stage musical, it was actually brilliant."

Another significant scriptural change was presenting the central male figure, Brian Roberts, played by Michael York, as an Englishman. Although true to the original Isherwood character, it differs from the Broadway *Cabaret*, in which he was an American named Cliff Bradshaw. The role of Fraulein Schneider, essayed by Lotte Lenya, was reduced almost to imperceptibility, thereby omitting much of the stage musical's comedy, which resulted from the landlady's semi-romantic bantering with Herr Schultz, the bourgeois Jewish shopkeeper, played on the stage by Jack Gilford, who never appears in the film. The anti-Semitism that clouded their relationship was transferred to the love affair between two new and younger characters, Fritz Wendel and Natalia Landauer, the daughter of a wealthy Jewish department store owner. This couple marries, whereas Lenya and Gilford did not. Distraught over the distinct possibility that the Nazis would outlaw "mixed" marriages between Jew and Gentile, each recognized the pain and sorrow they would invite if they dared to become husband and wife.

Because of the extensive rewriting of the original Joe Masteroff libretto, several stage songs were cut, although, mercifully, the major hits stayed intact, and two new songs were inserted. Dropped for the film were "Don't Tell Mama," "So What?," "I Don't Care Much" (actually written independently one year earlier for Barbra Streisand), "Meeskite," and "Why Should I Wake Up?" The lovely "Married (*Heiraten*)" was retained, although it is heard only briefly when Greta Keller sings it in the background over the radio. Also retained was the purposely insulting "love" song, "If You Could See Her." A startling example of sleaze masquerading as comedy, it is performed by Grey and a Kit Kat chorus girl dressed in a gorilla costume. In his eyes, Grey sings, she is a lovely creature even though, as he admits to the howling cabaret audience in the final line, her Jewishness undoubtedly makes her appear ridiculous and offensive to everyone else.

Accent on Realism. Rather than corrupting *Cabaret*'s original intent, the character and plot alterations amplify it. The picture is uncompromising in exposing the moral bankruptcy of a society on the cusp of disintegration and perversely contributing to the eventual ascent of Hitler and enactment of the "reforms" he promised would distinguish his "New Order." It also provides a fit prelude to the still greater horrors to be perpetuated by the Nazis, to which *The Sound of Music*, set at the end of the turbulent thirties, attests in much milder terms.

If anything, the film brings the impending fall of a great nation into far sharper focus than was attainable on the stage. The motion picture camera, with its unique ability to record unvarnished reality, makes the difference. Incident as well as speech is starkly realistic in 1972 terms, and particularly for a musical picture. Homosexuality is not only referred to, but also practiced (off-screen), and once-forbidden curse words are sprinkled throughout the script. Liza Minnelli is so heavily made up that her face often borders on the absurd, her false eyelashes competing for attention with the thick layers of eye shadow, long rainbow-colored fingernails, face-framing hats, and garish costumes.

In effect, the star is presented as a mockery of a silent screen vamp unable to distinguish the merely unconventional from the truly disgusting. Combining depravity and detachment, brooding and wistfulness, she remains essentially likable, no mean achievement for any actress, musical or dramatic, in such a part. At times so brittle as to be in serious jeopardy of breaking into pieces, at other times so self-indulgent as to appear indestructible, her Sally Bowles convincingly conveys extreme vulnerability lurking beneath the hard-boiled shell she has constructed as a defense against a cruel world. The Broadway Sally was more innocently kooky, a sort of sassy, fun-loving flapper seeking diversion in an occasional fling.

Similarly, the closeups of emcee Grey freeze the sight of his heavily rouged cheeks and perpetual smirk to the mind. That his face is shown through a distorting mirror at both the beginning and the end of the picture furnishes sufficient proof that nobody, least of all his appreciative Kit Kat fans, is willing to view the outside world as it actually is and call a halt to the nation's descent from democracy into dictatorship. Indeed, the future is the least of their worries, conveniently blotted from mind whenever they enter Grey's sordid escape hatch.

The underlying tragedy of both Grey and Liza is their disassociation from their families, with whom they might take refuge, as well as from any other repository of moral values capable of addressing their anxieties. Liza's mother is dead, and it becomes apparent that her father, whom she defines vaguely as a sort of roving ambassador continually involved in pressing matters of state, has little interest in her. Repeating the crazy-mirror closeup of Grey at the conclusion supports the film's premise that neither he nor anyone else is concerned over the fact that nothing much in their lives had changed over the intervening two hours.

With the equally disarming directness of *West Side Story*, the camera is relentless in revealing the total absence of even vestiges of respectability in Berlin's nightlife. The bevy of beefy chorus girls, constantly described by Grey as beautiful virgins, are really neither. Their blowsiness is apparent, as is their awkward cavorting that passes for dancing. Seen often only hazily through slits in the curtain of cigarette smoke, the patrons sit in somnambulant stillness except when applauding the skits or dialing table telephones to introduce themselves to an attractive lady of the evening, who for all they know is a transvestite, like the one who sidles up next to Michael York at a urinal.

The Kit Kat is not only an urban watering hole where the frustrated and despondent meet to shrug off the purposelessness of their lives. It is also a haven for the alienated, dispensing the false merriment that emcee Grey has institutionalized, a nether world where nonsense is in vogue; where young dreams dissolve into rubble; where people chuckle even at Grey's insipid jokes, cheer their favorite female mud wrestler on to victory, and find entertainment in despicable freak shows, all in hopes of substituting illusion for reality.

But the cabaret has at least one virtue. Contrasting starkly with the Nazi Party's efforts to smother freedom of expression, it is quite democratic when selecting subjects for ridicule.

Along with the Jews, the performers satirize Hitler's private army of brownshirted, jack-booted storm troopers (the SA 'or *Sturmabteilung*), with Grey appearing in drag, wearing a helmet atop his blonde wig. The unsophisticated pleasures of the rural peasant class are treated to equally devastating contempt in a Tyrolean routine that contrasts the chorus' harmless slapping of faces with the punches inflicted on the bloodied bodies of enemies of the Third Reich by Nazis just outside the cabaret doors. Married love is also subjected to ironic commentary in "Two Ladies," in which Grey consorts on stage with two chorus girls, at one point suggesting his sampling of their sexual favors while all three are covered with a sheet.

Where Tackiness Reigns. The rolling of the credits is accompanied not by music at first, but by the sounds of muffled voices, which gradually rise in volume until the camera focuses on the face of the master of ceremonies of Berlin's Kit Kat Club, played by Joel Grey. The voices were those of his audience, whom Grey welcomes and urges to leave all their troubles behind them. As he sings the opening song, the jaunty "Wilkommen," the camera engages in a short series of parallel-action scenes. Michael York (Brian Roberts) is seen stepping off a train at the city's railroad station and proceeding along the streets in search of a room to let. Scenes showing Grey leading the orchestra, also all-female, while the chorus dances in typical maladroit fashion to the tune periodically interrupt York's journey. An immediate contrast is drawn between the handsome, clean-cut Britisher and the chorines and instrumentalists, their faces as bizarrely camoflagued as Grey's with mascara, as if all were intent on concealing their misery under a thick coating of paint and powder.

Spotting a "Room for Rent" sign in the window of a boarding house, York enters it and meets Liza Minnelli (Sally Bowles), a broke but not yet broken young American expatriate with a zest for what she calls "divine decadence," who has lived there for almost three months. No ingenue, she nonetheless hopes to be introduced on the stage by none other than the great German director Max Reinhardt if, as she confides to York, sex and drugs don't get her first. She shows him the vacant room while explaining that she works at Grey's cabaret. Though the young man's finances are equally slim, he takes it for 50 marks a month, rather a hefty sum for a Ph.D. candidate on an extended holiday from Cambridge University, which Isherwood himself attended for a short time. It is York's plan to earn his keep by tutoring Berliners in English.

Liza, having easily surmounted what most likely was a straight-laced upbringing, is quite adept at affecting the devil-may-care pose of a gregarious, worldly young woman, and York instantly becomes infatuated with her. But she must hurry away, she tells him, to perform at the Kit Kat, that popular bunker of Berlin's bohemian underground.

She is next seen in a scanty black Dietrich-like costume, complete with high-heel boots and stockings rolled half way up her bare thighs, but wearing a derby instead of a top hat. Astride a chair, her only prop, she launches into the first of the new song interpolations, "Mein Herr," a sensual—and rare—paean to the dissolution, rather than the beginning, of a love affair that unquestionably encapsulates her own recent experience and elevates free love to be philosophically respectable. It was great fun while it lasted, she declares, implying, as Cole Porter once did, that it was just one of those things. More to the point, it was probably only the latest of such affairs, a romantic interlude now ended without regret or recrimination. In fact, Liza sings, she regards the breakup as salutary, since she is now again free to roam at will, love as she wishes, and resume her self-absorption uninterrupted by any commitment other than her wispy hope of someday becoming an actress.

York is in the audience that evening and meets Fritz Wepper (Fritz Wendel), who hires him as tutor. Later, York finds another employer in the person of Ralf Wolter (Herr Ludwig), who commissions him to translate his meritless unpublished novel, "Cleo, the Whip Lady," for 50 marks, sufficient to the pfennig to pay the first month's rent. To York the manuscript is little more than "pure pornography," which he is beginning to sense is the chief avocation of Berliners of both sexes.

With Liza acting as aggressor, relations between her and York begin their evolution from fascination to temptation, starting with her sister-like kiss on the cheek and brief but sultry tango to a phonograph record, both of which York greets with bemusement rather than the aroused sexuality she had expected. Admitting that male lovers are becoming more and more difficult to find, Liza interprets his passivity as undeniable evidence of his homosexuality. Her suspicion is confirmed when he concedes that lately his bisexual love life has consisted of "plenty of nothin,'" a surprising reference to the Gershwin song that would not be written until four years later, in 1935. Accustomed to snapping back from disappointment, she ungrudgingly accepts him as a friend. Undoubtedly, their relationship is at least partly autobiographical; in his early years in Germany, Isherwood entered into a homosexual relationship with a German working-class youth whom he later identified only by the name "Heinz." It was in his company that Isherwood fled Germany in 1933.

York's need to fatten his bankroll brightens markedly when he acquires a third pupil, the wealthy and appealing young Jewess, Marisa Berenson (Natalia Landauer). Liza takes an instant dislike of her partly because of her ladylike reserve, which contrasts so sharply with Liza's unconventional lifestyle, and partly because both York and Wendel ignore her to vie for Marisa's attention. What eludes Liza is that York by nature is politeness personified, and that the jobless Wendel is playing up to her as a result of having heard York describe her family as "stinking rich." Liza manages to command the attention of all three, however, when she opens a discourse on syphillis, commenting that her recent episodes of "screwing" may very well have infected her with the disease. As she had hoped, her monologue offends her listeners.

In one of the film's more pathetic, albeit touching, scenes, Liza falls into uncharacteristic self-pity over her father's not meeting her one afternoon as planned. To her, the incident is only the latest in a series of parental rebuffs that have always characterized their relationship. This one has similarly dampened her normally high spirits, which she tries to uplift by suggesting to York that she is most likely not worth caring about anyway, that she is "just nothing." Her display of sorrow, undoubtedly sincere, prods him into comforting her by praising her as an attractive young woman with abundant talent to realize her ambition. But it is not until he climbs into bed with her that Liza's distraught emotions are finally placated.

Woman in Love. Back the next night on the Kit Kat stage, Liza expresses her romantic fantasies in "Maybe This Time," an exuberant testimonial to her newly found happiness with York. Perhaps she has finally become a winner after all, in affairs of the heart if in nothing else. A few hours later, curiosity prods her into accepting Marisa's invitation to visit her in her home. Expecting to be quizzed on York's likes and dislikes, Liza is both astounded and pleased that her hostess' conversation centers exclusively on learning Liza's opinion of Wendel.

Lately, the apparently sex-starved young man has been showing more than casual interest in her, and what Marisa especially wants to know is whether he is simply a gigolo out to get his hands on the family fortune. She even reveals that, following York's man-to-man advice to be more assertive in his wooing, Wendel had "pounced" on her in an abrupt, and highly unwelcome, expression of infatuation, which minutes later he sought to legitimize by proposing marriage.

Marisa's confusion over whether the incident sprang from lust rather than deepening affection arouses Liza's sympathy, which becomes even more palpable when Marisa reveals that marrying a Christian is out of the question for her. Her Orthodox family would most likely frown upon it, and the increasingly virulent anti-Semitism infecting the country would be the cause of still greater grief. Hoping to soothe her with worthless advice, Liza limply recommends that if she cannot forget him, and will not "meet him on the sly," perhaps she should think about entering a convent. "They have Jewish nuns, you know," she explains.

At the cabaret, Liza joins Grey in a duet of "Money, Money," the film's second new song. Money was something the average German of the time had precious little of, and an overriding quest was to acquire as much as possible and hoard it. Basically an excellently crafted obscene song filled with references to money as the solution to all of life's problems, the lyric wallows in praise of those with plenty of it to buy their way out of misery. It is they who are uniquely able to lounge in comfort while weathering the economic storm by keeping their bellies fat, fuel in the furnace, shoes on their feet—and indulging in such pleasures as taking trips on yachts and contracting for call girl services.

Listening to the duet is the embodiment of German aristocracy, one Helmut Griem (Maxmillian von Heune), a handsome, cultured, and dapper young man, and the film's most corruptive character, indifferent to the deprivation of the German masses and so wealthy that he can afford to dine on caviar at breakfast. He had struck up an acquaintance with Liza in a laundry and accepted her invitation to visit the cabaret. York joins them at their table, but soon takes umbrage at Liza's flirting with Griem. Perhaps her objective is to make York jealous; more likely, her fawning over him is due to her assuming that anyone bearing the title of Baron is bound to know somebody of importance in the film industry.

Over the next few days, Griem responds to Liza's attentiveness by showering her with expensive gifts, in effect enticing her by providing clear insight into the advantages to be derived from friendship with a man with an abundance of money, and the inclination to spend it freely. He also presents York with a gold cigarette case as a bribe for his friendship, and invites both to spend several days at his estate.

Griem's commodious mansion introduces his guests to the luxuries most people only glimpsed on the pages of magazines catering to socialites. There, amid priceless antiques on display in cavernous rooms, where their every request is attended to immediately by uniformed domestics, the three characters delve briefly into the politics of the time. In a remarkable rendering of cynicism dueling with apathy, their individual comments condense the most prevalent opinions that were already dividing the German population on the issue of Nazism by distilling the essence of each with-

out exploring the complexities surrounding them.

To Max, the Nazis are a "gang of stupid hooligans," true, but at least they are serving the purpose of ridding the country of Communists, who threaten upper-class privileges, and most likely the aristocracy itself. If the Nazis themselves become too powerful, Germany will be able to "control them," he maintains. York, who later will be quick to denounce Nazism's aggressiveness and cruelty, offers only low-key denunciation. He is, after all, a British subject, free to leave Germany at will, and therefore not particularly worried about the country's potential threat to the rest of Europe. As for Liza, to be correctly described later by York as an "underage femme fatale," she is politically neutral, preferring to remain silent regarding which party should control the government. The Nazis, the Communists, the Weimar supporters—none attracts or revolts her. In her view, they are equally bad, equally good, deserving of only noninvolvement in their complex affairs.

Painfully aware that he is everything that Max is not—poor, unsophisticated, and unimpressive—yet also becoming increasingly stimulated in his presence, York proceeds to drink himself into a stupor. Apparently, he surmises with the unerring insight of the envious, Max enjoys flaunting his wealth by inviting Liza and him on an African safari, which is later cancelled by what Max describes as an urgent need to join his family on a trip to Argentina. Nor is Max the least hesitant to shoulder York aside trying to win her affection. The fact that he is married is no impediment to his sexual pursuits, since, as he proudly announces, he and his wife share a "special understanding" that allows each to seek outside companionship as desired. The result of this free-love arrangement is that Max has sexual relations that night with Liza, who is stunned the next morning to learn that he had also slept with York.

Of all the film's exposés of the powerful impact that the Nazis were exerting, none approaches the effectiveness of the song "Tomorrow Belongs to Me." Had it been written in Germany in the early thirties, it very well might have become as popular a Nazi anthem as the "Horst Wessel Lied," named in honor of one of the party's leading orators, who was shot to to death in early 1930, not by a political opponent, but by the jealous one-time pimp (Albrecht Höhler) of his prostitute girlfriend (Erna Jaenicke). Pumped up into a martyr-hero whose death would be avenged, Sturmfuehrer Wessel himself had written both melody and words, under the title "Die Fahne Höch." During the Nazi years, his song ranked second only to "Deutschland, Deutschland über Alles" in the hearts and minds of the faithful.

With a Song in Their Hearts. "Tomorrow Belongs to Me," sung reverentially by a handsome blond teenager (Oliver Collignon) the kind that later flooded the ranks of Hitler's Jugend, the melody is serenely lyrical rather than pulse-pounding militaristic as well as inordinately effective as a classic piece of propaganda. Featuring a stirring waltz melody that matches the lyric in poetic elegance, its low-key, almost casual affirmation of the inevitability of a Nazi takeover surely would have elevated the song to the stature of a national hymn in the early thirties. Its mesmerizing appeal to jingoism becomes scarily obvious when the patrons of an open-air beer garden become so infected with superpatriotism that they are compelled to rise one by one from their chairs and join the lad in singing it. Most likely neither Kander nor Ebb realized that the song would so precisely document the fervor with which all generations of Germans embraced the Nazi dogma. Luckily, they wrote it 21 years after Germany's unconditional surrender in World War II.

Meanwhile, the romance between Wendel and Marisa is experiencing disarray while proceeding cautiously toward fulfillment. It is obvious she loves him, but so is her fear of the reprisals they both might suffer if they marry. A further impediment arises when the fact that the Nazis have targeted the Landauer household as enemies becomes painfully apparent to Marisa. She sees the disapprobative word "Juden" scrawled on the front sidewalk of her house, near the dead body of her dog.

But that is only the first of two Nazi-inspired crudities visited on opponents of Hitlerian philosophy. York is savagely beaten and hospitalized after slapping a propaganda flyer from the hands of a Nazi functionary who had tried to jam it into his hand. Resentment is writ large on the dour faces of Nazis in the Kit Kat audience when the Fuehrer or the party is lampooned. Much to their misfortune, some Germans as late as 1931 regarded Hitler as more of a Charlie Chaplin comic figure than the dominant force in creating a "Third Reich" designed to be even more glorious than its two predecessors, one founded by Charlemagne, the other by Bismarck. Further fanning the flames of hatred are newspaper articles, like those in such newspapers as the venomously anti-Semitic *Volkischer Beobachter* and Julius Streicher's *Der Stürmer*, identifying Jewish bankers and Communists as co-conspirators in an alleged movement to seize all the national government's assets.

While revealing his innermost thoughts to York, Wendel admits to having been turned into a "lovesick fool" since meeting Marisa. He also tells his friend that he is a Jew, but has been posing as a Protestant in order to avoid whatever dire consequences knowledge of his birth religion might provoke among the nation's growing anti-Jewish element. Wendel's repeating his "confession" to Marisa is greeted with her acceptance of his proposal, and the couple is married under a synagogue canopy.

When Liza learns she is pregnant, York happily agrees to be the baby's father, despite her inability to assure him that he is the man who sired it, and he offers to marry her and relocate the family back in Cambridge. For once in her life, Liza actually seems genuinely pleased, rather than merely contented. As time passes, however, and York's enthusiasm dims in the light of his sexual ambivalence, she instinctively recognizes the telltale signs of the ending of another love affair, this one as temporary as all the others. Returning home late one evening, well after the Kit-Kat's closing time, she admits to having sold the fur coat Griem had given her to pay for a back-alley abortion. When York angrily demands to know why she had taken such a drastic step, she reverts to her more normal blend of disenchantment and cynicism, attributing it to just another of her "whims," which never require detailed explanation on her part.

She offers one anyway, coldbloodedly reviewing the myriad responsibilities of motherhood, which strike her as detrimental to achieving her acting goal, to which, incidentally, she expends absolutely no time or effort throughout the entire picture. She has no intention of being "tied down" to a playpen or washing diapers. She is, in fact, not the motherly type, nor is she the least interested in acquiring the talents that would turn her into one. Besides, she adds, if rearing the child would be the sole reason for their long-term togetherness, she and York in time would come to hate each other, and possibly the child as well. Irate at her excuse, delivered in dispassionate tones, York leaves the room. "Aw, shit!," Liza cries after falling in near despair on her bed. Her Berlin experiences, lurid but satisfactory, have smothered any hope she may have nourished of ever extricating herself from their influence.

Somewhat reluctantly shedding the mantle of husband and father, York decides to return to England. The one-time lovers' parting at the train station, in most films (like *Fiddler on the Roof* and *Since You Went Away*, 1944) played out with heartbreaking sentimentality, is impersonal, as if each felt compelled by formality rather than fondness to meet for a final time. Liza is no Jennifer Jones, tearfully chasing after the moving train to catch another glimpse of fiancé Robert Walker; nor has York pledged to marry the lady upon his return from war, which has yet to break out. With only a curt handshake and brief eye-to-eye contact, he and Liza say goodbye. "I'll see you," she says with only the slightest tinge of emotion, relieved in the certainty that their paths will never cross again.

Jubilantly, she retreats quickly back to her element, appearing for the final time on the Kit Kat stage. Her song, the effervescent and tremendously popular title tune, had already been heard in the film, but only in a few chorus turns and background snatches. Now she is ready to flesh it out, to give one of the best and peppiest production tunes of the 1960s all the attention and professionalism of which a great singer is capable. Rarely before, in any musical, has a performer more aptly embodied the final spectacular illumination of a collapsing star.

The cabaret is her home, she sings, the only place where she finds even a smidgen of happiness, and she urges all the equally disenchanted to join her there. She insists that they take a tip from her former roommate, Elsie, either a figment of her imagination or one-time fellow entertainer who has died. Her short life was as unpleasant and unfulfilling as Liza's. But even in her casket, Liza recalls, her chum's customary smile was so wide, so contagious, that she qualifies as the happiest corpse she has ever seen.

Cheers for Elsie, Liza seems to say. She lived life as best she could in view of the abysmally poor cards that an impersonal croupier had dealt her. But she trumped everyone else's hand, finding enjoyment in the unlikeliest of settings in the most perilous of recent times and always willing to share it with anybody, everybody.

The cabaret may not be heaven, but it's surely the closest either young woman will ever come to it.

All That Jazz (1979)

A Columbia picture. DIRECTOR: Bob Fosse; FIRST ASSISTANT: Wolfgang Glattes; SECOND ASSISTANT: Joseph Ray. EXECUTIVE PRODUCER: Daniel Melnick; ASSOCIATES: Kenneth Utt and Wolfgang Glattes. PRODUCER: Robert Alan Aurthur; SCREENWRITERS: Robert Alan Aurthur and Bob Fosse. FILM EDITOR: Alan Heim. PRODUCTION MANAGER: Kenneth Utt. PRODUCTION DESIGNER: Philip Rosenberg; FANTASY DESIGNER: Tony Walton. CINEMATOGRAPHER: Giuseppe Rotunno; ASSOCIATE: Bill Garroni. CHOREOGRAPHER: Bob Fosse; ASSISTANTS: Kathryn Doby and Gene Foote. SET DECORATORS: Edward Stewart and Gary Brink. SUPERVISING SOUND EDITOR: Maurice Schell; SOUND EDITORS: Jay Dranch, Bernard Hajdenberg, Sanford Rackow, and Stan Bochner. COSTUME DESIGNER: Albert Wolsky; WARDROBE: Max Solomon and Lee Austin III. MAKEUP: Fern Buchner. HAIRSTYLES: Romaine Greene. MUSIC ARRANGER AND CONDUCTOR: Ralph Burns; DANCE MUSIC ARRANGER: Arnold Gross. MUSIC EDITORS: Michael Tronick and La Da Productions. MUSICAL COORDINATOR: Stanley Lebowsky. SONGS: Various lyricists and composers. RUNNING TIME: 2 hours and 3 minutes. *Principal Players*: Roy Scheider (Joe Gideon). Jessica Lange (Angelique). Ann Reinking (Kate Jagger). Leland Palmer (Audrey Paris). Cliff Gorman (Davis Newman). Ben Vereen (O'Connor Flood). Deborah Geffner (Victoria). Erzsebet Foldi (Michelle). Michael Tolan (Dr. Ballinger). John Lithgow (Lucas Sergeant). *Major Academy Awards*: Best Film Editing; Art Direction; Costumes; Scoring. *Nominations*: Best Picture; Director; Actor (*Roy Scheider*); Original Screenplay; Cinematography.

Often spectacular, at times morbid and earthy, but innovative in choreography and cinematography throughout, *All That Jazz* is

Roy Scheider as Joe Gideon and Erzsebet Foldi as his daughter in Bob Fosse's semi-autobiographical *All That Jazz.*

the kind of musical movie that one either likes or dislikes intensely in an age that has largely substituted realism for fantasy and ballet for tap dancing. The choice depends on whether the viewer is a traditionalist or devotee of experimentation with dance, subject matter, and narrative, which as regards this musical film are provocative, daring, and purposely disjointed. Luckily for persons addicted to the Bob Fosse style, the featured dancers could hardly be better than they are in number after number.

Sometimes puzzling in presentation, the film is always uncompromisingly clear in detailing the degradation of a hard-living, hard-driving artist from the pinnacle of his profession into a graphic example of human wreckage. Toward the end, he is so physically and mentally weakened that he can never again hope to capitalize on the gifts on which his reputation rests. The profession that had enticed, challenged, coddled, and gratified the choreographer finally crushes him.

The film is one of a kind in that it depends entirely for effectiveness on character analysis rather than character development. The plot is not compelling, and the basically unattractive, self-indulgent lead is the sole focal point. He is the same at the end of the picture as at the beginning, although slightly happier by facing up to the inevitability of his own death with relief. He has not been the least adventurous, except in broadening the range of ensemble dancing, nor is his death lamented by very many who benefitted from his professional largesse.

All That Jazz is the only nominated musical to be given an "R" rating (*Cabaret* was a "PG"), which automatically excluded persons under 17 from listening to the abrasive, often vulgar, language and viewing several scenes containing bare-breasted young women. It is also the only Oscar contender to place all credits, even the names of the stars, at the end. Had the listings preceded the film, audiences would have been forewarned of its numerous studied attempts to shock. For among the participants are listed members of the "Cardiac Surgical

Team of St. Luke's Hospital Center in N.Y.C.," who perform an open-heart surgery with all the bloody trappings of slicing up what is perceived to be a human torso and plunging instruments deep into the crevices. Never before had any musical film gone quite that far in providing unnecessary realism.

Actually, one of the film's purposes was to open the screen to a unique new musical experience very much unlike anything anyone had seen before. "Biographies" of show people were hardly new by the late seventies, but no film had ever centered on a choreographer, who in earlier backstage musicals had been confined to a bit part as the impatient and exacting architect of chorus line routines. Even James Cagney in *Footlight Parade* combined the duties of dance director with those of producer, writer, and director. Nor had any previous musical film indulged so heavily in self-pity while performing autopsies on the stressful career of a talented but troubled artist who, while kindly toward dancing hopefuls, treated the women who loved him with shabbiness that created ever more resentment in them. Throughout the movie, Scheider is tortured by the conviction that he has done a poor job both as artist and as family man, unable to decipher where the stage work stops and life beyond the glare of the footlights begins.

Nourished at his height by the adulation of admiring fans, and then during his decline by artificial means, protagonist Roy Scheider is depicted as a creature of the theater, with which he carries on a love-hate relationship. The love arises from the creative challenges it poses, the hate from the self-destructiveness it exacts from persons strenuously devoted to experimenting with them. Scheider has learned that show business is indeed a jealous mistress, abiding no rivals and often frustrating the perfectionist forced into dealing with imperfect performers when trying to break new ground.

He wastes precious time assuring worried backers of his latest show that his innovations will click with the public, even though they doubt the merits of his deviating so widely from the norm. His endless practice sessions exhaust them as well as the dancers. Even when the latter manage to follow his instructions to the letter, the backers express fear that the routines are surely too offbeat to please more than the handful of avant-garde dance devotees willing to pay their way into his shows.

He must also contend with self-serving yes men and women whose quick agreement with his every suggestion casts doubt on their qualifications to judge; the envious play doctors like John Lithgow (Lucas Sergeant), whose advice and rewrites are given for free in hopes of being called on to replace Scheider in a subsequent production; and the hollowness of Ben Vereen (O'Connor Flood), a television personality who lumps the gifted with the shallow when dispensing lavish praise, hoping to gain the approbation of everyone connected with the theater.

A lifelong exponent of laissez-faire in show business, the iconoclastic choreographer is disturbed by anyone's interference in his attempts to breathe new excitement into dance. For good reason entertaining absolutely no doubt that he is master of his art, Scheider comforts himself following an anxiety crisis by squeezing medicinal drops into his bloodshot eyes, taking a shower, and gulping down another Dexedrine tablet with a shot of booze, which combined with his chain smoking and bedding down with numerous chorus girls (and possibly boys as well), reveal his desperate need to find the satisfaction he is no longer able to derive from his work. His determination to continue thus stiffened, he happily recites in Porky Pig fashion that "It's show time again, folks," indicating that, having restored faith in himself, he is back in business.

But Scheider's self-destructive bent naturally devalues his health. As the most frequently noted—and insightful—criticism of the film contends, within a short time his repetitious method of relieving tension becomes tiresome. Rather than empathy, his pops and gulps engender distaste for his habits and finally for Scheider himself. Viewers simply get to know him too well. But, as two of his financial supporters acutely observe, he is obsessed by a "deep-rooted fear of being conventional" and "of being regarded as ordinary, not special." He is not about to accept either designation with equanimity.

There is scant doubt that Scheider, a first-rate actor when given first-rate parts, does an extraordinary job as the anguished Joe Gideon, a stand-in for Bob Fosse, who directed, co-wrote, and choreographed the film. For 25 years the recipient of bountiful kudos for his heavily stylized dance configurations, performed in tandem with bizarre costumes and settings, Fosse began his career at age 13, appearing in vaudeville, burlesque, and seedy nightclubs, as the film points out (Keith Gordon plays him as a boy). In 1950s Hollywood, Fosse was a performer, and an excellent one, in several worthy musicals, dancing with Debbie Reynolds to Ira Gershwin and Burton Lane's "In Our United States" in *Give a Girl a Break*; Janet Leigh and Betty Garrett in Leo Robin and Jule Styne's musical revision of *My Sister Eileen;* and Ann Miller in Cole Porter's *Kiss Me Kate*. In Stanley Donen's 1944 movie-musical fantasy, *The Little Prince*, with equally inferior songs by Lerner and Loewe, Fosse danced the role of the Serpent.

On Broadway he won a Tony Award for choreographing *Pajama Game* (1954, made into a film in 1957), which contained Richard Adler and Jerry Ross' sexy "Steam Heat"; *Damn Yankees* (1955/1958), highlighted by the same writers' "Whatever Lola Wants"; and Betty Comden, Adolph Green, and Styne's *Bells Are Ringing* (1956/1960), among other musicals. As stage director as well as choreographer his works included the Pulitzer Prize-winning *How to Succeed in Business without Really Trying* (1961/1967), which he co-directed with Abe Burrows; *Sweet Charity* (1966/1969), a stunning musical adaptation of Fellini's film *Nights of Cabiria*; and *Chicago* (1975). His biggest year was 1973, when he won the Academy Award for directing *Cabaret*, two Tonys for *Pippin*, and an Emmy for *Liza with a "Z."* One of his last directorial assignments was the film drama *Star 80* (1983), starring Muriel Hemingway as the tragic seeker of a modeling career. None of his three wives, dancers Mary-Ann Niles, Joan McCracken, or Gwen Verdon, appears by name in *All That Jazz*. But it was *Dancin'*, produced on Broadway in 1978, that synthesized the best of the Fosse choreographic trademarks: the pelvic thrusts, jerky arm and leg gestures, scrunched shoulders, and roguish tips of derby hats that served the dual purpose of prop and adornment. As *All That Jazz* predicts, Fosse died of a heart attack in 1987, shortly after completing his chores on the unsuccessful show *Big Deal*.

Hoping for a Last Hurrah, Set in the Times Square of the 1970s, *All That Jazz* opens on Roy Scheider (Joe Gideon), who is trapped in a scheduling bind between winding up the editing of a film called "The Stand-Up" and the final touches on a forthcoming Broadway musical. Darting between the two daunting chores with diminishing enthusiasm, he lapses frequently into disillusionment over trying to improve both. Scheider is clearly the unintended victim of his own superb artistry, already displaying the abruptness and twitch of the harassed professional auditioning dancers for the musical while incessantly tinkering with the genuinely unfunny "comic" film monologue by Davis Newman, played by Cliff Gorman.

Typical of disturbed persons who prefer recalling the past to living wholly in the present and contemplating the future, Scheider conjures up visions of his earlier days to exorcise his growing recognition that extreme self-centeredness and frequent lapses in discipline are costing him the respect of his colleagues. To Jessica Lange, as the white-gowned beautiful and dreamlike Angelique, he confesses his sins, while to Ann Reinking, as his ex-wife Kate Jaggers, Leland Palmer (Audrey Paris), and Deborah Geffner (Victoria), he revives memories of his relations with them that have resulted in the mixed emotions that characterize their current regard for him. He has hurt them all, and yet his hold on their gratitude for assistance in building their careers remains firm. Also appearing intermittently is his mother, who tries to explain away his personality flaws as natural disruptions flowing from his genius, suggesting that they must be overlooked if not forgiven.

Veering more and more into total dysfunctionality when his recommendations are greeted with immediate, unanimous, and uncritical approval, Scheider falls into depression. The ready agreements proffered by his associates indicate to him that they are merely trying to humor him out of his instability, and he becomes more and more convinced that both the show and the film will bomb at the box office. The tension of trying to cure their artistic ills within deadline and budget finally takes its toll: he suffers several attacks of angina and is hospitalized, putting the musical on hold for four months and himself in serious doubt that he will ever recover sufficiently to continue in show business.

Warnings by his doctor Michael Tolan (Dr. Ballinger) that flirting with his nurse and partying with friends in his hospital room could lead to a coronary go unheeded by his celebrated patient. His heart operation, however, is successful, temporarily restoring Scheider's hope that he can soon return to work. Indeed, he falls into hallucinatory certainty that without him the musical will never open, unaware that his backers have been spending their time worrying not about his recuperation, but how much money his prolonged illness is costing them.

Already, "The Stand-Up" has received mixed reviews that have done little to soothe his fear of deteriorating infallibility. Self-doubt for the first time intrudes into what is supposed to be Scheider's post-operative rest period, driving him into wandering about the hospital corridors in search of escape. Orderlies are sent to find and return him to his room, where he suffers a severe relapse that documents the folly of his entertaining visions of recovery.

A brilliant Tony Walton-designed "fantasy" production number, highlighted by a superb backdrop awash in bright colors that seem to bleed like an ulcer across the screen, seals Scheider's fate. He sings his own swan song with Ben Vereen, in Felice and Boudleaux Bryant's song "Bye Bye Love," which had appeared one year earlier in *American Hot Wax*. Watching his performance with emotions ranging from indifference to satisfaction is an audience of past lovers and Broadway associates. Painfully few tears are shed over his impending departure from a disappointing life laden with grueling work schedules and unfulfilled lofty ambitions that have combined to insure a tragic end to his days of triumph. At the conclusion of the number, Scheider welcomes Jessica, now a symbol of the angel of death, as a friend who will at last put him out of his misery. No one will ever again hurt him, least of all himself.

Never before had a nominated musical since *The Hollywood Revue of 1929* of exactly 50 years earlier featured so many old songs interspersed with a few new ones. Curiously, not one of the many hit songs introduced in Fosse's own musicals is present. The opening number, "On Broadway," written by Barry Mann, Cynthia Weil, and long-time partners Jerry Lieber and Mike Stoller, and sung off-screen by George Benson, practically stops the show before it gets underway. The dancing by the chorus selected by Scheider to appear in his new musical in progress provides sufficient incandescence, generated by the precision of their steps and the effectiveness of the lighting. Not until an hour later will any *All That Jazz* musical number rival the electricity that the earlier selection sends from stage into audience. Again danced in vintage Fosse style, "Take Off with Us," written by Fred Tobias and *All That Jazz* musical coordinator Stan Lebowsky, displays a marvelous vivaciousness, courtesy of the scantily dressed chorus girls as airline stewardesses. The eroticism the number exudes, however, embarrasses Scheider's money men, who, one presumes, drop it from the show, which they eventually will be forced to pass along to other hands to complete.

Of particular interest is Peter Allen and Carole Bayer Sager's "Everything Old Is New Again," splendidly sung and danced in modified Fosse format by top-hatted Ann Reinking and 12-year-old Erzsebet Foldi, who is excellent in the role of Miss Reinking's and Scheider's daughter with stage aspirations of her own. Harry Nilsson's "A Perfect Day" is a minor piece, fully deserving of its anonymity, but adequately compensated for by the felicitous melange of old-time tunes, like Will J. Harris and Victor Young's "Sweet Sue," all written decades before *All That Jazz* was filmed. Most serve a purpose beyond treating the audience to reprises, sometimes delivered in fragmentary fashion, of songs largely forgotten by 1979.

Inserted to signal both Scheider's and the other singers' casual acceptance of his death, each old-time favorite is sung as a satiric commentary on the inevitability of his demise. For example, George Asaf and Felix Powell's "Pack Up Your Troubles in Your Old Kit Bag and Smile, Smile, Smile," a carryover from the World War I years, is sung by a black hospital attendant, played by Tiger Haynes, as an encouragement to Scheider to dismiss the recent problems he has endured. Death will soon relieve him of all of them, so what's the use of worrying.

Henry Creamer and Turner Layton's "After You've Gone," sung by Miss Palmer, lightly chastises Scheider for never appreciating the women who have loved him over the years, indicating that it is now too late for amends. Shelton Brooks's classic "Some of These Days," delivered by little Miss Foldi, reinforces the previous song's message by declaring that her father surely must rue his unfaithfulness, while Billy Higgins and W. Benton Overstreet's "There'll Be Some Changes Made," sung by Ann Reinking, jokingly slams the door on any plans the dying patient may have had of reforming his lifestyle by reminding him that it is far too late for that, too.

Likewise, the chorus rendition of Bert Kalmar, Harry Ruby, and Ted Snyder's "Who's Sorry Now?" pokes fun at Scheider's failing to realize that one day he would pay for his philandering by performing the number with the formality identified with the old-fashioned Ziegfeld Follies chorus line, which Fosse himself had contributed greatly to wipe out of existence.

And finally, when Scheider's body bag has been zipped closed, the most ironic musical interpolation is sung by the off-screen voice of Ethel Merman, which is heard in a joyful reprise of Irving Berlin's "There's No Business Like Show Business," which she had introduced in 1946 in *Annie Get Your Gun*. One can only agree with her ringing endorsement of the quirkiness of the theatrical professions. Considering the glory that once was Scheider's, and the tortured life that his total devotion to the business produced in its wake, the evidence that working in it is often a prescription for personal disaster rings loud and clear from the final scene.

Beauty and the Beast (1991)

A Walt Disney picture in association with Silver Screen Partners IV. DIRECTORS: Gary Trousdale and Kirk Wise. EXECUTIVE PRODUCER: Howard Ashman. PRODUCER: Don Hahn; ASSISTANT: Sarah McArthur. ANIMATION SCREENPLAY: Linda Woolverton. STORY: Brenda Chapman, Burny Mattinson, Brian Pimental, Joe Ranft, Kelly Asbury, Christopher Sanders, Kevin Harkey, Bruce Woodside, Tom Ellery, and Robert Lence. FILM EDITOR: John Carnochan. ART DIRECTOR: Brian McEntee. STORY SUPERVISOR: Roger Allers. VISUAL EFFECTS SUPERVISOR: Randy Fullmer. COMPUTER GRAPHICS IMAGES SUPERVISOR: Jim Hillin. SOUND: Terry Porter, Mel Metcalfe, David J. Hudson, and Doc Kane. SOUND EDITORS: Julia Evershade, Michael Benavente, Jessica Gallavan, J.H. Arrufat, and Ron Bartlett; ASSISTANTS: Sonya Pettijohn and Oscar Mitt. SUPERVISING MUSIC EDITOR: Kathleen Bennett. SONG ARRANGERS: Alan Menken and Danny Troub. VOCAL ARRANGER AND MUSICAL CONDUCTOR: David Friedman. SONGS AND SCORE ORCHESTRATORS: Danny Troub and Michael Starobin. ORIGINAL SCORE: Alan Menken. SONGS: Lyrics by Howard Ashman, music by Alan Menken. RUNNING TIME: 1 hour, 24 minutes. *Principal Character Animators*: Paige O'Hara (Belle). Bobby Benson (The Beast). Richard White (Gaston). Jerry Ohrbach (Lumiere). David Ogden Stiers (Cogsworth and Narrator). Angela Lansbury (Mrs. Potts). Bradley Michael Pierce (Chip). Rex Everhart (Maurice). Jesse Corti (LeFou). *Major Academy Awards*: Best Song ("Beauty and the Beast"); Scoring. *Nominations*: Best Picture; Songs ("Be Our Guest" *and* "Belle"); Sound.

The 30th in Disney's 59-year succession of full-length animated features, *Beauty and the Beast* has attained success of spectacular proportions on film and videocassette, as well as on the Broadway stage. An indisputable classic, it can also lay claim to being the Disney organization's most technologically perfect film, as well as the chief influence in the recent resurrection of the animated song-and-dance feature. Although the first full-length animated feature created entirely by computer would not appear until the release of Disney's *Toy Story* in 1995, the computer-designed images in *Beauty and the Beast* are unmatched in clarity by anything the studio had done previously, even if the spontaneity and much of the refreshing charm of the older hand-drawn characters had to be sacrificed to admit the new technology.

Matching the Academy Award-winning sound as a model of proficiency, the animation closely approximates live-action cinematography at its best, embellishing the narrative with a smoothly textured wide range of tracking, pans, and long- and medium-distance shots and close-ups that move the story forward in a manner that appears effortless to the casual viewer. The film's blending of the hilarious and the serious, the tender and the frightening, clearly shows that the new school of Disney craftsmen and women are every bit as accomplished at their specialties as the creators of the past.

Carrying on the studio's long-established tradition of teaching entertainingly, the film is a miracle of condensation, saying what it wants to in a succinct 84 minutes, the second shortest running time of any of the 38 nominated musicals. Like *42nd Street*, not a single frame is permitted to run one second longer than necessary. When it received nomination as the best picture of 1991, it called a halt to the 12-year hiatus that had descended on movie musicals, and the even longer one on the Disney organization. No musical had been nominated since 1979; nor had any Disney production ever been nominated, save for *Mary Poppins* in 1964, even though the organization had compiled an envious record over the years in the best song category, having introduced 19 nominees and six winners between the years 1940 and 1991.

Beauty and the Beast is the only fully animated feature-length film in the history of the Academy Awards to vie for the best picture award. This startling fact may well be judged inconceivable by movie fans, considering Disney's knack for producing first-rate pictures, whether they be all live, all animated, or part-live and part-animated. How, one might logically ask, did the Brothers Grimm's *Snow White and the Seven Dwarfs*, released in late 1937, miss out on nomination? Beautifully executed, the movies' first full-length animated cartoon surely deserved recognition at least as a runner up in the 1938 Oscar sweepstakes. The recipient of six decades' worth of popularity and renown, *Snow White* at the end of 1996 ranked as Disney's fifth biggest-grossing film of all time, accounting for $175 million, much of it generated at a time when children under 12 paid ten cents for a movie ticket. The same question can be asked of *Fantasia* (1940), another illustrious *Beauty and the Beast* predecessor, which still ranks as the most ambitious, innovative, and satisfying of all the studio's journeys into the world of fantasy.

To view either of these early films is to be transfixed by the artistry of its creators, which continues to astound with its ingenuity. Only *Beauty and the Beast* has equaled *Snow White* in mastering the complex art of retelling a classic romantic fairy tale in cartoon format through song lyrics as well as dialogue. *Snow White* is all sweetness and light; even the little princess' cruel stepmother is more ravishing than fearsome. *Fantasia*, like *Beauty and the Beast*, alternates between darkness and light, activating the characters, including Mickey Mouse (dubbed for the last time by Disney himself), by means of background music introduced by Deems Taylor and played by Leopold Stokowski's Philadelphia Symphony Orchestra. It twinkles with disconnected, abstract vignettes performed to the music of such diverse composers as Johann Sebastian Bach ("Toccata and Fugue in D Minor"), Tschaikovsky ("The Waltz of the Flowers"), Moussorgsky ("Night on Bald Mountain"), and Stravinsky ("Rite of Spring"). *Snow White*, thanks to its lyrical and quite popular songs, earned Academy Award nomination for best score; *Fantasia* failed to receive a single nomination.

Beauty and the Beast, on the other hand, was nominated for six awards, including the anomalous one of having no fewer than a trio of tunes vie for best song. Adding weight to the suspicion that worthy original movie songs have become so few in recent decades that the best song award should be discontinued, the film marked the first time that three songs from the same picture were considered by Academy voters. In the equally lean year of 1980, two songs from *Fame* were entered in the competition. In 1983, two from *Flashdance* and two others from *Yentl* received nomination, as did two from *Footloose* in 1984 and another two from *White Knights* in 1985. *Beauty and the Beast*'s title tune, written by Howard Ashman and Alan Menken, won the award over their "Be Our Guest" and "Belle."

Ashman and Menken, whose "Mean Green Mother from Outer Space," from *Little Shop of Horrors* (1986) was the team's first song to compete for the Oscar, were twice nominated for two songs from the same movie. "Kiss the Girl" and "Under the Sea" both came from Disney/Silver Screen Partners' *The Little Mermaid* (1989), and "Friend Like Me" and "A Whole New World" from *Aladdin* (1992).

Menken continues as Disney's chief contract composer, collaborating with lyricists Tim Rice on *Aladdin* (1992), *The Lion King* (1993), and *Pocahontas* (1995), and Stephen Schwartz on the songs for Disney's *The Hunchback of Notre Dame* (1996) following the untimely death of Ashman, an extraordinarily gifted lyricist, in 1991. In an unusual and touching postscript to a film, the final frame of *Beast* pays tribute to Ashman, who also served as executive producer, and "gave a mermaid her voice [a reference to his lyrics for Disney's *The Little Mermaid,* 1989] and a beast his soul."

The title *Beauty and the Beast* had twice been used previously to designate fantasy films. The first came along in 1946 for the French *La Belle et la Bête,* a marvelously taut story with symbolic trappings. Directed by Jean Cocteau, it was based on the still well-known 1757 fairy tale by Marie Leprince de Beaumont. Although not a musical, the superb background score by Georges Auric delightfully heightened the picture's textural impact. A simply terrible new version appeared in 1963, sporting a cast of virtual unknowns headed by the somewhat familiar B-picture character actor Arthur Franz.

On April 18, 1994, *Beauty and the Beast* followed *The Will Rogers Follies* into New York's newly renovated Palace Theatre in the heart of Times Square. To comprehend the prestige associated with that one-time Valhalla of American vaudeville, one need only recall Gene Kelly's deep chagrin at misreading, in *For Me and My Gal* (1942), the telegram from his agent, played by Keenan Wynn, informing the dancer that he and Judy Garland had been booked into the *Newark* Palace, not the New York Palace. Had it been the latter theater, Wynn explains patiently, the telegram would not have referred to it as the New York Palace. To all show biz hopefuls and the public at large, there was only one Palace, and it was never preceded by "New York" to distinguish it from the many other theaters in the country bearing the same name.

The Disney organization's initial legitimate stage play opened there with an advance sale of $5 million, a top ticket price of $65, and Terrence Mann and Susan Egan in the title roles. Helped greatly by the critical kudos generated by the film version, the libretto wisely adhered closely to Linda Woolverton's able screenplay. The transferral of the story of the spunky little French provincial miss, Belle, who frees a scary and melancholy Beast from an evil spell and returns him back to his former dashing self through the power of true love, soon became the most successful of all of Hollywood's comparatively recent reversals of the Hollywood tradition of turning stage pieces into films. At this writing, it was celebrating its third anniversary on Broadway, still mesmerizing adults

and children alike with its visual effects, which accounted for the musical's only Tony Award. Like *The Wizard of Oz* before it and *Pocahontas* after it, *Beauty and the Beast* has spun off a traveling ice show, and according to theatrical observers quite possibly represents only the first in a series of forthcoming Disney stage productions. Why else, they ask, would Disney spend $34 million to renovate Ziegfeld's old New Amsterdam, enlarging the seating capacity from 1,700 to 1,814, except to premiere more Disney movies or host more play versions of its movies. In fact, on May 15, 1997, the theater opened with Menken and Rice's musical oratorio *King David.* On June 15 the company's newest animated movie, *Hercules,* together with a live stage show and full orchestra, was moved into the New Amsterdam. There is also a stage spectacular based on Disney's *The Lion King.* With all this activity going on, surely a live presentation of *Mary Poppins* cannot be far behind.

Running two and one-half hours, including intermission, or almost twice as long as the film version, the Broadway *Beauty and the Beast* features a 38-member cast and cost Disney anywhere from the official figure of $11.9 million to unofficial estimates that range between $16 and $19 million, making it Broadway's most expensive property ever. More lumbering that inspired, it was festooned with tons of scenery and flashy costumes even more extravagant than Busby Berkeley's in that dance director's free-wheeling Warner Bros. days. And incandescent indeed was the high-tech lighting, along with a blinding arsenal of special effects that included ravening wolf packs tearing across the stage. The musical garnered some favorable reviews, even though three critics working for the vitally important *New York Times* found little to commend. Vincent Canby trashed it, summing up his disenchantment by equating it with "vulgarity." To Janet Maslin, the production displayed "nothing ... to suggest the film's magical atmosphere." To David Richards, it is a production where, for the most part, "simplemindedness prevails, cheerfully and unapologetically."

Strong words, certainly, to apply to any Disney production, but apropos in several respects. Giving human legs to the characters to tread the Palace floorboards was unable to compensate for the film's flawless animation. Attempting to rival the movie in pyrotechnics, helped along by computer-driven set changes and magical illusions, its special effects far too often fall flat on the stage, a major failing that is highly inconducive to conjuring up fantasy. Menken and Rice's addition of seven new inferior songs to the movie's six, largely for padding purposes, contributed little to extending the lyricality of the film score. In short, the stage piece can lay claim only to reviving the long-interrupted presentation of a sumptuous children's musical extravaganza reminiscent of *Babes in Toyland* and *A Yankee Circus on Mars*, which thrilled young audiences at the turn of the century. What it was unable to do was improve the quality that distinguished the movie. Films simply do a better job of conducting audiences on fantasy trips. Better to leave to the movies what they do best.

The Loveless Prince. "Once upon a time in a faraway land, a young prince lived in a shining castle. Although he had everything his heart desired, the prince was spoiled, selfish, and unkind. But then, one winter's night, an old beggar woman came to the castle and offered him a single rose in return for shelter from the bitter cold...."

So begins the fable of *Beauty and the Beast* as introduced by the off-screen voice of David Ogden Stiers while viewers are transported through a typical Edenlike forest wonderland brimming with rich hues of green and gold over to the prince's castle. There it stands, isolated and imposing, rising from a platform of craggy rocks and replete with the spires and turrets that have decorated such majestic dwellings since some storyteller created the first of them eons ago.

The prince, however, sneers at the gift and turns the beggar away. Her response is to warn him not to be deceived by appearance, for beauty is to be found within, not in a glamorous exterior, no matter how attractive it might appear to the eyes. But the prince again dismisses her, unimpressed by her philosophical ranting. Then, as if to prove that the age of miracles hadn't passed, the once-horrific creature turns into a beautiful enchantress. Startled at the sight, the prince

tries but fails to make amends for his rudeness. Perceiving that there is no love in his heart, she punishes him by transforming him from a handsome youth into a monstrous beast with as hideous a face as the Disney animators ever concocted.

She also places a powerful evil spell on the prince's servants, who lose their human identities to become pieces of furniture, crockery, and nicknacks. His housekeeper, Mrs. Potts (marvelously vocalized by Angela Lansbury) and her son, Chip (Bradley Michael Pierce) are now a teapot and tea cup, while his chef, Lumiere (Jerry Ohrbach), and butler, Cogsworth (David Ogden Stiers), appear respectively as a lighted candle holder and a mantle clock.

Ashamed and possibly a little fearful himself of his looks, the prince secludes himself in the castle. Only a magic mirror, presented by the beggar turned enchantress, provides him with the means to observe the world beyond the castle walls. Also given to the prince was an enchanted rose, enclosed inside a glass container, that is destined to bloom only until his 21st birthday. If, by the time the last petal falls, he learns to love another person, and earns her love for him, both he and his household staff will be restored to their pre-spell normalcy. Should he fail at the task set before him, he will be doomed to remain a beast forever.

Convinced that no woman could ever love such a horrible creature as he, the prince sulks menacingly along the corridors like a hirsute Quasimodo, alternating between fits of snarling anger and self-pitying depression. Not until the scene switches to a small provincial French village are viewers treated to the appealing face of heroine Belle (Paige O'Hara), a young raven-haired charmer on her way to the library, and to the picture's first song, "Belle." She is bored with the village, she sings, to say nothing of the villagers and their pettiness, small talk, and narrow interests. Unsurprisingly, they dislike her in return.

For one thing, with her nose always stuck in a book, Belle is looked upon as "strange," "odd," and "too different" to ever fit in with village life. But, as she confides to the bookseller (Alvin Epstein), books are important to her as the only means of entering into a much larger and far more thrilling world that she can visualize only in dreams. A new kind of Disney leading lady, Belle is a pragmatic romantic, un-popular with almost everyone, daring for a small-town girl, and resolute in the defense of her idiosyncratic father. Above all, she is will-ing to withhold a marriage commitment till the right man appears on the scene.

That a likely lover has yet to attract her eye is made abundantly apparent when she is ac-costed by Gaston (Richard White), a good-looking, muscular village boy, who offends her with his rudeness and conceit. Unquestionably an expert appraiser of beauty, Gaston is con-vinced that destiny has ordained his marriage to Belle, the prize catch among all the village's marriageable females. Refusing to take her pre-vious no's for an answer to his graceless court-ing, he serenades her with heartfelt praises of his masculinity and gorgeousness. As usual, none of his vocal pats on the back impress Belle. She has heard them all before, and far too often.

Belle turns her back on him to return home. There we meet her father, Maurice (Rex Everhart), whom she consistently has to defend as a genius among the villagers, who regard him as a certified crackpot. A sort of elderly Dr. Frankenstein, with his laboratory crammed with a myriad of sputtering, gyrating contrap-tions, he is putting the finishing touches on his newest invention, a mechanical log chopper. Certain that it will win the top award at a fair, he mounts the Rube Goldberg device on a wagon and prepares to make the trip, not in company with his eager daughter, but with his trusty horse.

On the way to the fair, however, master and horse meet terror in the form of a scarify-ing attack by a swarm of bats. The frightened horse runs away from the woods, leaving Mau-rice and his chopping machine alone on the snowy ground. His struggle to escape further danger proves to be futile when a pack of hun-gry wolves appears and chases him to the very gates of the prince's castle. Seeking safety, he sneaks inside, where he is welcomed by the hos-pitable Lumiere, who invites him to sit in the prince's comfortable armchair and warm him-self by the fire. As far as the Beast (Bobby Ben-son) is concerned, the old fellow is decidedly unwelcome. Spotting him in his chair, the monster flies into a rage and imprisons Mau-rice in a tower cell.

Meanwhile, die-hard optimist Gaston is paying another visit to Belle, so certain that his numerous physical assets will convert her into his wife and mother of the "six or seven sons" he wants that he has brought along a preacher, band, and village well-wishers to celebrate the wedding. But Belle crushes him once again, this time quite diplomatically by informing the swain that she really doesn't deserve to marry such a wonderful man—and then privately swearing never to do so in a reprise of "Belle" once he has left her sight.

When the horse returns to the house with-out her father and the machine, the animal re-sponds to her fears for his safety by carrying Belle on his back to the castle, which she en-ters with extreme trepidation and just a hint of delight. She had always hoped to meet a Prince Charming, and this seems to be the perfect site to find one. The sole observers to her entry are Lumiere, Cogsworth, and Mrs. Potts, who are overjoyed at the sight of a beautiful young woman roaming about the castle.

Perhaps, they happily suggest, she will be the agent for ending the spell that for the past 10 years has made the prince's and their own lives miserable. Henceforth, it will be their chief occupation to do all they can to have the Beast fall in love with her, and her with him. The Beast, too, will soon come to the realiza-tion that the lovely young lady could very well be the means of lifting the curse on him. What he will not know until much later is that in his calculated attempt to win her love by profess-ing his own for her, he will be speaking the truth.

Walking cautiously from room to room, Belle finally reaches her father's cell and en-courages him to flee with her back to their house. The Beast, however, disrupts their es-cape by blocking the exit. Nonetheless, mel-lowed by the sight of sweet Belle, he offers to release her father, provided that she vow to re-main forever with him in the castle. Despite her father's objections and her fear of the Beast, Belle agrees.

Maurice is released and the Beast escorts the girl to her room. No harm will come to her, he says, warning, however, that she must never enter the west wing of the castle. Al-though his tone is firm, his politeness toward her indicates that already his regard for his lovely and demure guest is changing from anger at her intrusion to compassion for the emotional distress he himself has inflicted on her. He even invites her to dine with him that evening in the huge banquet hall.

Back in the little village, Gaston and his comic sidekick, LeFou (Jesse Corti), are spending the time gulping down generous quaffs of mead in the local tavern. Finding an appreciative audience in the assembly of other tavern regulars, the happy hunk decides it is time to join LeFou in again praising his countless physical attributes, which they do in the clever and catchy production waltz, "Gaston." He is, LeFou attests, everybody's favorite guy, much admired and without parallel as a man among men who, as Gaston boasts, eats five dozen eggs every day for breakfast. Undoubtedly, in time he will triumph over Belle's refusal to wed him, the friends agree.

Suddenly, into the tavern bursts Maurice, eager to recruit volunteers to rescue Belle from the castle. None of them believes the old man's story about the horrible beast that has incarcerated her, preferring to ridicule it as another example of the endless tall tales fabricated in his demented mind. Not Gaston, however. A dedicated believer, he vows to get her out of the castle. Surely, he tells LeFou, the girl will marry him if only as repayment of his gallantry.

Meanwhile, in spite of his pledge to his three romantic advisers, Lumiere, Cogsworth, and Mrs. Potts, to control his temper when in Belle's presence, the Beast again explodes in anger when informed that she will not join him at dinner. His inference that Belle most likely detests him is validated when, via the magic mirror, he listens as Belle declares that she wants nothing to do with him, now or ever. He glances at the rose, which is continuing to shed its petals, a signal that time is running out on his hope of attracting a lover. But, then, how could a maiden as beautiful as she love a monster like him?

A Festive Occasion. A little later, hungry Belle creeps out of her room to join her candle holder, clock, and teapot friends in the kitchen. "Be Our Guest," they and a chorus of dishes, silverware, and glasses sing to her in a dazzling display of animated artistry.

After feasting on the culinary delights whipped up by gourmet chef Lumiere, Belle follows him and her other two friends on a tour of the castle. When they approach the west wing, a spur-of-the-moment whim leads Belle into thinking that now is her chance to see what it is the Beast is concealing there. Not knowing what horrors await her, she tiptoes up the stairs and into a dank and dusty room. But all she sees is a portrait of a young man whom she fails to recognize as the prince of long ago. Unlike Oscar Wilde's picture of Dorian Gray, also concealed from public view, which bore the brunt of that aristocrat's dissolute life while his face remained young and serene, the prince's portrait reveals the face of a very handsome young man. It is the prince himself who has undergone the terrifying transformation from human being to beast.

Transfixed by the portrait, she is routed from further contemplation by the Beast himself, who storms into the room and demands that she leave it. Gripped with fear, she rushes down the stairs and out the front door, jumps on her faithful horse, and rides into the woods. The wolf pack reappears, indicating eagerness to make a succulent meal of her with toothy snarls and clawing the air in anticipation. Luckily, their murderous intent is interrupted by the Beast, who resolves the conflict by defeating the animals in the most violent scene ever projected by the Disney organization. He himself is badly hurt in the combat, prompting grateful Belle to nurse the wounds of her savior. She is becoming more and more attracted to him, but wonders why. Could the real reason involve the sometimes mysterious workings of the human heart?

Back in the village Gaston is busily devising two plans to win Belle's love. First, in Plan A, he will threaten to send her father to an insane asylum unless she marries him. Since the entire village looks upon the old man as a "bit loony," and since Gaston has already bribed the asylum superintendent to lock Maurice up, Gaston has high hopes for success. Yet, should things go awry, there is always Plan B, under which he will summon up the courage to spirit her out of her castle prison. Dangerous, yes, but foolproof as well, certain to light the spark of love he wants so desperately to see in her eyes.

Moved by Belle's kindness on the battlefield, the Beast easily ingratiates himself with her by presenting his mammoth library to her as a gift and joining her in such pleasantries as feeding the birds. He also looks much better than before, thanks to the grooming services that Lumiere, Cosgworth, and Mrs. Potts have performed on him. They have even refined his table manners in anticipation that he will issue a second request for her to dine with him. He wants to confess his love but dreads what he feels will be her outright rejection. What he does not know is that she is already enamored of him, as she discloses in the song "Something There." Somehow, she sings, he does seem to have changed for the better, having dispensed with his former coarseness in favor of a gentility she had never detected.

That evening, they meet in the castle ballroom, Belle clad in a sparking green evening dress and the Beast looking—and acting—every inch the gentleman, where they dance to the lyrical Academy Award-winning theme song, "Beauty and the Beast." Observing them is Mrs. Potts, who sings the lyric off-screen as a testament to the uniting of two kindred spirits, so different in so many ways, yet able to turn what each had assumed was only close friendship into love.

Even though she has admitted she is happiest when in the Beast's presence, Belle still wants to help her father, who, the magic mirror has informed her, is struggling through the woods toward the castle to rescue her. Reluctantly, the Beast releases her so that she can go back to parent and home. Later, when asked by Cogsworth why he had done so, the Beast replies simply that "I love her." Jubilation arises in the hearts of Cogsworth, Lumiere, and even Mrs. Potts at hearing his explanation, although the level-headed teapot is quick to note that the lifting of the evil spell is not yet assured. True, she says, the prince has learned to love, but what about the other half of the bargain. Has Belle learned to love him in return?

Belle finds Maurice, who has passed out on the snow, and accompanies him back to their house. But trouble follows them through the front door. Egged on by the hoots and hollers of village neighbors, the superintendent arrives to take Maurice to the asylum. Gaston's offer to intercede to prevent her father's confinement is rejected out of hand by Belle, who is not exactly thrilled by the price she must pay for his freedom. So much for Plan A.

Growing more and more certain that Belle is in love with the Beast, jealous Gaston segues into backup Plan B and intensifies his demand that the villagers join him in attacking the monster in his lair by leading them in the rousing battle anthem, "The Mob Song." In it he attempts to gather a posse together by reciting some of the horrors the Beast will inflict on the villagers, like scooping up their children and carrying them off, unless they take steps to end his reign of terror.

Now united in the determination to rid their little world of the Beast, the villagers march behind Gaston up to the castle, batter down the main door, and rush about in search of their prey. The Beast, however, is not interested in either retaliation or capitulation. Nothing matters to him any more, he tells Chip, underscoring his despondency over Belle's seeming reluctance to reside with him in the castle. Hoping to compensate for the lack of leadership in opposing the invaders, pieces of crockery and furniture, including a dextrous Wardrobe Cabinet (Jo Anne Worley), combine forces to defeat them, with the lone exception of Gaston.

Spotting the Beast on a precipice, he confronts him bravely, preparing for the kill. But when the Beast happens to catch sight of Belle, who has returned to the castle, and of her anxious eyes while despairing of his safety, he suddenly becomes infused with the will to live. He parries Gaston's blows with a devastating counter attack that forces the young man to lose his grip and fall to his death. Yet, Gaston can claim at least partial victory. In their hand-to-hand combat, he had stabbed the Beast in the back. With tearful Belle at his side, the Beast dies, but not before hearing her say, "I love you," just as the last petal drops from the completely wilted rose.

The Beast's death consists of peeling off his horrid exterior, which is replaced by the figure of the graceful prince, mature and even more attractive than he was before the old beggar woman's visit. He has learned his lesson well, realizing now that the mighty redemptive value of loving another is vital to finding true happiness, which can be achieved only through admitting another human being into a heart where once upon a time self-centeredness prevailed.

Will their life together be happy? All romantic fairy tales promise such an ending, and so does *Beauty and the Beast*. Wasn't it Mrs. Potts who only minutes earlier had assured worried Chip that everything would work out just fine? She should know. She has only now been returned from a land of enchantment to become her former human self, along with her son, Lumiere and Cogsworth. Downstairs, Belle and the prince are again dancing to the strains of "Beauty and the Beast." And yes, they *are* happy—now and forevermore.

Appendix

Academy Award Nominations and Winners

Best Director

(WINNING DIRECTORS ARE DESIGNATED BY AN ASTERISK)

Harry Beaumont, *The Broadway Melody*, 1929
*George Cukor, *My Fair Lady*, 1964
Michael Curtiz, *Yankee Doodle Dandy*, 1942
*Bob Fosse, *Cabaret*, 1972; *All That Jazz*, 1979
Norman Jewison, *Fiddler on the Roof*, 1971
Walter Lang, *The King and I*, 1956
Robert Z. Leonard, *The Great Ziegfeld*, 1936
Ernst Lubitsch, *The Love Parade*, 1929
*Leo McCarey, *Going My Way*, 1944
*Vincente Minnelli, *Gigi*, 1958
*Carol Reed, *Oliver!*, 1968
*Jerome Robbins, *West Side Story*, 1961 (with Robert Wise)
Victor Schertzinger, *One Night of Love*, 1934
Robert Stevenson, *Mary Poppins*, 1964
King Vidor, *Hallelujah*, 1929
*Robert Wise, *West Side Story*, 1961 (with Jerome Robbins)
The Sound of Music, 1965

Best Picture

(WINNING FILMS ARE DESIGNATED BY AN ASTERISK; MUSICALS APPEAR IN BOLDFACE TYPE)

1927-28

The Last Command; The Racket; Seventh Heaven; The Way of All Flesh; *Wings

1928-29

Alibi; ***The Broadway Melody; The Hollywood Revue;** In Old Arizona; The Patriot

1929-30

*All Quiet on the Western Front; The Big House; Disraeli; The Divorcée; **The Love Parade**

1930-31

*Cimarron; East Lynne; The Front Page; Skippy Trader Horn

1931-32

Arrowsmith; Bad Girl; The Champ; Five Star Final; *Grand Hotel; **One Hour with You;** Shanghai Express; **The Smiling Lieutenant**

1932-33

*Cavalcade; A Farewell to Arms; **Forty-Second Street;** I Am a Fugitive from a Chain Gang; Lady for a Day; Little Women; The Private Life of Henry VIII; **She Done Him Wrong;** Smilin' Thru; State Fair

1934

The Barretts of Wimpole Street; Cleopatra; **Flirtation Walk; The Gay Divorcee;** Here Comes the Navy; The House of Rothschild; Imitation of Life; *It Happened One Night; **One Night of Love;** The Thin Man; Viva Villa; The White Parade

1935

Alice Adams; **The Broadway Melody of 1936;** Captain Blood; David Copperfield; The Informer; Les Miserables; The Lives of a Bengal Lancer; A Midsummer Night's Dream; *Mutiny on the Bounty; **Naughty Marietta;** Ruggles of Red Gap; **Top Hat**

1936

Anthony Adverse; Dodsworth; *The Great Ziegfeld; Libeled Lady; Mr. Deeds Goes to Town; Romeo and Juliet; San Francisco; The Story of Louis Pasteur; A Tale of Two Cities; **Three Smart Girls**

1937

The Awful Truth; Captains Courageous; Dead End; The Good Earth; In Old Chicago; *The Life of Emile Zola; Lost Horizon; **One Hundred Men and a Girl;** Stage Door; A Star Is Born

1938

The Adventures of Robin Hood; **Alexander's Ragtime Band;** Boys Town; The Citadel; Four Daughters; Grand Illusion; Jezebel; Pygmalion; Test Pilot; *You Can't Take It with You

1939

Dark Victory; *Gone with the Wind; Goodbye, Mr. Chips; Love Affair; Mr. Smith Goes to Washington; Ninotchka; Of Mice and Men; Stagecoach; **The Wizard of Oz;** Wuthering Heights

1940

All This and Heaven Too; Foreign Correspondent; The Grapes of Wrath; The Great Dictator Kitty Foyle; The Letter; The Long Voyage Home; Our Town; The Philadelphia Story; *Rebecca

1941

Blossoms in the Dust; Citizen Kane; Here Comes Mr. Jordan; Hold Back the Dawn; *How Green Was My Valley; The Little Foxes; The Maltese Falcon; One Foot in Heaven; Sergeant York; Suspicion

1942

The Invaders; Kings Row; The Magnificent Ambersons; *Mrs. Miniver; The Pied Piper; The Pride of the Yankees; Random Harvest; The Talk of the Town; Wake Island; **Yankee Doodle Dandy**

1943

*Casablanca; For Whom the Bell Tolls; Heaven Can Wait; The Human Comedy; In Which We Serve; Madame Curie; The More the Merrier; The Ox-Bow Incident; The Song of Bernadette Watch on the Rhine

1944

Double Indemnity; Gaslight; ***Going My Way;** Since You Went Away; Wilson

1945

Anchors Aweigh; The Bells of St. Mary's; *The Lost Weekend; Mildred Pierce; Spellbound

1946

*The Best Years of Our Lives; Henry V; It's a Wonderful Life; The Razor's Edge; The Yearling

1947

The Bishop's Wife; Crossfire; *Gentleman's Agreement; Great Expectations; Miracle on 34th Street

1948

*Hamlet; Johnny Belinda; The Red Shoes; The Snake Pit; The Treasure of the Sierra Madre

1949

*All the King's Men; Battleground; The Heiress A Letter to Three Wives; Twelve O'Clock High

1950

*All About Eve; Born Yesterday; Father of the Bride; King Solomon's Mines; Sunset Boulevard

1951

***An American in Paris;** Decision Before Dawn; A Place in the Sun; Quo Vadis; A Streetcar Named Desire

1952

*The Greatest Show on Earth; High Noon; Ivanhoe; Moulin Rouge; The Quiet Man

1953

*From Here to Eternity; Julius Caesar; The Robe; Roman Holiday; Shane

1954

The Caine Mutiny; The Country Girl; *On the Waterfront; **Seven Brides for Seven Brothers;** Three Coins in the Fountain

1955

Love Is a Many-Splendored Thing; *Marty; Mister Roberts; Picnic; The Rose Tattoo

1956

*Around the World in 80 Days; Friendly Persuasion; Giant; **The King and I;** The Ten Commandments

1957

*The Bridge on the River Kwai; Peyton Place; Sayonara; 12 Angry Men; Witness for the Prosecution

1958

Auntie Mame; Cat on a Hot Tin Roof; The Defiant Ones; ***Gigi;** Separate Tables

1959

Anatomy of a Murder; *Ben-Hur; The Diary of Anne Frank; The Nun's Story; Room at the Top

1960

The Alamo; *The Apartment; Elmer Gantry; Sons and Lovers; The Sundowners

1961

Fanny; The Guns of Navarone; The Hustler; Judgment at Nuremberg; ***West Side Story**

1962

*Lawrence of Arabia; The Longest Day; **The Music Man;** Mutiny on the Bounty; To Kill a Mockingbird

1963

America, America; Cleopatra; How the West Was Won; Lilies of the Field; *Tom Jones

1964

Becket; Dr. Strangelove or: How I Learned to Stop

Worrying and Love the Bomb; **Mary Poppins;** *My **Fair Lady;** Zorba the Greek

1965

Darling; Doctor Zhivago; Ship of Fools; *The **Sound of Music;** A Thousand Clowns

1966

Alfie; *A Man for All Seasons; The Russians Are Coming, The Russians Are Coming; The Sand Pebbles; Who's Afraid of Virginia Woolf?

1967

Bonnie and Clyde; **Doctor Doolittle;** The Graduate; Guess Who's Coming to Dinner; *In the Heat of the Night

1968

Romeo & Juliet; **Funny Girl;** The Lion in Winter; *Oliver!; Rachel, Rachel

1969

Anne of the Thousand Days; Butch Cassidy and the Sundance Kid; **Hello, Dolly!;** *Midnight Cowboy; Z

1970

Airport; Five Easy Pieces; Love Story; M*A*S*H; *Patton

1971

A Clockwork Orange; **Fiddler on the Roof;** *The French Connection; The Last Picture Show; Nicholas and Alexandra

1972

Cabaret; Deliverance; The Emigrants; *The Godfather; Sounder

1973

American Graffiti; Cries and Whispers; The Exorcist; *The Sting; A Touch of Class

1974

Chinatown; The Conversation; *The Godfather, Part II; Lenny; The Towering Inferno

1975

Barry Lyndon; Dog Day Afternoon; Jaws; Nashville; *One Flew Over the Cuckoo's Nest

1976

All the President's Men; Bound for Glory; Network; *Rocky; Taxi Driver

1977

*Annie Hall; The Goodbye Girl; Julia; Star Wars; The Turning Point

1978

Coming Home; *The Deer Hunter; Heaven Can Wait; Midnight Express; An Unmarried Woman

1979

All That Jazz; Apocalypse Now; Breaking Away; *Kramer vs. Kramer; Norma Rae

1980

Coal Miner's Daughter; The Elephant Man; *Ordinary People; Raging Bull; Tess

1981

Atlantic City; *Chariots of Fire; On Golden Pond; Raiders of the Lost Ark; Reds

1982

E.T. The Extra-Terrestrial; *Gandhi; Missing; Tootsie; The Verdict

1983

The Big Chill; The Dresser; The Right Stuff; Tender Mercies; *Terms of Endearment

1984

*Amadeus; The Killing Fields; A Passage to India; Places in the Heart; A Soldier's Story

1985

The Color Purple; Kiss of the Spider Woman; *Out of Africa; Prizzi's Honor; Witness

1986

Children of a Lesser God; Hannah and Her Sisters; The Mission; *Platoon; A Room with a View

1987

Broadcast News; Fatal Attraction; Hope and Glory; *The Last Emperor; Moonstruck

1988

The Accidental Tourist; Dangerous Liaisons; Mississippi Burning; *Rain Man; Working Girl

1989

Born on the Fourth of July; Dead Poets Society; *Driving Miss Daisy; Field of Dreams; My Left Foot

1990

Awakenings; *Dances with Wolves; Ghost; The Godfather, Part III; Good Fellas

1991

Beauty and the Beast; Bugsy; JFK; The Prince of Tides; *The Silence of the Lambs

1992

The Crying Game; A Few Good Men; Howards End; Scent of a Woman; *Unforgiven

1993

*Forrest Gump; Four Weddings and a Funeral; Pulp Fiction; Quiz Show; Shawshank Redemption

1994

The Fugitive; In the Name of the Father; The Piano; The Remains of the Day; *Schindler's List

1995

Apollo 13; Babe; *Braveheart; The Postman (Il Postino); Sense and Sensibility

1996

*The English Patient; Fargo; Jerry Maguire; Secrets and Lies; Shine

1997

As Good As It Gets; The Full Monty; Good Will Hunting; L.A. Confidential; *Titanic

1998

Elizabeth; Life Is Beautiful; Saving Private Ryan; *Shakespeare in Love; The Thin Red Line

1999

*American Beauty; The Cider House Rules; The Green Mile; The Insider; The Sixth Sense

2000

Chocolat; Crouching Tiger, Hidden Dragon; Erin Brockovich; *Gladiator; Traffic

Best Song

(WINNING SONGS ARE DESIGNATED BY
AN ASTERISK; MUSICAL FILMS
APPEAR IN BOLDFACE TYPE)

1934

Carioca (L: Edward Eliscu and Gus Kahn; M: Vincent Youmans), from **Flying Down to Rio**
*The Continental (L: Herb Magidson; M: Con Conrad), from **The Gay Divorcee**
Love in Bloom (L: Leo Robin; M: Ralph Rainger), from **She Loves Me Not**

1935

Cheek to Cheek (L&M: Irving Berlin), from **Top Hat**
Lovely to Look At (L: Dorothy Fields and James McHugh; M: Jerome Kern), from **Roberta**
*Lullaby of Broadway (L: Al Dubin; M: Harry Warren), from **Gold Diggers of 1935**

1936

Did I Remember (L: Harold Adamson; M: Walter Donaldson), from *Suzy*

I've Got You Under My Skin (L&M: Cole Porter), from **Born to Dance**
A Melody from the Sky (L: Sidney D. Mitchell; M: Louis Alter), from *Trail of the Lonesome Pine*
Pennies from Heaven (L: Johnny Burke; M: Arthur Johnston), from **Pennies from Heaven**
*The Way You Look Tonight (L: Dorothy Fields; M: Jerome Kern), from **Swing Time**
When Did You Leave Heaven (L: Walter Bullock; M: Richard A. Whiting), from **Sing, Baby, Sing**

1937

Remember Me (L: Al Dubin; M: Harry Warren), from **Mr. Dodd Takes the Air**
*Sweet Leilani (L&M: Harry Owens), from **Waikiki Wedding**
That Old Feeling (L: Lew Brown; M: Sammy Fain), from **Vogues of 1938**
They Can't Take That Away from Me (L: Ira Gershwin; M: George Gershwin), from **Shall We Dance**
Whispers in the Dark (L: Leo Robin; M: Frederick Hollander), from **Artists and Models**

1938

Always and Always (L: Chet Forrest and Bob Wright; M: Edward Ward), from *Mannequin* (Note: In a rare departure from traditional Academy Award practice, "Always and Always" [minus the lyric] had already been used as the background theme for MGM's *Double Wedding* in 1937.)
Change Partners (L&M: Irving Berlin), from **Carefree**
Cowboy and the Lady (L: Arthur Quenzer; M: Lionel Newman), from *Cowboy and the Lady*
Dust (M&L: Johnny Marvin), from *Under Western Stars*
Jeepers Creepers (L: Johnny Mercer; M: Harry Warren), from **Going Places**
Merrily We Live (L: Arthur Quenzer; M: Phil Craig), from *Merrily We Live*
A Mist Over the Moon (L: Oscar Hammerstein II; M: Ben Oakland), from *The Lady Objects*
My Own (L: Harold Adamson; M: James McHugh), from **That Certain Age**
Now It Can Be Told (L&M: Irving Berlin), from **Alexander's Ragtime Band**
*Thanks for the Memory (L: Leo Robin; Ralph Rainger), from **Big Broadcast of 1938**

1939

Faithful Forever (L: Leo Robin; M: Ralph Rainger), from **Gulliver's Travels**
I Poured My Heart Into a Song (L&M: Irving Berlin), from **Second Fiddle**
*Over the Rainbow (L: E.Y. Harburg; M: Harold Arlen), from **The Wizard of Oz**
Wishing (L&M: Buddy DeSylva), from *Love Affair*

1940

Down Argentina Way (L: Mack Gordon; M: Harry Warren), from **Down Argentine Way**

I'd Know You Anywhere (L: Johnny Mercer; M: James McHugh), from **You'll Find Out**

It's a Blue World (L&M: Chet Forrest and Bob Wright), from **Music in My Heart**

Love of My Life (L: Johnny Mercer; M: Artie Shaw), from **Second Chorus**

Only Forever (L: Johnny Burke; M: James V. Monaco), from **Rhythm on the River**

Our Love Affair (L&M: Roger Edens and Arthur Freed), from **Strike Up the Band**

Waltzing in the Clouds (L: Gus Kahn; M: Robert Stolz), from **Spring Parade**

*When You Wish Upon a Star (L: Ned Washington; M: Leigh Harline), from **Pinocchio**

Who Am I? (L: Walter Bullock; M: Jule Styne), from **Hit Parade of 1941**

1941

Baby Mine (L: Ned Washington; M: Frank Churchill), from **Dumbo**

Be Honest with Me (L&M: Gene Autry and Fred Rose), from *Ridin' on a Rainbow*

Blues in the Night (L: Johnny Mercer; M: Harold Arlen), from **Blues in the Night**

Boogie Woogie Bugle Boy (of Company B) (L: Don Raye; M: Hugh Prince), from **Buck Privates**

Chattanooga Choo Choo (L: Mack Gordon; M: Harry Warren), from **Sun Valley Serenade**

Dolores (L: Frank Loesser; M: Louis Alter) from **Las Vegas Nights**

*The Last Time I Saw Paris (L: Oscar Hammerstein II: M: Jerome Kern), from **Lady Be Good**

Out of the Silence (L&M: Lloyd B. Norlind), from *All American Co-Ed*

Since I Kissed My Baby Goodbye (L&M: Cole Porter), from **You'll Never Get Rich**

1942

Always in My Heart (L: Kim Gannon; M: Ernesto Lecuona), from *Always in My Heart*

Dearly Beloved (L: Johnny Mercer; M: Jerome Kern), from **You Were Never Lovelier**

How About You? (L: Ralph Freed; M: Burton Lane), from **Babes on Broadway**

I've Got a Gal in Kalamazoo (L: Mack Gordon; M: Harry Warren), from **Orchestra Wives**

I've Heard That Song Before (L: Sammy Cahn; M: Jule Styne), from **Youth on Parade**

Love Is a Song (L: Larry Morey; M: Frank Churchill), from **Bambi**

Pennies for Peppino (L: Chet Forrest and Bob Wright; M: Edward Ward), from **Flying with Music**

Pig Foot Pete (L: Don Raye; M: Gene dePaul), from **Hellzapoppin'**

There's a Breeze on Lake Louise (L: Mort Greene; M: Harry Revel), from **The Mayor of 44th Street**

*White Christmas (L&M: Irving Berlin), from **Holiday Inn**

1943

Change of Heart (L: Harold Adamson; M: Jule Styne), from **Hit Parade of 1943**

Happiness Is Jes a Thing Called Joe (L: E.Y. Harburg; M: Harold Arlen), from **Cabin in the Sky**

My Shining Hour (L: Johnny Mercer; M: Harold Arlen), from **The Sky's the Limit**

Saludos Amigos (L: Ned Washington; M: Charles Wolcott), from **Saludos Amigos**

Say a Pray'r for the Boys Over There (L: Herb Magidson; M: James McHugh), from *Hers to Hold*

That Old Black Magic (L: Johnny Mercer; M: Harold Arlen), from **Star Spangled Rhythm**

They're Either Too Young or Too Old (L: Frank Loesser; M: Arthur Schwartz), from **Thank Your Lucky Stars**

We Mustn't Say Goodbye (L: Al Dubin; M: James V. Monaco), from **Stage Door Canteen**

You'd Be So Nice to Come Home To (L&M: Cole Porter), from **Something to Shout About**

*You'll Never Know (L: Mack Gordon; M: Harry Warren), from **Hello Frisco, Hello**

1944

I Couldn't Sleep a Wink Last Night (L: Harold Adamson; M: James McHugh), from **Higher and Higher**

I'll Walk Alone (L: Sammy Cahn; M: Jule Styne), from **Follow the Boys**

I'm Making Believe (L: Mack Gordon; M: James V. Monaco), from **Sweet and Low Down**

Long Ago (and Far Away) (L: Ira Gershwin; M: Jerome Kern), from **Cover Girl**

Now I Know (L: Ted Koehler; M: Harold Arlen), from **Up in Arms**

Remember Me to Carolina (L: Paul Francis Webster; M: Harry Revel), from **Minstrel Man**

Rio de Janeiro (L: Ned Washington; M: Ary Barroso), from **Brazil**

Silver Shadows and Golden Dreams (L: Charles Newman; M: Lew Pollack) from **Lady Let's Dance**

Sweet Dreams, Sweetheart (L: Ted Koehler; M: M.K. Jerome), from **Hollywood Canteen**

*Swinging on a Star (L: Johnny Burke; M: James Van Heusen), from **Going My Way**

Too Much in Love (L: Kim Gannon; M: Walter Kent), from **Song of the Open Road**

The Trolley Song (L&M: Ralph Blane and Hugh Martin), from **Meet Me in St. Louis**

1945

Ac-Cen-Tchu-Ate the Positive (L: Johnny Mercer; M: Harold Arlen), from **Here Come the Waves**

Anywhere (L: Sammy Cahn; M: Jule Styne), from **Tonight and Every Night**

Aren't You Glad You're You? (L: Johnny Burke; M: James Van Heusen), from *The Bells of St. Mary's*

The Cat and the Canary (L: Ray Evans; M: Jay Livingston), from **Why Girls Leave Home**

Endlessly (L; Kim Gannon; M: Walter Kent), from **Earl Carroll Vanities**

I Fall in Love Too Easily (L: Sammy Cahn; M: Jule Styne), from **Anchors Aweigh**

I'll Buy That Dream (L: Herb Magidson; M: Allie Wrubel), from **Sing Your Way Home**

*It Might as Well Be Spring (L: Oscar Hammerstein II; M: Richard Rodgers), from **State Fair**

Linda (L&M: Ann Ronell), from *The Story of G.I. Joe*

Love Letters (L: Edward Heyman; M: Victor Young), from *Love Letters*

More and More (L: E.Y. Harburg; M: Jerome Kern), from **Can't Help Singing**

Sleighride in July (L: Johnny Burke; M: James Van Heusen), from **Belle of the Yukon**

So-o-o-o-o in Love (L: Leo Robin; M: David Rose), from **Wonder Man**

Some Sunday Morning (L: Ted Koehler; M: Ray Heindorf and M.K. Jerome), from *San Antonio*

1946

All Through the Day (L: Oscar Hammerstein II; M: Jerome Kern), from **Centennial Summer**

I Can't Begin to Tell You (L: Mack Gordon; M: James V. Monaco), from **The Dolly Sisters**

Ole Buttermilk Sky (L: Jack Brooks; M: Hoagy Carmichael), from *Canyon Passage*

*On the Atchison, Topeka and Santa Fe (L: Johnny Mercer; M: Harry Warren), from **The Harvey Girls**

You Keep Coming Back Like a Song (L&M: Irving Berlin), from **Blue Skies**

1947

A Gal in Calico (L: Leo Robin; M: Arthur Schwartz), from **The Time, Place and the Girl**

I Wish I Didn't Love You So (L&M: Frank Loesser), from *The Perils of Pauline*

Pass That Peace Pipe (L&M: Ralph Blane, Hugh Martin, and Roger Edens), from **Good News**

You Do (L: Mack Gordon; M: Josef Myrow), from **Mother Wore Tights**

*Zip-a-Dee-Doo-Dah (L: Ray Gilbert; M: Allie Wrubel), from **Song of the South**

1948

*Buttons and Bows (L&M: Ray Evans and Jay Livingston), from The Paleface

For Every Man There's a Woman (L: Leo Robin; M: Harold Arlen), from **Casbah**

It's Magic (L: Sammy Cahn; M: Jule Styne), from **Romance on the High Seas**

This Is the Moment (L: Leo Robin; M: Frederick Hollander), from **That Lady in Ermine**

The Woody Woodpecker Song (L&M: Ramey Idriss and George Tibbles), from *Wet Blanket Policy*

1949

*Baby, It's Cold Outside (L&M: Frank Loesser), from **Neptune's Daughter**

It's a Great Feeling (L: Sammy Cahn; M: Jule Styne), from **It's a Great Feeling**

Lavender Blue (L: Larry Morey; M: Eliot Daniel), from *So Dear to My Heart*

My Foolish Heart (L: Ned Washington; M: Victor Young), from *My Foolish Heart*

Through a Long and Sleepless Night (L: Mack Gordon; M: Alfred Newman), from *Come to the Stable*

1950

Be My Love (L: Sammy Cahn; M: Nicholas Brodszky), from **The Toast of New Orleans**

Bibbidy-Bobbidi-Boo (L&M: Mack David, Al Hoffman, and Jerry Livingston), from **Cinderella**

*Mona Lisa (L&M: Ray Evans and Jay Livingston), from *Captain Carey, USA*

Mule Train (L&M: Fred Glickman, Hy Heath, and Johnny Lange), from *Singing Guns*

Wilhelmina (L: Mack Gordon; M: Josef Myrow), from **Wabash Avenue**

1951

*In the Cool, Cool, Cool of the Evening (L: Johnny Mercer; M: Hoagy Carmichael), from **Here Comes the Groom**

A Kiss to Build a Dream On (L&M: Bert Kalmar, Harry Ruby, and Oscar Hammerstein II), from *The Strip*

Never (L: Eliot Daniel; M: Lionel Newman), from **Golden Girl**

Too Late Now (L: Alan Jay Lerner; M: Burton Lane), from **Royal Wedding**

Wonder Why (L: Sammy Cahn; M: Nicholas Brodszky), from **Rich, Young and Pretty**

1952

Am I in Love (L&M: Jack Brooks); from *Son of Paleface*

Because You're Mine (L: Sammy Cahn; M: Nicholas Brodszky), from **Because You're Mine**

*High Noon (Do Not Forsake Me, Oh My Darlin') (L: Ned Washington; M: Dimitri Tiomkin), from *High Noon*

Thumbelina (L&M: Frank Loesser), from **Hans Christian Andersen**

Zing a Little Zong (L: Leo Robin; M: Harry Warren), from **Just for You**

1953

The Moon Is Blue (L: Sylvia Fine; M: Herschel Burke Gilbert), from *The Moon Is Blue*

My Flaming Heart (L: Leo Robin; M: Nicholas Brodszky), from **Small Town Girl**

Sadie Thompson's Song (Blue Pacific Blues) (L: Ned Washington; M: Lester Lee), from *Miss Sadie Thompson*

*Secret Love (L: Paul Francis Webster; M: Sammy Fain), from **Calamity Jane**

That's Amore (L: Jack Brooks; M: Harry Warren), from **The Caddy**

1954

Count Your Blessings Instead of Sheep (L&M): Irving Berlin), from **White Christmas**

The High and the Mighty (L: Ned Washington; M: Dimitri Tiomkin), from *The High and the Mighty*

Hold My Hand (L&M: Jack Lawrence and Richard Myers), from *Susan Slept Here*

The Man That Got Away (L: Ira Gershwin; M: Harold Arlen), from **A Star Is Born**

*Three Coins in the Fountain (L: Sammy Cahn; M: Jule Styne), from *Three Coins in the Fountain*

1955

I'll Never Stop Loving You (L: Sammy Cahn; M: Nichola Brodszky), from **Love Me or Leave Me**

*Love Is a Many-Splendored Thing (L: Paul Francis Webster; M: Sammy Fain), from *Love Is a Many-Splendored Thing*

(Love Is) The Tender Trap L: Sammy Cahn; M: James Van Heusen), from *The Tender Trap*

Something's Gotta Give (L&M: Johnny Mercer), from **Daddy Long Legs**

Unchained Melody (L: Hy Zaret; M: Alex North), from *Unchained*

1956

Friendly Persuasion (Thee I Love) (L: Paul Francis Webster; M: Dimitri Tiomkin), from *Friendly Persuasion*

Julie (L: Tom Adair; M: Leith Stevens), from *Julie*

True Love (L&M: Cole Porter), from **High Society**

*Whatever Will Be, Will Be (Que Sera, Sera) (L&M: Jay Livingston and Ray Evans), from *The Man Who Knew Too Much*

Written on the Wind (L: Sammy Cahn; M: Victor Young), from *Written on the Wind*

1957

An Affair to Remember (L: Harold Adamson; M: Harry Warren), from **An Affair to Remember**

*All the Way (L: Sammy Cahn; M: James Van Heusen), from *The Joker Is Wild*

April Love (L: Paul Francis Webster; M: Sammy Fain), from *April Love*

Tammy (L&M: Ray Evans and Jay Livingston), from *Tammy and the Bachelor*

Wild Is the Wind (L: Ned Washington; M: Dimitri Tiomkin), from *Wild Is the Wind*

1958

Almost in Your Arms (L&M: Jay Livingston and Ray Evans), from *Houseboat*

A Certain Smile (L: Paul Francis Webster; M: Sammy Fain), from *A Certain Smile*

*Gigi (L: Alan Jay Lerner; M: Frederick Loewe), from **Gigi**

To Love and Be Loved (L: Sammy Cahn; M: James Van Heusen), from *Some Came Running*

A Very Precious Love (L: Paul Francis Webster; M: Sammy Fain), from *Marjorie Morningstar*

1959

The Best of Everything (L: Sammy Cahn; M: Alfred Newman), from *The Best of Everything*

The Five Pennies (L&M: Sylvia Fine), from **The Five Pennies**

The Hanging Tree (L: Mack David; M: Jerry Livingston), from *The Hanging Tree*

*High Hopes (L: Sammy Cahn; M: James Van Heusen), from *A Hole in the Head*

Strange Are the Ways of Love (L: Ned Washington; M: Dimitri Tiomkin), from *The Young Land*

1960

The Facts of Life (L&M: Johnny Mercer), from *The Facts of Life*

Faraway Part of Town (L: Dory Langdon; M: André Previn), from **Pepe**

The Green Leaves of Summer (L: Paul Francis Webster; M: Dimitri Tiomkin), from *The Alamo*

*Never on Sunday (L&M: Manos Hadjidakis), from *Never on Sunday*

The Second Time Around (L: Sammy Cahn; M: James Van Heusen), from **High Time**

1961

Bachelor in Paradise (L: Mack David; M: Henry Mancini), from *Bachelor in Paradise*

Love Theme from El Cid (The Falcon and the Dove) (L: Paul Francis Webster; M: Miklos Rozsa), from *El Cid*

*Moon River (L: Johnny Mercer; M: Henry Mancini), from *Breakfast at Tiffany's*

Pocketful of Miracles (L: Sammy Cahn; M: James Van Heusen), from *Pocketful of Miracles*

Town Without Pity (L: Ned Washington; M: Dimitri Tiomkin), from *Town Without Pity*

1962

*Days of Wine and Roses (L: Johnny Mercer; M: Henry Mancini), from *Days of Wine and Roses*

Love Song from Mutiny on the Bounty (Follow Me) (L: Paul Francis Webster; M: Bronislau Kaper), from *Mutiny on the Bounty*

Song from Two for the Seesaw (Second Chance) (L: Dory Langdon; M: André Previn), from *Two for the Seesaw*

Tender Is the Night (L: Paul Francis Webster; M: Sammy Fain), from *Tender Is the Night*

Walk on the Wild Side (L: Mack David; M: Elmer Bernstein), from *Walk on the Wild Side*

1963

*Call Me Irresponsible (L: Sammy Cahn; M: James Van Heusen), from *Papa's Delicate Condition*

Charade (L: Johnny Mercer; M: Henry Mancini), from *Charade*

It's a Mad, Mad, Mad, Mad World (L: Mack David; M: Ernest Gold), from *It's a Mad, Mad, Mad, Mad World*

More (L: Norman Newell; M: Riz Ortolani and Nino Oliviero), from *Mondo Cane*

So Little Time (L: Paul Francis Webster; M: Dimitri Tiomkin), from *55 Days at Peking*

1964

*Chim Chim Cher-ee (L&M: Richard M. and Robert B. Sherman), from **Mary Poppins**

Dear Heart (L: Jay Livingston and Ray Evans; M: Henry Mancini), from *Dear Heart*

Hush...Hush, Sweet Charlotte (L: Mack David; M: Frank DeVol), from *Hush...Hush, Sweet Charlotte*

My Kind of Town (Chicago Is) (L: Sammy Cahn; M: James Van Heusen), from **Robin and the Seven Hoods**

Where Love Has Gone (L: Sammy Cahn; M: James Van Heusen), from *Where Love Has Gone*

1965

The Ballad of Cat Ballou (L: Mack David; M: Jerry Livingston), from *Cat Ballou*

I Will Wait for You (L: Jacques Demy and Normal Gimbel; M: Michel Legrand), from **The Umbrellas of Cherbourg**

*The Shadow of Your Smile (L: Paul Francis Webster; M: Johnny Mandel), from *The Sandpiper*

The Sweetheart Tree (L: Johnny Mercer; M: Henry Mancini), from *The Great Race*

What's New Pussycat? L: Hal David; M: Burt Bacharach), from *What's New Pussycat?*

1966

Alfie (L: Hal David; M: Burt Bacharach), from *Alfie*

*Born Free (L: Don Black; M: John Barry), from *Born Free*

Georgy Girl (L: Jim Dale; M: Tom Springfield), from *Georgy Girl*

My Wishing Doll (L: Mack David; M: Elmer Bernstein), from *Hawaii*

A Time for Love (L: Paul Francis Webster; M: Johnny Mandel), from *An American Dream*

1967

The Bare Necessities (L&M: Terry Gilkyson), from **The Jungle Book**

The Eyes of Love (L: Bob Russell; M: Quincy Jones), from *Banning*

The Look of Love (L: Hal David; M: Burt Bacharach), from *Casino Royale*

*Talk to the Animals (L&M: Leslie Bricusse), from **Doctor Doolittle**

Thoroughly Modern Millie (L: Sammy Cahn; M: James Van Heusen), from **Thoroughly Modern Millie**

1968

Chitty Chitty Bang Bang (L&M: Richard M. and Robert B. Sherman), from *Chitty Chitty Bang Bang*

For the Love of Ivy (L: Bob Russell; M: Quincy Jones), from *For the Love of Ivy*

Funny Girl (L: Bob Merrill; M: Jule Styne), from **Funny Girl**

Star! (L: Sammy Cahn; M: James Van Heusen), from **Star!**

*The Windmills of Your Mind (L: Alan and Marilyn Bergman; M: Michel Legrand), from *The Thomas Crown Affair*

1969

Come Saturday Morning (L: Dory Previn; M: Fred Karlin), from *The Sterile Cuckoo*

Jean (L&M: Rod McKuen), from *The Prime of Miss Jean Brodie*

*Raindrops Keep Fallin' on My Head (L: Hal David; M: Burt Bacharach), from *Butch Cassidy and the Sundance Kid*

True Grit (L: Don Black; M: Elmer Bernstein), from *True Grit*

What Are You Doing the Rest of Your Life? (L: Alan and Marilyn Bergman; M: Michel Legrand), from *The Happy Ending*

1970

*For All We Know (L: Robb Royer and James Griffin [a.k.a. Robb Wilson and Arthur James]), from *Lovers and Other Strangers*

Pieces of Dreams (L: Alan and Marilyn Bergman; M: Michel Legrand), from *Pieces of Dreams*

Thank You Very Much (L&M: Leslie Bricusse), from **Scrooge**

Till Love Touches Your Life (L: Arthur Hamilton; M: Riz Ortolani), from *Madron*

Whistling Away the Dark (L: Johnny Mercer; M: Henry Mancini), from **Darling Lili**

1971

The Age of Not Believing (L&M: Richard M. and Robert B. Sherman), from **Bedknobs and Broomsticks**

All His Children (L: Alan and Marilyn Bergman; M: Henry Mancini), from *Sometimes a Great Notion*

Bless the Beasts & Children (L&M: Barry DeVorzon and Perry Botkin, Jr.), from *Bless the Beasts & Children*

Life Is What You Make It (L: Johnny Mercer; M: Marvin Hamlisch), from *Kotch*

*Theme from Shaft (L&M: Isaac Hayes), from *Shaft*

1972

Ben (L: Don Black; M: Walter Scharf), from *Ben*

Come Follow, Follow Me (L: Marsha Karlin; M: Fred Karlin), from *The Little Ark*

Marmalade, Molasses & Honey (L: Alan and Marilyn Bergman; M: Maurice Jarre), from *The Life and Times of Judge Roy Bean*

*The Morning After (L&M: Al Kasha and Joel Hirschhorn), from *The Poseidon Adventure*

Strange Are the Ways of Love (L: Paul Francis Webster; M: Sammy Fain), from *The Stepmother*

1973

All That Love Went to Waste (L: Sammy Cahn; M: George Barrie), from *A Touch of Class*

Live and Let Die (L&M: Paul and Linda McCartney), from *Live and Let Die*

Love (L: Floyd Huddleston; M: George Bruns), from **Robin Hood**

*The Way We Were (L: Alan and Marilyn Bergman; M: Marvin Hamlisch), from *The Way We Were*

Nice to Be Around (L: Paul Williams; M: John Williams), from *Cinderella Liberty*

1974

Benji's Theme (I Feel Love) (L: Betty Box; M: Euel Box), from *Benji*

Blazing Saddles (L: Mel Brooks; M: John Morris), from *Blazing Saddles*

Little Prince (L: Alan Jay Lerner; M: Frederick Loewe), from **The Little Prince**

*We May Never Love Like This Again (L&M: Al Kasha and Joel Hirschhorn), from *The Towering Inferno*

Wherever Love Takes Me (L: Don Black; M: Elmer Bernstein), from *Gold*

1975

How Lucky Can You Get (L&M: Fred Ebb and John Kander), from **Funny Lady**

*I'm Easy (L&M: Keith Carradine), from *Nashville*

Now That We're in Love (L: Sammy Cahn; M: George Barrie), from *Whiffs*

Richard's Window (L: Norman Gimbel; M: Charles Fox), from *The Other Side of the Mountain*

Theme from Mahogany (Do You Know Where You're Going To) (L: Gerry Goffin; M: Michael Masser), from *Mahogany*

1976

Ave Satani (L&M: Jerry Goldsmith), from *The Omen*

Come to Me (L: Don Black; M: Hanry Mancini), from *The Pink Panther Strikes Again*

*Evergreen (L: Paul William; M: Barbra Streisand), from **A Star Is Born**

Gonna Fly Now (L: Carol Connors and Ayn Robbins; M: Bill Conti), from *Rocky*

A World That Never Was (L: Paul Francis Webster; M: Sammy Fain), from *Half a House*

1977

Candle on the Water (L&M: Al Kasha and Joel Hirschhorn), from *Pete's Dragon*

Nobody Does It Better (L: Carole Bayer Sager; M: Marvin Hamlisch), from *The Spy Who Loved Me*

The Slipper and the Rose Waltz (He Danced with Me / She Danced with Me) (L&M: Richard M. and Robert B. Sherman), from **The Slipper and the Rose—The Story of Cinderella**

Someone's Waiting for You (L: Carol Connors and Ayn Robbins; M: Sammy Fain), from *The Rescuers*

*You Light Up My Life (L&M: Joseph Brooks), from *You Light Up My Life*

1978

Hopelessly Devoted to You (L&M: John Farrar), from **Grease**

*Last Dance (L&M: Paul Jabara), from *Thank God It's Friday*

The Last Time I Felt Like This (L: Alan and Marilyn Bergman; M: Marvin Hamlisch), from *Same Time, Next Year*

Ready to Take a Chance Again (L: Norman Gimbel; M: Charles Fox), from *Foul Play*

When You're Loved (L&M: Richard M. and Robert B. Sherman), from *The Magic of Lassie*

1979

*It Goes Like It Goes (L: Norman Gimbel; M: David Shire), from *Norma Rae*

The Rainbow Connection (L&M: Paul Williams and Kenny Ascher), from **The Muppet Movie**

It's Easy to Say (L: Robert Wells; M: Henry Mancini) from *10*

Through the Eyes of Love (L: Carole Bayer Sager; M: Marvin Hamlisch), from *Ice Castles*

I'll Never Say "Goodbye" (L: Alan and Marilyn Bergman; M: David Shire), from *The Promise*

1980

*Fame (L: Dean Pitchford; M: Michael Gore), from **Fame**

Nine to Five (L&M: Dolly Parton), from *Nine to Five*

On the Road Again (L&M: Willie Nelson), from **Honeysuckle Rose**

Out Here on My Own (L: Lesley Gore; M: Michael Gore), from **Fame**

People Alone (L: Wilbur Jennings; M: Lalo Schifrin), from *The Competition*

1981

*Arthur's Theme (Best That You Can Do) (L&M: Burt Bacharach, Carole Bayer Sager, Christopher Cross, and Peter Allen), from *Arthur*

Endless Love (L&M: Lionel Richie), from *Endless Love*

The First Time It Happens (L&M: Joe Raposo), from *The Great Muppet Caper*

For Your Eyes Only (L: Mick Leeson; M: Bill Conti), from *For Your Eyes Only*

One More Hour (L&M: Randy Newman), from *Ragtime*

1982

Eye of the Tiger (L&M: Jim Peterik and Frankie Sullivan III), from *Rocky III*

How Do You Keep the Music Playing? (L: Alan and Marilyn Bergman; M: Michel Legrand), from *Best Friends*

If We Were in Love (L: Alan and Marilyn Bergman; M: John Williams), from *Yes, Giorgio*

It Might Be You (L: Alan and Marilyn Bergman; M: Dave Grusin), from *Tootsie*

*Up Where We Belong (L: Will Jennings; M: Jack Mitzsche and Buffy Sainte-Marie), from *An Officer and a Gentleman*

1983

*Flashdance...What a Feeling (L: Keith Forsey and Irene Cara; M: Giorgio Moroder), from ***Flashdance***

Maniac (L&M: Michael Sembello and Dennis Matkosky), from ***Flashdance***

Over You (L&M: Austin Roberts and Bobby Hart), from *Tender Mercies*

Papa, Can You Hear Me? (L: Alan and Marilyn Bergman; M: Michel Legrand), from ***Yentl***

The Way He Makes Me Feel (L: Alan and Marilyn Bergman; M: Michel Legrand), from ***Yentl***

1984

Against All Odds (Take a Look at Me Now) (L&M: Phil Collins), from *Against All Odds*

Footloose (L&M: Kenny Loggins and Dean Pitchford), from ***Footloose***

Ghostbusters (L&M: Ray Parker, Jr.), from *Ghostbusters*

*I Just Called to Say I Love You (L&M: Stevie Wonder), from *The Woman in Red*

Let's Hear It for the Boy (L&M: Tom Snow and Dean Pitchford), from ***Footloose***

1985

Miss Celie's Blues (Sister) (L: Quincy Jones, Rod Temperton, and Lionel Richie; M: Quincy Jones and Rod Temperton), from *The Color Purple*

The Power of Love (L: Huey Lewis; M: Chris Hayes and Johnny Colla), from *Back to the Future*

*Say You, Say Me (L&M: Lionel Richie), from ***White Nights***

Separate Lives (L&M: Stephen Bishop), from ***White Nights***

Surprise, Surprise (L: Edward Kleban; M: Marvin Hamlisch), from ***A Chorus Line***

1986

Glory of Love (L: Peter Cetera and Diana Nini; M: Peter Cetera and David Foster), from *The Karate Kid Part II*

Life in a Looking Glass (L: Leslie Bricusse; M: Henry Mancini), from *That's Life*

Mean Green Mother from Outer Space (L: Howard Ashman; M: Alan Menken), from ***Little Shop of Horrors***

Somewhere Out There (L: Cynthia Weil; M: James Horner and Barry Mann), from *An American Tail*

*Take My Breath Away (L: Tom Whitlock; M: Giorgio Moroder), from *Top Gun*

1987

Cry Freedom (L&M: George Fenton and Jonas Gwangwa), from *Cry Freedom*

*(I've Had) The Time of My Life (L: Franke Previte; M: Frank Previte, John DeNicola, and Donald Markowitz), from ***Dirty Dancing***

Nothing's Gonna Stop Us Now (L&M: Albert Hammond and Diane Warren), from *Mannequin*

Shakedown (L: Harold Faltermeyer, Keith Forsey, and Bob Seger; M: Harold Faltermeyer and Keith Forsey), from *Beverly Hills Cops II*

Storybook Love (L&M: Willy DeVille), from *The Princess Bride*

1988

Calling You (L&M: Bob Telson), from *Bagdad Cafe*

*Let the River Run (L&M: Carly Simon), from *Working Girl*

Two Hearts (L: Phil Collins; M: Lamont Dozier), from *Buster*

1989

After All (L: Dean Pitchford; M: Tom Snow), from *Chances Are*

The Girl Who Used to Be Me (L: Alan and Marilyn Bergman; M: Marvin Hamlisch), from *Shirley Valentine*

I Love to See You Smile (L&M: Randy Newman), from *Parenthood*

Kiss the Girl (L: Howard Ashman; M: Alan Menken), from ***The Little Mermaid***

*Under the Sea (L: Howard Ashman; M: Alan Menken), from ***The Little Mermaid***

1990

Blaze of Glory (L&M: Jon Bon Jovi), from *Young Guns II*

I'm Checkin' Out (L&M: Shel Silverstein), from *Postcards from the Edge*

Promise Me You'll Remember (L: John Bettis; M: Carmine Coppola), from *The Godfather, Part III*

Somewhere in My Memory (L: Leslie Bricusse; M: John Williams), from *Home Alone*

*Sooner or Later (I Always Get My Man) (L&M: Stephen Sondheim), from *Dick Tracy*

1991

Be Our Guest (L: Howard Ashman; M: Alan Menken), from **Beauty and the Beast**

*Beauty and the Beast (L: Howard Ashman; M: Alan Menken), from **Beauty and the Beast**

Belle (L: Howard Ashman; M: Alan Menken), from **Beauty and the Beast**

(Everything I Do) I Do It for You (L: Bryan Adams and Robert John Lange; M: Michael Kamen), from *Robin Hood: Prince of Thieves*

When You're Alone (L: Leslie Bricusse; M: John Williams), from *Hook*

1992

Beautiful Maria of My Soul (L: Arne Glimcher; M: Robert Kraft), from *The Mambo Kings*

Friend Like Me (L: Howard Ashman; M: Alan Menken), from **Aladdin**

I Have Nothing (L: Linda Thompson; M: David Foster), from *The Bodyguard*

Run to You (L: Allan Rich; M: Jud Friedman), from *The Bodyguard*

A Whole New World (L: Tim Rice; M: Alan Menken), from **Aladdin**

1993

Again (L&M: Janet Jackson, James Harris III, and Terry Lewis), from *Poetic Justice*

The Day I Fall in Love (L&M: Carole Bayer Sager, James Ingram, and Cliff Magness), from *Beethoven's 2nd*

Philadelphia (L&M: Neil Young), from *Philadelphia*

*Streets of Philadelphia (L&M: Bruce Springsteen), from *Philadelphia*

A Wink and a Smile (L: Ramsey McLean; M: Marc Shaiman), from *Sleepless in Seattle*

1994

*Can You Feel the Love Tonight? (L: Tim Rice; M: Elton John), from **The Lion King**

Circle of Life (L: Tim Rice; M: Elton John), from **The Lion King**

Hakuna Matata (L: Tim Rice; M: Elton John), from **The Lion King**

Make Up Your Mind (L&M: Randy Newman), from *The Paper*

1995

*Colors of the Wind (L: Stephen Schwartz; M: Alan Menken), from **Pocahontas**

Dead Man Walking (L&M: Bruce Springsteen), from *Dead Man Walking*

Have You Ever Really Loved a Woman (L&M: Michael Kamen, Bryan Adams, and Robert John Lange), from *Don Juan DeMarco*

Moonlight (L: Alan and Marilyn Bergman; M: John Williams), from *Sabrina*

You've Got a Friend (L&M: Randy Newman), from *Toy Story*

1996

Because You Loved Me (L&M: Diane Warren), from *Up Close and Personal*

For the First Time (L&M: James Newton Howard, Jud J. Friedman, and Allan Dennis Rich), from *One Fine Day*

I Finally Found Someone (L: Bryan Adams and Robert Lange; M: Barbra Streisand and Marvin Hamlisch), from *The Mirror Has Two Faces*

That Thing You Do! (L&M: Adam Schlesinger), from *That Thing You Do!*

*You Must Love Me (L: Tim Rice; M: Andrew Lloyd Webber), from *Evita*

1997

Go the Distance (L: Alan Menken; M: David Zippel), from *Hercules*

How Do I Live (L&M: Diane Warren), from *Con Air*

Journey to the Past (L: Lynn Ahrens; M: Stephen Flaherty), from *Anastasia*

Miss Misery (L&M: Elliott Smith), from *Good Will Hunting*

*My Heart Will Go On (L: Will Jennings; M: James Horner), from *Titanic*

1998

A Bug's Life; Mulan; Patch Adams; The Prince of Egypt; *Shakespeare in Love

1999

Blame Canada (L&M: Trey Parker and Marc Shaiman), from *South Park: Bigger, Longer & Uncut*

Music of My Heart (L&M: Diane Warren), from *Music of the Heart*

Save Me (L&M: Aimee Mann), from *Magnolia*

When She Loves Me (L&M: Randy Newman), from *Toy Story 2*

*You'll Be in My Heart (L&M: Phil Collins), from *Tarzan*

2000

A Fool in Love (L&M: Randy Newman), from *Meet The Parents*

I've Seen It All (L: Lars von Trier and Sjon Sigurdsson; M: Bj_rk), from *Dancer in the Dark*

A Love Before Time (L: James Schamus; M: Jorge Calandrelli and Tan Dun), from *Crouching Tiger, Hidden Dragon*

My Funny Friend and Me (L: Sting; M: Sting and David Hartley), from *The Emperor's New Groove*

*Things Have Changed (L&M: Bob Dylan), from *Wonder Boys*

Music Scoring

(WINNING SCORES ARE DESIGNATED
BY AN ASTERISK; MUSICALS
APPEAR IN BOLDFACE TYPE)

1934

Best Score:

The Gay Divorcee (RKO Radio Studio Music Dept., Max Steiner, Head). Score by Kenneth Webb and Samuel Hoffenstein

The Lost Patrol (RKO Radio Studio Music Dept., Max Steiner, Head). Score by Max Steiner

*One Night of Love (Columbia Studio Music Dept., Louis Silvers, Head). Thematic music by Victor Schertzinger and Gus Kahn

1935

Best Score:

*The Informer (RKO Radio Studio Music Dept., Max Steiner, Head). Score by Max Steiner

Mutiny on the Bounty (Metro-Goldwyn-Mayer Studio Music Dept., Nat W. Finston, Head). Score by Herbert Stothart

Peter Ibbetson (Paramount Studio Music Dept., Irvin Talbot, Head). Score by Ernst Toch

1936

Best Score:

*Anthony Adverse (Warner Bros. Studio Music Dept., Leo F. Forbstein, Head). Score by Erich Wolfgang Korngold

The Charge of the Light Brigade (Warner Bros. Studio Music Dept., Leo F. Forbstein, Head). Score by Max Steiner

The Garden of Allah (Selznick International Pictures Music Dept., Max Steiner, Head). Score by Max Steiner

The General Died at Dawn (Paramount Studio Music Dept., Boris Morros, Head). Score by Werner Janssen

Winterset (RKO Radio Studio Music Dept., Nathaniel Shilkret, Head). Score by Nathaniel Shilkret

1937

Best Score:

The Hurricane (Samuel Goldwyn Studio Music Dept., Alfred Newman, Head). Score by Alfred Newman

In Old Chicago (20th Century-Fox Studio Music Dept., Louis Silvers, Head). Score: No composer credit

The Life of Emile Zola (Warner Bros. Studio Music Dept., Leo F. Forbstein, Head). Score by Max Steiner

Lost Horizon (Columbia Studio Music Dept., Morris Stoloff, Head). Score by Dimitri Tiomkin

Make a Wish (Principal Productions, Dr. Hugo Riesenfeld, Musical Director). Score by Dr. Hugo Riesenfeld

Maytime (Metro-Goldwyn-Mayer Studio Music Dept., Nat W. Finston, Head). Score by Herbert Stothart

*One Hundred Men and a Girl (Universal Studio Music Dept., Charles Previn, Head). Score: No composer credit

Portia on Trial (Republic Studio Music Dept., Alberto Colombo, Head). Score by Alberto Colombo

The Prisoner of Zenda (Selznick International Pictures Music Dept., Alfred Newman, Musical Director). Score by Alfred Newman

Quality Street (RKO Radio Studio Music Dept., Roy Webb, Musical Director). Score by Roy Webb

Snow White and the Seven Dwarfs (Walt Disney Studio Music Dept., Leigh Harline, Head). Score by Frank Churchill, Leigh Harline, and Paul J. Smith

Something to Sing About (Grand National Studio Music Dept., C. Bakaleinikoff, Musical Director). Score by Victor Schertzinger

Souls at Sea (Paramount Studio Music Dept., Boris Morros, Head). Score by W. Franke Harling and Milan Roder

Way Out West (Hal Roach Studio Music Dept., Marvin Hatley, Head). Score by Marvin Hatley

1938

Best Score:

***Alexander's Ragtime Band**, Alfred Newman

Carefree, Victor Baravalle

Girls School, Morris Stoloff and Gregory Stone

The Goldwyn Follies, Alfred Newman

Jezebel, Max Steiner

Mad About Music, Charles Previn and Frank Skinner

Storm over Bengal, Cy Feuer

Sweethearts, Herbert Stothart

There Goes My Heart, Marvin Hatley

Tropic Holiday, Boris Morris

The Young in Heart, Franz Waxman

Original Score:

*The Adventures of Robin Hood, Erich Wolfgang Korngold

Army Girl, Victor Young

Blockade, Werner Jenssen

Blockheads, Marvin Hatley

Breaking the Ice, Victor Young

The Cowboy and the Lady, Alfred Newman

If I Were King, Richard Hageman
Marie Antoinette, Herbert Stothart
Pacific Liner, Russell Bennett
Suez, Louis Silvers
The Young in Heart, Franz Waxman

1939

Best Score:
Babes in Arms, Roger Edens and Georgie Stoll
First Love, Charles Previn
The Great Victor Herbert, Phil Boutelje and Arthur Lange
The Hunchback of Notre Dame, Alfred Newman
Intermezzo, Lou Forbes
Mr. Smith Goes to Washington, Dimitri Tiomkin
Of Mice and Men, Aaron Copland
The Private Lives of Elizabeth and Essex, Erich Wolfgang Korngold
She Married a Cop, Cy Feuer
*Stagecoach, Richard Hageman, W. Franke Harling, John Leipold, and Leo Shuken
Swanee River, Louis Silvers
They Shall Have Music, Alfred Newman
Way Down South, Victor Young
Original Score:
Dark Victory, Alfred Newman
Eternally Yours, Werner Janssen
Golden Boy, Victor Young
Gone with the Wind, Max Steiner
Gulliver's Travels, Victor Young
The Man in the Iron Mask, Lud Gluskin and Lucien Moraweck
Man of Conquest, Victor Young
Nurse Edith Cavell, Anthony Collins
Of Mice and Men, Aaron Copland
The Rains Came, Alfred Newman
*The Wizard of Oz, Herbert Stothart
Wuthering Heights, Alfred Newman

1940

Best Score:
Arise, My Love, Victor Young
Hit Parade of 1941, Cy Feuer
Irene, Anthony Collins
Our Town, Aaron Copland
The Sea Hawk, Erich Wolfgang Korngold
Second Chorus, Artie Shaw
Spring Parade, Charles Previn
Strike Up the Band, Georgie Stoll and Roger Edens
*Tin Pan Alley, Alfred Newman
Original Score:
Arizona, Victor Young
The Dark Command, Victor Young
The Fight for Life, Louis Gruenberg
The Great Dictator, Meredith Willson
The House of Seven Gables, Frank Skinner
The Howards of Virginia, Richard Hageman
The Letter, Max Steiner
The Long Voyage Home, Richard Hageman

The Mark of Zorro, Alfred Newman
My Favorite Wife, Roy Webb
Northwest Mounted Police, Victor Young
One Million B.C., Werner Heymann
Our Town, Aaron Copland
*Pinocchio, Leigh Harline, Paul J. Smith, and Ned Washington
Rebecca, Franz Waxman
The Thief of Bagdad, Miklos Rozsa
Waterloo Bridge, Herbert Stothart

1941

Scoring of a Dramatic and Musical Picture:
All American Co-Ed, Edward Ward
*All That Money Can Buy, Bernard Herrmann
Back Street, Frank Skinner
Ball of Fire, Alfred Newman
Birth of the Blues, Robert Emmett Dolan
Buck Privates, Charles Previn
Cheers for Miss Bishop, Edward Ward
The Chocolate Soldier, Herbert Stothart and Bronislau Kaper
Citizen Kane, Bernard Herrmann
Dr. Jekyll and Mr. Hyde, Franz Waxman
*Dumbo, Frank Churchill and Oliver Wallace
Hold Back the Dawn, Victor Young
How Green Was My Valley, Alfred Newman
Ice-Capades, Cy Feuer
King of the Zombies, Edward Kay
Ladies in Retirement, Morris Stoloff and Ernst Toch
The Little Foxes, Meredith Willson
Lydia, Miklos Rozsa
Mercy Island, Cy Feuer and Walter Scharf
Sergeant York, Max Steiner
So Ends Our Night, Louis Gruenberg
The Strawberry Blonde, Heinz Roemheld
Sun Valley Serenade, Emil Newman
Sundown, Miklos Rozsa
Sunny, Anthony Collins
Suspicion, Franz Waxman
Tanks a Million, Edward Ward
That Uncertain Feeling, Werner Heymann
This Woman Is Mine, Richard Hageman
You'll Never Get Rich, Morris Stoloff

1942

Scoring of Dramatic/Comedy and Musical Picture:
Arabian Nights, Frank Skinner
Bambi, Frank Churchill and Edward Plumb
The Black Swan, Alfred Newman
The Corsican Brothers, Dimitri Tiomkin
Flying Tigers, Victor Young
Flying with Music, Edward Ward
For Me and My Gal, Roger Edens and Georgie Stoll
The Gold Rush, Max Terr (Revival, from 1925)
Holiday Inn, Robert Emmett Dolan
I Married a Witch, Roy Webb
It Started with Eve, Charles Previn and Hans Salter
Joan of Paris, Roy Webb

Johnny Doughboy, Walter Scharf
Jungle Book, Miklos Rozsa
Klondike Fury, Edward Kay
My Gal Sal, Alfred Newman
*Now, Voyager, Max Steiner
The Pride of the Yankees, Leigh Harline
Random Harvest, Herbert Stothart
The Shanghai Gesture, Richard Hageman
Silver Queen, Victor Young
Take a Letter, Darling, Victor Young
The Talk of the Town, Frederick Hollander and
   Morris Stoloff
To Be or Not to Be, Werner Heymann
*Yankee Doodle Dandy, Ray Heindorf and Heinz
   Roemheld
You Were Never Lovelier, Leigh Harline

1943

*Scoring of a Dramatic/Comedy Picture and Musical
   Picture:*
The Amazing Mrs. Holliday, Hans J. Salter and
   Frank Skinner
Casablanca, Max Steiner
The Commandos Strike at Dawn. Louis Gruenberg
   and Morris Stoloff
Coney Island, Alfred Newman
The Fallen Sparrow, C. Bakaleinikoff and Roy Webb
For Whom the Bell Tolls, Victor Young
Hangmen Also Die, Hanns Eisler
Hi Diddle Diddle, Phil Boutelje
Hit Parade of 1943, Walter Scharf
In Old Oklahoma, Walter Scharf
Johnny Come Lately, Leigh Harline
The Kansan, Gerald Carbonara
Lady of Burlesque, Arthur Lange
Madame Curie, Herbert Stothart
The Moon and Sixpence, Dimitri Tiomkin
The North Star, Aaron Copland
The Phantom of the Opera, Edward Ward
Saludos Amigos, Edward H. Plumb, Paul J. Smith,
   and Charles Wolcott
The Sky's the Limit, Leigh Harline
Something to Shout About, Morris Stoloff
*The Song of Bernadette, Alfred Newman
Stage Door Canteen, Frederic E. Rich
Star Spangled Rhythm, Robert Emmett Dolan
*This Is the Army, Ray Heindorf
Thousands Cheer, Herbert Stothart
Victory Through Air Power, Edward H. Plumb,
   Paul J. Smith, and Oliver Wallace

1944

*Scoring of a Dramatic/Comedy Picture and Musical
   Picture:*
Address Unknown, Morris Stoloff and Ernst Toch
The Adventures of Mark Twain, Max Steiner
Brazil, Walter Scharf
The Bridge of San Luis Rey, Dimitri Tiomkin
Casanova Brown, Arthur Lange

Christmas Holiday, Hans [J.] Salter
*Cover Girl, Carmen Dragon and Morris Stoloff
Double Indemnity, Miklos Rozsa
The Fighting Seabees, Walter Scharf and Roy Webb
The Hairy Ape, Michel Michelet and Edward Paul
Higher and Higher, C. Bakaleinikoff
Hollywood Canteen, Ray Heindorf
Irish Eyes Are Smiling, Alfred Newman
It Happened Tomorrow, Robert Stolz
Jack London, Frederic E. Rich
Kismet, Herbert Stothart
Knickerbocker Holiday, Werner R. Heymann and
   Kurt Weill
Lady in the Dark, Robert Emmett Dolan
Lady Let's Dance, Edward Kay
Meet Me in St. Louis, Georgie Stoll
The Merry Monahans, Hans [J.] Salter
Minstrel Man, Leo Erdody and Ferdie Grofé
None but the Lonely Heart, C. Bakaleinikoff and
   Hanns Eisler
The Princess and the Pirate, David Rose
Sensations of 1945, Mahlon Merrick
*Since You Went Away, Max Steiner
Song of the Open Road, Charles Previn
Summer Storm, Karl Hajos
Three Russian Girls, W. Franke Harling
Up in Arms, Lou Forbes and Ray Heindorf
Up in Mabel's Room, Edward Paul
Voice in the Wind, Michel Michelet
Wilson, Alfred Newman
Woman of the Town, Miklos Rosza

1945

*Scoring of a Dramatic/Comedy Picture and Musical
   Picture:*
*Anchors Aweigh, Georgie Stoll
Belle of the Yukon, Arthur Lange
The Bells of St. Mary's, Robert Emmett Dolan
Brewster's Millions, Lou Forbes
Can't Help Singing, Jerome Kern and Hans [J.]
   Salter
Captain Kidd, Werner Janssen
Enchanted Cottage, Roy Webb
Flame of the Barbary Coast, Dale Butts and Mor-
   ton Scott
G.I. Honeymoon, Edward J. Kay
Guest in the House, Werner Janssen
Guest Wife, Daniele Amfitheatrof
Hitchhike to Happiness, Morton Scott
Incendiary Blonde, Robert Emmett Dolan
The Keys of the Kingdom, Alfred Newman
The Lost Weekend, Miklos Rosza
Love Letters, Victor Young
Man Who Walked Alone, Karl Hajos
Objective Burma!, Franz Waxman
Paris-Underground, Alexander Tansman
Rhapsody in Blue, Ray Heindorf and Max Steiner
A Song to Remember, Miklos Rosza and Morris
   Stoloff

The Southerner, Werner Janssen
*Spellbound, Miklos Rosza
State Fair, Charles Henderson and Alfred Newman
The Story of G.I. Joe, Louis Applebaum and Ann Ronnell
Sunbonnet Sue, Edward J. Kay
This Love of Ours, Hans J. Salter
Three Caballeros, Edward Plumb, Paul J. Smith, and Charles Wolcott
Tonight and Every Night, Marlin Skiles and Morris Stoloff
Valley of Decision, Herbert Stothart
Why Girls Leave Home, Walter Greene
Woman in the Window, Hugo Friedhofer and Arthur Lange
Wonder Man, Lou Forbes and Ray Heindorf

1946

Scoring of a Dramatic/Comedy Picture and Musical Picture:
Anna and the King of Siam, Bernard Herrmann
*The Best Years of Our Lives, Hugo Friedhofer
Blue Skies, Robert Emmett Dolan
Centennial Summer, Alfred Newman
The Harvey Girls, Lennie Hayton
Henry V, William Walton
Humoresque, Franz Waxman
*The Jolson Story, Morris Stoloff
The Killers, Miklos Rosza
Night and Day, Ray Heindorf and Max Steiner

1947

Scoring of a Dramatic/Comedy Picture and Musical Picture:
The Bishop's Wife, Hugo Friedhofer
Captain from Castile, Alfred Newman
*A Double Life, Miklos Rosza
Fiesta, Johnny Green
Forever Amber, David Raksin
.Life with Father, Max Steiner
*Mother Wore Tights, Alfred Newman
My Wild Irish Rose, Ray Heindorf and Max Steiner
Road to Rio, Robert Emmett Dolan
Song of the South Daniele Amfitheatrof, Paul J. Smith, and Charles Wolcott

1948

Scoring of a Dramatic/Comedy Picture and Musical Picture:
*Easter Parade, Johnny Green and Roger Edens
The Emperor Waltz, Victor Young
Hamlet, William Walton
Joan of Arc, Hugo Friedhofer
Johnny Belinda, Max Steiner
The Pirate, Lennie Hayton
*The Red Shoes, Brian Easdale
Romance on the High Seas, Ray Heindorf
The Snake Pit, Alfred Newman
When My Baby Smiles at Me, Alfred Newman

1949

Scoring of a Dramatic/Comedy Picture and Musical Picture:
Beyond the Forest, Max Steiner
Champion, Dimitri Tiomkin
*The Heiress, Aaron Copland
Jolson Sings Again, Morris Stoloff and George Duning
Look for the Silver Lining, Ray Heindorf
*On the Town, Roger Edens and Lennie Hayton

1950

Scoring of a Dramatic/Comedy Picture and Musical Picture:
All About Eve, Alfred Newman
*Annie Get Your Gun, Adolph Deutsch and Roger Edens
Cinderella, Oliver Wallace and Paul J. Smith
The Flame and the Arrow, Max Steiner
I'll Get By, Lionel Newman
No Sad Songs for Me, George Duning
Samson and Delilah, Victor Young
*Sunset Boulevard, Franz Waxman
Three Little Words, André Previn
The West Point Story, Ray Heindorf

1951

Scoring of a Dramatic/Comedy Picture and Musical Picture:
Alice in Wonderland, Oliver Wallace
*An American in Paris, Johnny Green and Saul Chaplin
David and Bathsheba, Alfred Newman
Death of a Salesman, Alex North
The Great Caruso, Peter Herman Adler and Johnny Green
On the Riviera, Alfred Newman
*A Place in the Sun, Franz Waxman
Quo Vadis, Miklos Rosza
Show Boat, Adolph Deutsch and Conrad Salinger
A Streetcar Named Desire, Alex North

1952

Scoring of a Dramatic/Comedy Picture and Musical Picture:
Hans Christian Andersen, Walter Scharf
*High Noon, Dimitri Tiomkin
Ivanhoe, Miklos Rosza
The Jazz Singer, Ray Heindorf and Max Steiner
The Medium, Gian-Carlo Menotti
Miracle of Fatima, Max Steiner
Singin' in the Rain, Lennie Hayton
The Thief, Herschel Burke Gilbert
Viva Zapata! Alex North
*With a Song in My Heart, Alfred Newman

1953

Scoring of a Dramatic/Comedy Picture and Musical Picture:

Above and Beyond, Hugo Friedhofer
The Band Wagon, Adolph Deutsch
Calamity Jane, Ray Heindorf
***Call Me Madam**, Alfred Newman
5,000 Fingers of Dr. T., Frederick Hollander and Morris Stoloff
From Here to Eternity, Morris Stoloff and George Duning
Julius Caesar, Miklos Rosza
Kiss Me Kate, André Previn and Saul Chaplin
*Lili, Bronislau Kaper
This Is Cinerama, Lou Forbes

1954

Scoring of a Dramatic/Comedy Picture and Musical Picture:

The Caine Mutiny, Max Steiner
Carmen Jones, Herschel Burke Gilbert
Genevieve, Muir Mathieson
The Glenn Miller Story, Joseph Gershenson and Henry Mancini
*The High and the Mighty, Dimitri Tiomkin
On the Waterfront, Leonard Bernstein
***Seven Brides for Seven Brothers**, Adolph Deutsch and Saul Chaplin
The Silver Chalice, Franz Waxman
A Star Is Born, Ray Heindorf
There's No Business Like Show Business, Alfred and Lionel Newman

1955

Scoring of a Dramatic/Comedy Picture and Musical Picture:

Battle Cry, Max Steiner
Daddy Long Legs, Alfred Newman
Guys and Dolls, Jay Blackton and Cyril J. Mockridge
It's Always Fair Weather, André Previn
*Love Is a Many-Splendored Thing, Alfred Newman
Love Me or Leave Me, Percy Faith and Georgie Stoll
The Man with the Golden Arm, Elmer Bernstein
***Oklahoma!** Robert Russell Bennett, Jay Blackton, and Adolph Deutsch
Picnic, George Duning
The Rose Tattoo, Alex North

1956

Scoring of a Dramatic/Comedy Picture and Musical Picture:

Anastasia, Alfred Newman
*Around the World in 80 Days, Victor Young
The Best Things in Life Are Free, Lionel Newman
Between Heaven and Hell, Hugo Friedhofer
The Eddy Duchin Story, Morris Stoloff and George Duning

Giant, Dimitri Tiomkin
High Society, Johnny Green and Saul Chaplin
***The King and I**, Alfred Newman and Ken Darby
Meet Me in Las Vegas, Georgie Stoll and Johnny Green
The Rainmaker, Alex North

1957

Music Scoring:

An Affair to Remember, Hugo Friedhofer
Boy on a Dolphin, Hugo Friedhofer
*The Bridge on the River Kwai, Malcolm Arnold
Perri, Paul Smith
Raintree County, Johnny Green

1958

Scoring of a Dramatic/Comedy Picture and Musical Picture:

The Big Country, Jerome Moross
The Bolshoi Ballet, Yuri Faier and G. Rozhdestvensky
Damn Yankees, Ray Heindorf
***Gigi**, André Previn
Mardi Gras, Lionel Newman
*The Old Man and the Sea, Dimitri Tiomkin
Separate Tables, David Raksin
South Pacific, Alfred Newman and Ken Darby
White Wilderness, Oliver Wallace
The Young Lions, Hugo Friedhofer

1959

Scoring of a Dramatic/Comedy Picture and Musical Picture:

*Ben-Hur, Miklos Rozsa
The Diary of Anne Frank, Alfred Newman
The Five Pennies, Leith Stevens
L'il Abner, Nelson Riddle and Joseph J. Lilley
The Nun's Story, Franz Waxman
On the Beach, Ernest Gold
Pillow Talk, Frank DeVol
***Porgy and Bess**, André Previn and Ken Darby
Say One for Me, Lionel Newman
Sleeping Beauty, George Bruns

1960

Scoring of a Dramatic/Comedy Picture and Musical Picture:

The Alamo, Dimitri Tiomkin
Bells Are Ringing, André Previn
Can-Can, Nelson Riddle
Elmer Gantry, André Previn
*Exodus, Ernest Gold
Let's Make Love, Lionel Newman and Earle H. Hagen
The Magnificent Seven, Elmer Bernstein
Pepe, Johnny Green
***Song Without End**, Morris Stoloff and Harry Sukman
Spartacus, Alex North

1961

Scoring of a Dramatic/Comedy Picture and Musical Picture:
Babes in Toyland, George Bruns
*Breakfast at Tiffany's, Henry Mancini
El Cid, Miklos Rozsa
Fanny, Morris Stoloff and Harry Sukman
Flower Drum Song, Alfred Newman and Ken Darby
The Guns of Navarone, Dimitri Tiomkin
Khovanshshina, Dimitri Shostakovich
Paris Blues, Duke Ellington
Summer and Smoke, Elmer Bernstein
*West Side Story**, Saul Chaplin, Johnny Green, Sid Ramin, and Irwin Kostal

1962

Music Score—Substantially Original:
Freud, Jerry Goldsmith
*Lawrence of Arabia, Maurice Jarre
Mutiny on the Bounty, Bronislau Kaper
Taras Bulba, Franz Waxman
To Kill a Mockingbird, Elmer Bernstein
Scoring of Music—Adaptation or Treatment:
Gigot, Michel Magne
Gypsy, Frank Perkins
Jumbo, Georgie Stoll
*The Music Man**, Ray Heindorf
The Wonderful World of the Brothers Grimm, Leigh Harline

1963

Music Score—Substantially Original:
Cleopatra, Alex North
55 Days at Peking, Dimitri Tiomkin
How the West Was Won, Alfred Newman and Ken Darby
It's a Mad, Mad, Mad, Mad World, Ernest Gold
*Tom Jones, John Addison
Scoring of Music—Adaptation or Treatment:
Bye Bye Birdie, John(ny) Green
*Irma la Douce**, André Previn
A New Kind of Love, Leith Stevens
Sundays and Cybele, Maurice Jarre
The Sword in the Stone, George Bruns

1964

Music Score—Substantially Original:
Becket, Laurence Rosenthal
The Fall of the Roman Empire, Dimitri Tiomkin
Hush…Hush, Sweet Charlotte, Frank DeVol
*Mary Poppins**, Irwin Kostal
The Pink Panther, Henri Mancini
Scoring of Music—Adaptation or Treatment:
A Hard Day's Night, George Martin
Mary Poppins, Irwin Kostal
*My Fair Lady**, André Previn
Robin and the Seven Hoods, Nelson Riddle
The Unsinkable Molly Brown, Robert Armbruster,
Leo Arnaud, Jack Elliott, Jack Hayes, Calvin Jackson, and Leo Shuken

1965

Music Score—Substantially Original:
The Agony and the Ecstasy, Alex North
*Doctor Zhivago, Maurice Jarre
The Greatest Story Ever Told, Alfred Newman
A Patch of Blue, Jerry Goldsmith
The Umbrellas of Cherbourg [Les Parapluies de Cherbourg], Michel Legrand and Jacques Demy
Scoring of Music—Adaptation or Treatment:
Cat Ballou, Frank DeVol
The Pleasure Seekers, Lionel Newman and Alexander Courage
*The Sound of Music**, Irwin Kostal
A Thousand Clowns, Don Walker
The Umbrellas of Cherbourg [Les Parapluies de Cherbourg], Michel Legrand

1966

Original Music Score:
The Bible, Toshiro Mayuzumi
*Born Free, John Barry
Hawaii, Elmer Bernstein
The Sand Pebbles, Jerry Goldsmith
Who's Afraid of Virginia Woolf?, Alex North
Scoring of Music—Adaptation or Treatment:
*A Funny Thing Happened on the Way to the Forum**, Ken Thorne
The Gospel According to St. Matthew, Luis Enrique Bacalov
Return of the Seven, Elmer Bernstein
The Singing Nun, Harry Sukman
Stop the World—I Want to Get Off, Al Ham

1967

Original Music Score:
Cool Hand Luke, Lalo Schifrin
Doctor Doolittle, Leslie Bricusse
Far from the Madding Crowd, Richard Rodney Bennett
In Cold Blood, Quincy Jones
*Thoroughly Modern Millie**, Elmer Bernstein
Scoring of Music—Adaptation or Treatment:
*Camelot**, Alfred Newman and Ken Darby
Doctor Doolittle, Lionel Newman and Alexander Courage
Guess Who's Coming to Dinner, Frank DeVol
Thoroughly Modern Millie, André Previn and Joseph Gershenson
Valley of the Dolls, John Williams

1968

Best Original Score for a Motion Picture [Not a Musical]:
The Fox, Lalo Schifrin
*The Lion in Winter, John Barry
Planet of the Apes, Jerry Goldsmith

The Shoes of the Fisherman, Alex North
The Thomas Crown Affair, Michel Legrand
Best Score of a Musical Picture—[Original or Adaptation]:
Finian's Rainbow, adapted by Ray Heindorf
Funny Girl, adapted by Walter Scharf
***Oliver!**, adapted by John(ny) Green
Star!, Adapted by Lennie Hayton
The Young Girls of Rochefort [Les Demoiselles de Rochfort], Michel Legrand and Jacques Demy

1969

Best Original Score for a Motion Picture [Not a Musical]:
Anne of the Thousand Days, Georges Delerue
*Butch Cassidy and the Sundance Kid, Burt Bacharach
The Reivers, John Williams
The Secret of Santa Vittoria, Ernest Gold
The Wild Bunch, Jerry Fielding
Best Score of a Musical Picture [Original or Adaptation]:
Goodbye, Mr. Chips, adapted by John Williams
***Hello, Dolly!**, adapted by Lennie Hayton and Lionel Newman
Paint Your Wagon, adapted by Nelson Riddle
Sweet Charity, adapted by Cy Coleman
They Shoot Horses, Don't They?, adapted by John(ny) Green and Albert Woodbury

1970

Best Original Score:
Airport, Alfred Newman
Cromwell, Frank Cordell
*Love Story, Francis Lai
Patton, Jerry Goldsmith
Sunflower, Henry Mancini
(Best Original Song Score):
The Baby Maker (lyrics by Tylwyth Kymry; music by Fred Karlin)
A Boy Named Charlie Brown (lyrics by Rod McKuen, Bill Melendez, and Al Shean; music by Rod McKuen and John Scott Trotter; adapted by Vince Guaraldi)
Darling Lili (lyrics by Johnny Mercer; music by Henry Mancini)
***Let It Be** (lyrics and music by The Beatles)
Scrooge (lyrics and music by Leslie Bricusse; adapted by Ian Fraser and Herbert W. Spencer)

1971

(Best Original Dramatic Score):
Mary, Queen of Scots, John Barry
Nicholas and Alexandra, Richard Rodney Bennett
Shaft, Isaac Hayes
Straw Dogs, Jerry Fielding
*Summer of '42, Michel Legrand

Best Scoring: Adaptation and Original Song Score:
Bedknobs and Broomsticks (score by Richard M. and Robert B. Sherman; adapted by Irwin Kostal)
The Boy Friend (adapted by Peter Maxwell Davies and Peter Greenwell)
***Fiddler on the Roof** (adapted by John Williams)
Tchaikovsky (adapted by Dimitri Tiomkin)
Willy Wonka and the Chocolate Factory (score by Leslie Bricusse and Anthony Newley; adapted by Walter Scharf)

1972

Best Original Dramatic Score:
"images," John Williams
*Limelight, Charles Chaplin, Raymond Rasch, and Larry Russell (Revival, from 1952)
Napoleon and Samantha, Buddy Baker
The Poseidon Adventure, John Williams
Sleuth, John Addison
(Best Scoring: Adaptation and Original Song Score):
***Cabaret** (adapted by Ralph Burns)
Lady Sings the Blues (adapted by Gil Askey)
Man of La Mancha (adapted by Laurence Rosenthal)

1973

Best Original Dramatic Score:
Cinderella Liberty, John Williams
The Day of the Dolphin, Georges Delerue
Papillon, Jerry Goldsmith
A Touch of Class, John Cameron
*The Way We Were, Marvin Hamlisch
Best Scoring: Original Song Score and/or Adaptation:
Jesus Christ Superstar (adapted by André Previn, Herbert Spencer, and Andrew Lloyd Webber)
***The Sting** (adapted by Marvin Hamlisch)
Tom Sawyer (song score by Richard M. and Robert B. Sherman; adapted by John Williams)

1974

Best Original Dramatic Score:
Chinatown, Jerry Goldsmith
*The Godfather Part II, Nino Rota and Carmine Coppola
Murder on the Orient Express, Richard Rodney Bennett
Shanks, Alex North
The Towering Inferno, John Williams
Best Scoring: Original Song Score and/or Adaptation:
***The Great Gatsby** (adapted by Nelson Riddle)
The Little Prince (song score by Alan Jay Lerner and Frederick Loewe; adapted by Angela Morley and Douglas Gamley)
Phantom of the Paradise (song score by Paul Williams; adapted by Paul Williams and George Aliceson Tipton)

1975

Best Original Score:
Birds Do It, Bees Do It, Gerald Fried
Bite the Bullet, Alex North
*Jaws, John Williams
One Flew Over the Cuckoo's Nest, Jack Nitzsche
The Wind and the Lion, Jerry Goldsmith
Best Scoring: Original Song Score and/or Adaptation:
*Barry Lyndon (adapted by Leonard Rosenman)
Funny Lady (adapted by Peter Matz)
Tommy (adapted by Peter Townshend)

1976

Best Original Score:
Obsession, Bernard Herrmann
*The Omen, Jerry Goldsmith
The Outlaw Josey Wales, Jerry Fielding
Taxi Driver, Bernard Herrmann
Voyage of the Damned, Lalo Schifrin
Best Original Song Score and Its Adaptation or Best Adaptation Score:
*Bound for Glory (adapted by Leonard Rosenman)
Bugsy Malone (song score and its adaptation by Paul Williams)
A Star Is Born (adapted by Roger Kellaway)

1977

Best Original Score:
Close Encounters of the Third Kind, John Williams
Julia, Georges Delerue
Mohammad—Messenger of God, Maurice Jarre
The Spy Who Loved Me, Marvin Hamlisch
*Star Wars, John Williams
Best Original Song Score and Its Adaptation or Best Adaption Score:
***A Little Night Music** (adapted by Jonathan Tunick)
Pete's Dragon (song score by Al Kasha and Joel Hirschhorn; adapted by Irwin Kostal)
The Slipper and the Rose—The Story of Cinderella (song score by Richard M. and Robert B. Sherman; adapted by Angela Morley)

1978

Best Original Score:
The Boys from Brazil, Jerry Goldsmith
Days of Heaven, Ennio Morricone
Heaven Can Wait, Dave Grusin
*Midnight Express, Giorgio Moroder
Superman, John Williams
Best Adaptation Score:
***The Buddy Holly Story**, Joe Renzetti
Pretty Baby, Jerry Wexler
The Wiz, Quincy Jones

1979

Best Original Score:
The Amityville Horror, Lalo Schifrin
The Champ, Dave Grusin
*A Little Romance, Georges Delerue
Star Trek—The Motion Picture, Jerry Goldsmith
10, Henry Mancini
Best Original Song Score and Its Adaptation—or Best Adaptation Score:
***All That Jazz** (adaptation score by Ralph Burns)
Breaking Away (adaptation score by Patrick Williams)
The Muppet Movie (song score by Paul Williams and Kenny Ascher; adapted by Paul Williams)

1980

Best Original Score:
Altered States, John Corigliano
The Elephant Man, John Morris
The Empire Strikes Back, John Williams
*Fame, Michael Gore
Tess, Philippe Sarde
Best Adaptation Score:
("No award given this year due to insufficient eligible films.")

1981

Best Original Score:
*Chariots of Fire, Vangelis
Dragonslayer, Alex North
On Golden Pond, Dave Grusin
Ragtime, Randy Newman
Raiders of the Lost Ark, John Williams
(Best Original Song Score and Its Adaptation—or Adaptation Score):
("No award given this year due to insufficient eligible films.")

1982

Best Original Score:
*E.T. The Extra-Terrestrial, John Williams
Gandhi, Ravi Shanker and George Fenton
An Officer and a Gentleman, Jack Nitzsche
Poltergeist, Jerry Goldsmith
Sophie's Choice, Marvin Hamlisch
Best Original Score and Its Adaptation or Adaptation Score:
Annie (adaptation score by Ralph Burns)
One from the Heart (song score by Tom Watts)
*Victor/Victoria (song score by Henry Mancini and Leslie Bricusse; adapted by Henry Mancini)

1983

Best Original Score:
Cross Creek, Leonard Rosenman
Return of the Jedi, John Williams
*The Right Stuff, Bill Conti
Terms of Endearment, Michael Gore
Under Fire, Jerry Goldsmith
Best Original Song Score or Adaptation Score:
The Sting II (adaptation score by Lalo Schifrin)

Trading Places (adaptation score by Elmer Bernstein)
*Yentl (original song score by Michel Legrand and Alan and Marilyn Bergman)

1984

Best Original Score:
Indiana Jones and the Temple of Doom, John Williams
The Natural, Randy Newman
*A Passage to India, Maurice Jarre
The River, John Williams
Under the Volcano, Alex North
Best Original Song Score:
The Muppets Take Manhattan, Jeff Moss
*Purple Rain, Prince
Songwriter, Kris Kristofferson

1985

Best Original Score:
Agnes of God, George Delerue
The Color Purple, Quincy Jones, Jeremy Lubbock, Rod Temperton, Caiphus Semenya, Andrae Crouch, Chris Boardman, Jorge Calandrelli, Joel Rosenbaun, Fred Steiner, Jack Hayes, Jerry Hey, and Randy Kerber
*Out of Africa, John Barry
Silverado, Bruce Boughton
Witness, Maurice Jarre

1986

Best Original Score:
Aliens, James Horner
Hoosiers, Jerry Goldsmith
The Mission, Ennio Morricone
*'Round Midnight, Herbie Hancock
Star Trek IV: The Voyage Home, Leonard Rosenman

1987

Best Original Score:
Cry Freedom, George Fenton and Jonas Gwangwa
Empire of the Sun, John Williams
*The Last Emperor, Ryuichi Sakamoto, David Byrne, and Cong Su
The Witches of Eastwick, John Williams
The Untouchables, Ennio Morricone

1988

Best Original Score:
The Accidental Tourist, John Williams
Dangerous Liaisons, George Fenton
Gorillas in the Mist, Maurice Jarre
*The Milagro Beanfield War, Dave Grusin
Rain Man, Hans Zimmer

1989

Best Original Score:
Born on the Fourth of July, John Williams

The Fabulous Baker Boys, Dave Grusin
Field of Dreams, James Horner
Indiana Jones and the Last Crusade, John Williams
*The Little Mermaid, Alan Menken

1990

Best Original Score:
Avalon, Randy Newman
*Dances with Wolves, John Barry
Ghost, Maurice Jarre
Havana, Dave Grusin
Home Alone, John Williams

1991

Best Original Score:
*Beauty and the Beast, Alan Menken
Bugsy, Ennio Morricone
The Fisher King, George Fenton
JFK, John Williams
The Prince of Tides, James Newton Howard

1992

Best Original Score:
*Aladdin, Alan Menken
Basic Instinct, Jerry Goldsmith
Chaplin, John Barry
Howards End, Richard Robbins
A River Runs Through It, Mark Isham

1993

Best Original Score:
The Age of Innocence, Elmer Bernstein
The Firm, Dave Grusin
The Fugitive, James Newton Howard
The Remains of the Day, Richard Robbins
*Schindler's List, John Williams

1994

Best Original Score:
Forest Gump, Alan Silvestri
Interview with the Vampire, Elliot Goldenthal
*The Lion King, Hans Zimmer
Little Women, Thomas Newman
Shawshank Redemption, Thomas Newman

1995

Best Original Dramatic Score:
Apollo 13, James Horner
Braveheart, James Horner
Nixon, John Williams
*The Postman (Il Postino), Luis Bacalov
Sense and Sensibility, Patrick Doyle
Best Original Musical or Comedy Score:
The American President, Marc Shaiman
*Pocahontas, Alan Menken and Stephen Schwartz
Sabrina, John Williams
Toy Story, Randy Newman
Unstrung Heroes, Thomas Newman

1996

Best Original Dramatic Score:
The English Patient, Gabriel Yared
Hamlet, Patrick Doyle
Michael Collins, Elliot Goldenthal
Shine, David Hirschfelder
Sleepers, John Williams
Best Original Musical or Comedy Score:
Emma, Rachael Portman
The First Wives Club, Marc Shaiman
The Hunchback of Notre Dame, Alan Menken and
Stephen Schwartz
James and the Giant Peach, Randy Newman
The Preacher's Wife, Hans Zimmer

1997

Best Original Dramatic Score:
Amistad, John Williams
Good Will Hunting, Danny Elfman
Kundon, Philip Glass
L.A. Confidential, Jerry Goldsmith
Best Original Musical or Comedy Score:
Anastasia, Stephen Flaherty, Lynn Ahrens and David
Newman
As Good As It Gets, Hans Zimmer
*The Full Monty, Anne Dudley
Men in Black, Danny Elfman
My Best Friend's Wedding, James Newton Howard

1998

Best Original Dramatic Score:
Elizabeth, David Hirschfelder
*Life Is Beautiful, Nicola Piovani
Pleasantville, Randy Newman
Saving Private Ryan, John Williams
The Thin Red Line, Hans Zimmer
Best Original Musical or Comedy Score:
A Bug's Life, Randy Newman
Mulan, Matthew Wilder, David Zippel and Jerry
Goldsmith
Patch Adams, Marc Shaiman
The Prince of Egypt, Stephen Schwartz and Hans
Zimmer
*Shakespeare in Love, Stephen Warbeck

1999

Best Original Score
American Beauty, Thomas Newman
Angela's Ashes, John Williams
The Cider House Rules, Rachel Portman
*The Red Violin, John Corigliano
The Talented Mr. Ripley, Gabriel Yared

2000

Best Score
Chocolat, Rachel Portman
*Crouching Tiger, Hidden Dragon, Tan Dun
Gladiator, Hans Zimmer

Malena, Ennio Morricone
The Patriot, John Williams

Best Actor/Actress Winners in a Musical Film

Julie Andrews, *Mary Poppins*, 1964
Yul Brynner, *The King and I*, 1956
James Cagney, *Yankee Doodle Dandy*, 1942
Bing Crosby, *Going My Way*, 1944
Rex Harrison, *My Fair Lady*, 1964
Liza Minnelli, *Cabaret*, 1972
Luise Rainer, *The Great Ziegfeld*, 1936
Barbra Streisand, *Funny Girl*, 1968

Best Actor/Actress Nominees in a Musical Film

Julie Andrews, *The Sound of Music*, 1965; *Victor/Victoria*, 1982
Ann-Margaret, *Tommy*, 1975
Gary Busey, *The Buddy Holly Story*, 1978
Maurice Chevalier, *The Big Pond* and *The Love Parade*, 1929-30
Dan Dailey, *When My Baby Smiles at Me*, 1948
Dorothy Dandridge, *Carmen Jones*, 1954
Barry Fitzgerald, *Going My Way*, 1944
Judy Garland, *A Star Is Born*, 1954
Susan Hayward, *With a Song in My Heart*, 1952; *I'll Cry Tomorrow*, 1955
Gene Kelly, *Anchors Aweigh*, 1945
Deborah Kerr, *The King and I*, 1956
Bessie Love, *The Broadway Melody*, 1929
Shirley MacLaine, *Irma La Douce*, 1963
James Mason, *A Star Is Born*, 1954
Bette Midler, *The Rose*, 1979; *For the Boys*, 1991
Ron Moody, *Oliver!*, 1968
Grace Moore, *One Night of Love*, 1934
Peter O'Toole, *Goodbye, Mr. Chips*, 1969
Larry Parks, *The Jolson Story*, 1946
Debbie Reynolds, *The Unsinkable Molly Brown*, 1964
Mickey Rooney, *Babes in Arms*, 1939
Diana Ross, *Lady Sing the Blues*, 1972
Roy Scheider, *All That Jazz*, 1979
Lawrence Tibbett, *The Rogue Song*, 1930
Topol, *Fiddler on the Roof*, 1971
John Travolta, *Saturday Night Fever*, 1977

Best Actor/Actress Winners (Musical Performers in a Non-Musical Film)

Cher, *Moonstruck*, 1987
Joan Crawford (a dancer in early musical films), *Mildred Pierce*, 1945

Janet Gaynor, *Seventh Heaven, Street Angel,* and *Sunrise,* 1927-28

Ginger Rogers, *Kitty Foyle,* 1940

Jane Wyman (a singer/dancer early in her career), *Johnny Belinda,* 1948

Best Actor/Actress Nominees (Musical Performers in a Non-Musical Film)

Ann Blyth (a singer in later films), *Mildred Pierce,* 1945

Leslie Caron, *The L-Shaped Room,* 1963

Diahann Carroll, *Claudine,* 1974

Nancy Carroll, *The Devil's Holiday,* 1930

Joan Crawford, *Possessed,* 1947; *Sudden Fear,* 1952

Bing Crosby, *The Country Girl,* 1954

Doris Day, *Pillow Talk,* 1959

Irene Dunne, *Cimarron,* 1931; *Theodora Goes Wild,* 1936; *The Awful Truth,* 1937; *Love Affair,* 1939; *I Remember Mama,* 1948

Janet Gaynor, *A Star Is Born,* 1937

Angela Lansbury (a singer in several MGM films), *Gaslight,* 1944; *The Picture of Dorian Gray,* 1945

Liza Minnelli, *The Sterile Cuckoo,* 1969

Walter Pidgeon (a baritone in early filmed operettas), *Mrs. Miniver,* 1942; *Madame Curie,* 1943

Mickey Rooney, *The Human Comedy,* 1943

Frank Sinatra, *The Man with the Golden Arm,* 1955

Barbra Streisand, *The Way We Were,* 1973

Gloria Swanson (a singer in early filmed operettas), *Sadie Thompson,* 1927-28; *The Trespasser,* 1929-30; *Sunset Boulevard,* 1950

Jane Wyman, *The Yearling,* 1946; *The Blue Veil,* 1951; *Magnificent Obsession,* 1954

Best Supporting Actor/ Actress Winners in a Musical Film

George Chakiris, *West Side Story,* 1961

Barry Fitzgerald, *Going My Way,* 1944

Joel Grey, *Cabaret,* 1972

Rita Moreno, *West Side Story,* 1961

Best Supporting Actor/Actress Nominees in a Musical Film

Mikhail Baryshnikov, *The Turning Point,* 1977

Carol Channing, *Thoroughly Modern Millie,* 1967

Gladys Cooper, *My Fair Lady,* 1964

William Demarest, *The Jolson Story,* 1946

Charles Durning, *The Best Little Whorehouse in Texas,* 1982

Stuart Erwin, *Pigskin Parade,* 1936

Frederick Forrest, *The Rose,* 1979

Leonard Frey, *Fiddler on the Roof,* 1971

Jean Hagen, *Singin' in the Rain,* 1952

Stanley Holloway, *My Fair Lady,* 1964

Walter Huston, *Yankee Doodle Dandy,* 1942

Amy Irving, *Yentl,* 1983

Miliza Korjus, *The Great Waltz,* 1938

Peggy Lee, *Pete Kelly's Blues,* 1955

Daniel Massey, *Star!,* 1968

Kay Medford, *Funny Girl,* 1968

Robert Preston, *Victor/Victoria,* 1982

Thelma Ritter, *With a Song in My Heart,* 1952

Lesley Ann Warren, *Victor/Victoria,* 1982

Jack Wild, *Oliver!,* 1968

Peggy Wood, *The Sound of Music,* 1965

Best Supporting Actor/ Actress Winners (Musical Performers in a Non-Musical Film)

Don Ameche, *Cocoon,* 1985

James Dunn, *A Tree Grows in Brooklyn,* 1945

Burl Ives, *The Big Country,* 1958

Frank Sinatra, *From Here to Eternity,* 1953

Best Supporting Actor/- Actress Nominees (Musical Performers in a Non- Musical Film)

Fred Astaire, *The Towering Inferno,* 1974

Theodore Bikel, *The Defiant Ones,* 1958

Joan Blondell, *The Blue Veil,* 1951

Cher, *Silkwood,* 1983

Bobby Darin, *Captain Newman, M.D.,* 1958

Judy Garland, *Judgment at Nuremberg,* 1961

Shirley Jones, *Elmer Gantry,* 1960

Lotte Lenya, *The Roman Spring of Mrs. Stone,* 1961

Jack Oakie, *The Great Dictator,* 1940

River Phoenix, *Running on Empty,* 1988

Mickey Rooney, *The Bold and the Brave,* 1956; *The Black Stallion,* 1979

Ann Southern (a singer in 1930s films), *The Whales of August,* 1987

Russ Tamblyn, *Peyton Place,* 1957

Ethel Waters, *Pinky,* 1949

Bibliography

Alpert, Hollis. *Broadway!: 125 Years of Musical Theatre*. New York: Arcade, 1991.

ASCAP Biographical Dictionary, 4th Edition. New York: Bowker, 1980.

Astaire, Fred. *Steps in Time*. New York: Harper, 1974.

Atkinson, Brooks. *Broadway*. New York: Macmillan, 1970.

Balliett, Whitney. *American Popular Singers*. New York: Oxford, 1979.

Barnes, Ken. *Sinatra and the Great Song Stylists*. New York: Ian Allen, 1972.

_____. *The Crosby Years*. New York: St. Martin's, 1981.

Barrett, Mary Ellin. *Irving Berlin: A Daughter's Memoir*. Simon & Schuster, 1995.

Baum, John. *Notes on a Cowardly Lion*. New York: Knopf, 1969.

Behr, Edward. *The Good Frenchman: The True Story of the Life and Times of Maurice Chevalier*. New York: Villard, 1993.

Benjamin, Ruth, and Arthur Rosenblatt. *Movie Song Catalogue: Performers and Supporting Crew for the Songs Sung in 1460 Musical and Nonmusical Films, 1928-1988*. Jefferson, N.C.: McFarland, 1993.

Bordman, Gerald. *American Musical Theatre*. New York: Oxford, 1984.

Bradley, Edwin M. *The First Hollywood Musicals: A Critical Filmography of 171 Features, 1927 through 1932*. Jefferson, N.C.: McFarland, 1996.

Buxton, Frank, and Bill Owen. *Radio's Golden Age: The Programs and the Personalities*. New York: Easton, 1966.

Carnes, Mark C. *Past Imperfect: History According to the Movies*. Holt, 1995.

Catalog of Copyright Entries, 1929-39; 1944-45; 1954, 1956, 1958; 1961-62, 1964; 1968; 1971- 72; 1979; 1993. Washington, D.C.: Government Printing Office.

Chevalier, Maurice. *The Man in the Straw Hat: My Story*. New York: Crowell, 1949.

Conrad, Earl. *Billy Rose: Manhattan Primitive*. New York: World, 1968.

Crosby, John. *Out of the Blue*. New York: Simon & Schuster, 1952.

Eames, John Douglas. *The M-G-M Story*. New York: Crown, 1975.

Edwards, Anne. *Streisand*. Boston: Little, Brown & Co., 1997.

Engel, Lehman. *The American Musical Theatre*. New York: CBS Legacy, 1967.

Eyles, Allen. *The World of Oz*. Tucson, Ariz.: HP Books, 1985.

Eyman, Scott. *Ernst Lubitsch: Laughter in Paradise*. New York: Simon & Schuster, 1993.

Farnsworth, Marjorie. *The Ziegfeld Follies*. London: Peter Davies, 1956.

Fordin, Hugh. *The World of Entertainment*. Garden City, N.Y.: Doubleday, 1975.

Fricke, John, Jay Scarfone, and William Stillman. *The Wizard of Oz*. Warner, 1989.

Giles, Sarah. *Fred Astaire: His Friends Talk*. New York: Doubleday, 1988.

Gottfried, Martin. *All His Jazz: The Life and Death of Bob Fosse*. New York: Bantam, 1990.

Green, Stanley. *Ring Bells! Sing Songs!: Broadway Musicals of the 1930's*. New Rochelle, N.Y.: Arlington House, 1971.

_____. *The Rodgers and Hammerstein Story*. New York: John Day, 1963.

_____, and Burt Goldblatt. *Starring Fred Astaire*. New York: Dodd, Mead, 1973.

Grossman, Barbara W. *Funny Woman: The Life and Times of Fannie Brice*. Bloomington, Ind.: Indiana University, 1991.

Grun, Bernard. *Prince of Vienna*. New York: Putnam, 1957.

Hamm, Charles. *Irving Berlin: Songs from the Melting Pot: The Formative Years, 1907-1914*. New York: Oxford, 1997.

Harris, Warren G. *Audrey Hepburn*. New York: Simon & Schuster, 1994.

Hay, Peter. *MGM: When the Lion Roars*. Atlanta: Turner, 1991.

Henderson, Amy, and Dwight Blocker Bowers. *Red Hot & Blue: A Smithsonian Salute to the American Musical*. Washington, D.C.: Smithsonian, 1996.

Henderson, Mary C. *Theater in America: 200 Years of Plays, Players, and Productions*. New York: Abrams, 1988.

Herman, Jerry, and Marilyn Stasio. *Showtune*. New York: Donald I. Fine-Penguin, 1996.

Jablonski, Edward. *Alan Jay Lerner: A Biography*. New York: Holt, 1996.

Juran, Robert A. *Old Familiar Faces: The Great Char-*

acter *Actors and Actresses of Hollywood's Golden Era.* Sarasota, Fla.: Movie Memories, 1996.

Katkov, Norman. *The Fabulous Fanny.* New York: Knopf, 1953.

Katz, Ephraim. *The Film Encyclopedia.* New York: Putnam's, 1979.

Lahr, Frank Joslyn, and Russell P. MacFall. *To Please a Child: A Biography of L. Frank Baum, Royal Historian of Oz.* Chicago: Reilly & Lee, 1961.

McCabe, John. *George M. Cohan: The Man Who Owned Broadway.* Garden City, N.Y.: Doubleday, 1982.

Meredith, Scott. *George Kaufman and His Friends.* Garden City, N.Y.: Doubleday, 1974.

Merman, Ethel, and George Eells. *Merman.* New York: Simon & Schuster, 1978.

Minnelli, Vincente. *I Remember It Well.* Garden City, N.Y.: Doubleday, 1974.

Mitchell, Otis C. *Hitler Over Germany: The Establishment of the Nazi Dictatorship (1918-1934).* Philadelphia: Institute for the Study of Human Issues, 1983.

Monush, Barry, ed. *International Motion Picture Almanac.* New York: Quigley, 1994.

Moore, John. *You English Words: A Book About Them.* New York: Dell, 1961.

Mordden, Ethan. *The Hollywood Musical.* New York: St. Martin's, 1981.

Morehouse, Ward. *Matinee Tomorrow: Fifty Years of Our Theater.* New York: Whittlesey, 1949.

Pallot, James, and the editors of CineBooks. *The Movie Guide.* New York: Berkley, 1995.

Pleasants, Henry. *The Great American Popular Singers.* New York: Simon & Schuster, 1974.

Robinson, Ray. *American Original: A Life of Will Rogers.* Oxford, 1996.

Rodgers, Richard. *Musical Stages.* New York: Random House, 1975.

Rogers, Ginger: *Ginger, My Story.* New York: HarperCollins, 1991.

Schwartz, Charles. *Gershwin: His Life and Music.* New York: Bobbs-Merrill, 1973.

Sennett, Ted. *Warner Brothers Presents: The Most Exciting Years—From* The Jazz Singer *to* White Heat. Secaucus, N.J.: Castle Books, 1971.

Spaeth, Sigmund. *A History of Popular Music in America.* New York: Random House, 1948.

Taylor, Deems. *Some Enchanted Evenings.* New York: Harper, 1953.

Walker, John, ed. *Halliwell's Film Guide.* New York: Harper, 1995.

Kimball, Robert T., and Alfred Simon, eds. *The Gershwins.* New York: Atheneum, 1973.

Waters, Edward N. *Victor Herbert: A Life in Music.* New York: Macmillan, 1955.

Wilder, Alex. *American Popular Song: The Great Innovators, 1900-1950.* New York: Oxford, 1972.

Index